The oral history reader

D0092160

Oral history has had a significant impact upon historical practice in the second half of the twentieth century. It has democratized the study of the past by recording the experience of people who have been 'hidden from history'. *The Oral History Reader*, edited by Robert Perks and Alistair Thomson, is an international anthology of key writings about the theory, method and use of oral history. This collection examines how oral history has challenged the practice of history and explores developments and debates in the field through classic and recent articles.

Arranged in thematic parts, *The Oral History Reader* details issues in the theory and practice of oral history, from the creation of oral evidence through to data analysis. Highlighting the complexity of historical relationships and testimony, this collection covers key debates in the post-war development of oral history including: the problems posed by interviewing, issues of ethics, the politics of empowerment, analytical strategies for interpreting memories, and the concerns of archiving and public history. Each part contains an introduction which contextualizes the selection by reviewing key issues and relevant literature. Extensive cross-referencing and indexing provide aids to research.

The Oral History Reader is an essential resource for students of oral history as well as practitioners. This comprehensive volume illustrates similarities and differences in oral history work around the world and details the many subjects to which oral history has made a contribution.

Robert Perks is Curator of Oral History, the British Library National Sound Archive, London. **Alistair Thomson** is a lecturer in the Centre for Continuing Education, University of Sussex.

The oral history reader

Edited by Robert Perks and
Alistair Thomson

Routledge
Taylor & Francis Group

LONDON AND NEW YORK

First published 1998
by Routledge
11 New Fetter Lane, London EC4P 4EE

Simultaneously published in the USA and Canada
by Routledge
29 West 35th Street, New York, NY 10001

Reprinted 2000, 2002, 2003, 2004

Routledge is an imprint of the Taylor & Francis Group

© Editorial matter and selection, 1998 Robert Perks and Alistair Thomson.
Individual contributions, the contributors (see individual chapters).

Typeset in Times by RefineCatch Limited, Bungay, Suffolk
Printed and bound in Great Britain by St Edmundsbury Press Ltd,
Bury St Edmunds, Suffolk

British Library Cataloguing in Publication Data
A catalogue record for this book is available from the British Library

Library of Congress Cataloguing in Publication Data
A catalogue record for this book has been requested

ISBN 0–415–13351–3
ISBN 0–415–13352–1 (pbk)

Contents

Introduction

In the second half of the twentieth century, oral history – 'the interviewing of eye-witness participants in the events of the past for the purposes of historical reconstruction'[1] – has had a significant impact upon contemporary history as practised in many countries. While interviews with members of social and political elites have complemented existing documentary sources, the most distinctive contribution of oral history has been to include within the historical record the experiences and perspectives of groups of people who might otherwise have been 'hidden from history', perhaps written about by social observers or in offical documents, but only rarely preserved in personal papers or scraps of autobiographical writing.[2] Through oral history interviews, working-class men and women, indigenous peoples or members of cultural minorities, amongst others, have inscribed their experiences on the historical record, and offered their own interpretations of history. More specifically, interviews have documented particular aspects of historical experience which tend to be missing from other sources, such as personal relations, domestic work or family life, and they have resonated with the subjective or personal meanings of lived experience.

Oral history has challenged the historical enterprise in other ways. Oral historians have had to learn skills required for the creation of recorded interviews, and to draw upon different intellectual disciplines – including sociology, anthropology, psychology and linguistics – to better understand the narratives of memory. Most significantly, oral history is predicated on an active human relationship between historians and their sources, which can transform the practice of history in several ways. The narrator not only recalls the past but also asserts his or her interpretation of that past, and in participatory oral history projects the interviewee can be a historian as well as the source. Moreover, for some practitioners oral history has not just been about making histories. In certain projects a primary aim has been the empowerment of individuals or social groups through the process of remembering and reinterpreting the past, with an emphasis on the value of process as much as historical product.

In challenging orthodoxies about historical sources, methods and aims, oral history has generated fierce debates; for example about the reliability of memory and the nature of the interview relationship, or more generally about the relationships between memory and history, past and present. By bringing together some of the best writings by practitioners in the field, this *Oral History Reader* explores the issues at stake in these debates and the distinctive nature and contribution of oral history.

The *Oral History Reader* is intended as a core text for undergraduate and postgraduate students who are using oral history, and as a resource for oral history practitioners working in a wide variety of fields, including academic research and community history, museum and public history projects, archives and libraries, reminiscence work and education, and in the media. The *Reader* is not a handbook which details the practical nuts and bolts of doing oral history, though there are practically orientated articles within each section (for beginners, this book might best be used alongside one of the oral history handbooks available in most countries and listed in our Select Bibliography at the end of the volume). Nor does the *Reader* argue for a particular 'right' way to do oral history. The contributors draw upon diverse oral history experiences to explore issues in the theory and practice of oral history, from the creation of oral evidence through to data analysis and historical production. They highlight the complexity of the oral history relationship, the richness of oral testimony, and the extraordinary variety of ways of interpreting the past and making histories using oral sources.

We have arranged *The Oral History Reader* in five thematic parts, each of which focuses on a related set of issues and which take the reader through the different stages of oral history. Part I, 'Critical developments', includes a selection of articles which represent key debates in the post-war development of oral history, from arguments about the value and validity of oral evidence through to more sophisticated explorations of memory, narrative and subjectivity, and the significant contributions of feminism. In Part II, 'Interviewing', the contributions introduce a variety of different interview experiences and approaches, and consider issues posed by the oral history relationship. The articles in 'Advocacy and empowerment' explore some of the ways in which oral history interviews and publications can be used to empower individual narrators and particular social groups, and highlight the politics of oral history. Part IV on 'Interpreting memories' covers a variety of analytical strategies which historians have brought to bear on oral testimony, and Part V 'Making histories' moves from the concerns of archiving and transcription through to the practical, ethical and interpretative issues that arise as we use oral testimony to make histories in a wide variety of forms: in books and exhibitions, on stage and in school projects, in radio, film or multimedia. In each of these parts an introduction contextualizes the selection, noting significant issues and reviewing the relevant literature.

Rather than structuring *The Oral History Reader* around particular historical subjects – such as labour history or women's history – we have tried to ensure that most of the subjects to which oral history has made a significant contribution are represented in one or several of the articles. The index allows readers to trace subjects which cut across our arrangement of the book, and to follow up their own areas of interest.[3] Inevitably, many of the articles in the *Reader* relate to the concerns of more than one section, and the index thus enables users to find references to a particular issue which occur in different sections.

The index also provides a guide to the different countries and regions represented in oral history projects discussed by contributors. One of the aims of *The Oral History Reader* is to provide an international collection of writings which introduce the range of ways in which oral history is used in different countries, suggesting common and distinctive features and showing how the shared concerns of oral history are faced in rather different ways in diverse cultural and national contexts.

In his article 'Movement Without Aim', published in 1975 and reproduced in the initial section 'Critical developments', North American oral historian Ron Grele lamented the rather limited critical discussion among oral historians about the theoretical and methodological issues underpinning their work. That charge could not be levelled at oral historians in the late 1990s; in our research for this *Reader* we turned up a wealth of insightful recent writing in which oral historians reflect on their practice in different parts of the world. Our problem has been to narrow the selection down.

Some of our selection criteria were pragmatic considerations. We decided that we would only include previously published material (about half from books and half from journals, as it turned out, with two conference papers on subjects which had been covered less effectively in the literature), but were keen to include pieces which are out of print or not readily available. We did not have a budget for translation and so were limited to pieces published in English, though we were fortunate to be offered a translation of the French Canadian article on archiving by Jean-Pierre Wallot and Normand Fortier. Apart from the opening section on critical developments we favoured recent publications, though other sections do include a number of older pieces with continuing relevance for oral historians. In order to open up the *Reader* to as wide a range of different experiences and perspectives as possible, we opted for a larger number of shorter pieces (or extracts from longer articles), and we decided to limit our selection to one contribution per author. For a number of notable oral historians who have published extensively in the field our selection was not necessarily the 'best' piece they had written, but the publication which best fitted the needs of the *Reader*. For example, Alessandro Portelli's 'The death of Luigi Trastulli: memory and the event',[4] is a classic exploration of individual and social remembering, but it is not included here because a short extract from the long article would not have worked, because we had several other excellent pieces exploring similar issues, and because Portelli's shorter article, 'What makes oral history different', which is included in 'Critical developments', is a fine introductory analysis of oral history's distinctive features.

Other criteria took shape as we scanned oral history journals, monographs, conference papers and edited collections, as well as other journals with occasional contributions about oral history. We wanted to use pieces written in lively and engaging prose, which would be relatively free of unexplained jargon and accessible to students and practitioners with different levels of oral history experience and theoretical understanding. Wherever possible we have opted for writings which are grounded in the author's own oral history practice, and which use examples from interviews. We have also favoured writings which situate critical reflection on practice within the relevant historiographical literature, and which therefore introduce readers to the concerns and approaches of other oral historians. In many cases there were several equally apt and effective pieces about a particular oral history concern – for example the interview relationship – and our final selection was influenced by an attempt to achieve a balance, across the *Reader* as a whole, in terms of geographical spread and historical subject matter.

There are some gaps in our selection. This is an English-language publication primarily aimed at an English-speaking readership, and it includes a strong selection of writings from North America, Britain, Australasia and Africa, with a smaller number of articles from continental Europe and Latin America. For continental Europe we were limited to publications already translated into English, and though the works by Luisa Passerini and Alessandro Portelli which are included have been enormously influential they represent only the tip of the significant contribution which oral historians from the Continent have made to the field over the last thirty years.[5] Of greater concern to us has been the difficulty of finding appropriate English-language pieces from Latin America, a region which has seen the vibrant development of oral history projects and publications in recent years.[6] We would strongly support the translation and publication of an English-language anthology of writings from Latin American oral history experience.

In the course of our research we also found that certain aspects of oral history practice are under-represented in the literature. Of particular note is the rather limited range of reflective writing about radio, video and television oral history, and about the work of oral historians in museums, libraries and archives. By contrast, there is an extensive and impressive literature about oral history interviewing and about the uses of oral testimony as a historical source.

In our editing of the selection we have standardized reference styles, and we have reduced the length of the longer pieces by choosing self-contained extracts or by deleting discursive footnotes. Wherever possible we have left the contributions in their original form.[7] Deletions from original texts are represented thus, [. . .], and explanatory editorial notes are also contained within square brackets. We thank the authors and original publishers for their cooperation. We also thank our oral history colleagues from around the world who have provided invaluable advice about the structure and selection for this collection – in particular: Dora Schwarzstein (Argentina); Rosie Block,

Heather Goodall, Paula Hamilton and Janis Wilton (Australia); Sonia Maria de Freitas and Daisy Perelmutter (Brazil); Joanna Bornat, Graham Dawson, Donny Hyslop and Dan Weinbren (Britain); Richard Lochead (Canada); Tuula Juvonen (Finland); Anna Green and Megan Hutching (New Zealand); Belinda Bozzoli and Jonathan Grossman (South Africa); Rena Benmayor, David Dunaway, Jim Fogerty, Michael Frisch, Sherna Berger Gluck, Ron Grele, Anne Ritchie, Don Ritchie, Rebecca Sharpless, Linda Shopes and Andor Skotnes (USA). Thanks also to participants in workshops about the *Reader* held in 1996 at the International Oral History Conference in Göteborg, and the Oral History Association Conference in Philadelphia.

NOTES

1 R.J. Grele, 'Directions for oral history in the United States', in D.K. Dunaway and W.K. Baum (eds), *Oral History: An Interdisciplinary Anthology*, Walnut Creek, Altamira Press, 1996, p. 63.
2 S. Rowbotham, *Hidden from History*, London, Pluto, 1973.
3 For surveys of oral history literature on particular historical subjects, see the bibliographies listed in our Select Bibliography, and P. Thompson, *The Voice of the Past: Oral History*, Oxford, Oxford University Press, 1988, pp. 274–283.
4 A. Portelli, 'The death of Luigi Trastulli: memory and the event', in *The Death of Luigi Trastulli and Other Stories: Form and Meaning in Oral History*, Albany, State University of New York Press, 1991, pp. 1–26.
5 See, for example, P. Thompson and N. Burchardt (eds), *Our Common History: The Transformation of Europe*, London, Pluto, 1982; R. Samuel and P. Thompson (eds), *The Myths We Live By*, London, Routledge, 1990; the chapters by Karen Hartewig (Germany), Danièle Voldman (France) and Alessandro Portelli (Italy) in D.K. Dunaway and W.K. Baum (eds), *Oral History: An Interdisciplinary Anthology*, Walnut Creek, Altamira Press, 1996; and the journals *BIOS* (Germany) and *Historia y Fuente Oral* (Spain).
6 See, for example, D. Schwarzstein (ed.), *La Historia Oral*, Buenos Aires, Centro Editorial de América Latina, 1991; M. de Moraes Ferreira and J. Amado (eds), *Usos & Abusos da História Oral*, Rio de Janeiro, Fundaçâo Getulio Vargas, 1996; and the chapters by Eugenia Meyer (Mexico and the Caribbean) and Dora Schwarzstein (Latin America) in Dunaway and Baum (eds), *Oral History*.
7 We have not changed the gender-specific pronouns used by some authors in the 1970s.

ACKNOWLEDGEMENT

The publishers would like to thank all those for their kind permission to reproduce their material. Complete sources are given in the opening of each chapter.

Part I

Critical developments:
introduction

This section does not attempt to survey the national or regional histories of oral history, which are readily available in other publications.[1] Paul Thompson, among others, charts the prehistory of the modern oral history movement, explaining that historians from ancient times relied upon eyewitness accounts of significant events, until the nineteenth-century development of an academic history discipline led to the primacy of archival research and documentary sources, and a marginalization of oral evidence. Gradual acceptance of the usefulness and validity of oral evidence, and the increasing availability of portable tape recorders, underpinned a revival of oral history after the Second World War. The timing and pattern of this revival differed markedly around the world. For example, the first organized oral history project was initiated by Allan Nevins at Columbia University in New York in 1948, and his interest in archival recordings with white male elites was representative of early oral history activity in the United States. In Britain in the 1950s and 1960s oral history pioneers were more interested in recording the experiences of so-called 'ordinary' working people – George Ewart Evans, for example, determined to 'ask the fellows who cut the hay'[2] – and this interest fused with political commitment to a 'history from below' amongst many social historians in Britain and around the world from the 1960s. Yet although the points of genesis and patterns of development for oral history have varied from one country to another, there are sets of ideas and debates which have proved to be critical in shaping contemporary approaches to oral history, and which have influenced oral historians around the world. The readings in this section outline and explore some of these critical developments.

Alex Haley's best-selling books, *Autobiography of Malcolm X* (first published in 1965) and *Roots: The Saga of an American Family* (1976), encouraged black Americans to explore their past and helped to popularize oral history and family history in the United States.[3] Our first extract is from a talk which Haley gave to an early meeting of the United States Oral History Association, published in the very first issue of the Association's journal *Oral History Review* in 1973. Haley describes the transmission of memories within his African-American family, and the oral traditions which are preserved in precise detail and retold by the *griot* or historical storyteller of a West African tribal community. Critics have questioned the accuracy of the evidence which Haley used to link his African and American ancestors.[4] Despite these concerns, Alex Haley's writing reminds us – as does Samuel Schrager in a later section of this *Reader* – that oral history recording taps into a vast, rich reservoir of oral traditions sustained through family, community and national memories.[5] Haley's experience evokes the passion and commitment of early oral historians as they set out to uncover and record those traditions.

Paul Thompson, a social historian at the University of Essex, played a leading role in the creation of the British Oral History Society in the early 1970s and the subsequent development of an international oral history movement from the end of that decade. His book, *The Voice of the Past: Oral History*, became a standard textbook for oral historians around the world when it was first published in 1978.[6] As a socialist, Thompson was committed to a history which drew upon the words and experiences of working-class people. Yet he also sought to defend oral history against critics who claimed that memory was an unreliable historical source, and determined to prove the legitimacy and value of the approach. In the extract from *The Voice of the Past* which we use here, Thompson explains how oral history has transformed both the content of history – 'by shifting the focus and opening new areas of enquiry, by challenging some of the assumptions and accepted judgements of historians, by bringing recognition to substantial groups of people who had been ignored' – and the processes of writing history, breaking 'through the barriers between the chroniclers and their audience; between the educational institution and the outside world'. For many practitioners, recording experiences which have been ignored in history and involving people in exploring and making their own histories, continue to be primary justifications for the use of oral history.

Michael Frisch, a lecturer in History and American Studies at the State University of New York in Buffalo, suggested rather different possibilities for oral history in an essay first published in a student magazine in 1972, brought to a wider audience through the *Oral History Review* in 1979, and reprinted here. Writing about Studs Terkel's influential book, *Hard Times: An Oral History of the Great Depression*,[7] Frisch argued against the attitude that oral memory was 'history as it really was', and asserted that memory – 'personal and historical, individual and generational' – should be moved to centre stage 'as the object, not merely the method, of oral history':

> What happens to experience on the way to becoming memory? What happens to experiences on the way to becoming history? As an era of intense collective experience recedes into the past what is the relationship of memory to historical generalization?

Used in this way, oral history could be 'a powerful tool for discovering, exploring, and evaluating the nature of the process of historical memory – how people make sense of their past, how they connect individual experience and its social context, how the past becomes part of the present, and how people use it to interpret their lives and the world around them'.[8] Over the next two decades these concerns about the connections between memory and history, and between individual and collective historical consciousness, would become central to the work of many oral historians.

By the late 1970s, oral history was well established in archival projects and amongst academic and community historians in many parts of the world. Yet this success, and both the methods and politics of oral history, had sparked serious challenges, ranging from fierce criticisms by traditional documentary historians to sophisticated re-evaluations of aims and approaches from within the emergent field.[9] In 'Movement without aim: methodological and theoretical problems in oral history', first published in 1975 and reproduced here, Ron Grele outlined some of the North American debates concerning the reliability of memory and the representativeness of individual testimony, about research standards in interviewing, comparisons between written and oral sources, and whether or not interview testimony was just another historical source or was interpretative history in its own right. Grele's survey concludes with a call for more theoretical introspection about the end product of the 'conversational narrative' produced in the interview. He argues that oral historians should explore three significant relationships: the linguistic and 'performative' aspects of an interview, and the connections between individual and social historical consciousness. The interdisciplinarity which characterizes Grele's writing – in this and other influential articles – would become an important feature of oral history literature in the following decades.[10]

Grele and a number of North American oral historians met up with their European counterparts at the First International Conference on Oral History held in Essex, England, in 1979. This meeting was to be the first of many international exchanges, and was a catalyst for the publication of an *International Journal of Oral History* (from 1980) and a series of collaborative, international oral history anthologies.[11] At that initial Essex conference, Luisa Passerini's opening paper, subsequently published as 'Work ideology and consensus under Italian fascism' and extracted here, sought to transcend the earlier debates about the value and validity of oral history.[12] Most significantly, she highlighted the role of subjectivity in history – the conscious and unconscious meanings of experience as lived and remembered – and showed how the influences of public culture and ideology upon individual memory might be revealed in the silences, discrepancies and idiosyncrasies of personal testimony. Passerini's pioneering work on subjectivity and silences is one of the most widely referenced contributions to the literature of oral history, and is used by several contributors to the section 'Interpreting memories' in this *Reader*.

Another Italian, Alessandro Portelli, challenged the critics of oral history and so-called 'unreliable memories' head-on in 1979 by arguing that 'what makes oral history different' – orality, narrative form, subjectivity, the 'different credibility' of memory, and the relationship between interviewer and interviewee – should be considered as strengths rather than as weaknesses, a resource rather than a problem. Portelli's article, reproduced here in full, is a subtle exploration of 'the peculiarities of oral history' and an ideal introduction for newcomers to the field.[13]

In the late 1970s and early 1980s some socialist historians were particularly critical of the notion that the method of oral history was necessarily radical and democratic. Luisa Passerini cautioned against the 'facile democratisation' and 'complacent populism' of oral history projects which encouraged members of oppressed groups to 'speak for themselves', but which did not see how memories might be influenced by dominant histories and thus require critical interpretation.[14] At the Centre for Contemporary Cultural Studies in Birmingham, the Popular Memory Group developed a similar critique of British oral history in an article about 'popular memory' which is extracted here. The Group situated professional and other historical practices within the much wider process of 'the social production of memory', and argued that public struggles over the construction of the past are profoundly significant both in contemporary politics and for individual remembering. For example, oral history as used within the community and women's history movements could be a significant resource for making more democratic and transformative histories.[15] Yet the Popular Memory Group concluded that this radical potential was often undermined by superficial understandings of the connections in oral testimony between individual and social memory and between past and present, and by the unequal relationships between professional historians and other participants in oral history projects. The Popular Memory Group's writing highlights the political possibilities and contradictions for oral history projects which have a radical agenda, a theme which is explored in the section on 'Advocacy and empowerment' in this *Reader*.[16]

Oral history and feminist history have enjoyed a symbiotic connection since the late 1960s. Interviews with women have provided an invaluable source for uncovering and exploring experiences which have been, in Sheila Rowbotham's resonant phrase, 'hidden from history', and for challenging historical interpretations based upon the lives and documentation of men.[17] Feminist oral historians have also made significant contributions to theoretical and methodological developments in oral history, illuminating issues about oral history relationships and the interconnections between language, power and meaning.[18] In the concluding article of this section, Canadian historian Joan Sangster explores feminist debates about the social construction of memory, the ethical dilemmas of the oral history relationship, and theoretical dilemmas posed by post-structuralist and post-modernist approaches to language and representation. She argues in conclusion that 'without a firm grounding of oral narratives in their material and social context, and a probing analysis of the relationship between the two, insights on narrative form and on representation may remain unconnected to any useful critique of oppression and inequality'. Sangster's work represents the attempt by many contemporary oral historians to link theoretical sophistication about narrative and memory with the political commitment to the history of oppressed and marginal groups which motivated the first generation of feminist and socialist oral historians.

As Joan Sangster and other authors in this section note, much of the best practice in oral history has been interdisciplinary, with practitioners drawing upon approaches to interviewing and interpretation which have been developed in different academic contexts and disciplines. Some of the more influential interdisciplinary literature is referenced in subsequent sections, though it is worth noting here the significant parallel developments over the last decade within qualitative and life history research (much of which crosses traditional disciplinary boundaries), such as life story sociology,[19] auto/biographical approaches in literary studies,[20] anthropology,[21] cultural studies,[22] narrative psychology,[23] linguistics and communication studies,[24] and related work which explores the relationships between identity, memory and personal narrative.[25] While theoretical and methodological developments in each of these fields have enriched the practice of oral history, oral historians themselves, as represented by the authors in this and other sections, have made substantial contributions to the theory, method and politics of qualitative research through their interdisciplinary reflections on interview relationships and ways of interpreting and using oral testimony.

NOTES

1 See P. Thompson, 'Historians and oral history', in *The Voice of the Past: Oral History*, Oxford, Oxford University Press, 1988, pp. 22–71; C.T. Morrissey, 'Why call it oral history? Searching for early uses of a generic term', *Oral History Review*, 1980, vol. 8, pp. 20–48; the chapters by Allan Nevins, Louis Starr and Ronald J. Grele (United States), Eugenia Meyer (Mexico and the Caribbean), Paul Thompson (Britain), Karen Hartewig (Germany), Danièle Voldman (France), Alessandro Portelli (Italy) and Dora Schwarzstein (Latin America) in D.K. Dunaway and W.K. Baum (eds), *Oral History: An Interdisciplinary Anthology*, Walnut Creek, Altamira Press, 1996 (many of these articles were initially published in *BIOS*, Special Issue, 1990); L. Douglas and P. Spearitt, 'Talking history: the use of oral sources', in W. Mandle and G. Osborne (eds), *New History: Studying Australia Today*, Sydney, Allen & Unwin, 1988, pp. 59–68; R. Lochead, 'Preface', in N. Fortier, 'Guide to Oral History Collections in Canada', published in *Canadian Oral History Association Journal*, vol. 13, 1993; P. la Hause, 'Oral history and South African studies', *Radical History Review*, 1990, nos. 46–47, pp. 346–356; R. Jamieson, 'Aspects of oral history projects and archives in New Zealand, the United States and the United Kingdom', *Oral History*, 1990, vol. 20, no. 2, pp. 53–60. The various national oral history journals which are cited in the Select Bibliography reference other national and regional surveys, and see also references in R. Perks, *Oral History: An Annotated Bibliography*, London, British Library National Sound Archive, 1990.

2 G.E. Evans, *Ask the Fellows Who Cut the Hay*, London, Faber, 1956. See also

Evans's anthology, *Spoken History*, London, Faber, 1987. For later but comparable developments in Australia see M. Loh and W. Lowenstein, *The Immigrants*, Melbourne, Hyland House, 1977; and W. Lowenstein, *Weevils in the Flour: An Oral Record of the 1930s Depression in Australia*, Melbourne, Hyland House, 1978. See references in note 7 to the work of Studs Terkel in the United States.

3 A. Haley, *Autobiography of Malcolm X*, Harmondsworth, Penguin, 1968; and *Roots: The Saga of an American Family*, London, Hutchinson, 1977.

4 See Thompson, *The Voice of the Past*, pp. 24–26.

5 On family memory and history see the articles by Kikumura and Borland in later sections of this *Reader*, and T. Harevan, 'The search for generational memory', *Daedalus*, 1978, vol. 106, pp. 137–149. On oral tradition in non-literate societies see: J. Vansina, *Oral Tradition as History*, Madison, University of Wisconsin Press, 1985; J.C. Miller (ed.), *The African Past Speaks: Essays on Oral Tradition and History*, Folkestone, Dawson, 1980; D. Henige, *Oral Historiography*, London, Longman, 1982; J. Binney, 'Maori oral narratives, Pakeha written texts: two forms of telling history', *New Zealand Journal of History*, 1987, vol. 21, no. 1, pp. 16–28; R. Finnegan, *Oral Tradition and the Verbal Arts*, London, Routledge, 1991; J. Cruikshank, 'Oral tradition and oral history: reviewing some issues', *Canadian Historical Review*, 1994, vol. 75, no. 3, pp. 403–418; E. Tonkin, *Narrating Our Pasts: The Social Construction of Oral History*, Cambridge, Cambridge University Press, 1995.

6 A revised edition published in 1988 expanded the initial chapters about the history and achievements of oral history, and explored new thinking about memory, subjectivity and psychoanalysis.

7 *Hard Times* was first published in New York by Pantheon Books in 1970. Other important works by this American pioneer of oral history include: *Division Street, America*, Penguin, Harmondsworth, 1970, and *'The Good War': An Oral History of World War Two*, Penguin, Harmondsworth, 1986.

8 M. Frisch, *A Shared Authority: Essays on the Craft and Meaning of Oral and Public History*, Albany, State University of New York Press, 1990, p. 188. On the relationships between memory and history see, among others: A. Thomson, M. Frisch and P. Hamilton, 'The memory and history debates: some international perspectives', *Oral History*, 1994, vol. 22, no. 2, pp. 33–43; D. Thelen, *Memory and American History*, Bloomington, Indiana University Press, 1990; D. Middleton and D. Edwards (eds), *Collective Remembering*, London, Sage, 1990; J. Le Goff, *History and Memory*, New York, Columbia University Press, 1992; K. Darian-Smith and P. Hamilton (eds), *Memory and History in Twentieth Century Australia*, Melbourne, Oxford University Press, 1994.

9 Among early critics were: William Cutler III, 'Accuracy in oral history interviewing', *Historical Methods Newsletter*, 1970, no. 3, pp. 1–7; B. Tuchman, 'Distinguishing the significant from the insignificant', *Radcliffe Quarterly*, 1972, no. 56, pp. 9–10 (these two articles are reproduced in Dunaway and Baum (eds), *Oral History*); E. Powell, 'Old men forget', *The Times*, 5 November 1981; P. O'Farrell, 'Oral history: facts and fiction', *Oral History Association of Australia Journal*, 1982–83, no. 5, pp. 3–9.

10 See also Grele's edited collection: *Envelopes of Sound: The Art of Oral History*, New York, Praeger, 1991.

11 See, for example: P. Thompson and N. Burchardt (eds), *Our Common History: The Transformation of Europe*, London, Pluto, 1982; R. Samuel and P. Thompson (eds), *The Myths We Live By*, London, Routledge, 1990. There have been several successors or alternatives to the *International Journal of Oral History*, which lapsed in the late 1980s: *Life Stories/Recits de Vie*, Colchester, Biography and Society Research Committee, International Sociological Association, 1985–1989; R. Grele (ed.), *Subjectivity and Multi-Culturalism in Oral History, The*

International Annual of Oral History, New York, 1992; *International Yearbook of Oral History and Life Stories*, Oxford, Oxford University Press, 1992–1996; *Memory and Narrative*, London, Routledge, from 1997.

12 See also, L. Passerini, *Fascism in Popular Memory: The Cultural Experience of the Turin Working Class*, Cambridge, Cambridge University Press, 1987.

13 See also A. Portelli, *The Death of Luigi Trastulli and Other Stories: Form and Meaning in Oral History*, Albany, State University of New York Press, 1991.

14 L. Passerini, 'Work ideology and consensus under Italian fascism', *History Workshop*, 1979, no. 8, p. 84. Louise Tilly also criticized oral historians' atheoretical and individualist tendencies, though from a more conventional academic standpoint, in her article, 'People's history and social science history', *Social Science History*, 1983, vol. 7, no. 4, pp. 457–474, reprinted with responses from leading oral historians in the *International Journal of Oral History*, 1985, vol. 6, no. 2, pp. 5–46. For a comparable Australian critique see J. Murphy, 'The voice of memory: history, autobiography and oral memory', *Historical Studies*, 1986, vol. 22, no. 87, pp. 157–175.

15 A contemporary overview of oral history's radical potential is provided in the introduction to J. Green, 'Engaging in people's history: the Massachusetts History Workshop', in S.P. Benson *et al.* (eds), *Presenting the Past: Essays on History and the Public*, Philadelphia, Temple University Press, 1986, pp. 337–359.

16 For a critique of the Popular Memory Group, see T. Lummis, *Listening to History: The Authenticity of Oral Evidence*, London, Hutchinson, 1987.

17 Sheila Rowbotham, *Hidden from History*, London, Pluto, 1973.

18 The key text for feminist oral history is S. Berger Gluck and D. Patai (eds), *Women's Words: The Feminist Practice of Oral History*, New York and London, Routledge, 1991. See also Personal Narratives Group, *Interpreting Women's Lives: Feminist Theory and Personal Narratives*, Bloomington and Indianapolis, Indiana University Press, 1989; M. Stuart, 'You're a big girl now: subjectivities, oral history and feminism', *Oral History*, 1994, vol. 22, no. 2, pp. 55–63; *Frontiers: A Journal of Women's Studies,* special issue on 'Women's oral history', 1977, vol. 2, no. 2; special issue on 'Women's oral history II', 1983, vol. 7, no. 2; the three women's history issues of *Oral History*: 1977, vol. 5, no. 2; 1982, vol. 10, no. 2; and 1993, vol. 21, no. 2; *Canadian Oral History Association Journal*, 1991, no. 11, special issue on 'Women and oral history'; and the articles by Anderson and Jack, Borland, Bozzoli, Kennedy and Shostak in this *Reader*.

19 See D. Bertaux (ed.), *Biography and Society: The Life History Approach in the Social Sciences*, Beverly Hills, Sage, 1981; K. Plummer, *Documents of Life: An Introduction to the Problems and Literature of a Humanistic Method*, London, Allen & Unwin, 1983; 'Autobiography and Society' issue of *Sociology*, 1993, vol. 27, no. 1; *Auto/Biography* journal (from 1992). On oral history and interdisciplinarity see M. Chamberlain and P. Thompson, 'Introduction: Genre and narrative in life stories', *Memory and Narrative*, 1997, vol. 1.

20 See J. Olney (ed.), *Studies in Autobiography*, New York, Oxford University Press, 1988; J. Swindells (ed.), *The Uses of Autobiography*, London, Taylor & Francis, 1995; A. Portelli, *The Text and the Voice*, New York, Columbia University Press, 1994; and the North American journals *Biography* and *Journal of Narrative and Life History*.

21 See L.L. Langness and G. Frank, *Lives: An Anthropological Approach to Biography*, Novato, California, Chandler & Sharp, 1981; J. Okely and H. Callaway (eds), *Anthropology and Autobiography*, London and New York, Routledge, 1992; S. Mintz, 'The anthropological interview and the life history', in Dunaway and Baum (eds), *Oral History*, pp. 298–305.

22 R. Johnson *et al.* (eds), *Making Histories: Studies in History-writing and Politics*, London, Hutchinson, 1982; C. Steedman, *Past Tenses: Essays on Writing,*

Autobiography, History, London, Rivers Oram Press, 1992; R. Samuel, *Theatres of Memory: Past and Present in Contemporary Culture*, London, Verso, 1994.

23 See W.M. Runyan, *Life Histories and Psychobiography: Explorations in Theory and Method*, New York and Oxford, Oxford University Press, 1982; T.R. Sarbin (ed.), *Narrative Psychology: The Storied Nature of Human Conduct*, New York, Praeger, 1986; and R. Josselson and A. Leiblich (eds), *Narrative Study of Lives*, Newbury Park, Sage, from 1993.

24 See E. McMahan, *Elite Oral History Discourse: A Study of Cooperation and Coherence*, Tuscaloosa, University of Alabama Press, 1989; R.J. Grele, 'A surmisable variety: interdisciplinarity and oral testimony', in Grele, *Envelopes of Sound*, pp. 156–195; C. Joyner, 'Oral history as communicative event', in Dunaway and Baum (eds), *Oral History*, pp. 292–297.

25 D. Carr, *Time, Narrative and History*, Bloomington, Indiana University Press, 1986; G.C. Rosenwald and R.L. Ochberg (eds), *Storied Lives: The Cultural Politics of Self-Understanding*, New York and London, Yale University Press, 1992; B. Ross, *Remembering the Autobiographical Past: Descriptions of Autobiographical Memory*, Oxford, Oxford University Press, 1992; M. Freeman, *Rewriting the Self: History, Memory, Narrative*, London and New York, Routledge, 1993. See also references in note 8.

1 Black history, oral history and genealogy

Alex Haley

The late Alex Haley is best known as the co-author of *Autobiography of Malcolm X* (1965) and author of *Roots: The Saga of an American Family* (1976). Extracted from *Oral History Review*, 1973, vol. 1, pp. 1–17, by permission of the Oral History Association.

When I was a little boy I lived in a little town which you probably never heard of called Henning, Tennessee, about fifty miles north of Memphis. And I lived there with my parents in the home of my mother's mother. And my grandmother and I were very, very close. Every summer that I can remember growing up there in Henning, my grandmother would have, as visitors, members of the family who were always women, always of her general age range, the late forties, early fifties. They came from places that sounded pretty exotic to me – Dyersburg, Tennessee, Inkster, Michigan – places like that, St. Louis, Kansas City. They were like Cousin Georgia, Aunt Plus, Aunt Liz, so forth. And every evening, after the supper dishes were washed, they would go out on the front porch and sit in cane-bottomed rocking chairs, and I would always sit behind grandma's chair. And every single evening of those summers, unless there was some particularly hot gossip that would overrule it, they would talk about otherwise the self same thing. It was bits and pieces and patches of what I later would learn was a long narrative history of the family which had been passed down literally across generations.

As a little boy I didn't have the orientation to understand most of what they talked about. Sometimes they would talk about individuals, and I didn't know what these individuals were often; I didn't know what an old massa was, I didn't know what an old missus was. They would talk about locales; I didn't know what a plantation was. And then at other times, interspersed with these, they'd talk about anecdotes, incidents which had happened to these people or these places. The furthest-back person that they ever talked about was someone whom they would call 'The African'. And I know that the first time I ever heard the word Africa or African was from their mouths, there on the front porch in Henning.

I think that my first impression that these things they spoke of went a long way back, came from the fact that they were wrinkled, greying, or completely grey in some cases, and I was a little boy, three, four, five, and now and then when some of them would get animatedly talking about something, they would fling their finger or hand down towards me and say something like 'I wasn't any bigger than this young 'un here'. And the very idea that someone as old and wrinkled as she had at one time been no older than I was just blew my mind. I knew it must be way, way back that they were talking about.

When they were speaking of this African, the furthest-back person of all, they would tell how he was brought on a ship to this country to a place they pronounced as 'Naplis'. And he was bought off this ship by a man whose name was John Waller, who had a plantation in a place called Spotsylvania County, Virginia. And then they would tell how he was on this plantation and he kept trying to escape. The first three times he escaped he was caught and given a worse beating than previously as his punishment. And then the fourth time he escaped he had the misfortune to be caught by a professional slave catcher. And I grew up hearing how this slave catcher decided to make an example of him. And I grew up hearing how he gave the African the choice either to be castrated or to have a foot cut off. And the African chose the foot. And I grew up hearing how his foot was put against a stump, and with an ax was cut off across the arch. It was a very hideous act. But as it turned out that act was to play a very major role in the keeping of a narrative down across a family for a long time.

The reasons were two. One of them was that in the middle 1700s in Virginia, almost all slaves were sold at auction. A male slave in good condition would bring on the average about $750. At the end of every slave auction they would have what they called the scrap sale, and those who were incapacitated, ill, or otherwise not so valuable for market, would be sold generally for amounts of $100 or less in cash. And this particular African managed to survive and then to convalesce, and he posed then to his master an economic question. And his master decided that he was crippled and he hobbled about, but he still could do limited work. And the master decided that he would be worth more kept on that plantation than he would be worth sold away for cash of less than $100. And that was how it happened that this particular African was kept on one plantation for quite a long period of time.

Now that came at a time when, if there was any single thing that probably characterizes slaves, it was that they had almost no sense of what we today know and value and revere as family continuity. And the reason simply was that slaves were sold back and forth so much. Characteristically slave children would grow up without an awareness of who their parents were, and particularly male parents. This African, now kept on the plantation by his master's decision, hobbling about and doing the limited work he could, finally met and mated with another slave on that plantation, and her name (in the stories told by my grandmother and the others on the front porch in Henning) was Bell the big house cook. And of that union was born a little girl who was given the name Kizzy. As Kizzy got to be four or five or so, this African would take that little girl by the hand, and he would take her around and point out to her various natural objects, and he would tell her the name for that thing – tree, rock, cow, sky, so forth. The names that he told her were instinctively in his native tongue, and to the girl they were strange phonetic sounds which in time, with repetitive hearing, the girl could repeat. He would point at a guitar and he would make a single sound as if it were spelled *ko*. And she came in time to know that *ko* was guitar in his terms. There were other strange phonetic sounds for other objects. Perhaps the most involved of them was that contiguous to the plantation there was a river, and whenever this African would point out this river to his daughter Kizzy he would say to her '*Kamby Bolongo*'. And she came to know that *Kamby Bolongo* in his terms meant river.

There was another thing about this African which is in the background of all the Black people in this country, and that was that whoever bought them off the slave ship, when they got them to a plantation, about their first act was giving them an Anglicized name. For all practical purposes that was the first step in the psychic dehumanization of an individual or collectively of a people. And in the case of this particular African his master gave him the name Toby. But whenever any of the other adult slaves would address him as Toby, this African would strenuously rebuff and reject it and he would tell them his name was '*Kin-tay*', a sharp, angular two-syllabic sound that the little girl Kizzy came to know her father said was his name.

And there was yet another thing about this African characteristic of all those original Africans in our background, and that was that they had been brought from a place where they spoke whatever was their native tongue, and brought to this place where it became necessary to learn English for sheer survival's sake. And gradually, haltingly, all those original Africans learned a word here, a phrase there, of the new tongue – English. As this process began to happen with this African, and he began to be able to express himself in more detailed ways, he began to tell his little daughter Kizzy little vignettes about himself. He told her, for instance, how he had been captured. He said that he had not been far away from his village chopping wood to make himself a drum when he had been set upon by four men, overwhelmed, and taken thusly into slavery. And she came to know along with many other stories the story of how he was chopping wood when he was captured.

To compress what would happen over the next decade, the girl Kizzy stayed on the plantation in Spotsylvania County directly exposed to her father who had come directly from Africa, and to his stories, until she had a considerable repertoire of knowledge about him from his own mouth. When the girl Kizzy was sixteen years of age, she was sold away to a new master whose name was Tom Lea and he had a much smaller plantation in North Carolina. And it was on this plantation that after a while the girl Kizzy gave birth to her first child, a boy who was given the name George. The father was the new master Tom Lea. And as George got to be four or five or so, now it was his mother Kizzy who began to tell him the stories that she heard from her father. And the boy began to discover the rather common phenomenon that slave children rarely knew who their fathers were, let alone a grandfather. He had something which made him rather singular. And so it was with considerable pride the boy began to tell his peers the story of his grandfather; this African who said his name was *Kin-tay*, who called a river *Kamby Bolongo*, and called a guitar *ko* and other sounds for other things, and who said that he had been chopping wood when he was set upon and captured and brought into slavery.

When the boy George got to be about twelve, he was apprenticed to an old slave to learn handling the master's fighting gamecocks. And this boy had innate, green thumb ability for fighting gamecocks. By the time he was in his mid-teens he had been given (for his local and regional renown as an expert slave handler and pitter of fighting gamecocks) the nickname he would take to his grave decades later – Chicken George.

When Chicken George was about eighteen he met and mated with a slave girl. And her name was Matilda, and in time Matilda gave birth to seven children. Now for the first time that story which had come down from this African began to fan out within the breadth of a family. The stories as they would be told on the front porch in Henning by grandma and the others were those of the winter evenings after the harvest when families would entertain themselves by sitting together and the elders would talk and the young would listen. Now Chicken George would sit with his seven children around the hearth. The story was that they would roast sweet potatoes in the hot ashes, and night after night after night across the winters, Chicken George would tell his seven children a story unusual among slaves, and that was direct knowledge of a great-grandfather; this same African who said his name was *Kin-tay*, who called the river *Kamby Bolongo*, and a guitar *ko*, and who said that he was chopping wood when he was captured.

Those children grew up, took mates and had children. One of them was named Tom. And Tom became an apprenticed blacksmith. He was sold in his mid-teens to a man named Murray who had a tobacco plantation in Alamance County, North Carolina. And it was on this plantation that Tom, who became that plantation's blacksmith, met and mated with a slave girl whose name was Irene and who was the plantation weaver. And Irene also in time bore seven children. Now it was yet another generation, another section of the state of North Carolina and another set of seven children who would sit in yet another cabin, around the hearth in the winter evenings with the sweet potatoes in the hot ashes. And now the father was Tom telling his children about something virtually unique in the knowledge of slaves, direct knowledge of a great-great-grandfather, this same African, who said his name was *Kin-tay*, who called the river *Kamby Bolongo*, who said he was chopping wood when he was captured, and the other parts of the story that had come down in that way.

Of that second set of seven children, in Alamance County, North Carolina, the youngest was a little girl whose name was Cynthia, and Cynthia was my maternal grandmother. And I grew up in her home in Henning, Tennessee, and grandma pumped that story into me as if it were plasma. It was by all odds the most precious thing in her life – the story which had come down across the generations about the family going back to that original African.

I stayed at grandma's home until I was in my mid-teens. By that time I had two younger brothers, George and Julius. Our father was a teacher at small black land grant colleges about the South and we began now to move around wherever he was teaching. And thus I went to school through two years of college. When World War II came along I was one of the many people who thought that if I could hurry and get into an organization of which I had recently heard called the US Coast Guard, that maybe I could spend the war walking the coast. And I got into the service and to my great shock rather suddenly found myself on an ammunition ship in the Southwest Pacific, which was not at all what I had in mind. But when I look back upon it now, it was the first of a series of what seemed to be accidental things, but now seem to be part of a pattern of many things that were just meant to be, to make a certain book possible, in time. On the ships in the Coast Guard, totally by accident, I stumbled into the long road to becoming a writer. It was something I had never have dreamed of. [. . .]

[MANY YEARS LATER]

One morning, I was in the British Museum and I came upon something, I had vaguely heard of it, the Rosetta Stone. It just really entranced me. I read about it, and I found how, when this stone was discovered in 1799, it seemed to have three sets of texts chiseled into the stone: one of them in Greek characters, which Greek scholars could read, the second in a then-unknown set of characters, the third in the ancient hieroglyphics which it was assumed no one would ever translate. Then I read how a French scholar, Jean Champollion, had come along and had taken that second unknown set of script, character for character, matched it with the Greek and finally had come up with a thesis he could prove – that the text was the same as the Greek. And then in a superhuman feat of scholarship he had taken the terribly intricate characters of the hieroglyphics and cross matched them with the preceding two in almost geometric progression, and had proved that too was the same text. That was what opened up to the whole world of scholarship, all that hitherto had been hidden behind the mystery of the allegedly undecipherable hieroglyphics.

And that thing just fascinated me. I would find myself going around London doing all sorts of other things and at odd times I would see in my mind's eye, almost as if it were projected in my head, the Rosetta Stone. And to me, it just had some kind of special significance, but I couldn't make head or tail of what it might be. Finally I was on a plane coming back to this country, when an idea hit me. It was rough, raw, crude, but it got me to thinking. Now what this scholar worked with was language chiseled into the stone. And what he did was to take that which had been unknown and match it with that which was known, and thus found out the meaning of what hitherto had been unknown. And then I got to thinking of an analogy: that story always told in our family that I had heard on the front porch in

Henning. The unknown quotient was those strange phonetic sounds. And I got to thinking, now maybe I could find out where these sounds came from. Obviously these strange sounds are threads of some African tongue. And my whole thing was to see if maybe I could find out, just in curiosity, what tongue did they represent. It seemed obvious to me what I had to do was try to get in touch with as wide a range of Africans as I could, simply because there were many, many tongues spoken in Africa. I lived in New York, so I began doing what seemed to me logical. I began going up to the United Nations lobby about quitting time. It wasn't hard to spot Africans, and every time I could I'd stop one. And I would say to him my little sounds. In a couple of weeks I stopped a couple of dozen Africans, each and every one of which took a quick look, quick listen to me, and took off. Which I well understand; me with a Tennessee accent trying to tell them some African sounds, I wasn't going to get it.

I have a friend, a master researcher, George Sims, who knew what I was trying to do and he came to me with a listing of about a dozen people renowned for their knowledge of African linguistics. And one who intrigued me right off the bat was not an African at all, but a Belgian. Educated at England, much of it at the School of Oriental and African Studies, he had done his early work living in African villages, studying the language or the tongue as spoken in those villages. He had finally written a book called in French, *La Tradition Orale*.[1] His name: Dr Jan Vansina, University of Wisconsin. I phoned Dr Vansina. He very graciously said I could see him. I got on a plane and flew to Madison, Wisconsin, with no dream of what was about to happen. In the living room of the Vansinas that evening I told Dr Vansina every little bit I could remember of what I'd heard as a little boy on the front porch in Henning. And Dr Vansina listened most intently. And then he began to question me. Being himself an oral historian, he was particularly interested in the physical transmission of the story down across the generations. And I would answer everything I could. I couldn't answer most of what he asked. Around midnight, Dr Vansina said, 'I wonder if you'd spend the night at our home,' and I did stay there. The following morning, before breakfast, Dr Vansina came down with a very serious expression on his face; I was later to learn that he had already been on the phone with colleagues, and he said to me: 'The ramifications of what you have brought here could be enormous.' He and his colleagues felt almost certain that the collective sounds that I had been able to bring there, which had been passed down across the family in the manner I had described to him, represented the Mandinka tongue. I'd never heard the word. He told me that that was the tongue spoken by the Mandingo people. He began then to guess translate certain of the sounds. There was a sound that probably meant cow or cattle; another probably meant the bow-bow tree, generic in West Africa. I had told him that from the time I was knee-high I'd heard about how this African would point to a guitar and say *ko*. Now he told me that almost surely this would refer to one of the oldest of the stringed instruments among the Mandingo people, an instrument made of a gourd covered with goat skin, a long neck, 21 strings, called the *kora*. He came finally to the most involved of the sounds that I had heard and had brought to him – *Kamby Bolongo*. He said without question in Mandinka, *bolongo* meant river; preceded by *Kamby* it probably would mean Gambia River. I'd never heard of that river.

It was Thursday morning when I heard those words; Monday morning I was in Africa. I just had to go. There was no sense in messing around. On Friday I found that of the numerous African students in this country, there were a few from that very, very small country called Gambia. And the one who physically was closest to me was a fellow in Hamilton College, Clinton, New York. And I hit that campus about 3:30 Friday afternoon and practically snatched Ebou Manga out of an economics class and got us on Pan American that night. We flew through the night to Dakar, Senegal, and there we got a light plane that flew over to a little airstrip called Yundum – they literally had to run monkeys off the runway to get in there. And then we got a van and we went into the small city of Bathurst, the capital of Gambia. Ebou Manga, his father Alhaji Manga (it's a predominantly Moslem culture there), assembled a group of about eight men, members of the government, who came into the patio of the Atlantic Hotel, and they sat in kind of a semi-circle as I told them the history that had come down across the family to my grandmother and thence to me; told them everything I could remember.

And when I finished, the Africans irritated me considerably because *Kamby Bolongo*, the sounds which had gotten me specifically to them, they tended almost to poo-poo. They said, 'Well, of course *Kamby Bolongo* would mean Gambia River; anyone would know that.' What these Africans reacted to was another sound: a mere two syllables that I had brought them without the slightest comprehension that it had any particular significance. They said, 'There may be some significance in that your forefather stated his name was *Kin-tay*.' I said, 'Well, there was nothing more explicit in the story than the pronunciation of his name, *Kin-tay*.' They said, 'Our oldest villages tend to be named for those families which founded those villages centuries ago.' And then they sent for a little map and they said, 'Look, here is the village of Kinte-Kundah. And not too far from it is the village of Kinte-Kundah-Janneh-Ya.' And then they told me about something I never had any concept existed in this world. They told me that in the back country, and particularly in the older villages of the back country, there were old men called *griots*, who are in effect walking, living archives of oral history. They are the old men who, from the time they had been in their teen-ages, have been part of a line of men who tell the stories as they have been told since the time of their forefathers, literally down across centuries. The incumbent *griot* will be a man usually in his late sixties, early seventies, and underneath him will be men separated by about decade intervals, sixty, fifty, forty, thirty, twenty, and a teen-age boy, and each line of *griots* will be the experts in the story of a major family clan; another line of *griots* another clan; and so on for dozens of major clans. Another line of *griots* would be the experts in the history of a group of villages. Another would go into the history of the empires which had preceded it, and so forth. And the stories were told in a narrative, oral history way, not verbatim, but the essential same way they had been told down across the time since the forefathers. And the way they were trained was that the teen-age boy was exposed to that story for forty or fifty years before he would become the oral historian incumbent.

It astounds us now to realize that men like these, in not only Africa but other cultures, can literally talk for days, telling a story and not repeating themselves, and telling the details in the most explicit detail. The reason it astounds us is because in our culture we have become so conditioned to the crush of print that most people in our culture have almost forgotten what the human memory is capable of if it is trained to keep things in it. These men, I was told, existed in the back country. And the men there told me that since my forefather had said his name was *Kin-tay* they would see what they could to do help me.

I came back to this country enormously bewildered. I didn't know what to do. It embarrasses me to say that up to that time I really hadn't thought all that much about Africa. I knew where it was and I had the standard cliché images of it, the Tarzan Africa and stuff like that. Well, now it was almost as if some religious zealotry came into me. I just began to devour everything I could lay eyes on about Africa, particularly slavery. I can remember after reading all day I'd sit on the edge of a bed at night with a map of Africa, studying the positions of the countries, one with relation with the other.

It was about six weeks later when an innocuous looking letter came to me which suggested that when it was possible I should come back. I was back over there as quickly as I possibly could make it. The same men, with whom I had previously talked rather matter-of-factly, told me that the word had been put out in the back country and that there had indeed been found a *griot* of the Kinte clan. His name, they said, was Kebba Kanga Fofana. When I heard there was such a man I was ready to have a fit. Where is he? I figured from my experience as an American magazine writer, the government should have had him there with a public relations man for me to talk to. And they looked at me oddly and they said, he's in his village.

I discovered at that point that if I was to see this man, I was going to have to do something I'd never dreamed before: I would have to organize a safari. It took me three days to rent a launch to get up the river, lorry, Land-Rover to take supplies by the back route, to hire finally a total of fourteen people, including three interpreters, four musicians (they told me in the back country these old oral historians would not talk without music in the background), bearers and so forth. And on the fourth day we went vibrating in this launch up the Gambia River. I was very uncomfortable. I had the feeling of being alien. I had the queasy feeling of what do they see me as, another pith-helmet? We got on up the river to a little village called Albreda on the left bank. And then we went ashore. And now our destination by foot was a village called Juffure where this man was said to live.

There's an expression called 'the peak experience'. It is that which emotionally nothing in your life ever can transcend. And I know I have had mine that first day in the back country in black West Africa. When we got up within sight of the village of Juffure the children who had inevitably been playing outside African villages, gave the word and the people came flocking out of their huts. It's a rather small village, only about seventy people. And villages in the back country are very much today as they were two hundred years ago, circular mud huts with conical thatched roofs. And from a distance I could see this small man with a pillbox hat and an off-white robe, and even from a distance there was an aura of 'somebodiness' about him. I just knew that was the man we had come to see. And when we got closer the interpreters left our party and went straight to him. And I had stepped unwittingly into a sequence of emotional events that always I feel awkward trying to describe, simply because I never ever verbally could convey the power, the physical power, of emotional occurrences.

These people quickly filtered closely around me in kind of a horseshoe design with me at the base. If I had put up my hands I would have touched the nearest ones on either side. There were about three, four deep all around. And the first thing that hit me was the intensity of the way they were staring at me. The eyes just raped. The foreheads were forward in the intensity of the staring. And it was an uncomfortable feeling. And while this was happening there began to occur inside me a kind of feeling as if something was turgid, rolling, surging around. And I had this eerie feeling that I knew inside me why it was happening and what it was about, but consciously I could not identify what had me so upset inside. And after a while it began to roll in: it was rather like a galeforce wind that you couldn't see but it just rolled in and hit you – bam! It was enough to knock you down. I suddenly realized what so upset me was that I was looking at a crowd of people and for the first time in my life every one of them was jet black. And I was standing there rather rocked by that, and in the way that we tend to do if we are discomforted we drop our glance. And I remember dropping my glance, and my glance falling on my own hand, my own complexion, in context with their complexion. And now there came rolling in another surging galeforce thing that hit me perhaps harder than the first one. A feeling of guilt, a feeling rather of being hybrid, a feeling of being the impure among the pure.

And the old man suddenly left the interpreters, walked away, and the people as quickly filtered away from me and to the old man. And they began a very animated talking, high metallic Mandinka tongue. One of the interpreters, his name was A.B.C. Salla, whispered in my ear and the significance of what he whispered probably got me as much as all the rest of it collectively. He said, 'They stare at you so because they have never seen a black American.' And what hit me was they were not looking at Alex Haley, writer, they didn't know who he was, they couldn't care less. But what they saw me as was a symbol of twenty-five millions of us over here whom they had never seen. And it was just an awesome thing to realize that someone had thrust that kind of symbolism upon me. And there's a language that's universal. It's a language of gestures, noises, inflections, expressions. Somehow looking at them, hearing them, though I couldn't understand a syllable, I knew what they were talking about. I somehow knew they were trying to arrive at a consensus of how did they collectively feel about me as a symbol for them of all the millions of us over here whom they never had seen. And there came a time when the old man quickly turned. He walked right through the people, he walked right past three interpreters, he walked right up to me, looking piercingly into my eyes and spoke in Mandinka, as if instinctively he felt I should be able to understand it. And the translation came from the side. And the way they collectively saw me, the symbol of all the millions of us black people here whom they never had seen was, 'Yes, we have been told by the forefathers that there are many of us from this place who are in exile in that place called America and in other places.' And that was the way they saw it.

The old man, the *griot*, the oral historian, Kebba Kanga Fofana, seventy-three rains of age (their way of saying seventy-three years, one rainy season a year), began now to tell me the ancestral history of the Kinte clan as it had been told down across the centuries, from the times of the forefathers. It was as if a scroll was being read. It wasn't just talk as we talk. It was a very formal occasion. The people became mouse quiet, rigid. The old man sat in a chair and when he would speak he would come up forward, his body would grow rigid, the cords in his neck stood out and he spoke words as though they were physical objects coming out of his mouth. He'd speak a sentence or so, he would go limp, relax, and the translation would come. Out of this man's head came spilling lineage details incredible to behold. Two, three centuries back. Who married whom, who had what children, what children married whom and their children, and so forth, just unbelievable. I was struck not only by the profusion of details, but also by the biblical pattern of the way they expressed it. It would be something like: 'and so and so took as a wife so and so and begat and begat and begat', and he'd name their mates and their children, and so forth. When they would date things it was not with calendar dates, but they would date things with physical events, such as, 'in the year of the big water he slew a water buffalo', the year of the big water referring to a flood. And if you wanted to know the date calendar-wise you had to find when that flood occurred.

I can strip out of the hours that I heard of the history of the Kinte clan (my forefather had said his name was *Kin-tay*), the immediate vertical essence of it, leaving out all the details of the brothers and the cousins and the other marriages and so forth. The *griot* Kebba Kanga Fofana said that the Kinte clan had been begun in a country called Old Mali. Traditionally the Kinte men were blacksmiths who had conquered fire. The women were potters and weavers. A branch of the clan had moved into the country called Mauretania. It was from the country of Mauretania that a son of the clan, whose name was Kairaba Kunta Kinte (he was a *Marabout*, which is to say a holy man of the Moslem faith), came down into the country called the Gambia. He went first to a village called Pakali n'Ding. He stayed there for a while. He went next to a village called Jiffarong; thence he went to a village called Juffure. In the village of Juffure the young *Marabout* Kairaba Kunta Kinte took his first wife, a Mandinka maiden whose name was Sireng. And by her he begat two sons whose names were Janneh and Saloum. Then he took a second wife; her name, Yaisa. And by Yaisa he begat a son whose name was Omoro. Those three sons grew up in the village of Juffure until they came of age. The elder two, Janneh and Saloum, went away and started a new village called Kinte-Kundah Janneh-Ya. It is there today. Literally translated it means 'The Home of Janneh Kinte'. The youngest son, Omoro, stayed in the village until he had thirty rains, and then he took a wife, a Mandinka maiden, her name Binta Kebba. And by Binta Kebba, roughly between 1750 and 1760, Omoro Kinte begat four sons, whose names were Kunta, Lamin, Suwadu and Madi.

By the time he got down to that level of the family, the *griot* had talked for probably five hours. He had stopped maybe fifty times in the course of that narrative and a translation came into me. And then a translation came as all the others had come, calmly, and it began, 'About the time the king's soldiers came.' That was one of those time-fixing references. Later in England, in British Parliamentary records, I went feverishly searching to find out what he was talking about, because I had to have the calendar date. But now in back country Africa, the *griot* Kebba Kanga Fofana, the oral historian, was telling the story as it had come down for centuries from the time of the forefathers of the Kinte clan. 'About the time the king's soldiers came, the eldest of these four sons, Kunta, went away from this village to chop wood and was seen never again.' And he went on with his story.

I sat there as if I was carved out of rock. Goose-pimples came out on me I guess the size of marbles. He just had no way in the world to know that he had told me that which meshed with what I'd heard on the front porch in Henning, Tennessee, from grandma, from Cousin Georgia, from Aunt Liz, from Cousin Plus, all the other old ladies who sat there on that porch. I managed to get myself together enough to pull out my notebook, which had in it what grandma had always said. And I got the interpreter Salla and showed it to him and he got rather agitated, and he went to the old man, and he got agitated, and the old man went to the people and they got agitated.

I don't remember it actually happening. I don't remember anyone giving an order, but those seventy people formed a ring around me, moving counter-clockwise, chanting, loudly, softly, loudly, softly, their bodies were close together, the physical action was like drum majorettes with their high knee action. You got the feeling they were an undulating mass of people moving around. I'm standing in the middle like an Adam in the desert. I don't know how I felt; how could you feel a thing like that? And I remember looking at the first lady who broke from that circle (there were about a dozen ladies who had little infant children slung across their backs), and she with a scowl on this jet black face, broke from that circle, her bare feet slapping against the hard earth, came charging in towards me. And she took her baby and roughly thrust it out. The gesture said, 'Take it!' and I took the baby and I clasped it, at which point she snatched it away and another lady, another baby, and I guess I had clasped about a dozen babies in about two minutes. It would be almost two years later at Harvard when Dr Jerome Bruner told me, you were participating in one of the oldest ceremonies of humankind called 'the laying on of hands'; that in their way they were saying to you, 'through this flesh which is us, we are you, and you are us'. There were many, many other things that happened in that village that day, but I was particularly struck with the enormity of the fact that they were dealing with me and seeing me in the perspective of, for them, the symbol of twenty-five millions of us black people in this country whom they never had seen. They took me into their mosque. They prayed in Arabic which I couldn't understand. Later the crux of the prayer was translated, 'Praise be to Allah for one long lost from us whom Allah has returned.' And that was the way they saw that.

When it was possible to leave, since we'd come by water, I wanted to go out over the land. My five senses had become muted, truncated. They didn't work right. If I wanted to feel something I would have to squeeze to register the sense of feeling. Things were misty. I didn't hear well. I would become aware the driver sitting right by me was almost shouting something and I just hadn't heard him up to that point. I began now, as we drove out over the back country road, with drums distantly heard around, to see in my mind's eye, as if it were being projected somehow on a film, a screen almost, rough, ragged, out of focus, almost a portrayal of what I had studied so, so much about: the background of us as a people, the way that ancestrally we who are in this country were brought out of Africa. [. . .]

NOTE

1 J. Vansina, *De la Tradition Orale: Essai de Methode Historique*, Belgique, Tervuren, 1961. Translated as *Oral Tradition: A Study in Historical Methodology*, Chicago, Routledge & Kegan Paul, 1965.

2   The voice of the past
Oral history

Paul Thompson

Paul Thompson is Research Professor at the University of Essex. © Paul Thompson 1978, 1988. Extracted from P. Thompson, *The Voice of the Past: Oral History*, Oxford, Oxford University Press, 1988 (second edition) by permission of Oxford University Press.

All history depends ultimately upon its social purpose. This is why in the past it has been handed down by oral tradition and written chronicle, and why today professional historians are supported from public funds, children are taught history in schools, amateur history societies blossom, and popular history books rank among the strongest bestsellers. Sometimes the social purpose of history is obscure. There are academics who pursue fact-finding research on remote problems, avoiding any entanglement with wider interpretations or contemporary issues, insisting only on the pursuit of knowledge for its own sake. They have one thing in common with the bland contemporary tourism which exploits the past as if it were another foreign country to escape to: a heritage of buildings and landscape so lovingly cared for that it is almost inhumanly comfortable, purged of social suffering, cruelty, and conflict to the point that a slavery plantation becomes a positive pleasure. Both look to their incomes free from interference, and in return stir no challenge to the social system. At the other extreme the social purpose of history can be quite blatant: used to provide justification for war and conquest, territorial seizure, revolution and counter-revolution, the rule of one class or race over another. Where no history is readily at hand, it will be created. South Africa's white rulers divide their urban blacks between tribes and 'homelands'; Welsh nationalists gather at bardic eisteddfods; the Chinese of the cultural revolution were urged to construct the new 'four histories' of grass-roots struggle; radical feminists looked to the history of wet-nursing in their search for mothers without maternal instinct. Between these two extremes are many other purposes, more or less obvious. For politicians the past is a quarry for supportive symbols: imperial victories, martyrs, Victorian values, hunger marches. And almost equally telling are the gaps in the public presentation of history: the silences in Russia on Trotsky, in West Germany on the Nazi era, in France on the Algerian war.

Through history ordinary people seek to understand the upheavals and changes which they experience in their own lives: wars, social transformations like the changing position of youth, technological changes like the end of steam power, or personal migration to a new community. Family history especially can give an individual a strong sense of a much longer personal lifespan, which will even survive their own death. Through local history a village or town seeks meaning for its own changing character and newcomers can gain a sense of roots in personal historical knowledge. Through political and social history taught in schools children are helped to understand, and accept, how the political and social system under which they live came about, and how force and conflict have played, and continue to play, their part in that evolution.

The challenge of oral history lies partly in relation to this essential social purpose of history. This is a major reason why it has so excited some historians, and so frightened others. In fact, fear of oral history as such is groundless. We shall see later that the use of interviews as a source by professional historians is long-standing and perfectly compatible with scholarly standards. American experience shows clearly enough that the oral history method can be regularly used in a socially and politically conservative manner; or indeed pushed as far as sympathy with Fascism in John Toland's portrait of *Adolf Hitler* (New York, 1976).

Oral history is not necessarily an instrument for change; it depends upon the spirit in which it is used. Nevertheless, oral history certainly can be a means for transforming both the content and the purpose of history. It can be used to change the focus of history itself, and open up new areas of inquiry; it can break down barriers between teachers and students, between generations, between educational institutions and the world outside; and in the writing of history – whether in books, or museums, or radio and film – it can give back to the people who made and experienced history, through their own words, a central place.

Until the present century, the focus of history was essentially political: a documentation of the struggle for power, in which the lives of ordinary people, or the workings of the economy or religion, were given little attention except in times of crisis such as the Reformation, the English Civil War, or the French Revolution. Historical time was divided up by reigns and dynasties. Even local history was concerned with the administration of the hundred and parish rather than the day-to-day life of the community and the street. This was partly because historians, who themselves then belonged to the administering and governing classes, thought that this was what mattered most. They had developed no interest in the point of view of the labourer, unless he was specifically troublesome; nor – being men – would they have wished to inquire into the changing life experiences of women. But even if they had wished to write a different kind of history, it would have been far from easy, for the raw material from which history was written, the documents, had been kept or destroyed by people with the same priorities. The more personal, local, and unofficial a document, the less likely it was to survive. The very power structure worked as a great recording machine shaping the past in its own image.

This has remained true even after the establishment of local record offices. Registers of births and marriages, minutes of councils and the administration of poor relief and welfare, national and local newspapers, schoolteachers' log books – legal records of all kinds are kept in quantity; very often there are also church archives and accounts and other books from large private firms and landed estates, and even private correspondence from the ruling land-owner class. But of the innumerable postcards, letters, diaries, and ephemera of working-class men and women, or the papers of small businesses like corner shops or hill farmers, for example, very little has been preserved anywhere.

Consequently, even as the scope of history has widened, the original political and administrative focus has remained. Where ordinary people have been brought in, it has been generally as statistical aggregates derived from some earlier administrative investigation. Thus economic history is constructed around three types of source: aggregate rates of wages, prices, and unemployment; national and international political interventions into the economy and the information which arises from these; and studies of particular trades and industries, depending on the bigger and more successful firms for records of individual enterprises. Similarly, labour history for long consisted of studies on the one hand of the relationship between the working classes and the state in general, and on the other of particular but essentially institutional accounts of trade unions and working-class political organizations; and, inevitably, it is the larger and more successful organizations which normally leave records or commission their own histories. Social history has remained especially concerned with legislative and administrative developments like the rise of the welfare state; or with aggregate data such as population size, birth rates, age at marriage, household and family structure. And among more recent historical specialisms, demography has been almost exclusively concerned with aggregates; the history of the family, despite some ambitious but ill-judged attempts to break through to a history of emotion and feeling, has tended to follow the lines of conventional social history; while at least until quite recently women's history has to a remarkable extent focused on the political struggle for civil equality, and above all for the vote.

There are, of course, important exceptions in each of these fields, which show that different approaches are possible even with the existing sources. And there is a remarkable amount of unexploited personal and ordinary information even in official records – such as court documents – which can be used in new ways. The continuing pattern of historical writing probably reflects the priorities of the majority of the profession – even if no longer of the ruling class itself – in an age of bureaucracy, state power, science, and statistics. Nevertheless, it remains true that to write any other kind of history from documentary sources remains a very difficult task, requiring special ingenuity. It is indicative of the situation that E.P. Thompson's *The Making of the English Working Class* (1963) and James Hinton's *The First Shop*

Steward's Movement (1973) each depended to a large extent on reports by paid government informers, in the early nineteenth century and First World War respectively. When socialist historians are reduced to writing history from the records of government spies, the constraints imposed are clearly extreme. We cannot, alas, interview tombstones, but at least for the First World War period and back into the late nineteenth century, the use of oral history immediately provides a rich and varied source for the creative historian.

In the most general sense, once the life experience of people of all kinds can be used as its raw material, a new dimension is given to history. Oral history provides a source quite similar in character to published autobiography, but much wider in scope. The overwhelming majority of published autobiographies are from a restricted group of political, social, and intellectual leaders, and even when the historian is lucky enough to find an autobiography from the particular place, time, and social group which he happens to need, it may well give little or no attention to the point at issue. Oral historians, by contrast, may choose precisely whom to interview and what to ask about. The interview will provide, too, a means of discovering written documents and photographs which would not have otherwise been traced. The confines of the scholar's world are no longer the well-thumbed volumes of the old catalogue. Oral historians can think now as if they themselves were publishers: imagine what evidence is needed, seek it out and capture it.

For most existing kinds of history, probably the critical effect of this new approach is to allow evidence from a new direction. The historian of working-class politics can juxtapose the statements of the government or the trade union headquarters with the voice of the rank and file – both apathetic and militant. There can be no doubt that this should make for a more realistic reconstruction of the past. Reality is complex and many-sided; and it is a primary merit of oral history that to a much greater extent than most sources it allows the original multiplicity of standpoints to be recreated. But this advantage is important not just for the writing of history. Most historians make implicit or explicit judgements – quite properly, since the social purpose of history demands an understanding of the past which relates directly or indirectly to the present. Modern professional historians are less open with their social message than Macaulay or Marx, since scholarly standards are seen to conflict with declared bias. But the social message is usually present, however obscured. It is quite easy for a historian to give most of his attention and quotations to those social leaders whom he admires, without giving any direct opinion of his own. Since the nature of most existing records is to reflect the standpoint of authority, it is not surprising that the judgement of history has more often than not vindicated the wisdom of the powers that be. Oral history by contrast makes a much fairer trial possible: witnesses can now also be called from the under-classes, the unprivileged, and the defeated. It provides a more realistic and fair reconstruction of the past, a challenge to the established account. In so doing, oral history has radical implications for the social message of history as a whole.

At the same time oral history implies for most kinds of history some shift of focus. Thus the educational historian becomes concerned with the experiences of children and students as well as the problems of teachers and administrators. The military and naval historian can look beyond command level strategy and equipment to the conditions, recreations, and morale of other ranks and the lower deck. The social historian can turn from bureaucrats and politicians to poverty itself, and learn how the poor saw the relieving officer and how they survived his refusals. The political historian can approach the voter at home and at work; and can hope to understand even the working-class conservative, who produced no newspapers or organizations for investigation. The economist can watch both employer and worker as social beings and at their ordinary work, and so come closer to understanding the typical economic process, and its successes and contradictions.

In some fields, oral history can result not merely in a shift in focus, but also in the opening up of important new areas of inquiry. Labour historians, for example, are enabled for the first time to undertake effective studies of the ill-unionized majority of male workers, of women workers, and of the normal experience of work and its impact on the family and the community. They are no longer confined to those trades which were unionized, or those which gained contemporary publicity and investigation because of strikes or extreme poverty. Urban historians similarly can turn from well-explored problem areas like the slums to look at other typical forms of urban social life; the small industrial or market town, for example, or the middle-class surburb, constructing the local patterns of social distinctions, mutual help between neighbours and kin, leisure and work. They can even approach from the inside the history of immigrant groups – a kind of history which is certain to become more important in Britain, and is mainly documented only from outside as a social problem. These opportunities – and many others – are shared by social historians: the study of working-class leisure and culture, for example; or of crime from the point of view of the ordinary, often undetected and socially semi-tolerated poacher, shoplifter, or work-pilferer.

Perhaps the most striking feature of all, however, is the transforming impact of oral history upon the history of the family. Without its evidence, the historian can discover very little indeed about either the ordinary family's contacts with neighbours and kin, or its internal relationships. The roles of husband and wife, the upbringing of girls and boys, emotional and material conflicts and dependence, the struggle of youth for independence, courtship, sexual behaviour within and outside marriage, contraception and abortion – all these were effectively secret areas. The only clues were to be gleaned from aggregate statistics, and from a few – usually partial – observers. The historical paucity which results is well summed up in Michael Anderson's brilliant, speculative, but abstract study of *Family Structure in Nineteenth-Century Lancashire* (1971): a lop-sided, empty frame. With the use of interviewing, it is now possible to develop a much fuller history of the family over the last ninety years, and to establish its main patterns and changes over time, and from place to place, during the life cycle and between the sexes. The history of childhood as a whole becomes practicable for the first time. And given the dominance of the family through housework, domestic service, and mother-hood in the lives of most women, an almost equivalent broadening of scope is brought to the history of women.

In all these fields of history, by introducing new evidence from the under-side, by shifting the focus and opening new areas of inquiry, by challenging some of the assumptions and accepted judgements of historians, by bringing recognition to substantial groups of people who had been ignored, a cumula-tive process of transformation is set in motion. The scope of historical writ-ing itself is enlarged and enriched; and at the same time its social message changes. History becomes, to put it simply, more democratic. The chronicle of kings has taken into its concern the life experience of ordinary people. But there is another dimension to this change, of equal importance. The process of writing history changes along with the content. The use of oral evidence breaks through the barriers between the chroniclers and their audience; between the educational institution and the outside world.

This change springs from the essentially creative and co-operative nature of the oral history method. Of course oral evidence once recorded can be used by lone scholars in libraries just like any other type of documentary source. But to be content with this is to lose a key advantage of the method: its flexibility, the ability to pin down evidence just where it is needed. Once historians start to interview they find themselves inevitably working with others – at the least, with their informants. And to be a successful interviewer a new set of skills is needed, including an understanding of human relation-ships. Some people can find these skills almost immediately, others need to learn them; but in contrast to the cumulative process of learning and amass-ing information which gives such advantage in documentary analysis and interpretation to the professional historian well on in life, it is possible to learn quite quickly to become an effective interviewer. Hence historians as field-workers, while in important respects retaining the advantages of profes-sional knowledge, also find themselves off their desk, sharing experience on a human level. [. . .]

The co-operative nature of the oral history approach has led to a radical questioning of the fundamental relationship between history and the com-munity. Historical information need not be taken away from the community for interpretation and presentation by the professional historian. Through oral history the community can, and should, be given the confidence to write its own history.

[. . .] oral historians have travelled a long way from their original aim – and there is, undoubtedly, some danger of conflict between the two. On the level of the interview itself, for example, there have been telling criticisms of a relationship with informants in which a middle-class professional determines who is to be interviewed and what is to be discussed and then disappears with a tape of somebody's life which they never hear about again – and if they did, might be indignant at the unintended meanings imposed on their words. There are clear social advantages in the contrasting ideal of a self-selected group, or an open public meeting, which focuses on equal discussion and encourages local publication of its results; and of individual recording sessions which are conversations rather than directed interviews. But there are also drawbacks in the alternative.

The self-selected group will rarely be fully representative of a community. It is much more likely to be composed from its central groups – people from a skilled working-class or lower middle-class background. The local upper class will rarely be there, nor will the very poor, the less confident especially among women, or the immigrant from its racial minority. A truer and socially more valuable form of local oral history will be created when these other groups are drawn in. Its publications will be much more telling if they can juxtapose, for example, the mistress with the domestic servant, or a millowner with the millworkers. It will then reveal the variety of social experience in the community, the groups which had the better or the worse of it – and perhaps lead to a consideration of what might be done about it. Local history drawn from a more restricted social stratum tends to be more complacent, a re-enactment of community myth. This certainly needs to be recorded and a self-sufficient local group which can do this is undoubtedly helping many others besides itself. But for the radical historian it is hardly sufficient. History should not merely comfort; it should provide a challenge, and understanding which helps towards change. For this the myth needs to become dynamic. It has to encompass the complexities of conflict. And for the historian who wishes to work and write as a socialist, the task must be not simply to celebrate the working class as it is, but to raise its consciousness. There is no point in replacing a conservative myth of upper-class wisdom with a lower-class one. A history is required which leads to action: not to confirm, but to change the world.

In principle there is no reason why local projects should not have such an object, while at the same time continuing to encourage self-confidence and the writing of history from within the community. Most groups will normally contain some members with more historical experience. They certainly need to use tact; to undervalue rather than emphasize their advantage. But it is everybody's loss in the long run if they disown it: their contribution should be to help the group towards a wider perspective. Similar observations apply in the recording session where the essential need is mutual respect. A superior, dominating attitude does not make for a good interview anyway. The oral historian has to be a good listener, the informant an active helper. As George Ewart Evans puts it – 'although the old survivors were walking books, I could not just leaf them over. They were persons.'[1] And so are historians. They have come for a purpose, to get information, and if ultimately ashamed of this they should not have come at all. A historian who just engages in haphazard reminiscence will collect interesting pieces of information, but will throw away the chance of winning the critical evidence for the structure of historical argument and interpretation.

The relationship between history and the community should not be one-sided in either direction: but rather a series of exchanges, a dialectic, between information and interpretation, between educationists and their localities, between classes and generations. There will be room for many kinds of oral history and it will have many different social consequences. But at bottom they are all related.

Oral history is a history built around people. It thrusts life into history itself and it widens its scope. It allows heroes not just from the leaders, but from the unknown majority of the people. It encourages teachers and students to become fellow-workers. It brings history into, and out of, the community. It helps the less privileged, and especially the old, towards dignity and self-confidence. It makes for contact – and thence understanding – between social classes, and between generations. And to individual historians and others, with shared meanings, it can give a sense of belonging to a place or in time. In short it makes for fuller human beings. Equally, oral history offers a challenge to the accepted myths of history, to the authoritarian judgement inherent in its tradition. It provides a means for radical transformation of the social meaning of history.

NOTE

1 *Oral History*, 1973, vol. 1, no. 4, p. 57.

3   Oral history and *Hard Times*

A review essay

Michael Frisch

Michael Frisch lectures in History and American Studies at the State University of New York, Buffalo. Reprinted from *Oral History Review*, 1979, vol. 7, pp. 70–79, by permission of the Oral History Association. Originally published in *Red Buffalo*, 1972, vol. 1, nos. 2/3.

Studs Terkel's book, *Hard Times*, is subtitled *An Oral History of the Great Depression*, and it offers a good base for exploring a number of problems inherent in doing, reading, and thinking about oral history, and for understanding why these problems matter. It is, perhaps, appropriate to the topic to begin with some comments about this paper's own genesis and history.

Hard Times is a massive compilation of more than 150 self-portraits of American lives – culled from hundreds more – centred on the experience of the 1930s. The interviews were conducted, edited, and arranged by Studs Terkel, the remarkable Chicago radio personality whose special gift for getting all sorts of people to talk about themselves was so profoundly demonstrated in *Division Street: America*. The people of *Hard Times* range widely, from New Deal officials and famous businessmen and artists to anonymous farmers, workers, and plain people. Terkel also includes a number of interviews with young people who can, of course, only talk about the Depression in terms of what they have read or been told, and who therefore enable us to see the book's topic in terms of received memory as well as given. To read through the enormous range of personality and experience presented in the book is to encounter, in a sort of multimedia exposure, the depth and drama of life in the Depression. As has virtually every other reader, I found it moving, poignant, intense, human, and instructive.

Shortly after a first reading, I noticed that the cover of my paperback edition said, in a blurb from *Newsweek*, 'It will resurrect your faith in all of us to read this book.' The inside front cover, quoting *Saturday Review*, called the book 'A huge anthem in praise of the American Spirit.' These intrigued me considerably, because I found the book more depressing than anything else in its overall implications. It had all the moving force of life, I felt, which is why it could so profoundly suggest the Depression's destructive impact on the lives people lived, the personalities that emerged, and on the abilities individuals retained to understand what was happening to them. Rather than 'resurrecting my faith in all of us', the book seemed to show why Americans find it so hard to examine their culture and institutions critically, even when massive breakdowns make such examination imperative. And it seemed an anthem in praise of the American Spirit only in the sense of showing the tremendous self-preservative power of a threatened culture, as revealed in and through people whose experiences posed fundamental threats to the society's premises. Perhaps I should not have been surprised at the book's inspiring such different readings, but the contrast suggested that something more was at work than simply a difference of politics or perspective. I went back to the book, and to the full reviews, in order to see whether they contained more fundamental questions, questions about what oral history has to teach and about how, as a particular form of history, it can be read or misread.

The text of reviews in *Time*, *Newsweek*, *Saturday Review*, the *New Yorker*, the *Nation*, and the *New York Review of Books* indicates the paperback blurbs were not unrepresentative. With only two exceptions, which I address shortly, the critics saw the vitality and struggle and life so apparent in the interviews as emblematic of America itself; they located the book's inspirational quality in the 'startling decency' of its people, and the capacity of their comments to connect us with deep cultural sources of redemptive, transcending energy. In the *New Yorker*, for example, L.E. Sissman calls *Hard Times* 'a folk-song composed by American voices to celebrate and commemorate the 1930s', a song which has its center in 'a sense of solidarity in adversity, a willingness to reach out to others, an ability to see others not as households of accreted possessions but as naked human beings. In the birth of that paradoxical nation was the rebirth of some elemental historical principles: truth, justice, and equality.'

Beyond the repeated litany of inspiration, one is struck by how the reviewers so inspired seem to share a particular notion of the nature of the book, almost apart from its contents and meaning. In the first place, they treat the interviews as reflecting a distant and discrete historical phenomenon, as being literally evidential of the 1930s, with the critic's job being the provision of a contrastive, contemporary perspective. This explains why the particular atmosphere of 1970 figures so centrally in the reviews. The fragment from Henry Resnick's piece in the *Saturday Review*, quoted earlier, reads in full: 'Americans have little reason to be proud of their country these days, but in *Hard Times* Studs Terkel has given us what amounts to a huge anthem in praise of the American Spirit. [It has] an almost mythic quality.' Faced with 'the hopelessness and squalor of contemporary life', he said, we need the book to 'put us back in touch with our elemental humanity'. The sources of this need are suggested by the way the critics generally understood Terkel's conversations with young people. Rather than taking these as illustrating the complex process of historical memory and generational transfer, they saw them only as revealing the character of the young people themselves. Writing in a year of protest, of Kent State and Cambodia, Geoffrey Wolf in *Newsweek* thus discovered the 'startling decency' of Terkel's people in relation to the arrogance and insensitivity he reads in contemporary youth, and he observed acidly that 'memory is long, but curiosity is not'.

There are other senses in which the critical comments imply a common view of *Hard Times* and, by extension, oral history. It is revealing, for example, to observe that critics so concerned with the relevance of the book for the present generally ignore the fact that the interviews were conducted only recently; the people who spoke to Terkel so movingly of the past were also trying to live in and understand the 1960s. Thus the basic historicality of the interviews – the degree to which they involve historical statements rather than, or in addition to, historical evidence – was barely alluded to in the reviews being considered. In fact, rather than exploring the oral testimonies as forms of history the tendency was to perceive them as something of a counterhistorical way of understanding the past. The critics described the book in terms of literature rather than history, comparing it frequently to Oscar Lewis and Truman Capote. Resnick's article even saw Terkel as challenging the hegemony of history as a form of knowledge, predicting that 'dedication to the truth as fact will be supported by more and more historians as the fundamentals of historiography encounter increasing threats in the form of books like *Hard Times*'.

The critics, this suggests, understand the book as history mainly in the sense of telling it 'like it was'. 'As history the book may be weak on the why', observed *Time*, 'but it can hardly be matched by any scholarly work in giving a sense of what it was like at that time'. Thus oral history enables us to see history, according to this view, as more or less direct and unmediated experience, rather than as the abstracted and ordered rendering of objective historical intelligence.

Two reviews in the batch did not share this notion of oral history, and significantly, these were the only two that did not find the book a confirmation and celebration of the American spirit and character. In the *New Yorker*, Murray Kempton focused on the variable relation people could have to their own experience in the past – 'who noticed what was happening and who didn't' – and what has happened to this sense over time. Exploring the gap between what was felt and what was said in the interview, he sought to locate the controlling level of experience where many levels exist simultaneously and are selectively remembered. He concluded that the Depression 'did not teach us what it should have . . . there is a gaiety in these recollections which ought to have been more transfiguring yet wasn't', and he tried to explore why. Nelson Algren, writing in the *Nation*, looked even more closely at the speakers themselves, rather than at the content of their recollections, and concluded that 'the author has provided us with a definitive report on the psychological recoil of a generation that suffered a failure of nerve'.

The contrast among the reviews confirmed for me the notion that reading oral history depends, more than in most historical writing, on the deeper assumptions one has about the nature of the evidence and the form. Because most of the critics seem at least partially to have misconstrued *Hard Times* owing to an uncritical approach to the book's method, it appeared that one good way to get more deeply into the book might be to look at its historical nature, rather than its content per se. Therefore, I propose to use *Hard Times* as a way of demonstrating the need for a more self-conscious and reflective sense of the nature of oral history, what it has to teach, and what questions the reader is obligated to bring to it. That this perspective leads to a more critically analytic view of cultural processes than does one which sees oral history as direct experience is, I hope to show, far from coincidental.

The discussion so far would reduce to a simple truism were it not for a compelling paradox: oral history is of such self-evident importance and interest that it has proven difficult for people to take it very seriously. By this I mean that those interested in history, culture, and politics have responded so intuitively to recent work in oral history that they have not generally stopped to think about what it is, on levels beyond the obvious, that makes it so worth pursuing. In part, this is because proponents of oral history, particularly in America, are somewhat prisoners of its own methodological past.

In quasi-formal terms, American oral history came into its own through Allan Nevins's project at Columbia University, the main focus of which was on political and diplomatic history, and the main work of which was the 'debriefing' of the Great Men before they passed on. Its nature was explicitly archival, informational, and elitist. This work has profoundly shaped recent interest in oral history, although in a largely negative and reactive way: critics saw the focus on great decisionmakers as a part of the traditional bias toward the articulate and powerful, and calls for history 'from the bottom up' found a swift focus in oral history, a form that seemed to fit the object of transcending evidential biases that sustained the elitist perspective. However, while the bottom-up approach seems to promise generically different insights for oral history – by exploring, for example, common shared experiences in preference to individualized and unique actions – these have not yet generated a really clear sense of any special nature and role for oral history. To the extent that oral history has produced such a sense, it has come in work on traditional and folk societies and centers on a view of oral tradition as a distinct type of historical thinking and transference. But in Western society, where culture is so penetrated by literacy, communication, and self-consciousness as to make such notions of oral tradition of dubious application, oral history has not gone much beyond the traditional focus of historical work.

Accordingly, most of us have casually assumed that oral history does one of two things, or perhaps both. First, it functions as a source of historical information and insights, to be used, in traditional ways, in the formulation of historical generalizations and narratives. In this sense, the oral method and the interest in the inarticulate do swing the flashlight of history into a significant, much neglected, and previously unknowable corner of the attic, but they still assume a more traditional sense of the object and nature of explanation. On the other hand, oral history can be understood as a way of bypassing historical interpretation itself, avoiding all the attendant elitist and contextual dangers. It seems to provide a way to communicate with the past more directly, to be presented with a somehow purer image of direct experience.

The prevailing choices can thus be concisely understood as that of 'more history' or, in that special sense, 'no history'. It is risky to associate these leanings with particular positions of other spectrums: Allan Nevins and Staughton Lynd, for example, share the sense of the informational and archival purposes of oral history, while, as we have just seen, conservative journalists are just as likely to take the 'pure experience' position as are radicals who might more usually be expected to endorse it as a way of demystifying and reclaiming from historians the experience of the people. In any event, 'more' or 'no' history seem to represent the poles between which the common notion of oral history hangs in a state of vagueness. Having said this, I wish to return to *Hard Times*, because in spite of its friendly critics, I think it can be seen as outlining a way to transcend these categories, and a way to discover the role for oral history in modern society.

Studs Terkel suggests this in the book's first sentence. 'This is a memory book, rather than one of hard fact and precise statistic', he writes. In prefatory notes, he muses more personally on this theme: the book is 'about Time as well as a time', he says: 'heroes and dragons of a long-gone day were old men, some vigorous, some weary, when I last saw them. Some have died'. And in the introduction he quotes Steinbeck's Pa Joad as saying 'He's tellin' the truth, awright. The truth for him. He wasn't making nothin' up.' Adds Terkel, referring to the people of *Hard Times*, 'in their rememberings are their truths'. From the start, then, Terkel distances the book from the kinds of oral history discussed so far. Were we searching either for information or a pure sense of how it 'really' was, both the intense subjectivity of his form and the thirty-year lag would disqualify the interviews from being taken seriously.

But Terkel is clearly not apologizing; rather, he is suggesting that these factors are the strength and uniqueness of the book, in that they force us to look at what the interviews actually represent, rather than at what they can not claim to be. In these terms, the question of memory – personal and historical, individual, and generational – moves to center stage as the object, not merely the method, of oral history. The questions that emerge can be thought of in the following general forms, focused on process and change: What happens to experience on the way to becoming memory? What happens to experience on the way to becoming history? As an era of intense collective experience recedes into the past, what is the relationship of memory to historical generalization? These questions, so basic to thinking about how culture and individuality interact over time, are the sort of questions that oral history is peculiarly, perhaps uniquely, able to penetrate.

The best way to show this is to indicate how many different things are going on in the book, how many different methods the interviews suggest for studying how experience, memory, and history act on lives over time. In somewhat schematic form, the interviews with young people can represent one end of the spectrum of possibilities: here, the Depression takes the form of pure and abstracted memory, wildly subjective and selective. An interview with Christopher Lasch holds down the other end, for he speaks as the abstracted voice of professional history, generalizing with calm confidence and cool breadth about the painful experience bubbling through the surrounding pages. Pure memory, then, with all its faults, and pure history, with all its limitations. All the other interviews lie somewhere between, and accordingly require the most careful reading.

To this end, I suggest three questions that can help in exploring the complexity of the interviews. What sort of person is speaking? What sort of thing is he or she talking about? What sort of statements about it are being made? The range of possible answers to each of these can serve as axes for mapping the territory between the poles, for sensing the possible combinations in which people relate and integrate the dimensions of past and present experience.

Who is speaking? Intuitively, most of us are primarily sensitive to the social class or status of the speaker, particularly if our interest is in oral history's ability to work from the bottom up. Perhaps more important, however, is the way the speaker functioned historically, in relation to the overall experience with which the book is concerned. Some of Terkel's people speak of private and anonymous lives, historical in their generality rather than their particularity. Others, however, were more precisely 'actors' in historically visible forums, and their subjectivity thus has important public and self-conscious dimensions. Generally, this spectrum of private and public experience and subjectivity parallels the spectrum of power and position, but with important exceptions: rich people who lived quite privately and unselfconsciously; labor organizers, workingmen, and a remarkable revivalist preacher whose proletarian experience is rooted to a major extent in a public dimension well beyond their own subjectivity.

What is being talked about? Responses can be crudely sorted out according to the way they deal with things actually experienced as opposed to things observed at some remove, or experienced in only the most general terms. What this implies is a more complicated spectrum of particularity and generality, ranging from detailed anecdotal reporting of personal incidents, to the abstracted discussion of general conditions and experiences. In these terms, the interviews show no categorical relationship to the social nature of the speakers – powerful politicians are as likely to give a heavily anecdotal account as are barely literate workers to generalize freely about 'how it was' at some time, and vice versa. Interviews with two psychiatrists show in a different way what this concern means. One looks back and discusses his practice, his problems, his professional activity, and his personal perspective as seen through his work. The other discusses the psychic patterns he found himself facing in his patients and generalizes about their significance. Both interviews offer insights into the men and the Depression, yet they are quite different examples of the 'evidence' oral history can produce, and they need to be understood, qualified, and digested in different ways.

What are they saying about it? This has to do with the sorts of statements people make; it seems to me the most problematic and yet the most crucial category. At what distance, in what ways, for what reasons, and in what patterns do people generalize, explain, and interpret experience? What cultural and historical categories do individuals use to help understand and present a view of experience? How are we to understand the variable weave of pure recall and reflective synthesis – historical statements as well as historical information – that characterize almost all of the interviews? All these may sound like very abstract matters, but together with the other questions I think they form the core of Terkel's 'memory book', and lie close to the source of its enormous energy. By showing people trying to make sense of their lives at a variety of points in time and in a variety of ways, by opening this individual process to view, the oral history reveals patterns and choices that, taken together, begin to define the reinforcing and screening apparatus of the general culture, and the ways in which it encourages us to digest experience.

The perspective afforded by the questions I have suggested helps clarify the substantive lessons of the book, and Terkel notes some of these explicitly. (It is again significant to note that his own clues were apparently uninteresting to critics who had little sensitivity to the complexity of his method.) Despite the systemic and general nature of the Depression – more precisely because of it, of course – people tended to view their problems in atomized, alienating ways. Shame, a sense of personal failure, unavoidable obsession with personal concerns, paralytic insecurity in several dimensions – all these are repeatedly described as the predominant personal responses. Translated somewhat, this can be understood as the perception of collective, historical experience in the form of idiosyncratic personal experience, with all the attendant psychic scarring, searing memory, and sense of crushing responsibility. Anyone who has wondered why the Depression crisis did not produce more focused critiques of American capitalism and culture, more sustained efforts to see fundamental structural change, will find more evidence in the interior of these testimonies than in any other source I know. By seeing people turn history into biographical memory, general into particular, we see how they tried to retain deeper validation of their life and society, and how they deferred the deeper cultural judgment implied by the Depression crisis.

The interviews also show these dynamics remaining central to the way the people live with their history over time. The further the generalizations are located from the crisis itself – people reflecting about it, rather than remembering how they thought about it themselves – the greater the tendency to present the past experience in a variety of romanticized modes. Having never been well-connected with the history, memory continues to function as a creator of distance, not merely as an expression of it. The interviews with youth show this most directly, for their hazy sense of the Depression owes much to what their parents have not remembered and have not told them. But far more than fading memory is involved here. As many of the young people say, and as most of the interviews confirm, current realities have affected the transferal process crucially, just as they influenced the views of the journalists discussed earlier. Contemporary pressures and sensitivities encourage people to screen their memories in a selective, protective, and above all didactic fashion. Sometimes this comes across as a moving tribute to the pain of living, sometimes as a desperate weapon in what has been called 'the shootout at generation gap'. But whatever their tone, and whatever their limits as history in traditional terms, these responses are fascinating in what they reveal about historical memory patterns as cultural documents themselves.

Contemporary contexts, in this sense, operate as a sort of rearguard attack on the structure of memory, and the needs of validation begin to work in a way paradoxically inverse to their effects on the understanding of initial experience. Failure forced people to reduce general experiences to personal terms, the intense pain thereby sheltering them from deeper, more profoundly threatening historical truths; survival, however, seems to encourage them to elevate personal and biographical generalization into historical terms, at once a self-validating message and a culturally validating legacy for the next generations. The 'real' history has thus been doubly filtered by time and subsequent experience before it reaches Terkel's tape recorder, and contradictions of the culture are thus doubly masked.

These comments just begin to suggest ways in which the interviews can be studied for insights into cultural and historical processes. The crucial point is the centrality of the dimensions these questions locate, to the understanding of oral history, particularly in a self-conscious advanced society. Rather than the 'more history' or the 'no history' discussed earlier, this approach promises unique insights that are profoundly historical in a somewhat special sense. By studying how experience, memory, and history become combined in and digested by people who are the bearers of their own history and that of their culture, oral history opens up a powerful perspective; it encourages us to stand somewhat outside of cultural forms in order to observe their workings. Thus it permits us to track the elusive beats of consciousness and culture in a way impossible to do within, and this, I think, is at the heart of the variant readings of *Hard Times* with which this chapter began.

To develop this critical perspective, to look for significance on this level of oral history, is to argue that the medium of the retrospective biography is in some ways its message. But only implicitly. Perhaps the greatest danger in modern historical studies is the fascination with new methodology, which makes exciting new forms of evidence seem to exhibit self-evident and unequivocal significance. More careful work in most areas, however, quickly shows that the questions to be asked are by no means obvious, the uses of the materials by no means self-evident, and the results to be obtained by no means necessarily meaningful. What matters, rather, are the insights and questions that the historian brings. The same is just beginning to be realized about oral history. Although it is so tempting to take historical testimony to be history itself, a tendency reinforced by the discomfort intellectuals feel at being intellectuals, the very documents of oral history really suggest a very different lesson. To the extent that *Hard Times* is any example, the interviews are nearly unanimous in showing the selective, synthetic, and generalizing nature of historical memory itself. And far from being restricted to the histor-ian's study, these capacities are shown to be not only present, but central in the way we all order our experience and understand the meaning of our lives. There seems to be no reason why, in order to decipher the meaning of mem-ory, historians should feel uncomfortable about applying the same reflective, generalizing intelligence to the documents of oral history.

4 Movement without aim

Methodological and theoretical problems in oral history

Ronald J. Grele

Ronald J. Grele is Director of the Columbia University Oral History Research Office. Extracted from R.J. Grele, *Envelopes of Sound: The Art of Oral History*, Chicago, Precedent Publishing, 1985 (original edition, 1975), pp. 127–154, by permission of Greenwood Publishing Group Inc., Westport, Conn., USA.

During the past ten years the collection of oral testimony as an ancillary technique of historical study has expanded rapidly. Both in terms of number of persons interviewed and number of projects established, the growth of what is rather loosely called 'oral history' has been steadily accelerating.[1] So too has its reputation, if the report of the American Historical Association committee on the state of the AHA and its recommendations are taken as an example of opinion in the profession at large.[2] Despite this growth and the evidence that more and more historians are using the oral history interview in their own work, there has been little serious discussion of oral history by historians. The dominant tendency has been to be overly enthusiastic in public print, and deeply suspicious in private conversation. Neither attitude speaks directly to the issues which should be raised by the use of oral interviewing for historical purposes.

Examples of the historian's enthusiasm for oral history abound. Typical of this reaction were the reviews of Studs Terkel's *Hard Times* and Professor T. Harry Williams' biography of Huey Long.[3] The praise of such works, while in many ways justified, also contains a lack of perspective because, as Michael Frisch notes in the most thoughtful review of *Hard Times* that I have found, 'oral history is of such self-evident importance and interest that it has proven difficult for people to take it seriously'. By this Frisch means

> that those interested in history, culture and politics have responded so intuitively to recent work in oral history that they have not generally stopped to think about what it is, on levels beyond the obvious, that makes it so worth pursuing.[4]

Despite this uncritical acceptance of the results of the use of oral testimony, there is evidence of skepticism about and doubt and distrust of oral history among professional historians – those paid to write and teach history. Surfacing only occasionally, these doubts are institutionalized within the profession in the organization and conventions of our practice. Few history departments either teach or encourage field work in oral interviewing or oral history. Few departments are willing to accept either the financial or intellectual responsibilities of oral history projects. More telling is the fact that while the collection and editing of manuscripts or personal correspondence has long been considered a legitimate task both for Ph.D. candidates and established scholars, no history department that I know of would grant a doctorate to one of its students in return for the submission of a set of thoroughly documented and well-conducted oral histories, and few historians would receive wide applause for the publication of carefully edited interviews such as is regularly done in other disciplines. In short, what the profession is saying is that oral history is not a respected practice of history.

This attitude is neither new nor unique. In a period of declining job opportunities, historians have taken a very limited view of their professional domain. 'Had Clio's inspiration been sufficient, we would have now but one social scientific discipline. Its name would be history.'[5] This has not, however, been the case. Historians have allowed the training of librarians, archivists, and bibliographers to pass by default to others. And so it has been with oral history – snubbed by the profession, oral historians have, for the most part, turned to librarians and archivists for support and sustenance. They, in turn, have been much more hospitable,[6] thus of course reinforcing the suspicions of most historians who, with the best intentions in the world, cannot conceive of librarians and archivists as significant initiators of serious scholarship.

Some of the professional historians' doubts about oral history do surface occasionally when historians are called upon to evaluate such works as the interviews of historians conducted by Professors Garraty and Cantor.[7] These criticisms are however usually too gentlemanly and rarely ask questions about the methodological limits of oral history, even where one would expect it. Professors Cantor and Garraty, in their interviews, have shown little regard for the interviewing techniques developed by other disciplines such as anthropology, sociology, folklore, or even of industrial relations. They and others do tend to ask the same ill prepared and badly formulated questions with surprising regularity. As for *Hard Times*, one must question the editing techniques used by Terkel, his cryptic questions and the nature of the historical memories of his informants. As Terkel himself notes, his work is not history but memory, and he is searching not for fact, but the truth behind the fact. Such distinctions raise serious theoretical problems which have not, in the main, been addressed by professional historians. There are also major questions to be raised about such works as that of Professor Williams, which rely so heavily upon documents which will be unavailable for alternative readings by other scholars for years to come.

To be fair, it must be noted that among a few historians, serious concern about these issues has been raised. William Cutler of Temple University has been particularly articulate in warning oral historians about the vagaries of memory and in questioning some of our basic assumptions about the effect of cultural milieu and other influences on the validity of oral testimony.[8] Charles Morrissey, Gould Colman and Saul Benison have continually accented the need for scholarly standards for oral history and have raised other serious methodological questions.[9]

Despite these warnings and the public approval given to them, oral history has in a large part remained cursed, in the words of Gershon Legman's critique of folklore, with an 'endless doodling with insignificant forms and [an] ignorance of meaning to the people who transmit material'.[10] The quality of oral history interviews varies too widely, as even a cursory examination of the now available Columbia University Oral History Office materials reveals (although this harsh criticism must be tempered by a reminder that Columbia is one of the few oral history projects which has attempted to make its interviews widely available). Few oral historians are forced to submit their work to public criticism. Many interviewers are poorly trained and far too many are willing to settle for journalistic standards of usefulness. In many projects, much too little time is devoted to the research necessary to prepare for an interview. Oral historians are still prone to rush out and ask how it happened without spending the arduous months plowing through related written materials. Worse yet, their sponsors often encourage this attitude and practice. There is much room for speculation about the reliability of the products of such activities.

In this situation, the professional historian has had little to offer in the way of constructive criticism. Eight years ago, Donald Swain noted the 'need for . . . greater attention to the problems of oral history on the part of practicing historians'.[11] Little has been done to answer that need. As noted earlier, historians have not raised the pertinent historiographical questions about oral history when dealing with major works using the technique. In most cases, they have simply turned their responsibilities over to others and hoped for the best, and when they have offered criticism or comment, their remarks have usually been informed by a myopic paper or book fetishism, inadequate definitions of their own standards of judgement, and a hostility towards and reluctance to understand other social science disciplines.[12]

Generally the criticisms that have so far been leveled at oral history can be classified into three categories; interviewing, research standards for preparation, and questions of historical methodology. The oral historian should be able to deal with the first set of these criticisms rather easily, for there is an already adequate bibliography and an already existent body of knowledge concerning interviewing and questioning techniques available to those interested.[13] While much of the literature may not prepare the interviewer for the almost confessional nature and the various other responses engendered in the open interview, as Richard Sennett and Jonathan Cobb note,[14] there is no reason why an interviewer, if well prepared, cannot gain control over these techniques.

The second category of problems, those centering on research standards, can be met most forcibly simply by insisting that the highest standards of research and training be expected of oral historians. These are problems faced by all historians and the same canons of practice should apply. Sources should be checked, documentation should be provided, evidence must be weighed carefully. In this sense, oral history interviewing does not represent any major deviation from the methodology of other forms of historical research. There is no other solution to this problem, 'except in the exercise of that personal judgement which the historian has to apply to any source of information'.[15] To insure such practice, those historians called upon to review works based on oral histories should insist on a review of the interviews used for documentation.

Questions of method cannot be dismissed so easily. As the most cogent critics have noted, there are real and serious issues to be faced by the practitioners of oral history. Many of these issues are not, however, those specifically noted by historians. When historians claim that oral history interviewees are not statistically representative of the population at large or any particular segment of it,[16] they raise a false issue and thereby obscure a much deeper problem. Interviewees are selected, not because they present some abstract statistical norm, but because they typify historical processes. Thus, the questions to be asked concern the historian's concept of a historical process (i.e.: his own conception of history) and the relevance of the information garnered to that particular process. The real issues are historiographical, not statistical.

Another erroneous caveat of the profession concerns the primacy of written testimony to oral testimony. Oral history, runs the typical argument, 'cannot rank with an authentic diary, with a contemporary stock report, or with an eyewitness account transcribed on the day of the event'. But, we are told, 'it is probably to be ranked above contemporary hearsay evidence'.[17] Not only does this criticism ignore the problems of accuracy faced by historians who use written testimony; it ignores a growing literature on the analysis of oral testimony for historical purposes.[18] The usefulness of any source depends upon the information one is looking for, or the questions one seeks to answer. It is quite possible to argue, as Ruth Finnegan has, that oral testimony or 'literature' has its own characteristics and is not to be understood by the application of literary standards of judgement.[19] In some cases, oral testimony can be more full and accurate than written testimony. For, as Plato noted in regard to works of art, and by extension written documents, 'You would think they were speaking as if they were intelligent, but if you ask them about what they are saying and want to learn [more], they just go on saying one and the same thing forever.'[20] Thus criticisms of oral testimony often miss their mark because they fail to realize that to seriously critique any form, it is necessary to understand precisely what it is one is about to evaluate.

The same qualifications must be applied to those criticisms which question the accuracy of memory or the intrusion of subjective or social biases.[21] It all depends upon the questions one is seeking to answer. A linguist searching for the linguistic range, context and style of the language of ethnic Americans, is interested in a different kind of accuracy than that of a historian.[22] So too health researchers or those interested in sexual behavior.[23] Obviously, the careful interviewer does try, as Cutler suggests, to overcome these problems, yet it should be understood that not all the historical uses of information are covered by the conventional questions of historians.[24]

Important as many of these questions may be, they are still simply questions of method and depend in large part upon a theoretical frame of reference for their meaning and for their answers, and it is at this level that the lack of serious analysis of oral history interviews has had its most deleterious effects. The sad condition of our theoretical knowledge about oral history, and the lack of serious efforts to think through exactly what an oral interview is or should be, how it is to be analyzed, or for what purposes, has resulted in a situation of endless activity without goal or meaning. As a result, oral history has not become a tool for a serious analysis of the culture. It has continued as a movement without aim, with all the attendant problems of such a situation.

The two most significant debates over the nature of oral history are those articulated by Cutler and Benison, and Staughton Lynd and Jesse Lemisch. Since all four have at least tried to grapple with the larger theoretical and historiographical questions raised by interviewing, it is proper here to note the issues they raise. In the first case, Cutler argues that an oral history interview as it exists in final form – a transcript – is 'raw material similar to any other source'.[25] Benison, however, has argued that an oral history is an autobiographical memoir and, duly noting the creative role of the historian-interviewer, sees it as 'a first interpretation, filtered through a particular individual experience at a particular moment of time'. It is, he argues, a first ordering, 'a beginning of interpretation although not an end'.[26] In the second debate, Lynd has argued that oral history is history itself, in the form of an articulating consciousness. Impressed with the very real opportunities offered by oral history for the history of the 'inarticulate', and by the dynamic of the interview situation, he has called for a new, radical use for oral history. In answer, Lemisch takes a more traditional view of an oral history interview as a limited document upon which is constructed a new historical synthesis.[27]

Neither of these discussions has, however, resulted in any serious reformulation of the thinking about oral history among oral historians themselves or others in the profession. Both discussions also center upon a number of questionable assumptions which so far have not been challenged. Cutler and Lemisch, in their view of oral history interviews as sources and documents, seem to have confused these interviews, which are a form of oral testimony, with written manuscript sources. Unlike these traditional sources, oral history interviews are constructed, for better or for worse, by the active intervention of the historian. They are a collective creation and inevitably carry within themselves a pre-existent historical ordering, selection and interpretation. Unlike letters, records, archival materials or other manuscript sources, they are created after the fact, by historians – thus they are very singular documents indeed.

On the other hand, while Benison and Lynd recognize the active role of the historian-interviewer, their analyses suffer from differing, albeit equally limited frames of reference. Benison, as articulate and creative as is his analysis of oral history, is still reluctant to see the interviews as end products complete unto themselves.[28] Still bound by the book fetishism of historical study, Benison does not tell us why the written narrative of a historian with proper footnotes to his interview ranks higher in accuracy or interpretation than the interviews themselves. It may be that, even admitting the excellence of the biography of Huey Long, or the sometimes useful commentary in *The Hidden Injuries of Class* and other works using oral histories, in the long run the interviews themselves will prove much more useful to scholars than the texts grafted upon them.

This is, of course, the most useful of Lynd's insights but unfortunately, by stressing the consciousness-raising potential of the interview, he seems to have confused the moment of presentation with the material presented, and history as process with history as study, discipline or cognitive action. In addition, there would seem to be wide theoretical gaps between interviewing, consciousness and 'praxis' which, for a Marxist especially, have to be articulated more precisely.

For all these reasons, these debates and discussions, while worthwhile and refreshing, have not begun to yield the kind of theoretical introspection which oral history needs. Such introspection must begin with the object at hand – the interview as an end product – what it is and what it should be, for it is only in this framework that we can begin to discuss what kinds of information we are getting, what is it that structures an interview, and how it should be conducted. To initiate a tentative discussion of these points is the aim of the rest of this chapter.

The first question which must be asked, before we can begin the kind of analysis oral history needs, concerns the nature of the end product which is created by the oral historian and his subject – the interview. For reasons already noted, the final product of oral history is not a monograph or historical narrative based upon interviews as sources. The interviews may be used for such work, but all the prideful boasting about how many historians use our work for their own publications should not obscure the fact that the focus of oral history is to record as complete an interview as possible – an interview which contains, within itself, its own system of structures, not a system derived from the narrow conventions of written history.

If this is the case, and I strongly believe it is, we must then try to define rather precisely what the form of the completed interview is. For reasons which Professor Tedlock has already explained, the final form of the interview is not a transcript, no matter how beautifully typed or indexed. Neither is it, except in the most limited of mechanical aspects, a tape, for the tape is simply a reproduction of the verbal (or visual and verbal, if videotape is used) aspects of a particular set of structures or patterns, behind which exists some human relationship.

Given the active participation of the historian-interviewer, even if that participation consists of only a series of gestures or grunts, and given the logical form imposed by all verbal communication, the interview can only be described as a conversational narrative: conversational because of the relationship of interviewer and interviewee, and narrative because of the form of exposition – the telling of a tale.[29]

These narratives, while some may be constructed as chronological tales of personal remembrances of events, are not autobiographies, biographies or memories.[30] The recorded conversations of oral history, it must be repeated, are joint activities, organized and informed by the historical perspectives of both participants and therefore, as Professor Jan Vansina pointed out to me in an earlier conversation in regard to Alex Haley's *Autobiography of Malcolm X*, they are not really autobiographies. No matter what the construction of the narrative, the product we create is a conversational narrative and can only be understood by understanding the various relationships contained within this structure.[31]

The relationships in an oral history interview (conversational narrative) are of three types or sets, one internal and two external.[32] The first unites each element, word or sign to all of the others in the interview. It relates the words to one another to create a whole. It is the linguistic, grammatical, and literary structure of the interview, and while mainly the object so far of a formal linguistic analysis, if read properly, this relationship provides one of the most exciting methods of analysis possible in oral history.[33]

The second set of relationships is that which is created by the interaction of the interviewer and interviewee. Again, as psychologists, sociologists and especially those, like Erving Goffman, who are interested in small group interaction have shown, these relations are also highly structured, and if analyzed properly can add wide dimensions to our understanding of exactly what kind of communication is taking place within the interview and what meaning is being conveyed.[34] Contained within this relationship are those aspects of the interview which can be classified as performance. Since the interview is not created as a literary product is created, alone and as a result of reflective action, it cannot be divorced from the circumstances of its creation, which of necessity is one of audience participation and face to face confrontation.[35] To analyze an oral interview properly as a conversational narrative, we must combine an analysis of the social and psychological relationships between the participants, and their appropriateness to the occasion, with our historical analysis.

The third set of relationships present in the interview is more abstract, less studied, and therefore more elusive to define, although of far more importance to us as historians. When we interview someone, he not only speaks to himself and to the interviewer, but he also speaks through the interviewer to the larger community and its history as he views it. This is a dialogue, the exact nature of which is difficult to define. There are seemingly two relationships contained in one – that between the informant and the historian, and that between the informant and his own historical consciousness.

The first of these relations is in large measure engendered by the historian, for it is his curiosity, not that of the historical actor, which both the questions and the explanations seek to justify. In most cases the informant has acted as if his views of historical processes were a given reality in his world, and he has not thought them out until faced with the necessity to do so by the interview.[36] The relation that thus emerges is both relative and equivalent. It is relative in that the informant's view of history (its use, its structure, a system of cause, etc.) are developed only in relation to the historian's view of that process, while the historian's organization of his questions (the structure of the interview) is in turn developed in response to the answers of the interviewee. Each view is thus a standard of reference for the other. The relationship is also equivalent in the sense that when it is finally articulated, the questions, asked and unasked, and the answers given, form an historical view equal to and independent of that of the historian.

The second relation, that of the informant to what he or she views as the history of the community, is probably the most clearly articulated aspect of the interview and also the most difficult to grasp, for it is only one part of a much broader cultural vision and cognitive structure, and demands a very special type of reading to analyze. To read the narrative properly, to discover this relation and the cultural vision which informs it, we must give the interview the same kind of reading which Jacques Lacan has given to Freud or which Louis Althusser has given to Marx,[37] a method of reading Althusser terms 'symptomatic'.

While few of us or our interviewees, will create narratives or analyses as rich, as complex, or as theoretically sophisticated as those of Freud or Marx, our interviews, as I have tried to show, are far more complex than we usually assume. If read properly, they do reveal to us hidden levels of discourse – the search for which is the aim of symptomatic reading.[38] If read (or really listened to) again and again, not just for facts and comments, but also, as Althusser suggests, for insight and oversights, for the combination of vision and nonvision, and especially for answers to questions which were never asked, we should be able to isolate and describe the problematic which informs the particular interview.

It is at the level of this problematic – the theoretical or ideological context within which words and phrases, and the presence or absence of certain problems and concepts is found[39] – that we find the synthesis of all of the various structural relationships of the interview, as well as the particular relation of the individual to his vision of history. What we are here discussing is not simply a Weltanschauung, but a structural field in which men live their history and which guides their practice or action. Within this problematic, a view of history plays a key role, and provides for the oral historian a crucial tool of both creation and analysis.

In one of the most profound and important essays in American historio-graphy, Warren Susman has brilliantly outlined how, '[t]he idea of history itself, special kinds of historical studies and various attitudes towards history always play – whether intelligently conceived or not – a major role within a culture'. What we call a 'worldview' [substitute problematic], Susman argues, 'always contains a more or less specific view of the nature of history', and 'attitudes towards the past frequently become facts of profound consequences for the culture itself'.[40]

Noting that 'the idea of history itself belongs to a special kind of social and cultural organization', what we usually call 'contract societies', in which the social order must be explained, rationalized or reasonably ordered, Sus-man argues that 'it is history which can [most] reasonably explain the origin, the nature and the function of various institutions and their interaction. History seems able to point the direction in which a dynamic society is moving. It brings order out of the disordered array of the consequences of change itself.'[41]

To history, over which no one person or group has a monopoly, Susman contrasts societies in which myth predominates, status societies, where the 'world view' is dominated by deeply believed myths whose articulation is usually the prerogative of a special class of people, usually priests.[42] Myth, with its utopian vision, its sacerdotal nature, its elements of authority in answer to ignorance, doubt or disbelief, functions as a cohesive element in a society, in contrast to history which, because it explains the past in order to offer ways to change the future and serves as the basis of political philosophy, becomes an ideological tool to alter the social order. Thus while actual consequences follow from each view of the world it is history, in its most ideological form, which offers a plan for social action.

As Susman notes, the historical vision of the past does not replace a mythic vision; rather, in historical societies they exist in dialectical tension with one another and by combination and interaction, they produce a variety of his-torical visions. These, as Susman demonstrates in American historiography, can become the basis for a morphology of historical thought;[43] a morphology which in turn becomes an accurate gauge of the tendencies of social integra-tion or differentiation in the culture itself, and an index of the potency or impotency of the institutions of that society to further the cultural vision of the masses of people in the society.

All of this is important to the historian, and especially to the oral historian because this analysis allows us to focus our interviews upon the crucial elem-ent of the cognitive thought of the member of the culture with whom we are particularly concerned. We can thus use the idea of history and its relation to myth and ideology as the central aim of our interviews to grasp the deeper problematic of the interviewee. To do this, however, we must first recognize the crucial role played by ideologies in modern society, and develop a methodology for the analysis of the structure and function of ideology.

An ideology is more than simply a political program. As discussed by

Susman and defined by Althusser, it is ideology which structures the consciousness of individuals and their conceptions of their relations to the conditions of existence, and which governs their actions and practices through an array of apparatuses such as the family, the church, trade unions, systems of communication as well as modes of conduct and behavior. It is the basic conceptualization of the relations of a class-based society.[44] It is therefore crucial to an understanding of the dynamics of the culture – learned patterns of behavior.

The key to the understanding of the function of ideology lies in the concept of 'hegemony' as developed by Antonio Gramsci[45] for it is through hegemony – the 'spontaneous loyalty that any dominant social group obtains from the masses by virtue of its intellectual prestige and its supposedly superior function in the world of production'[46] – that ideology attains its importance as a mechanism of class rule and finds expression in popular beliefs.[47] With a broad definition of ideology, and a proper understanding of the theory of hegemony, its limits, and the roles played by a view of historical change in the development of an ideology, the oral historian should be able to synthesize his analyses of the three sets of relations contained in the interview, for the socio or paralinguistic structure, patterns of behavior and theory of history are all united within the concept of ideology.

Earlier in this volume (*Envelopes of Sound*, Chapter II) Alice Kessler Harris noted her experiences in interviewing women who had migrated to the United States, and the contradiction between their actions within their families and their discussion of changing family patterns. Buried beneath this contradiction is a deeper structure of historical cognition which proclaims the necessity of progress in history and the participation of the immigrant in that progress. Thus history and myth have been synthesized into a dynamic view of life which if analyzed with care can explain many, if not most, of the tensions of immigrant life in America. In cases such as this, by concentrating our interviews on a series of questions aimed at the articulation by the interviewee of his views of historical change, causality, the evolution of institutions, and his view of the way in which the past has been ordered and rationalized, and upon which the future predicted, we can begin to explain the particular ideological context of the interview. We can also understand how and to what degree our informants have accepted the hegemonic view of the culture – in this case the idea of progress.

Such a use of the idea of history to gain an understanding of ideology and thus an understanding of the dynamics of the history of the culture is, of course, not limited to oral history. The special methods of oral history do, however, make such a procedure especially useful in structuring and analyzing our interviews.

Oral history, almost alone among the various practices of historiography is heavily dependent upon fieldwork, which means that not only can we come back again and again to our sources and ask them to tell us more, but we can also explore the varieties of historical visions in far greater detail and amid radically changing historical conditions. Indeed, just as in the case mentioned above, it is the interviewing experience itself which can reveal the contradiction between ideology, myth and reality. By careful observation and understanding of this experience we can add a depth to our historical understanding which is never revealed in the written record.

Also, alone among our peers our documents exist in the realm of sound and vision as well as printed record. If carefully prepared and symptomatically read we should be able to bring to our historical study the powerful analytical tools of more advanced disciplines such as linguistics and anthropology. There would seem to be no theoretical reason why historical documents of this type cannot be subject to the same type of analysis given to other interviews in other professions.

To do this, however, we need a larger and more general concept of historical cognition, because without some larger context within which to place the information we gather, and the various aspects of the interview – linguistic, performatory, and cognitive – which will synthesize these structures, we risk not only the possibility of misunderstanding what is happening in the interview, but also of misunderstanding what is being said and why. It is only the larger context which makes the information conveyed in an interview unambiguous.

Also, if we fail to see our interviewees as bearers of a culture and thus people with their own view of the past, be it formed as part of a hegemonic ideology, or in opposition to that ideology, or as some combination of myth and ideology, or even a secret history, we will, because the information must be structured, infuse our own vision of the past into the interview. Such a situation is exactly what we do not want to do. Our aim is to bring to conscious articulation the ideological problematic of the interviewee, to reveal the cultural context in which information is being conveyed, and to thus transform an individual story into a cultural narrative, and thereby, to more fully understand what happened in the past. While this can only be done through the interplay of the various conceptions of the past held by both the interviewer and the interviewee, the particular present ideological conceptions of the interviewer should not structure that articulation.[48]

Concentration upon the interplay of ideology and various conceptions of history is also of special importance to the oral historian because such a methodology is what distinguishes him from other field workers who use interviews, such as psychologists, anthropologists and folklorists. As historians we are trained to understand and analyze the varieties of historical thought and their cultural context, and thus oral history interviewing is simply an extension of that training into the field.[49]

This view of the role of ideology in uniting the various structural elements of the oral history interview also provides oral historians with a method of dealing with the vexing problem of historical memory. Our problem, as anyone who has done extensive interviewing will readily admit, is not, except in odd cases, the problem of forgetfulness but rather the problem of being overwhelmed with reminiscences and memories flowing in uninterrupted and seemingly unrelated fashion.[50] If we view memory as one form or vehicle of historical cognition and if we examine our interviews carefully for a view of the problematic which informs these memories, we can begin to grasp the deeper structures which organize this seemingly unorganized flow of words, and then so direct our questioning and other responses to develop as full an interview as possible.

Finally, as field workers we should, in general, hold to the view that 'the methods of collecting which are to be most encouraged are those which will supply the greatest amount of reliable information', in the sense of providing a systematic view of the creative activities of mankind.[51] That systematic view, in many cases, can only be developed by the oral historian because the past, as it has existed, has never asked the pertinent questions about its own systematic view of the world – i.e., its own ideology and its own myth.

Such a view of the role of oral history – the search for the ideological and mythic matrix of the cultural consciousness of the society through the development of the idea of history – should not be taken to imply that the oral historian is now free to ignore the written records of facts and events in order to fly with the winds of grand theory. Rather it should be a call for oral historians to realize the potential of their work, and to take it seriously enough to become even more rigorous in their use of materials. Both theory and rigorous practice are necessary if oral history is, in the words of Henry Glassie, to contribute to 'a revolution in diachronic theorizing and to the development of an understanding of what people really did in the past'.[52]

NOTES

1 The most current survey, G. Shumway, *Oral History in the United States: A Directory*, New York, Columbia University Press, 1970, lists 230 projects. Since this compilation is already out of date the figure is probably closer to 450.
2 American Historical Association, *Newsletter*, 1972, vol. X, no. 5, p. 21.
3 See especially R. Rhodes's review of 'Hard Times', *New York Times Book Review*, April 19, 1970, p. 1, and G.B. Tindall's review of 'Huey Long', *American Historical Review*, 1970, vol. 75, p. 1792.
4 M. Frisch, 'Oral history and *Hard Times*: a review essay', *Red Buffalo*, n.d., nos. 2 and 3.
5 H. Glassie, 'A folkloristic thought on the promise of oral history', *Selections from the Fifth and Sixth National Colloquia on Oral History*, New York, Oral History Association, 1971, p. 54.
6 O.W. Bombard, 'A new measure of things past', *American Archivist*, 1955, vol. 18, p. 156. A.R. Stephans, 'Oral history and archives', *Texas Librarian*, 1967, vol. 29, pp. 203–214. M.J. Zachert, 'The implication of oral history for librarians', *College and Research Libraries*, 1968, vol. 29, pp. 101–103. Some have even argued that oral history is too important to leave to historians: see R.A. Bartlett, 'Some thoughts after the Third National Colloquium on Oral History', *The Journal of Library History*, 1969, vol. 4, pp. 169–172 and D.B. Nunis, Jr, 'The library and oral history', *California Librarian*, 1961, vol. 22, pp. 139–144.

7   See especially Peter Gay's discussion of N.F. Cantor, *Perspectives on the European Past: Conversations With Historians*, in *American Historical Review*, 1972, vol. 77, no. 5, pp. 1404–1405.

8   W.W. Cutler III, 'Accuracy in oral interviewing', *Historical Methods Newsletter*, 1970, no. 3, pp. 1–7.

9   C.T. Morrissey, 'On oral history interviewing', in L.A. Dexter (ed.), *Elite and Specialized Interviewing*, Evanston, Northwestern University Press, 1970, pp. 109–118. G. Colman, 'A call for more systematic procedures', *American Archivist*, 1965, vol. 28, no. 1, pp. 79–83. S. Benison, 'Reflections on oral history', *American Archivist*, 1965, vol. 28, no. 1, pp. 71–77.

10 As quoted in K.S. Goldstein, *A Guide for Field Workers in Folklore*, London, Herbert Jenkins, 1964, fn. p. 6.

11 D.C. Swain, 'Problems for practitioners of oral history', *American Archivist*, 1965, vol. 28, no. 1, p. 64.

12 Professor Gay discusses *Conversations with Historians* as textbook supplement or rival. Susanne Paul of the New York Women's Collective criticizes oral history as being 'elitist' without defining that term, and without any realization that even interviews with members of the working class if done from a certain ideological stance are 'elitist'. Remarks at the Sixth Annual Colloquia on Oral History. See also, 'Is oral history really worthwhile?', in C. Lord (ed.), *Ideas In Conflict: A Colloquium on Certain Problems in Historical Society Work in the United States and Canada*, Harrisburg, Pa., American Association for State and Local History, 1958.

13 See E.E. Maccoby and N. Maccoby. 'The interview: a tool of social science', in G. Lindzey (ed.), *The Handbook of Social Psychology*, Cambridge Mass., Addison-Wesley Publishing Company, 1954, vol. I, pp. 449–487, and Goldstein, *Guide for Field Workers in Folklore*. An updated and annotated bibliography of relevant works can be found in W.H. Banaka, *Training in Depth Interviewing*, New York, Harper & Row, 1970, pp. 162–189.

14 R. Sennett and J. Cobb, *The Hidden Injuries of Class*, New York, A.A. Knopf, 1972, p. 24.

15 C. Storm-Clark, 'The miners, 1870–1970, a test case for oral history', *Victorian Studies*, 1971, vol. XV, no. 1, p. 73. For an excellent discussion of the problem of accuracy in oral history in an actual fieldwork situation, see pp. 69–74.

16 Cutler, 'Accuracy in oral interviewing', pp. 6–7, L. Eaton, 'Book review, two Chicago architects and their clients', *Historical Methods Newsletter*, 1972, vol. 5, no. 4, p. 169.

17 V.D. Bornet, 'Oral history *can* be worthwhile', *American Archivist*, 1955, vol. 18, p. 244.

18 The classic work in this field is J. Vansina, *Oral Tradition; A Study in Historical Methodology* (translated by H.M. Wright), London, Routledge & Kegan Paul, 1965. See especially Section III. See also Storm-Clark, 'The miners', p. 73.

19 R. Finnegan, *Oral Literature in Africa*, Oxford, The Clarendon Press, 1970, p. 1. See also: G. Ewart Evans, *Tools of Their Trade: An Oral History of Men at Work, c. 1900*, New York, Taplinger Publishing Co., 1970, p. 18.

20 As quoted in Finnegan, *Oral Literature in Africa*, p. 11.

21 Cutler, 'Accuracy in oral interviewing', pp. 1–2.

22 For an example of the concerns of socio-linguists see J.A. Fishman (ed.), *Readings in the Sociology of Language*, The Hague, Mouton and Company, 1968. An example of an especially interesting use of interview materials is W. Labov. 'Phonological correlates of social stratification', *American Anthropologist*, 1964, vol. 66, part 2, pp. 164–176.

23 K. Marquis, 'Effects of social reinforcement on health reporting in the household interview', *Sociometry*, 1970, vol. 33, no. 2, pp. 203–215. P.H. Gebhard, 'Securing

sensitive personal information by interviews', *Selections from the Fifth and Sixth National Colloquia on Oral History*, pp. 63–79.

24 Also, as noted by S. Benison, 'Oral history and manuscript collecting', *Isis*, 1962, vol. 53, pp. 113–117, the collection of untruth is often as valuable as what passes for truth.

25 Cutler, 'Accuracy in oral interviewing', p. 7.

26 S. Benison, 'Oral history: a personal view', in E. Clark (ed.), *Modern Methods in the History of Medicine*, New York, Oxford University Press, 1971, p. 291.

27 The Lynd–Lemisch debate took place at a meeting of the Radical Caucus of the American Historical Association at its annual meeting in New York in 1971. For a fuller exposition of Lynd's views see 'Guerrilla history in Gary', *Liberation*, 1969, vol. 14, pp. 17–20, and 'Personal histories of the early CIO', *Radical America*, 1971, vol. 5, no.3, pp. 50–51.

28 Benison, 'A personal view', p. 293.

29 G.N. Gordon, *The Languages of Communication: a Logical and Psychological Examination*, New York, Hastings House, 1969, pp. 111–127. E. Rumics, 'Oral history: defining the term', *Wilson Library Bulletin*, 1966, vol. 40, pp. 602–605.

30 For more precise definitions of these terms see R. Pascal, *Design and Truth in Autobiography,* London, Routlege & Kegan Paul, 1960.

31 'Structure': 'a systematic whole of self-regulating transformations.' J. Piaget, *Structuralism* (translated and edited by C. Maschler), New York, Basic Books Inc., 1970, p. 44.

32 From a reading of R. Barthes, *Critical Essays*, translated by R. Howard, Evanston, Northwestern University Press, 1972, pp. 51–58, 203–211.

33 See for example W. Labov, *The Social Stratification of English in New York City*, Washington DC, Center for Applied Linguistics, 1966. One of the most exciting attempts to use linguistic analysis for cultural history, which also attempts a needed historiographical reconstruction in labor history, is R.P. Baker, 'Labor history, social science and the concept of the working class', *Labor History*, 1973, Winter, pp. 95–105. See also F. Berry, *The Physical Voice of Poetry*, Oxford, Oxford University Press, 1962. For a brief but cogent discussion of linguistic theory and its relations to contextual meaning see D.I. Slobin, *Psycholinguistics*, Glenview, Ill., Scott, Foresman & Company, 1971.

34 A. Benjamin, *The Helping Interview*, Boston, Houghton Mifflin & Company, 1969. E. Goffman, *Relations in Public: Microstudies of the Public Order*, New York, Basic Books Inc., 1971.

35 Finnegan, *Oral Literature in Africa*, pp. 2, 9–10.

36 H. Stretton, *The Political Sciences*, New York, Basic Books Inc., 1969, pp. 14–15. See also R. Blythe, *Akenfield: Portrait of an English Village*, New York, Pantheon, 1969, p. 20.

37 J. Lacan, *The Language of the Self: The Function of Language in Psychoanalysis* (edited and translated by A. Wilden), Baltimore, Johns Hopkins Press, 1968. L. Althusser and E. Balibar, *Reading Capital* (translated by B. Brewster), New York, Pantheon, 1970.

38 Althusser and Balibar, *Reading Capital*, pp. 16–17, 316.

39 Ibid.

40 W. I. Susman, 'History and the American intellectual: uses of a usable past', *American Quarterly*, 1964, vol. 16, part 2, p. 243.

41 Ibid., p. 244. For two interesting examples of this function of history see the Introduction, by Alice Kessler Harris, to R.J. Grele, *Envelopes of Sound: The Art of Oral History*, Chicago, Precedent Publishing, 1985.

42 Susman, 'History and the American intellectual', p. 244. See the discussion of the role of the myth among the Fon and Ashanti in Finnegan, *Oral Literature in Africa*, p. 365. See also W.R. Bascom, 'The forms of folklore: prose narratives', *Journal of American Folklore*, 1965, vol. 78, p. 4.

43 That this view of the tension between myth and history may have wider implications is seen in the remarkably similar distinction drawn by C. Levi-Strauss, *The Savage Mind*, Chicago, Chicago University Press, 1966, pp. 231–234.
44 L. Althusser, *Lenin and Philosophy and Other Essays*, New York, Monthly Review Press, 1971, pp. 143–161.
45 A. Gramsci, *The Modern Prince and Other Essays*, New York, International Publishers, 1959.
46 J. Cammett, *Antonio Gramsci and the Origins of Italian Communism*, Stanford, Stanford University Press, 1967, pp. 204–206.
47 A.S. Kraditor, 'American radical historians and their heritage', *Past and Present*, 1972, no. 56, p. 139.
48 It is exactly this lack of context which mars such works as *Huey Long*. See R.G. Sherill's review in *The Nation*, November 3, 1969, p. 209.
49 This is not to imply that the analysis of ideology cannot be united with the formal analysis of culture as used in other disciplines. See especially M. Godelier, 'Systeme, structure et contradiction dans "Le Capital"', *Les Temps Moderns*, 1966, vol. 22, pp. 828–865. See also Piaget, *Structuralism*, pp. 120–134, and the remarkable tour de force of Anthony Wilden in Lacan's *The Language of the Self*, pp. 302–311.
50 Cutler, 'Accuracy in oral interviewing', pp. 2–4, cites evidence of forgetfulness, but the studies upon which this judgment is based, as well as others in the field of memory, are so narrowly 'experimental' or behavioral that they tell us little about the actual functioning of historical memory. For example, see the reports in D. A. Norman (ed.), *Memory and Attention: An Introduction to Human Information Processing*, New York, John Wiley & Sons, 1968. For a more complex discussion of oral history and memory see Frisch, 'Oral history and *Hard Times*', pp. 288–231.
51 Goldstein, *A Guide for Field Workers in Folklore*, p. 5.
52 Glassie, 'A folkloristic thought on the promise of oral history', p. 57.

5   Work ideology and consensus under Italian fascism

Luisa Passerini

Luisa Passerini is Professor of History at the European University in Florence. Extracted from *History Workshop*, 1979, no. 8, pp. 84–92, by permission of Oxford University Press.

Oral history has until recently been engaged in two major battles with the established tradition of historiography. The first of these of course has been the struggle to ensure acceptance of the validity of oral sources for European history, and to accord them the same importance as other sources. Among the gains on this front one might mention the critique undertaken of other sources,[1] not to speak of a series of works of oral history which have at least demonstrated the equal worth of oral and other sources. The second is the attempt to widen the horizons of historical research, whether in the sense of including new spheres of reality (such as daily life, and the experiences of oppressed and subordinate social strata), or that of amplifying and clarifying the political aims and objectives within historical writing.[2] These battles have by no means been won as yet, and much remains to be done in developing existing initiatives. However in these two fields the direction of oral historical research is clear, and the debate is well advanced.

These developments of oral history, and our awareness of its shortcomings – by no means few – require us to undertake the task of redefining our aims. Amongst the gravest of the inadequacies of oral history, I would suggest, is the tendency to transform the writing of history into a form of populism – that is, to replace certain of the essential tenets of scholarship with facile democratisation, and an open mind with demagogy. Such an approach runs the risk of constructing oral history as merely an alternative ghetto, where at last the oppressed may be allowed to speak. In order to counteract this tendency towards a complacent populism (and the simple description which appears to be intrinsic to it), we must elaborate ways of using oral sources which take account of two interrelated requirements. First, we have thus far made a predominantly factual use of oral sources, and have been concerned in particular with such spheres as methods of work, relationships between parents and children, and the experience of community life. This is indeed not far removed from the use customarily made of most other sources. This is not enough. We cannot afford to lose sight of the peculiar specificity of oral material, and we have to develop conceptual approaches – and indeed insist upon that type of analysis – which can succeed in drawing out their full implications. Above all, we should not ignore that the raw material of oral history consists not just in factual statements, but is pre-eminently an expression and representation of culture, and therefore includes not only literal narrations but also the dimension of memory, ideology and subsconscious desires.

The second consideration is that thus far our critique of the positivist and historicist conception of history – or at least of its residue, as represented in various tendentious conceptions – has been, so to speak, an external one. That is, we have juxtaposed oral history to the customary tradition of European historiography. This critique should necessarily question the content of the latter's categories, however, and the use of sources which they imply. Historicism, inspired by the positivist tradition, has been happy to borrow interpretative categories from the social sciences, many of which were taken over with the illusory belief of 'reproducing' society itself. Society was conceived simply as a series of given facts, to be discovered and described, even though they might be partially immaterial constructs such as ethical codes and religious beliefs. Utilising this framework, then, the historian treats the sources as fragments through which the past 'as it really was' may be reconstructed.[3]

I consider it highly productive, in seeking to come to terms with both the problems outlined above, to assume that oral sources refer to and derive from a sphere which I have chosen to call subjectivity. By this I wish to connote that area of symbolic activity which includes cognitive, cultural and psychological aspects. The terms used to define this area more narrowly are generally confused and vague because of the overlapping meanings and subtle differences of emphasis which have been attached to their typical conceptualisations, such as mentality, ideology, culture, world-view (*Weltanschauung*), and consciousness. In comparison with these, subjectivity has the advantage of being a term sufficiently elastic to include both the aspects of spontaneous subjective being (*soggettività irriflessa*) contained and represented by attitude, behaviour and language, as well as other forms of awareness (*consapevolezza*) such as the sense of identity, consciousness of oneself, and more considered forms of intellectual activity. The importance of this term, moreover, is that it embraces not only the epistemological dimension but also that concerned with the nature and significance of the political. In this paper I wish to touch only briefly on the wider debate implied by the utilisation of these categories, but nevertheless believe it to be of great importance that the writing of history should today take account of this problem of subjectivity and subjective liberation.

These concerns first emerged during the 1920s in the theoretical reflections on social and political revolutions (notably Lukacs, Korsch), but did not really fully develop in character until the inter-war period. The fragmentation of the workers' movement under fascism and the defeat of their hopes for a subjective liberation – particularly in those countries where they had formally taken power – constitute the most dramatic elements. But there are other changes which began in the same period, particularly in the 1930s, such as the growing propensity for political and economic factors to intervene in the daily life of the individual, which equally require us to undertake reformulation. During the 1960s this problem was more or less explicitly brought to the forefront of our attention by various social movements; youth, the women's movement and ethnic and linguistic minorities have all and in a variety of ways (some indeed even displaying the politics of reaction) raised the question of liberty in the mental and personal sphere. Various historical processes, including the development of intellectual disciplines such as psychology, have made this aspect of the problem even more relevant to our contemporary concerns: how far and in what way does coercion take place in the sphere of subjectivity? Even if we accept that coercion always has a material basis, what is it that leads the oppressed to accept their oppression in cultural and psychological terms, even to the point of praising it and preferring it to any struggle for change?

The events of 1968 marked the point at which the problem burst fully into the open. It was clear then that the past analyses concerning the categorisation and emancipation of consciousness undertaken with respect to the history of the workers' movement of the Third International were inadequate: they failed to examine the transformations which had taken place in the structures for the satisfaction of the workers' needs, and in the relationships between the individual and power.[4] The clues which we are able to derive from social reality, at times intuitively, through the discipline of oral history need now to be harvested, selected, arranged and freed from their ambiguity. I consider it indeed a matter of political urgency, facing as we do a situation where we have so little theoretical grasp in such fields as the manipulation of information, or the passions of such a social stratum as youth, as it shifts from apathy to violence and terrorism. I also hope that in pursuing these questions, social historians will point out that subjective reality also has its own history, and a multi-faceted relationship with institutional power.

It is my own intention in this paper to seek to contribute to the discussion of a highly contentious issue, namely the attitude of the Italian working class towards fascism, by drawing on a collated selection of oral sources. These represent, I would argue, a manifestation of a subjective reality which enables us to write history from a novel dimension unconsidered by traditional historiography. This will avoid its narrow concern with piling up facts and its failure to make explicit the political nature of all historical writing, while also presenting in the concept of subjectivity a tool of analysis peculiarly appropriate to social history. [. . .]

It is not easy to apply to a working class which underwent 20 years of the Mussolini regime the stereotype of a class immediately and totally antagonistic to the existing order. Nevertheless some post-World War II historiography has revealed a tendency to remain faithful to the image of a spontaneously anti-fascist working class, unquestioningly loyal to the workers' traditions handed down from generation to generation and unchanged by the dictatorship. (This attitude is particularly noticeable as far as the working class of Turin is concerned, with its political heritage of factory occupations, the experience of workers' councils, and the relationship with Gramsci's *Ordine Nuovo*).

From that historiography, in spite of its validity at certain levels, one receives the impression of an uninterrupted core of anti-fascism present in the working class, from an irreducible opposition and refusal to participate in fascism to a tireless ability to give shelter to the militant anti-fascist organisations of those in exile. This vision indeed corresponds with that of the notion of a continuity without conflicts between the class and its historic organisations: as Luraghi, for example, says,

> the communists . . . felt behind them, solid and ready, the vast reserve of the forces of the working class, wholly and clearly lined up in hostility against fascism.[5]

This image, allowed to slip only as regards *qualche consenso*[6] (some consensus) with the Ethiopian war, makes it impossible to understand the tragedy of a working class which was denied by the corporatist regime even the very name of *class*.

Such is the approach of this historiography, that it has seemed possible to explain the innumerable failures of clandestine activity solely on the basis of spies and infiltration, without referring to the narrow basis and archaic nature of such attempts, and in particular ignoring the need for mass struggle.[7] One does not wish to detract from the value of these forms of struggle, which indeed prepared for the mass struggle of the Resistance, but one should underline the real problems of the conflict against fascism. As S. Lunadei Girolami has written,

> through what process of subjective transformation . . . does the action of the clandestine opposition come to be a majority activity amongst the Turin proletariat in 1943, from its virtual negligibility in 1934?[8]

On the contrary, however, contemporary opponents of fascism acknowledged – albeit here and there in the triumphal tones of political propaganda[9] – the existence of serious problems of indifference, of apathy particularly amongst young workers, of a lack of communication between the generations, and of a disjuncture between action on the economic level and its political implications. A classic example is the analysis by Togliatti, who really brought to light towards the end of 1934 the hold which fascism had on the working class. He suggested that the strength of this grasp was attained through satisfaction of certain basic and elementary needs, which had been ignored by the old socialism, such as better material conditions, social assistance, cultural and sports activity:

> It is time to stop thinking that workers should not have sport. Even the smallest material advances are not despised by workers. The worker always

seeks each minute betterment of his conditions; even the very fact of having a room to go into at night and being able to listen to the radio is something to be pleased about. We cannot attack the worker who accepts entrance to that room, for the sole reason that on the door is inscribed the mark of fascism.[10]

Togliatti also pointed towards the possibility that despite their strong reservations there would nevertheless be a progressive adaptation towards fascism amongst old workers and senior political cadres through habit and routine.[11]

There was thus in Togliatti an awareness of the ambivalence which resulted from the material needs of the masses and their propensity to be manipulated either in a revolutionary direction or towards an acceptance of the partial satisfaction of their needs by fascism and capitalism. This awareness certainly ran the risk of unduly emphasizing the initiative of the party in the face of the inertia of the masses, but fundamentally it is an essential premise for understanding the condition of the working class under fascism. The point had been emphasized by Wilhelm Reich when he indicated the ambivalence between the masses' historically conditioned, passive psychological and cultural structures on the one hand, and the latent potentialities arising from their 'real' needs on the other.[12] This sense of ambivalence has however been lost sight of in the most recent debate on the consensus under fascism, which has touched on – even if somewhat tangentially – the involvement of the working class. [. . .]

[In this debate] we see a refusal to admit that the working class has undergone an internalisation of its defeat, by virtue of the coercion of its subjectivity (false consciousness?), which would happily be admitted if it were the result of a *material* coercion. At the level of historiography this implies that one is no longer capable of recognising that the defeat has been internalised and rationalised, and also that there were pre-existing subjective bases onto which the consensus under fascism has been grafted.

It was this lack of recognition which for a long time prevented me from understanding the oral sources I had collected on the working class in Turin between the wars, and from ordering them systematically. I realize now that I was continuing to pose questions of my sources which I had inferred from the existing debate on consensus and fascism. I originally attributed the difficulties mainly to the discrepancy between local and national history, and between the individual and his or her epoch. These problems are accentuated by the fact that my research is still in progress, and that the samples I give here are not fully representative of the Italian working class in the interwar period. I have drawn in this paper on the life-stories of some 60 individuals, in all some 100 hours of tape-recorded interviews,[13] which I have compared with about 110 published life-stories of workers.[14]

However, I have anticipated a fuller study with this present analysis, as it has enabled me to clarify the precise directions for a more definitive review of the topic. I trust that a larger and more representative sample will not invalidate this current work, since the hypotheses are mainly related to the types of ideologies and mentalities that declined or emerged during the period under consideration. In this sense I think this work bears some resemblances to anthropology, although the ambition is to place working-class culture in a historical perspective. This is also why I have given preference, in the choice of interviews to be quoted at length, to the ones I conducted myself, which included some sort of participant observation.

The present sample is composed of workers belonging to two sets of generations: the first includes those born before 1910 and the second those born between 1910 and 1925. This is an interim distinction, drawn from the existing literature on the subject of generations and fascism. Male informants had all been factory workers for at least part of their lives; this was the case also for some of the women. A number of them however were daughters, wives, sisters, mothers of workers and/or had been involved in the putting-out system. Most informants were born in Turin or had immigrated within the first half of the 1930s. A small number of them lived and worked in smaller towns near Turin (Asti, Pinerolo). The life-stories have been collected in two phases: a first one, of free narration, sometimes very short, according to the informant's desire; a second one, led on the basis of general questions concerning daily activities. Questions of the following kind were also asked: 'What do you remember of the period before the last war?'

This method of procedure, seeking to obtain from informants the most spontaneous type of reply by reducing direct questions to a minimum, has produced primary source material which is by no means easy to interpret. In particular it has elicited replies with scant significance for any historiography which is predominantly concerned with establishing 'what really happened'. At a first reading my sources gave, for the problem of consensus, enigmatic replies. It was clear that I did not know how to read them – in the sense of interpreting their message – and that I did not understand them. Let me indicate here briefly the sort of preliminary typology which I have drawn up in the process of seeking to interpret the readings, which has on the one hand tried to take oral sources as accurate statements about given facts which need to be unveiled, and on the other has accepted traditional concepts of consent and dissent based either on the total separation or on the confusion between different forms of subjectivity, and between different spheres such as daily life and politics. Not having criticised the operational implications of an inherited conception of history, I was unable to receive any satisfying answer to our questions, and I am not referring to questions posed to the informants in order to produce interviews. I am thinking of the questions which emerge while analysing interviews. Oral sources refuse to answer certain kinds of questions; seemingly loquacious, they finally prove to be reticent or enigmatic, and like the sphynx [*sic*] they force us to reformulate problems and challenge our current habits of thought.

Indeed, I received what to my ears were either irrelevant or inconsistent answers. 'Irrelevant' answers were mainly of two sorts: silences and jokes.

Anecdotes and jokes deserve a special study: the general meaning they conveyed was that there existed an irreverent attitude towards the regime and that this attitude was most of the time brutally curbed.[15] There were two types of silences: (*a*) whole life-stories were told without any reference to fascism, except for casual ones (while talking about other events considered essential for one's life). For instance, one woman told how she used to meet her boyfriend who was in a prison for teenagers:

> They used to come to Via Passo Buole – there was fascism then, you see, and they were put through their gym drills – to Via Passo Buole they used to come, those boys, they'd come out all regimented for the drills, and so we'd go straight across to them. 'Cause we'd got to know who they were, looking out from our windows.[16]

This seemed to be an interviewee with little or no political interest. A second type of silence can be found in (*b*) interviews with person having some perception of the encroachment of institutional power upon their lives. Life-stories of such persons often present a striking chronological gap between 1922–23 (1925 at the latest) and the outbreak of World War II. Beppino, born in 1897, a Lancia worker, who later became a manager in a smaller factory, narrates his life up until his military service and his return to work after the Great War:

> Then there was the occupation of the factories and at that point they [the workers on strike] came in there, into the Lancia, and kicked us out and made us leave. In those days there weren't all those buildings there, but fields, real fields, and so we fled into them, split up and then went back to our homes. When all that was over, we went back to work and we worked normally again. Well, of course life was full of fear and anxiety because inside the factory there were always all these fascists who could point their fingers at any Tom, Dick or Harry. And then when you left in the evening there were always groups of fascists waiting and they'd beat somebody up, so we were always worried. There was one bloke who worked near me, who was the personnel manager's son and always had a gun in the drawer and as we were in the same team, I had this gun in the drawer near to me and it was none too pleasant; in any case we went on like this. Then the bombing started, and when the bombs started here, in Via Di Nanni we got bombed too, in the house where I lived.[17]

The extraordinary thing about this testimony is that it refers, with the exception of the last sentence, entirely to a period no later than 1925. With the last sentence the story suddenly jumps to World War II. Afterwards he goes on to talk about the postwar period.

Up to now I have been referring to spontaneous parts of the interviews. When questioned more directly, the interviewees recalled usually the period of fascism's rise to power with all its atrocities (sometimes by hearsay, if they were then too young) and World War II. Memory reached its highest pitch about 1943–45: Resistance, war and liberation have left a mark, although sometimes negative, like one of disapproval and fear:

> On the 25th of July – says a worker – when fascism fell I was in bed and heard people shouting. I went to the window to see the people in the streets: they were shouting, destroying the emblems and pulling down the fascist headquarters; then I went back to bed because it was better to keep clear of them, 'cause they are all hypocrites and they'd all been on the fascists' side before and then they were all against them.[18]

A question mark still remains for those 15–20 years between 1922–25 and 1941–43. Whatever the justifications, this self-censorship is evidence of a scar, a violent annihilation of many years in human lives, a profound wound in daily experience.

'Inconsistent' answers are such in the sense that they manifest a discrepancy with what are considered the main historical events and processes. Interviewees speak very little about any form of organised leisure, almost do not mention fascist trade unions, do not seem to remember anything about assistance and social security, and so on. By and large they speak about their jobs, marriage and children, narrating a daily life apparently indifferent to fascism.[19] On the other hand, it has been noticed that even the traditional concept of anti-fascism is too narrow, if compared with the issues emerging from the oral sources.[20] But can such discrepancies be interpreted solely as signs of ordinary people's estrangement from fascism? On the contrary, I believe they originate in incorrect formulations of problems.

Irrelevancies and discrepancies must not be denied, and should be taken to indicate in the first place that some important operation has been forgotten by the historian. History, like other social sciences, must 'transform the concepts which it brings, as it were, from outside, into those which the object has of itself, into what the object, left to itself, seeks to be'.[21] It may sometimes be necessary, in order to do that, to make a detour and try to consider the object from a wider point of view. Oral sources seek to be taken as forms of culture and testimonies of its changes over time. But we must strive to develop a concept of culture which can embrace the reality of daily life. Oral sources start to speak more clearly, even on consensus, in the context of those 'bedrock assumptions, responses and notions' (as opposed to 'specific public ideals, deliberately propagated') among which Tim Mason includes reverence for the family and religion.[22] I would add, at least for the period under consideration, attitudes towards work. The acceptance of alienated work relations, of the apparently free and equal exchange between worker and employer, involves internalized acceptance of social hierarchies. Ideologies of work, whether expressed in thought or in behaviour, can be considered one of the main channels of individual acceptance of authority, already existing in the period of the liberal state. [. . .]

NOTES

1 See P. Thompson, 'Problems of method in oral history', *Oral History*, 1973, vol. 1, no. 4, pp. 1–55.
2 See R. Samuel, 'People's history', in R. Samuel (ed.), *Village Life and Labour*, London, Routledge, 1975.
3 For a critique of history as mere reconstruction, see, e.g., G. Stedman Jones, 'From historical sociology to theoretical history', *The British Journal of Sociology*, 1976, vol. XXVII, no. 3; and G. Mensching, 'Zeit and fortschritt in den geschichts-philosophischen Thesen Walter Benjamins', in P. Bulthaup (ed.), *Materialien zu Benjamins Thesen 'Ueber den Begriff der Geschichte'*, Frankfurt-am-Main, 1975.
4 On this subject see the interesting debate by F. Cerutti, D. Claussen, H.-J. Krahl, O. Negt, A. Schmidt, *Geschichte und Klassenbewusstsein heute*, Amsterdam, 1971.
5 R. Luraghi, 'Momenti della lotta antifascista in Piemonte negli anni 1926–43', *Movimento di liberazione in Italia*, Turin, 1954, p. 20.
6 D. Zucaro, *Cospirazione operaia. Resistanza al fascismo in Torino Milano Genova, 1927–43*, Turin, 1965, p. 183.
7 Luraghi in fact stresses the point that the communists were the only ones to elaborate legal forms of struggle, such as participation in the fascist trade unions.
8 S. Lunadei Girolami, 'Partito comunista e classe operaia a Torino 1929–34', *Annali della Fondazione Luigi Einaudi*, 1970, vol. IV, p. 162.
9 For example, the periodical published by the communists exiled in Paris, *Stato operaio*, alternates such tones with more realistic views of the situation.
10 P. Togliatti, *Lezioni sul fascismo*, Rome, 1970, p. 108.
11 Ibid., p. 113.
12 W. Reich, 'Zur anwendung der psychoanalyse in der geschichtsforschung', *Zeitschrift für politische Psychologie und Sexualökonomie*, Copenhagen, 1934.
13 The original tapes are part of two collections: one at the Istituto di Storia, Facoltà di Magistero, Università di Torino (tapes belonging to that collection will be referred to with the abbreviation ISM, followed by numbers and letters indicating the position in that archive) and the other at the Galleria d'Arte Moderna of Turin (GAM). In the quotations from the transcripts I have used pseudonyms in order to guarantee, where requested, the anonymity of the informants. The following are the main signs used in the transcripts:

> . . .   suspension, hesitation of the voice;
> [. . . . . .]   parts have been cut in the quotation;
> —   —   parenthetical expressions.

14 They are included in the following books: E. Vallini, *Operai del nord*, Bari, 1957; A. Pizzorno, *Comunità e razionalizzazione*, Turin, 1960; D. Montaldi, *Militanti politici di base*, Turin, 1971; P. Crespi, *Esperienze operaie*, Milan, 1974; A. M. Bruzzone/R. Farina, *La Resistenza taciuta*, Milan, 1976; B. Guidetti-Serra, *Compagne*, 2 vols., Turin, 1977.
15 So far jokes have been considered simply as symbolic compensations to impotence: cf. E.R. Tannenbaum, *The Fascist Experience, Italian Society and Culture 1922–1945*, New York, 1972, ch. IX. They might be studied as a specific part of a culture and of its reactions and changes under Fascism.
16 GAM. The interviewee was born in 1919, in Veneto, immigrated to Turin in 1930; she worked in three small factories since then.
17 ISM, TO/SP/10.
18 Antonio T., born in Turin in 1911, cf. E. Vallini, *Operai del nord*, p. 254.
19 Such discrepancy has been evidenced by the documents collected for the exhibition on 'Working-class culture and daily life in Borgo San Paolo' (a borough of Turin) between the wars. See the essay by G. Levi, D. Pianciola, B. Bianco,

A. Frisa, M. Gribaudi, S. Cavallo, E. Gennuso, C. Savio, 'Cultura operaia e vita quotidiana in borgo San Paolo', in the exhibition catalogue, *Torino tra le due guerre*, Turin, 1978, pp. 2–45.

20 See G. Miccoli, 'Contadini del cuneese e storia delle classi subalterne', *Bollettino dell' Instituto Regionale per la storia del movimento di liberazione nel Friuli-Venezia Giulia*, 1977, vol. V, nos. 2–3, pp. 66–71; and M. Isenghi, 'Valori popolari e valori "ufficiali" nella mentalità del soldato tra le due guerre mondiali', *Quaderni storici*, 1978, no. 38, pp. 701–709.

21 See the essay by T. Adorno, in Th. W. Adorno, K.R. Popper, R. Dahrendorf, J. Habermas, H. Albert, H. Pilot, *The Positivist Dispute in German Sociology*, London, 1976.

22 T. Mason, 'Women in Germany, 1925–40: family, welfare and work: conclusion', *History Workshop*, 1976, no. 2, p. 32.

6 What makes oral history different

Alessandro Portelli

Alessandro Portelli holds a Chair in American Literature at the University of Rome. Reprinted from A. Portelli, *The Death of Luigi Trastulli and Other Stories: Form and Meaning in Oral History*, State University of New York Press, Albany, 1991, pp. 45–58, by permission of the State University of New York Press. A first version, 'Sulla specificità della storia orale', appeared in *Primo Maggio* (Milano, Italy), 1979, vol. 13, pp. 54–60, reprinted as 'The peculiarities of oral history' in *History Workshop*, 1981, no. 12, pp. 96–107.

'Yes,' said Mrs. Oliver, 'and then when they come to talk about it a long time afterwards, they've got the solution for it which they've made up themselves. That isn't awfully helpful, is it?' 'It is helpful,' said Poirot . . . 'It's important to know certain facts which have lingered in people's memories although they may not know exactly what the fact was, why it happened or what led to it. But they might easily know something that we do not know and that we have no means of learning. So there have been memories leading to theories . . .

> Agatha Christie, *Elephants Can Remember*

His historical researches, however, did not lie so much among books as among men; for the former are lamentably scanty on his favorite topics; whereas he found the old burghers, and still more their wives, rich in that legendary lore, so invaluable to true history. Whenever, therefore, he happened upon a genuine Dutch family, snugly shut up in its low-roofed farmhouse, under a spreading sycamore, he looked upon it as a little clasped volume of black-letter and studied it with the zeal of a book-worm.

> Washington Irving, 'Rip Van Winkle'

MEMORIES LEADING TO THEORIES

A specter is haunting the halls of the academy: the specter of oral history. The Italian intellectual community, always suspicious of news from outside – and yet so subservient to 'foreign discoveries' – hastened to cut oral history down to size before even trying to understand what it is and how to use it. The method used has been that of charging oral history with pretensions it does not have, in order to set everybody's mind at ease by refuting them. For instance, *La Repubblica*, the most intellectually and internationally oriented

of Italian dailies rushed to dismiss 'descriptions "from below" and the artificial packages of "oral history" where things are supposed to move and talk
by themselves', without even stopping to notice that it is not *things*, but
people (albeit people often considered no more than 'things') that oral history
expects to 'move and talk by themselves'.[1]

There seems to be a fear that once the floodgates of orality are opened,
writing (and rationality along with it) will be swept out as if by a spontaneous uncontrollable mass of fluid, amorphous material. But this attitude
blinds us to the fact that our awe of writing has distorted our perception of
language and communication to the point where we no longer understand
either orality or the nature of writing itself. As a matter of fact, written and
oral sources are not mutually exclusive. They have common as well as
autonomous characteristics, and specific functions which only either one can
fill (or which one set of sources fills better than the other). Therefore, they
require different specific interpretative instruments. But the undervaluing
and the overvaluing of oral sources end up by cancelling out specific qualities, turning these sources either into mere supports for traditional written
sources, or into an illusory cure for all ills. This chapter will attempt to
suggest some of the ways in which oral history is intrinsically different, and
therefore specifically useful.

THE ORALITY OF ORAL SOURCES

Oral sources are *oral* sources. Scholars are willing to admit that the actual
document is the recorded tape; but almost all go on to work on the transcripts, and it is only transcripts that are published.[2] Occasionally, tapes are
actually destroyed: a symbolic case of the destruction of the spoken word.

The transcript turns aural objects into visual ones, which inevitably implies
changes and interpretation. The different efficacy of recordings, as compared
to transcripts – for classroom purposes, for instance – can only be appreciated
by direct experience. This is one reason why I believe it is unnecessary to give
excessive attention to the quest for new and closer methods of transcription.
Expecting the transcript to replace the tape for scientific purposes is equivalent to doing art criticism on reproductions, or literary criticism on translations. The most literal translation is hardly ever the best, and a truly faithful
translation always implies a certain amount of invention. The same may be
true for transcription of oral sources.

The disregard of the orality of oral sources has a direct bearing on interpretative theory. The first aspect which is usually stressed is origin: oral
sources give us information about illiterate people or social groups whose
written history is either missing or distorted. Another aspect concerns content: the daily life and material culture of these people and groups. However,
these are not specific to oral sources. Emigrants' letters, for instance, have the
same origin and content, but are written. On the other hand, many oral
history projects have collected interviews with members of social groups who

use writing, and have been concerned with topics usually covered by the standard written archival material. Therefore, origin and content are not sufficient to distinguish oral sources from the range of sources used by social history in general; thus, many theories of oral history are, in fact, theories of social history as a whole.[3]

In the search for a distinguishing factor, we must therefore turn in the first place to form. We hardly need repeat here that writing represents language almost exclusively by means of segmentary traits (graphemes, syllables, words, and sentences). But language is also composed of another set of traits, which cannot be contained within a single segment but which are also bearers of meaning. The tone and volume range and the rhythm of popular speech carry implicit meaning and social connotations which are not reproducible in writing – unless, and then in inadequate and hardly accessible form, as musical notation.[4] The same statement may have quite contradictory meanings, according to the speaker's intonation, which cannot be represented object- ively in the transcript, but only approximately described in the transcriber's own words.

In order to make the transcript readable, it is usually necessary to insert punctuation marks, which are always the more-or-less arbitrary addition of the transcriber. Punctuation indicates pauses distributed according to gram- matical rules: each mark has a conventional place, meaning, and length. These hardly ever coincide with the rhythms and pauses of the speaking subject, and therefore end up by confining speech within grammatical and logical rules which it does not necessarily follow. The exact length and position of the pause has an important function in the understanding of the meaning of speech. Regular grammatical pauses tend to organize what is said around a basically expository and referential pattern, whereas pauses of irregular length and position accentuate the emotional content, and very heavy rhyth- mic pauses recall the style of epic narratives. Many narrators switch from one type of rhythm to another within the same interview, as their attitude toward the subjects under discussion changes. Of course, this can only be perceived by listening, not by reading.

A similar point can be made concerning the velocity of speech and its changes during the interview. There are no fixed interpretative rules: slowing down may mean greater emphasis as well as greater difficulty, and acceler- ation may show a wish to glide over certain points, as well as a greater familiarity or ease. In all cases, the analysis of changes in velocity must be combined with rhythm analysis. Changes are, however, the norm in speech, while regularity is the norm in writing (printing most of all) and the pre- sumed norm of reading: variations are introduced by the reader, not by the text itself.

This is not a question of philological purity. Traits which cannot be con- tained within segments are the site (not exclusive, but very important) of essential narrative functions: they reveal the narrators' emotions, their par- ticipation in the story, and the way the story affected them. This often involves attitudes which speakers may not be able (or willing) to express otherwise, or elements which are not fully within their control. By abolishing these traits, we flatten the emotional content of speech down to the supposed equanimity and objectivity of the written document. This is even more true when folk informants are involved: they may be poor in vocabulary but are often richer in range of tone, volume and intonation than middle-class speakers who have learned to imitate in speech the monotone of writing.[5]

ORAL HISTORY AS NARRATIVE

Oral historical sources are *narrative* sources. Therefore the analysis of oral history materials must avail itself of some of the general categories developed by narrative theory in literature and folklore. This is as true of testimony given in free interviews as of the more formally organized materials of folklore.

For example, some narratives contain substantial shifts in the 'velocity' of narration, that is, in the ratio between the duration of the events described and the duration of the narration. An informant may recount in a few words experiences which lasted a long time, or dwell at length on brief episodes. These oscillations are significant, although we cannot establish a general norm of interpretation: dwelling on an episode may be a way of stressing its importance, but also a strategy to distract attentions from other more delicate points. In all cases, there is a relationship between the velocity of the narrative and the meaning of the narrator. The same can be said of other categories among those elaborated by Gérard Genette, such as 'distance' or 'perspective', which define the position of the narrator toward the story.[6]

Oral sources from nonhegemonic classes are linked to the tradition of the folk narrative. In this tradition distinctions between narrative genres are perceived differently than in the written tradition of the educated classes. This is true of the generic distinction between 'factual' and 'artistic' narratives, between 'events' and feeling or imagination. While the perception of an account as 'true' is relevant as much to legend as to personal experience and historical memory, there are no formal oral genres specifically destined to transmit historical information; historical, poetical, and legendary narratives often become inextricably mixed up.[7] The result is narratives in which the boundary between what takes place outside the narrator and what happens inside, between what concerns the individual and what concerns the group, may become more elusive than in established written genres, so that personal 'truth' may coincide with shared 'imagination'

Each of these factors can be revealed by formal and stylistic factors. The greater or lesser presence of formalized materials (proverbs, songs, formulas, and stereotypes) may measure the degree in which a collective viewpoint exists within an individual's narrative. These shifts between standard language and dialect are often a sign of the kind of the control which speakers have over the narrative.

A typical recurring structure is that in which standard language is used overall, while dialect crops up in digressions or single anecdotes, coinciding with a more personal involvement of the narrator or (as when the occurrences of dialect coincide with formalized language) the intrusion of collective memory. On the other hand, standard language may emerge in a dialect narrative when it deals with themes more closely connected with the public sphere, such as politics. Again, this may mean both a more or less conscious degree of estrangement, or a process of 'conquest' of a more 'educated' form of expression beginning with participation in politics.[8] Conversely, the dialectization of technical terms may be a sign of the vitality of traditional speech and of the way in which speakers endeavor to broaden the expressive range of their culture.

EVENTS AND MEANING

The first thing that makes oral history different, therefore, is that it tells us less about *events* than about their *meaning*. This does not imply that oral history has no factual validity. Interviews often reveal unknown events or unknown aspects of known events; they always cast new light on unexplored areas of the daily life of the nonhegemonic classes. From this point of view, the only problem posed by oral sources is that of verification (to which I will return in the next section).

But the unique and precious element which oral sources force upon the historian and which no other sources possess in equal measure is the speaker's subjectivity. If the approach to research is broad and articulated enough, a cross section of the subjectivity of a group or class may emerge. Oral sources tell us not just what people did, but what they wanted to do, what they believed they were doing, and what they now think they did. Oral sources may not add much to what we know, for instance, of the material cost of a strike to the workers involved; but they tell us a good deal about its psychological costs. Borrowing a literary category from the Russian formalists, we might say that oral sources, especially from nonhegemonic groups, are a very useful integration of other sources as far as the *fabula* – the logical, causal sequence of the story – goes; but they become unique and necessary because of their *plot* – the way in which the story materials are arranged by narrators in order to tell the story.[9] The organization of the narrative reveals a great deal of the speakers' relationships to their history.

Subjectivity is as much the business of history as are the more visible 'facts'. What informants believe is indeed a historical *fact* (that is, the fact that they believe it), as much as what really happened. When workers in Terni misplace a crucial event of their history (the killing of Luigi Trastulli) from one date and context to another, this does not cast doubts on the actual chronology, but it does force us to arrange our interpretation of an entire phase of the town's history. When an old rank-and-file leader, also in Terni, dreams up a story about how he almost got the Communist Party to reverse its strategy after World War II, we do not revise our reconstructions of political debates within the Left, but learn the extent of the actual cost of certain decisions to those rank-and-file activists who had to bury into their subconscious their needs and desires for revolution. When we discover that similar stories are told in other parts of the country, we recognize the half-formed legendary complex in which the 'senile ramblings' of a disappointed old man reveal much about his party's history that is untold in the lengthy and lucid memoirs of its official leaders.[10]

SHOULD WE BELIEVE ORAL SOURCES?

Oral sources are credible but with a *different* credibility. The importance of oral testimony may lie not in its adherence to fact, but rather in its departure from it, as imagination, symbolism, and desire emerge. Therefore, there are no 'false' oral sources. Once we have checked their factual credibility with all the established criteria of philological criticism and factual verification which are required by all types of sources anyway, the diversity of oral history consists in the fact that 'wrong' statements are still psychologically 'true' and that this truth may be equally as important as factually reliable accounts.

Of course, this does not mean that we accept the dominant prejudice which sees factual credibility as a monopoly of written documents. Very often, written documents are only the uncontrolled transmission of unidentified oral sources (as in the case of the report on Trastulli's death, which begins: 'According to verbal information taken. . .'). The passage from these oral '*ur*-sources' to the written document is often the result of processes which have no scientific credibility and are frequently heavy with class bias. In trial records (at least in Italy, where no legal value is accorded to the tape recorder or shorthand transcripts), what goes on record is not the words actually spoken by the witnesses, but a summary dictated by the judge to the clerk. The distortion inherent in such procedure is beyond assessment, especially when the speakers originally expressed themselves in dialect. Yet, many historians who turn up their noses at oral sources accept these legal transcripts with no questions asked. In a lesser measure (thanks to the frequent use of shorthand) this applies to parliamentary records, minutes of meetings and conventions, and interviews reported in newspapers: all sources which are legitimately and widely used in standard historical research.

A by-product of this prejudice is the insistence that oral sources are distant from events, and therefore undergo the distortion of faulty memory. Indeed, this problem exists for many written documents, which are usually written some time after the event to which they refer, and often by nonparticipants. Oral sources might compensate chronological distance with a much closer personal involvement. While written memoirs of politicians or labor leaders are usually credited until proven to be in error, they are as distant from some aspects of the event which they relate as are many oral history interviews, and only hide their dependence on time by assuming the immutable form of a 'text'. On the other hand, oral narrators have within their culture certain aids to memory. Many stories are told over and over, or discussed with members of the community; formalized narrative, even meter, may help preserve a textual version of an event.

In fact, one should not forget that oral informants may also be literate. Tiberio Ducci, a former leader of the farm workers' league in Genzano, in the Roman hills, may be atypical: in addition to remembering his own experience, he had also researched the local archives. But many informants read books and newspapers, listen to the radio and TV, hear sermons and political speeches, and keep diaries, letters, clippings, and photograph albums. Orality and writing, for many centuries now, have not existed separately: if many written sources are based on orality, modern orality itself is saturated with writing.

But what is really important is that memory is not a passive depository of facts, but an active process of creation of meanings. Thus, the specific utility of oral sources for the historian lies, not so much in their ability to preserve the past, as in the very changes wrought by memory. These changes reveal the narrators' effort to make sense of the past and to give a form to their lives, and set the interview and the narrative in their historical context.

Changes which may have subsequently taken place in the narrators' personal subjective consciousness or in their socio-economic standing, may affect, if not the actual recounting of prior events, at least the valuation and the 'coloring' of the story. Several people are reticent, for instance, when it comes to describing illegal forms of struggle, such as sabotage. This does not mean that they do not remember them clearly, but that there has been a change in their political opinions, personal circumstances, or in their party's line. Acts considered legitimate and even normal or necessary in the past may be therefore now viewed as unacceptable and literally cast out of the tradition. In these cases, the most precious information may lie in what the informants *hide*, and in the fact that they *do* hide it, rather than in what they *tell*.

Often, however, narrators are capable of reconstructing their past attitudes even when they no longer coincide with present ones. This is the case with the Terni factory workers who admit that violent reprisals against the executives responsible for mass layoffs in 1953 may have been counterproductive, but yet reconstruct with great lucidity why they seemed useful and sensible at the time. In one of the most important oral testimonies of our time, *Autobiography of Malcolm X*, the narrator describes very vividly how his mind worked before he reached his present awareness, and then judges his own past self by the standards of his present political and religious consciousness. If the interview is conducted skillfully and its purposes are clear to the narrators, it is not impossible for them to make a distinction between present and past self, and to objectify the past self as other than the present one. In these cases – Malcolm X again is typical – *irony* is the major narrative mode: two different ethical (or political, or religious) and narrative standards interfere and overlap, and their tension shapes the telling of the story.

On the other hand, we may also come across narrators whose consciousness seems to have been arrested at climactic moments of their personal experience: certain Resistance fighters, or war veterans; and perhaps certain student
militants of the 1960s. Often, these individuals are wholly absorbed by the
totality of the historical event of which they were part, and their account
assumes the cadences and wording of *epic*. The distinction between an ironic
or an epic style implies a distinction between historical perspectives, which
ought to be taken into consideration in our interpretation of the testimony.

OBJECTIVITY

Oral sources are not *objective*. This of course applies to every source, though
the holiness of writing often leads us to forget it. But the inherent nonobjec-
tivity of oral sources lies in specific intrinsic characteristics, the most important being that they are *artificial, variable, and partial*.

Alex Haley's introduction to *Autobiography of Malcolm X* describes how
Malcolm shifted his narrative approach not spontaneously, but because the
interviewer's questioning led him away from the exclusively public and official
image of himself and of the Nation of Islam which he was trying to project.
This illustrates the fact that the documents of oral history are always the
result of a relationship, of a shared project in which both the interviewer and
the interviewee are involved together, if not necessarily in harmony. Written
documents are fixed; they exist whether we are aware of them or not, and do
not change once we have found them. Oral testimony is only a potential
resource until the researcher calls it into existence. The condition for the
existence of the written source is emission; for oral sources, transmission: a
difference similar to that described by Roman Jakobson and Piotr Bogatyrev
between the creative processes of folklore and those of literature.[11]

The content of the written source is independent of the researcher's need
and hypotheses; it is a stable text, which we can only interpret. The content of
oral sources, on the other hand, depends largely on what the interviewer puts
into it in terms of questions, dialogue, and personal relationship.

It is the researcher who decides that there will be an interview in the first
place. Researchers often introduce specific distortions: informants tell them
what they believe they want to be told and thus reveal who they think the
researcher is. On the other hand, rigidly structured interviews may exclude
elements whose existence or relevance were previously unknown to the interviewer and not contemplated in the question schedule. Such interviews tend
to confirm the historian's previous frame of reference.

The first requirement, therefore, is that the researcher 'accept' the informant, and give priority to what she or he wishes to tell, rather than what the
researcher wants to hear, saving any unanswered questions for later or for
another interview. Communications always work both ways. The interviewees
are always, though perhaps unobtrusively, studying the interviewers who
'study' them. Historians might as well recognize this fact and make the best

of its advantages, rather than try to eliminate it for the sake of an impossible (and perhaps undesirable) neutrality.

The final result of the interview is the product of both the narrator and the researcher. When interviews, as is often the case, are arranged for publication omitting entirely the interviewer's voice, a subtle distortion takes place: the text gives the answers without the questions, giving the impression that a given narrator will always say the same things, no matter what the circumstances – in other words, the impression that a speaking person is as stable and repetitive as a written document. When the researcher's voice is cut out, the narrator's voice is distorted.

Oral testimony, in fact, is never the same twice. This is a characteristic of all oral communication, but is especially true of relatively unstructured forms, such as autobiographical or historical statements given in an interview. Even the same interviewer gets different versions from the same narrator at different times. As the two subjects come to know each other better, the narrator's 'vigilance' may be attenuated. Class subordination – trying to identify with what the narrator thinks is the interviewer's interest – may be replaced by more independence or by a better understanding of the purposes of the interview. Or a previous interview may have simply awakened memories which are then told in later meetings.

The fact that interviews with the same person may be continued indefinitely leads us to the question of the inherent incompleteness of oral sources. It is impossible to exhaust the entire memory of a single informant; the data extracted with each interview are always the result of a selection produced by the mutual relationship. Historical research with oral sources therefore always has the unfinished nature of a work in progress. In order to go through all the possible oral sources for the Terni strikes of 1949 to 1953, one ought to interview in depth several thousand people: any sample would only be as reliable as the sampling methods used, and could never guarantee against leaving out 'quality' narrators whose testimony alone might be worth ten statistically selected ones.

The unfinishedness of oral sources affects all other sources. Given that no research (concerning a historical time for which living memories are available) is complete unless it has exhausted oral as well as written sources, and that oral sources are inexhaustible, the ideal goal of going through 'all' possible sources becomes impossible. Historical work using oral sources is unfinished because of the nature of the sources; historical work excluding oral sources (where available) is incomplete by definition.

WHO SPEAKS IN ORAL HISTORY?

Oral history is not where the working classes speak for themselves. The contrary statement, of course, would not be entirely unfounded: the recounting of a strike through the words and memories of workers rather than those of the police and the (often unfriendly) press obviously helps (though not automatically) to balance a distortion implicit in those sources. Oral sources are a necessary (not a sufficient) condition for a history of the nonhegemonic classes; they are less necessary (though by no means useless) for the history of the ruling classes, who have had control over writing and leave behind a much more abundant written record.

Nevertheless, the control of historical discourse remains firmly in the hands of the historian. It is the historian who selects the people who will be interviewed; who contributes to the shaping of the testimony by asking the questions and reacting to the answers; and who gives the testimony its final published shape and context (if only in terms of montage and transcription). Even accepting that the working class speaks through oral history, it is clear that the class does not speak in the abstract, but speaks *to* the historian, *with* the historian and, inasmuch as the material is published, *through* the historian.

Indeed, things may also be the other way around. The historian may validate his or her discourse by 'ventriloquizing' it through the narrator's testimony. So far from disappearing in the objectivity of the sources, the historian remains important at least as a partner in dialogue, often as a 'stage director' of the interview, or as an 'organizer' of the testimony. Instead of discovering sources, oral historians partly create them. Far from becoming mere mouthpieces for the working class, oral historians may be using other people's words, but are still responsible for the overall discourse.

Much more than written documents, which frequently carry the impersonal aura of the institutions by which they are issued – even though, of course, they are composed by individuals, of whom we often know little or nothing – oral sources involve the entire account in their own subjectivity. Alongside the first person narrative of the interviewee stands the first person of the historian, without whom there would be no interview. Both the informant's and the historian's discourse are in narrative form, which is much less frequently the case with archival documents. Informants are historians, after a fashion; and the historian is, in certain ways, a part of the source.

Traditional writers of history present themselves usually in the role of what literary theory would describe as an 'omniscient narrator'. They give a third-person account of events of which they were not a part, and which they dominate entirely and from above (above the consciousness of the participants themselves). They appear to be impartial and detached, never entering the narrative except to give comments aside, after the manner of some nineteenth-century novelists. Oral history changes the writing of history much as the modern novel transformed the writing of literary fiction: the most important change is that the narrator is now pulled into the narrative and becomes a party of the story.

This is not just a grammatical shift from the third to the first person, but a whole new narrative attitude. The narrator is now one of the characters, and the *telling* of the story is part of the story being told. This implicitly indicates a much deeper political and personal involvement than that of the external narrator. Writing radical oral history, then, is not a matter of ideology, of subjective sides-taking, or of choosing one set of sources instead of another. It is, rather, inherent in the historian's presence in the story, in the assumption of responsibility which inscribes her or him in the account and reveals historiography as an autonomous act of narration. Political choices become less visible and vocal, but more basic.

The myth that the historian as a subject might disappear in the objective truth of working-class sources was part of a view of political militancy as the annihilation of all subjective roles into that of the full-time activist, and as absorption into an abstract working class. This resulted in an ironical similarity to the traditional attitude which saw historians as not subjectively involved in the history which they were writing. Oral historians appear to yield to other subjects of discourse, but, in fact, the historian becomes less and less of a 'go-between' from the working class to the reader, and more and more of a protagonist.

In the writing of history, as in literature, the act of focusing on the function of the narrator causes this function to be fragmented. In a novel such as Joseph Conrad's *Lord Jim*, the character/narrator Marlow can recount only what he himself has seen and heard; in order to tell the 'whole story', he is forced to take several other 'informants' into his tale. The same thing happens to historians working with oral sources. On explicitly entering the story, historians must allow the sources to enter the tale with their autonomous discourse.

Oral history has no unified subject; it is told from a multitude of points of view, and the impartiality traditionally claimed by historians is replaced by the partiality of the narrator. 'Partiality' here stands for both 'unfinishedness' and for 'taking sides': oral history can never be told without taking sides, since the 'sides' exist inside the telling. And, no matter what their personal histories and beliefs may be, historians and 'sources' are hardly ever on the same 'side'. The confrontation of their different partialities – confrontation as 'conflict', and confrontation as 'search for unity' – is one of the things which make oral history interesting.

NOTES

1 B. Placido in *La Repubblica*, 3 October 1978.
2 One Italian exception is the Istituto Ernesto De Martino, an independent radical research organization based in Milan, which has published 'sound archives' on long-playing records since the mid-1960s – without anyone in the cultural establishment noticing: see F. Coggiola, 'L'attivitá dell'Istituo Ernesto de Martino', in D. Carpitella (ed.), *L'etnomusicologia in Italia*, Palermo, Flaccovio, 1975, pp. 265–270.
3 L. Passerini, 'Sull'utilità e il danno delle fonti orali per la storia'. Introduction to Passerini (ed.), *Storia Orale. Vita quotidiana e cultura materiale delle classi subalterne*, Torino, Rosenberg & Sellier, 1978, discusses the relationship of oral history and social history.
4 On musical notation as reproduction of speech sounds, see G. Marini, 'Musica

popolare e parlato popolare urbano', in Circolo Gianni Bosio (ed.), *I giorni cantati*, Milano, Mazzotta, 1978, pp. 33–34. A. Lomax, *Folk Song Styles and Culture*, Washington DC, American Association for the Advancement of Sciences, 1968, Publication no. 88, discusses electronic representation of vocal styles.

5 See W. Labov, 'The logic of non-standard English', in L. Kampf and P. Lauter (eds.), *The Politics of Literature*, New York, Random House, 1970, pp. 194–244, on the expressive qualities of non-standard speech.

6 In this article, I use these terms as defined and used by G. Gennete, *Figures III*, Paris, Seuil, 1972.

7 On genre distinctions in folk and oral narrative, see D. Ben-Amos, 'Categories analytiques et genres populaires', *Poétique*, 1974, no. 19, pp. 268–293; and J. Vansina, *Oral Tradition*, Harmondsworth, Penguin Books, [1961], 1973.

8 For instance, G. Bordoni, Communist activist from Rome, talked about family and community mainly in dialect, but shifted briefly to a more standardized form of Italian whenever he wanted to reaffirm his allegiance to the party. The shift showed that, although he accepted the party's decisions, they remained other than his direct experience. His recurring idiom was 'There's nothing you can do about it.' See Circolo Gianni Bosio, *I giorni cantati*, pp. 58–66.

9 On fabula and plot see B. Tomaševskij, 'Sjužetnoe postroenie', in *Teorija literatury. Poetika*, Moscow-Leningrad, 1928; Italian trans., 'La costruzione dell'intreccio', in T. Todorov (ed.), *I formalisti russi*, Torino, Einaudi, 1968, published as *Théorie de la littérature*, Paris, Seuil, 1965.

10 These stories are discussed in chapters 1 and 6 of A. Portelli, *The Death of Luigi Trastulli*, Albany, State University of New York Press, 1991.

11 R. Jakobson and P. Bogatyrev, 'Le folklore forme spécifique de creation', in R. Jakobson, *Questions de poétique*, Paris, Seuil, 1973, pp. 59–72.

7 Popular memory
Theory, politics, method

Popular Memory Group

This essay, written by Richard Johnson and Graham Dawson, was based on the collective work in 1979 and 1980 of the Popular Memory Group at the Centre for Contemporary Cultural Studies, University of Birmingham (England). The Group at that time consisted of Michael Bommes, Gary Clarke, Graham Dawson, Jacob Eichler, Thomas Fock, Richard Johnson, Cim Meyer, Rebecca O'Rourke, Rita Pakleppa, Hans-Erich Poser, Morten Skov-Carlsen, Anne Turley and Patrick Wright. Extracted with permission from R. Johnson *et al.* (eds.), *Making Histories: Studies in History-writing and Politics*, London, Hutchinson, 1982.

> Must become historians of the present too.
> (Communist Party Historians' Group Minutes, 8 April 1956)

In this article we explore an approach to history-writing which involves becoming 'historians of the present too'. It is important to stress 'explore'. We do not have a completed project in 'popular memory' to report. We summarize and develop discussions which were intended as an initial clarification. These discussions had three main starting-points. First, we were interested in the limits and contradictions of academic history where links were attempted with a popular socialist or feminist politics. Our main example here was 'oral history', a practice that seemed nearest to our own preoccupations. Second, we were attracted to projects which moved in the direction indicated by these initial criticisms. These included experiments in popular autobiography and in community-based history, but also some critical developments with a base in cultural studies or academic historiography. Third, we tried [. . .] to relate problems of history-writing to more abstract debates which suggested possible clarifications.

What do we mean, then, by 'popular memory'? We give our own provisional answers in the first part of this essay. We define popular memory first as an *object of study* but, second, as a *dimension of political practice*. We then look, in the second part, at some of the resources for such a project, but also sketch its limits and difficulties. [. . .]

POPULAR MEMORY AS AN OBJECT OF STUDY

The first move in defining popular memory is to extend what we mean by history-writing (and therefore what is involved in historiographical comment). [. . .] to expand the idea of historical production well beyond the limits of academic history-writing. We must include *all* the ways in which a sense of the past is constructed in our society. These do not necessarily take a written or literary form. Still less do they conform to academic standards of scholarship or canons of truthfulness. Academic history has a particular place in a much larger process. We will call this 'the social production of memory'. In this collective production everyone participates, though unequally. Everyone, in this sense, is a historian. As Jean Chesneaux argues, professionalized history has attempted to appropriate a much more general set of relationships and needs: 'the collective and contradictory relationship of our society to its past' and the 'collective need' for guidance in the struggle to make the future.[1] We have already noted a similar stress in Christopher Hill's work: the recognition of a larger social process in which 'we ourselves are shaped by the past' but are also continually reworking the past which shapes us.[2] The first problem in the pursuit of 'popular memory' is to specify the 'we' in Hill's formulation or 'our society' in Chesneaux's. What *are* the means by which social memory is produced? And what practices are relevant especially outside those of professional history-writing?

It is useful to distinguish the main ways in which a sense of the past is produced: through public representations and through private memory (which, however, may also be collective and shared). The first way involves a public 'theatre' of history, a public stage and a public audience for the enacting of dramas concerning 'our' history, or heritage, the story, traditions and legacy of 'the British People'. This public stage is occupied by many actors who often speak from contradictory scripts, but collectively we shall term the agencies which construct this public historical sphere and control access to the means of publication 'the historical apparatus'. We shall call the products of these agencies, in their aggregate relations and combinations at any point of time, 'the field of public representations of history'. In thinking about the ways in which these representations affect individual or group conceptions of the past, we might speak of 'dominant memory'. This term points to the power and pervasiveness of historical representations, their connections with dominant institutions and the part they play in winning consent and building alliances in the processes of formal politics. But we do not mean to imply that conceptions of the past that acquire a dominance in the field of public representations are either monolithically installed or everywhere believed in. Not all the historical representations that win access to the public field are 'dominant'. The field is crossed by competing constructions of the past, often at war with each other. Dominant memory is produced in the course of these struggles and is always open to contestation. We do want to insist, however, that there are real processes of domination in the historical field. Certain representations achieve centrality and luxuriate grandly; others are marginalized or excluded or reworked. Nor are the criteria of success here those of truth: dominant representations may be those that are most ideological, most obviously conforming to the flattened stereotypes of myth.

[. . .] the various sites and institutions do not act in concert. To make them sing, if not in harmony at least with only minor dissonances, involves hard labour and active intervention. Sometimes this has been achieved by direct control (censorship for example) and by a violent recasting or obliteration of whole fields of public history. More commonly today, in the capitalist West, the intersections of formal political debates and the public media are probably the crucial site. Certainly political ideologies involve a view of past and present and future. Ranged against powers such as these, what price the lonely scholar, producing (also through commercial channels) the one or two thousand copies of the latest monograph?!

There is a second way of looking at the social production of memory which draws attention to quite other processes. A knowledge of past and present is also produced in the course of everyday life. There is a common sense of the past which, though it may lack consistency and explanatory force, none the less contains elements of good sense. Such knowledge may circulate, usually without amplification, in everyday talk and in personal comparisons and narratives. It may even be recorded in certain intimate cultural forms: letters, diaries, photograph albums and collections of things with past associations. It may be encapsulated in anecdotes that acquire the force and generality of myth. If this is history, it is history under extreme pressures and privations. Usually this history is held to the level of private remembrance. It is not only unrecorded, but actually silenced. It is not offered the occasion to speak. In one domain, the modern Women's Movement well understands the process of silencing and is raising the 'hidden' history of women's feelings, thoughts and actions more clearly to view. Feminist history challenges the very distinction 'public'/'private' that silences or marginalizes women's lived sense of the past. But similar processes of domination operate in relation to specifically working-class experiences, for most working-class people are also robbed of access to the means of publicity and arc cqually unuscd to the male, middle-class habit of giving universal or 'historic' significance to an extremely partial experience. But we are only beginning to understand the class dimensions of cultural domination, partly by transferring the feminist insights. Nor is this only a question of class or gender positions. Even the articulate middle-class historian, facing the dominant memory of events through which he has actually lived, can also be silenced (almost) in this way. One telling example is the difficulty of writers of the New Left in speaking coherently about the Second World War:

> One is not permitted to speak of one's wartime reminiscences today, nor is one under any impulse to do so. It is an area of general reticence: an unmentionable subject among younger friends, and perhaps of mild ridicule among those of radical opinions. All this is understood. And one understands also why it is so.
>
> It is so, in part, because Chapman Pincher and his like have made an uncontested take-over of all the moral assets of that period; have coined the war into Hollywood blockbusters and spooky paper-backs and

television tedia; have attributed all the value of that moment to the mythic virtues of an authoritarian Right which is now, supposedly, the proper inheritor and guardian of the present nation's interests.

I walk in my garden, or stand cooking at the stove, and muse on how this came about. My memories of that war are very different.[3]

This is followed by a reassuringly confident passage which is a classic text for studying the popular memory of the 1940s, but the struggle is intense, the victory narrow, and the near-silencing of so strong and masculine a voice in the shape of its domestication is very revealing.

It is this kind of recovery that has become the mission of the radical and democratic currents in oral history, popular autobiography and community-based publishing. We will look at these attempts to create a socialist or democratic popular memory later in the argument. But we wish to stress first that the study of popular memory cannot be limited to this level alone. It is a necessarily *relational* study. It has to take in the dominant historical representation in the public field as well as attempts to amplify or generalize subordinated or private experiences. Like all struggles it must needs have two sides. Private memories cannot, in concrete studies, be readily unscrambled from the effects of dominant historical discourses. It is often these that supply the very terms by which a private history is thought through. Memories of the past are, like all common-sense forms, strangely composite constructions, resembling a kind of geology, the selective sedimentation of past traces. As Gramsci put it, writing about the necessity of historical consciousness for a Communist politics, the problem is ' "knowing thyself" as a product of the historical process to date which has deposited in you an infinity of traces, without leaving an inventory'. Similarly the public discourses live off the primary recording of events in the course of everyday transactions and take over the practical knowledge of historical agents. It is for these reasons that the study of 'popular memory' is concerned with *two* sets of relations. It is concerned with the relation between dominant memory and oppositional forms across the whole public (including academic) field. It is also concerned with the relation between these public discourses in their contemporary state of play and the more privatized sense of the past which is generated within a lived culture.

POPULAR MEMORY AS A POLITICAL PRACTICE

[. . .] The political uses of history do seem to us more problematic even from a Marxist perspective. This is especially the case when history is defined as 'the study of the past'. We have come to see this as one of the key features of professional history, and indeed, of historical ideologies. Certainly it is deeply problematic from the viewpoint of 'popular memory'. For memory is, by definition, a term which directs our attention not the past but to *the past–present relation*. It is because 'the past' has this living active existence in the present that it matters so much politically. As 'the past' – dead, gone or only *subsumed* in the present – it matters much less. This argument may be clarified if we compare a number of approaches to the political significance of history. [. . .]

The construction of traditions is certainly *one* way in which historical argument operates as a political force though it risks a certain conservatism; similarly any adequate analysis of the contemporary relations of political force has to be historical in form as well as reaching back to more or less distant historical times. It must also attempt to grasp the broader epochal limits and possibilities in terms of a longer history of capitalist and patriarchal structures. What we may insist on in addition is that all political activity is intrinsically a process of historical argument and definition, that all political programmes involve some construction of the past as well as the future, and that these processes go on every day, often outrunning, especially in terms of period, the preoccupations of historians. Political domination involves historical definition. History – in particular popular memory – is a stake in the constant struggle for hegemony. The relation between history and politics, like the relation between past and present, is, therefore, an *internal* one: it is about the politics of history and the historical dimensions of politics. [. . .]

The formation of a popular memory that is socialist, feminist and antiracist is of peculiar importance today, both for general and for particular reasons. Generally, as Gramsci argued, a sense of history must be one element in a strong popular socialist culture. It is one means by which an organic social group acquires a knowledge of the larger context of its collective struggles, and becomes capable of a wider transformative role in the society. Most important of all, perhaps, it is the means by which we may become selfconscious about the formation of our own common-sense beliefs, those that we appropriate from our immediate social and cultural milieu. These beliefs have a history and are also produced in determinate processes. The point is to recover their 'inventory', not in the manner of the folklorist who wants to preserve quaint ways for modernity, but in order that, their origin and tendency known, they may be *consciously* adopted, rejected or modified.[4] In this way a popular historiography, especially a history of the commonest forms of consciousness, is a necessary aspect of the struggle for a better world.

More particularly, the formation of a popular socialist memory is an urgent requirement for the 1980s in Britain. Part of the problem is that traces of a politicized memory of this kind chart, on the whole, a post-war history of disillusionment and decline. In particular, there is a sense of loss and alienation so far as the Labour Party is concerned. But the problem is deeper than this difficulty (which, even now, the socialist revival within and outside the Labour Party may be lessening). For what are to be the forms of a new socialist popular memory? A recovery of Labour's past will hardly do; nor is it helpful to chart the struggles only of the male, skilled, white sectors of the working class who have formed the main subjects of 'labour history' to this day. We need forms of socialist popular memory that tell us about the situation and struggles of women and about the convergent and often antagonistic history of black people, including the black Britons of today. Socialist popular memory today has to be a *newly constructed enterprise*; no mere recovery or re-creation is going to do. Otherwise we shall find that nostalgia merely reproduces conservatism.

RESOURCES AND DIFFICULTIES

Resources

The resources for such a project are great but they are also, in important ways, very disorganized, systematically disorganized that is, not merely 'lacking organization'. This has much to do with the diverse social origins of different kinds of resources and the immense difficulties of their combination. For many resources have, in the last two decades, been created through the critical work of academic practitioners – especially, in our field, historians, sociologists, philosophers and so on, dissatisfied with the limits and ideologies of their professional discipline. 'Cultural studies' has developed along these lines, but belongs to a very much wider field of radical and feminist intellectual work where much of the stress has been, till lately, upon theoretical clarification and development. But there have been important breaks outside the academic circles too, or in a tense relation to them. They have been most commonly connected to adult education (especially the WEA) or to schoolteaching or to post-1968 forms of community action. The principal aim of these tendencies has been to democratize the practices of authorship; in the case of 'history' to lessen or remove entirely the distance between 'historian' and what Ken Worpole has called 'the originating constituency'. The characteristic products of this movement have been popular autobiographies, orally based histories, histories of communities and other forms of popular writing. But it has also developed a characteristic critique of academic practice that stresses the inaccessibility even of left social history in terms both of language and price, and the absorption of authors and readers in the product (book or journal) rather than the process by which it is produced and distributed. Partly because of the stress on 'language' and the commitment to 'plain speech', oral-historical or popular-autobiographical activists are often deeply critical of the dominant forms of theory. It is this division that is, in our opinion, a major source of disorganization. The tensions between the 'activist' and 'academic' ends of radical historical tendencies are explosive to a degree that is often quite destructive. They are often qualitatively less productive than directly cross-class encounters in which working-class people directly interrogate academic radicals. Even so there is a beginning of useful connections between academic 'critics' and community activists (who are not always different persons); where patience holds long enough on either side there are the beginnings of a useful dialogue. Some of this can be traced in the pages of *History Workshop Journal*, the conference volume to History Workshop 13 and in the writings, especially, of some authors whose experience spans an 'amateur' and 'professional' experience.[5] In general History Workshop (as journal and as 'movement') has been distinguished by its attempt to hold together these two unamiable constituencies along with other groups under the banner of 'socialist' or 'people's' history. In this sense History Workshop is the nearest thing we have to an *alternative* 'historical apparatus', especially if its own recently-formed federation is placed alongside the older Federation of Worker Writers and Community Publishers.[6] In what follows we want simply to note some developments, within and outside the History Workshop movement that seem to us already to point towards the study of popular memory.

It is oral history – the evocation and recording of individual memories of the past – which seems, at first sight, nearest to the popular memory perspective, or one aspect of it. In fact the term oral history embraces a very large range of practices only tenuously connected by a 'common' methodology. What interests us most about oral history is that it is often the place where the tension between competing historical and political aims is most apparent: between professional procedures and amateur enthusiasm, between oral history as recreation (in both senses) and as politics, between canons of objectivity and an interest, precisely, in subjectivity and in cultural forms. Later, we want to illustrate these tensions by looking at the early work of the oral and social historian Paul Thompson.[7] [. . .]

In focusing part of our argument around Thompson's work, we do not mean to imply that there are not alternative models. Other adaptations of oral history are, indeed, much nearer to our own concerns. We would cite for example the critique of oral history, in its more empiricist forms, to be found in Luisa Passerini's work.[8] Her pursuit of the structuring principles of memory and of forgetfulness, her concern with representation, ideology and subconscious desires, her focus on 'subjectivity' as 'that area of symbolic activity which includes cognitive, cultural and psychological aspect',[9] and her understanding of subjectivity as a ground of political struggle, all bring her work very close to British traditions of cultural studies, especially where they have been influenced by feminism. Her critique of oral history seems to us much more radical than its sometimes guarded expression might suggest. And we agree absolutely with her criticisms of English debates for the failure to connect oral history as a *method* with more general theoretical issues.[10] The beginnings of her analysis of popular memories of Italian fascism in Turin mark a large advance on most thinking about the cultural and political (as opposed to merely 'factual') significance of oral history texts.

Although there is a beginning of a more self-reflexive mood in Britain, the strengths here lie more in a developed practice of popular history, often building on the social and labour history traditions. This is the case, for example, with the most stunning single work drawing on evoked memories of participants – Ronald Fraser's *Blood of Spain*.[11] The lessons of this book for future practice lie more in the way it is written than in any self-conscious

prescriptions by the author, a long-time practitioner of oral history or 'qualitative sociology'. What we found interesting in *Blood of Spain* was the use of
oral remembered material in something like the form in which it is first
evoked: not as abstracted 'facts' about the past, but as story, as remembered
feeling and thought, as personal account. The whole book is woven from
such stories and retrospective analyses, sometimes quoted, sometimes para-
phrased, clustered around the chronology of the Spanish Civil War or the
make-or-break issues that were debated and literally fought out in its course.
There is a sense in which Fraser's interviewees actually 'write' *Blood of Spain*
by providing the author with the cellular form of the larger work: innumerable tiny personal narratives from which is woven a larger story of heroic
proportions and almost infinite complication. *Blood of Spain* is history
through composite autobiography, the re-creation of experience in the form
of a thousand partial and warring viewpoints.[12]

But it is arguable that the most significant development has been the growth
of community history, popular autobiography and working-class writing
more generally, where the terms of authorship have been more completely
changed. In one sense, *all* these texts and projects are evidence for the forms of
popular memory; they are all about the relation of past to present, whether
self-consciously 'historical' or not. Some projects, however, have specifically
focused on these themes: the chronologically-ordered sequence of accounts
of work in Centreprise's *Working Lives*, part of the *People's Autobiography of
Hackney*, is one example,[13] the work of the Durham Strong Words Collective,
especially *Hello Are You Working?* (about unemployment) and *But the World
Goes on the Same* (about past and present in the pit villages) is another.[14] The
Durham work is especially organized around contrasts of 'then' and 'now',
often viewed through inter-generational comparisons. As the editors put it:

> The past exerts a powerful presence upon the lives of people in County
> Durham. The pit heaps have gone but they are still remembered, as is the
> severity of life under the old coal owners and the political battles that were
> fought with them. As they sit, people try to sort things out in their minds –
> how *were* things then? How different are they now? And why?[15]

Different from either of these projects are the politically located, culturally
sensitive projects around history and memory that have developed within the
contemporary Women's Movement. There is already a strong past–present
dialogue at work within contemporary feminism. [. . .] Much feminist history
also draws on oral materials, sometimes using them in innovative ways.[16] The
autobiographies evoked by Jean McCrindle and Sheila Rowbotham, and
published as *Dutiful Daughters*, are framed by the editors' feminism and by a
distinctive politics of publication. The aim is to render private feminism
oppression more public and more shared, thereby challenging dominant
male definitions and the silencing of women.[17] Works like this continue a long
feminist tradition of writing about past and present through autobiographical form. We might also note in this collection, in the Durham work, in

Jeremy Seabrook's *What Went Wrong?* and elsewhere the beginnings of an interest in a specifically socialist popular memory. It was interesting that both *Dutiful Daughters* and *What Went Wrong?* were the subjects of 'collective reviews' at History Workshop 14.[18]

Not all relevant practices and debates belong to what would usually be thought of as 'historical' work. Indeed, there is a real danger that 'History', who is often a very tyrannous Muse, will draw the circumference of concerns much too narrowly. That is one reason why the broader categories – black, or women's or working-class 'writing' for example – are sometimes preferable. Even here, though, there are unhelpful limitations: the commitment, for example, to the *printed* word and the tendency to neglect other practices including the critique of dominant memory in the media. It is here that debates on 'popular memory' which come out of a completely different national and theoretical tradition are so important, especially debates in France around Michel Foucault's coinage of 'popular memory' as a term.[19] French debates focus on such issues as the representation of history in film and around the 'historical' policies of the French state – for example the Ministry of Culture's promotion of popular history and archival retrieval during the official Heritage Year of 1979.[20] Another important French voice for us has been Jean Chesneaux's *Pasts and Presents: What is History For?*, a militant and sometimes wildly iconoclastic attack on French academic history, including academic social history written by Marxists.

One importance of the French debates is that they have directed attention to the possibility of radical cultural practice of an 'historical' kind outside the writing of history books.[21] It is important to note developments of this kind in film, community theatre, television drama and radical museum work. The film *Song of the Shirt*, the television series *Days of Hope*, the television adaptation of Vera Brittain's *Testament of Youth* and the strong historical work of radical theatre groups like 7:84, Red Ladder and The Monstrous Regiment are examples of 'history-making' often with a real popular purchase, yet usually neglected by historians. Innovations in this area are intrinsic to popular memory both as a study and a political practice. They should certainly receive as much interest and support from socialist and feminist historians as the latest historical volume, or the newest issue of 'the journal'.

Difficulties and contradictions

What, then, are some of the difficulties in realizing the potential of these resources? Oral history and popular autobiography have, after all, now been around for some time, initially generating a real excitement. Why have the political effects been fairly meagre? What are the remaining blocks and inhibitions here?

There are, perhaps, four main areas of difficulty. Very often these have to do with the tensions that exist between the academic or professional provenance of new practices and their adaptation to a popular politics. We will summarize the four areas of difficulty briefly here. [. . .]

The first set of difficulties is epistemological in character. They arise from the ways in which 'historical' objects of study are defined. They revolve around the empiricism of orthodox historical practice. They are not purely technical matters for philosophers to adjudicate. The historian's empiricism is a real difficulty. It blocks political progress. That is why it is so important to return to these questions once more, showing the political effects of this persistently empiricist stance.

The second set of difficulties derive initially from the form in which the 'raw material' of oral history or popular autobiography first arises: the *individual* testimony, narrative or autobiography. This poses, in a very acute form, the problem of the individual subject and his or her broader social context. In what sense is individual witness evidence for larger social changes? How can these changes themselves be understood, not as something that evades human action, but also as the product of human labour, including this individual personality? This difficulty runs through the oral history method and through the autobiographical form. It is also reflected in larger divisions of genres: history, autobiography, fiction (with its particular experiential truth). Such diversions in turn encapsulate hierarchies of significance. The oral-historical witness or the autobiographer, unless held to be a personage of exceptional public power, speaks only for herself; it is the historian who, like the Professor in *Lucky Jim*, speaks literally for 'History'. Some resolution of this persistent problem, some way of thinking the society of individuals, would be an important additional resource.

We have already touched on a third set of difficulties: the tendency to identify the object of history as 'the past'. This largely unquestioned feature of historical common sense has extremely paradoxical results when applied to oral history or popular autobiography. Indeed it shows us that this definition cannot be held without a radical depoliticization of the practice of research. What is interesting about the forms of oral-historical witness or autobiography are not just the nuggets of 'fact' about the past, but the whole way in which popular memories are constructed and reconstructed as part of a *contemporary* consciousness. In this section we will look at some of the characteristic ways in which a sense of the past has been constructed in private memories.

The fourth set of difficulties is more fundamental. It concerns not just the manifest intellectual and theoretical blockages, but the social relations which these inhibitions express. In oral history and in similar practices the epistemological problem – how historians are going to use their 'sources' – is also a problem of human relationships. The practice of research actually conforms to (and may in practice deepen) social divisions which are also relations of power and of inequality. It is cultural power that is at stake here, of course, rather than economic power or political coercion. Even so research may certainly construct a kind of economic relation (a balance of economic and cultural benefits) that is 'exploitative' in that the returns are grossly unequal ones. On the one hand there is 'the historian', who specializes in the production of explanations and interpretations and who constitutes himself as the most active, thinking part of the process. On the other hand, there is his 'source' who happens in this case to be a living human being who is positioned in the process in order to yield up information. The interviewee is certainly subject to the professional power of the interviewer who may take the initiative in seeking her out and questioning her. Of course, the problem may be solved rhetorically or at the level of personal relations: the historian may assert that he has 'sat at the feet of working-class witnesses' and has learnt all he knows in that improbable and uncomfortable posture. It is, however, *he* that produces the final account, *he* that provides the dominant interpretation, *he* that judges what is true and not true, reliable or inauthentic. It is his name that appears on the jacket of his monograph and his academic career that is furthered by its publication. It is he who receives a portion of the royalties and almost all the 'cultural capital' involved in authorship. It is his *amour propre* as 'creator' that is served here. It is his professional standing among his peers that is enhanced in the case of 'success'. In all this, at best, the first constructors of historical accounts – the 'sources' themselves – are left untouched, unchanged by the whole process except in what they have given up – the telling. They do not participate, or only indirectly, in the educational work which produces the final account. They may never get to read the book of which they were part authors, nor fully comprehend it if they do.

We have deliberately overdrawn this case, to make the point polemically. But we do not describe an untypical situation for the more professionalized types of oral-historical practice. The question is what are the wider effects of such social divisions? Are they transformable? To what extent, locally, fragilely, have they already been transformed? And what are the difficulties and opportunities involved in further transformations? Much is at stake here. We are discussing a particular form of class relation (that between working-class people and sections of the professional middle class) and how it can be transformed into a more equal alliance. It is an alliance that happens to have a crucial one in the history of left politics and one which is certainly central to the future of socialism and feminism today. [. . .]

NOTES

1 J. Chesneaux, *Pasts and Futures or What is History For?*, London, Thames & Hudson, 1978, especially pp. 1 and 11.
2 C. Hill, *Change and Continuity in Seventeenth Century England*, London, Weidenfield & Nicolson, 1974, p. 284.
3 E.P. Thompson, *Writing by Candlelight*, London, Merlin, 1980, pp. 130–131.
4 Q. Hoare and G. Nowell-Smith (eds and trans.), *Selections from the Prison Notebooks of Antonio Gramsci*, London, Lawrence & Wishart, 1971, *passim* but especially pp. 324–325.

5 See especially the debate between K. Worpole, J. White and S. Yeo in R. Samuel (ed.), *People's History and Socialist Theory*, London, Routledge & Kegan Paul, 1981, pp. 22–48.
6 The FWWCP was founded in 1976 and 'links some twenty or more working class writers' workshops and local publishing initiatives around the country'. For a useful account of the history of History Workshop see R. Samuel, 'History Workshop, 1966–80,' in Samuel, *People's History*, pp. 410–417.
7 [See pp. 221–227 and 231–234 of the original article – eds.]
8 L. Passerini, 'Work ideology and consensus under Italian fascism', *History Workshop Journal*, 1979, no. 8, pp. 82–108; L. Passerini, 'On the use and abuse of oral history' (mimeo translated from L. Passerini (ed.), *Storia Orale: Vita Quotidiana e Cultura Materiale delli Classe Subalterne*, Torino, Rosenberg & Sellier, 1978. We are grateful to the author for sending us a copy of this paper. See also her position paper given at History Workshop, 13: 'Oral history and people's culture' (mimeo, Nov.–Dec. 1979).
9 Passerini, 'Italian fascism', p. 83.
10 Passerini, 'Use and abuse', pp. 7–8.
11 R. Fraser, *Blood of Spain: The Experience of Civil War 1936–39*, London, Allen Lane, 1979. See also R. Fraser, *Work: Twenty Personal Accounts*, 2 vols, Harmondsworth, Penguin, 1967.
12 We are grateful to Bill Schwarz for sharing his responses to this book.
13 'A people's autobiography of Hackney', *Working Lives*, 2 vols., Hackney WEA and Centreprise, n.d. For Centreprise more generally see K. Worpole, *Local Publishing and Local Culture: An Account of the Centreprise Publishing Project 1972–77*, London, Centreprise, 1977, and *Centreprise Report*, December 1978.
14 K. Armstrong and H. Beynon (eds), *Hello, Are you Working? Memories of the Thirties in the North East of England*, Durham, Strong Words, 1977; Strong Words Collective, *But the World Goes on the Same: Changing Times in Durham Pit Villages*, Durham, Strong Words, 1979. We are grateful to Rebecca O'Rourke for introducing us to the work of this collective.
15 Strong Words, *But the World Goes on the Same*, p. 7.
16 For example, the use of autobiographical material in J. Liddington and J. Norris, *One Hand Tied Behind Us*, London, Virago, 1978.
17 J. McCrindle and S. Rowbotham (eds), *Dutiful Daughters*, Harmondsworth, Penguin, 1979.
18 J. Seabrook, *What Went Wrong? Working People and the Ideals of the Labour Movement*, London, Gollancz, 1978.
19 M. Foucault, 'Interview', in *Edinburgh '77 Magazine* (originally published in French in *Cahiers du Cinéma*, 1974). See also *Radical Philosophy*, 1975, no. 16.
20 P. Hoyau, 'Heritage year or the society of conservation', *Les Révoltes Logiques* (Paris), 1980, no. 12, pp. 70–77. See also the report on *Cahiers du Forum – Histoire* in *Les Révoltes Logiques*, 1979–80, no. 11, p. 104, a group with similar interests and aims to our own.
21 Hence the debate in Britain on radical filmic practices and historical drama. See, for example, C. MacCabe, 'Memory, phantasy, identity: *Days of Hope* and the politics of the past', *Edinburgh '77 Magazine*; K. Tribe, 'History and the production of memories', *Screen*, 1977–8, vol. xvii, no. 4; C. McArthur, *Television and History*, London, British Film Institute, 1978.

8 Telling our stories

Feminist debates and the use of oral history

Joan Sangster

Joan Sangster is Professor of History and Women's Studies at Trent University, Peterborough, Ontario. Extracted from *Women's History Review*, 1994, vol. 3, no. 1, pp. 5–28, with permission from the author and *Women's History Review* (Triangle Journals Ltd).

> When people talk about their lives, people lie sometimes, forget a little, exaggerate, become confused, get things wrong. Yet they are revealing truths . . . the guiding principle for [life histories] could be that all auto-biographical memory is true: it is up to the interpreter to discover in which sense, where, and for what purpose.[1]

For almost two decades, feminist historians have played an important role within the profession stimulating new interest in, and debate surrounding, oral history.[2] The feminist embrace of oral history emerged from a recognition that traditional sources have often neglected the lives of women, and that oral history offered a means of integrating women into historical scholarship, even contesting the reigning definitions of social, economic and political importance that obscured women's lives. The topics potentially addressed through oral history; the possibilities of putting women's voices at the centre of history and highlighting gender as a category of analysis; and the prospect that women interviewed will shape the research agenda by articulating what is of importance to *them*; all offer challenges to the dominant ethos of the discipline. Moreover, oral history not only redirects our gaze to overlooked topics, but it is also a methodology directly informed by interdisciplinary feminist debates about our research objectives, questions, and use of the interview material.[3]

Although both popular and scholarly historical works have increasingly embraced oral history as a methodology able to expose ignored topics and present diversified perspectives on the past, there lingers some suspicion that oral sources may be inappropriate for the discipline. As one labour historian recently pointed out, it would be unthinkable for historians to host a conference session asking 'written sources: what is their use?'[4] Yet one still finds that question posed for oral history. Consideration of whether oral sources are 'objective', it appears, still worries the profession – even for those using oral history.[5]

While the biases and problems of oral history need to be examined – as do the limitations of other sources – my intention is not to retrace these older debates, but rather to examine some of the current theoretical dilemmas encountered by feminist historians employing oral history. Rather than seeing the creation of oral sources as biased or problematic, this creative process can become a central focus for our research: we need to explore the construction of women's historical memory. Asking why and how women explain, rationalise and make sense of their past offers insight into the social and material framework within which they operated, the perceived choices and cultural patterns they faced, and the complex relationship between individual consciousness and culture.[6]

For feminist historians, two other questions are pressing: what are the ethical issues involved in interpreting other women's lives through oral history, and what theoretical approaches are most effective in conceptualising this methodology? The latter question is especially timely in the light of recent post-structuralist scepticism that we can locate and describe a concrete and definable women's experience, separate from the cultural discourses constructing that experience.[7]

I wish to explore these three interrelated issues using examples from my own oral history research on the lives of wage-earning women in the large factories of Peterborough, Canada, from 1920 to the end of the Second World War. [. . .]

ORAL HISTORY AND THE CONSTRUCTION OF WOMEN'S MEMORIES

If we are to make 'memory itself the subject of study',[8] our interviews must be carefully contextualised, with attention to who is speaking, what their personal and social agenda is, and what kind of event they are describing. We need to unearth the underlying assumptions or 'problematic' of the interview, and to analyse the subtexts and silences, as well as the explicit descriptions in the interview.[9] We need to avoid the tendency, still evident in historical works, of treating oral history only as a panacea designed to fill in the blanks in women's or traditional history, providing 'more' history, compensating where we have no other sources, or 'better' history, a 'purer' version of the past coming, unadulterated, from the very people who experienced it.[10] The latter approach erroneously presents oral histories as essentially unmediated, ignoring the process by which the researcher and the informant create the source together; it may also obscure the complicated questions of how memory is constructed, to what extent oral sources can ever reveal the objective experience of people, and whether oral histories should be seen as expressions of ideologies – whether dominant, submerged, oppositional – given to us in the form of personal testimony.

It is also crucial that we ask how gender, race and class, as structural and ideological relations, have shaped the construction of historical memory. The exploration of oral history must incorporate gender as a defining category of analysis, for women often remember the past in different ways in comparison with men. Some studies, Gwen Etter-Lewis points out, have found that 'women's narratives' are more liable to be characterised by 'understatements, avoidance of the first person point of view, rare mention of personal accomplishments and disguised statements of personal power'.[11] Similarly, a French oral historian noted that the women she interviewed were less likely than men to place themselves at the centre of public events; they downplayed their own activities, emphasising the role of other family members in their recollections.[12] Furthermore, women's 'embeddedness in familial life' may also shape their view of the world, and even their very consciousness of historical time.[13] In my study, for instance, many women reconstructed the past using the bench-marks of their family's life-cycle – as does Amelia, described below, whose recollections of a major textile strike are woven around, and indeed are crucially influenced by, her memory of her wedding.

Class, race and ethnicity, other writers have shown, create significant differences in how we remember and tell our lives: in some instances, these influences overshadow gender in the construction of memory. Cultural values shape our very ordering and prioritising of events, indeed our notions of what is myth, history, fact or fiction.[14]

In my study, class shaped people's recollections in stark, as well as subtle, ways. Not surprisingly, managers remember history differently than workers; a manager in one factory described the period when the company explored relocation to other cities in search of lower wages as 'an interesting'[15] time of travel and experimentation as he knew his job would be salvaged. But workers in the plant who faced job loss remember that same period as 'stressful'[16] and uncertain. On a more subtle level, in this workplace, many women's reticence to speak forcefully as critics of, or experts on, their workplace contrasted markedly to managers' strong sense of pre-eminence on these issues; these contrasting styles reflected the confidence shaped by both class and gender inequalities.

One's past and current political ideology also shape the construction of memory. Women who were more class conscious, militant trade unionists did not hesitate to criticise managers and they presented workplace conditions in a more critical light than other workers. Interviewees' knowledge of my ideological sympathies, combined with their own, could also shape the interview. A male trade union official I interviewed tended to remember his life story around the theme of himself as a progressive socialist, battling more conservative unionists. Suspecting I was a feminist, his role *vis-à-vis* the defence of women's rights in the union became aggrandised in his interview, beyond my own reading of the written record.

The influences of class, gender, culture or political worldview on memory may reveal themselves through both content and the narrative form of the interview. While recent writing on oral history draws heavily on post-structuralist theory to explore narrative form and the way in which subjectivity is created, similar themes have preoccupied oral history theorists for some time. Almost twenty years ago, Ronald Grele suggested we uncover the theme which suffuses the life history, the 'script' around which an informant shapes the presentation of their life. Amelia, for instance, though now comfortable, grew up in the 1930s in a poor farming family; at 15 she was forced to leave school to work in a textile mill. Throughout the interview, she criticised current social values, often by contrasting her youth – characterised by hard work and selfless dedication to her family – to the current selfish, affluent youth. Whether or not she was influenced by a conservative philosophy that distrusted modern trends, or whether she wished to understand her relative success as a result of hard work, or whether she was hurt by the seeming neglect by the younger members of her family – or all of the above – the point is that this critical worldview came to colour her description of the working conditions she had seen in the textile factory.

Oral history may also illuminate the collective scripts of a social group, revealing, for instance, how and why people's memories of their workplaces or communities are created.[17] Many workers I interviewed who were employed at a factory which embraced paternalism as a labour relations strategy, emphasised the 'family-like'[18] atmosphere at the plant, and the way in which the patriarchal and charismatic company head saw himself as a father figure. Their descriptions of the rise and decline of the firm were recounted in the form of an epic family drama, with the eventual economic decline of the factory actually compared to a family breakup. Their way of remembering indicates the assimilation, at some level, of the familial metaphors employed by the company to promote its paternalism.

Other ingredients of the narrative form, such as expression, intonation and metaphors also offer clues to the construction of historical memory. When I asked one woman how her family survived during the time she and her father were on strike in 1937, she could not remember. It is possible, first, that the family went on welfare but that she has forgotten because it was a humiliating experience for some people. Later in the interview, however, she made a casual *aside*, noting her mother 'sewed at home for extra money'.[19] Her mother may have supported the family during the strike, but her work in the informal economy (like that of many women) was undervalued, remembered as an afterthought, indeed almost forgotten.

Revelations may also come from silences and omissions in women's stories.[20] The realisation that discrimination based on religion is not socially desirable led many women I interviewed initially to deny any religious rivalry in their workplaces; yet one such woman, when describing a different issue – the foreman intervening in a bitter dispute on the line – admitted that severe Catholic and Protestant taunting had initiated the disagreement. One of the most telling examples of silences is the way in which women reacted to the subject of violence. In response to questions about sexual harassment at work (often I did not begin by using that modern term) or about women's freedom on the streets after work, women seldom spoke of women's vulnerability to violence. Others purposely contrasted the absence of violence when they were younger to contemporary times: in their youth, they claimed, women could walk home alone at night, they were not bothered at work, and violence against women was rare.

Yet, from other sources and research, I knew that violence in the streets, and in women's homes, was very much a part of daily life. I came to understand women's silence in a number of ways: for one thing, a few women's veiled and uncomfortable references to harassment indicated that some working women, especially in the 1930s, saw harassment as an unfortunate but sometimes obligatory part of the workplace that one could not change and did not talk about. Secondly, it is not only that feminism has made us more aware of harassment and thus provided us with a vocabulary to describe it, but also that similar experiences were labelled differently in the past, often with the term 'favouritism'. Third, a denial of violence was sometimes an externalisation of women's ongoing painful fears about violence, and a comforting means of idealising a chivalrous past in contrast to the more visible violence of today.

Finally, in order to contextualise oral histories, we also need to survey the dominant ideologies shaping women's worlds; listening to women's words, in turn, will help us to see how women understood, negotiated and sometimes challenged these dominant ideals. For example, perceptions of what was proper work for young women are revealed as women explain the images, ideas and examples upon which they constructed their ambition and work choices. Ideals of female domesticity and motherhood, reproduced in early home life, the school and the workplace, and notions of innate physical differences, for instance, were both factors moulding young women's sense of their limited occupational choices in both blue and white collar work in the 1930s.[21] Interviews may also indicate when women questioned these dominant ideals, as a few notable women described how and why they made the unusual decision not to marry, to work after marriage, or to attempt a non-traditional job.

Understanding the ideological context may help to unravel the apparently contradictory effects of ideology and experience. Why, for example, when I interview women who worked during the Second World War, do they assume that the war had a liberating effect on women's role in the workplace, even when they offer few concrete examples to substantiate this? As Ruth Pierson points out, sex segregation and gender hierarchy persisted in the Canadian wartime workforce, despite rhetoric to the contrary. Why this contradiction between women's positive memory of new opportunities during the war, and the reality of persisting discrimination?[22] One answer may be the powerful and hegemonic influence of a popular and mystifying ideology of 'the people's war' – the notion that women were breaking down gender roles – on the very construction of women's memory.[23] Secondly, oral history may reveal women's own definitions of liberation, which actually diverge from those utilised by historians. In this small city, women saw the wartime abandonment of the marriage bar in local factories as a small revolution for working women. Historians, on the other hand, have based their assessments of continuing inequality on the maintenance of a gendered division of labour during and after the war.

In using oral history as a means of exploring memory construction, then, careful attention to the processes of class and gender construction is needed, as is an understanding of ideological context shaping women's actions. In order to understand the formation of women's gendered consciousness and memory, however, we must also acknowledge our *own* influence on the shape of the interview.

ETHICAL DILEMMAS: FOR HISTORIANS TOO

It is important to acknowledge how our own culture, class position and political worldview shapes the oral histories we collect, for the interview is a historical document created by the agency of *both* the interviewer and the interviewee. Many of us originally turned to oral history as a methodology with the radical and democratic potential to reclaim the history of ordinary people and raise working-class and women's consciousness. As feminists, we hoped to use oral history to empower women by creating a revised history '*for* women',[24] emerging from the actual lived experiences of women. Feminist oral history has often implicitly adopted (though perhaps not critically theorised about) some elements of feminist standpoint theory in its assumption that the distinct material and social position of women produces, in a complex way, a unique epistemological vision which might be slowly unveiled by the narrator and historian.[25]

'Representing the world from the standpoint of women', while a laudable feminist aim, may still be difficult to accomplish. As well as the thorny theoretical question of our ability to adequately locate women's experience (discussed below) there are two other concerns. Are we exaggerating the radical potential of oral history, especially the likelihood of academic work changing popular attitudes? Even more important, are we ignoring the uncomfortable ethical issues involved in using living people as a source for our research?

Some years ago, feminist social scientists mounted a critique of interview relationships based on supposed 'detachment' and objectivity, but in reality on unequal power and control over outcome. As a solution, sociologists like Ann Oakley proposed the laudable aim of equalising the interview, making it a more cooperative venture.[26] Yet, in attempting this, we may be simply masking our own privilege. While a detached objectivity may be impossible, a false claim to sisterhood is also unrealistic. As Janet Finch has argued, a romanticisation of oral history research that ignores the fact that we are often 'trading on our identity – as a woman, a professional'[27] – to obtain information is unacceptable. Judith Stacey also points out that feminist research is inevitably enmeshed in unequal, intrusive and potentially exploitative relationships, simply by virtue of our position as researchers and that of other women, with less control over the finished product, as 'subjects' of study.[28] I agree. Nor will renaming these relationships with terms implying a sharing of power completely erase our privilege.[29] After all, we are using this material for the purpose of writing books which are often directed, at least in part, to academic or career ends. I gained access to women's memories not as a friend, but as a *professional historian*.

These ethical issues are visibly highlighted through the conflicting interpretations which may be embraced by my informants and myself. By necessity, historians analyse and judge, and in the process, we may presume to understand the consciousness of our interviewees. Yet our analysis may contradict women's self-image, and our feminist perspective may be rejected by our interviewees. Would women who worked in the paternalist factory I studied agree to the very word paternalist as a description of their relationship to management? Would workers in low paid textile work accept language like subordination or exploitation to describe their status in the family or workplace? The answer to the latter two questions may be no.

While I had every intention of allowing women to speak about their *own* perceptions, if my interpretation and theirs diverged, mine would assume precedence in my writing. We can honour feminist ethical obligations to make our material accessible to the women interviewed, never to reveal confidences spoken out of the interview, never to purposely distort or ridicule their lives, but in the last resort, it is our privilege that allows us to interpret, and it is our responsibility as historians to convey their insights using our own – as the opening quotation to this article indicated. Even feminists like Judith Stacey and Daphne Patai, who offer trenchant critiques of the unequal interview relationship, do not recommend abandoning this methodology; in the last resort, they see the potential for feminist awareness and understanding outweighing the humbling recognition that it is currently impossible to create an ideal feminist methodology which negates power differences.

These debates have usually taken place between sociologists and anthropologists, less often with historians' participation. Why? Is it related to the fact that, as Ruth Pierson argues, until recently, we have undertheorised our work[30] Is it possible that our traditional disciplinary training – especially an emphasis on empirical methods and a tendency to objectify our sources, but also the preference of the discipline *not* to work with living subjects – has obscured these questions from our view? We might be less concerned about imposing our interpretations on women's voices if we were dealing with a written source; we are particularly sensitive about judging women because of the personal relationship – however brief – established between ourselves and our interviewees. But this is not necessarily positive for it may lead us to shy away from critical conclusions about their lives.

Other limitations in our historical training may also obscure these ethical questions. Is the study of people of different time periods, cultures and classes so taken for granted that we have not questioned the power inherent in writing across these boundaries? As Pierson notes on the current, troubling question of who has the 'right' to write whose history, if historians cannot study women of different backgrounds who have less power, we may be reduced to writing autobiography.[31] Perhaps the mere fact of historical time – again, inherent in the discipline – helps to distance us, if only in an illusory way, from the issue of unequal relationships. When I interview wage-earning women about their experience in the 1930s, the age gulf allows both of us detachment from the subject we are discussing, which then sanctions the license to interpret and judge.

In the last resort, I wonder how much soul searching is useful: is endless debate self-indulgent, sometimes an *ex post facto* justification of our work, and does our concern with interviewing women from other backgrounds sometimes take on a condescending tone?[32] Perhaps it is important not to definitely answer, but rather to be ever aware of these questions: we need to continually analyse the interview as an interactive process, examine the context of the interview, especially inherent power imbalances, and always evaluate our own ethical obligations as feminists to the women we interview.

THEORETICAL DILEMMAS

While it is important to explore the interview as a mediated source, moulded by the political and social worldview of the author and subject, I think we should beware of recent trends to see oral history embodying innumerable contingencies and interpretations. When more traditional historians questioned the reliability of oral sources, suggesting that interviews are more fiction than fact, they may not have realised that they were echoing the tenets of some post-structuralist analyses which explore the relationship between language, subjectivity, and the construction of cultural meanings and social organisation.

While linguistic theories are far from new in the interdisciplinary field of oral history, the more recent turn to post-structuralism suggests a more intensive concern with both linguistic structure and cultural discourses determining oral narratives, as well as a scepticism about any direct relationship between experience and representation. This theorising has enriched our understanding of oral history, but it may also pose the danger of overstating the ultimate contingency, variability and 'fictionality' of oral histories and the impossibility of using them to locate a women's past which is 'real and knowable'.[33]

Since the mid-1980s, oral historians have increasingly examined language 'as the invisible force that shapes oral texts and gives meaning to historical events'.[34] This approach is evident in the recent *Women's Words*, whose editors urge us to consider 'the interview as a linguistic, as well as a social and psychological event'.[35] While the book's contributions range widely in their perspective, substantial attention is paid to narrative form and language; one author urges the embrace of 'deconstruction' rather than mere 'interpretation' of the text.[36] In other works, the emphasis on language has been taken to more extreme conclusions, resulting in the denigration of historical agency: one such writer claims that the 'narrative discourses available in our culture ... structure perceptual experience, organize memory ... and purpose-build the very events of a life'. Our life stories then come to 'reflect the cultural models available to us', so much so that we become mere 'variants on the culture's canonical forms'.[37]

Practitioners of oral history have been more visibly influenced by the post-structuralist turn in anthropology and by some literary theory than by similar historical debates. In anthropology, life histories are being re-evaluated as post-structuralist voices emphasise the power-laden, complex process of *constructing* the oral narratives; one author suggests that life histories 'provide us with a conventionalized gloss on a social reality that ... we cannot know ... We may be discussing the dynamics of narration rather than the dynamics of society'.[38] Similarly, works like *Writing Culture* have stressed the creation of an indeterminate reality by the observed and the observer, well summed up by the conclusion that we can only hope for 'a constructed understanding of the constructed native's constructed point of view'.[39]

Of course, post-structuralism has also stimulated debate in historical circles, with feminists apparently sympathetic or at least divided, and some working-class historians more critical.[40] Feminist historians have been understandably attracted to the challenge to androcentric epistemologies, critiques of essentialism, concerns with language and representation, and the analysis of power suggested by some post-structuralist writing.[41] Nonetheless, critics have cautioned against the inherent idealism in some post-structuralist theory and the abandonment of the search for historical causality and agency, not to mention a sense of political despair when the very notions of exploitation and oppression are deconstructed so completely as to be abandoned.[42]

These debates – which cannot be explored in detail here – have important implications for the way in which we interpret our interviews, confront the ethical questions of the power-laden interview and consider the concept of experience. New attention to language and the way in which gender is itself shaped through the discourses available to us can offer insight as we analyse the underlying form and structure of our interviews. Reading our interviews on many levels will encourage us to look for more than one discursive theme and for multiple relations of power based on age, class, race and culture as well as gender.

On the ethical question of the inherent inequality of this methodology, however, post-structuralist writing is less useful. As Judith Stacey persuasively argues, the post-modern strategy of dealing with ethical questions in ethnography is inadequate because it highlights power imbalances we knew to exist, but does not suggest any way of acting to ameliorate them. Post-structuralist anthropologists, for instance, suggest the process of 'evoking' rather than describing narratives through 'cooperative' dialogue, fragmentary or polyphonic discourse[43] as an alternative to their own power of authorship. As critics point out, however, these tactics can also veil and deny power: they can involve 'self reflection, perhaps self preoccupation, but not self criticism'.[44] Privilege is not negated simply by inclusion of other voices, or by denial of our ultimate authorship and control. Solutions that disguise power are not helpful to the historical profession in particular, which still needs to face and debate the question of power inherent in historical writing.

Finally, there is also the troubling and seemingly unsolvable problem of 'experience'. Exploring and revaluing women's experience has been a cornerstone of feminist oral history, but the current emphasis on differences between women – in part encouraged by post-structuralist writing – has posed the dilemma of whether we can write across the divides of race, class and gender about other women's experiences, past or present. In the case of oral history, Ruth Pierson implies that we should be 'as close as possible' to the oppressed group being studied, preferably a member of that group. If we are not, we should concentrate on the exterior context of women but avoid with 'epistimal humility' a presumption to know women's interioriality.[45] This raises troubling questions for me: just how close should we be to the subjects we are interviewing? Across the boundaries of sexual orientation, race, ethnicity, disability, class and age, can we score two out of six and still explore subjectivity? Where are the boundaries and under what circumstances can they shift? Secondly, separating exterior context from inner lives is extremely difficult. Does my assertion that women's ambition was socially constructed not emerge from precisely that presumptuous supposition about the relationship between context and interior life. Will we not impoverish our historical writing if we shy away from attempts to empathetically link women's inner and outer lives?

Also, is experience itself a construction of the narratives available to us in our culture? The concept of experience is not without its problems in history and feminist theory; it has been used to justify essentialism and to create a homogeneous 'woman' whose existence is enigmatic.[46] But what are the consequences of ignoring a concept which allows women to 'name their own lives'[47] and struggles, and thus validates a notion of real, lived oppression which was understood and felt by women in the past?

Related concerns were voiced over a decade ago by Louise Tilley, in her critique of oral history shaped by literary theory and used to study subjectivity, and her counter-endorsement of a materialist oral history, used to study social relations.[48] But can these two aims be so easily separated? Can the interview not be interpreted with a keen materialist and feminist eye to context, and also informed by post-structuralist insights into language? The cultural construction of memory would still be a focus of inquiry, posed within a framework of social and economic relations and imperatives. While it is important to analyse *how* someone constructs an explanation for their life, ultimately there are patterns, structures, systemic reasons for those constructions which must be identified to understand historical causality.[49] Polarities between subjectivity and social relations, or between a dated 'older' generation of women doing oral history who supposedly naively accepted the 'transparency' of their interviewees' accounts and the new 'complex' approach influenced by theory[50] may not be justified – and ironically creates precisely the kind of 'conceptual hierarchy which post-structuralism is supposed to decentre'.[51] [. . .]

CONCLUSION

My conclusions are shaped by both the moral stance of Denise Riley's assertion that, in the interests of a feminist praxis, we must lay political claim to women's experience of oppression,[52] and secondly, by a belief that post-structuralist insights must be situated in a feminist materialist context. While an emphasis on language and narrative form has enhanced our understanding of oral history, I worry about the dangers of emphasising form over context, of stressing deconstruction of individual narratives over analysis of social patterns, of disclaiming our duty as historians to analyse and interpret women's stories. Nor do we want to totally abandon the concept of experience, moving towards a notion of a de-politicised and 'unknowable' past. We do not want to return to a history which either obscures power relationships or marginalises women's voices. Without a firm grounding of oral narratives in their material and social context, and a probing analysis of the relation between the two, insights on narrative form and on representation may remain unconnected to any useful critique of oppression and inequality. [. . .]

NOTES

1 Personal Narratives Group, 'Truths', and L. Passerini, 'Women's personal narratives: myths, experiences, and emotions', in Personal Narratives Group (eds), *Interpreting Women's Lives: Feminist Theory and Personal Narratives*, Bloomington, Indiana University Press, 1989, pp. 261, 197.

2 For example: Women's History Issue, *Oral History: the Journal of the Oral History Society*, 1977, vol. 5, no. 2; special issues of *Frontiers* in 1977 and 1983; M. Chamberlain and P. Thompson, 'International Conference on Oral History and Women's History', *Oral History Review*, 1984, vol. 12, no. 1, S. Gluck, 'Introduction', in *Rosie the Riveter Revisited*, Boston, Twayne Publishers, 1987; S. Diamond, 'Women in the B.C. labour movement', *Canadian Oral History Association Journal*, 1983, vol. 6. On women's studies see J. Humez and L. Crimpacker, 'Using oral history to teach women's studies', *Oral History Review*, 1977, (summer); K. Anderson, K. Armitage, S. Jack and D. Wittner, 'Beginning where we are: feminist methodology in oral history', in J. Nielsen (ed.), *Feminist Research Methods*, 1990, Boulder, Westview Press.

3 S. Geiger, 'What's so feminist about women's oral history?' *Journal of Women's History*, 1990, vol. 2, no. 1, pp. 169–170.

4 W. Roberts, 'Using oral history to study working class history'. Paper presented at the Canadian Oral History Association Conference, Toronto, 1991.

5 H. Hodysk and G. McIntosh, 'Problems of objectivity in oral history', *Historical Studies in Education*, 1989, vol. 1, no. 1.

6 My argument here is indebted to R. Grele, *Envelopes of Sound*, Chicago, Precedent Publishing, 1975.

7 The term post-structuralist is an umbrella expression, actually referring to a number of theoretical positions. In this article I deal primarily with theories

shaped by linguistic and deconstructive approaches, which explore the construction of subjectivity and cultural meaning through language. As Chris Weedon argues, these positions generally argue that 'experience has no inherent essential meaning'. See C. Weedon, *Feminist Practice and Post-structuralist Theory*, Oxford, Basil Blackwell, 1987, p. 34.

8 M. Frisch, 'The memory of history', *Radical History Review*, 1981, no. 25, p. 16. See also M. Frisch and D. Watts, 'Oral history and the presentation of class consciousness', *International Journal of Oral History*, 1980, vol. 1, no. 20.

9 These warnings come from Grele, *Envelopes of Sound.*

10 M. Frisch, 'Report on the International Conference on Oral History', *Oral History Journal,* 1983, p. 8. See also his 'The memory of history'. Both older and some newer articles reflect these tendencies. See, for example, E. Silerman, *The Last Best West: Women on the Alberta Frontier, 1880–1930*, Montreal, Eden Press, 1984; and M. Culpepper, 'Views from fourscore and more: youth and maturation in the oral histories of elderly women', *International Journal of Oral History*, 1989, vol. 10, no. 3.

11 G. Etter-Lewis, 'Black women's life stories: reclaiming self in narrative texts', in S. Berger Gluck and D. Patai (eds), *Women's Words: the Feminist Practice of Oral History*, New York, Routledge, Chapman & Hall, 1991, p. 48. This does not appear to be the case in J. Cruikshank's analysis of Northern Canadian native women's histories in *Life Lived Like a Story*, Vancouver, UBC Press, 1992. The importance of culture in shaping women's narratives is thus also crucial.

12 This is reflected overtly in language: women tended to use 'on', men, 'je'. I. Bertaux-Wiame, 'The life history approach to internal migration: how men and women came to Paris between the wars', in P. Thompson (ed.), *Our Common History; the Transformation of Europe*, New Jersey, Humanities Press, 1982.

13 S. Geiger, 'Life histories', *Signs*, 1986, p. 348.

14 See C. Salazar, 'A third world women's text: between the politics of criticism and cultural politics', in *Women's Words*, 1991; D. Sommer, 'Not just a personal story', in B. Brodski and C. Schenck (eds), *Life/Lines: Theorizing Women's Autobiography*, Ithaca, Cornell University Press, n.d.; J. Cruickshank, 'Myth and tradition as narrative framework', *International Journal of Oral History*, 1988, vol. 9, no. 3. I have chosen to emphasise class and gender in this article because the city I am studying was overwhelmingly homogeneous in ethnic composition.

15 Interview with M.H., 18 July 1989.

16 Interview with M.A., 27 June 1989.

17 On collective scripts see J. Bodnar, 'Power and memory in oral history: workers and managers at Studebaker', *Journal of American History*, 1989, vol. 75, no. 4.

18 Interview with C.E., 27 June 1989. This issue is dealt with in more detail in my 'The softball solution: male managers, female workers and the operation of paternalism at Westclox', *Labour/Le Travail*, 1993, no. 32.

19 Interview with R.M., 27 August 1989.

20 For discussion of silences and jokes see L. Passerini 'Work ideology and working-class attitudes to Fascism', in Thompson (ed.), *Our Common History*, 1982.

21 This conclusion, which is detailed elsewhere, is supported in an article on women teachers of this period which also uses oral histories. See C. Reynolds, 'Hegemony and hierarchy: becoming a teacher in Toronto, 1930–80', *Historical Studies in Education*, 1990, vol. 2, no. 1.

22 R. Roach Pierson, *They're Still Women After All: the Second World War and Canadian Womanhood*, Toronto, McClelland & Steward, 1986. For a popular Canadian book which stresses women's positive memories see J. Bruce, *Back the Attack! Canadian Women during the Second World War, at Home and Abroad*, Toronto, Macmillan, 1985. For a scholarly discussion of women's memories and

how 'women were changed by war work in subtle and private ways', S. Gluck, *Rosie the Riveter Revisited: Women, the War and Social Change*, Boston, Twayne Publishers, 1987, p. 269.

23 See Grele, *Envelopes of Sound*, for discussion of how notions of hegemony and ideology may be useful in analysing oral histories. On the use of hegemony see also J. Lears, *American Historical Review*, 1985, vol. 90, no. 3.

24 My conscious re-shaping of D. Smith's words from *The Everyday World as Problematic*, Boston, Northeastern Press, 1987.

25 Here, I am not only referring to Smith, noted above, but also N. Hartstock, 'The feminist standpoint: developing the ground for a specifically feminist historical materialism', in S. Harding (ed.), *Feminist Methodology*, Bloomington, Indiana University Press, 1987. See also A. Jaggar, *Feminist Politics and Human Nature*, Totowa, Rowman & Allanheld, 1983, pp. 369–371; and S. Harding, *The Science Question in Feminism*, Ithaca, Cornell University Press, 1986, chs 6 and 7.

26 A. Oakley, 'Interviewing women: a contradiction in terms', in H. Roberts (ed.), *Doing Feminist Research*, London, Routledge & Kegan Paul, 1981.

27 J. Finch, 'It's great to have someone to talk to: the ethics and politics of interviewing women', in C. Bell and H. Roberts (eds), *Social Researching: Politics, Problems, Practice*, London, Routledge & Kegan Paul, 1984, p. 78.

28 J. Stacey, 'Can there be a feminist ethnography?', in Gluck and Patai, *Women's Words*. See also D. Patai, 'US academics and Third World women: is ethical research possible?', in *Women's Words*.

29 See Personal Narrative Group, *Interpreting Women's Lives*, p. 201, for the recommendation we replace 'researcher-subject' with 'life historian-producer'.

30 R. Roach Pierson, 'Experience, difference, dominance and voice in the writing of Canadian women's history', in K. Offen, R. Roach Pierson and J. Rendall (eds), *Writing Women's History: International Perspectives*, Bloomington, Indiana University Press, 1991.

31 Ibid.

32 For example in K. Olsen and L. Shopes, 'Crossing boundaries, building bridges: doing oral history with working-class women and men', in Gluck and Patai, *Women's Words*, one author notes that she puts her working-class interviewees 'at ease' with a measure of self-disclosure: yet, the example she selects leaves me somewhat unsettled: 'Informants are more willing to reveal their own experience when they learn that I have shared many of the family problems that plague them – a father who was chronically unemployed, a son whose adolescent acting-out included run-ins with juvenile services, a troubled marriage that ended in divorce' (p. 194). Are there certain 'assumptions' about working-class life inherent in this statement? For a critique of proceeding from such assumptions about 'representativeness' see Geiger, 'What's so feminist about women's oral history?'

33 L. Tilly, 'Gender, women's history, social history and deconstruction', *Social Science History*, 1989, vol. 13, no. 4, p. 443.

34 G. Etter-Lewis, 'Reclaiming', in Gluck and Patai, *Women's Words*, p. 44.

35 S. Gluck and D. Patai, 'Introduction', in their edited book *Women's Words*, p. 9.

36 G. Etter-Lewis, 'Black women's life stories', in Gluck and Patai, *Women's Words*, p. 44.

37 J. Bruner, 'Life as narrative', *Social Research*, 1987, p. 54.

38 V. Crapanzano, 'Life histories', *American Anthropologist*, 1984, vol. 86, no. 4, p. 955.

39 V. Crapanzano, 'Hermes' dilemma: the masking of subversion in ethnographic description', in J. Clifford and S. Marcus (eds), *Writing Culture: the Politics and Poetics of Ethnography*, Berkeley, University of California Press, 1986, p. 74. For a feminist critique of this book see F. Mascia-Lees, P. Sharpe and C. Ballerino

Cohen, 'The post-modernist turn in anthropology: cautions from a feminist perspective', *Signs*, 1989, vol. 15, no. 1.

40 For a taste of this discussion see J. Scott, *Gender and the Politics of History*, New York, Columbia University Press, 1988; D. Riley, *Am I That Name: Feminism and the Category of 'Woman' in History*, Minneapolis, University of Minnesota Press, 1988; J. Newman, 'History as usual?: feminism and the new historicism', in H. Veeser (ed.), *The New Historicism*, London, 1989, and *Radical History Review*, 1989, no. 43. See the replies to Scott in *The International Journal of Labour and Working Class History*, 1987, no. 31, and critical reviews of her book, *Women's Review of Books*, 6 January 1989, and *Signs*, 1989, vol. 15, no. 4. For a critique by a working-class historian see B. Palmer, *Descent into Discourse*, Philadelphia, Temple University Press, 1990, or for a Marxist critique, E. Wood, *The Retreat from Class*, London, Verso, 1986.

41 Indeed, some of these insights have been inspired by feminist writing. See J. Flax, 'Post modernism and gender relations in feminist theory', *Signs*, 1987; L. Alcoff, 'Cultural feminism versus post-structuralism', *Signs*, 1988, vol. 13, no. 3. L. Gordon also points to ways in which some 'new' insights of post-structuralism are not really very new in her review of Scott in *Signs*, 1990, vol. 15, no. 4. Her conclusion applies to the field of oral history.

42 D. Tress, 'Comment on Flax's postmodernism and gender relations in feminist theory', *Signs*, 1988, vol. 14, no. 1, p. 197. For other semi-critical assessments see also M. Valverde, 'Poststructuralist gender historians: are we those names', *Labour/Le Travail*, 1990, vol. 25; M. Walzer, 'The politics of Foucault', in D. Hoy (ed.), *Foucault: a Critical Reader*, Oxford, Basil Blackwell, 1986; M. Jehlen, 'Patrolling the borders', *Radical History Review*, 1989, vol. 43, and a far more severe critique, N. Hartstock, 'Foucault on power: a theory for women?', in L. Nicholson (ed.), *Feminism and Postmodernism*, New York, Routledge, 1990.

43 S. Tyler, 'Post-modern ethnography: from document of the occult to occult document', in Clifford and Marcus, *Writing Culture.*

44 Mascia-Lees *et al.*, 'The post-modernist turn in anthropology'. These authors are understandably sceptical of some post-modern theories implying that 'verbal constructs (voices) do not relate to reality, that truth and knowledge are contingent, that no one subject position is possible' (p. 15) developed by Western, white academic men at precisely the moment these men are being challenged by women's and Third World voices.

45 Pierson, 'Experience', pp. 91–94.

46 M. Barrett, 'The concept of difference', *Feminist Review*, 1987.

47 L. Stanley, 'Recovering women in history from feminist deconstruction', *Women's Studies International Forum*, 1990, vol. 13, nos. 1–2.

48 L. Tilly, 'People's history and social science history'. See the responses in *International Journal of Oral History*, 1985, vol. 6, no. 1. This was also well characterised as a debate between hermeneutic and ethnographic methods in oral history by D. Bertaux and M. Kohli, 'The life story approach: a continental view', *Annual Review of Sociology*, 1984, vol. 10. Again analyses of linguistic structure and narrative form, and explorations of how the writer 'creates' the historical document are both long-standing concerns in oral history.

49 See Cruikshank's (1988) examination of myth, narrative form and social and economic structures in 'Myth and tradition as narrative framework'.

50 Gluck and Patai, *Women's Words*, 'Introduction'.

51 P. Stevens Sangren, 'Rhetoric and authority of ethnography: post-modernism and the social reproduction of texts', *Current Anthropology*, 1988, vol. 29, no. 3, pp. 405–424.

52 Riley, *Am I That Name?*

Part II

Interviewing: introduction

The point when historians began to use interviews to gather information absent in documentary and printed sources, and whether this can be characterized as 'oral history interviewing', has been much debated.[1] Journalists routinely used interviews from the middle of the nineteenth century onwards and by the turn of this century social investigators valued interview evidence. Amongst historians, after generations of hostility towards interview data, the emergence of the oral history movement since 1945 has forced a reassessment, as Part I of this volume has shown. Portable tape recorders liberated us from laborious note-taking, and the *frisson* of excited discovery that marks early writings espousing oral history interviewing as the key to discovering more about the past, has given way to a more acute discussion of the interview relationship. It is this discussion that we explore in this section. If there is an emphasis on audio interviewing to the detriment of video techniques, this is partly because of the paucity of good writings on video interviewing and partly because it is considered in Part V.[2]

Charles Morrissey's piece which opens this section was published nearly thirty years ago and although its focus is ostensibly on elite and political interviewing,[3] there is little that many oral history practitioners would quibble with today. He rightly argues that it is impossible to reduce interviewing to a set of techniques or rules, but none the less summarizes the kind of practical advice which is to be found in a plethora of oral history handbooks: the value of preparation, the importance of establishing a rapport and intimacy, of listening and of asking open-ended questions, not interrupting, allowing for pauses and silences, avoiding jargon, probing, minimizing the presence of the tape recorder and so on.[4]

What has changed in the intervening years, with oral history techniques being taken up all over the world, has been a gradual awareness that the interviewing relationship is both significantly more complex and culturally specific: that the methods taken for granted by oral historians in the North can be wholly inappropriate for researchers in the South. This is the focus of Hugo Slim and Paul Thompson's piece on collecting oral testimony in developing countries, in which they characterize the one-to-one interview as a 'dangerously intimate encounter' and emphasize the value of group remembering. Drawing on the work of anthropologists, they point out that in certain societies storytelling has a season (often winter) and that researchers need to be aware of local hierarchies and 'norms relating to turn-taking' which may differ markedly from interviewing in the North.[5] They also explore the applicability of a variety of interview approaches: family-tree interviewing, single-issue testimony, diary interviewing, focus groups and community interviews. Whilst other oral historians have written of eliciting memories through introducing photographs[6] and objects[7] into the interview, Slim and Thompson highlight the value of visual techniques when gathering testimony in communities unfamiliar with the interview form: time-lines, maps and diagrams become expressions of personal and collective memory.

These are techniques that Jan Walmsley finds similarly valuable in working with people with learning disabilities, though she sees them as supplementary to the life story or 'biographical chronology' form of interviewing that many oral historians now espouse as the most effective means of contextualizing specific experiences. For Walmsley, life story interviews with people with learning difficulties present a challenge and she emphasizes that adaptations have to be made to the research process if the interviewer's aims are to be fully explained and disempowered people are to have a voice.[8] She found that one-to-one interviews are not always possible and that her interviewees often have carers functioning as participant intermediaries, who in some cases try to control the content and circumstances of the interview.

Ensuring informed consent is never straightforward in any interview context, and in recent years oral history groups and associations around the world have attempted to address the moral issue of ownership by rendering the power relationship inherent to the interview situation into codes of ethics and interview guidelines.[9] Early oral historians tended to see themselves as professionals, slightly aloof from the data-gathering process, where they merely needed to ask sensible questions to extract useful information. Most of the pieces in Part II represent more recent thinking, in which the interview is viewed as a co-construction, a dynamic process of interactivity where there is a recognition that the interviewer takes a major role in shaping the interview.

In this context the issue of 'insider–outsider' interviewing is central to Akemi Kikumura's reflections on interviewing her own mother, an Issei woman from Japan who immigrated to the United States in 1923. Whilst 'outsider' status is believed to accord objectivity and detachment, an 'insider' perspective has the benefits of special insight otherwise obscure to outsiders. She concludes, in this case, that her mother would *only* have spoken openly to her because she was an 'insider' family member: 'No! You don't disclose your soul to *tanin* [a non-relative]'; and argues that the dichotomy is a false one. She shows that it is possible to be simultaneously an insider (a family member) and an outsider (generationally and culturally remote from her mother's Japanese upbringing).[10]

Belinda Bozzoli also explores 'insider interviewing' in an extract from

Women of Phokeng, a study of black South African women which seeks to assess the 'consciousness of the powerless' in a society of 'inequality and brutality'. She picks up the issues around culturally specific interviewing raised by Slim and Thompson and goes on to argue that her colleague Mmantho Nkotsoe's successful interviewing was due to her 'insider' status as a local, black female, speaking the same dialect as her interviewees and from the same class.[11] She observes that a spontaneous and unstructured questioning approach of informal exchanges had yielded the most revealing results.[12] Yet she also found that the interaction between interviewer and interviewee affected the women's remembering.

Kathryn Anderson and Dana Jack take this a stage further by arguing that in 'uncovering women's perspectives' the interviewer needs to shift from 'information gathering to interaction', moving beyond facts to subjective feelings, by listening more carefully not only to what is said but what is meant.[13] When interviewing women we need to learn to listen 'in stereo', they argue, to women's dominant *and* muted channels of thought.[14] Although as interviewers we are active participants in the process, we need to be acutely aware of our own agendas, setting aside preconceived structures and interpretations which might directly impact on the interview. We must be vigilant to discrepancies between what is said through the conventions of ordinary social conversation and the meanings that lie beneath. Listening for 'meta-statements' or reflections, for silences and for internal consistency, becomes vital.

We close Part II with a piece about an aspect of interviewing which often preoccupies novice interviewers: traumatic remembering. Naomi Rosh White has interviewed Jewish Holocaust survivors and discusses some of the 'difficulties in telling' where there is no shared world, no shared values, when words are not enough to describe such horror. In listening for language, as Anderson and Jack and others encourage us to do,[15] words like 'cold' and 'hungry' take on different meanings in the setting of a death camp. These meanings can only be guessed at by the interviewer. Indeed some writers, including Elie Wiesel, have suggested that the Holocaust is so traumatic and so utterly removed from 'normal' human experience that it can never be spoken about directly, it can only be evoked through silence.[16] Listening for silences, as much as for words, becomes central to the interviewing relationship, providing new layers of meaning.

Amongst Holocaust survivors there is a compelling desire to 'bear witness' (as there is amongst survivors from the Soviet 'gulag' and Central American refugees featured in Part III), and White argues that this 'shatters the conventional boundaries ... and prohibitions against disclosure'. The need to speak out to prevent similar attrocities from happening again, forces us to shift our understanding of the relationship between private memory and public memory, where the private takes precedence.[17]

Ultimately every interview is different and each person brings something unique to the relationship as it evolves. As Beatrice Webb has said: 'A spirit of adventure, a delight in watching human beings as human beings quite apart from what you can get out of their minds, an enjoyment of the play of your own personality with that of another, are gifts of rare value in the art of interviewing.'[18]

NOTES

1 For example: P. Thompson, *The Voice of the Past: Oral History*, Oxford, Oxford University Press, 1988; C. Morrissey, 'Why call it oral history? Searching for early use of a generic term', *Oral History Review*, 1980, vol. 8, pp. 20–48; C. Silvester (ed.), *The Penguin Book of Interviews: An Anthology from 1859 to the Present Day*, London, Viking, 1993.

2 An important exception is T.A. Shorzman, *A Practical Introduction to Video-history: The Smithsonian Institution and Alfred P. Sloan Foundation Experiment*, Florida, Krieger, 1993, which surveys the field. Also Brad Jolly, *Videotaping Local History*, Nashville, American Association for State and Local History, 1982.

3 A. Seldon and J. Pappworth, *By Word of Mouth: 'Elite' Oral History*, London, Methuen, 1983, surveys this field very effectively. On the challenges of political interviewing see Blee (Chapter 28), and C. Romalis, 'Political volatility and historical accounts: tiptoeing through contested ground', *Canadian Oral History Association Journal*, 1992, vol. 12, pp. 25–29.

4 For example: R. Perks, *Oral History: Talking about the Past*, London, The Historical Association, 1995; V.R. Yow, *Recording Oral History: A Practical Guide for Social Scientists*, London, Sage, 1994; D. Ritchie, *Doing Oral History*, New York, Twayne, 1995; M. Hutching, *Talking History: A Short Guide to Oral History*, Wellington, New Zealand, Bridget Williams Books/Historical Branch of the Department of Internal Affairs, 1993; B. Robertson, *Oral History Handbook*, third edition, Adelaide, Oral History Association of Australia (South Australia Branch), 1994; P. Hayes, *Speak for Yourself*, Namibia, Longman, 1992; E.D. Ives, *The Tape-Recorded Interview: A Manual for Field Workers in Folklore and Oral History*, Knoxville, University of Tennessee Press, 1980; E.G. Mishler, *Research Interviewing: Context and Narrative*, Cambridge, Mass., Harvard University Press, 1986. Morrissey offers a valuable and amusing blow-by-blow critique of an interview in 'John Hawkes on tape: The paradox of self-identity in a recorded interview', *International Journal of Oral History*, 1985, vol. 6, no. 1.

5 See for example E. Tonkin, *Narrating Our Pasts: The Social Construction of Oral History*, Cambridge, Cambridge University Press, 1992; T.A.C. Royal, *Te Haurapa: An Introduction to Researching Tribal Histories and Traditions*, Wellington, New Zealand, Bridget Williams Books/Historical Branch of the Department of Internal Affairs, 1992; and R. Finnegan, *Oral Tradition and the Verbal Arts*, London, Routledge, 1991. It is worth adding that an understanding of these norms has proved equally valuable for researchers working with different cultural groups in the North, see N. North, 'Narratives of Cambodian refugees: issues in the collection of refugee stories', *Oral History*, 1995, vol. 23, no. 2 , pp. 32–39.

6 J. Modell and C. Brodsky, 'Envisioning Homestead: using photographs in interviewing', in E.M. McMahan and K. Lacey Rogers (eds), *Interactive Oral History Interviewing*, Hilldale, N.J., Erlbaum, 1994, pp. 141–161.

7 For example G.E. Evans, 'Approaches to interviewing', *Oral History*, 1973, vol. 1, no. 4, pp. 56–71.

8 The US context for oral history and disability is explored by Hirsch (Chapter 18). For the British context see S. Humphries and P. Gordon, *Out of Sight: The Experience of Disability 1900–1950*, Plymouth, Northcote, 1993; M. Potts and R. Fido, *A Fit Person To Be Removed*, Plymouth, Northcote, 1991.

9 Oral History Association, *Evaluation Guidelines*, Los Angeles, OHA, 1992; A. Ward, *Oral History, Copyright and Ethics*, Colchester, Oral History Society, 1995; National Oral History Association of New Zealand, *Code of Ethical and Technical Practice*, in Hutching, *Talking History*, pp. 71–72; *Oral History Association of Australia Journal*, 1993, vol. 15: special issue on 'Publicity and privacy: balancing the interests in oral history'. See also V.R. Yow, 'Ethics and interpersonal relationships in oral history research', *Oral History Review*, 1995, vol. 22, no. 1, pp. 51–66; Yow, *Recording Oral History*, pp. 84–115; A. Lynch, 'The ethics of interviewing', *Canadian Oral History Association Journal*, 1979, vol. 4, no. 1, pp. 4–9; and J. Guy and M. Thabane, 'The Ma-Rashea: a participant's perspective', in B. Bozzoli (ed.), *Class, Community and Conflict*, Johannesburg, Ravan, 1987. On power relations in interviewing see the pieces by Friedlander (Chapter 26) and Blee (Chapter 28).

10 On family interviewing see C. Parekowhai, 'Korero taku whaea: Talk my Aunt. Learning to listen to Maori women', *Oral History in New Zealand*, 1992, no. 4, pp. 1–4; L. Shopes, 'Using oral history for a family history project', and T. Harevan, 'The search for generational memory', both in D.K. Dunaway and W.K. Baum (eds), *Oral History: An Interdisciplinary Anthology*, second edition, London, Altamira Press, 1996, pp. 231–240 and pp. 241–256; also *Oral History Association of Australia Journal*, 1981–2, no. 4: special issue on 'Family and local history'. On interviewing friends see M. Zukas, 'Friendship as oral history: a feminist psychologist's view', *Oral History*, 1993, vol. 21, no. 2, pp. 73–79; P. Cotterill, 'Interviewing women: issues of friendship, vulnerability and power', *Women's Studies International Forum*, 1992, vol. 15, nos. 5/6, pp. 593–606; M. Stuart, 'And how was it for you, Mary? Self, identity and meaning for oral historians', *Oral History*, 1993, vol. 21, no. 2, pp. 80–83. More generally see J. Stanley, 'Including the feelings: personal political testimony and self-disclosure', *Oral History*, 1996, vol. 24, no. 1, pp. 60–67.

11 The issue of interviewing in a second language and through an interpreter is explored in M. Andrews, 'A monoglot abroad: working through problems of translation', *Oral History*, 1995, vol. 23, no. 2, pp. 47–50; and North, 'Narratives of Cambodian refugees'.

12 Whether it is helpful to have a questionnaire or question structure has been much debated. See Thompson, *The Voice of the Past*, Chapter 7 for a summary; also P. Thompson, 'Tony Parker: writer and oral historian', *Oral History*, 1994, vol. 22, no. 2, pp. 64–73.

13 On feminist interviewing see Sangster (Chapter 8) for an overview, and the other essays in the excellent anthology by S.B. Gluck and D. Patai (eds), *Women's Words: The Feminist Practice of Oral History*, London, Routledge, 1991; also A. Oakley, 'Interviewing women: a contradiction in terms', in H. Roberts, *Doing Feminist Research*, London, Routledge, 1981, pp. 30–61; R. Edwards, 'Connecting method and epistemology: a white woman interviewing black women', *Women's Studies International Forum*, 1990, vol. 13, no. 5, pp. 477–490; J. Scanlon, 'Challenging the imbalances of power in feminist oral history: developing a take-and-give methodology', *Women's Studies International Forum*, 1993, vol. 16, no. 6, pp. 639–645; A. Janson, 'Respecting silences: recording the lives of immigrant women', *Oral History in New Zealand*, 1990/1, no. 3, pp. 11–13.

14 I. Bertaux-Wiame, 'The life story approach in the study of internal migration', *Oral History*, 1979, vol. 7, no. 1, pp. 26–32, discusses how men and women reminisce in different ways.

15 R.J. Grele, 'History and the languages of history in the oral history interview: who answers whose questions and why', in E.M. McMahan and K. Lacey Rogers (eds), *Interactive Oral History Interviewing*, Hilldale, N.J., Erlbaum, 1994, pp. 141–161; E.M. McMahan, *Elite Oral History Discourse: A Study of Cooperation and Coherence*, Tuscaloosa, University of Alabama, 1989.

16 E. Wiesel, *One Generation After*, New York, Simon & Shuster, 1970. L.L. Langer, *Holocaust Testimonies: The Ruins of Memory*, Newhaven, Yale University Press, 1991, is an essential text on the Holocaust and oral history.

17 For a summary of the public–private debate see A. Thomson, *Anzac Memories: Living with the Legend*, Oxford, Oxford University Press, 1994; and his piece in Part IV (Chapter 25).

18 B. Webb, *My Apprenticeship*, Cambridge, Cambridge University Press, 1979 (reprint of 1926 edition), p. 411, see also pp. 361–363 on interviewing.

9   On oral history interviewing

Charles T. Morrissey

Charles T. Morrissey is Oral History Consultant for Baylor College of Medicine and the Howard Hughes Medical Institute. He was President of the Oral History Association, 1971–2. Reprinted from L.A. Dexter (ed.), *Elite and Specialised Interviewing*, Northwestern University Press, Evanston, Ill., 1970, pp. 109–118.

The more I've discussed oral history with various people, the more I've become impressed with the fact that techniques and other aspects of oral history vary with the type of person you're interviewing. My experience with political figures might be different from someone who is interviewing people in medical research, scientists, early alumni of the University of California, or people in other professions. Likewise, with any large category of people there are individual variations. I interviewed fat old tired congressmen and bright young men who came to Washington with John F. Kennedy, in some cases younger than me. It is an unusual experience to be interviewing someone on Kennedy who is not yet thirty-one years old.

A lot depends on the interviewer, and I'm talking now about a single interviewer. We have tried team interviewing, but I'm rather lukewarm about it. In some cases it's worked out well, but it all depends on the person you're talking to. To some people, three is a crowd; others enjoy having several people around the table. For the most part, however, we prefer one interviewer facing one interviewee. We think that works out best.

A lot depends on the interviewer's background: how much prior research he's done; how many interviews he's already conducted; that is, how many interviews he's conducted on the subject that he's going to discuss with the person before him today. Did he have a preliminary, exploratory interview in which to discuss the project and procedures? That very definitely has an influence on how he would conduct the interview.

How much control does he have over the situation confronting him? Once, I went to interview a senator [Jacob Javits], and was told I could have only twenty minutes with him. Then I was kept waiting forty minutes before getting into his office, so obviously this is a factor. When you're rushing for an airplane, if you've done four interviews and you have a fifth one coming up, you're not in the best of shape to really focus on the fifth one. (I've done as many as five in a single day, in a city away from home). You're tired, you're run-down, you're confused, and in some cases you can't remember if the person you're interviewing said something to you five minutes ago, or if somebody you interviewed earlier in the day said something to you; that very definitely affects your technique. A lot depends on how much control you have over your situations.

Let me say that to reduce interviewing to a set of techniques is, as one person put it, like reducing courtship to a formula. Gould Colman has pointed this out; Elizabeth Dixon has pointed this out in some of the things she's written about the UCLA project. There is a danger of too much reliance on tools and not relying sufficiently on old-fashioned intuition as to which tool to use in which situation.

It's very easy to be critical of how someone does an interview. You've probably heard the story of the football player who ran back the opening kickoff of a game for a touchdown. The coach called him off the field and criticized him for not doing things right. He cut the wrong way; he used the wrong arm to straight-arm somebody, and so forth; and the player said, 'How was it for distance, Coach?'

We should truly play it by ear, so what follows is meant to be taken in a cautious, tentative way. It will sound much more didactic than it is intended. Nevertheless, I want to distill my experience with interviewing about ninety people on the Kennedy project and about fifteen on the Truman project.

We had what we called volunteer interviewers at the outset of the Kennedy project, about 135 of them, who did a total of about 300 interviews. When I say volunteers, I mean journalists, people in the administration, colleagues of people to be interviewed, friends, all sorts of arrangements, put on a kind of person-to-person, informal basis. There were two other interviewers working with me full time on the Kennedy project, and it was my responsibility to train them and supervise their work.

In dealing with both President Truman and President Kennedy, our interest was episodic. We'd interview a person on his association with each of these presidents. We were not strictly autobiographical in getting his whole story. This obviously has problems; when you interview someone like Averell Harriman, you'd like to get the whole story. But our purpose was to focus on the Kennedy chapter or the Truman chapter and hope that, someday, somebody will get the rest. We just couldn't do everything.

One of the things we emphasized was to let the interviewee talk. It's his show. Let him run with the ball. As Louis Starr said, 'A good interviewer is a good listener'. Oftentimes we would start by saying, 'When did you first meet John Kennedy?' or 'When did you come into his orbit?' He would take off, usually chronologically; this might turn into a topical treatment, just running on haphazardly; I would sit and listen. There's a value to this because he's volunteering what's foremost in his recollections.

While this was going on, I would often sit with a notepad and pencil, just writing one or two words about things he had covered, or things I wanted to come back to. Before the interview started, I would tell him that I would take notes, in the sense of trying to get down just a word here or a word there, or perhaps asking him later for the correct spelling of a name he mentioned. We always carried a notepad with us when we went on an interview.

After he had run through his story, I would often go back and interlace my questions with what he had already said, trying to probe deeply into certain matters, raising points he missed, asking for examples of generalizations he had given.

In phrasing our questions, we found it most important to leave them open-ended, that is, not to indicate in the phrasing of the question the answer you expected to get. We would not offer alternatives and say, 'Was it this way or that?' or 'Was it either this way or that way?' We would try to state the question in such a way as to get him to pick his own alternative, because he might come up with one that we had not anticipated. We would avoid the loaded word. On the film of the interview done at Berkeley, that word 'lobby-ist' bothered me. Some people aren't 'lobbyists': they are 'public relations consultants', 'industrial representatives', or something else. We would try very desperately not to impress our own conclusions on the answers the man was giving. It is very hard to restrain yourself, but one way we would try to do it would be to phrase our question, 'To what extent was such and such so?' not, 'Was such and such so?' We would not try to build a case like a lawyer trying to build a case in a courtroom. I used to advise people to read the Warren Report, because so many times the attorney would say, 'This is the way it was, wasn't it?' and the witness would say, 'Yes' or 'No'. And right down the page, the answers are yes or no. We went at it saying, 'Tell us how it was; describe it in your own words', to let the interviewee volunteer what he thought was important.

I advise people to read the transcripts of Lawrence Spivak's program, 'Meet the Press', and then do it just opposite from the way he does it. Those transcripts are available, incidentally. It is worthwhile to see how someone can phrase a tricky question in trying to trip up someone being interviewed on that program.

We would of course avoid jargon, and for academic people that's difficult. Many people in Washington don't like academic people and don't under-stand academic publications because of the jargon. Dean Acheson, among others, has spoken very forcefully on this point.

We would try to focus in our interviews on the dynamics of how policy was developed, the actual development of policies. This may seem obvious to us, but many of these volunteer interviewers we had on our project would ask a man in 1964 or '65 how he appraised policy developed back in '61 and '62. We wanted to know how that policy developed, and then, perhaps, conclude with his appraisal of it. One guideline I would stress, perhaps above all others, is that a good interviewer should pursue *in detail*, constantly asking for examples, constantly asking people to illustrate points they are making.

A good interviewer should not allow intimations to pass into the record without elaboration: specifically what did the person mean by such and such? We would try to keep our questions brief and pointed. At most, a question, in our opinion, should occupy no more than two sentences: one sentence to say, 'this is why I'm going to ask you this question', and then, 'This is the question

I'm asking you', ending the question with a question mark, and then sitting, biting the lip, keeping quiet, letting the man think (hopefully), letting him answer the question. It's difficult to endure, that embarrassing silence that bothers so many of us socially when we talk.

In oral history one of the great dangers is for the interviewer to feel that he has to keep talking until the interviewee tries to get a word in edgewise. I think, sometimes, the interviewer tends to rush things. We should let the interviewee set his own pace; if it is slow, from our viewpoint, nonetheless it is his pace. We should let him go at his own rate. With the volunteer interviewers in the Kennedy project, we found, time after time, that they were rushing the man from one point to another, and we actually had cases of the man saying, 'Just a minute, can I say something about that last point, before you rush on?'

People often ask about mike fright. Are people afraid of the mike and the tape-recording equipment? Our experience with the Kennedy volunteer interviewers was that *they* were more scared of the equipment than were the people being interviewed. Most of the people being interviewed were familiar with microphones; they had spoken publicly; they had dictated their own letters into dictaphones, and so forth. However, many of the volunteer interviewers were new to operating tape-recording equipment and were uneasy with it. They didn't know whether they were doing the right thing, whether the volume was high enough, whether the mike was close enough, and this sort of thing. It bothered and affected the quality of the interview.

When there were very tough questions to be asked, we learned to postpone the tough ones until the interview was well under way. Obviously, we wanted to establish good rapport; the longer the interview lasted, more times than not, the man would relax, open up, and even enjoy the occasion. Likewise, if we asked tough questions, the man might take offense, and that would affect the remainder of the interview. The definition of a tough question varies for different people. Some people were offended when we raised the question of John Kennedy's religion as a factor in the 1960 election, which strikes us as a very normal question for a political scientist or historian to ask about. Also, if we had several tough questions to ask, we would never ask them consecutively. We would ask one, handle it, and then try to move the interview into an area we wanted the man to talk about, so he would relax and enjoy it; then perhaps later, we would come back to another tough one.

In phrasing the tough ones we often did what book reviewers do: 'Some readers might object to the author's tendency to do such and such', which really means, 'I object to his tendency to do such and such.' We'd say, 'Some people have reported that you got into difficulty on such and such a project.' In other words, we're asking him to answer these anonymous people who aren't in the room.

Constantly in our interviews, if we had an important subject we wanted to cover, we would return to it from different angles. Let's say we were interested in the West Virginia primary of 1960; so we'd ask about it, why Kennedy defeated Humphrey. Later, if we were talking about how the Kennedy campaign was organized, we might move back into West Virginia from a different angle, such as the Kennedy organization in West Virginia and how it was set up. If later we were talking about public-opinion polls, we'd move into the West Virginia primary from that angle; if we were talking about campaign finances, we'd move in from there; and if we were talking about the relationship between John Kennedy and Hubert Humphrey throughout their political careers, we'd move in from there. We were always amazed at how a different approach on a different topic would produce new information. The danger, in other words, is to think a matter has been entirely discussed when you cover it once, drop it, and then don't come back.

In the course of all this, we would try to find out how good the man's memory was. We would throw in little questions, sometimes, to test it. For example, if he mentioned the name of a person named Lawrence, we'd say 'Is that the Lawrence that was governor of Pennsylvania or the Lawrence who writes for *U.S. New and World Report*?' And we would say, 'Did that happen before or after something else happened?' And these little clues someday, we assume, will help the researcher who's reading the transcript or listening to the tapes to decide how much weight he should put on the testimony of this person.

Likewise, we would try to find out, indirectly, how close the person was to the events he was discussing, if he was intimately involved or on the periphery. We tried to ask questions to bring this out. And many times somebody would admit, 'Well, no, I wasn't there when that happened, but I heard about it afterwards.' And that of course has great bearing on how much weight a historian should put on it.

We tried to find out who was involved in a certain matter – let's suppose, how the Peace Corps speech was prepared in the 1960 campaign. Who was where? Who worked on what draft? and so forth. This obviously has leads for the future; and in interviewing other people you can ask them about it.

We would also ask a lot of these people what other evidence would exist for the things they were talking about. Would there have been a memorandum on the subject? Or did some newspaperman with entrée have something reliable in his column on that particular subject? Did he keep a diary? Was there exchange of correspondence on it? And, as a result, in the long run the oral history transcripts at the Kennedy Library will say an awful lot about the documentation in conventional written sources pertaining to the Kennedy Administration.

We would try not to miss the obvious, even if it seemed silly to cover the obvious. For example, somebody would say, 'I was responsible for getting voters registered in the Mexican precincts of Los Angeles.' Well, to him, I suppose, this was an obvious task, but we wanted to know exactly how you go about it. Where do you start? What do you do? And we'd ask him to elaborate on some of these procedures that people in public office and public affairs conduct.

We'd often use documents in our interviews; that is, if the man's memory was poor, let's say on the 1948 campaign, I'd have an itinerary of where Truman spoke in that campaign, each stop, right through the day. Or we'd present a picture of the people who were present at a certain occasion. By seeing the people who were there, he might say, 'Oh yes, this fellow helped us with the draft of such-and-such.' Or we'd show him newspaper columns and say, 'How does this represent your impressions of how such-and-such happened?

On other occasions, we'd set up a hypothetical adversary. This is a technique that Forrest Pogue of the George Marshall Library has used. He'd say to someone, 'You were present when Roosevelt died, and someday someone is going to write a book saying Roosevelt was murdered. How would you answer that?' And of course the fellow would offer all sorts of evidence in response to it.

There were many times when we were stuck. We were covering matters we didn't know much about, so we'd rely on the old-fashioned journalistic technique of who, what, when, where, how, why, and so forth.

Also, constantly in the course of interviewing we would try to put ourselves in the position of the person being interviewed. We'd try to visualize the web he operated in, if he had worked with people in Congress, in the White House, in the Bureau of the Budget, and in other departments, the press, lobbyists, or the Democratic National Committee. We would try to visualize how he must have operated with all these other people in Washington, and in that way try to think of questions that would perhaps bring to light some of these relationships.

We'd also try to put ourselves in the place of other students who would be interested in what this person had to say, and suddenly the oral historian becomes an economist or sociologist, or he says, 'If I were a biographer of John Kennedy, what could this person offer about the biography of Kennedy? If I'm a student of public administration, what can he offer about certain procedures that were conducted?'

We'd ask ourselves. 'How does this fellow spend his day? Where does his time go?' And if you could figure that out, you could figure out what questions to put to him.

We sent our transcripts back to be edited by the person interviewed. In the eyes of many people, this is considered to be indulgence to the interviewee. We used it as a second opportunity to ask questions we didn't think to ask in the first interview. We would ask for the elaboration. We'd clip a question to the side of the page and say, 'Senator, could you give an example of this?' In some cases, if a man had not covered a subject in the transcript, we would leave a blank section. 'Would you mind writing in ink some more on this?' With that blank paper in front of him when he went through the transcript, sometimes he would actually sit there and fill it up with two hundred and fifty words or so, and contribute some material that was valuable.

Also, if you chicken out in an interview and don't ask the tough questions, you can always ask them when you send the transcript back to be edited. I think the key question in assessing an oral history transcript is really not how much material does it provide for history, but rather, how well did the interviewer do with the circumstances affecting him and the material he had to work with? You can't blame the interviewer if the interviewee has a bad memory. But you can blame the interviewer if he doesn't take advantage of every opportunity available to him. And it seems to me that's the key question. If the interviewer did the best he could with what he had, you can't blame him for the results. If he did less than that, you can blame him, and I think he should be blamed appropriately. [. . .]

Interviewing, in conclusion, is very difficult when you think that the good interviewer must know his stuff; he must be listening to what the man is saying; he must think of more questions to ask; he must be thinking of what the question was he just asked, to make sure the man is answering it. He must know what's already been covered; know what he has yet to cover. He must anticipate where he's going to go if the man, while he's talking, indicates he's about through with the subject; and in anticipating where the conversation is going to go, he must in his mind be beginning to try to formulate the next question so it will come out well-phrased. It's a very difficult business. Anyone who does it successfully is probably so successful that he should himself be interviewed.

10 Ways of listening

Hugo Slim and Paul Thompson, with Olivia Bennett and Nigel Cross

Hugo Slim was Senior Overseas Research Officer for Save the Children Fund, and is now Director, Centre for Development and Emergency Planning (CENDEP) at Oxford Brookes University. Paul Thompson is Research Professor at the University of Essex. Olivia Bennett is Director, Oral Testimony Programme, Panos Institute, London. Nigel Cross was Research Director of the Sahel Oral History Project, and is now Executive Director of the Panos Institute, London. Extracted with permission from Hugo Slim and Paul Thompson, with Olivia Bennett and Nigel Cross (eds), *Listening for Change: Oral History and Development*, London, Panos, 1993, pp. 61–94. This book was published as part of the Panos Institute's Oral Testimony Programme, which explores and illustrates the potential of oral testimony in the development process; and gathers, publishes and amplifies the views and experiences of individuals and communities in the South on specific development themes.

[. . .] While the interview is now a common form of enquiry and communication in the West – where a job interview is a prerequisite for most employment, the media feature endless interviews, both informative and entertaining, and few people escape having to take part in polls and questionnaires – this is by no means a universal experience. As British anthropologist Charles Briggs has observed, in some societies the interview is not an established type of speech event, and there can often be an incompatibility between standard interview techniques and indigenous systems of communication.[1] This incompatibility can create problems for people who, as interviewees, are forced to express themselves in an unfamiliar speech format. In particular, the interview form has a tendency to put unnatural pressure on people to find ready answers, to be concise and to summarise a variety of complex experiences and intricate knowledge.[2] It may also mean that researchers and interviewers unwittingly violate local communication norms relating to turn-taking, the order of topics for discussion or various rituals attached to storytelling. In some societies, individual interviews are considered dangerously intimate encounters. In others, the recounting of group history can be a sacred ritual and certain people must be consulted before others. Sometimes a number of clearly prescribed topics should be used to start proceedings, while other topics may be taboo, or should not be introduced until a particular level of intimacy and trust has been achieved.

In many societies, community or clan history is the vested interest of particular people or a designated caste, such as the *griots* of West Africa.

They will often adapt their account to a particular audience, tailoring it to focus on the ancestors of their listeners. Alongside the right to tell, there is often a reward: payment in cash or kind for the teller. Storytelling may also have a seasonal dimension. In Ladakh, for example, winter is the time for telling stories. It is considered an inappropriate activity during the busy summer months when the agricultural workload is at its peak, as a local saying makes clear: 'As long as the earth is green, no tale should be told.'[3] It would be an ill-prepared and disappointed oral testimony project that set out to collect traditional stories in Ladakh during the summer!

There may also be special rituals of rendition which require certain elders to act as witnesses and checks on the history or stories being recounted. The proper setting for the recounting of a community history may be a feast with a minimum number present. Such conditions affect the collection of oral history and can sometimes even make it impossible, as Lomo Zachary, a Sudanese researcher, found when he tried to gather information about the origins and relations of various Ugandan clans living as refugees in South Sudan:

> I approached several clan historians but all were asking me for a 'Calabash' – meaning some liquor . . . After requesting some liquor most told me that they were unable to narrate me any stories because there were no esteemed witnesses or observers. Usually when such clan histories are told to clansmen or a group of interested young clansmen there is someone also well versed in the clan history who makes corrections when necessary. Sometimes they have long debates on a controversial item in the history. For example, the storyteller might skip or include a false family line of a particular clansman. Here the observer or witness has to interpose immediately with concrete proofs . . . So all gave me a similar response: 'My son, I am indeed grateful for your wise request for knowing where we originated from, how we have come to be separated and how we handle our affairs. I could have given you an elaborate history of our people but as you know, we are all scattered at this time. We have lost all our animals. There are no more tribal palavers where our people could be gathered . . . It could be during such sittings that our wise children could now put down all our cultures and traditions. Please accept my sincere apologies.'[4]

It is critically important to be aware of these different conceptual and cultural dimensions to interviewing and to historical information. A vital part of any preparation for an oral testimony project should involve learning about the norms of what Briggs describes as people's 'communicative repertoire': its particular forms, its special events, its speech categories and its taboos.[5] The most fundamental rule is to be sensitive to customary modes of speech and communication and allow people to speak on their own terms.

METHODS OF COLLECTION

There are a number of different kinds of interview. The most wide-ranging form is the individual life story. This allows a person to narrate the story of his or her whole life in all its dimensions: personal, spiritual, social and economic. Another kind is the single-issue interview which seeks to gain testimony about a particular aspect or period of a person's life. The object might be to hear about someone's working life, perhaps with an emphasis on indigenous knowledge, or to listen to their experiences during an event or episode such as a famine or a time of conflict or displacement. In addition to individual interviews, oral testimony can also be collected in focus group discussions, community interviews or by diary interviewing. When choosing the method(s) to be employed, it is important to bear in mind the objectives of the project and the kind of testimony required.

Life story interviews

These are normally private, one-to-one encounters between interviewer and narrator. Sessions should be held at a time convenient to the interviewee and in a suitable location, preferably somewhere which offers seclusion, comfort and familiarity. There is often no better place than the narrator's home.

In some societies, a one-to-one interview may not be acceptable, particularly for women, and one or more observers will need to be present. This can serve the additional function of testing and cross-checking information as observers interrupt to challenge or correct the interviewee. However, it can also mean that information is distorted. In some situations observers can act as censors and indeed may be there specifically to intimidate: husbands observing wives; parents observing children; or officials observing a community living in fear or repression.[6] While it is important to conform to the communicative repertoire of the people being interviewed, it pays to be aware that there may be more dubious aspects to observation and extra participation. Gender can also be an inhibiting factor and as a general rule interviewer and narrator should be the same sex.[7] [. . .]

An average life story interview may need two or three sessions and can take anything from one to eight hours. Breaking up the interview into separate sessions gives people time to remember and explore the past and makes recollection more of a process than an occasion. It takes the pressure off a single session, when the narrator might feel obliged to cram everything in. Things triggered in one session can be reflected upon by the narrator in peace and then brought to the next. The interviewer can similarly benefit from the pause between sessions.

It is important to remember that a life story interview can often have a profound effect on the interviewee, who may never have told anyone their memories before and certainly is unlikely to have recalled their whole life in the course of a few hours. For most people, recounting their life story is a positive, if emotional, experience from which they can gain much satisfaction and a renewed sense of perspective, but the listener should always ensure that the narrator is comfortable at the end of the interview and is surrounded by the support they need, whether from family or friends.

Family-tree interviewing

In the course of a life story interview, the narrator will describe many members of his or her family from contemporary or previous generations. These people will obviously be mentioned largely in terms of their impact on the narrator. However, it is possible to focus on these other family members in more depth by asking the narrator to supply second-hand accounts of their relatives' lives. This technique is perhaps best described as family-tree interviewing. [. . .]

It obviously takes up much more time, but it does give an interesting ripple effect to any study. It is perhaps most useful when one is looking for trends, rather than the specific detail of direct personal experience. An alternative, which is still more time-consuming but also a more direct measure of change, is to interview two generations from the same family.

Single-issue testimony

Single-issue interviews may be carried out on a one-to-one or group basis, and focus on a specific aspect of the narrator's life. As such they can be shorter than a life story, but more detailed. Single-issue interviews can yield valuable insights for many development and relief activities. They are the main method of learning about a particular event, such as drought, or for an investigation into a particular area of knowledge or experience. For example, they might involve interviewing farmers about land use and water conservation methods, or a traditional healer about botany and plant use. They require the interviewer to have more detailed background or technical knowledge of the subject matter than is necessary for a more wide-ranging life story.

Diary interviewing

Diary interviewing is a method which is increasingly being used by social scientists. It involves selecting a sample of people who contribute regular diary entries as part of a continuing and long-term study of social trends. Such a study might ask people to report on specific issues or it might seek more general life story material. The participants make a commitment to keep a written or oral, tape-recorded diary. Entries might be made on a daily, weekly, monthly or annual basis, and are then sent in and analysed centrally, over time.

Alternatively, diary interviewing can involve a less rigorous procedure whereby the participant is interviewed at key moments over a period of time. In a study of indigenous agricultural practices, for example, these might include particular times during the cropping calendar such as land preparation, sowing, weeding, harvesting and threshing. In a more general life story study, such moments might include religious festivals, rites of passage or different stages of educational or working life. The objective of diary interviewing is therefore to collect a running progress of a person's experience over time and not just retrospectively.

Group interviews

Oral testimony can also be collected through group work. Indeed, in many societies, group interviews may be more in keeping with the customary ways of communicating. If the concept of a one-to-one interview seems unusual or unnatural, the format of group discussions or public meetings may be more familiar and oral testimony collection can be adapted accordingly.

Groups can bring out the best and the worst in people. Sometimes, by taking the focus off individuals, they make them less inhibited, but the opposite can occur just as easily. A group may subtly pressurise people towards a socially acceptable testimony or a mythical representation of the past or of a current issue which everyone feels is 'safe' to share and which may be in some sense idealised. Communal histories gathered in this way can involve a powerful process of myth construction or fabulation which misrepresents the real complexity of the community. At worst, this can develop into a persistent false consciousness which can only tolerate the good things, and remembers 'how united we all were', or which exaggerates the totality of suffering and recalls 'how bad everything was'.[8] The voices of the less confident, the poorer and the powerless, are less likely to be heard, and so the variety of experience and the clashes and conflicts within a community may well remain hidden.

But groups can also be especially productive, as members 'spark' off one another. Memories are triggered, facts can be verified or checked, views can be challenged and the burning issues of the past can be discussed and argued about again in the light of the present. Group work can also increase rapport between project workers/interviewers and the community, encouraging people to come forward for one-to-one sessions if appropriate. Two kinds of group work are appropriate to oral testimony collection: small focus group discussions and larger community interviews.

Focus group discussions developed as an important part of market research, but are now used widely on an inter-disciplinary basis as a means of assessing attitudes and opinions. In this context, they are a particularly useful forum for discussing both the past and the major issues of the day. Focus groups are particularly appropriate for collecting testimony from people who may be very reserved on a one-to-one basis, but draw confidence from being in a familiar group. Children are a good example of this.

The idea is to bring a group together – preferably between five and twelve people – to discuss a particular issue or a number of issues. They should be a homogeneous group made up of participants of the same sex and largely equal in social status, knowledge and experience so that confidence is generally high and no-one feels threatened. The discussion should last for one to two hours, with the participants sitting comfortably and facing each other in a circle. Several consecutive sessions can be held if necessary.

Social scientist Krishna Kumar notes that the main emphasis on a focus group is the interaction between the participants themselves, and not that between participants and interviewer.[9] Focus groups are therefore guided by a 'moderator' rather than an interviewer, whose role is to steer the discussion and ask some probing questions by adopting a posture of 'sophisticated naïveté'. This encourages the group to talk in depth with confidence, but also to be ready to spell things out for the outsider. The moderator's role also involves countering the two main constraints on a focus group: dominance of the proceedings by so-called 'monopolisers'; and a sense of group pressure which can build up from a majority viewpoint and which then discourages a minority of participants from expressing their views.

Community interviews involve larger groups and may resemble public meetings more than group discussions. Their emphasis is different, too. The main interaction of a community interview is between the interviewer and the community. The ideal size is around thirty people, but no more, and two interviewers will be needed for such an event. Their role is a directly questioning one, but they must still take responsibility for balancing participation in the meeting with guiding the interview. Having two interviewers can be confusing and their respective roles should be well defined in advance of the interview, to ensure that they do not speak at the same time or interrupt each other's train of enquiry.

The advantage of a community interview is the opportunity it provides for gathering a wide cross-section of people together at one time. This is particularly useful at the outset of a project, for example, when background information is being collected or future interviewees are being sought and selected. It is also useful midway or at the end of the process of collecting interviews, when certain details or views need to be tested or checked. It can provide the occasion for a number of 'straw polls' and hand counts in order to learn how many people share experiences or hold similar views. Finally, both group and community meetings are especially useful for the 'return' of oral testimony. They can act as a review mechanism and can encourage decision-making based on the testimonies collected. [. . .]

PROPS AND MNEMONICS

Questions are not the only way to inspire a narrator and jog the memory. Physical objects, such as old tools, photographs and traditional costumes or artefacts, can provide the focus for a more detailed testimony or group discussion. A farmer will often be more eloquent when holding an implement and describing its function. A refugee may find much more to say when looking at a picture of home. However, any prop should be carefully chosen, otherwise they will tend to distract the narrator and divert the interview instead of giving it depth.

One prop which is central to the communicative repertoire of Native Americans is the talking-stick.[10] This is a ritual stick which lies in the centre of any group of people who are there to talk or listen, whether it be at a political meeting or a storytelling session. In order to speak a person must go into the centre of the circle and pick up the stick. The speaker must then hold it while they talk and replace it when they stop. The stick places certain responsibilities upon speaker and listeners alike. It requires the latter to listen actively and patiently, but also tends to curb excessive talkativeness on the part of garrulous speakers and gives courage to the shy. Similar indigenous speech rituals should be employed wherever they exist.

Revisiting a place and conducting an interview *in situ* or during a 'walk-about' can also free the mind and allow someone to recall the past more easily. Such walkabouts might include: visiting a sparsely wooded watershed which used to be a forest, in order to discuss environmental history and change; returning to a mine or factory which used to be a place of work, to discuss child labour; or examining an abandoned and broken pump, to discuss irrigation techniques and land use.[11]

Role play can also be useful as a mnemonic or memory aid, particularly in groups, but also in one-to-one interviews (if you had been the elder what would you have done?). Role play not only releases memory through the re-enacting of situations or events (a certain dance, a typical working day, a particularly important meeting), but also allows people to be less inhibited as they narrate events under the cover of a different persona. Hearing old stories is another good way to jog the memory, and a song or tune from the past can be particularly evocative, taking the mind right back to the time the interviewer is investigating.

VISUAL TECHNIQUES

While props and mnemonics help to jog people's memories, some visual techniques may assist them to express the past more clearly. Many oral testimony projects rely on straightforward interviewing alone, but additional visual methods can be helpful when testimony is being gathered among groups unfamiliar with the interview form. Creating a diagram or making a model can take the place of a potentially awkward personal interaction between interviewer and narrator; or may complement, assist or encourage people's verbal performance. Such material can then be displayed alongside the testimony in any report, exhibition or book resulting from a project.

Robert Chambers has described a range of techniques which can be used by rural people and development workers to give expression to various aspects of the past or recent past. These include time lines and biographies (including ethno-biographies); historical maps and models; historical transects; and trend diagrams and estimates.[12] Older people in the community usually play a key role in providing and shaping the relevant historical information in these techniques.

A *time line* is a list of key events, changes and 'landmarks' in the past, written up in chronological order on a large sheet of paper. It is often a useful way of putting an individual's or a community's history into perspective by identifying the broad framework of events which shaped their past. It can therefore be a good way into a life story interview or focus group discussion and may also provide the basis for the interview map. Figure 1 shows a time line produced by a village in Tamil Nadu, India, stretching from 1932 to 1990.[13]

A visual *biography* is a similar kind of chart which traces the 'life' of a particular phenomenon, whether it be a famine, a certain crop or diet, or the

1932	– TANK UNDERTAKEN BY GOVT
1935–1946	– ESTABLISHMENT OF VERANDA SCHOOL BY GOVT
1947	– INDEPENDENCE
1948	– 16 WERE DIED DUE TO CHOLERA, FAMINE
1954	– ROAD, RHATCHED SCHOOL
1956–1964	– CYCLONE, FLOODS
1966	– NEW SCHOOL BUILDING
1968	– AGAIN CHOLERA, 4 WERE DIED
1970	– ELECTRICITY FACILITY, BRIDGE 100 FAMILIES MIGRATED BECAUSE OF SEVERE DROUGHT
1977	– ESTABLISHMENT OF NOON-MEAL CENTER
1978	– COMMUNITY WELL, 2 BORE WELL FOR DRINKING PURPOSE
1983	– TIN P
1984	– ELECTION BOYCOTT. ONE MORE BORE WELL. DRINKING WATER OVERHEAD TANK. STREET TAPS BY GOVT
1984–1985	– NON FORMAL EDUCATION BY GOVT
1987	– SPEECH
1989	– GROUP HOUSES FOR 20 HARIJANS
1990	– HEAVY CROP DAMAGE BECAUSE OF FLOOD

Figure 1 Time line: Tamil Nadu, India, 1932–1990

development of a kind of technology. These biographies are particularly useful for single-issue histories and can form the framework for the interview.

Maps can be drawn on paper or on the ground with sticks, chalks, pens or paints. Those worked on the ground can be photographed or transcribed on to paper before they are destroyed. Maps of the past are particularly useful in illustrating ecological histories and showing previous land-use patterns, plant and animal coverage. Figure 2 shows the landscape change over the past twenty-five years in Abela Sipa Peasant Association in Ethiopa.[14]

Three-dimensional *historical models* using local materials have aided discussion on erosion and other environmental and agricultural concerns. In another example described by Chambers, villagers from Seganahalli in Karnataka, India, made two models on the ground. One showed their watershed as they remembered it fifty years earlier with trees growing on the rocky hills, and the other as they saw it now, with no trees and serious erosion. The striking difference between the two models began an important debate about what should be done, in which the models were used to present and explore the various options.[15] Thus historical analysis can be the trigger to development debate and it can also be used to generate so-called 'dream' models and maps, expressions of people's hopes for the future which can then form the basis of development action. *Historical transects* are another kind of diagram which represent changing conditions through time. Again they have traditionally been used in agro-ecosystem analysis and are usually compiled by walking through an area with some of the older inhabitants and recording their recollections of various conditions at key moments identified by the

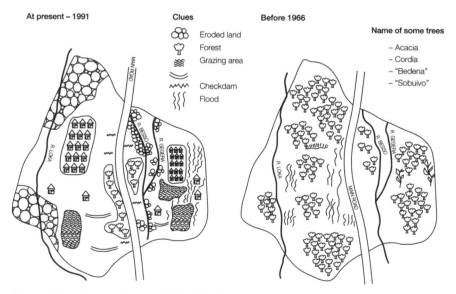

Figure 2 Landscape change: Abela Sipa Peasant Association, Ethiopia

time line. Figure 3 is a transect through time illustrating land-use trends in a village in East Java.[16]

Three main kinds of chart have been used by rural people to estimate or measure change and historical trends: counters, pie charts and straight-forward trend lines. Stones, seeds or pieces of stick can be used as *counters* representing absolute or relative values. People can pile up these counters along a simple time line to express absolute values for things like harvest yields, price changes or population changes. They can also place counters in a matrix diagram to express relative values or scores which indicate certain differences over time. For example, one matrix might allow a narrator to express her preferences for certain crops and income-generating activities during five key years in the past.

Pie charts drawn on paper or the ground are another useful way by which people can express relative values and how these changed over time. Figure 4 shows two pie charts made by three elderly farmers which illustrate changing

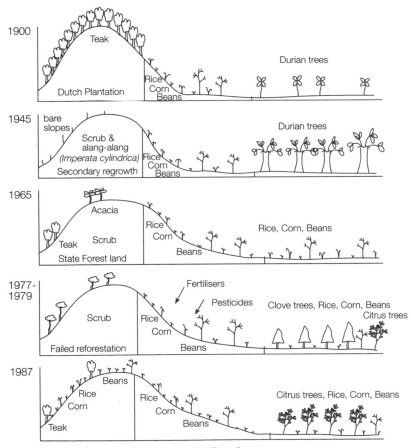

Figure 3 Land-use trends in a village in East Java

cropping and land-use patterns in a village near Dehra Dun, Uttar Pradesh, India, between 1950 and 1990.[17]

Trend lines are simple graphs in which people use a curved line to illustrate historic trends. A normal histogram or bar-chart can be used for the same purpose. Figure 5 shows a trend line drawn in the dust by an old farmer in Mahbubnagar district, Andhra Pradesh, India. The lines illustrate the increasing and decreasing trends relating to farmyard manure, pests, soil fertility,

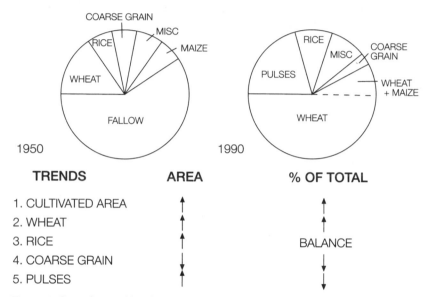

Figure 4 Cropping and land-use patterns in a village near Dehra Dun, Uttar Pradesh, India, 1950–1990

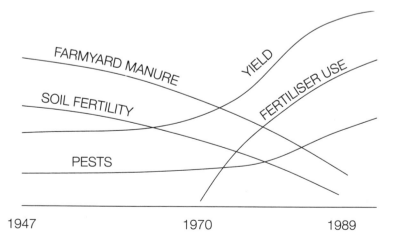

Figure 5 Trend line for Mahbubnagar district, Andhra Pradesh, India, 1947–1989

fertiliser and yields over forty years.[18] Participatory diagrams are another way in which people can describe a past event and the processes it generated (flow diagrams) or the effect it had on their lives (impact diagrams).[19]

NOTES

1 C. Briggs, *Learning How to Ask: A Sociolinguistic Appraisal of the Role of the Interview in Social Science Research*, Cambridge, Cambridge University Press, 1986.
2 J. Mitchell and H. Slim, 'Listening to rural people in Africa: the semi-structured interview in rapid rural appraisal', *Disasters*, 1991, vol. 15, no. 1.
3 H. Norberg-Hodge, *Ancient Futures: Learning From Ladakh*, London, Rider Books, 1991, p. 36.
4 Lomo Zachary in a letter to Ken Wilson, Refugee Studies Programme, Oxford, 1987.
5 Briggs, *Learning How to Ask*.
6 J. Mitchell and H. Slim, 'Interviewing amidst fear', Unpublished paper, Rural Evaluations, 1990.
7 See also the introduction to N. Cross and R.Barker (eds), *At The Desert's Edge: Oral Histories from the Sahel*, London, Panos Books, 1991.
8 See J. Bornat, 'The communities of community publishing', *Oral History*, 1992, vol. 20, no. 2.
9 K. Kumar, 'Conducting group interviews in developing countries', AID Program Design and Evaluation Methodology Report No. 8, US Agency for International Development, Washington, 1987.
10 The details about the Native American talking-stick are taken from a talk given by the American storyteller, Richard Cupidi, at Intermediate Technology's 1992 Annual Public Meeting, London.
11 See R. Chambers, 'Shaping the past: people's maps, models and diagrams in local historical analysis and planning', a paper presented to the National Life Story Collection's conference on Oral History and Development, London, November 1991.
12 See, for example, R. Chambers, 'Rural appraisal: rapid, relaxed and participatory', IDS Discussion Paper 311, Institute of Development Studies, Sussex, England, 1992.
13 J. Devararam, *et al.*, 'PRA for rural resource management', *RRA Notes*, 1991, no. 13, cited in Chambers, 'Shaping the past'. IIED training materials and *RRA Notes* are useful sources of information on PRA and RRA methods in practice.
14 'Farmer participatory research in north Omo, Ethiopia', a report on a training course in Rapid Rural Appraisal, Soddo, July 1991, IIED and FARM Africa, London, cited in Chambers, 'Shaping the Past'.
15 Chambers, 'Shaping the Past'.
16 J.N. Pretty, J.A. McCracken, D.S. McCauley and C. Mackie, *Agroecosystem Training and Analysis in Central and East Java, Indonesia*, London, IIED, 1988.
17 A. Venu Prasad, in Chambers, 'Shaping the Past'.
18 Chambers, 'Shaping the Past'.
19 See J. Theis and H. Grady, 'PRA for community development', IIED and SCF (UK), 1991; and R. Leurs, 'A resource manual for trainers and practitioners of PRA', Overseas Aid Group, Birmingham University, UK, 1993.

11 Life history interviews with people with learning disabilities

Jan Walmsley

Jan Walmsley is a Senior Lecturer in the School of Health and Social Welfare at the Open University in Britain. This article is reprinted with permission from *Oral History*, 1995, vol. 23, no. 1, pp. 71–77.

This paper describes a life history research project with people with learning disabilities (mental handicap). I discuss the methods adopted for the research, and compare them with other approaches in life history research. I argue that because most people with learning disabilities have minimal literacy skills certain adaptations of method have to be made. These adaptations may have insights to offer other researchers because they highlight important and problematic issues: explaining the research, enabling people to 'have a voice', and offering feedback and a final say to research participants. Sally French[1] suggests that improvements to the environment to give access to disabled people can be of benefit to all. Similarly, some of the issues raised in this research can inform life history research with a wide range of people.

The aim of the research was to discover what experiences people with learning disabilities have, and have had, of caring and being cared for.[2] A life history approach was chosen as people's experiences of care are related to their biographies. Their circumstances influence their opportunities to care for others, as well as determining the kind of care they have received in their lives. People with learning disabilities are often portrayed as people who receive care, not people who give it. Yet this is not always the whole picture. Some people with learning disabilities give care, as well as receive it. Through personal testimony it is possible to challenge the myth of dependence, and demonstrate that they see themselves as giving, taking and reciprocating care, support and help.

LIFE HISTORIES IN RESEARCH WITH DISABLED PEOPLE

Disabled people have been marginalised in biographical research, in particular in oral history. Humphries and Gordon write: 'The experience of physical disability in Britain during the first half of the century is almost completely undocumented'[3] and Joanna Bornat found few disabled people represented in the 'communities of community publishing'.[4] No examples of work with people with learning disabilities are mentioned in Paul Thompson's extensive review of the practice of oral history.[5] Yet it is important to recognise the experiences of disabled people as distinctive, and to add their voices to those of other 'outsiders' whose viewpoints have not appeared in conventional histories. A beginning has been made. Some anthologies exist, compiled and edited by disabled women, in particular.[6] These focus on the experience of being disabled, rather than on the historical contexts in which people have lived.

Gerber[7] dates the tradition of asking people with *learning* disabilities to speak to researchers about their lives to Bogdan and Taylor's life history of Ed Murphy, a man labelled as mentally retarded.[8] He describes this as 'an essential step in recasting social welfare policy' and links it to a process in which minority or oppressed groups are finding a voice.[9] Bogdan and Taylor drew radical conclusions from this work, concluding, 'Our research suggests . . . that the concept of mental retardation is not just less than useful, it is seriously misleading.'[10]

Three recent examples of work which draws on the personal testimonies of people with learning disabilities demonstrate the variety of work now being undertaken. The first of these, *Know Me As I Am*,[11] is an anthology, similar to the anthologies compiled by disabled women described above. The editors discovered that people's common human experiences override the label they have been given, 'It challenges our assumptions and stereotypes even when we think we have none'.[12] The second example, *A Fit Person to be Removed*,[13] draws on oral history accounts from patients to reconstruct the experience of being in a mental handicap hospital (colony) in the twentieth century. The emphasis is on being labelled and the consequences of that; spending long periods in an institution shut away from the rest of the world. The third example, *Parenting under Pressure*,[14] uses a life story approach to explore the lives of parents with learning disabilities. The authors found this approach altered their perceptions of parents with learning disabilities, and conclude that the problems they experience are as much to do with poverty and prejudice as they are due to their individual deficits.

In trying to categorise these approaches Armstrong's summary is useful: 'The complete life history attempts to cover the entire sweep of the subject's life experience. It is inevitably long, many sided and complex . . . The multiple biographies approach, by abstracting dominant themes, makes it possible to generalise to one type by showing that certain biographies have, for all the idiosyncrasy, some common elements.'[15]

Oral history tends to focus on a historical question, and use oral evidence to help answer it. It is, in its pure form, a more focused approach than the life history.[16] Potts and Fido's *A Fit Person to be Removed* is oral history in a way that other research cited here is not, because it seeks to answer an essentially historical set of questions about life in an institution through the testimonies of those who lived there.

Placing my own research within the rich context of work which draws on people's life stories is complex. It has most in common with multiple life histories like Booth and Booth's *Parenting under Pressure*, where the stories are used to contribute to an analysis which abstracts dominant themes, but it also draws on oral history in that there is a 'focus on the way in which historical time and place and personal experiences are lived out by individual(s)'.[17]

PARTICULAR CHALLENGES IN LEARNING DISABILITY RESEARCH

Compiling life histories of people with learning disabilities is unlike superficially similar projects such as the Jewish Women in London Group's *Generations of Memories*[18] and the Hall Carpenter Archive's *Inventing Ourselves: Lesbian Life Stories*.[19] In these collections, the contributors wrote their own stories, a task few adults with learning difficulties can undertake unaided. In addition, learning disability is an ascribed characteristic which, at least at present, has negative overtones. It is not a label people bear with pride, unlike, say, being a Jewish woman or, sometimes, being a lesbian. Some researchers cited here concluded that being a person with a learning disability is most akin to being a human being.[20] Yet people are labelled, and it does affect their lives, as Potts and Fido's book shows. There is an argument, well rehearsed amongst oppressed groups, that reclaiming one's history is an important step in understanding and learning to celebrate one's identity.[21] Joanna Ryan wrote of people with learning disabilities, 'What history they do have is not so much theirs as the history of others acting either on their behalf or against them'.[22] Reclaiming that history is important in enabling people to set their lives in a broader context and to comprehend them; it is a step towards empowerment.

In undertaking this research I faced distinct challenges. One of these was working as a non-disabled researcher. A strong theme in disability research currently is the importance of disabled people setting the agenda.[23] This poses an additional challenge, especially in learning disability. It would, I believe, be unrealistic at this time to expect people with learning disabilities to record their history unaided. Even to scholars it is a relatively unexplored field, lacking the glamour of mental illness which is now well researched. People with learning disabilities lack the formal skills required of historians, often even basic ones such as literacy. Oral history and personal testimonies are one way, but without a basic map it is hard to make sense of them. As Patricia Hill Collins observed in relation to Black people, 'groups unequal in power are correspondingly unequal in their ability to make their standpoint known to themselves and others'.[24]

A second challenge is related to the question 'what history?' It is possible to reconstruct the history of mental handicap services through documentary sources, both primary and secondary. Yet this history is not known to people with learning disabilities, often even at a basic level. No one I interviewed had heard of the 1913 Mental Deficiency Act, the legislation to have attracted most attention from historians. It remained in force until 1959, and was the legislative framework which influenced people's early lives, but its existence was unknown to them. This made relating people's accounts to the history, and using one's own knowledge of that history to prompt questions somewhat problematic, though this is recommended in all basic oral history texts.[25]

A third challenge was that most methods employed in oral history and life history research rely on respondents having literacy skills: the introductory letter; the return of the transcript for correction; the provision of the finished account. In working with people with learning disabilities different approaches were required, based on tape recordings and face to face meetings. It is this challenge that is the main focus of this article.

RESEARCH METHODS

In carrying out life history interviews with people with learning disabilities I struggled to adapt mainstream research methods advocated by oral historians and life history researchers to make it possible for them to relate their own life stories. In this article I focus on four main aspects: explaining the research; power and involvement in the interview; the interview process and negotiating meanings.

None of these issues are new to life history or oral historians, though working with people with learning disabilities presented them in quite a stark way.

Explaining the research

Actually finding people to interview and telling them about the project was a taxing process. Surprisingly little is written about this in standard texts. The advice is often confined to construction of sampling frames and the virtues of insider or outsider status for the researcher. Advice also includes sending an introductory letter, or making a preliminary phone call.

People with learning disabilities often are not on the phone, and may be unable to read letters and notices. I am based in a university and do not have direct access to service users. Making contact was not straightforward. On the whole, people taking part were contacted and briefed through intermediaries (MENCAP, Adult Training Centre workers, friends, social workers, adult education tutors). This meant that I was not fully in control of the circumstances in which people were approached, with problematic results. For example, I planned to interview people in their forties, but eventually extended my sampling frame to include thirty to seventy year olds because intermediaries either forgot the age bracket, or were not sure of people's ages.

Working through intermediaries extended the chain of communication about the research. In one instance the project had to be explained to five people before I got to speak to Eileen, the interviewee. The original contact was an adult education tutor who referred me to the Adult Training Centre where I spoke to the receptionist, the key worker, the deputy manager who in turn consulted with the woman's family. Only then was Eileen herself asked, by her key worker.

After some pilot interviews I decided that an information sheet was needed as the process of explaining to intermediaries was both time consuming and somewhat erratic. Using some data obtained in pilot interviews I drew up an illustrated information sheet. This sheet gave intermediaries information about the research which they could show to potential interviewees and provided a starting point for discussion in the interview itself. It also found another unexpected use as participants showed it to other people to explain what they were doing. One interviewee, Gary, took it away to show his mother.

The information sheet also had limitations. It may have constrained the research, giving people a set of fairly concrete ideas to respond to which may not correspond with their experiences. In one instance it appeared patronising. Alison, for example, was critical of the way she had been approached and argued that she would have preferred to respond in writing to a set of pre-set questions, rather than in a face to face interview where she had felt exposed and vulnerable. This throws an interesting light on the school of thought, associated with feminist research, which advocates free ranging interviews where the interviewee sets the research agenda.[26]

There was a tension between allowing interviewees free rein, and at the same time informing them about the research to the extent that they could make an informed choice about consent. This tension was made more acute when the approach was made through others. Alison (see above) in reflecting on why she had agreed to be interviewed said, 'I didn't want to let Hazel (tutor) down.' In using Hazel to make contact with Alison I had unwittingly compromised her. When Alison subsequently became distressed about our initial interview it was Hazel who bore the brunt of her distress, not I.

It was not always clear that the person involved was actually consenting to be interviewed, so much as feeling she had no choice. It is a pitfall in research with people with learning disabilities that interviews for assessment and other purposes are fairly commonplace. Bercovici observes: 'It took many months to convince "natives" of this system that the researcher was not part of the collaborative network they saw as an immutable part of life . . . they had no social type in their classification system that corresponded to the identity the researcher wanted them to perceive and understand'.[27] Atkinson, describing her research interviews, furnishes some insights into her interviewees' perceptions of her: one said to his social worker, 'She must be very important, asking us all these questions'.[28] After I had consulted five people about interviewing Eileen it might have been hard for her to refuse.

The information sheet was no guarantee of avoiding the researcher being viewed as a professional service provider. It did serve to differentiate the research from other interview situations, and to set out a contract specifying how many meetings, the choice of confidentiality, and the type of feedback people could expect.

However, consent issues remained problematic, especially where, as was often the case, people had little idea of what research is, and what use it may be put to. Of the twenty-two people I interviewed only Alison challenged me beyond the polite, 'you doing a project?' level of query.

The practicalities of working with many people with learning disabilities are currently such that far from undertaking 'emancipatory research',[29] the researcher must police her own ethical stance. To achieve a level of understanding of research to the extent that people could challenge the researcher directly was beyond the scope of a small scale research project such as this, though might be a worthy enterprise in its own right.

Except for a few cases I am certain that people were very hazy about my intentions in interviewing them, though this may not be unique to adults with learning difficulties. As McCall and Simmonds observed, 'What motives, what alien causes, would lead a man to turn on his brethren with an analytic eye?'[30] How many people invited to take part in any research really know what is going on? Perhaps it is not just people with learning disabilities who are confused by this esoteric activity.

Involvement and power in the interview relationship

The importance of developing rapport with informants has been well documented both in research relating to learning disability and in qualitative research more generally.[31] In this research some strategies were particularly helpful with people with learning disabilities.

Like others, I found that it took time to build trust. The first time I met Anna, a woman in her fifties, I obtained little information as it was the first time she had been tape recorded and she asked me to play back our taped conversation seven times within fifty minutes. The interview ended with my promising to let her have a copy of the tape, and she insisted that I name the time I would return with it, despite some reluctance on my part. When I returned as agreed she was ready to show me her photos, and she rewarded me with as much information as she could recall.

On one occasion I felt I may have been too successful in establishing rapport. Janet Finch recounts how easy it was for her to gain the confidence of the clergy wives she interviewed. They were lonely, and welcomed the chance to talk.[32] Alison confided more in me than she subsequently felt was good for her, and became quite distressed. Why this happened I can only guess, but one reason may be that as an experienced counsellor I knew how to establish rapport quickly, and to persist with subjects that appear to be sensitive. And Alison herself was an experienced counsellee; she knew the role well.

Most texts on interviewing recommend that the interviewee is seen alone: 'Nearly always it is best to be alone with an informant'.[33] I found that this was not always possible, and adopted a policy of involving other people at the request of the interviewee. The first person I interviewed, Isobel, had been briefed by her adult education tutor in advance, but was very nervous when we met, and made an excuse to end the interview after thirty minutes. However, after I'd switched off the tape, she hinted that she'd like her boyfriend there next time. I duly collected Barry before our next interview and the conversation flowed, they were reluctant to end the interview, and Barry subsequently became an interviewee in his own right. He commented on his importance: 'she might feel better when I'm here, more confident' and Isobel added, 'keep me company'.

Involvement of a third person undoubtedly adds a new dimension to the interview. The researcher can observe a social relationship which casts light on the interviewee's situation. Beryl sat in on two interviews with her friend Eileen. Eventually I realised that Beryl, no less than staff and family, was determined that Eileen stay in the Adult Training Centre she had attended for twenty-five years. When Eileen and I discussed the possibility of her doing some voluntary work with children Beryl intervened with a series of good reasons why she should not: 'children can be horrible, hit you', 'your dad would be upset', 'you're better off in the Centre'. I realised how hard it was for Eileen to make any changes in her life when her friend joined the chorus of voices keeping her where she was.

It is important that the choice of companion is made by the interviewee. Jacqueline, a woman in her forties living with her widowed mother, was contacted through her mother who was present at both interviews. I could not persuade Mrs M to allow me to speak to her daughter alone, and Mrs M's voice was the only one I heard.

The social relations of research have been a preoccupation in feminist research for many years. Mies argues that when people from 'underprivileged groups are being interviewed by people from a socially higher stratum it has been observed that the data thus gathered often reflect "expected behaviour" rather than "real behaviour"'.[34] More recently disabled people have begun to challenge traditional research into disability as being oppressive rather than enlightening.[35]

I belong to a higher social stratum than the interviewees, and I am not disabled. I was aware that this could influence the research, and that the relative powerlessness of the interviewees could distort their perception of me. It is hard to document this. One instance, however, is indicative. Lynne lived with her father, and emphasised in our interviews how much she wanted to move into her own place. This was such a strong theme that I am convinced she perceived me as someone who could help her achieve such a move. It was so powerful a message that after our second interview I contacted an acquaintance in the Social Services Department to ask whether Lynne could get any help. In a sense Lynne was right; I was powerful enough to pick up the phone to someone who could help her.

Ethics aside, I am uncertain how problematic such misunderstandings are. Dean and Foot Whyte argue that there is no such thing as truth telling in interviews; whatever the interviewee tells you is informative.[36] Stimson[37] proposes that 'life histories will be influenced by the social situation in which they are told'. The problem lies more in not always knowing what social situation people think they are in, in an interview; what kind of impression are they trying to convey; and why.

Within limits interviewees did exercise power. Anna had me switching the tape recorder on and off for her which was not behaviour I had chosen. Isobel arranged for me to collect Barry and take him to her house for an interview. When we arrived she was having a personal review meeting with her social worker. Barry was ushered in to join her and I was left sitting outside the house. I was told later that she had probably used me as a means of getting Barry to the review! In that situation she had exercised power, and I was thwarted. These instances correspond with Stimson and Webb's findings[38] that in doctor–patient interactions the patient exercises power: to ignore the doctor's advice, to recast the story in a light favourable to them, to withhold information. The doctor, like the researcher, apparently is the one with the power; but it is not as straightforward as it appears.

The interview process

In order to ensure that people were aware of the research focus and its purpose I tried to support the process throughout with concrete information. With a fairly abstract research question it is not as straightforward as it was for George Ewart Evans who used to take along a work tool to stimulate memory.[39]

My starting point was the illustrated information sheet. The first interview was loosely structured, using prompts from the information sheet. After this I transcribed the tape and developed two diagrams, a 'life map' (Figure 1) and a 'network diagram' (Figure 2). The life map illustrates key points in the individual's biography, for example date of birth, schooling, changes of residence. The network diagram contains information about the people currently in the participant's social networks, with an indication of the degree of reciprocity. If a relationship is primarily one in which the participant receives care an arrow points towards the participant, and vice versa. Two way arrows indicate a reciprocal relationship.

These 'life maps' and 'network diagrams' provided a basis for the follow-up interview. I talked through the diagrams with the interviewees and pursued any omissions, ambiguities or contradictions. The advantage of diagrams was that they could be shown to participants to see what information has been derived from their words. I saw them as research tools, forcing me to summarise data, and to try to make sense of it in a way people could understand.

In this way I was able to clarify points which were unclear in the first interview, and to make corrections. People's inability to read once more put the onus on me to be painstaking in checking understanding; yet it was valuable because it gave the opportunity to elaborate on points touched on in

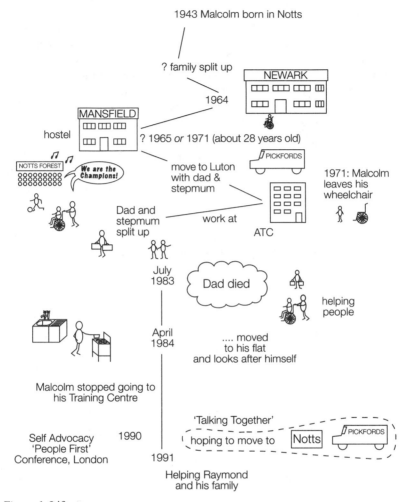

Figure 1 Life map

the first interview. For example, Gary had glossed over the reasons for his going into hospital in our first interview, but it appeared on the 'life map'. As we went over this he explained further:

> I stayed at home for quite a long time and then I went on there (the ATC), and then I went to Bromham (hospital) for me fits. It's a long story really because where me fits are, with all the tablets I used to take, I used to take more tablets than I do now and I used to get very bad tempered and shout and swear and turn nasty so they sent me to Bromham for me medication and me tempers. I was only supposed to be there for seven weeks but I was there for quite a long time.

> (GH Interview September 1992)

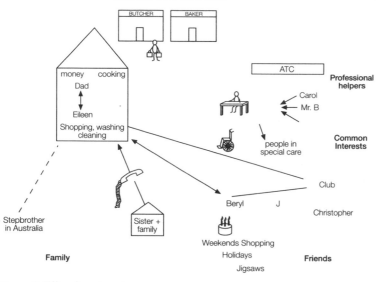

Figure 2 Eileen's network

Photographs were a good support. If we met in people's own homes they showed me the photos on the walls, and talked about them. If we were in another setting I encouraged people to bring photos to our second meeting, and to talk about who was in them, where they were when they were taken, and what was going on. Anna was vague about her past life, but the photos helped establish some kind of chronology, and introduced new people, like her neighbour's daughter. They also corroborated some of the things she had told me, for example the importance of her friend Helen whom she sees infrequently. There were photos of Anna and Helen smiling as they exchanged Christmas gifts, and Helen was present at Anna's birthday celebration.

Concreteness was also expressed verbally. 'Care' and 'caring' are jargon words. People did not ever use them in describing relationships. Instead they used the terms 'helping' or, less often, 'looking after'. I tried to reflect this in the information sheet, following the pilot interviews. This practice, of using people's own terms rather than imposing language from an academic culture, is based on Glaser and Strauss's concept, 'grounded theory'.[40]

A final prompt was the 'story'. To end the relationship I compiled a brief life story based on the interview data using, as far as possible, the informant's own words. Once more, this was usually delivered face to face. The utility of the 'story' as a means of checking accuracy varied. Eileen, for example, used the opportunity to correct one or two names, and the date when she left school. By contrast, Alanna used the opportunity to say what she wanted for the future:

Jan: What about the ending? I didn't know how to end it, what about the future?

Alanna: I'd like mum if she lives that long to get to know me better . . . I don't know, I think other mothers let their daughters do what they want to do and I think I'm a bit left behind if you know what I mean. I'm doing what my mum wants me to do . . .

In effect, Alanna was saying something very important about herself and her wish to assert her adult status to her mother, providing an important insight with which to end our relationship.

Research interviews with people with learning disabilities throw up similar issues to other research relationships. All interviewers have to develop rapport, to ponder how they are perceived by the interviewee, and to check accuracy. The relative powerlessness of many people with learning disabilities and their inability to read forced me to tackle those issues in a slightly different way. These lessons may have wider implications.

Negotiating meanings

Finally, my research gave me cause to consider negotiated meanings. Much research literature recently has emphasised the importance of leaving the 'ownership' of the research with the participants: 'Recently the practice has developed, particularly amongst anthropologists, of giving a draft of the report to research participants and asking them to comment on its validity'.[41] In my own research I did this by drawing up life maps and network diagrams, summarising the research information in a 'story', and working through it with them.

I consciously omitted the normal oral history practice of returning the transcript to people[42] because of the weight of reading, though I gave a copy of the tape as a memento.

The 'story' has limitations as a way of giving 'ownership' to the interviewees because only the individual's account is available. I, as researcher, had an overview of all the interviews. The individual only knew of her own contribution and the guarantee of confidentiality requires that this remains the case. I have discussed elsewhere the difficulties of feeding back research findings to a group of research participants who know one another.[43] Opie identifies another difficulty: 'such a (co-authorship) relationship is difficult to achieve when participants, while constituting a community of interest, do not form a close knit physical community'.[44] Only some interviewees knew one another, and to constitute them as a group for the purpose of sharing research findings would be impractical as well as presenting a major challenge to my powers of explaining. Overall, although interviewees had the final word on their own 'story', they had no means of controlling the interpretations I subsequently made of their experiences as related to me. They have had no direct say in this paper, for example.

A second limitation is more personal. The Jewish Women in London Group comment in their introduction: 'For most of the women being presented some time later with, as one of us put it, an "autobiography that they had not written" was a disturbing experience and added another dimension to the vexed question of "finding a voice" '.[45] Only one of my interviewees, Alison, expressed reservations about having her 'story' presented to her. Because she can read I posted it to her in advance of our meeting. She described graphically the experience of reading it for the first time; finding a private moment, making herself a coffee, taking a deep breath, and . . . In the end, she rewrote it for me and we jointly finalised the draft. Alison asked why she could not have written it herself. There is no doubt she could have done so, but she alone of the twenty-two had the writing skills to produce such an account. The others relied on me to do so, and questioned little. The 'story' was already one step removed from the immediate interview account. It had the authority of the written word, albeit mediated by a face to face meeting. Perhaps it required more confidence than most people had to challenge the authority of print.

SUMMARY

In this research I adapted tried and tested methods in life history research to suit the interviewees. How far are these generalisable to other research of this nature?

The main contribution is, I believe, the commitment to clarity about the research in explaining it to interviewees. The particular circumstances of many people with learning difficulties mean that questions about their lives are both familiar, in the form of assessment interviews, case conferences and reviews, and unfamiliar, in that they are unlikely to have a concept of 'research' as an activity. I am not satisfied that I achieved a high level of understanding of my research, or its goals but I began to move towards that. If an interview is seen as a social situation in which both participants work to construct a version of the 'truth', then the importance of the interviewee understanding her role becomes paramount. Otherwise, the researcher may see a version of the truth, but she is unclear about what has influenced that particular portrayal.

A second important observation relates to the current orthodoxy that research must be owned by those researched. In principle, this is a worthy goal; in practice I found it almost impossible to achieve. I am certain that none of the people I interviewed would have thought of asking the questions which I sought to answer, questions about how biography and history have interacted to produce their unique experiences. Yet I believe that it is important to ask those questions so that in the longer term people may come to have an understanding of the 'life course', the subtle interaction of accident of birth, specific historical time and social policy which have combined to produce a set of unique experiences. The challenge will be to find ways of telling people what I discovered in a way that they can comprehend. It is a challenge I have yet to tackle.

NOTES

1 Sally French in Workbook 3 of *The Disabling Society*, Buckingham, Open University, 1993.
2 Some of the research findings are published in J. Walmsley, 'Contradictions in Caring', *Disability, Handicap and Society*, 1993, vol. 8, no. 2.
3 S. Humphries and P. Gordon, *Out of Sight: The Experience of Disability 1900–1950*, Plymouth, Channel Four/Northcote Press, 1992, p. 9.
4 J. Bornat, 'The communities of community publishing', *Oral History*, 1992, vol. 20, no. 2, pp. 23–31.
5 P. Thompson, *The Voice of the Past*, second edition, Oxford, Oxford University Press, 1988.
6 J. Campling, *Images of Ourselves*, London, Routledge & Kegan Paul, 1981; J. Morris, *Able Lives*, Women's Press, 1989, are examples.
7 D. Gerber, 'Listening to disabled people: the problem of voice and authority' in R.B. Edgerton's 'The Cloak of Competence', *Disability, Handicap and Society*, 1990, vol. 5, no. 1, pp. 3–23.
8 R. Bogdan and S. Taylor, 'The judges not the judged: an insider's view of mental retardation', *American Psychologist*, 1976, vol. 31, pp. 47–52.
9 Gerber, 'Listening to disabled people', p. 4.
10 R. Bogdan and S. Taylor, *Inside Out: The Social Meaning of Mental Retardation*, University of Toronto Press, 1982.
11 D. Atkinson and F. Williams (eds), *Know Me As I Am*, London, Hodder & Stoughton, 1990.
12 Ibid., p. 7.
13 M. Potts and R. Fido, *A Fit Person to be Removed*, Plymouth, Northcote Press, 1991.
14 T. Booth and W. Booth, *Parenting under Pressure: Mothers and Fathers with Learning Difficulties*, Buckingham, Open University Press, 1994.
15 P. Armstrong, *The Use of the Life History Method in Social and Educational Research*, Newland Papers no. 7, University of Hull, 1982, p. 10.
16 Thompson, *The Voice of the Past*, p. 72.
17 Jewish Women in London Group, *Generations of Memories*, London, Women's Press, 1989, p. 9.
18 Jewish Women in London Group, *Generations of Memories*, 1989.
19 Hall Carpenter Archives, *Inventing Ourselves: Lesbian Life Stories*, London, Routledge, 1989.
20 Bogdan and Taylor, 'The judges not the judged', and *Inside Out*; Atkinson and Williams, *Know Me As I Am*.
21 See, for example, S. Rowbotham, *Hidden from History*, London, Pluto, 1981, and Jewish Women in London Group, *Generations of Memories*.
22 J. Ryan and F. Thomas, *The Politics of Mental Handicap*, London, Free Association Books, 1987, p. 85.
23 G. Zarb, 'On the road to Damascus: first steps towards changing the relations of disability research production', *Disability, Handicap and Society*, 1992, vol. 7, no. 2, pp. 157–166.
24 P. Hill Collins, *Black Feminist Thought: Knowledge, Consciousness and the Politics of Empowerment*, Unwin Hyman, 1990.
25 Thompson, *The Voice of the Past*.
26 Such advice is current orthodoxy in feminist research; see K. Anderson and

D. Jack, 'Learning to listen: interview techniques and analysis', in S. Gluck and D. Patai (eds), *Women's Words*, London, Routledge, 1991.

27 S. Bercovici, 'Qualitative methods and cultural perspectives in the study of de-institutionalisation', in R. Bruininks, C. Meyers, B. Sigford and C. Lakin (eds), *Deinstitutionalisation and Community Adjustment of Mentally Retarded People*, Monograph of the American Association of Mental Deficiency, 1981, no. 4, p. 139.

28 D. Atkinson, 'Research interviews with people with mental handicaps', in A. Brechin and J. Walmsley (eds), *Making Connections*, London, Hodder & Stoughton, 1989.

29 M. Oliver, 'Changing the social relations of research production?', *Disability, Handicap and Society*, 1992, vol. 7, no. 2, pp. 157–166.

30 G. McCall and J. Simmonds, *Issues in Participant Observation*, Addison Wesley, 1969.

31 R. Bogdan and S. Taylor, *An Introduction to Qualitative Research Methods*, John Wiley, 1984; J. Cornwell and B. Gearing, 'Biographical interviews with older people', *Oral History*, 1990, vol. 17, no. 1, pp. 36–43.

32 J. Finch, 'It's great to have someone to talk to', in C. Bell and H. Roberts (eds), *Social Researching: Politics, Problems and Practice*, London, Routledge & Kegan Paul, 1984.

33 Thompson, *The Voice of the Past*, p. 205.

34 M. Mies, 'Towards a methodology for feminist research', in G. Bowles and R. Duelli Klein (eds), *Theories of Women's Studies*, London, Routledge & Kegan Paul, 1983, p. 123.

35 Oliver, 'Changing the social relations of research production', and Zarb, 'On the road to Damascus'.

36 J. Dean and W. Foot Whyte, 'How do you know if the informant is telling the truth?' in J. Bynner and K. Stribley (eds), *Social Research: Principle and Procedures*, London, Longman, 1978.

37 G. Stimson, 'Biography and retrospection: some problems in the study of life histories'. Paper delivered at the British Sociological Association's Conference, April 6–9, 1976.

38 G. Stimson and B. Webb, *Going to see the Doctor*, London, Routledge & Kegan Paul, 1975.

39 Thompson, *The Voice of the Past*, pp. 204 205.

40 B. Glaser and A. Strauss, *The Discovery of Grounded Theory*, Aldine Press, 1967.

41 A. Opie, 'Qualitative research, appropriation of the "other" and feminism', *Feminist Review*, 1992, no. 40, pp. 52–69.

42 Thompson, *The Voice of the Past*, p. 216.

43 J. Walmsley, 'Adulthood and people with mental handicaps: report of a research project', *Mental Handicap Research*, 1991, vol. 4, no. 2, pp. 141–154.

44 Opie, 'Qualitative research', p. 63

45 Jewish Women in London Group, *Generations of Memories*, p. 15.

12 Family life histories

A collaborative venture

Akemi Kikumura

Akemi Kikumura has taught at UCLA and the University of Southern California, appeared on television and films, and published short stories. Reprinted from *Oral History Review*, 1986, vol. 14, pp. 1–7 by permission of the Oral History Association.

As an anthropologist, an area of inquiry that has always intrigued me is cultural continuity and change. In my attempt to gain greater insight and understanding into this phenomenon, particularly as it applied to Japanese Americans, I had decided to use the life history approach, focusing on the life experiences of my mother, an Issei woman from Hiroshima, Japan, who had immigrated to the United States in 1923.

There were many questions that remained for me about my mother. As the youngest member in a family of ten girls and three boys, I knew very little about my family's past. So much had happened in my family history before I was born, much of which was no longer discussed, especially those stories about Japan before World War II and the concentration camp experience. And so I wondered: What was her life like in Japan? Why did she leave her homeland? How did she manage to cope with the extraordinary hardships that she faced in her everyday life? What specific factors allowed her to remain minimally acculturated after living in America for fifty years? It took me over four years, hundreds of interview hours, and a trip to Japan to see my parents' relatives before many of the answers to these questions slowly unfolded. What emerged from my years of research was a book called *Through Harsh Winters*.[1]

Today more and more researchers in various disciplines are using the life history approach as a method of inquiry. Accordingly, in this essay I would like both to share some of the advantages and limitations faced by me in my research as an 'insider' and to discuss some of the methodological issues and problems that face all of us who attempt to convey the reality of other people's experiences by using the life history method.

The issue surrounding the advantages and limitations of the 'outsider' and 'insider' perspectives has provided volumes of dialogue between social scientists of various disciplines over the past decades. On the one hand, advocates for the outsider perspective generally argue that access to authentic knowledge is more obtainable because of the objectivity and scientific detachment with which one can approach one's investigation as a nonmember of the group. On the other hand, proponents of the insider perspective claim that group membership provides special insight into matters (otherwise obscure to others) based on one's knowledge of the language and one's intuitive sensitivity and empathy and understanding of the culture and its people.

Both perspectives confront the researcher with a different set of problems. However, I agree with Robert Merton: 'We no longer ask whether it is the Insider or the Outsider who has monopolistic or privileged access to social truth; instead, we begin to consider their distinctive and interactive roles in the process of truth seeking'.[2] Since both perspectives have the possibility of distortions and preconceptions of social reality, it is the role of the researcher to evaluate the distinctive advantages and limitations of each perspective in relationship to the problem of research at hand.

Given the purpose of my research and the kinds of data I wanted to collect, I firmly believe that my study could not have been completed by anyone other than a member of my immediate family. When I asked my mother if she would have revealed her life experiences to anyone other than a family member, she replied, 'No! You don't disclose your soul to *tanin* (a nonrelative).' According to my mother, an outsider is anyone who is *tanin* – that is, anyone who is not related to the family, whether Japanese or not. My mother's attitudes exemplify the importance of uncovering the life history participant's own definition of the terms 'insider' and 'outsider', since these definitions could affect the kinds of information gathered and the interactional process within the interview sessions themselves.

Even within the family structure, there are those who would be better life historian candidates than others. I believe that my role as the youngest member of the family proved to be beneficial to the data-collecting process. I am viewed by my older sisters as a neutral force in the family since half of them were married and out of the household by the time I was an adolescent. Personal grudges and sibling rivalry did not have time to fester because of the wide age differences that existed between us. In my mother's eye, I am the 'baby' no matter how old I become. My relationship with my mother has been more like one between grandmother and grandchild because of the forty years that separate us. Unlike some of the other sisters, my relationship with her was relatively conflict-free.

However, being an insider (in my case, a member of the family) did limit my access to certain types of information. As an insider, the life history participant oftentimes assumes that you already know about past events and do not need to be told. This was anthropologist Delmos Jones's problem when he was conducting research among blacks in Denver, Colorado. Jones discovered, with the help of students who were mostly white, that some of the women from the rural South craved a particular kind of dirt during pregnancy – knowledge about which he was previously unaware and possibly did not uncover because of the assumption by the informants that he already knew about such health practices.[3]

This problem was magnified in my case since I am a member of the family.

I therefore decided to stop the life history narrative approximately twenty years before the actual time of data collection. Events occurring after that time, I quickly discovered, were often recalled by her with an economy of detail since she assumed that I was old enough to remember them, in some case more clearly than she.

Notwithstanding my insider status, I feel that the objectivity with which the outsider approaches research was not totally abandoned. In many ways, I was simultaneously an outsider as well as an insider. The distinctions that separated me from my mother were our generational and cultural differences. Generationally, my mother is an Issei; I am a Nisei. Chronologically, the generational difference is even greater because of the forty years that separate us. But more than the years, the greater gulf that existed between us consisted of cultural differences. She was a woman of Meiji Japan, born in an era when Confucian ethics tenaciously gripped the moral fabric of that country; I was born in one of America's concentration camps during World War II, a time when Japanese Americans tried very hard to disassociate themselves from their Japanese half, widening the cultural gap between Issei and Nisei even more.

The differences that lay between my mother and myself grew even wider since the isolated Japanese American world of family and community to which she found herself confined seemed so far removed from the white world I had to live in. It was my older sisters to whom I turned and with whom I identified when it came to matters outside of the family. But in the process of collecting my mother's life history, I was allowed the privilege of becoming an insider into her world, filling in with new awareness the tremendous generational and cultural gap that had separated us before.

A problem area that all life historians face is the reliability and validity of our data. How do we know what our life history participant tells us is correct? Several techniques that the life historian can use to assess the reliability of collected information are observation, interviewing others and checking their account against the collected data, and asking the same question more times than one, or in different ways, over a long period of time.

The advantage that anthropologists have is knowing and interacting with the people they study over an extended period of time. Anthropologists usually go into the field and study a people and their culture for a minimum of one year. It seems apparent that the longer one remains in the field, the greater the reliability and validity of information one gathers. As L.L. Langness and Gelya Frank state in their book *Lives*, 'It is difficult to sustain a web of falsehoods over a long period and anthropologists also have the advantage of often being able to match up statements and observations on the spot.'[4]

In my own case, I was able to observe my mother in various settings over an extended period of time which allowed me to check her description of events with what actually occurred. Direct observation also allowed me to fill in her own account with greater detail. For example, at the time of my interview sessions, my mother was extremely dissatisfied with my brother because she felt that he was not living up to his role expectations as the only surviving son. He had little contact with my sisters and their children; he made infrequent visits to see my mother, and he had not made any plans for taking care of her after her retirement. After one of his rare visits, she said to me, 'I got angry with him and told him off – told him how he has been neglecting his responsibilities.' But on several occasions after this conversation, I had the opportunity to be at her house when he came to visit her. Minutes before he arrived, she expressed only the joy she felt of seeing him again and never gave him the slightest indication that she was dissatisfied with his behavior. The large discrepancy between her own account of what she said and what I had actually observed made me begin to question whether she had, in fact, made any negative statements to my brother. After checking my account with other sisters, I found their experiences, and consequent doubts, to be similar to my own. Thus, during my research I relied heavily upon information provided by other members of the family as a technique to assess the reliability of her information.

Another technique I used was to repeatedly ask her the same question over a long period of time. By doing this, I not only was able to check and recheck for possible discrepancies, but at the same time I was able to elicit further information that enriched her narrative. The concentration camp experience was one area where I used this technique quite often. Initially, she was hesitant to discuss this part of her life with me. Over the years I continued to ask her about the camps, and it was only through repetitive questioning that I was able to piece together this sparsely recollected period of her life.

The last issue that I would like to raise is, in my opinion, one of the most important in the life history process. Langness and Frank emphasize that the life history is a collaborative venture and that the outcome 'is the result of a dual input from two individuals with their own past experiences, biases, interests, needs and motives'.[5] It has been suggested that anthropologists undergo psychoanalysis before entering the field in order to better understand their own personality and how it affects and influences the data collection process and the interpretation and analysis of that data. I am not suggesting that we, as life historians, all undergo psychoanalysis before we begin our research, but I do believe that we must carefully examine our needs and motives for conducting research as well as the needs and motives of our life history participant.

When I asked my mother about her motives for agreeing to tell me about her life experiences and to have them printed in a book, she claimed that they stemmed from her desire to establish a bridge of understanding between the Issei, who often lead isolated and lonely lives, and the younger generations, whom she felt had to learn from the Issei. But probably the real motive for telling me her life history was a more personal one. She wanted to pass down to me, the younger generation, her youngest daughter, the important lessons in life, knowledge that she felt would lead me on the 'right path to life'. With that thought in mind, she selectively recalled the events in her life that she wanted to relate to me.

Three of the most important lessons that she emphasized were the concepts of *gaman* (to persevere at all costs), *on* (to repay the debt you owe to others, especially to your parents), and to be *giri gatai* (a person who has a sense of duty and gratitude). These were concepts that had helped her, and many Issei, cope with the hardships that they faced in America.

As for myself, the real motive for delving into my family's past was to learn more about myself and to feel a greater sense of continuity with my family. The life history turned out to be a very transformative experience for me, for in the process, I was able to reshape many of the negative images that society had ascribed to people of color and I was drawn closer to my mother, my family, and my community. By peeling away the layers of secrecy, shame, and guilt obscured by a history of cultural genocide, racism, and discrimination, and by placing my mother's life within a broader social, historical, and cultural context, I began to reexamine and reinterpret old beliefs I held about her and, finally, to redefine my own self-concept within a more positive framework.

NOTES

1 A. Kikumura, *Through Harsh Winters: The Life of a Japanese Immigrant Woman*, Novato, Calif., Chandler & Sharp, 1981.
2 R. Merton, 'Insiders and outsiders: a chapter in the sociology of knowledge', *American Journal of Sociology*, 1972, vol. 78 (July), pp. 9–47.
3 D.J. Jones, 'Toward a native anthropology', *Human Organization*, 1979, vol. 29 (Winter), pp. 251–259.
4 L.L. Langness and G. Frank, *Lives: An Anthropological Approach to Biography*, Novato, Calif., Chandler & Sharp, 1981, p. 44.
5 Ibid., p. 61.

13 Interviewing the women of Phokeng

Belinda Bozzoli

Belinda Bozzoli is Professor and Head of Sociology at the University of Witwatersrand, South Africa. Extracted from Belinda Bozzoli with Mmantho Nkotsoe, *Women of Phokeng: Consciousness, Life Strategy and Migrancy in South Africa, 1900–1983*, London, James Currey, 1991, by permission of Ravan Press.

> *My name is Nkotsoe. I am a girl from Mabeskraal, the nearby village. I think you know that village.*
>
> Yes I do. My name is Ernestina Mekgwe. I was born here in Phokeng and brought up here also.[1]

The twenty-two women whose interviews are analysed [in *Women of Phokeng*] were all residents of Phokeng, an old and typically Tswana settlement, now in the officially designated and legally 'independent' homeland of Bophuthatswana. Their stories exemplify some of the complexities involved in the formation of modern South Africa. Born at the turn of the century, they grew up in a rural economy that was both viable and resilient, but one that had already had to make significant adaptations to survive the newly emerging order of the times. Many of them became migrants to the city, however, in their early twenties, as migrancy became both an economic necessity and an institutionalised expectation. For many, what were planned as temporary sojourns in the city lasted for up to forty years, during which they lived a life defined by family, work, and community, a life that was only partially proletarian in character. In the end, they returned to their village to live as pensioners and grandmothers in the 'homeland' of Bophuthatswana.

The women were interviewed, up to four times each, by Mmantho Nkotsoe – also a black South African woman – who, as she says, was born in a 'nearby village'. The conversations between Mmantho and the women were recorded as part of a larger oral history project (the Oral Documentation Project, or ODP) initiated at the University of the Witwatersrand in 1979. Some one thousand oral histories of black and some white South Africans, mainly from the countryside of the Transvaal, have been collected since the project began.

The ODP has focussed on the life experiences of rural black South Africans in the Transvaal, and has a variety of analytical and geographical focal points. Methodologically, it adopted a pragmatic and eclectic approach.[2] No fixed procedure for obtaining life stories was decided upon in advance; researchers and interviewers worked together to construct a viable set of ground rules as the material was being collected and problems emerged.

Fundamental to the ODP was the initial decision that interviews with rural people, often barely literate and certainly unfamiliar with the English language, needed to be undertaken in the vernacular, preferably without the presence of a translator or other intervening party. Setswana- or Sesotho-speakers were the obvious candidates for the role of interviewer in the case of the Transvaal, and the ODP has over the years employed a succession of interviewers fluent in either or both of these languages, who would undertake interviews in collaboration with a researcher or team of researchers, and then transcribe the tapes and translate them into English. The ODP archives have been used by a variety of authors and interpreted in a range of different ways. Some have used them as a source of information not obtainable elsewhere;[3] others have used selected interviews as the basis for essays on individual life experiences;[4] and a major biography of the ODP's most loquacious informant is under way.[5] This study has chosen a different means of interpreting the material, which was generated as a result of specific choices over time about the direction the interviewing should take.

Mmantho Nkotsoe, a university graduate, was trained by the ODP, and she and our initial research team – Tim Couzens, Charles van Onselen, and I – worked cooperatively on the project during 1981–1983. Her mandate was to find interesting elderly women who lived in the countryside and to record the stories of their lives. At first, the intention of the study was simply to record the stories of those whose lives are hidden from history; Mmantho was asked to travel around the Transvaal from village to village, and enquire whether any of the elderly women of the village would be willing to talk to her. She was working together with the other similarly trained oral historians in the ODP, but she alone has been asked to interview only women (the others interviewed men or women). Mmantho was given guidance as to the kinds of sociological questions which the study of the lives of African women in South Africa might involve. She was introduced to modern feminist literature, to the comparative literature on African women, and to the history of women in South Africa. She was trained to record life stories in roughly chronological sequence, and to prompt her informants with indirect questions about issues that she and we considered to be particularly interesting or informative. She was not, however, asked to administer anything like a structured interview schedule in the early stages of the project; when appropriate, she was to allow her informant to guide the interview.

In the early part of the project, Mmantho interviewed women from Potchefstroom, Kuruman, Vryburg and Phokeng.[6] But she developed a particularly striking rapport with the Phokeng women. Using her native Setswana to speak to Setswana-speaking informants, she elicited from the first few women from this particular place life stories and statements of world views that rang with intimacy. One obvious reason for this was Mmantho's own background in the neighbouring village. Now, of course, she was a University-trained historian and sociologist. But to the women she was interviewing, as will become evident in the body of this study, she was almost a kinswoman, a young girl, a child to some, who wanted to know the stories of the past. Thus, what to positivists might seem to be Mmantho's weakness (her subjective involvement in the lives of the informants, and their perception of her as having a particular meaning in their lives) proved to be her greatest strength. It was in the light of this that Mmantho was then asked to continue her interviewing only with women from Phokeng, and to focus her questions more directly on their specific experiences. In the subsequent months, the full twenty-two life stories of women living in Phokeng, in their late seventies and early eighties, were collected. These provide the basis for this study, a remarkably coherent collection of stories with a similarity of context that enabled this 'cohort' of women to be examined using sociological more than biographical tools.

This collection of stories has been both reported and interpreted somewhat unconventionally. The life stories have been treated as texts, imperfectly reflecting lives, and more accurately revealing 'cultural and psychological myth',[7] rather than as sources or 'gobbets' of useful answers to key questions, as the positivist approach might have it. While the 'texts' have not been given full priority over the 'context' in poststructuralist fashion, literary methods of analysis have certainly been brought to bear upon them.[8] The seventy or so bare transcripts that make up the twenty-two life histories have been subjected to a variety of different readings; they have been treated variously as documents, narratives, stories, histories, incoherent ramblings, interlinked fragments of consciousness, conversations, and/or recitals of fact.[9] Each of these ways of looking at them has revealed a different set of meanings.

The first, and most conventional, use to which they have been put has been as reflections of the history of the places and times experienced by the women interviewed – they have indeed provided us with 'more history'. The history of Phokeng – a relatively unknown village, in an underresearched part of South Africa – is undoubtedly illuminated by the recollections of the women who have lived there.[10] The conversations throw light on the way of life in early peasant and sharecropping households, the standard of living attained, the sexual division of labour that prevailed, the history of schooling, family relations, ethnic divisions, and particular Bafokeng struggles, for example. As the women migrate, they are drawn into relationships that are far better documented by other researchers. But we may still see their stories as sources of information about the conditions of labour in domestic service, wages, networks of support, and social relations, as well as about the nature of life in freehold townships such as Sophiatown and Alexandra during the interwar years in particular. Of course the interviewees tend to romanticise their childhood, to get dates wrong, to abandon all chronology, and simply to forget. The reading of these transcripts has involved the craft of sifting the valid piece of information from the invalid, the weak informant from the strong one. But what source of sociological and historical information does not involve these processes? Can we assume that the witnesses to government commissions of enquiry, or the government officials and public figures who write official letters to one another – sources that have all the grave respectability required of historians' footnotes – are freer of the sins of bias and distortion than the women of Phokeng? Thus, as with any source of information, there are crucial times and places where the informants interviewed here can and do provide valid, important, and useful insights, which might emerge as much in spite of their intentions as because of them. Of course these testimonies need to be read with a critical eye and with enough knowledge of the context to make it possible to sift the gold of true evidence from the bulk of ideology, poor memory, and wilful misleading that occurs. But it would be a poor researcher who did not perform this sifting process with every source available to her.

[*Women of Phokeng*] will have failed, however, if it is read as yet another contribution to the detailed understanding of 'what happened' – whether in Phokeng, Parkview, or Pimville. It is not designed to add, in incremental fashion, to our store of information about sharecroppers or peasants, servants or beerbrewers, although it does reveal a lot of interesting detail about these things. But more importantly, these texts have revealed themselves to be unsurpassed sources for revealing otherwise hidden forms of consciousness. In the case of interviews such as these, which take the form of a dynamic conversation, expressions of consciousness and social identity are evident which do not normally find their way into the kinds of sources and methods conventionally used – where black South Africans are in any case thinly represented, and women hardly at all.[11] How has this aspect of interpretation of the texts occurred?

The very intimacy and interactiveness of the interviews has lent them a special character, and the study has not pretended that these life stories were obtained through the sterile means of removing the interviewer as far as possible from any involvement in the interaction, and turning her into the 'absent' listener. Instead, the interaction itself is analysed here,[12] and the book acknowledges the transcripts of these interviews for being precisely what they are – records of conversations between black South Africans of differing backgrounds and levels of education, but with sufficient similarities between them to lend authenticity, richness, and depth to what is being said. As such, the interviews reveal things about the women and their mentalities that would otherwise remain opaque. Mmantho's questions as well as the women's answers are usually included, as are fairly lengthy extracts in which the full flow of their interaction is revealed. We see how even the most canny of informants tells Mmantho, the educated young girl from the nearby village, a little about her childbearing and marital experiences. Mmantho allays the suspicions of most of her informants about her political credentials in a culture riddled with suspicion and fear. It is Mmantho who draws out of her subjects stories of home and work that many white, or male, or 'outsider' researchers might struggle to obtain, even using the most 'scientific' of methods. Let us examine more carefully the various components of this process of interaction, in order to help us understand what precisely it is that these interviews are capable of yielding.

The interviews are not treated as having a clearly defined beginning and end, as perhaps a pseudoscientific interpretation of them might suggest.[13] Of course they have boundaries – between the 'formal' period of actual interviewing, where questions are asked and answers recorded, and the 'informal' preliminaries, interludes, and lengthy farewells which surround and cushion what some think of as the 'actual' interview. But both the informal and the formal parts of the interaction have their functions, and are interpreted as part of the text – again providing us with insight into the kinds of people being interviewed. In the former, for example, Mmantho establishes the crucial rapport discussed above; in the latter, she requires the interviewee to respond to her questioning initiatives, to submit to a certain degree to the authority she claims to possess. In these conversations it becomes clear that what is formally recorded is informed and indeed inspired by what is not. Many of the insights these interviews give us are not derived from any clear-cut and formalised set of interview questions; nor are they insights that any interviewer, administering the same set of questions, could have gained. Rather, they are a product of the unique formal and informal exchanges between this particular interviewer and her interviewees.

Mmantho herself brings particular characteristics to bear upon the situation. The fact that she is 'a girl from Mabeskraal, the nearby village' is perhaps the most important of these[14] – the focus on Phokeng was selected at an early stage in the study precisely because of Mmantho's ability to call upon common understanding between herself and her interviewees from this particular place. As the 'local girl', Mmantho can appeal to common conceptions of space, community, boundary, property, history, hierarchy and culture, both on the broad level (she is a Tswana too) and on a local level (she knows Mrs X who lives down the road; her sister went to Y school, which Mrs J's daughter went to, or of which Mrs M has heard). These are areas where her knowledge of the society is more experiential and intuitive than learnt. On the level of class, too, Mmantho is not an outsider – for she shows great sensitivity to and empathy for those whom she interviews, in spite of her better education. Mmantho 'knows what is going on' in Phokeng. The interviews display a sense of conversation and intimacy between interviewer and interviewee, which is obviously aided by Mmantho's fluent use of rural Setswana. The interviews are replete with references to Tswana words, some with a local meaning, to surnames, clan names, and regional realities.[15] Her local origins allow a particular type of interview to emerge, one rich in local detail, and one which allows us to 'overhear' interactions. This means that what is taken for granted between Mmantho and her interviewee is often of as much significance as what is regarded as of unusual and extraordinary value by both of them. The structure that both parties almost unconsciously attribute to Bafokeng society and the world around it is one that contains categories which are of great interest to the sociologist. Often, as suggested earlier, social scientific categories of analysis prove inappropriate for, or have to be adapted to fit, reality as it is perceived locally. This is not to say there are not hidden, invisible structures that common consciousness does not perceive. Of course there are – and part of Mmantho's quest was to discover them. But often these hidden forces are better understood by starting with the common consciousness of existing forces, than by assuming that categories derived from other contexts are appropriate by virtue of their theoretical pedigree. In the interviews, the women assume that Mmantho is aware of such matters as the boundaries of the community, its inner workings, and the roles it attributes to its members, as well as a whole range of other matters they feel she 'knows', assumptions that give us a lot to work with. Sometimes this rapport fails, and the interviewee gets irritated with Mmantho because she hasn't indicated the common ground the subject thought they both possessed; or Mmantho finds her question gets the 'wrong' answer, because she has assumed common ground that does not exist.

Mmantho is also black, and to the white outsider, the interviews sometimes read like private conversations.[16] Interviewees will sometimes express a hostility towards whites that they feel Mmantho will understand. At other times they confide in her, with a sense of amazement, about the extraordinary behaviour displayed by whites. Elsewhere, they show simple interest, treating her as a source of potentially important and useful information about whites – what can you tell me about these people? The impression given is that whites are mysterious, they come in a variety of different 'types',[17] and their behaviour requires constant explication. There are, it is assumed, nice whites and not-so-nice ones.[18] Whites are the outside category in these interviews, blacks the inside one. 'We blacks' is a commonly used phrase, for example. Mmantho herself does not indulge in exchanging information about 'good' and 'bad' whites. But her interviewees assume she is a ready listener to such information because of the assumption of a common universe.

Thirdly, Mmantho is also a woman. Common womanhood is appealed to less frequently than Tswana-ness or blackness as a basis for mutual understanding. But Mmantho was trained to ask questions about the female experience, and about relations between men and women. Although the sociological categories she brings to bear on the interviews do not always 'work',[19] there are few examples of places in the interviews where such questions are brushed off or ignored. Rather, interviewees participate eagerly in discussions of such matters as how 'women get rich through farming',[20] how 'men do not worry about women who dislike arranged marriages',[21] or how women took out their breasts and showed them to the police, shouting 'you were fed from this breast'.[22] Perhaps the fact that Mmantho is a good fifty to sixty years younger than her informants made them less than forthcoming about the details of childbirth, or about the role of prostitution in township life – and the study is unable to pursue the issue of sexuality beyond a limited sphere. Still, childbirth rituals, fears of rape, and the difficulties of arranged marriage are issues raised by several of the women.

Mmantho's youth often causes her to be subjected to the older women's homilies about the evils of the younger generation, the virtues of the good old days, and the decline of moral and ethical standards. They like Mmantho because she shows respect towards them, and because she does not objectify them as 'old people'. Reminiscences are often treated by the women as opportunities for them to educate the younger girl about the culture, history, and achievements of her own people, and to draw her into an acknowledgement of the failures of the present. Her high level of education, while often treated as something to be valued, is assumed by some of the women to render Mmantho ignorant of local history and culture. She combines, therefore the roles of a learned authority, whose questions must be answered, and an ignorant junior, who must be told about reality. At the same time, some of the women prefer to present themselves to Mmantho in terms they know will be understood by a younger, modern person.

The very interviewing technique used by Mmantho – the pursuing, in as near chronological order as possible, of the trajectory of the life of each woman through her experiences as a young girl, a married woman, a peasant and an urban worker, a mother and a churchgoer – also contributed to the special character of the interviews. Mmantho was sensitive, for example, to the fact that most 'ordinary people', especially less educated ones, do not think of their lives as an elaborate curriculum vitae, arranged in chronological order and divided up into neat compartments such as work, home, and leisure.[23] Her interviewing technique adapted itself to the rambling style of many interviewees, to the fact that personal histories are a jumble and that they contain inconsistencies; or to occasions when the interviewee herself would wish to lead the discussion at certain crucial points rather than allow herself to be led – all of which would be anathema to the positivist. The consciousness of the interviewees is most often revealed, here, where they are not necessarily being 'led' by Mmantho, but when they make unsolicited or seemingly irrelevant statements, in the 'wrong' chronological order, about matters they consider to be important. Often it is what is spontaneous about the interviews that is most revealing.[24]

Some of these special characteristics of Mmantho as an interviewer were very clearly highlighted when, after the first thirty or so interviews were completed, we decided to 'advance' to a more 'scientific' stage in the research, by devising and administering a more formal questionnaire, based on the findings of the first interviews. The questionnaire was designed to overcome the problems of inconsistency between the interviewees – all would now be asked the same set of questions in the same order – and of major gaps that existed in the testimonies. The resulting more tightly structured interviews were factually informative, and probably, in case it appears that this book lacks any commitment to structure whatsoever, essential in giving us a bank of information common to all members of this 'cohort' of women. But they lacked qualitative insights. They told us about the ages and dates of birth of each member of the informants' families, for example, but informants failed to take the opportunity to make their own statements, answer their own questions, lead the interview, or give their own opinions. The interviews became less interactive, more one-sided. Subjectivity vanished. The terms of reference were dictated by myself; Mmantho became simply the channel of my structured views, and the resulting words of the informants were often static and shallow, although Mmantho managed to make more imaginative use of the questionnaire than seemed possible.

This problem became even more obvious when Mmantho left the project, and the final round of questionnaires was administered by a second interviewer who, although black and with every intention of sympathy, was male, from an entirely different region and social class from the Phokeng women, and not a native Setswana speaker. The women failed to respond to the questions with more than yes or no answers in some cases; and some expressed feelings of resentment and anxiety about being interviewed. The rapport was lacking, the women became reticent, and they presented themselves to him in less open a manner.

Thus when we look at each interview as the text of a conversation between Mmantho and another woman, we are able to ask questions about the self perception of older Tswana women *vis-à-vis* the younger generation, or about the boundaries of common identity established between interviewer and interviewee, which suggest something about the meaning of being a 'Tswana', a woman, a black, or a Mofokeng. We can probe how the relating of historical tales and details is seen as an important and socially underestimated activity, or how complex is the matter of the value given the high level of education of a woman like Mmantho.

Besides the process of interaction that produced the texts, the interviewees themselves have brought certain personal and individual qualities to the interviews, which add to their value. It should be said that the interviewees here were all informed that their stories were to be recorded, translated, and made fully available to scholars. The women who agreed to participate did so for a variety of reasons, each of which leaves its mark on the kind of interview they give. Some agreed because they believed they had an interesting and important story or series of stories to tell. They show a sense of their place in history, and their significance as historical actors. Naomi Setshedi, for example, stops Mmantho and changes the direction of the interview completely at times, with the sense that she knows important things that Mmantho is not particularly good at getting at. Others believe that by participating in the interview some aspect of their lives will perhaps be bettered. One woman refused to be reinterviewed, claiming that 'nothing had come' of her previous interviews, so why, she asked, should she be interviewed again. Some treat the interview as an occasion to tell Mmantho all the things they have been longing to convey to the younger generation – either about the lost past, their own lost dignity, or about the lost struggles that achieved things which the younger generation now take for granted. The women regard themselves 'as stores of information and history'. They talk about times long ago, and about old practices, sometimes patronising Mmantho with a cultural heritage she 'should' know about, but at other times simply telling her that there are things she has not heard of.

The women are almost all keen to be interviewed. They wish their village and their people to be known. They place a value on history, on recording the deeds of people, and on genealogy. They display a feeling that the past contains truths and inspirations that the present has crushed. As 'ordinary' women, few interviewees give Mmantho the sense that they might think they are not worthy of being interviewed,[25] although it might be Mmantho's special status as an interviewer that brings their self-confidence and assertiveness to the fore.

Each interviewee constructs her life story in a different way. The different personalities of the interviewees of course affect their responses. But there are also ideological and cultural perceptions that have a social determination, varying from person to person. While the least successful interviewees treat the interview as something rather official, answering questions in a static, monosyllabic way and giving even Mmantho the status of an outsider, denied access to the interviewee's inner feelings, the best become story tellers, creating a series of well told anecdotes.[26] In telling stories, the informants construct the past in ways that place them at the centre of important events, and convey to us what they think is important about their lives – the pleasure or horror of living in Sophiatown, their courage, or their trauma, in difficult circumstances; and what type of person they wish to present themselves as being. Certain character 'types' emerge, whether by the artful design of the interviewee or as a reflection of different social patterns of identity. The 'Mayibuye' woman, who saw Christianity and education as a means to other ends, who took part in social protest, rebelled against arranged marriage, and has a coherent sense of her reasons for her various dissatisfactions, may be distinguished from the more conservative church-going woman, who tends to accept authority, to be overwhelmed by defeat, and to show a suspicion of social movements, for example. The study does not often try to label each individual woman as such. It is difficult to do so without obscuring the way in which the women's stories are also repositories of different fragmented components of consciousness and identity; the same woman who presents herself as having a rather clear sense of herself as a 'Mayibuye' woman, also reveals aspects of her identity as a tribeswoman, churchgoer, wife, mother, daughter, township dweller, and so on. What the study attempts to reveal are the patterns of interplay between the consistent and fragmented aspects of identity, the myriad building blocks out of which a particular individual is constructed, and the larger patterns she might try to present. We ask when and why it is that at certain times, identity appears to cohere. Does it have to do with the presence of an 'organic intellectual' (in Gramsci's terms) who seeks to and is able to organise consciousness?[27] The study does not seek to suggest that the presence of a variety of aspects of identity confirms the currently fashionable view that all subjectivity is 'decentred', but suggests that there is an interplay between the self and its multiple components, an interplay that may be historically examined, and which involves processes of social interaction and ideological creativity. [. . .]

NOTES

1 Ernestina Mekgwe, interviewed by Mmantho Nkotsoe (MN) on 11–9–1981, p. 1, University of the Witwatersrand African Studies Institute Oral Documentation Project, Womens' Project [hereafter ODP WP].

2 As far as its theoretical background is concerned, in the early stages of the Oral Documentation Project, authors such as P. Thompson, *The Voice of the Past: Oral History*, Oxford, Oxford University Press, 1978, and T. Rosengarten, *All God's Dangers*, New York, Avon Books, 1974, proved influential – more so, perhaps, than the existing Africanists who had worked with oral sources. The women's project in particular was influenced by the work of such Western scholars as Ann Oakley and Lillian Rubin, both of whom gave the voices of ordinary women a prominent place earlier than most.

3 Perhaps using the 'more history' approach. See, for example, H. Bradford, *A Taste of Freedom: the ICU in Rural South Africa, 1924–1930*, New Haven, Yale University Press, 1987.

4 See, for example, T. Keegan, *Facing the Storm: Portraits of Black Lives in Rural South Africa*, Cape Town, David Philip, 1988; M. Nkadimeng and G. Relly, 'Kas Maine: the story of a black South African agriculturist', in B. Bozzoli (ed.), *Town and Countryside in the Transvaal*, Johannesburg, Ravan Press, 1983; and T. Matsetela, 'The life story of Nkgona Mma Pooe: aspects of sharecropping and proletarianisation in the northern Orange Free-State 1890–1930', in S. Marks and R. Rathbone (eds), *Industrialisation and Social Change in South Africa*, London, Longman, 1982.

5 C. van Onselen is writing a biography of Kas Maine, who was a sharecropper.

6 Tapes of these early interviews are lodged in the ODP, but, with the exception of the Phokeng tapes, do not form part of this study.

7 D.E. Faris, 'Narrative form and oral history: some problems and possibilities', *International Journal of Oral History*, 1980, vol. 1, no. 3, p. 172.

8 I am grateful to Isabel Hofmeyr and Stephen Clingman for having drawn me into these analytical approaches, although they bear no responsibility for my failings in this respect.

9 R. Grele suggests that oral history interviews are in fact 'conversational narratives' – a useful notion which approximates that used here, although perhaps it does not capture quite the range of ways in which the text of an oral history may be used. See R. Grele, 'Movement without aim: methodological and theoretical problems in oral history', in R. Grele (ed.), *Envelopes of Sound: Six Practitioners Discuss the Method, Theory and Practice of Oral History and Oral Testimony*, Chicago, Precedent Publishers, 1985.

10 There are a few studies of Phokeng and the surrounding area. N. Mokgatle's *Autobiography of an Unknown South African*, London, University of California Press, 1971, includes important material on the oral traditions and early history of Phokeng.

11 See L. Passerini, 'Italian working class culture between the wars: consensus to fascism and work ideology', *International Journal of Oral History*, 1980, vol. 1, no. 1, pp. 8–10. Discussions of method are all too rare in Southern African studies.

12 I am not a symbolic interactionist, although this approach has proved useful – the

ideas of Erving Goffman in particular have helped in the treatment of the 'conversations'.

13 However, in the physical sciences, too, we are told that great innovations and discovery often occur outside of what is formally defined as the 'experimental situation.'.

14 This is one of many examples of the interviewees mentioning Mmantho's background, some of which appear in the body of the study. In another, Rosinah Setsome says to Mmantho, 'You come from a local area' (ODP WP, MN interview with Rosinah Setsome, 12–9–1981, p. 17), while elsewhere mention is made of Mmantho's school, her surname, and the likelihood that she will know some of the people being discussed.

15 Mrs Setshedi engages in a long discussion with her about the Setshedi clan, in which she assumes Mmantho has a knowledge of African history, and particularly of the Difaqane (early nineteenth-century wars between the Nguni and other ethnic groups in Southern Africa), and of its effects upon the Bafokeng.

16 It should be stressed that at no stage was the impression given to the interviewees that these conversations were, or would remain, private. They knew full well their purpose. The tone of intimacy simply arises as a result of Mmantho's skill and acceptability to her subjects.

17 Jews, Germans, Boers, English, and policemen are the main ones.

18 See, for a comparative example, P. Mayer's analysis of the attitudes of a sample of Sowetan blacks, in his '"Good" and "Bad" Whites', a paper presented to the Conference on South Africa in the Comparative Study of Class, Race and Nationalism, New York, 1982.

19 It was most frequently Western-derived feminist categories of analysis that proved difficult to transfer into this African setting – but more generally it was a case, as Passerini suggests, of existing social scientific concepts needing to be re-thought in the light of oral evidence.

20 ODP WP, MN interview with Ernestina Mekgwe, 11–9–1981, p. 2.

21 Ibid., pp. 14–15.

22 Ibid., p. 46.

23 It is important for positivistically inclined sociologists to recognise that questionnaire/survey methods of research were devised and evolved in Western settings, with high levels of literacy, good basic data from which to draw samples and construct questions, and the incorporation of even the poorer strata into a technocratic culture. People are used to filling in forms and ordering their perceptions. Even in those settings such methods have severe limitations. One of the reasons why sociological studies in South Africa have so often confined themselves to the white, middle class, literate, or dominant populations is that the discipline's own major heritage is faulty. These flawed instruments can barely be used amongst non-Western, peasant peoples, about whom basic raw data are almost entirely unknown, with low levels of literacy and a low level of absorption of technocratic values. African sociologists would do well to look to the discipline's non-positivistic heritage, and its social anthropological offshoot, for insight into performing research in such settings.

24 Luisa Passerini found it significant in the 'spontaneous' part of her interviews with Italian workers who had lived through Fascism, that they remained silent about the fact of Fascism itself – an important form of self-censorship which, she says, is 'evidence of a scar, a violent annihilation of many years in human lives and memories, a profound wound in daily experience' (Passerini, 'Italian working-class culture', p. 9).

25 This is in strong contrast with the experiences of interviewers in many Western settings, where the kind of silences Passerini refers to appear to be common amongst poorer people who may have experienced harsh repression or taken part

in strikes or other forms of protest without a sense of pride. See, for example, L. Shopes, 'Oral history and community involvement: the Baltimore Neighbourhood Heritage Project', in S.P. Benson *et al.* (eds), *Presenting the Past*, Philadelphia, Temple University Press, 1986.

26 I am grateful to Mike Kirkwood for first pointing out the rich storytelling capacities of particular interviewees, and for his creative editing of one of the woman's stories. See 'The story of Mrs S', *Staffrider*, 1984, vol. 6, no. 1. For an analysis of this essay and other life stories run in *Staffrider* see A. Oliphant, 'Staffrider magazine and popular history: the opportunities and challenges of personal testimony', *Radical History Review*, 1990 (Winter), pp. 46–47.

27 This concept is linked to those of 'inherent' and 'derived' ideologies mentioned above; Gramsci's idea was that particular knowledgeable and educated thinkers close to the working and poorer classes – the organic intellectuals – would be able to transform the incoherent 'inherent' set of ideas into a more coherent and socially useful ideology.

14 Learning to listen

Interview techniques and analyses

Kathryn Anderson and Dana C. Jack

Kathryn Anderson and Dana Jack are both professors at Fairhaven College, Western Washington University. Reprinted from Sherna Berger Gluck and Daphne Patai (eds), *Women's Words: The Feminist Practice of Oral History*, London, Routledge, 1991, pp. 11–26, with permission.

Oral history interviews provide an invaluable means of generating new insights about women's experiences of themselves in their worlds. The spontaneous exchange within an interview offers possibilities of freedom and flexibility for researchers and narrators alike. For the narrator, the interview provides the opportunity to tell her own story in her own terms. For researchers, taped interviews preserve a living interchange for present and future use; we can rummage through interviews as we do through an old attic – probing, comparing, checking insights, finding new treasures the third time through, then arranging and carefully documenting our results.

Oral interviews are particularly valuable for uncovering women's perspectives. Anthropologists have observed how the expression of women's unique experience as women is often muted, particularly in any situation where women's interests and experiences are at variance with those of men.[1] A woman's discussion of her life may combine two separate, often conflicting, perspectives: one framed in concepts and values that reflect men's dominant position in the culture, and one informed by the more immediate realities of a woman's personal experience. Where experience does not 'fit' dominant meanings, alternative concepts may not readily be available. Hence, inadvertently, women often mute their own thoughts and feelings when they try to describe their lives in the familiar and publicly acceptable terms of prevailing concepts and conventions. To hear women's perspectives accurately, we have to learn to listen in stereo, receiving both the dominant and muted channels clearly and tuning into them carefully to understand the relationship between them.

How do we hear the weaker signal of thoughts and feelings that differ from conventional expectations? Carolyn Heilbrun urges biographers to search for the choices, the pain, the stories that lie beyond the 'constraints of acceptable discussion'.[2] An interview that fails to expose the distortions and conspires to mask the facts and feelings that did not fit will overemphasize expected aspects of the female role. More important, it will miss an opportunity to document the experience that lies outside the boundaries of acceptability.

To facilitate access to the muted channel of women's subjectivity, we must inquire whose story the interview is asked to tell, who interprets the story, and with what theoretical frameworks. Is the narrator asked what meanings she makes of her experiences? Is the researcher's attitude one of receptivity to learn rather than to prove preexisting ideas that are brought into the interview? In order to learn to listen, we need to attend more to the narrator than to our own agendas.

INTERVIEW TECHNIQUES: SHEDDING AGENDAS
Kathryn Anderson

My awareness of how both personal and collective agendas can short-circuit the listening process developed while scanning oral histories for the Washington Women's Heritage Project. This statewide collaborative effort received major support from the National Endowment for the Humanities and the Washington Commission for the Humanities to develop educational workshops and to produce a traveling exhibit documenting women's lives in interviews and historical photographs. The first stage of the project involved training dozens of interviewers in a series of oral history workshops held throughout the state. A typical workshop provided information on equipment, processing tapes, interviewing techniques, and a crash course in the new women's history scholarship. Prospective interviewers left with a manual, which included Sherna Gluck's 'Topical Guide for Oral History Interviews with Women'.[3]

To select excerpts for the exhibit, we reviewed dozens of interviews produced by project staff and workshop participants along with hundreds of interviews housed in archives and historical societies. We found them filled with passages describing the range and significance of activities and events portrayed in the photographs. To our dismay and disappointment, however, most of them lacked detailed discussions of the web of feelings, attitudes, and values that give meaning to activities and events. Interviewers had either ignored these more subjective dimensions of women's lives or had accepted comments at face value when a pause, a word, or an expression might have invited the narrator to continue. Some of us found discrepancies between our memories of interviews and the transcripts because the meaning we remembered hearing had been expressed through intense vocal quality and body language, not through words alone.

We were especially confused that our interviews did not corroborate the satisfactions and concerns other historians were discovering in women's diaries and letters, or the importance of relationships social scientists were uncovering in women's interviews. To understand why, I scrutinized the interviews with rural women that I had done for the project, paying special attention to interview strategies and techniques. My expectations that the interviews would give rural women a forum to describe their experiences in their own terms and to reflect on their experiences as women in the specific context of Washington state were thwarted to some extent by three factors: the project's agenda to document women's lives for the exhibit; an incomplete conversion from traditional to feminist historical paradigms; and the conventions of social discourse.

While the project's general goal was to accumulate a series of life histories, my special task was to discover women's roles in northwest Washington farming communities. Project deadlines and the need to cover a representative range of experiences combined to limit interviews to no more than three hours. In retrospect, I can see how I listened with at least part of my attention focused on producing potential material for the exhibit – the concrete description of experiences that would accompany pictures of women's activities. As I rummage through the interviews long after the exhibit has been placed in storage, I am painfully aware of lost opportunities for women to reflect on the activities and events they described and to explain their terms more fully in their own words.

In spite of my interest at the time in learning how women saw themselves as women in specific historical contexts, the task of creating public historical documents as well as the needs of the project combined to subvert my personal interests and led to fairly traditional strategies. As a result, my interviews tended to focus on activities and facts, on what happened and how it happened. They revealed important information about the variety of roles women filled on Washington farms, and how they disguised the extent and importance of their contributions by insisting that they were just 'helping out' or 'doing what needed to be done'. Left out, however, was the more subjective realm of feelings about what made these activities fun or drudgery, which ones were accompanied by feelings of pride or failure. The resulting story of what they did tells us something about the limitations under which they operated but less about the choices they might have made. My interests were not incompatible with the project's goals but my methods often failed to give women the opportunity to discuss the complex web of feelings and contradictions behind their familiar stories.

My background included both women's history and interpersonal communication, but no specific training in counseling. My fear of forcing or manipulating individuals into discussing topics they did not want to talk about sometimes prevented me from giving women the space and the permission to explore some of the deeper, more conflicted parts of their stories. I feared, for good reasons, that I lacked the training to respond appropriately to some of the issues that might be raised or uncovered. Thus, my interview strategies were bound to some extent by the conventions of social discourse. The unwritten rules of conversation about appropriate questions and topics – especially the one that says 'don't pry!' – kept me from encouraging women to make explicit the range of emotions surrounding the events and experiences they related. These rules are particularly restrictive in the rural style I had absorbed as a child on an Iowa farm. In a context where weather, blight, pests, and disease were so crucial to productivity and survival, conversation often tended towards the fatalistic and pragmatic; we certainly did not dwell on feelings about things beyond our control. As I interviewed rural women, the sights, sounds, and smells of a farm kitchen elicited my habits of a rural style of conversation and constrained my interview strategies.

Another interviewer experienced tensions between project goals and rules of conversation in a different context for different reasons. As she interviewed Indian women from various Washington tribes, she felt torn between a need to gather specific information and an awareness of appropriate relationships between young and old: the rules she had learned as an Indian child prohibited questioning elders, initiating topics, or disagreeing in any form, even by implying that a comment might be incomplete. When, as in these instances, interviewer and narrator share similar backgrounds that include norms for conversation and interaction, interview strategies must be particularly explicit to avoid interference.

Although I approached the interviews with a genuine interest in farm women's perceptions of themselves, their roles, and their relationships in the rural community, I now see how often the agenda to document farm activities and my habit of taking the comments of the farm women at face value determined my questions and responses. Both interfered with my sensitivity to the emotionally laden language they used to describe their lives. My first interview with Elizabeth illustrates a lost opportunity to explore her discussion of the physical and mental strains of multiple roles.[4] We had been talking about her relationships with her mother and half-sister when she offered the following:

> I practically had a nervous breakdown when I discovered my sister had cancer, you know; it was kind of like knocking the pins [out from under me] – and I had, after the second boy was born, I just had ill health for quite a few years. I evidently had a low-grade blood infection or something. Because I was very thin, and, of course, I kept working hard. And every fall, why, I'd generally spend a month or so being sick – from overdoing, probably.

Instead of encouraging further reflection on the importance of her relationship with her sister or on the difficulties of that period in her life, my next question followed my imperative for detailing her role on the farm: 'What kind of farming did you do right after you were married?'

Elizabeth was a full partner with her husband in their dairy farm and continued to play an active role as the farm switched to the production of small grains. Her interview has the potential of giving us valuable information about the costs incurred by women who combined child-rearing and housework with the physical labor and business decisions of the farm. It also suggests something of the importance of relationships with family and close friends in coping with both roles. The interview's potential is severely limited, however, by my failure to encourage her to expand upon her spontaneous reflections and by my eagerness to document the details of her farming activity. Not until later did I realize that I do not know what she meant by 'nervous breakdown' or 'overdoing'. The fact that other farm women used the same or similar terms to describe parts of their lives alerted me to the need for further clarification. I now wish I had asked her to tell me in her own words of the importance of the relationship with her sister and why its possible loss was such a threat.

Later in the same interview I was more sensitive to Elizabeth's feelings about the difficulty of combining roles, only to deflect the focus from her experience once again. She was telling me how hard it was to be a full partner in the field and still have sole responsibility for the house:

> This is what was so hard, you know. You'd both be out working together, and he'd come in and sit down, and I would have to hustle a meal together, you know. And that's typical.

How did you manage?

> Well, sometimes you didn't get to bed till midnight or after, and you were up at five. Sometimes when I think back to the early days, though, we'd take a day off, we'd get the chores done, and we'd go take off and go visiting.

Was that typical? Neighbors going to visit each other after the chores were done?

While Elizabeth was telling me how she managed, I was already thinking about patterns in the neighborhood. My first question had been a good one, but, by asking about what other people did, my next one told her that I had heard enough about her experience. The two questions in succession have a double message: 'Tell me about your experience, but don't tell me too much'. Part of the problem may have been that even while I was interviewing women I was aware of the need to make sense of what they told me. In this case, the scholar's search for generalizations undermined the interviewer's need to attend to an individual's experience. Ideally, the processes of analysis should be suspended or at least subordinated in the process of listening.

If we want to know how women feel about their lives, then we have to allow them to talk about their feelings as well as their activities. If we see rich potential in the language people use to describe their daily activities, then we have to take advantage of the opportunity to let them tell us what that language means, 'Nervous breakdown' is not the only phrase that I heard without asking for clarification. Verna was answering a question about the relationship between her mother and her grandmother when she said:

> It was quite close since my mother was the only daughter that was living. My grandmother did have another daughter, that one died. I didn't know it until we got to working on the family tree. My mother was older than her brother. They were quite close. They worked together quite well when it

would come to preparing meals and things. They visited back and forth a lot.

Her answer gave several general examples of how the closeness was manifested, but what did Verna mean when she described a relationship as 'close' twice in a short answer? What did her perception of this relationship mean to her? My next question asked, instead, for further examples: 'Did they [your grandparents] come to western Washington because your parents were here?'

Even efforts to seek clarification were not always framed in ways that encouraged the interviewee to reflect upon the meaning of her experience. Elizabeth was answering a question about household rules when she was a child and commented: 'My mother was real partial to my brother because, of course, you know that old country way; the boy was the important one.' My question 'How did her partiality to the brother show?' elicited some specific examples, but none of a series of subsequent questions gave her an opportunity to reflect upon how this perception affected her understanding of herself and her place in the family.

A final example from Verna's interview illustrates the best and the worst of what we are trying to do. Her statement is a powerful reflection upon her roles as a mother; the subsequent question, however, ignores all the emotional content of her remarks:

> Yes. There was times that I just wished I could get away from it all. And there were times when I would have liked to have taken the kids and left them someplace for a week – the whole bunch at one time – so that I wouldn't have to worry about them. I don't know whether anybody else had that feeling or not, but there were times when I just felt like I needed to get away from everybody, even my husband, for a little while. Those were times when I would maybe take a walk back in the woods and look at the flowers and maybe go down there and find an old cow that was real gentle and walk up to her and pat her a while – kind of get away from it. I just had to, it seems like sometimes . . .

Were you active in clubs?

As the above portion of her remarks indicates, Verna was more than willing to talk spontaneously about the costs of her choice to combine the roles of wife, mother, and diligent farm woman. Perhaps she had exhausted the topic. If not, my question, even though it acknowledged the need for support at such times, certainly did not invite her to expand upon the feelings that both she and I knew might contradict some notion of what women ought to do and feel. She was comfortable enough to begin to consider the realities beyond the acceptable façade of the female role, but my question diverted the focus from her unique, individual reflections to the relative safety of women's clubs and activities, a more acceptable outlet for such feelings. In this case, my ability to listen, not Verna's memory, suffered from the constraints of internalized cultural boundaries. Until we can figure out how to release the brakes that these boundaries place on both hearing and memory, our oral histories are likely to confirm the prevailing ideology of women's lives and rob women of their honest voices.

What I learned by listening carefully to my interviews is that women's oral history requires much more than a new set of questions to explore women's unique experiences and unique perspectives; we need to refine our methods for probing more deeply by listening to the levels on which the narrator responds to the original questions. To do so we need to listen critically to our interviews, to our responses as well as to our questions. We need to hear what women implied, suggested, and started to say but didn't. We need to interpret their pauses and, when it happens, their unwillingness or inability to respond. We need to consider carefully whether our interviews create a context in which women feel comfortable exploring the subjective feelings that give meaning to actions, things, and events, whether they allow women to explore 'unwomanly' feelings and behaviors, and whether they encourage women to explain what they mean in their own terms.

When women talk about relationships, our responses can create an opportunity to talk about how much relationships enriched or diminished life experiences. When women talk about activities or events, they might find it easy to take blame for failures, but more sensitive responses may also make it possible to talk about feelings of competence or pride, even for women who do not consider such qualities very womanly. When women talk about what they have done, they may also want to explore their perceptions of the options they thought they had and how they feel about their responses. We can probe the costs that sometimes accompany choices, the means for accommodating and compensating for such costs, and how they are evaluated in retrospect. We can make it easier for women to talk about the values that may be implicit in their choices or feelings. When women reveal feelings or experiences that suggest conflict, we can explore what the conflict means and what form it takes. We can be prepared to expect and permit discussion of anger. If our questions are general enough, women will be able to reflect upon their experience and choose for themselves which experiences and feelings are central to their sense of their past.

The language women use to explore the above topics will be all the richer when they have ample opportunity to explain and clarify what they mean. When they use words and phrases like 'nervous breakdown', 'support', 'close', 'visiting', and 'working together', they should have an opportunity to explain what they mean in their own terms. With letters and diaries we can only infer what individuals mean by the language they use; with oral interviews we can ask them. As they discuss examples, the particularities of their experiences often begin to emerge from behind the veil of familiar and ambiguous terms.

As a result of my discussions with Dana, a trained therapist, I have developed a new appreciation for oral history's potential for exploring questions of self-concept and [self]-consciousness, for documenting questions of value and meaning in individuals' reflections upon their past. Important distinctions remain between oral history and therapeutic interviews, but as we shed our specific agendas the women we interview will become freer to tell their own stories as fully, completely, and honestly as they desire.

INTERVIEW ANALYSES: LISTENING FOR MEANING
Dana Jack

I have been using oral interviews in research on depression among women and on moral reasoning among practicing attorneys.[5] In broad terms, both studies examine the interactions among social institutions, social roles, and women's consciousness. The women I interviewed are grappling with ideas about relationships, self-worth, career, and personal integrity in the context of society-wide changes in women's roles. As I listened to a woman's self-commentary, to her reflection upon her own thoughts and actions, I learned about her adaptation to her particular relationships and historical circumstances, especially her adaptation to the ideas of 'good lawyer', 'good wife', 'good woman', to which she tried to conform.

I listened with an awareness that a person's self-reflection is not just a private, subjective act. The categories and concepts we use for reflecting upon and evaluating ourselves come from a cultural context, one that has historically demeaned and controlled women's activities. Thus, an exploration of the language and the meanings women use to articulate their own experience leads to an awareness of the conflicting social forces and institutions affecting women's consciousness. It also reveals how women act either to restructure or preserve their psychological orientations, their relationships, and their social contexts. This was true for two very different studies and populations – depressed women and practicing lawyers.

The first, and the hardest, step of interviewing was to learn to listen in a new way, to hold in abeyance the theories that told me what to hear and how to interpret what these women had to say. Depressed women, for example, told stories of the failure of relationships, an inability to connect with the person(s) with whom they wanted to experience intimacy. These were the expected stories, predicted by existing models, and the temptation was to interpret the stories according to accepted concepts and norms for 'maturity' and 'health'. Because psychological theories have relied on men's lives and men's formulations for these norms, they explain women's psychological difference as deviant or 'other'.[6] The interview is a critical tool for developing new frameworks and theories based on women's lives and women's formulations. But we are at an awkward stage: old theories are set aside or under suspicion and new ones are still emerging. We must therefore be especially attentive to the influences that shape what we hear and how we interpret. How do we listen to an interview when we have rejected the old frameworks for interpretation and are in the process of developing new ones? How can an interview pull us beyond existing frameworks so that we stretch and expand them?

First, we must remember that the researcher is an active participant in qualitative research. My initial training was as a therapist, and the practice of listening to others while also attending to my own response to them has helped in conducting interviews. Theodore Reik calls this quiet involvement of the self 'listening with the third ear'.[7] As a researcher, I have learned that critical areas demanding attention are frequently those where I think I already know what the woman is saying. This means I am already appropriating what she says to an existing schema, and therefore I am no longer really listening to *her*. Rather, I am listening to how what she says fits into what I think I already know. So I try to be very careful to ask each woman what she means by a certain word, or to make sure that I attend to what is missing, what literary critics call the 'presence of the absence' in women's texts – the 'hollows, centers, caverns within the work-places where activity that one might expect is missing . . . or deceptively coded.'[8]

And what is it that is absent? Because women have internalized the categories by which to interpret their experience and activities, categories that 'represent a deposit of the desires and disappointments of men',[9] what is often missing is the woman's own interpretation of her experience, or her own perspective on her life and activity. Interviews allow us to hear, if we will, the particular meanings of a language that both women and men use but that each translates differently. Looking closely at the language and the particular meanings of important words women use to describe their experience allows us to understand how women are adapting to the culture within which they live. When their behavior is observed from the outside, depressed women are called passive, dependent, masochistic, compliant, and victimized by their own learned helplessness. Yet, when I listened to the women's self-reflection, what became clear was that behind the so-called passive behavior of depressed women was the tremendous cognitive activity required to inhibit both outer actions and inner feelings in order to live up to the ideal of the 'good' woman, particularly the good wife. Statements such as 'I have to walk on eggshells in dealing with my husband', and 'I have learned "don't rock the boat"' show awareness of both their actions and their intended effects: not to cause discord.[10]

How do we listen to interviews without immediately leaping to interpretations suggested by prevailing theories? The first step is to immerse ourselves in the interview, to try to understand the person's story from her vantage point. I found that three ways of listening helped me understand the narrator's point of view. The first was to listen to the person's *moral language*. In the depression study, I heard things like: 'I feel like I'm a failure', 'I don't measure up', 'I'm a liar, a cheat, and I'm no good.' In the lawyer study, when lawyers were describing fulfilling the obligations of role, we heard statements such as: 'It's like being forced into a sex relationship you didn't anticipate. It's a screw job. It feels horrible to do something that you wouldn't do normally.'

Or 'I have to contradict myself depending on what role I'm taking . . . it's sort of professional prostitution.' Or finally, 'Sometimes you feel almost like a pimp or something . . . [I]t felt sleazy to cut the truth that finely.'

Although very different in tone, these moral self-evaluative statements allow us to examine the relationship between self-concept and cultural norms, between what we value and what others value, between how we are told to act and how we feel about ourselves when we do or do not act that way. In a person's self-judgement, we can see which moral standards are accepted and used to judge the self, which values the person strives to attain. In the depression study, this was the key to learning about gender differences in the prevalence and dynamics of depression. Negative self-judgement affecting the fall in self-esteem is considered to be one of the key symptoms of depression. Research by Carol Gilligan and her colleagues indicates that women and men often use differing moral frameworks to guide their perception and resolution of moral problems.[11] Listening to the moral language of depressed women illuminated both the standards used to judge the self and the source of their despair. The women considered the failure of their relationships to be a *moral* failure; their sense of hopelessness and helplessness stemmed from despair about the inability to be an authentic, developing self within an intimate marriage while also living up to the moral imperatives of the 'good woman'.

Attending to the moral standards used to judge the self allows the researcher to honor the individuality of each woman through observing what values she is striving to attain. An oral interview, when structured by the narrator instead of the researcher, allows each woman to express her uniqueness in its full class, racial, and ethnic richness. Each person is free to describe her idiosyncratic interaction between self-image and cultural norms. Each person can tell us how she comes to value or devalue herself. During the interview, the researcher's role is to preserve and foster this freedom, and to restrict the imposition of personal expectations. When the woman, and not existing theory, is considered the expert on her own psychological experience, one can begin to hear the muted channel of women's experience come through.

In analyzing the depression study, for example, I heard how women use the language of the culture to deny what, on another level, they value and desire. A key word for depressed women is 'dependency'. Psychologists consider depressed women to be excessively dependent upon their relationships for a sense of self and self-esteem. But when I looked at how depressed women understand dependence, and how their negative evaluation of themselves as dependent affects their self-perception and their actions, the concept was cast in a new light.

In a first interview with a thirty-three-year-old depressed woman, the issue of dependence was central and problematic: 'You know, I'm basically a very dependent person to start with. And then you get me married and tied down to a home and start not working . . .'

Asked what she meant by dependent, she responded:

I like closeness. I like companionship. I like somebody, an intimate closeness, even with a best friend. And I've never had that with my husband . . .
Sometimes I get frustrated with myself that I have to have that, you know.

I look at other people that seem so self-sufficient and so independent. I
don't know – I just have always needed a closeness. And maybe I identified
that as dependency.

. . . [S]ince I've been married I realize it's kind of a negative thing to be
that way. I've tried to bury that need for closeness. And so I guess that has
also contributed to a lot of my frustrations.

Saying that she 'had been feeling that my need for intimacy and my need for
that kind of a deep level of friendship or relationships with people was sort of
bad', this woman began 'to believe there was something the matter with me'.
In her attempt to bury her needs for closeness, she revealed the activity
required to be passive, to try to live up to self-alienating images of 'today's
woman'.

This interview contains an implicit challenge to prevalent understandings
of dependence. Looking closely, we are able to see how this woman has
judged her feelings against a dominant standard that says to need closeness
makes one dependent, when one should be able to be self-sufficient and
autonomous. Further, she reflects upon her own experience, her capabilities,
and her needs not from the basis of who she is and what she needs but in
terms of how her husband and others see her. Her capacity for closeness and
intimacy goes unacknowledged as strength. Rather than a failure of the husband's response, the problem is identified as her 'neediness'. If a researcher
went into this interview with the traditional notion of dependence in mind,
s/he would find the hypothesis that depressed women are too dependent confirmed. But if one listens to the woman's own feelings about dependence, her
confusion about what she knows she needs and what the culture says she
should need, one begins to see part of the self-alienation and separation from
feelings that is a key aspect of depression.

The second way of listening that allowed me to hear the voice of the
subject instead of my own preconceptions was to attend to the subject's *meta-
statements*. These are places in the interview where people spontaneously stop,
look back, and comment about their own thoughts or something just said.

For example, in the lawyer study, a woman is answering the question,
'What does morality mean to you?':

. . . [I]t seems to me anything that raises to mind hurting other people or
taking things away from other people or some sort of monetary gain for
oneself . . . And I suppose just how we interact with each other, if there's a
contentiousness or bad feelings or bad blood between some people, that
raises some moral issues because I guess I see us all as having a bit of a
moral obligation to be nice to each other and to get along. *So – do I sound
much like a litigator?*

Meta-statements alert us to the individual's awareness of a discrepancy within the self – or between what is expected and what is being said. They inform the interviewer about what categories the individual is using to monitor her thoughts, and allow observation of how the person socializes feelings or thoughts according to certain norms.[12] Women lawyers made many more meta-statements than men, indicating they were 'watching' their own thinking. Because women have come into a legal system designed by men, for men, and because they still face discrimination, it is easy for them to develop an 'onlooker' attitude of critical observation toward themselves.[13] This woman looks at herself being looked at in law and notices the difference. Second, these remarks show how powerfully a stereotypic image of the successful, adversarial lawyer divides them from their personal experience and makes some women, early in their careers, question their ability within law. Finally, such comments reveal the lack of public validation of frameworks that women use to understand and value their own feelings and experiences.[14]

The third way of listening was to attend to the *logic of the narrative*, noticing the internal consistency or contradictions in the person's statements about recurring themes and the way these themes relate to each other. I listened to how the person strings together major statements about experience so I could understand the assumptions and beliefs that inform the logic and guide the woman's interpretation of her experience.

A woman I call Anna, age fifty-four, hospitalized twice for major depression, provides an example of a contradiction within the logic of her narrative, a contradiction that points to conflicting beliefs. Anna says:

> I was telling my daughter-in-law, 'I guess I was just born to serve others.' But we shouldn't be born to serve other people, we should look after ourselves.

Anna constructs the most important issues in her life – how to balance the needs of her self with the needs of others – as an either/or choice that presents her with loss on either side. The choice is either loss of self or loss of other. Such dichotomous thinking leaves Anna with feelings of hopelessness about how to resolve the conflicts in the relationships, and restricts her perception of choice.

On the surface, Anna's statement simply pits the traditional female role against the new 'me first' ethic of self-development. But, looking more deeply, one sees that she describes two visions of relationship: either isolation or subordination. Through Anna's construction of her possibilities in relationship, one gains a glimpse of how specific historical ideas about women's roles and women's worth affect her own depression. Anna's vision of her self in relationship as either subordinated or isolated is profoundly influenced by a social context of inequality and competition. When unresolved personal issues intersect with conflicting social ideals that limit women's lives, that intersection increases the difficulty of forming a positive and realistic vision of self toward which one can strive.

Rather than conclude, as do cognitive theories of depression, that cognitive errors 'cause' depression, observing this dichotomous thinking led me to see how the female social role is structured in thought and works to constrict women's perceptions of their relationships and their choices. Such logic of the narrative allowed me to see how a woman deals with conflicting cultural ideas, and how easy it is to feel depression as a personal failure rather than to recognize its social and historical aspects.

CONCLUSION

The process of sharing and critiquing our interviews has helped us sharpen our listening skills and improve our interviewing methods so that narrators feel more free to explore complex and conflicting experiences in their lives. Because of our divergent disciplinary interests, we have changed in different ways. The historian has become more alert to the subjective dimensions of events and activities; the psychologist has gained greater awareness of how the sociohistorical context can be read between the lines of a woman's 'private' inner conflict. Both are more determined to discover how individual women define and evaluate their experience in their own terms.

Realizing the possibilities of the oral history interview demands a shift in methodology from information gathering, where the focus is on the right questions, to interaction, where the focus is on process, on the dynamic unfolding of the subject's viewpoint. It is the interactive nature of the interview that allows us to ask for clarification, to notice what questions the subject formulates about her own life, to go behind conventional, expected answers to the woman's personal construction of her own experience. This shift of focus from data gathering to interactive process affects what the researcher regards as valuable information. Those aspects of live interviews unavailable in a written text – the pauses, the laughter – all invite us to explore their meaning for the narrator. The exploration does not have to be intrusive; it can be as simple as 'What did that [event] mean for you?'

This shift in focus, from information (data) gathering to interactive process, requires new skills on the researcher's part. In our view, it stimulates the development of a specific kind of readiness, the dimensions of which have been sketched in this paper. As Anderson has suggested, its most general aspects include an awareness that (1) actions, things, and events are accompanied by subjective emotional experience that gives them meaning; (2) some of the feelings uncovered may exceed the boundaries of acceptable or expected female behavior; and (3) individuals can and must explain what they mean in their own terms. Jack described three ways of listening during the interview that sharpen the researcher's awareness of the feelings and thoughts that lie behind the woman's outwardly conventional story: (1) listening to the narrator's moral language; (2) attending to the meta-statements; and (3) observing the logic of the narrative. Incorporating these insights has helped us learn how to remain suspended and attentive on a fine line between accomplishing our research goals and letting the subject be in charge of the material in the interview.

While by no means conclusive or inclusive, the following points suggest further ways to sharpen our attentiveness to the interactive process of the interview:

A. Listening to the narrator
   1 If the narrator is to have the chance to tell her own story, the interviewer's first question needs to be very open-ended. It needs to convey the message that in this situation, the narrator's interpretation of her experience guides the interview. For example, in the depression study, Jack started with, 'Can you tell me, in your own mind what led up to your experience of depression?'
   2 If she doesn't answer the interviewer's question, what and whose questions does the woman answer?
   3 What are her feelings about the facts or events she is describing?
   4 How does she understand what happened to her? What meaning does she make of events? Does she think about it in more than one way? How does she evaluate what she is describing?
   5 What is being left out, what are the absences?

B. Listening to ourselves
   1 Try not to cut the narrator off to steer her to what our concerns are.
   2 Trust our own hunches, feelings, responses that arise through listening to others.
   3 Notice our own areas of confusion, or of too great a certainty about what the woman is saying – these are areas to probe further.
   4 Notice our personal discomfort; it can become a personal alarm bell alerting us to a discrepancy between what is being said and what the woman is feeling.

Oral history interviews are unique in that the interaction of researcher and subject creates the possibility of going beyond the conventional stories of women's lives, their pain and their satisfactions, to reveal experience in a less culturally edited form. But despite the value of this focus on the oral history interview in its dynamic, interactive form, we must offer one word of caution. The researcher must always remain attentive to the moral dimension of interviewing and aware that she is there to follow the narrator's lead, to honor her integrity and privacy, not to intrude into areas that the narrator has chosen to hold back.[15] This is another part of the specific kind of readiness the researcher brings to the interview: a readiness to be sensitive to the narrator's privacy while, at the same time, offering her the freedom to express her own thoughts and experiences, and listening for how that expression goes beyond prevailing concepts.

NOTES

Public discussion of this collaborative work began at the National Women's Studies Association Conference held in Seattle, Washington, in June 1985 and continued with coauthors Susan Armitage and Judith Wittner in the *Oral History Review*, 1987, vol. 15 (Spring), pp. 103–127.

1 See S. Ardener (ed.), *Perceiving Women*, New York, John Wiley & Sons, 1975, pp. xi–xxiii. In that volume see also E. Ardener, 'Belief and the problem of women', pp. 1–27, and H. Callan, 'The premise of dedication: notes towards an ethnography of diplomats' wives', pp. 87–104.

2 C. Heilbrun, *Writing a Woman's Life*, New York, W.W. Norton & Company, 1988, pp. 30–31.

3 'Women's oral history resource section', *Frontiers*, 1977, vol. 2 (Summer), pp. 110–118.

4 K. Anderson and others, interviews for the Washington Women's Heritage Project, Center for Pacific Northwest Studies, Western Washington University, Bellingham, Washington. In the following account, two interviews from the collection are cited: interview with Elizabeth Bailey, 1 July 1980; interview with Verna Friend, 31 July 1980.

5 D. C. Jack, 'Clinical depression in women: cognitive schemas of self, care and relationships in a longitudinal study', unpublished doctoral dissertation, Harvard University, 1984; and D. C. Jack, 'Silencing the self: the power of social imperatives in female depression', in R. Formanek and A. Gurian (eds), *Women and Depression: A Lifespan Perspective*, New York, Springer Publishing Co., 1987. The lawyer study is in R. Jack and D.C. Jack, *Moral Vision and Professional Decisions: The Changing Values of Women and Men Lawyers*, New York, Cambridge University Press, 1989.

6 C. Gilligan, *In a Different Voice*, Cambridge, Mass., Harvard University Press, 1982.

7 T. Reik, *Listening with the Third Ear*, New York, Farrar Straus Giroux, 1948.

8 C. Heilbrun and C. Stimpson, 'Theories of feminist criticism: a dialogue', in J. Donovan (ed.), *Feminist Literary Criticism*, Lexington, Ky., The University Press of Kentucky, 1975, pp. 61–73.

9 K. Horney, *Feminine Psychology*, New York, W.W. Norton & Company, 1967, p. 56.

10 Jack, 'Clinical depression in women', p. 177.

11 Gilligan, *In a Different Voice*. See also C. Gilligan, J. Taylor and J. Ward (eds), *Mapping the Moral Domain*, Cambridge, Mass., Harvard University Pres, 1989.

12 See A. Russell Hochschild, 'Emotion work, feeling rule, and social structure', *American Journal of Sociology*, 1979, vol. 85 (November), pp. 551–575.

13 The onlooker phenomenon is described by M. Westkott, *The Feminist Legacy of Karen Horney*, New Haven, Conn., Yale University Press, 1986.

14 J. Baker Miller, *Toward a New Psychology of Women*, Boston, Beacon Press, 1976, writes 'When . . . we can think only in terms given by the dominant culture, and when that culture not only does not attend to our own experiences but specifically denies and devalues them, we are left with no way of conceptualizing our lives. Under these circumstances, a woman is often left with a global, undefined sense that she must be wrong' (p. 57).

15 The American Psychological Association (APA) has adopted ethical standards for the treatment of research subjects that provide some guidelines for thinking through issues of researcher intrusiveness. A copy of the APA Ethical Principles may be obtained from the APA Ethics office, 1200 17th Street NW, Washington, DC 20036.

15 Marking absences

Holocaust testimony and history

Naomi Rosh White

Naomi Rosh White is an Associate Professor in the Department of Anthropology and Sociology at Monash University, Melbourne, Australia. Reprinted from *Oral History Association of Australia Journal*, 1994, no. 16, pp. 12–18 with permission from Naomi Rosh White and the OHAA.

> To set oneself the task of bringing back to life the hallucinatory reality of a single human being, in a single camp, borders on sacrilege. The truer the tale, the more fictitious it appears. The secret must remain inviolate. Once revealed, it becomes myth, and can only be tarnished, diminished. In the end, words lose their innocence, their power to cast a spell. The truth will never be written. Like the Talmud, it will be transmitted from mouth to ear, from eye to eye. By its uniqueness, the Holocaust defies literature. We think we are describing an event, we transmit only its reflection. No one has the right to speak for the dead, no one has the power to make them speak. No image is sufficiently demented, no cry sufficiently blasphemous to illuminate the plight of a single victim, resigned or rebellious, walking silently toward death, beyond anger, beyond regret.[1]

What does it mean to apply notions of the private or the secret to victims' recollections of their experiences during the Holocaust? This dichotomy rests on a distinction which we take to be self-evident: namely a distinction between our 'role', 'persona' or 'mask' on the one hand and our individual consciousness and inner life on the other. In common usage, the private or secret suggest areas of life to be kept from the scrutiny of others, or which may be exposed only in intimate relationships or within relationships of trust. These concepts can also be understood to apply to thoughts or actions which, if made known to others, may attract censure. Finally, the private and secret can be taken to refer to that which may be disturbing to the listener and which is therefore silenced. Many of these understandings relating to permissible disclosure inhibit the content and process of giving Holocaust testimony.

But at a more fundamental level survivor testimony challenges, and in some respects, shatters the conventional boundaries between the private and the public. Survivors' accounts deal with the devastating consequences of ideologies of hatred and repression, with the perversion of power and with a civility dissolved by fear, self-interest or apathy. This testimony reveals a world of grotesque cruelty and barbarism. Survivors present us with stark, harrowing images of suffering. Their memories touch the raw centre of evil and of pain. These recollections move us beyond the problematical (and some would say arbitrary) distinction between the political and the personal, beyond consideration of prohibitions against disclosure, to reflection about the limits of representation. We are confronted not with the question of whether information is being withheld, but with the problem of how one might convey experiences and feelings for which words cannot be found.

In this paper I will explore some of the difficulties facing those who testify about the Holocaust. Secondly, I will suggest a way of thinking about the significance of this testimony for survivors and for their listeners. In addressing these issues, I will be moving between two claims: on the one hand, that Holocaust testimony can only allude to what are, ultimately, unspeakable truths; and on the other hand, that this testimony contains truths which are significant not only as historical sources but which are fundamental to individual and collective identity.

THE SPEAKER: DIFFICULTIES IN TELLING

Holocaust testimony presents us with searing images of suffering, despair and pain. Sometimes these feelings are attached to particular events and actions etched indelibly in memory. Survivor testimony reveals persistent and corrosive self-inquisition and a universe of unimaginable cruelty. Woven through this testimony is an inchoate sense of horror and despair, a sense of disorientation about the individual's being in the world.

> I couldn't understand any of it. It was like a blow on the head. I didn't even know where I was . . . I was in shock, as if I'd been hypnotised, ready to do whatever I was told. I was so muddled, so horrified . . .[2]
> (Testimony from a survivor who was forced to deal with the dead in the crematoria in Auschwitz)

The inside is inconceivable, even to those who were there. The victims' accounts of discrete events are often marked by absences: of idiom, of moral context and most powerfully, the absence of those who did not survive. Because of this, writers such as Elie Wiesel suggest that the Holocaust can never be written or spoken about directly. It can only be evoked obliquely, or through silence – because it is impossible to testify from inside the Holocaust world; the inside has no voice.

Communication about experience is constituted by shared symbols and is embedded in cultural practices. It is a social transaction, the meaning of which emerges through the mutual efforts of both speaker and listener. But the concentrationary universe represents a profound violation of conventional social relations and cultural practices. It is a universe in which coercion, deliberately induced disorientation and the 'logic of destruction' structured daily life, where the structure of social relations was designed to systematically destroy victims' intentionality and agency. The disjunction between the world of the Holocaust survivor and the listener, with its associated absence of shared 'sense-making practices'[3] has significant consequences for the ease with which the survivor can speak about his or her experiences. One is confronted with the implications of the limits of language.

Language is a tool for making sense of experience. But it can also violate the meaning of this experience, subverting and distorting what it is being used to represent. The use of terms such as 'special treatment' or 'Final Solution' for the processes of genocidal mass murder provide examples of self-conscious political decisions to use language in order to deceive and mis-inform. But distortions can also arise from the ways meaning is derived from usage in everyday discourse. When survivors bear witness to their experiences during the Holocaust, and when listeners (be they social scientists, historians or others) struggle to understand this testimony, both are confronted by this potential violation.

When listening to survivors speak about their experiences during the war we are left with the sense that ultimately our language fails us. The words we have available to us are inadequate to the task of conveying the systematic humiliation and degradation experienced by European Jews during World War 2; they cannot express the complex, anguished feelings and mental imagery of the survivor. As one writer put it, 'We need new categories because the Holocaust is not a "relapse into barbarism", not a "phase in historical dialectic", nor is it a radical-but-merely-"parochial" catastrophe. It is a total rupture.'[4]

Primo Levi describes the linguistic implications of this rupture from the vantage point of his time in Auschwitz. He writes,

> Just as our hunger is not that feeling of missing a meal, so our way of being cold has need of a new word. We say 'hunger', we say 'tiredness', 'fear', 'pain', we say 'winter', and they are different things. They are free words, created and used by free men who lived in comfort and suffering in their homes. If the Lagers (concentration camps) had lasted longer a new, harsh language would have been born; and only this language could express what it means to toil the whole day in the wind, with the temperature below freezing, wearing only a shirt, underpants, cloth jacket and trousers, and in one's body nothing but weakness, hunger and knowledge of the end drawing nearer.[5]

THE LISTENER: DIFFICULTIES IN HEARING

In addition to language hindering the survivor there is the interaction with the listener, or more particularly, the 'unhearing' listener. The following interchange between two interviewers and a woman called Hanna illustrates the difficulty posed by the unhearing listener. Hanna is a survivor who experienced two deportations to Auschwitz, as well as imprisonment in other concentration camps. As the interview draws to a close, the discussion turns to how Hanna survived.

Interviewer: You were able to survive because you were so plucky . . .

Hanna: No dear, no dear, no . . . no, I had no . . . How shall I explain to you? I know that I had to survive, even running away, even being with people constantly, especially the second part, the second time, being back in Auschwitz. That time I had determined already to survive – and you know what? It wasn't luck, it was stupidity.

(At this the two interviewers laugh deprecatingly, overriding her voice with their 'explanation', as one calls out, 'You had a lot of guts!')

Hanna: (simultaneously) No, no, no, no, there were no guts, there was just sheer stupidity. I just, you know . . . (More laughter from the interviewers.)[6]

The intelligibility of survivors' testimony depends on the listener as much as it does on the speaker. Stories or accounts of experience make sense, or are seen to be plausible if they draw on shared background knowledge and a common vocabulary of motives. This common ground does not exist for the survivors and listeners who were spared the survivors' experiences.

At other times, competing agendas fracture the testimony which has been offered. Drawing on the perspective provided by psychoanalysis, Dominick LaCapra has noted:

The Holocaust presents the historian with transference in the most traumatic form conceivable – but in a form that will vary with the difference in subject position of the analyst. Whether the historian or analyst is a survivor, a relative of survivors, a former Nazi, a former collaborator, a relative of former Nazis or collaborators, a younger Jew or German distanced from more immediate contact with survival, participation or collaboration, or a relative 'outsider' to these problems will make a difference even in the meaning of statements that may be formally identical.[7]

Dori Laub, a psychoanalyst who has taken oral testimony from many survivors while collecting material for the Video Archive for Holocaust Testimony at Yale, writes about the debate provoked when a group of historians, psychoanalysts and artists viewed a videotaped interview with a woman in her late sixties. This woman was narrating her experiences in Auschwitz, in particular, her memories as a witness of the Auschwitz uprising.

'All of a sudden', she said, 'we saw four chimneys going up in flames, exploding. The flames shot into the sky, people were running. It was unbelievable.'[8]

In fact, only one chimney had been blown up, not four. Because of this error, the historians in the group were loathe to give credence to the woman's testimony. Her memory was fallible, they argued. The facts must be correct, particularly in light of revisionist views about the Holocaust.

Others saw the matter differently. They took the view that every survivor of the Holocaust has a different story to tell, not because people's experiences varied, but because the individual ways in which they as victims and survivors grasped and related their experiences comprise the actual core of their story. They argued that the woman was testifying not to the number of chimneys which were destroyed, but to something else more radical, more crucial: the reality of an unimaginable occurrence. One chimney blown up was as incredible as four. The woman was testifying to an event which momentarily shattered the framework of overwhelming oppression.[9]

Because of these difficulties (and for many other reasons as well), there are survivors who have remained silent. For some, silence has its source in the pain from which the survivor seeks protection. For others, silence is a way of respecting those who died. It can separate the private from the public.

> I will be doing everyday duties, living everyday life, but my mind will be in a different world. At that time I live with the feelings I imagine my parents and sisters had before they died. I go into a different part of myself, a part I never speak about. It has nothing to do with anyone else.
>   It's mine.[10]

Silence can be a sanctuary which protects speakers from themselves and from their listeners. It encloses feelings and experiences which may attract censure because they are unfamiliar, alien or threatening to the listener. The sense of impotence and powerlessness experienced by the targets of the Nazi programme of genocide, feelings of having been defiled, diminished and humiliated may remain unspoken because the listener's response may be disbelief, contempt, abandonment, misunderstanding or pity. Sometimes, the survivor who speaks of this Holocaust world sees in the eyes of those who listen a judgement that perhaps the survivor should have acted differently. As Primo Levi writes,

> Consciously or not, (the survivor) feels accused and judged, compelled to justify and defend himself.

Silence also protects the listener.

GIVING TESTIMONY: TRANSFORMING THE UNSPOKEN TO THE SPOKEN

And yet survivors do speak. Sometimes feelings and experiences are revealed haltingly – a phrase, a word. At other times, images and incidents are captured in an anguished flood of stories. When Holocaust survivors do speak about their experiences, we are made aware of how past and present sit adjacent in memory, sliding unpredictably between foreground and background. Experiences return with dazzling immediacy. Images appear in dreams; they interrupt daily activities. As one survivor to whom I spoke said,

> Something happens and you feel breathless, or you start cringing. Seconds later, you realise there is no need for the feeling of panic or fear. It's a feeling which skips past quickly. It's important only at that moment. Then it passes.[11]

Or another,

> What happens from time to time is a short, vivid flash of something I have previously not thought about. Just a second. A train station, a street, a particular corner of the camp. It's like a photograph. And then I forget about it again.[12]

The survivors speak about intensely experienced feelings and fleeting, vivid images. How might these sharply etched feelings and images, and the events and actions which have an enduring, tenacious presence in memory, become articulated? For those who do speak, what is involved in transforming an interior life which is unspoken, to the spoken?

The origins of the word 'testimony' offer us a clue. 'Testimony' derives from the Latin for 'witness'. In turn, 'witness' draws on notions of seeing and becoming conscious or aware. To testify is therefore to make knowledge, both about oneself and about one's world.[13] Becoming aware entails the interpretation and attribution of meaning to experience. Some theorists argue that events or acts become meaningful only *after* they have occurred, and *after* they have been grasped reflectively.[14]

The following account by one of the people whom I interviewed about his war-time experiences graphically illustrates this connection between testifying and knowledge, between experience and meaning. The account refers to an incident in which the interviewee (then seventeen years old) had been captured and included in a deportation of Jews. During the ensuing journey, he and two others seized an opportunity to escape by jumping from the moving train. My interviewee was the second to jump. The third person was sighted and shot. The interviewee says of that incident:

> When I was running away, things were going so quickly that it was only later on that I could interpret what I had registered. The first interpretation was not mine. When I went back to the ghetto, I told my cousin and my uncle what happened. As I told them the story they interpreted what I was describing. I had not been interpreting what was happening to me. I think that at the time I registered certain scenes like a camera. It is only later that they become emotionally coloured.

Lawrence Langer, in his book about Holocaust testimony, also draws on the distinction between meaning and experience with his reference to the abstractness of a recovered truth – *vrai* – and the concreteness of an experienced moment – *veridique*.[15] But despite his acknowledgement of this distinction, Langer does not accept the view that the process of testifying involves the attribution of meaning to experience.

According to Langer, survivors' testimony deals first and foremost with the concreteness of the experienced moment. The retelling is a process of reliving. In recounting what is conventionally understood to be the past, Langer argues that the survivor re-enters a Holocaust world which is ever-present. The resulting testimony eschews the chronicler's notion of time and the narrative historian's reliance on 'plot'. Often, the story does not have a recognisable or familiar structure. It may be disjointed, lacking an angle of vision or a consistent world view in accordance with which the events and people in the story are evaluated. Holocaust testimony reveals the undiminished immediacy or actuality of survivors' experiences during the Holocaust: 'The witness plunges into a buried past to rescue the private truths of the event.'[16]

Langer's argument challenges the view that the retelling of events is part of the process of giving them meaning. According to him, when victims of the Holocaust speak about their experiences during the war they are not engaged in the process of reflection. Their experiences are not 'done with' or finished. No meaning can be wrung from their experiences, no sense can be made of them. Rather, the memories they invoke are repositories for unresolved, continuing pain and suffering. Therefore, from Langer's view, the unspoken becomes spoken without the mediation of reflection. Without reflection, there is no creation of boundaries in the act of telling, so notions of the secret or the private are irrelevant to Holocaust testimony. The listener remains positioned outside the process of re-living past events and feelings.

But in retelling the events of the past, the survivor is not immersed solely in that past. He or she concurrently occupies the everyday world of the listener, as well as that 'other' world under Nazi rule. This duality suggests an additional mode in which survivors bear witness, resulting in two distinctive, but complementary, types of testimony. The first is the type characterised by its immediacy and the absence of reflection. (This is the type of testimony described by Langer.) The other arises from the survivor's location in the post-war world. This form of testimony incorporates reflection on experiences and interpretation of them by the survivor for the listener (or, on occasion, by the listener for the survivor).

TESTIMONY AND IDENTITY

I would now like to turn to another way of thinking about Holocaust testimony. This approach moves us away from the difficulties inherent in articulating the unspeakable to reflection on the connection between oral testimony and history. Earlier I suggested that testifying is integral to the process of coming to know. In this section of the paper I wish to pursue this connection between testimony and knowledge in relation to the construction of personal and collective identity. That is, I will examine testimony as a means through which individuals come to know themselves. I will also discuss how testimony contributes to collective identity, to the group coming to know itself.

In a novel called *Imagining Argentina* by Lawrence Thornton, the principal character (whose name is Carlos), discovers a couple living in isolation in the desolate pampas region of Argentina. He learns that the couple are survivors of the Holocaust. During one of their conversations, the couple show Carlos photos taken when they were liberated from the concentration camp.

'How did you survive?' Carlos asks them.

'We survived', they answered, 'because we knew we were not what you see in those pictures'.[17]

In bearing witness about the war, the survivor takes charge of his or her own image, personal narrative and therefore, identity. In testifying about their experiences, the survivors recreate themselves, establishing threads of continuity with whom they were before the war and who they have become subsequently. The process of testifying can enable survivors to experience feelings of grief and of hope, as well as offering them an unfolding knowledge of themselves.[18] Moving from silence into speech is a gesture of defiance that heals, that makes new life and new growth possible. It is that act of speech, of 'talking back', that is the expression of moving from object to subject.[19] The narratives also commemorate those who did not survive.

Tony Morrison describes the fusion of memory, telling one's story and knowledge. She is talking about the writer, but what she says can also be applied to the survivor who is bearing witness. She writes:

You know, they straightened out the Mississippi River in places, to make room for houses and livable acreage. Occasionally the river floods these places. 'Floods' is the word they use, but in fact it is not 'flooding'; it is remembering. Remembering where it used to be. All water has a perfect memory and is forever trying to get back to where it was. Writers are like that: remembering where we were, what valley we ran through, what the banks were like, the light that was there and the route back to our original place. It is emotional memory – what the nerves and the skin remember, as well as how it appeared.[20]

There are commentators who take the view that this process of recalling the events of the Holocaust is not redemptive for the survivors, and that they are inevitably living with fractured selves. Langer, for instance, writes that when victims of the Nazi regime talk about their experiences, they draw on different kinds of memory, each of which reveals a distinctive, essentially damaged aspect of the self.

Langer identifies five associations of memory and self. The first he calls 'deep memory' which connects with the 'buried self'.

I have the feeling that the 'self' who was in the camp isn't me, isn't the person who is here, opposite you. No, it's too unbelievable. And everything that happened to this other 'self', the one from Auschwitz, doesn't touch me now, *me*, so distinct are deep memory and common memory.[21]

There is 'anguished memory' which recovers the sense of being divided, of living in more than one world at the same time. 'Humiliated memory' reveals a 'besieged self' unable to act during the war and now, because memory and the process of narrating offer no rescue from uncompensated and uncompensatable loss, no possibility of transforming stories of unredeemable atrocity to triumphant accounts of survival.[22] The 'impromptu self' is expressed in the struggle between memories of violation and feelings of intactness. As one survivor puts it,

You can't be normal. As a matter of fact, I think we are not normal because we are so normal.[23]

Finally, Langer writes about 'unheroic memory', which reveals the 'diminished self', with its deprivation of moral agency and its partially traumatised or maimed self esteem. Langer therefore writes about the persistence of a fractured, fragmented self. But even though he does not see the process of remembering as empowering or as contributing to personal integration, Langer acknowledges the essential connection of this process to the innermost recesses of the self.

In contrast to the position adopted by Langer, one could argue that the process of speaking about the Holocaust is integral to the construction and maintenance of self and identity. Identity is the name we give to the different ways we are positioned by, and position ourselves in narratives of the past. To the extent that the world of the death camps is wrought anew through survivors' testimony, continuity is restored to a personal history that has been severed. Continuity is also restored to the group.

Reflection on the past, and the restless, continuing search for ways to give form to this past leads to another way of thinking about the significance of Holocaust testimony. Communally shared ways of making-sense of experience are constitutive of people's social and psychological being. Among other things, they enable people to not only account for themselves to themselves and others when required to do so, but also enable them to appreciate how they are placed in relation to those around them. They enable action and also constrain it by teaching people to act and talk only in ways appropriate to their momentary position or status in relation to others around them.[24] [. . .]

The capacity to remember and the desire to listen establishes a continuity which is an essential element of individual and social life. In telling stories, survivors (with their listeners) structure and give significance to experience, fusing past and present, memory and contemporary understandings. And what memory is to the individual, history is to the group. By listening to stories about the Holocaust, we each become engaged in its events. The listener becomes a participant, involved with the speaker, contacting the terror that was experienced, raging at its injustice, grieving with its victims.

Many survivors say that one reason for holding on to life in the camps was the desire to bear witness. One woman who I interviewed said,

> When I was so sick that I could no longer move, one of the women who was working in the kitchen came with some coffee for me. I was fading in and out of consciousness, and I could hear the other women talking about the fact that I was dying. But I felt I wanted to live. I have to live. I have to let the world know what is happening.[25]

Our role as listeners to these stories cannot be overestimated. Totalitarian regimes are horrifying not only because of their violations of human dignity, but because they engender the fear that nobody might remain to bear witness to the past and that this bearing of witness will have no listeners. Enslavement of a citizenry begins when its members are denied their memories and when they are deprived of an audience for this memories. As Elie Wiesel said,

> I will tell my son that all the fires, all the pain, will be meaningless, if he in turn will not transmit our story to others, to his friends and one day to his own children ... A moral society must have the strength to [hear] these accounts, just as their authors have the strength to [give] them. For a moral society must remember ... If we stop remembering, we stop being.[26]

NOTES

1 E. Wiesel, *One Generation After*, New York, Simon & Shuster, 1970, p. 16.
2 Cited in S. Felman, 'The return of the voice: Claude Lanzmann's Shoah', in S. Felman and D. Laub M.D. (eds), *Testimony: Crises of Witnessing in Literature, Psychoanalysis and History*, New York, Routledge, 1992, p. 231.
3 J. Shotter, 'Social accountability and the social construction of "you"', in J. Shotter and K. Gergen (eds), *Texts of Identity*, London, Sage, 1993, p. 143.
4 E. Fackenheim, *To Mend the World: Foundations of Post-Holocaust Jewish Thought*, New York, Schocken, 1989, p. 250.
5 P. Levi, *If This is a Man*, (trans. S. Woolf), p. 129.
6 L. Langer, *Holocaust Testimonies: the Ruins of Memory*, New Haven, Yale University Press, 1991, pp. 63–64.
7 D. LaCapra, 'Representing the Holocaust: reflections on the historian's debate' in S. Friedlander (ed.), *Probing the Limits of Representation: Nazism and the 'Final Solution'*, Cambridge, Mass., 1992, p. 110.
8 J.E. Young, *Writing and Rewriting the Holocaust: Narrative and the Consequences of Interpretation*, Bloomington, Indiana University Press, 1990, p. 39.
9 Felman and Laub, *Testimony*, p. 58.
10 N. Rosh White, *From Darkness to Light: Surviving the Holocaust*, Ringwood, Collins Dove, 1988, p. 221.
11 Ibid., p. 221
12 Ibid., p. 219.
13 Young, *Writing and Rewriting the Holocaust*, p. 19.
14 A. Schutz, *The Phenomenology of the Social World*, Evanston, Northwestern University Press, 1967, p. 52.

15 Langer, *Holocaust Testimonies*, p. 42.
16 Ibid., p. 148, p. 157.
17 L. Thornton, *Imagining Argentina*, London, Bloomsbury, 1987.
18 Felman and Laub, *Testimony*, p. 60.
19 B. Hooks, 'Talking back', in R. Ferguson, M. Gover and T.T. Minh-ha (eds), *Out There: Marginalization and Contemporary Culture*, Cambridge, Mass., MIT Press, 1990, p. 340.
20 T. Morrison, 'The site of memory', in Ferguson *et al.*, p. 305.
21 Charlotte Delbo, cited in Langer, *Holocaust Testimonies*, p. 5.
22 Langer, *Holocaust Testimonies*, p. 84, p. 109–110.
23 Cited in ibid., p. 141.
24 Shotter, 'Social accountability', p. 142.
25 White, *From Darkness to Light*, p. 138.
26 E. Wiesel, *One Generation After*. (I have merged excerpts from two of Elie Wiesel's speeches and inserted the words in brackets so that they refer to oral rather than written accounts).

Part III

Advocacy and empowerment: introduction

Knowledge and understanding of the past has a profound impact upon contemporary social and political life. Though the use of recorded interviews is not necessarily a radical historical intervention in itself, many oral historians aim to effect social and political change through their work. We might use oral testimony alongside other sources to recover neglected or silenced accounts of past experience, and as a way of challenging dominant histories which underpin repressive attitudes and policy (see for example the chapters by Blee or Kennedy in Part IV). We might seek a more direct impact by involving interviewees in the process of interpreting their lives and the changes in the world around them. The chapters in this section explore a range of ways in which oral history has been empowering for individuals and a tool for advocacy by social groups and political movements.

In the opening article Joanna Bornat outlines the development in Britain of a social movement which has linked academic oral historians, community publishing and reminiscence work in care settings. She notes the crucial recognition in the 1960s and 1970s that remembering could be a valuable and affirming process for older adults. Developments in the psychology of old age had challenged an orthodoxy that reminiscence or 'life review' was 'an abnormal or pathological activity, something to be discouraged', and suggested instead that guided remembering could have therapeutic benefits and might contribute to 'reality orientation'.[1] Bornat describes the explosion of British interest in reminiscence work with older people in the 1980s, in residential homes and hospitals, in social welfare fieldwork, and through adult education and self-help groups. In turn, the emphasis on the value of remembering for older adults (or for narrators of any age) which characterizes reminiscence work, made oral historians more aware that their interviewees were not just research sources, but might be profoundly affected – for better or worse – by the experience of remembering in an interview situation.

Though the links between oral history and reminiscence work are especially strong in Britain, and to a lesser extent in Australia and New Zealand, there are oral history projects and writings from other parts of the world which relate to themes introduced by Bornat. A number of recent anthologies explore the theory and practice of reminiscence work in different settings, and outline debates about therapeutic and other outcomes.[2] In an article on 'Reminiscence as literacy', reproduced in part in the final section of this *Reader* (Chapter 33), Jane Mace considers issues in a community education project with older adults. Other practitioners have explored the role of oral history in community education and literacy projects for adults of all ages, in which the writing and telling of life stories has been used to develop skills and strengthen personal and collective identities.[3]

Schools have provided an important context for intergenerational oral history projects in many countries. In our second extract Eliot Wigginton explains the origins and methods of Foxfire, a hugely successful and influential secondary school oral history project and magazine based in the Southern Appalachian region of the United States.[4] The Foxfire project turned high school 'into something positive and productive instead of the opposite' for teenage students. Oral history infused the history curriculum with life and significance and involved students with very different skills and academic abilities, thus offsetting teenage alienation from school and society. Foxfire helped to engender respect across the generations – combating stereotypes about age and race, for example – and instilled self-esteem in students who gained positive affirmation of their culture and roots. School oral history projects can be empowering for students, and for participants of all ages from surrounding communities who are reminded that their life experiences are of historical interest and social value.[5]

Articles in other sections of this *Reader* show how oral history can be a significant resource for political groups and emergent social movements: in the women's movement (Anderson and Jack, Sangster and Bozzoli),[6] for trade unionists and working class communities (Friedlander, and Nethercott and Leighton, who also explore how oral history can be used to foster collective understandings and commitment within geographic communities which have suffered economic or social dislocation),[7] for indigenous peoples (Flick and Goodall, and Shostak),[8] for immigrant and ethnic communities (Haley and Kikumura),[9] in gay and lesbian politics (Kennedy)[10] and for people with learning disabilities (Walmsley).[11] Here Karen Hirsch explains how the comparatively recent use of oral history in disability studies 'could allow yet another group to find a voice, could lead to a new view of local and social history, and could help create a deeper understanding of cultural conditions which affect everyone' (p. 214). Hirsch's survey of disability oral history offers parallels with the ways in which oral history has been used by other social groups: to recover the experiences of the silenced; to assert new ways of understanding past and present; to engage members of an oppressed group in projects which explore experiences of both injustice and self-assertion in their life histories.[12] She notes, however, that there are significant tensions, between a celebration of individual achievement and the exploration of social patterns of discrimination, and between scholarship and advocacy. Elsewhere in this *Reader* the Popular Memory Group (Chapter 7), Katherine Borland (Chapter 27) and Kathleen Blee (Chapter 28) offer a cautionary note about the dilemmas and difficulties of radical oral history, asking if and how it is possible to create 'a shared authority' (to use Michael Frisch's resonant phrase) in oral history research and interpretation.[13]

William Westerman's chapter provides an example of the direct use of oral history in a particular political struggle, that of the Central American refugees who use their own life story testimonials to educate North Americans about the situation in their countries, and to gain financial and political support. Westerman shows how these testimonials were constructed for maximum political effect and presented through a range of narrative forms: as performance, in writing, and etched into the bodies of victims of torture. Apart from gaining support for their cause, the narrators attain therapeutic benefits and public affirmation through telling their stories. The process of 'bearing witness' – by refugees and other victims of social and political oppression – can thus be empowering for individual narrators, and can generate public recognition of collective experiences which have been ignored or silenced. It can also have direct social and political outcomes, as evidenced in the land rights struggles of indigenous peoples.[14]

In totalitarian regimes power is maintained in part through the control of memory. In her study of 'The Gulag in memory', Irina Sherbakova explains how the past was continually reinvented by the Soviet regime and describes the fitful process of liberalization which made it possible to challenge those fabrications. Using interviews she has conducted since the 1970s with survivors of the Soviet prison and labour camps, Sherbakova evokes the impact of fear and distortion upon individual remembering, and how survivors have been torn between the urge to speak out and the danger of talk. Remembering is a process of struggle for survivors, and in the social and political life of a nation. Organized movements of survivors and the families of victims – such as the Memorial organization – have supported the difficult processes of individual and collective remembering. Throughout Central and Eastern Europe, oral history has been used as one resource for the identification and excavation of mass graves, as a way of 'rehabilitating' the reputations and rights of victims of persecution, and as evidence in court actions against the perpetrators of injustice (the work of the Truth and Reconciliation Commission in South Africa offers an international comparison).[15] Like Naomi Rosh White's exploration of Holocaust testimony (Chapter 15), or Alistair Thomson's work with war veterans (Chapter 25), Sherbakova's article shows how oral history can play a role in helping individuals and societies to remember and make better sense of traumatic pasts.

The two final chapters in this section demonstrate how oral history can serve a functional role which empowers individuals and communities. In a number of countries in the South oral history is used alongside development projects to ensure that foreign aid interventions – for example new agricultural technologies – draw upon local knowledge and complement traditional land use (in fact, these aims and approaches are not dissimilar to those of the more sensitive urban redevelopment projects in the industrialized

North).[16] Nigel Cross and Rhiannon Barker introduce the SOS Sahel Oral History Project, which records stories from men and women in sub-Saharan Africa about their changing environment and ways of life: 'we did not set out to accumulate facts, but rather to find the stories, to improve the techniques for their collection and, most important of all, to demonstrate their value and utility'. In effect, memories of effective social relations and land use are used as a resource for community and environmental survival.

Sanjiv Kakar also demonstrates the utility of life stories, in his account of the uses of oral history in leprosy projects in India. Interviews with villagers provide essential information about the local conditions and attitudes which shape the experience of leprosy, and ensure that eradication strategies are appropriate for particular communities. Indeed, oral history projects have helped to break down the silence and stigma which surrounds leprosy, and interviewees have become activists in community health and education schemes. Kakar also shows how the oral testimony of leprosy patients can 'enable a more sensitive reading of colonial records' and 'help to fill in the gaps within colonial histories' which denied the experience of leprosy patients in the community. This two-way use of both oral and written life histories – to improve historical understanding *and* contemporary care strategies – is a significant recent development in health and welfare practice in many countries.[17] Though such professional uses for oral history seem far removed from its origins in community, academic and archival projects, respect for the life stories of people who might otherwise have been ignored – by history, by society, in professional practice – is a powerful common thread.

NOTES

1 See R. Butler, 'The life review: an interpretation of reminiscence in the aged', *Psychiatry*, February 1963, vol. 26, pp. 67–76.

2 J. Bornat (ed.), *Reminiscence Reviewed: Perspectives, Evaluations, Achievements*, Buckingham, Open University Press, 1994; B.K. Haight and J.D. Webster (eds), *The Art and Science of Reminiscing: Theory, Research, Methods and Applications*, Washington, DC, Taylor & Francis, 1995; see also M. Kaminsky, *The Uses of Reminiscence: New Ways of Working With Older Adults*, New York, Haworth Press, 1984; H.R. Moody, 'Twenty-five years of the life review: Where did we come from? Where are we going?', in *Journal of Gerontological Studies*, 1988, vol. 12, pp. 7–21; *Oral History*, 1989, vol. 17, no. 2, special issue on 'Reminiscence'; *Oral History Association of Australia Journal*, 1990, no. 12, special issue on 'Oral history and social welfare'.

3 See, for example, J. Lawrence and J. Mace, *Remembering in Groups: Ideas From Reminiscence and Literacy Groups*, London, Oral History Society, 1980; R. Benmayor, 'Testimony, action research, and empowerment: Puerto Rican women and popular education', in S. Berger Gluck and D. Patai (eds), *Women's Words: The Feminist Practice of Oral History*, New York and London, Routledge, 1991, pp. 159–174; M. Breen and D. Sobel, *Popular Oral History and Literacy*, Toronto, Storylinks, 1991.

4 See E. Wigginton (ed.), *The Foxfire Books*, vols 1–10, New York, Anchor Press, Doubleday, 1972–93.

5 On oral history in schools see: A. Redfern, *Talking in Class: Oral History and the National Curriculum*, Colchester, Oral History Society, 1996; B. Lanman and G. Mahaffy, *Oral History in the Secondary School*, Los Angeles, Oral History Association, 1988; *Oral History Association of Australia Journal*, 1986, no. 8, special issue on 'Oral history, children and schools'. See also the article by Alistair Ross (Chapter 37, this volume).

6 See also Gluck and Patai, *Women's Words* (especially Part IV, 'Community and Advocacy').

7 See also: J. Green, 'Engaging in people's history: the Massachusetts History Workshop', in S.P. Benson, *et al.* (eds), *Presenting the Past: Essays on History and the Public*, Philadelphia, Temple University Press, 1986, pp. 337–359; L. Niethammer, 'Oral history as a channel of communication between workers and historians', in P. Thompson (ed.), *Our Common History: The Transformation of Europe*, London, Pluto, 1982, pp. 23–37; S. Linqvist, 'Dig where you stand', *Oral History*, 1979, vol. 7, no. 2, pp. 26–30. On oral history with geographical communities, see also L. Shopes, 'Oral history and community involvement: the Baltimore Neighbourhood Heritage Project', in Benson, *et al.*, *Presenting the Past*, pp. 249–262; J. Bornat, 'The communities of community publishing', *Oral History*, 1992, vol. 20, no. 2, pp. 23–31; J. Modell and C. Brodsky, 'Envisioning Homestead: using photographs in interviewing', in E. McMahan and K.L. Rogers (eds), *Interactive Oral History Interviewing*, Hillsdale, N.J., Lawrence Erlbaum, 1994, pp. 141–161; R. Samuel, 'Oral history and local history', *History Workshop*, 1976, no. 1, pp. 191–208.

8 See also: H. Goodall, 'Colonialism and catastrophe: contested memories of nuclear testing and measles epidemics at Ernabella', in K. Darian-Smith and P. Hamilton (eds), *Memory and History in Twentieth Century Australia*, Melbourne, Oxford University Press, 1994, pp. 55–76; P. Taylor, *Telling It Like It Was: A Guide to Aboriginal and Torres Strait Islander History*, Canberra, Institute of Aboriginal and Torres Strait Islander Studies, 1996, pp. 33–89; M. King, 'New Zealand oral history: some cultural and methodological considerations', *New Zealand Journal of History*, 1978, vol. 12, no. 2, pp. 104–123.

9 See also R. Benmayor and A. Skotnes (eds), *International Yearbook of Oral History and Life Stories, Vol. III, Migration and Identity*, Oxford, Oxford University Press, 1994; G.Y. Okihiro, 'Oral history and the writing of ethnic history', in D.K. Dunaway and W.K. Baum, *Oral History: An Interdisciplinary Anthology*, second edition, Walnut Creek, Altamira Press, 1996, pp. 199–214; L. Serikaku, 'Oral history in ethnic communities: widening the focus', *Oral History Review*, 1989, vol. 17; C.H. Bailey, 'Precious blood: encountering inter-ethnic issues in oral history research, reconstruction, and representation', *Oral History Review*, 1990, vol. 18, pp. 61–108; *Oral History Association of Australia Journal*, 1984, no. 6, special issue on 'Migrant oral histories'; *Oral History*, 1980, vol. 8, no. 1, special issue on 'Black oral history'; *Oral History*, 1993, vol. 21, no. 1, special issue on 'Ethnicity and oral history'; *Canadian Oral History Association Journal*, 1989, no. 9, special issue on 'Oral history and ethnicity'.

10 See also: Hall Carpenter Archives, *Inventing Ourselves: Lesbian Life Stories*, and *Walking After Midnight: Gay Men's Life Stories*, both London, Routledge, 1989; T. Nightingale, 'Hidden histories: oral research on gay and bisexual men', *Oral History in New Zealand*, 1994, no. 6, pp. 11–13; G. Wotherspoon, *City of the Plain: History of a Gay Sub-Culture*, Sydney, Hale & Iremonger, 1991; E. Lapovsky Kennedy and M. Davis, *Boots of Leather, Slippers of Gold: The History of a Lesbian Community*, New York, Routledge, 1993.

11 See also: R. Fido and M. Potts, ' "It's not true what was written down": experience of life in a mental hospital', *Oral History*, 1989, vol. 17, no. 2, pp. 31–34; D. Atkinson, ' "I got put away": group-based reminiscence with people with learning difficulties', in Bornat, *Reminiscence Reviewed*, pp. 96–104.

12 Note that oral history has also been used to understand the power and ideology of elites. See, for example, C. Courtney and P. Thompson (eds), *City Lives: The Changing Face of British Finance*, London, Methuen, 1997; M. Roper, *Masculinity and the British Organisation Man Since 1945*, Oxford, Oxford University Press, 1994.

13 M. Frisch, *A Shared Authority: Essays on the Craft and Meaning of Oral and Public History*, Albany, State University of New York Press, 1990.

14 A. McGrath, ' "Stories for country": oral history and Aboriginal land claims', *Oral History Association of Australia Journal*, 1987, no. 9, pp. 34–46; J. Cruikshank, 'Oral tradition and oral history: reviewing some issues', *Canadian Historical Review*, 1994, vol. 75, no. 3, pp. 403–418.

15 See also L. Passerini (ed.), *International Yearbook of Oral History and Life Stories, Vol. I, Memory and Totalitarianism*, Oxford, Oxford University Press, 1992; R. Perks, 'Ukraine's forbidden history: memory and nationalism', *Oral History*, 1993, vol. 21, no. 1, pp. 43–52.

16 See H. Slim and P. Thompson (eds), *Listening For a Change: Oral History and Development*, London, Panos, 1993; O. Bennett, 'Review article: oral testimony as a tool for overseas development', *Oral History,* 1995, vol. 23, no. 1, pp. 89–92. For a comparable project in the North, see *People, History and Change in Birmingham's Heartlands*, Birmingham, Birmingham Museums and Art Gallery/ Birmingham Heartlands Development Corporation, 1993.

17 See *Oral History*, 1995, vol. 23, no. 1, special issue on 'Health and welfare'; Bornat, *Reminiscence Reviewed*; R.P. Martin, *Oral History in Social Work*, Newbury Park, Sage, 1995.

16 Oral history as a social movement

Reminiscence and older people

Joanna Bornat

Joanna Bornat is a Senior Lecturer in the School of Health and Social Welfare at the Open University in Britain. Reprinted from *Oral History*, 1989, vol. 17, no. 2, pp. 16–20, with permission.

In a recent radio programme[1] the poet Stephen Spender, who is now in his eighties, described himself as feeling like a spaceman landed on Earth from another planet. He has knowledge he can't communicate because all his contemporaries are left behind.

To hear Stephen Spender talk is to be reminded of the distance which sometimes stretches between generations. It's a distance which can feel painful if it means a feeling of exclusion and the loss of a sense of value. But it can be a distance to be appreciated if it helps to understand differences in experience and if it makes us search harder for continuities between generations.

It seems as if Stephen Spender has somehow missed out on the widespread interest in reminiscence and oral history which has spread throughout the British Isles. It is *so* widespread and so much a part of working and living with older people that, for someone like myself who has been carried along in the midst of what seems like a social transformation, it is difficult to realise how anyone could still be untouched by it.

In what follows I want to chronicle this movement and to evaluate its importance for older people, particularly those older people who are given care and support. Inevitably my examples are going to come from Britain because that is where I live and work and inevitably what I talk about is liable to be translated through my own experience.

What I want to talk about is a movement with very recent origins. Fifteen years ago or so there was little to show in history books, in social work textbooks or in publishing, of any idea that ordinary older people's life experience might be of interest or of any value. There were few exceptions. Writing in 1960, Susan Hale a retired psychiatric social worker, told of her delight in listening to elderly people in the Brixton area of South London talk about their memories of fifty to sixty years before. Noel Streatfield, the children's author, felt it was important in 1956 to let her readers know about life 'fifty years ago' and Stephen Peet in his late 1960s BBC television series *Yesterday's Witness* pioneered the filming of ordinary people talking about their memories of events, some forgotten, some only partially remembered.[2]

About ten years ago there were three rather isolated areas of work which quite separately were beginning to make an impact, but which had yet to influence each other. In history, psychology and in community publishing during the 1960s and early 1970s some new and challenging ideas were beginning to take shape. They generated ideas which, when they came together in the early 1980s, were to change care work practice with elderly people, widen learning opportunities across the age range and produce a rich yield of historical evidence from all corners of the British Isles. I want to begin with a brief account of the development of those three areas of work.

ORAL HISTORY ORIGINS

Oral history, treating recollection of experience as valid evidence, has its own long history, as Paul Thompson has shown.[3] Traditionally, and until the mid nineteenth century, historians regarded spoken testimony with as much reverence as they treated documents recording events, laws and customs. Indeed the recollections of the famous, rich and influential in society have always had a place in accounts of wars, political change and custom. The place of the diary and of memoirs of politicians and opinion leaders has rarely been challenged by historians whose skills include deciphering documents and piecing together the past from written records. This practice left us with a history that was narrow in content and often uncritical in method. The personal accounts which remained to us represented only a narrow range of social and economic viewpoints tending to concentrate on what was public and political at the highest levels of society. Daily life, insofar as it was chronicled through parish and census records and the detailed surveys of Booth and Rowntree, was passed through the filter of bureaucratic form filling or of record keeping of observers external to the daily lives under scrutiny. There were few accounts from women, from minorities, from deviant groups and in content the bias neglected accounts of family life, social customs, working life, old age, neighbourhood, community and undocumented events hidden from history.

Oral history turns the historian into an interviewer and changes the practice of the historian into a personal interaction with the past within living memory. Listening to someone describe their first day at work, school days, participation in unofficial strikes, childbirth, courtship, housework, historians have learned to broaden ideas of what history is about. It was in the late 1960s that oral history began to establish itself in Britain. At that time, two large surveys, at the Universities of Essex and Kent[4] used interviews with a large sample of older people as respondents. These led to many other research projects[5] and to writing which made use of the memories of elderly people to explain areas of the past previously unrecorded. It was significant for the development of oral history that the more successful and long lasting of those two university-based initiatives was in a department of sociology. This theoretical context gave oral history in Britain a distinctively humanistic bias which contributed to its later broadening out into less formally academic areas of work and research.[6]

For those of us who were involved in the early days of the mid 1970s, it was an exciting time. The search for oral evidence made research a lively and emotional experience. Documents like newspapers, census reports and minute books seemed dull in comparison with the words of eye-witnesses to the past. Studs Terkel, in his autobiography, evokes that electricity of personal contact when he describes meeting Bertrand Russell and 'shaking the hand of the man who shook the hand of the man who shook the hand of Napoleon'.[7]

Looking back to the early seventies what seems remarkable now is the fact that we oral historians took so long to realise that what we were involved in was a two-way process. It was a relationship with people who were parting with something which was personal and often very private. Too many of us saw the interviewee as just another source of evidence to be extracted.[8] We turned on the tape recorder and we encouraged an outpouring of the past. The content of our training was in techniques akin to managing the atmosphere of the broadcaster's green room. We were to put interviewees at ease, we were to be sensitive to their needs, we were to preserve an atmosphere of hospitality and never to forget our thank you letters. It was well intentioned but with one aim in mind: the eliciting of 'usable' material.

Inevitably it was the interviewee who reminded the historian that this was a shared experience. The retired West Riding textile worker who thanked *me* for asking her questions about her days as a young factory worker made me realise that oral history can be enjoyable and exciting on both sides of the microphone. In the second edition of *Voice of the Past* Paul Thompson acknowledges this shift in awareness amongst some oral historians. Writing ten years on, he brings out the importance of the interview in the life of an older person and points up the responsibility of the historian to understand and empathise with the strong emotions which an interview may evoke.[9]

COMMUNITY PUBLISHING ORIGINS

At about the same time as oral history methods were beginning to have an impact on the world of historical research, there were other developments going on. Community publishing evolved in the early 1970s with a form and content which opened up new possibilities for access to audiences and to new writers. In many respects community publishing represents the 1970s expression of the University Settlement movement of over a hundred years earlier. In the 1970s teachers, graduates, community activists living and working in the more deprived areas of inner cities encouraged working class people to write and produce their own art and literature. The Centerprise Publishing Project is one such enduring example. In an account of their first five years' work, Centerprise showed how people in the London Borough of Hackney devoured the pamphlets of autobiography and reminiscence which, amongst others, a dressmaker, a shoemaker and a cab driver had written.[10] Dot Starn's *When I was a Child*, published in 1973, sold 1,000 copies in its first three months. Arthur Newton's *Years of Change* sold 400 copies in four years. Other community groups in Bristol, Manchester and Brighton were at the same time publishing local people's writing and finding a mass readership amongst people who could identify with childhood experiences of family life, growing up, migration to England, finding work and struggling through, when it was written by their contemporaries and described streets, experience and even individual people they could remember. Ordinary people became their own historians and biographers and many took an active part in editing, designing and promoting their books.

These community publishing projects and countless others since have been funded by a variety of sources, by local government, charitable trusts, commercial sponsors, and latterly and most ironically, as a response to widespread unemployment, by central government, thanks to the Manpower Services Commission's short-lived Community Programme. They developed and refined a medium for reminiscence, the cheaply produced illustrated booklet. From towns and cities the length and breadth of the British Isles, there is now an enormous literature of people's history published in this format.[11] Almost exclusively this has been written by older people or edited from accounts recorded with their help.

Community publishing projects trace their history in England back through 300 years of pamphleteering, through the radical and dissenting tradition of debating political and social issues. Publishing short and cheaply produced booklets which are easily distributed and written in a style which is immediately understood and responded to has involved community publishers in challenging the official version of who the book-buying public is. When Centerprise opened its doors to the public in 1971 there was only one bookshop in the borough of Hackney. In Tower Hamlets and Lambeth there were none at all. The example of Centerprise was followed in many towns during the 1970s and following their example, libraries and museums have now taken on themselves the function of book producers and distributors. The network of outlets for community publishing continues to grow.

PSYCHOLOGY OF OLD AGE ORIGINS

The third area in which new ideas were taking shape during the 1960s and 1970s was in the psychology of old age. This change has been discussed in detail by people more qualified than me, elsewhere.[12] Starting in the United States, psychologists interested in the ageing process began to question the idea that reminiscing was an abnormal or pathological activity, something to be discouraged. Robert Butler published a paper in 1963 which was to excite and interest those working with more frail elderly people.[13] He used the idea of 'life review' and argued for a perspective which accepts looking back over a past life as a normal and universal experience in old age. Rose Dobrof, a New York social worker, has described the impact of these ideas on practice:

> I remember well being taught by our consulting psychiatrists and the senior social work staff about the tendency of our residents to talk about childhood in the shtetls of East Europe or arrival at Ellis Island or early years on the Lower East Side of New York. At best this tendency was seen as an understandable, although not entirely healthy preoccupation with happier times, understandable because these old and infirm people walked daily in the shadow of death. At worst, 'living in the past' was viewed as pathology – regression to the dependency of the child, denial of the passage of time and the reality of the present, or evidence of organic impairment of the intellect. It was even said that remembrance of things past, could cause or deepen depression among our residents, and God forgive us, we were to divert the old from their reminiscing through activities like bingo and arts and crafts.[14]

Partly in response to the very great enthusiasm which Robert Butler's work gave rise to, Peter Coleman's later influential study, *Ageing and Reminiscence Processes*, argues for a more qualified perspective on reminiscence as therapy.[15] His research found older people who were unwilling or unhappy reminiscers.

THE EMERGENCE OF RECALL

During the 1970s three areas of work were emerging. Each of these involved older people and each emphasised the importance of recalling the past. These three areas might have developed independently, they might have had little impact beyond the boundaries of influence of their various practitioners. In order for the qualitative and quantitative leap forward to have taken place, something else needed to happen.

What was needed was some kind of evidence that older people willingly took part in recalling the past, that there was enjoyment and that change and development could be observed as a result of this activity. This evidence needed to be witnessed and reproduced by people working with groups of older people or with individuals on a one-to-one basis.

Without wanting to sound too dramatic, or monocausal, I want to argue that the one event which was to draw attention to oral history with older people was the publication in November 1981 of Help the Aged's tape/slide programme *Recall*. The simplicity and apparent comprehensiveness of sequences of images and sounds covering the first eighty years of the twentieth century made *Recall* an instant success. Hundreds of sets of the package sold in the first few years and it continues to sell well today, even in the face of several competing formats and versions.

Recall's immediate origins were in none of the three areas of work so far described. It began in 1977 as the Reminiscence Aids Project run by an architect, Mick Kemp,[16] in what was then the Department of Health and Social Security. His particular responsibility was the environment of elderly people with mental infirmity. Funding for the project lasted until 1979 when a change of government brought an end to qualitative and long-term research not only in the DHSS but also arguably elsewhere in the British Isles. It was at that point that Help the Aged took over.

Regrettably I cannot go into the whole story of *Recall* here. I simply want to stress why I think the package has become such a milestone in the development of 'reminiscence work', as it has come to be known. Firstly, because of the way it originated, *Recall* encouraged an open-ended approach to the whole process of oral history work with older people. Secondly, because of its format, the package made it possible for anyone, whatever their background, to become an oral historian of some kind.

Recall's origins lie in the arts. As an architect, Mick Kemp was interested in the meaning of the environment for mentally frail older people. His project workers were art students with an interest in images and self-expression. For them history was something which older people generated or could be encouraged to create, giving the right cues and stimuli. The philosophy behind *Recall* was very much one which gave equal validity to the memories of all older people. As an historian who came in at a later stage in the development of the packages I well remember conflicts between those whose main concern was to evoke responses, and those people, like me, who wanted both to evoke and *inform*. Thus an early version of the First World War sequence focussed almost exclusively on life in the trenches since this was what the elderly men they met talked about. After discussion amongst members of the production team and further testing with groups of older men, and women, the sequence finally included images of women's work and life on the home front. *Recall* in its final form invites recognition of past events and experience, but it also stirs up what may have been forgotten and it introduces the idea of differing experience and perspective on the past.

The second point I want to draw from the *Recall* experience concerns opening up opportunities to more people to become oral historians. Care staff and community workers with a background in historical research can reasonably be expected to be few in number. and even those who have an interest in local history find that they have no opportunity to follow their interest within working hours. History is not a subject area for social or health services training. What *Recall* provided and still provides is a technologically simple means to explore the past. This opens up possibilities to residential, community and hospital care staff and to anyone else who can find a slide projector, cassette player and a screen or white wall. Slide/tape production has, in my opinion, many advantages over video. It allows for larger images, it can easily be interrupted with a clear still picture and it requires fairly low level technology.

Equipped with *Recall*'s slide/tape packages, staff-led reminiscence sessions took off in homes and centres all over the British Isles. The idea caught on not just because the packaging was simple and the images and sounds highly evocative. The impact of *Recall* lay in the responses of the audiences and groups of older people. Very quickly the issue became not just one of how to show *Recall*, but how to manage and develop work with groups convened to watch and take part. The evidence that reminiscing is stimulating and enjoyable was immediately available.

REMINISCENCE: A MOVEMENT

Recall is not the whole story of course. Oral history, community publishing and life review were having their own impact with groups of workers and older people at this time. *Recall* had captured a market of interested people who it seems were awaiting an opportunity to explore the memories of the older people they knew. What followed over the next eight years in Britain at least was something like an explosion of interest in reminiscence work with older people. There have been several local editions of *Recall*, there have been television programmes, radio programmes, videos, training packs, large scale exhibitions like *Exploring Living Memory*, workshops, journal articles, conferences, courses, booklets, plays, films, almost every possible medium has been explored. Inevitably reminiscence work developed a systemisation and 'reminiscence therapy' became the talking point amongst workers caring for older people. Courses emerged with freelancing practitioners offering training in this new area of work.

The impact on oral history, community publishing and in psychology has been selective. Perhaps because some of the most enthusiastic proponents of reminiscence work with older people were also oral historians, it's possible to say that in Britain, with some exceptions, oral historians have taken a rather different approach to colleagues in other continental European countries. We'd like to think we've sustained an awareness of the meaning of reminiscence in the lives of older people. For some of us the separation between oral history and reminiscence risks the distancing of older people in the process and weakens their control over what is produced. The pursuit of oral history is a goal which we all share, whether we work as individual researchers of any age or in groups with older people. Reminiscence work implies a more active role for those whose memories are sought and it introduces goals and objectives which can be personal, social and, of course, historical.

Community publishing contributed a format and a basis for the dissemination of the outcomes of reminiscence in the early days and it has continued with this role. For about five years the extra cash and energy which unemployment projects like the Community Programme injected into the scene have made sure that there is scarcely a town in the country which has not had some kind of reminiscence project. Now that the Community Programme has been replaced by a less flexible and less generously funded scheme, many of these projects have been literally shelved. Still, in some towns and areas local authorities and arts bodies continue to direct cash towards reminiscence and oral history groups.[17]

REMINISCENCE: THE DEBATE ABOUT THERAPY

Within psychology and in work with more frail elderly people debates continue. Surprisingly, given the extent to which reminiscence work has been taken up in homes and hospitals around Britain there has been very little research and evaluation into its outcomes for older people. But perhaps it is because of the general level of enthusiasm and the sense of being part of something akin to a social movement that there tend to be strong claims for the positive benefits of the work, and very few pauses for comparison or reflection.

A recent paper brought together in a critical review much of the evidence from the work of psychologists working in the field of reminiscence with older people. Susan Thornton and Janet Brotchie looked at clinical and experimental evidence for therapeutic outcomes for reminiscence activities with elderly people.[18] Their conclusions confirm what some of us had suspected. Based on available evidence there is no safe case to be made for reminiscence on its own bringing about change in the mental abilities of elderly people who may be experiencing depression or low self esteem as a result of organic illness.

Early in the days of the Reminiscence Aids Project there had been a hope that somehow by encouraging the use of memories, mentally frail people would somehow improve their grip on reality. More recently experimental research has shown small improvements in some measures of functioning amongst non-confused elderly people,[19] but it isn't clear that the results can always be shown to be directly the result of reminiscing. The strong case for a therapy status for reminiscence has yet to be found or proved.

Does the lack of status as a therapy matter? As Andrew Norris points out, simply awarding reminiscence work the title of therapy would only mean that it joined a number of other similarly dubiously labelled activities. Within the context of hospitals, gardening has become 'horticultural therapy', reading is 'bibliotherapy' and listening to or playing music or 'music therapy'.

There may be good reasons for avoiding the label therapy. Again Andrew Norris argues that 'the main function of labelling . . . seems to be to validate (these activities) as legitimate activities in which professional people are entitled to engage'. Taken further, Mike Bender argues[20] it could mean that *only* professionally qualified people are entitled to take up activities labelled as therapies. This would certainly have unhappy outcomes for the practice of reminiscence work.

One of the strengths of reminiscence work with older people is its openness in terms of process and skill base. Following Andrew Norris it is possible to see reminiscence work as being utilised in a range of therapeutic approaches.

He argues for a role for a reminiscence approach in bereavement counselling, insight based psychotherapy, in cognitive therapy, in reality orientation with people suffering from dementia, in providing stimulation for confused elderly people and in goal planning in more behavioural models of psychotherapy.[21] By avoiding the label of therapy we can continue to enjoy the advantages of working flexibly and in a variety of settings.

I'd like to go on to develop this point further in relation to three areas of work: reminiscence activities in residential homes and hospitals, older people's learning and finally, enhancing the understanding of issues facing some older people.

REMINISCENCE WORK IN RESIDENTIAL HOMES AND HOSPITALS

Psychologists, nurses and occupational therapists working in hospitals and residential care workers and social workers in community based settings have all found reminiscence work useful and appropriate with groups and with individual elderly people.[22] Approaches vary. John Adams talks eloquently about the way his continuing care ward was transformed by the introduction of posters from the First World War as talking points. The elderly women on the ward talked about their experiences of the Blitz, visitors stayed on, maintenance men lingered to hear stories. Many of these women had only a fragmentary account to give of their past lives because of their present confused states. It was through the stimulus of reminiscence and by staff and relatives picking up on comments about their pasts that a more detailed, and more sensitive picture of their earlier lives began to unfold.[23]

At Claybury Hospital in north east London, people with depressive illnesses have been encouraged to write scrapbooks and include photographs of themselves as a means to self-discovery and restoring confidence and renewed insights into themselves and family members.[24] Mel Wright and Martin Truelove, social workers in South London and Bradford have used reminiscence projects with housebound elderly people. In South London a newsletter focussed on life on an inter-war housing estate and encouraged a small group of housebound people who otherwise had little contact to share memories of the early years of the estate. In Bradford, volunteers were recruited to take down the memories of housebound elderly people. In one case this resulted in 10,000 words of testimony from a post-war refugee.[25]

Groupwork with elderly people has become incorporated into the life of some homes and hospitals. It is perhaps inevitable, if regrettable, that reminiscence has occasionally been left to become just another panacea or passing time activity in some institutions. Now that it's possible to buy boxes of photographs and reminiscence stimuli, in some homes there is a fairly routinised approach to reminiscence. The 'memories' group tends to take its place alongside bingo and crafts. I want to go on to talk about learning aspects for older people shortly. At this stage what I would prefer to highlight are what can be positive outcomes for older people and staff in a caring context.

Early on in *Recall*'s development it was suggested that the programme could have some use in training staff.[26] It is probably true to say that the implications for caring relationships were not fully realised at first. Eight years later things look very different. Most people who have responsibility and involvement in training care staff and others agree that insights gained from reminiscence sessions have had a profound effect on the relationships of staff and the elderly people they work with. As far as one senior nursing officer is concerned reminiscence work is even seen as an opportunity to reward grades of staff whose jobs are undervalued and unpaid.[27] Working on training days and workshops with carers in the statutory, voluntary and private sectors, time and again there are reminders of just how valued and rewarding reminiscence group work has become.

Amongst the best and most committed carers, interests lie in de-routinising reminiscence activities. In group sessions these workers are their best en-thusers and resourcers. Some have become part-time researchers into memorabilia and local history, others give accounts of sessions which have brought out the most reticent group member. In some homes and hospitals, knowledge of individual past lives has led to outings and visits, closer staff and relatives involvement and shared experiences from personal histories.[28]

Successful reminiscence work depends less on the accurate remembering of the past and more on the process of exchange and listening. It is this under-standing which has captured the interest and commitment of people working with more frail and dependent elderly people.

OLDER PEOPLE'S LEARNING

Within educational gerontology debates concentrated at first on the *rights* of older people to participate in learning and have more recently moved on to look at issues which are related more closely to practice and to the curric-ulum. One type of practice which is argued as having most relevance and attraction for older learners is the self-help group. It is seen as being appropriate because it encourages reflection and negotiation.[29] The self-help approach correlates well within the life styles and experience of older learners since it assumes:

> a non-prescriptive attitude, issue centred curricula, problem posing, praxis, continuous negotiation, shared responsibility for learning, valuing process, dialogue, openness, mutual respect and integrated thinking and learning.[30]

Within adult education circles, the advantages of self-help, learner directed work are widely accepted. To what extent older people have wholeheartedly adopted these ideals is less certain. For many, the experience of formal learn-ing is likely to have been along the lines of the transmission model. This is the model which operates with the assumption that the teacher has knowledge and the learners are without knowledge.

It may be the case that some older learners find it difficult to recognise educational processes in the open structure of self-help, with its emphasis on the validation of personal experience and a shared negotiation of what is to be learned. However, it has been my experience along with others that reminiscence work offers almost unequalled opportunities to older people to successfully incorporate self-help and learner led work into their learning.[31]

During the last few years reminiscence work with groups of older people has developed sufficiently to the point that there now exist models of work which leaders and group members can borrow from. In particular the learning processes which tutors from the adult literacy movement provide, show insights into the kinds of dialogue and mutual exploration which a group leader might hope to encourage amongst older learners embarking on some kind of reminiscence project.[32]

There are examples from varied contexts, including continuing care wards of hospitals, groups of more active older people, the role of drama and intergenerational work.[33] In almost all cases, the characteristics which I quoted earlier have been guiding principles. Reminiscence work is observably an encouragement to people to define their own scope of work, to focus on issues which directly affect their lives, to share the need to organise and progress the group, to value each other's contributions and to develop personally and as group members. My experience working with a north London group which has produced its own publication brought out all these aspects of learning.[34]

Of course it would be unreasonable to pretend that reminiscence work does not still raise issues and problems. There is the problem of maintaining group solidarity while attempting to include conflicting and sometimes divisive memories and experiences.[35] Many published projects are superb testimonies to the effective solidarity of white working class culture. Some of the best and most challenging work has been carried out by groups who have a strong message to put across. And as reminiscence work is now successfully developing with encouraging and inspiring outcomes amongst members of minority ethnic groups, it is true to say that the range of perspective has never been wider.[36] Exploring Living Memory, which on three occasions hosted an across London exhibition and festival of life-history, illustrates the powerful impact of displaying co-existing perspectives of the past. Groups which produced exhibitions came from all over London and from many ethnic and culturally distinct communities. Exploring Living Memory events are compulsive viewing and certainly represented a will to acknowledge and celebrate differences.[37] It is within groups that there seems to be persisting boundaries to a closer sharing of some aspects of the past.

It is, however, in the development of groups, in the management of dominating versions of the past, in the resolution of conflicts and, above all, in group response to expressions of pain and the revival of past griefs that much of the real tension of reminiscence work with older people lies. For some people it may become too much; they may withdrawn from a group or refuse to participate. For others, it's important for the painful experience to be re-lived and shared. Group leaders have to be alert and sensitive to changes in mood. And there may be times when a 'non-prescriptive' attitude has to be shed, if racist and excluding comments are to be outlawed.

Reminiscence work with older people, when viewed from a learning per-spective, offers opportunities for personal and group change. With a focus on reminiscence, curriculum development in adult education follows. The cook-ery class may decide to explore and try out shared knowledge of recipes. The crafts class may decide to work together on a wall-hanging which depicts change in their community or memories of childhood. The north London group which I worked with found that they had a common interest in the preservation of local open spaces of land and water. The result, an additional summer short course on ecology, included visits to a reclaimed area and to offices of Thames Water.

UNDERSTANDING ISSUES FACING SOME OLDER PEOPLE

I want to conclude with a brief look at interesting developments in using reminiscence, or a life history approach, with older people who may be facing problems in their lives.

It is becoming more widely accepted amongst people caring and working with older people that knowledge of an individual life history makes an important contribution to their care plans. The gerontologist Malcolm Johnson has argued the case for a biographical approach to assessing prefer-ences and choices in community care.[38] In a current action research project he and colleagues at the Open University are exploring ways of incorporating a life history approach into assessing appropriate decisions for older people requiring support in the community. The project has identified a number of areas in which this approach could be useful. These include eliciting older people's attitudes to, for example, residential care, understanding family relationships, finding out about relationships between carers and the older person, discovering kinds of help which would be unacceptable, relating to and understanding people labelled 'difficult' and learning how people coped with past difficulties and hardships.[39]

Some research which begins from a similar position has been carried out by Andrew Sixsmith who looks at the meaning of 'home' for older people. He describes his motivation as being to find out what older people want, rather than treating their lives as a series of problems to be solved. Interviewing people about their feelings about home, he concludes that home plays an important part in older people's sense of having a history. It presents a resource for coping and it has symbolic value for the preservation of independence, individuality and identity.[40]

These two projects are examples of work which values reminiscence and which consequently is helping to focus attention on the older person, centring on them, their feelings and emotions, when it comes to negotiating change and understanding choices and preferences.

CONCLUSION

Underlying the argument in this article is the assumption that recall of the past is a normal part of human mental activity. It is something people do throughout their lives. In old age, however, it has a more developed role and perhaps more significant outcomes.

With more of life to be recalled the range of reminiscence activities is of course possibly greater amongst older than amongst younger people. There is a greater range in terms of content and possibly too, in terms of process, since at a later stage in life, reminiscences may be imparted to the young as part of one's role as an older person in society, as part of normal ageing and as part of that process of resolution and self-recognition which seems to accompany the later stages of life.

But there is another reason why it is important to acknowledge the role of the past in older people's lives. The past has a habit of recurring and older people's witness enables us to understand the lessons from this. The past recurs in two ways: it recurs within individual lives and it recurs over time within all our lives.

Within lives, the past may recur in painful recall. Recently a picture in the social work journal *Community Care*[41] illustrated a short story about young ex-offenders from Birmingham who, as an alternative to custody, were burying symbols of their past in a remote part of South-West Ireland. Setting aside the symbolism of this act in terms of Anglo-Irish relations, the story struck me with its hopeless trust in the idea of a rootless present or a clean sheet for the future.

In their old age, will these young people still be able to bury their past mentally as well as physically? Another recent press article suggests that this may not be easy. Eugene Heimler, a psychotherapist working in north London, has spent time listening to the stories of elderly Holocaust survivors who still need to meet and talk about their experience. More recently he has found himself talking not just to people who went through the death camps as he did, but also to their children who, now adult, need to understand their parents' experience for themselves.[42]

In common with other oral historians in interview situations, Freda Millett of Oldham in Lancashire found herself confronting bitterness and resentment when she interviewed one elderly man. She was interested in children's homes which had been set up in the early years of this century and was struck by the degree of control which Boards of Guardians held over the lives of children and parents. The man she spoke to was in his eighties and had lived in one of the homes. He had only the memory of a young woman who visited him until he was three. He had one postcard from Australia signed 'mother' and quite late in life heard that his mother had left him a bungalow in Australia in her will. He was bitter and felt all his life that he had been abandoned. Freda's work with the records of the Boards of Guardians and her interviews with staff and children helped her to be able to convince this man that his mother had quite probably been unable to go against the powers of the Guardians. Her apparent abandonment was an unwilling act. It was Freda Millett's sensitive work which helped him, later in life, to finally overcome some of his bitter feelings towards his mother.[43]

My final point relates to the way the past recurs within all our lives. One thing which reminiscence enables us to do is to recognise forms of repetition in history. Making links between the past and the present is more than an academic exercise sometimes. Amongst the group I worked with in north London was a woman who had lived in temporary accommodation at the end of the Second World War. She was amongst thousands of Londoners who were put into requisitioned flats and hotels while they waited to be rehoused. She told us about their struggles, demonstrations and final delight in being given new flats. The significance of her story was not lost on the group. Their housing estate has many empty flats which are boarded up and unlet. Only yards away are homeless families living in cramped and unhealthy conditions in hotel bedrooms. It almost seemed as if history was repeating itself were it not for the fact that today there is no large scale public housing programme to solve these families' accommodation problems.

It seems to me that we ignore the communications of spacemen like Stephen Spender at our peril. Reminiscence is an activity which has outcomes which may go far beyond individual memory if we can all develop the capacity to listen and learn.

NOTES

1 The programme was an edition of *Desert Island Discs* originally broadcast on 7 April 1989.
2 S. Hale, 'The horse buses stopped north of the Rye', *Case Conference*, 1960, vol. 7, no. 6; N. Streatfield (ed.), *The Day Before Yesterday: Firsthand Stories of Fifty Years Ago*, London, Collins, 1956; J. Cameron, *Yesterday's Witness: a Selection from the BBC Series*, London, British Broadcasting Corporation, 1979.
3 P. Thompson, *The Voice of the Past*, Oxford, Oxford University Press, 1978.
4 The two surveys were set up and run by Professor Theo Barker at the University of Kent and by Paul Thompson at the University of Essex.
5 See. L. Davidoff and B. Westover (eds), *Our Work, Our Lives, Our Words: Women's History and Women's Work*, London, Macmillan, 1986. See also back issues of *Oral History.*
6 See K. Plummer, *Documents of Life: an Introduction to the Problems and Literature of a Humanistic Method*, London, Allen & Unwin, 1983, for a discussion of the development of a life history approach in sociology.
7 Studs Terkel, *Talking to Myself: A Memoir of My Times*, London, Harrap, 1986, p. 64.

8 See for example discussions noted in L. Moss and H. Goldstein (eds), *The Recall Method in Social Surveys*, London, University of London Institute of Education, 1979.

9 P. Thompson, *The Voice of the Past*, second edition, Oxford, Oxford University Press, 1988, pp. 59 ff.

10 *Local Publishing and Local Culture: an account of the work of the Centerprise publishing project, 1972–1977*, Centerprise, Centerprise Publishing Trust, London, 1977.

11 The list of publications is too long to be included here. See back issues of *Oral History* for titles, places and dates of publication.

12 See P. G. Coleman, *Ageing and Reminiscence Processes: Social and Clinical Implications*, Chichester, Wiley, 1986; A. Norris and M.A. El Eilah, 'Reminiscence groups: a therapy for elderly patients and their staff', *Oral History*, 1983, vol. 11, no. 1; J. Adams, 'Reminiscence in the geriatric ward – an undervalued resource', *Oral History*, 1984, vol. 12, no. 2.

13 R. Butler, 'The Life Review: an interpretation of reminiscence in the aged', *Psychiatry*, 1963, vol. 26.

14 R. Dobrof, 'A time for reclaiming the past', *Journal of Gerontological Social Work*, Special Double Issue on The Uses of Reminiscence, 1984, vol. 7, nos 1/2.

15 Colman, *Ageing and Reminiscence Processes*, 1986, ch. 10.

16 *Recall – a Handbook*, London, Help the Aged Education Department 1981.

17 Examples of local and central government funding include £5,000 funding for a project in Yate, Bristol and full-time posts for oral historians at Bradford and Southampton Museums and Art Galleries and at the National Sound Archive.

18 S. Thornton and J. Brotchie, 'Reminiscence: a critical view of the empirical literature', *British Journal of Clinical Psychology*, 1987, vol. 26.

19 A. Hobbs, 'A study to determine some effects of Help the Aged's *Recall* audio-visual programme', Unpublished Dip. Psych. dissertation, The British Psychological Society, Leicester. M. Bender, 'Practical uses of reminiscence', Paper given at SW PSIGE Conference, Bristol, 1988.

20 M. Bender, 'Reminiscence: applications and limitations', *PSIGE Newsletter*, 1989, No. 29.

21 A. Norris, 'Reminiscence based psychotherapeutic work with elderly people', paper presented at the Winter Meeting of the Belgian Society of Gerontology and Geriatrics, Ostend, February 1989.

22 See for example J. Adams, 'Anamnesis in dementia: restoring a personal history', *Geriatric Nursing*, September/October 1986; J. Adams, 'Ghosts of Christmas past', *Nursing Times*, 14 December 1988, vol. 84, no. 50; H. Griffiths and A. Burford, 'Thanks for the memories', *Nursing Times*, 7 September 1988, vol. 84, no. 36; A. Thompson, 'Times past', *Nursing Times*, 8 February 1989, vol. 85, no. 6. It is interesting to note that Validation Theory as devised and advocated by Naomi Feil makes use of personal history and biography. See G.M.M. van Amelsvoort Jones, 'Validation therapy: a companion to reality orientation', *The Canadian Nurse*, March 1985; and C. Bleathman and I. Morton, 'Validation therapy with the demented elderly', *Journal of Advanced Nursing*, 1988, vol. 13.

23 J. Adams, 'Reminiscence in the geriatric ward'.

24 A. Nance, 'Reminiscence with the elderly in hospitals', in *Living Memories: Recalling and Recording the Past*, London History Workshop and Thames Television, 1988.

25 M. Wright, 'Priming the past', *Oral History*, 1986, vol. 14, no. 1; M. Truelove, contribution to Oral History Society Annual Conference, University of Bradford, April 1988, see account in *Oral History*, 1988, vol. 16, no. 1.

26 Help the Aged Education Department, 1981.
27 Senior Nursing Manager, Frank Rugeley, in communication with the author.
28 See F. Gibson, *Using Reminiscence: a Training Pack*, London, Help the Aged, 1989.
29 P. Allman, 'Self help learning and its relevance for learning and development in later life', in E. Midwinter (ed.), *Mutual Aid Universities*, London, Croom Helm, 1984.
30 Quoted in C. Hamby, 'Learning later: does andragogy cater for qualitative differences in learning of older people?', *Journal of Educational Gerontology*, 1988, vol. 3, no. 2.
31 J. Bornat, 'Oral history and adult education practice with older people', Paper presented at the Winter Meeting of the Belgian Society of Gerontology and Geriatrics, Ostend, February 1989; J. Liddington, 'One in four: who cares? education and older adults', in K. Ward and R. Taylor (eds), *Adult Education and the Working Class: Education for the Missing Missions*, London, Croom Helm, 1986. I am grateful to my former colleague, Maureen Cooper at the ILEA Education Resource Unit for Older People who has discussed many of these ideas with me.
32 S. Shrapnel Gardener, *Conversations with Strangers*, London, Write First Time/ Adult Literacy and Basic Skills Unit, 1986: J. Lawrence and J. Mace, *Remembering in Groups: Ideas from Reminiscence and Literacy Work*, London, Exploring Living Memory/Oral History Society, 1987.
33 See P. Duffin, 'Reminiscence at the sharp end', *Oral History*, 1989, vol. 17, no. 1; S. Purkis, *Oral History in Schools*, University of Essex, Oral History Society, n.d.; A. Ross, 'Children becoming historians: an oral history project in a primary school', *Oral History*, 1984, vol. 12, no. 2; S. Jones and C. Major, 'Reaching the public: oral history as a survival strategy for museums', *Oral History*, 1986, vol. 14, no. 2; C. Dallat and F. Gibson, 'The Playback Project: a walk into history', *Oral History*, 1987, vol. 15, no. 2; A. Hill, 'Oral history and multicultural education', *Oral History*, 1987, vol. 15, no. 2; L. Beevers, S. Moffat, H. Clark and S. Griffiths, *Memories and Things: Linking Museums and Libraries with Older People*, WEA West of Scotland District, 1988. See also the work of the Age Exchange Theatre Company which has, since 1982, resulted in plays and drama work drawing on reminiscence and which has involved older people in creation and, at times, productions.
34 Bornat, 'Oral history and adult education practice'.
35 For an anthropological view of these conflicts see H. Hazan, *The Limbo People: a Study of the Constitution of the Time Universe Among the Aged*, London, Routledge, 1980.
36 See for example, Writings by Asian Women, *Breaking the Silence*, London, Centerprise, 1984; C. Adams (ed.), *Across Seven Seas and Thirteen Rivers: Life Stories of Pioneer Sylheti Settlers in Britain*, London, THAP books, 1987; J. Duff and L. Watson, *Boris the Studio Photographer 1900–1985*, London, Museum of the Jewish East End, n.d.
37 K. Worpole, 'The history lark', *Oral History*, 1984, vol. 12, no. 2; J. Bornat, 'Exploring living memory: photos and issues', in P. Holland and J. Spence, *Domestic Photography*, London, Camden Press, 1990.
38 M. Johnson, 'That was your life: a biographical approach to later life', in J.M.A. Munnichs and W.J.A. van den Heuvel (eds), *Dependency and Interdependency in Old Age*, The Hague, Martinus Nijhoff, 1976.
39 B. Gearing and T. Dant. 'Doing biographical research', in S. Peace (ed.), *Researching Social Gerontology: Concepts, Methods and Issues*, London, Sage/British Society of Gerontology, London, 1990.
40 A.J. Sixsmith, 'The meaning and experience of "Home" in later life', Paper

presented at the British Society of Gerontology annual conference, University of Swansea, 1988.

41 *Community Care*, 18 August, 1988.

42 C. Driver, 'Life after the death camps', *Guardian*, 1 May, 1989.

43 F. Millett's paper 'Scattered homes' was presented to the Oral History Society's annual conference at the University of Bradford, 1988.

17 Reaching across the generations
The Foxfire experience

Eliot Wigginton

The schoolteacher Eliot Wigginton was founder of the Foxfire Project. Extracted from David Stricklin and Rebecca Sharpless (eds), *The Past Meets the Present: Essays on Oral History*, Lanham, Md., University Press of America, 1988, pp. 27–41, by permission of Rebecca Sharpless, Institute for Oral History, Baylor University.

STUMBLING ONTO ORAL HISTORY

[. . .] I've got to start, first of all, with a little story and it has to do with putting together the first issue of *Foxfire* magazine in 1966. And it has to do with the fact that, as part of that process, I had students doing a good bit of writing. The idea of putting a magazine out was not to document a lot of material but simply to give students a reason for wanting to pay attention to the writing that they were doing. And if there were an audience out there and their work was going to be published, it stood to reason to me that they would put some more energy into it than they would have otherwise. If you look at the first issue of *Foxfire* magazine, you'll see my first year's language-arts curriculum unfold before your eyes, because on the first few pages there are some haiku poems and those are followed by a few essays defending the use of a couple of novels that I was teaching in my class, one being *To Kill a Mockingbird* and the other one being *Lord of the Flies*, both of which almost got me fired. And you'll see a speech that a student gave to a local Rotary Club about the American teenager and what he stands for in 1966.

You'll see this hodgepodge, potpourri of stuff accompanied by a list of home remedies and a list of superstitions because, it seemed to me, that that was one way to involve all the students in the process of putting this magazine together. Everybody could go home and collect a couple of superstitions. And so the assignment was to do that. And we posted those lists on the wall in the classroom and added to them on a daily basis and eliminated the duplications, the idea being to save me from the agony of having to read compositions like 'What I Did Over My Summer Vacation'. The idea was to collect material that would really be fun to share with each other. I told the kids, 'I want good superstitions.' You know, I knew a little bit about that part of the country. I was partly raised there. I said, 'I don't want superstitions like, if you break a mirror you're gonna have seven years of bad luck. I want the good stuff like, if you kill a toad, your cow will give bloody milk, and things like that.' So the kids began to bring all this material together.

Meanwhile, they were also collecting donations from people in the community to get up enough money to print the first issue. They collected $440. That little act of generosity on the part of those community people, by the way, has now grown into an operation in Rabun County that has an annual budget of $475,000 a year and encompasses a whole range of activities. At any rate, in the process of the kids going out into the community and collecting not only remedies and superstitions and money, they also ran into people like Sara Rickman who said, 'You know, if you guys are going to put out a magazine about Rabun County, you really ought to have some of the good stuff from the county in there because that's the only way it's going to sell.' She said 'Like my father-in-law, for example, used to be the old sheriff in Rabun County. He was sheriff when the Bank of Clayton was robbed in 1936', one of *our* big events. She said, 'You ought to really put stories like that in there, too.'

So four students and I left after school one day and went to see Luther Rickman and said, 'Luther, I've heard there's this great story about the time the bank was robbed.' And his eyes lit up and he leaned back in his chair – he was sitting in front of his wood heater – and he said, 'Well, I's getting a shave and a haircut in Roy Mize's barber shop when the Zade Sprinkle gang came into town.' And this wonderful story unfolded about the Zade Sprinkle boys who came in in a Model T and went into the hardware store first with a little toy pistol they had and robbed the guns and ammunition they needed to go next door and hold up the bank and, at the same time, stole a big, fifty-pound keg of roofing nails with the big heads, and went into the bank and got thirty-six hundred bucks, jumped in the car and went out of town, threw the nails out on the road and blew the tires off of Luther's sheriff's car. He came chasing them in his barber's cloth and foam on his face. It's a wonderful story.

We got back to school and I said, 'Now, there's a composition assignment.' And the students that had been with me told the story to the kids in the class and I said, 'Okay, that's your composition assignment for this week', and they handed in their papers. And I said, 'The best one we'll print.' And none of the stories were any good any more. Basically what they were were things like, 'Luther Rickman was the sheriff when the bank was robbed and he finally tracked the robbers down and caught them and got the money back.' And we sat around for days thinking about that, saying, What in the hell happened to that story? because all of a sudden it wasn't worth printing – trying to figure out what we were going to do.

Finally one of the kids said, 'Well we could go to Bob Edwards and get a tape recorder.' Bob Edwards runs a little local Kodak shop. We didn't have any money, didn't have a camera, didn't have a tape recorder, didn't have anything. So we went to Bob Edwards, and Bob said, 'Yeah, I'll loan you one and if you like it you can buy it later. You don't have to pay me now but if you want to take it go ahead and take it.' Four of us went to see Luther Rickman one night after supper and said, 'Luther, you've got to tell us that story again.' And so Luther sat back and said, 'Well, I's gettin' a shave and a haircut –' and it all came right back out again, and it was all intact. And the next day I played that thing for every one of my classes. The kids clapped and cheered, and all of a sudden we had a good story again. And they transcribed that tape recording, and it appeared in the first issue of *Foxfire* magazine. Later on, about two years after that point, we found out that somebody had called that kind of stuff oral history! [. . .]

MEMORIES AND FRIENDSHIPS

But we also found that there were other values that came from these experiences. They did tend to be *memorable* for students for whom high school was not a particularly memorable experience in a positive sense. There's a wonderful poem by Richard Brautigan from a book called *Rommel Drives On Deep into Egypt*. And the concluding lines of the poem are: 'My teachers could have ridden with Jesse James for all the hours they stole from me.'[1] If you talk to any of those kids who were involved in that first set of interviews, though, one of the high points of their high-school experience will be the interview with Luther Rickman and his wife sitting around that old wood stove. *That* material sticks and has consequence and lives on in a collective memory that turns high school into something positive and productive instead of the opposite.

We also found that there were enormously close friendships that developed. To introduce these, Luther, for example, became a friend. And Luther was responsible for our creating one of the most interesting articles we ever put together where he went out and found for us a number of different moonshiners that he had arrested at one point or another in his career. He had those moonshiners tell us all the tricks that they used to keep him from being able to find their stills. And then he revealed from his point of view what he had done to actually find them and capture them. They'd be saying things like: 'And we knew we had Luther this time.' And Luther would look at them and say, 'Yeah, but I knew that this was going on.' This really magical set of things began to happen, and Luther and I and the students became closer and closer friends as he got into the spirit of this whole thing. And at his funeral people that I had never met before – still don't know who they were – kept coming up to me and to some of the students that were there saying, 'You know, the last couple of years of Luther's life he believed that this kind of thing you folks were doing with him was some of the most valuable stuff that ever happened in his life and that's all he talked about.'

The same thing happened with a funeral I went to for Buck Carver, who was one of the moonshiners, and became one of our closest friends, one of the typical country funerals, where there are hundreds of people gathered in a funeral parlor and flowers piled to the ceiling on these racks. And, of course, we sent flowers. But I went down there with Chet Welch, one of my kids who went on to Georgia Tech. We had interviewed Buck for years. There are pictures in the *Foxfire* magazine of Buck in my classroom with the kids gathered around in this tight circle. His wife came and got me and took me over to the casket, and she said, 'I want to show you something. See those flowers right down there? Those are the ones that you guys sent. Those are from Foxfire and we moved all the other flowers and put these up beside the casket because we knew that Buck would have wanted it that way.' And so that kind of thing begins to happen. And family members come back and say, 'You know, we've got a six-year-old now that never met his grandmother and we'd like to have copies of those tapes, by the way, if you wouldn't mind, so that he can hear his grandmother talk' – or copies of photographs. And that happens constantly.

Later we began to uncover other values that have to do more primarily with curriculum design, and that's what I'm going to be focusing on specifically later in the symposium. But they have to do with things like the lessons that can come from this fact-versus-opinion kind of situation that so often crops up in oral history. We did a major issue of the magazine on cock fighting, for example, which is a big sport in our part of the world. And one of the people that we interviewed said, 'You've got to understand that this has been around for a long, long time. I mean, this is stuff that has real precedent. You know, George Washington even fought chickens on the lawn of the White House.' And we printed it right on, no problem. The kids got a letter from this guy in New England that said, 'You guys need to know that the White House wasn't built then.' And that creates in kids' minds a sense of or an awakening to history that hadn't quite been there before and the propriety of things that I think is important, on the need for checking things, and how you deal with something when it isn't true.

Another nice thing that came out of this activity in terms of schoolwork, too, is that in high school there's this incredible pecking order. Certain students get to do everything and other students get to do very little. And one of the magical aspects of this whole area of endeavor is that virtually anybody can play a part and make a valuable contribution, and it doesn't have anything to do with strength or looks or popularity or money or whether or not you have a car or any of those other trappings of adolescent prestige. Those all fall by the wayside in a situation like this; everybody can pitch in and play a part, which is another one of the values I think is so important, and also the whole fact that the older people that we interview give their friendship and give their affection to kids who often are floundering in terms of self-esteem and self-worth, and they give their affection unconditionally. That's really nice to see a kid who thinks that nobody likes him responding to someone like an Aunt Arie Carpenter, for example.

VALUES, CULTURE, AND COMMUNITY

I have some things that other people have written that might help put all this in even more perspective. We recently suffered through a year-long evaluation by a man named John Puckett who was getting his Ph.D. in education at

UNC-Chapel Hill. He lived with us for a year and made notes every day, interviewed over five hundred people: former students, current students, administration officials, peer teachers, all the rest of the community, everybody. The comments that were made about this experience by former students were made completely independently of me or anybody else; it was just John and the former student together. And we uncover in the process of reading some of these quotations still other values that emerge from this kind of activity, one of them being, for example, that the barriers between young people and old people and a reluctance to associate with them in the initial stages in meaningful ways come tumbling down. This is a quotation John Puckett got from Mike Cook.[2] It says:

> I saw a lot of beautiful things in old folks that had to do with Foxfire, which was a starting point for my communication with older people. It opened my ears to really hear what they were saying. That's the beginning of a road you start down that leads you to finding out that those folks who seem so different are people like you who've seen a lot of things and done a lot of things that you haven't. I regret that my grandfather died before I learned to talk to old people, which I learned to do when I was in Foxfire.

Or from Faye Carver, who said:

> I had always felt uncomfortable with them, not knowing what to say or do. I guess Foxfire taught me that they're people, too, not just something to be stared at and ignored. It seemed like every old person I saw, I knew they had a story. I knew they had a history. And just about every one of them had a history to be proud of and it made me want to know what that history was. Every one of them that I experienced had some knowledge that they could pass on that could help you in some way.

Or from Myra Queen: 'I got kind of a city mentality sometimes, especially being with dorm students.' There are a lot of city kids that are moving into Rabun County; it's turning into a second-home development community. 'You'd want to be like them. They'd laugh at an old person wearing overalls, and I'd laugh too, just to be kind of like them.' She was a community student – a country girl – and it's the city kids that she was going to school with that would laugh at these folks. She'd feel like she had to laugh at her own people also because obviously that was the appropriate thing to do.

> Foxfire showed that those old people weren't just dumb old hillbillies, that they were smarter and had a lot more common sense than people were giving them credit for. It made me feel proud to be a part of that, a part of a culture that they came out of. I never really ever knew what my heritage was until I got into Foxfire. It seems like I had a lot more in common with these older people than I had thought. It was like you've got a thumb here but you've never paid any attention to it. It was like something that's been there but I never realized it was part of me.

It's the same kind of value that comes, by the way, as students begin to uncover aspects of their own culture that they hadn't realized. It is routine for me to get final examination papers from my students that say, as Teresa Cook said last spring, 'Until I got into Foxfire, I didn't know I was from the southern Appalachian region', much less how to spell it, of course.

There are also things like human strength and values that students begin to appreciate and pick up on. The cause of some of this came out in a story from one of the people who was interviewed for the magazine *Foxfire*, fall 1984. There's a great sign on the back of that issue, by the way: 'If you go to hell it's your fault.' This is an old man in Kentucky that makes those roadside signs you see when you're driving down the highway that say, 'Jesus is coming.' That was one of them. Inside the same magazine there's an article about a woman named Carolyn Stradley. Allison Adams interviewed her. And one of the stories that Carolyn felt was important to share with Allison was one that goes: 'One particular Christmas (I guess I was about eleven or twelve); I had been by myself.' You have to know about Carolyn that her mother died and her father left; she was left alone to raise herself when she was a young teenager, and she lived by herself and raised herself alone in the mountains.

Daddy was down here in the city with his friends and Eldon was away. I had got a Christmas tree and at school we had colored little strips of paper and glued them into chains. It was Christmas Day, but I felt very much alone . . . so I thought, 'Well, it's Christmas and there's gonna be good spirit and good cheer at the preacher's house.' I walked across the field, crossed the creek on a footlog, and then back up through another field to his house. When I went in I didn't feel any kind of uncomfortableness. Their house was so nice and warm, and I was cold. I didn't have a fire [at my house] that day and I was wet. [On my way over,] I'd slipped off the footlog and fallen down into the creek – just like a kid will. The smells of the turkey and dressing and all that food had my mouth watering. You've got to look at an eleven-year-old kid to understand what I'm saying. Anyway, I went in and the only thing I could think was, 'Oh, boy! I'm gonna get something to eat . . .'

And then all the family went in [to eat]. [I stood back because] I would never go into anyone's kitchen without being asked. Then the pastor came out and pulled me aside and he told me, 'Carolyn, I don't get to spend much time with my family alone and I'd prefer to have this time and I would appreciate it if you could come back later.' See, he'd been working in Atlanta some and preaching on Sundays up [in Youngcane]. He didn't say, 'Would you leave?' He said, 'Come back later', but I knew what he meant. I'll tell you what. That was probably the only man I've ever hated in my life. That man was an A-number-one hypocrite. I disliked him then and I dislike him today, and he's dead . . .

And from that day on, I vowed that I would *never* ask for anything from anyone for as long as I live. I'm still pretty strict about that. I've found that you have to ask for some things, but you don't beg for anything. To communicate and survive in this world, you have to ask in some way, but you never beg for anything. I haven't, and with God's help I won't. I'll beg God for help and forgiveness but not another human being. Even all that time that Arthur [my husband] was sick, we never had one penny of welfare![3]

Experiences like that and stories like that affected Allison in a pretty profound way. She went on to Agnes Scott College, majoring in English, and really developed a sense of the value of that human communication and what people have and the magic that stories can have and weave around you that she's probably going to make [it] her life's work.

I can also share with you the kind of respect that the kids develop for the strength and resilience that humans have. In the introduction to an article that Kyle Conway wrote for the magazine, he talks about a fellow named Roy Roberts, who is eighty-nine years old. Roy was a former sheriff also up in Madison County, North Carolina. And Roy is this amazingly energetic person who through his life ran general stores. Roy was the first conservationist in our part of the world, I guess. Roy had these general stores and everybody that bought at the general store traded, of course, for goods. They'd come and get a pocketknife and they'd trade eggs and beans and that sort of thing. Often when the eggs came in they were spoiled, but he wouldn't know that until after the trade had been made. So he'd candle the eggs and he'd pick the ones out that were spoiled an set them aside. Then he developed a satellite business around those eggs that had to do with raising skunks. He raised skunks and sold skunks to people and fed the eggs to the skunks, and everything went around and around and around. It's a long story. It takes reading the article to get the full import of it, but he had about thirty related businesses, each of which fed off the others. And he became the southern Appalachian mountaineer's version of a millionaire, making a steady income when everybody else was living on potatoes.

Kyle writes in the introduction about Roy, 'Then he went back to the shelter', this little picnic shelter he's got, 'and sat around the cement picnic tables and he began to show us how to make some of the toys he used to play with when he was a child.' This is after six solid hours of interview. This is getting way up into the evening. We've had supper.

The directions he gave us will appear in a Foxfire Press book about toys and games. That's when the fun began. As he would remember things, he'd get excited and his eyes would light up. Once he had found the right wood, he sat and whittled while he reminisced until late in the night. After showing us how to make two different kinds of whistles and a pop gun, he decided he needed a different stick of wood. So off he went, romping through the woods at ten o'clock at night with no flashlight in the pitch black darkness. He left us sitting there dead tired and sleepy-eyed, wondering what was going on. We could hear him thrashing around and breaking branches. By the time we'd figured out what was going on and had started out after him, he was already back with a satisfied grin on his face holding a perfect stick for the next toy.

We were ready to call it a day but he was just getting started. We finally got to bed after he showed us how to make a fly gun.

Roy was waiting for us when we woke up the next morning. He'd been up for hours and he had already fed the squirrels that come every day to the roof of his springhouse on wooden poles he has running from a nearby tree. He had even made another toy that morning that shot little wooden pegs.

We made some more tape recordings and a water gun. Then we drove ten miles over the mountains to see Roy's abandoned charcoal kilns and his old stores.

He used to produce charcoal for the Asheville market.

He had us struggling to keep up with him as he pointed out different features. After that, Roy took us to some land he used to own and he showed us a lake and a dam he had built himself. We straggled behind him as he marched up and down hills and through the woods.

Finally, all of our film was used and all our tapes were full, so we packed up and headed for home. We were all worn out and slept all the way. They say times flies. Well I don't think even time can keep up with Roy Roberts.[4]

There are also things that happen as students encounter older people and the certainty of death and the usefulness that older people have even in their later years. A quotation from John Puckett again:

Working with Foxfire made me see that the old mountain people were strong and useful people who weren't afraid of dying. Seeing that they still had useful lives helped me get over the fear of death that I had seen as the next step after getting old. That had been the only thing I had seen about being old and it frightened me but that fear's laid to rest. [. . .]

NOTES

1 R. Brautigan, 'The memoirs of Jesse James', in *Rommel Drives On Deep into Egypt*, New York, Delacorte, 1970.
2 J. Puckett, 'Foxfire: mediating the twain', Ph.D. diss., The University of North Carolina at Chapel Hill, 1985.
3 C. Stradley, 'The worst feeling was being alone, never really feeling like I belonged', *Foxfire*, 1984, no. 18, pp. 184–185.
4 K. Conway, Introduction to 'I done some work in my time', by R. Roberts, *Foxfire*, 1985, no. 19, pp. 4 and 7.

18 Culture and disability

The role of oral history

Karen Hirsch

Karen Hirsch is Program Director at Paraquad Inc., an Independent Living Center in St Louis, Missouri. Extracted from *Oral History Review*, 1995, vol. 22, no. 1, pp. 1–27, by permission of the Oral History Association.

Today, people with different kinds of disabilities are working together and discovering their political potential, as witnessed in the passage of the American with Disabilities Act (ADA) of 1990. The growth of a disability rights movement raises many questions about the history of disabled Americans and the cultural meaning of disability for both disabled and nondisabled citizens.

Compared to the impact on historical studies of the Black freedom movement and the women's movement, however, the disability rights movement has so far had little effect on historical scholarship. Peter Stearns described in 1983 how social historians 'mean to leave nothing out in their remaking of our map of the past'.[1] But to date, few historians have included disability issues as an integral part of their thinking and writing.[2] Paul Thompson argues that all history serves a social purpose, and that since 'the nature of most existing records is to reflect the standpoint of authority, it is not surprising that the judgement of history more often than not vindicated the wisdom of the powers that be'. Since people with disabilities constitute one of the most powerless groups of individuals in any society, it is also not surprising that disability issues have not been broadly dealt with in historical writings.

But Thompson also notes that while 'oral history is not necessarily an instrument for change' it often leads to a 'shift of focus' in which the point of view of the less powerful players in a social context also get a chance to express themselves. This suggests that the use of oral histories in disability studies could allow yet another group to find a voice, could lead to a new view of local and social history, and could help create a deeper understanding of cultural conditions which affect everyone.[3]

Disability studies is a growing interdisciplinary field. Within it, a small but growing number of scholars are becoming interested in culture and disability, and some are beginning to study disability history and to use oral history interviews to shed light on past events still alive in the memories of people. This article considers two main issues raised by this work: (1) The need to include disability issues as an analytic category in historical scholarship, in the 'total history' that social historians aspire to produce,[4] and

(2) The role of oral history in the development of disability studies and disability history.

In what ways could knowledge about disability issues shed light on our understanding of American history and culture? What are the implications of thinking about people with disabilities as a group? What are the theoretical models of disability that shape the cultural conditions in which disability policies and services are established and implemented? What are the essential aspects of disability history? Do people with diverse disabilities share similar cultural experiences? What are some defining issues that disability historians could pursue as they stake out the initial terrain of disability history? A tentative synthesis of disability history will be put forth, suggesting some issues that could help future scholars consider where disability history might begin and end, and where related but still distinct concerns begin to overlap.

Questions concerning disability and culture represent new territory for many scholars, because the disciplines that traditionally have been concerned with disability do not deal well with the impact of cultural contexts, while scholars in the humanities have rarely included 'disability' in their analytical framework. The introduction of a disabled/nondisabled dimension in historical studies brings to light new issues not revealed by familiar categories such as gender, class, race, ethnicity, age, occupation, or rural versus urban settings.

Social historians, for example, could begin to rethink much of the evidence about disability that they have inadvertently collected but largely ignored. Archival collections holding papers about slaves, coal mining towns, family and kinship ties, tenant farmers, labor conditions – any collections by social information about the past – are likely to include bits and pieces of disability experiences. Incorporating these would change our view of traditional historical topics, leading to new questions and new ways of thinking about the past.

To appreciate this, it is helpful to consider familiar works in social history with the disability perspective in mind. This way of reading *Like a Family: The Making of a Southern Cotton Mill World* – one of many examples that could have been chosen – suggests that questions about disability experiences in the mill workers' lives could have provided an additional dimension for the authors' hypothesis that the mill village functioned as an extended family, with the support given to individual families in the case of an illness or accident showing how this social network functioned.[5] Illnesses, accidents, or even the death of a family member represent temporary periods of stress, but disability is a long term, more permanent situation. Did the mill village provide emotional and material support when a child with Down syndrome was born? What would the support be for a worker several years after he permanently lost the ability to contribute his share to the common good of village life? Had such questions been included, the research for this book could have provided a more complete perspective on the Southern cotton mill world.

Folklorists, like historians, have collected much material regarding disabilities that they have not categorized in that way. For example, blues collections could be systematically searched for information about disability experiences. and folkloric archives and interviews may be especially rich sources for studying how issues of language, consciousness, and memory figure in the representation of disability in such cultural settings.[6]

Scholars in fields like medicine, rehabilitation, public health, psychology, and special education, have long traditions of dealing with issues related to poor health, illness, birth defects, and traumas caused by accidents. But their accounts do not generally comprise disability history, though they may contribute relevant background information. This is because the 'medical model' with its emphasis on evaluation, diagnosis, prescription, isolation, treatment, cure and prognosis, has dominated both theory and practice in the 'helping professions' that deal with disabled people. The prevailing notion has been that a disability was like an illness that the medical and psychological professions needed to deal with.

The need for a broader cultural and historical approach to disability studies has only recently begun to be recognized. Disability scholars are beginning to call for a change in the 'constricted and myopic thinking that has long characterized . . . the study of disability'. Some claim that it is comparable to 'confusing gynecology with the study of women in society, or dermatology with the study of racism'.[7] This model and the concomitant 'sick role' have relegated people with disabilities to a passive role which often does not permit them to control crucial aspects of the services they need or even the choices they must make in their own lives.[8]

The disability rights movement was in part born out of the desire of disabled people to demedicalize their lives and take control over their own destinies. This impulse has had its parallel in scholarship. For while medical historians have occasionally conceived their studies to include the relevant intellectual, political, and economic history, they have rarely given space to the voices of the patients, the clients, the recipients of services. While these areas of historical inquiry are beginning to benefit from adding the perspectives of disabled individuals in the roles of clients, students, patients, or consumers, their primary focus remains the history of medicine or of the professions – not a broader disability history focused on the everyday life experiences of people with disabilities.[9] This disability history – the story of what life experiences with a disability have been like for different people in different places and at different times – is a field in its infancy: there is no established historical approach with a defined body of literature and a list of distinguished contributors.

The reasons for this go deeper than historiography. The central aspect of disability history is the experience – individual and social – of living with a disability. This cumulative experience is varied, complex, and shifting as life itself, and it is intimately mixed up with the all the human milestone events of birth, growth, maturation, procreation, aging, and death. Why, then, has the experience of disability been largely absent from most examinations of human cultures? Perhaps the deepest reason is fear – individual fear of losing bodily worth and function, and societal fear that a large number of disabled individuals might somehow endanger the future of the human species. In an age when medical advances permit an increasing number of individuals who would once have died instead to survive as people with disabilities, it is becoming more and more important to overcome the fear of a 'different' bodily experience, to uncover the history of disabled people, to explore the cultural meaning of disability, to end the oppression of people with disabilities.

Oral history has a crucial role to play in the emergence of this kind of disability history. Oral history interviews with disabled people are adding a viewpoint that has been ignored partly because it has been assumed that disabled people do not have an articulate view of their circumstances that differs from other views. Scholars in the humanities are just beginning to discover that disabled people have a unique perspective on life informed by their disability experiences. And in the process, oral history projects [. . .] can help shape our understanding of broader issues in American history and culture.

Paul Longmore, for example, has documented recently a long-forgotten story of a group of unemployed disabled job applicants, refused employment by the Works Progress Administration (WPA) in the 1930s because of their disabilities, who staged a protest to make their case public.[10] The history of the WPA may not be extensively re-written because of this re-discovery, but it is significant enough to merit mention in discussions of who benefited directly from the New Deal and who did not. While some WPA officials, like the directors of the Federal Writers' Project, tried to define American culture and identity in 'pluralistic' and 'inclusive' terms, there were groups like disabled citizens who were being left out.[11]

The struggle to be fully included as citizens with equal rights is still going on, and is one impetus behind the disability rights movement. As a general matter, disability scholarship involves issues in which scholarship and advocacy are inevitably intertwined.[12] The growth of disability studies as an academic field and the emergence of disability history at once reflect and speak to recent improvements in the political and social status of disabled people. As a result, disability activists have recently begun to work for the establishment of oral history projects or other cultural disability studies. Until the ADA they may well have been too preoccupied with legal, political, and policy issues, but now there is a growing sense that it is time to move beyond questions of services, accessibility, policies and legislation. The number of disability scholars beginning to focus their attention on topics concerning disability and culture is thus increasing, and at many major disability conferences activists regularly organize sessions on culture and disability.

In all of this work, the question of what kind of group people with disabilities constitute is central, and has practical and political as well as academic implications, particularly for oral history. Scholars involved in developing a new approach to disability policy have long been working to establish the idea that people with disabilities do constitute a group – that they should not be considered only as individuals with private problems, but should also be given the legal status of a minority discriminated against as a group.[13] In this context, however, might the collecting of oral histories and the studying of life histories or what folklorists call personal experience narratives present a throwback to the individual rather that the collective point of view? This concern is perhaps one reason why disability activists have so far been only marginally interested in the development of a comprehensive oral history program dealing with disability experiences.

Another reason may lie in the fact that so far most of the literature based on interviews with disabled individuals has not demonstrated the empowering shift of focus that Paul Thompson describes in *The Voice of the Past*.[14] Published collections of stories based on interviews with disabled people are not necessarily 'oral histories', although there is historical information in them. Some examples of these works are *The Hidden Minority* (1977) by Sonny Kleinfield, *Voices: Interviews with Handicapped People* (1981) by Michael Orlansky and William Heward, and *Ordinary Moments: The Disabled Experience* (1984) by Alan Brightman.[15] Published with the explicit purpose of allowing people with disabilities to speak for themselves, these interviews do not serve the same function for the disability community as oral histories collected about other groups. Although the people in these collections are speaking about their disability experiences, they do not relate their stories to place or time periods, and they do not describe public events that influenced their individual lives. The presence of a disability in each individual's life story is not sufficient to create a sense of a group with shared experiences. Instead, the stories seem to reinforce a notion of individual coping and personal adjustments. These volumes fall into the 'try harder', 'suffer through', and 'I'm just like everybody else', genres that reflect the preoccupation in American culture with individual achievements and individualistic solutions.

This kind of disaggregation of the group into isolated individuals does not seem to happen to other groups whose cultural connections and historical significance are being portrayed through oral history collections. The question remains of whether or not stories collected by oral history scholars and given a more historical context and focus would reveal a group identity among a diverse and random collection of people with disabilities.

Lay observers as well as scholars often argue that disabled people are better off not being considered a group, because that would inevitably lead to increased discrimination. Segregation at all levels in society, and incarceration of disabled people into large institutions, is seen as the result of considering people with disabilities as a group instead of treating them as individuals. The assumption seems to be that prejudice against people with disabilities is inevitable; it cannot be eliminated or reduced.

This static and ahistorical view of disability characterizes most disability scholarship to date. For example, Erving Goffman's work on the management of a 'spoiled identity', frequently cited in research related to disability issues, assumes that in Western Cultures a disability will always be interpreted as a stigma for the individual to cope with. But disability history, like the work being done by historian David Gerber on disabled war veteran and actor Harrold Russell, documents changes over time in the social climate in which real people with disabilities develop their skills of self-presentation.[16] To be sure, there are changes in such skills within an individual person's life, caused by maturation and experience. However, the changes that Goffman does not take into account are the changes in the political and social status of disabled people as a group, which allow individuals to start at different points and push further the rejection of disability as a stigma.

While there is a need to acknowledge and understand the differences that exist among disabled individuals and sub-groups, there is a more basic need to recognize that disability activists are consciously building a positive sense of an inclusive disability community in which the idea of disability as stigmatizing is rejected, and in which people accept each other across disability categories thus affirming a shared sense of human value and dignity. In this context, disability oral history projects can be expected to document how competent disabled individuals experience being 'reassured' by their non-disabled friends or colleagues that they are not seen as disabled, handicapped, members of 'that' group.[17]

The question of what kind of group people with disabilities constitute begs the prior question of who has the power to define the category. One frequently debated current issue concerns language: which is the preferable term, 'disabled' or 'handicapped'? Today most members of the disability community prefer to be called 'disabled', in part because they feel that 'handicapped' was a label chosen by the professionals, not by themselves.[18]

What people with disabilities need is a community of peers and a disability identity that is voluntary and constructed by themselves, not one prescribed from the outside by others. Mildred Blaxter, in *The Meaning of Disability*, says that in 'most countries, the tendency has always been to structure a social segregation, providing separate facilities and encouraging the disabled to interact primarily with their own minority group'.[19] She may not be using the term 'minority group' in the same way that a social or cultural historian would, but she is expressing the idea that to the general public, people with disabilities constitute a group that somehow belong together. Only in the wake of the black civil rights movement is it possible to accept that this kind of discriminating assignment to a minority group status outside the mainstream of society and turn it into a political and legal advantage.

One of the immediately applicable lessons from work on women's oral history is the need to acknowledge differences among categories while continuing to explore issues and characteristics shared across subgroups.[20] Like women, people with disabilities exist within and among every other cultural group, and like other minority groups, disabled people are 'singled out from others in the society in which they live for differential and unequal treatment'.[21] Like women and other minority groups, disabled citizens are 'distinguished by their exclusion from full participation in the society, their debarment from certain economic, political, and social opportunities'.[22] Other similarities include the 'restricted scope of their occupational and professional advancement', and the general tendency to treat them 'as members of a category, irrespective of their individual merits'.[23] Feminist scholars have discovered the need to study the interaction between gender and such other factors as class and ethnicity; likewise disability scholars must consider the areas where gender, ethnicity, and class intersect with disability to make up the total lived experience [. . .]

For American history in general, it is time to embrace disability as a category for analysis and as a perspective indispensable for a complete picture. Disability issues, however, could easily end up being presented by those who presume to speak for their disabled patients, clients, students, or children. It is hard to overstate how resistant and pervasive is the cultural assumption that people with disabilities cannot speak for themselves. Thus while there are many oral history projects that need to be done, the most important are those that deal with disability experiences as they have been lived by disabled people, and that can give voice and interpretive authority to people with disabilities themselves, not only to their advocates, their teachers, or their parents.

To this end, several questions bearing on interpretive authority are crucial. Are the projects conceived, carried out, and interpreted within an intellectual framework that allows people with disabilities to focus on barriers or accessibility, on segregation or integration, on discrimination or equal opportunities? Or are the studies dealing with disability experiences conceptually situated within the theoretical and applied research traditions of the 'medical model' with its emphasis on the individual's diagnosis, treatment, cure, and psychological adjustment? The two ways of framing disability experiences presented here differ from the two poles of authority Michael Frisch describes as represented by the oral historian and the narrator. But, to use his term, the authority to interpret disability experiences is 'sharable' between an oral historian and a disabled narrator when the oral historian has enough background to recognize the difference in ideology that exists between the medical establishment and the 'helping professions' on the one hand, and the disability rights movement on the other.[24]

Disability issues have been so invisible in historical scholarship for so long that it will take a keen historical sense indeed to begin to unearth that history.[25] Some [. . .] studies [. . .] examine disability experiences as if they did not vary from place to place, or change over time. Scholars using oral history interviews to examine the cultural meaning of disability experiences need the best background information possible in order to sort out the confusing interplay between ancient assumptions about the relationship between body and mind, and the expanding achievements expected of disabled people, achievements made possible through modern medicine and technology. Is the cultural assumption that it takes a 'sound body' to possess a 'sound mind' perhaps responsible for some of the pervasively negative attitudes toward people with disabilities? Is it perhaps also one reason why the medical model is so hard to shake even outside of medical contexts?

Oral history interviews with disabled people have an untested capacity to explore how disabled people react to these contradictory expectations, in that disabled people live their daily lives with the tension described here, and are confronted with a large number of theories about their self-images, adjustments to loss of function, overcompensations, and expected frustrations caused by environmental and attitudinal barriers. But because there is practically no written disability history, most of these theories, including some formulated by activists in the disability rights movement, are too simplistic to reveal, much less sort out, the tensions between ancient ideas and modern expectations.

Some of the disability oral history projects described in this article suggest an increase over time in social awareness among disabled individuals. While the disabled demonstrators from the 1930s cared about each other, they did not extend their concerns for unemployment among other groups of disabled people. The sit-ins in 1977, however, succeeded in part because of co-operation across different disability groups. The increasing social awareness among disabled people can be seen in other unexplored chapters of disability history as well. As a social movement, the disability rights movement has become increasing inclusive and aware of the need to associate with all kinds of other minority groups. Contact with the disability rights movement has helped many disabled individuals start working as advocates, not only for themselves, but for disabled peers and the cause in general. Disability rights has become an international concern. When the students at Gallaudet protested the installment of a hearing president who did not know how to sign, deaf people from all over America and the rest of the world, and other subgroups of the disability community voiced their support.[26] The ADA became law because many different disability groups worked together.[27]

Rejection of the idea that disability is stigmatizing may be a cultural trend closely related to an increased acceptance of and care for each other among disabled people. It may also be associated with the growth of disability studies and disability history. Historian Idus A. Newby has suggested 'that sea changes in historical treatment of social groups occur only when basic improvements take place in the status of the groups themselves. The abatement of popular prejudice serves, as it were, to legitimize the group and facilitate a new, more sympathetic look at its history.'[28] For people with disabilities it is important to participate in the development of this new look at their history. Disability activists need to advocate for oral history projects, to participate in local history projects, and to work with and work as disability scholars in focusing the questions, interpreting the findings, and developing the language and images that can begin to give the disability community its history.

NOTES

1 P. Stearns, 'The new social history: an overview', in J.B. Gardner and G. Rollie Adams (eds), *Ordinary People and Everyday Life: Perspectives on the New Social History*, Nashville, The American Association for State and Local History, 1983, p. 7.

2 Two notable exceptions are historians Paul K. Longmore and John S. Schuchman. See for example P.K. Longmore, 'Uncovering the hidden history of people with disabilities', *Reviews in American History*, 1988, vol. 15, pp. 355–364, and J.S. Schuchman, 'Silent movies and the deaf community', *Journal of Popular Culture*, 1984, vol. 17, pp. 58–78.

3 P. Thompson, *The Voice of the Past: Oral History*, Oxford, Oxford University Press, 1988, pp. 2–6.

4 Stearns, 'New social history', p. 7.

5 J.D. Hall, J. Lelondis, R. Korstad, M. Murphy, L.A. Jones, C.B. Daly, *Like a Family: The Making of a Southern Cotton Mill World*, Chapel Hill, N.C., The University of North Carolina Press, 1988.

6 See for example, H. Halpert, 'Legends of the cursed child', in W.S. Walker (ed.), *Whatever Makes Papa Laugh: A Folklore Sheaf Honoring Harold W. Thompson*, Cooperstown, N.Y., New York Folklore Society, 1958, pp. 72–81, and S.S. Eberly, 'Fairies and the folklore of disability: changelings, hybrids and the solitary fairy', *Folklore*, 1988, vol. 99, pp. 58–77, as well as P.K. Longmore, 'A note on language and the social identity of disabled people', *American Behavioral Scientist*, 1985, vol. 28, pp. 419–423.

7 M.G. Eisenberg, C. Griggins and R.J. Duval, *Disabled People as Second Class Citizens*, New York, Springer Publishing Company, 1982, p. xiii.

8 For a discussion of the medical model, see G. DeJong, 'Defining and implementing the independent living concept', in N.M. Crewe and I.K. Zola (eds), *Independent Living for Physically Disabled People*, San Francisco, Jossey-Bass Publishers, 1987, pp. 15–18.

9 See for example, S.M. Rothman, 'The doctors did better than the patients', review of B. Bates, *Bargaining for Life: A Social History of Tuberculosis*, The New York Times Book Review, 19 July 1992, pp. 10–11.

10 T. Johnston, 'Breaking another set of stereotypes. Beyond screen villains: Paul Longmore puts disability minorities into historical perspective', *Stanford Observer*, May–June 1991, p. 5.

11 J. Hirsch, 'Portrait of America: the Federal Writers' Project in an intellectual and cultural context', Ph.D. diss., University of North Carolina at Chapel Hill, 1984.

12 See for example, R. Benmayor and others, *Stories to Live By: Continuity and Change in Three Generations of Puerto Rican Women*, Centro de Estudios Puertorriqueños Working Paper Series, New York, Centro de Estudios Puertorriqueños at Hunter College of the City University of New York, 1987.

13 See E. Berkowitz, *Disabled Policy, America's policy for the handicapped*, Cambridge, Cambridge University Press, 1989, pp. 188–189, 265; H. Hahn, 'Civil rights for disabled Americans: the foundation of a political agenda', in A. Gartner and T. Joe (eds), *Images of the Disabled, Disabling Images*, New York, Praeger Publishers, 1987, pp. 181–203; C. Liachowitz, in *Disability as a Social Construct, Legislative Roots*, Philadelphia, The University of Pennsylvania Press, 1988.

14 Thompson, *Voice of the Past*.

15 S. Kleinfield, *The Hidden Minority: A Profile of Handicapped Americans*, Boston, Little, Brown & Company, 1977; M. Orlansky and W. Heward, *Voices: Interviews with Handicapped People*, Columbus, Charles E. Merrill Publishing Company, 1981; A. Brightman, *Ordinary Moments: The Disabled Experience*, Baltimore: University Park Press, 1984.

16 D. Gerber, 'Anger and Affability: the rise and representation of a repertory of self-presentation skills in a World War II disabled veteran', *Journal of Social History*, Fall 1993, vol. 27, pp. 5–28.
17 K. Hirsch, 'Studying culture', *The Disability Rag*, May/June 1987, pp. 38–39.
18 Liachowitz, *Disability as a Social Construct.*
19 M. Blaxter, *The Meaning of Disability: A Sociological Study of Impairment*, New York, Neale Watson Academic Publications, 1976, pp. 196–197.
20 S. Berger Gluck and D. Patai (eds), *Women's Words, The Feminist Practice of Oral History*, New York, Routledge, 1991.
21 L. Wirth, 'The problem of minority groups', in R. Linton (ed.), *The Science of Man in the World Crisis*, New York, Columbia University Press, 1945, pp. 347–350.
22 W.H. Chafe, *Women and Equality: Changing Patterns in American Culture*, Oxford, Oxford University Press, 1977, p. 4.
23 Wirth, 'The problem of minority groups', pp. 347–350.
24 M. Frisch, *A Shared Authority: Essays on the Craft and Meaning of Oral and Public History*, Albany, State University of New York Press, 1990.
25 This idea is expressed by Paul Longmore in his article 'Uncovering the hidden history of people with disabilities', *Reviews in American History*, September 1987, pp. 355–364.
26 J.R. Gannon, *The Week the World Heard Gallaudet*, Washington, DC, Gallaudet University Press, 1989, p. 79 and *passim.*
27 See for example M. Johnson, 'Americans with Disabilities Act: a new day for disability rights', *The Disability Rag*, July/August 1988; I. and M. Yeager, photos, 'ADA: the signing', *Mainstream, Magazine of the Able Disabled*, September 1990, pp. 10–11.
27 I. A. Newby, *Plain Folk in the New South. Social Change and Cultural Persistence, 1880–1915*, Baton Rouge, Louisiana State University Press, 1989, p. 9.

19 Central American refugee testimonies and performed life histories in the Sanctuary movement

William Westerman

At the time of writing William Westerman was completing a doctorate at the University of Pennsylvania on Quaker involvement in refugee issues. © William Westerman, 1994. Extracted from R. Benmayor and A. Skotnes (eds), *International Yearbook of Oral History and Life Stories, vol. III: Migration and Identity*, Oxford, Oxford University Press, 1994, pp. 167–181, by permission of Oxford University Press.

To testify is to bear witness, to tell what you have seen or felt. A religious experience, perhaps, or a crime. Then to come forward and speak. To deliver the word.

December 1987. We are standing in the Cathedral of San Salvador, El Salvador, tape recorders in hand. There are around two hundred people occupying the Cathedral, just dispersed with tear gas and rubber hoses from the National Ministry of Justice. Young men are taking off their shirts to allow witnesses to photograph the red welts on their backs from the beatings. Scattered among the people in the church, at the doors, in the pews, and before us, dressed in black, their heads covered by white scarves, are the women of COMADRES, the Committee of Mothers and Relatives of Political Prisoners, Disappeared, and Assassinated of El Salvador. They are standing on the front steps of the Cathedral with banners and megaphones, telling all of San Salvador of the injustices they have witnessed. They are blocking the doors, making sure only those who bring no harm can enter. Who are you? they ask us. A North American delegation. Come on in.

One woman stands before us, and our tape recorders and cameras. She tells us why she is there, about the demonstration violently disrupted by the police. She tells us that a 22-year-old baker had been found dead just several days earlier. He had been held for a brief time in one of the political prisons. They found his corpse, the body mutilated, the skin peeled back in strips from his arms and his thighs, burns from a live wire tied around his tongue. She and the other women of COMADRES were protesting at the Justice Department to demand why.

She asks if we would like to hear her personal testimony. Yes, we tell her, shaking, while our eyes check the doors guarded by the other women for security. She gives us her testimony, and tells us about those in her family she has lost to the death squads, the police, and the government. A daughter. A son. A grandchild. She will go on fighting, speaking out, she says, until the end, until she finds justice, because she has nothing else left to live for. Only a hope that one day there will be justice, one day she might not live to see. Still, she speaks.

Most of us North Americans in the Cathedral that day had previously heard these stories, these testimonies, but without having been to Central America. Since 1980 we had been hearing these accounts across the United States, in churches and synagogues, schools and union halls. They had been brought north to us, on foot, by bus, by plane, by hundreds of thousands of refugees from El Salvador and Guatemala. In the words of one Arizona priest, in 1980 for the first time:

> Not only were there people who came here [to the church] daily for food, for handouts, that were stranded, but there were a new breed of people who came and not only were without food and clothing, but had a story to tell. And it was that story of horror, of terror, from not Mexico but from El Salvador, and from Guatemala, that demanded a new pastoral response.[1]

They came by the thousands: as many as 750,000 fleeing death squads and war in El Salvador which left over 75,000 dead; fleeing massacres, assassinations, torture and repression, hunger and disease in Guatemala, which left at least 30,000 dead as well as up to another 70,000–100,000 'disappeared', killed and buried in clandestine cemeteries.

All the refugees came with stories, histories of why they left and how they arrived. But a select few, at least a thousand, came forward in some way, and began to tell their life stories in public, to North Americans, as a way of informing the US (and Canadian) public about the repression in El Salvador and Guatemala, repression largely funded by our own US Government.

Most of those who came forward to speak during the years 1982 to 1987 were affiliated with the well-known Sanctuary movement, a loose conglomeration of over four hundred congregations which sponsored, transported, and provided legal, medical, and other assistance to Central American refugees, many of whom were undocumented.[2] Though protected by the Geneva Conventions ratified by the US Senate and the US Refugee Act of 1980, most were considered unwelcome by the Reagan and Bush administrations, under which fewer than 3 per cent could obtain political asylum.[3] Some refugees only spoke because they had to, to a judge or lawyer during deportation proceedings, if they got that far. But others, some associated with Sanctuary and some not, spoke out and continue to speak out in public, and these have included union leaders, students, human-rights workers, health workers, businesspeople, peasants. Many spoke out, in the hopes that, as one Salvadoran said to me, 'Once these people listen to us, I believe that they are not going to be the same anymore.'[4] In other words, they hoped that the US public would be moved to act and to question their own government, just as they had done in their home countries.

Those refugees who chose to go public were mostly between eighteen and thirty-five years of age, reflecting in part the age of those who had been most involved politically. Rather than deliver a political 'analysis', the refugees usually delivered a life history in public, which they themselves referred to as 'testimony', a direct translation of the Spanish *testimonio*, or 'personal experience'. These testimonies, lasting between twenty and forty-five minutes in length, were delivered in Spanish, through an interpreter, or preferably in English, since translators became notorious for their errors or failure to capture subtle shades of meaning. English also became the language of choice because North American listeners were more inclined to pay attention and be directly affected by hearing a testimony in their own language. When Spanish was used, it was more formal than usual conversational Central American Spanish, with fewer colloquialisms and clearer pronunciation, both because this accommodated the translators, who often spoke Spanish as their second language, and because the testimony took on the nature of a formal oration.

Such testimony could be given in a variety of contexts, usually in religious settings. Most commonly the personal testimony was a formal component of the ceremony in which the refugee was welcomed into sanctuary. On those occasions, it might also have been released in written form. But testimony would also have been given in a variety of other situations: in private house meetings and gatherings, in elementary and secondary schools, at colleges and universities, in churches and synagogues, in union halls, in law offices, at governmental hearings, even at fashion shows, and on regional tours to areas where there were interested people, but no formal sanctuary communities. It could also have been given in the course of a formal interview with a reporter or with an ethnographer, as in my case as part of a long-term, field-based study.

We can now safely say that testimony was effective, because of the rapid growth in the Sanctuary movement and other Central American solidarity movements during the early 1980s. The Sanctuary movement in the southwest US actually grew out of the experience of listening to the stories of refugees just having crossed the border. A number of Sanctuary workers I interviewed remembered distinctly the first time they ever heard a refugee speak and could relate to me the story they heard. Word of mouth, personal visits, and refugee narratives were responsible for the participation of most of the active congregations. The Sanctuary movement might possibly have grown anyway had there not been personal testimony, but the success in converting the sceptical and the 'apolitical' to a politicized stance, as well as the involvement of the religious sector in the larger Central American Solidarity movement, was largely due to the strength of a few individuals who learnt to speak out, to bear witness to the injustice they had known and were committed to end.

What emerged was an overall consistent traditional pattern to these narratives. Testimony was always in the first person, with episodes concerning third parties – children, siblings, parents – mentioned, but usually only in relation to the speaker. Most examples I heard and compared showed the same structure, including six definite sections: (1) introduction and background, (2) life and activity in the home country, (3) persecution, (4) escape, (5) exile, and (6) analysis and call to action.[5] This is the general chronological pattern, too. This structure was found to be the most successful with North American audiences. While the structure seems intuitive, the choice of autobiography was instead cultural and practical, as Central Americans realized North Americans were much more willing to listen to personal experiences than political discussion. Fundamental parts of the story would not be omitted, but short episodes, details, and descriptions could be lengthened, shortened, or dropped altogether, depending on the audience. The important themes and episodes, according to one refugee, are those 'which are marked in your life'.[6]

Certain historical episodes (such as the military take-over of El Salvador's National University, the assassination and funeral of Archbishop Oscar Romero, or fleeing from aerial bombardments, to name a few) were part of the experience of so many people that they recurred as traditional motifs. Other, more personal episodes were of course unique to the teller, such as a story of capture and torture, but similar thematically to those told by others. Thus each testimony was personal, yet commented upon the larger social picture.

Rather than existing in isolation, these testimonies were each part of that larger mural of the recent history of Central America, and they corroborated one another by offering overlapping perspectives of the same historical event. Indeed, considerable interchange and story-sharing did go on among refugees in the United States. The structure of having two or more refugees in one evening's house or church meeting made such public interaction unavoidable, but also refugees worked together in human rights and church offices and socialized together, trading experiences informally and analysing speaking strategies more formally in business meetings. Discussions among refugees yielded pointers and suggestions, with less experienced speakers learning about form, and these same newer arrivals giving updates on recent political developments at home. Though individual experiences were often different, through refugee interactions testimonies become 'traditional' in their structure.

In the case of Central America refugee narratives, each story was the story of an individual, but only moved people to action when placed within the context of an entire nation of similar testimonies. Hearing one testimony was not sufficient. Nor was content alone the significant feature, and eventually it became important for North Americans not only to hear a variety of refugee testimonies but to visit Central America and hear the testimonies of those who had not left and who continued (and continue) to experience repression on a day-to-day basis while struggling for justice. And it became important for Central Americans in the United States to develop a speaking style that would engage listeners, without making an audience feel threatened or become bored. That meant concentrating on human, anecdotal narrative and removing political commentary that could be construed as inflammatory or accusatory.

More recent research, including a brief trip to El Salvador in 1987, made me aware that testimony in North America was merely that *testimonio* in Central America which had been brought north. In other words, the concept of testimony was not devised in and for the United States, though the idea of delivering testimony to North Americans *in their own country and language* was. As a verbal form conveying historical or eyewitness information, thousands of people continue to speak out in El Salvador and Guatemala, painting a canvas so large and complex that together it gives an oral historical portrait of a people at war, seeking justice.[7] What went on in the United States, the testimony from those who had left or escaped, was only a small part of a larger phenomenon. [. . .]

Why did (and do) these people speak out, and why did they speak out in the form that they did, that is, telling their personal history? For one thing, these personal narratives were also religious testimony within the framework of the widely practised theology of liberation. This radical reinterpretation of official, standard religion emphasizes the liberation of the poor and oppressed from the repressive situations and societies in which they live. Developed at the grass-roots level since Pope John XXIII, and becoming widely practised in Latin America since 1972, it became closely linked with the liberation movements in Nicaragua, El Salvador, and Guatemala, and elsewhere in Latin America.[8] Liberation theology focuses on the active role of the community and the individual in ending the sinful state of oppression and violence perpetrated by the state and in building the Kingdom of God on earth. This religious interpretation is not limited to theory alone, but also demands action.

Testimony, then, became one such form of action. The conversion experience of liberation theology is known as 'conscientization': the process of becoming conscious of the often unjust political and social reality and its root causes. In bringing the message of liberation theology to North America, refugees had to first make North Americans aware of the social, economic, and political conditions in Latin America, as well as of the political reality in the United States and the role of the US Government in maintaining conditions as they are throughout Latin America.

Clearly, the personal testimony in this context was indeed religious, and one essential purpose of giving testimony was to bring about the conscientization in North Americans. Most of the refugee speakers were devoutly Roman Catholic, and many had backgrounds in the practice of liberation theology in the Christian base communities, the local study- or worship-groups through which the popular church is organized. Giving testimony and denouncing oppression is therefore one way of being a good Christian. The refugees asked North Americans for a similar conversion, such that US citizens would side not with the oppressors (the governments of the United States, El Salvador, and Guatemala) but with the oppressed. The refugees asked for – and in many cases secured – a commitment to social change and social justice.

Also from liberation theology comes an idea central to testimony and crucial for its success: the creation of solidarity between North and Central Americans, between the middle and upper classes of the North, and the poor and oppressed in Latin America (as well as, I might add, the poor and oppressed in the North, too). The Central Americans were more than aware of the distance between the two cultures; that distance is in itself responsible for the problem of North American apathy and ignorance concerning the US Government's actions or its heavy involvement in Central American affairs (up to $1.5 million US tax dollars a day were spent in El Salvador alone for some years, for example, not to mention the deployment of US military advisers in combat, US funding of the Nicaraguan *contras*, and the militarization of Honduras). Refugee testimony was personal and included the essential function of conveying a part of the history that was not recorded in the official media of the state and dominant culture.

In order to achieve this awakening, intimacy needed to be created[9] and personal identification with the refugee became essential. The refugee had to present himself or herself as a complete, three-dimensional, feeling human being in order to show, quite simply, that the war and repression had very real victims. By performing their life histories, the refugees presented themselves as fully human; and as they described their pain and their experience they encouraged identification, sympathy, and empathy, leading, they hoped, to action on the part of the listeners. In the words of one Salvadoran in Philadelphia, 'The [North American] people, they can feel us, you know, they can – they can hear us, they can see us, they can *think* [of us] . . . human beings – we have been suffering that, that situation.'[10] Testimony was, in an oft-quoted phrase of Archbishop Oscar Romero, 'the voice of the voiceless', and in North America it had the additional feature of making these statistics human.

Intimacy and personal identification ideally led to more politicized solidarity, going beyond empathy to concrete work on behalf of the poor and oppressed. Paulo Freire, the Brazilian educator and theorist, writes that the:

> oppressor is solidary with the oppressed only when he stops regarding the oppressed as an abstract category and sees them as persons who have been unjustly dealt with, deprived of their voice, cheated in the sale of their labor – when he stops making pious, sentimental, and individualistic gestures and risks an act of love.[11]

Speaking itself became one way to render the oppressed no longer as abstractions, but as representatives of all too real human suffering in Central America. Speaking, and committed listening, became one such risky act of love, a love which in the words of theologian Gustavo Gutiérrez, 'seeks also to liberate the oppressors from their own power, from their ambition, and from their selfishness . . . One loves the oppressors by liberating them from their inhuman condition as oppressors, by liberating them from themselves.'[12] Refugee testimony was a manifestation of this act of love, even when it involved disagreement or conflict.

The functions of testimony, then, were fourfold. First, speaking itself was a political act, an act of denouncing the injustice from which the refugees fled. It was also a religious act, a way of concretizing faith so that it transcended belief to include action as a manifestation of that belief. Thirdly, testimony created solidarity between the refugees and those representatives of a people whose government was held responsible for creating refugees in the first place, and in turn, that solidarity led to further political action by US citizens. And fourthly, there was and continues to be a therapeutic function, in the sense that speaking out is a way of making sense of a destructive, violent past, a past in which one often felt victim, and of triumphing over that experience, turning it into a motivation for living and working in the pursuit of certain social ideals. One Salvadoran told me that when he first entered this country he had hoped to remain anonymous, but his outlook changed after being encouraged to speak out. For him, it was a way of overcoming feelings of helplessness and depression.[13] I would also say that, significantly, testimony need not have been a spoken narrative. I have heard songs of personal experience, seen narrative embroidered tapestries from refugee camps, and have heard refugees mention 'testimony of life', that is, when one gives one's life for the purpose of social justice, as in the case of a martyred priest or nun.

Testimony can be visual too; one refugee asked me in Spanish (the first time I ever met him, in fact), 'You want my testimony? This is my testimony', and he pulled up his sleeve to reveal a deep gouged out scar from a bullet wound in his shoulder, received, as I later found out, when he was taken out to a garbage dump with other prisoners, lined up and shot.

Testimony is about people rising from a condition of being victims, objects of history, and taking charge of their history, becoming subjects, actors in it. History no longer makes them; they make it, write it, speak it. On one level, this concerns the everyday struggle to stay alive. But this also concerns at another level the role of the individual in history, and how all of us depict that experience in our narratives. Anthropologist Barbara Myerhoff, in describing a life-history class among elderly Jews in Los Angeles, commented that:

> Conditions sometimes make the members of a generational cohort acutely self-conscious, and then they become active participants in their own history; they provide their own sharp, insistent definitions of themselves, their own explanations for their past and their destiny. They are then knowing actors in a historical drama which they themselves script, rather than subjects in someone else's study.[14]

Becoming the subject, the 'active participant' in one's one history requires, according to Freire, questioning, speaking out, being critical of one's own life.[15] Freire has written, in his earlier *Pedagogy of the Oppressed* – that:

> There is no true word that is not at the same time a praxis. Therefore to speak a true word is to transform the world . . .
>
> Human existence cannot be silent, nor can it be nourished by false words, but only by true words, with which men transform the world. To exist, humanly, is to *name* the world, to change it . . . Men are not built in silence, but in word, in work, in action-reflection.
>
> But while to say the true word – which is work, which is praxis – is to transform the world, saying that word is not the privilege of some few men, but the right of every man.[16]

Testimony was, and in Latin America continues to be, precisely this, the naming of the world by denouncing the oppression, the beginning of dialogue between Central and North Americans, and the liberation of individuals, and eventually a people, through the process of becoming historical narrators, and thus actors. Testimony is a word that transforms, but moreover, a word that emerges from the critical examination of one's own life by those deeply involved in the shaping of history. To give testimony is to bear witness; it is to tell the unofficial story, to construct a history of people, of individual lives, a history not of those in power, but by those confronted by power, and becoming *em*powered.

Finally, at the risk of romanticizing refugee testimony, I would like to make the argument that this utilitarian speech was also a folk art form and that it subscribed to a traditional aesthetic which was both conscious and well defined. The terms 'art' and 'aesthetic' can be misleading, suggesting the creation of pleasure or beauty. But certainly folklorists recognize that not only can the utilitarian be art but functional qualities can also render something aesthetic. With folk art, the judgement of what is 'good' or aesthetic' often rests with the community itself, and this was very true of refugee testimony. Good testimony, as defined by the refugees, was that which was most effective in moving the audience to a new level of understanding or action. The good speaker, like a good story-teller, was responsive to the different interests of each audience. He or she would have prepared those topics to be emphasized and would have decided on the level of political analysis to be included, for example, concentrating on repression against workers in a talk to a labour union audience. What would make the content or structure 'good' was the effect the talk had on the audience, to move them, motivate them, make them reflect. The best testimony was that which was easy to understand, got the point across, and reached people on an emotional and moral as well as intellectual level. That required having an important story to tell, and understanding how to turn that personal experience into something that others – people who in this case were linguistically, culturally, politically, often religiously, and economically different – could appreciate. The testimony was more important than the abilities of the speaker, the process of subsequent action ultimately more important.

Unlike many forms of narrative story-telling, the goal was not to come up with, in folklorist Richard Bauman's words, 'artful texts, identified on independent formal grounds',[17] though many testimonies were beautiful in the sense of being emotionally moving. But as this was a group of people speaking from a politically marginal position, most often in broken English or poorly translated Spanish, their materials were determined by necessity and their aesthetic ideals by political as well as cultural and religious factors. Without recognizing that, we might fail to appreciate what is good or beautiful – that is, artistic – in these narratives and might miss their message altogether. Furthermore the performers could 'be both admired and feared – admired for their artistic skill and power and for the enhancement of experience they provide, feared because of the potential they represent for . . . transforming the *status quo*'.[18] That status quo could be of course political, but also personal, since the refugees implicitly (and sometimes explicitly, later) asked for commitment and action in everyday life that North Americans generally were unprepared – and may otherwise have felt unable – to give. Though in some ways this separated them from the North American population to whom they were talking, such narratives helped to establish them as representatives of the struggles for social justice that were being waged back in their countries of origin. Thus there was a tension between allying themselves with the North Americans with whom they had to, wanted to, work everyday, and remaining distinct, Salvadorans and Guatemalans with their own histories, identities, and experiences that were separate from those of their North American audiences.

In that context, inflammatory speeches which emphasized too much political analysis would have been threatening to a North American audience and were dismissed by refugees as ineffective. Often, it was the most personal, and most understated talks that had the most impact. John A. Robinson has noted that one possible motivation for telling a personal narrative is 'to instigate action . . . in a way that avoids preaching or invoking one or another type of authority'.[19] Such narratives can be one method of accomplishing this because the 'very typicality of an incident . . . recommends it for narration, rather than its remarkableness'. This may be particularly true when the action in the narrative is typical for the speaker, but not for the audience. Hence, 'commonplace activities may excite great interest in listeners who are unfamiliar with the sphere of life to be discussed'.[20] By personalizing the history of Central American, then, the refugees could offer authority without being seen as authoritarian. And, it was the unfortunately commonplace quality of the episodes which made testimony so effective. The atrocities and the poverty described are part of the everyday life of Central Americans. Thus a narrative told in an understated, almost offhand manner could actually be more effective than a fiery speech, since the content had not been presented as something remarkable. The implication was that the miserable situation was almost normal, but still not acceptable. If it were not seen as normal, such acts of violence and oppression would seem isolated and would to some extent not be cause for such alarm or concentrated political activity in response.

We can also therefore begin to understand these refugees as historical actors by looking further at the genre of performed life history. The life histories became powerful tools in the construction of a more just society when wielded by devoted performers skilled in their use. As Myerhoff notes, such actors '"make" themselves . . . an activity which is not inevitable or automatic but reserved for special people and special circumstances'.[21] If, in Dell Hymes's words, the acceptance of responsibility determines a 'breakthrough into performance', then testimony was an example of performance *par excellence*. They accepted – even grabbed – responsibility 'not only for knowledge but also for performance . . . [in order] to shape history'[22] and not only for verbal performance but for historical performance as well. By being witnesses from Central America, they earned the right to be authentic speakers, the right to take on that responsibility. Their tradition demanded of its bearers careful attention to an aesthetic, sensitivity to an audience, the memory of the past, a view to the future, and considerable bravery just to assume the responsibilities of performance.

NOTES

1 Interview with Fr Matthews (pseudonym), Nogales, Arizona, 2 August 1986. Because of the legal history of the Sanctuary movement and people involved in it, although some people were willing to allow me to use their names, I have made the choice – preferring to err on the side of safety – to use pseudonyms.
2 By 1988 the structure of personal testimony began to change, at least outside the south-western, border areas of the country. The focus shifted away from 'protecting the refugee' to defending the right of the civilians, and especially the displaced, back home. As interest in the Sanctuary movement waned (some congregations remained active into the 1990s), the focus on publicly performed life stories faded too.
3 For the best summary of the legality of Salvadoran and Guatemalan refugees, see I. Bau, *This Ground is Holy*, Mahwah, N.J., 1985, pp. 39–56.
4 Interview with Diego (pseudonym), Los Angeles, California, 11 August 1986.
5 Which could really be two sections, depending on the individual. In order to determine exactly, it would be necessary to examine linguistic and paralinguistic markers, such as particles and pauses, to see exactly how each speaker structured the narrative and where the 'sections' were divided. The outline I have provided above refers primarily to a plot structure, rather than a linguistic one.
6 A comment made to me by Gregorio (pseudonym), a Salvadoran in Philadelphia, in 1986.
7 Collections and examples include M. Argueta, *One Day of Life*, (trans by B. Brow), New York, 1983 (orig. published 1980), the testimony of a Salvadoran peasant woman in novel form; A. Hernandez, *León de Piedra*, El Salvador, 1981; M. López Vigil (ed.), *Marxismo y cristianismo en Morazán: Testimonio del Padre Rogelio*, El Salvador, 1987; examples published in R. Golden and M. McConnell, *Sanctuary: The New Underground Railroad*, Maryknoll, N.Y., 1986; R. Menchú,

234 Advocacy and empowerment

I . . . *Rigoberta Menchú*, (ed. by E. Burgos-Debray, trans. by A. Wright), London, 1984; and V. Montejo, *Testimony: Death of a Guatemalan Village* (trans. by V. Perera, Willimantic, Conn., 1987.

8 Two of the best introductions to liberation theology in Latin-American politics are P. Berryman, *The Religious Roots of Rebellion*, Maryknoll, N.Y., 1984; and P. Lernoux, *Cry of the People*, New York, 1980.

9 Part of this process, then, is what S.K. Dolby-Stahl calls the creation of intimacy. 'The higher the percentage of "private" folklore embedded in a story, the more likely the creation of intimacy is a major motivation for the storytelling' ('A literary-folkloristic methodology for the study of meaning in personal narrative', *Journal of Folklore Research*, 1985, vol. 22, pp. 47–48). The motivations for creating the intimacy in this case are significant. In order to overcome the cultural, linguistic, historical, and political differences, some sense of a 'shared inner life' between Central and North Americans had to be created.

10 Gregorio, 1986.

11 P. Freire, *Pedagogy of the Oppressed* (trans. by M.B. Ramos), New York, 1970 (first published 1968), pp. 33–35.

12 G. Gutiérrez, *A Theology of Liberation* (trans. by Sister C. Inda and J. Eagleson), Maryknoll, N.Y., 1973 (first published 1971), pp. 275–276.

13 Personal interview with Diego, Los Angeles, 11 August 1986. His experience was by no means unique. See also I. Agger and S. B. Jensen, 'Testimony as ritual and evidence in psychotherapy for political refugees', *Journal of Traumatic Stress*, 1990, vol. 3, pp. 115–130; and A.J. Cienfuegos and C. Monelli, 'The testimony of political repression as therapeutic instrument', *American Journal of Orthopsychiatry*, 1983, vol. 53, pp. 43–51.

14 B. Myerhoff, 'Telling one's story', *Center Magazine*, 1980, vol. 13, no. 2. p. 22.

15 P. Freire, *The Politics of Education*, (trans. by D. Macedo and L. Slover), South Hadley, Mass, 1985, p. 199.

16 Freire, *Pedagogy*, pp. 75–76.

17 R. Bauman, 'Verbal art as performance', *American Anthropologist*, 1975, vol. 77, p. 293.

18 Ibid., p. 305.

19 J.A. Robinson, 'Personal narratives reconsidered', *Journal of American Folklore*, 1981, vol. 94, p. 61.

20 Ibid., p. 62.

21 Myerhof, 'Telling', p. 22.

22 D. Hymes, '*In Vain I Tried to Tell You*', Philadelphia, 1981, p. 134.

20 The Gulag in memory

Irina Sherbakova

Irina Sherbakova is a freelance Moscow journalist. © Irina Sherbakova, 1992. Reprinted from L. Passerini (ed.), *International Yearbook of Oral History and Life Stories vol. I: Memory and Totalitarianism*, Oxford, Oxford University Press, 1992, pp. 103–115, by permission of Oxford University Press.

The uniqueness of our Soviet situation lies in the decades through which historical truth within our country lived on only through underground memory. Publications which appeared in the West, broadcasts from foreign radio stations, and manuscripts secretly circulated in samizdat form only began to seep through comparatively widely as recently as the 1960s and 1970s. Before that there was only silence, or at the most, rare whispers between intimates, because to tell anyone about the prisons and concentration camps was deadly dangerous.

I began collecting accounts of the Stalinist camps myself in the mid-1970s. At first I only recorded women whom I knew well as close family friends: often I had listened to their stories since my childhood. Gradually the circle of people I was recording widened, as I was sent from one person to another. I started to use a tape recorder in 1978. Altogether, I have now recorded 250 ex-prisoners. Sometimes I have listened to someone for months, but with others I have only talked for a few hours. The interviewees fall into several groups, but the largest number are 'victims of 1937', imprisoned at the height of the terror, followed by those convicted in the renewed repressions of the late 1940s and early 1950s. A much smaller group of my interviewees started their prison lives in the 1920s. The first of them all was imprisoned in 1919, and the last in 1953. Two-thirds of them are women, which may well be a typical proportion of survivors generally. In terms of nationality, the majority are Russian, one-third are Jewish, and the rest are Polish, German, Latvian, Armenian, and so on. As to social background, the majority come from the urban intelligentsia – doctors, teachers, scholars, students, or journalists – while others were party workers or from the armed forces.

For the Soviet regime, memory itself was intrinsically a serious threat. The entire history of the past, and above all of the revolution and the civil war, was rewritten and mythologized. Memory was made to function in a truly Orwellian style: what had been peace was now declared war, and the Soviet version of memory became oblivion.

The time span of many decades, compared with just twelve years of Nazi power in Germany, has shaped the character of memory and recollection.

Those who fell before the waves of repression in the 1920s – beginning with members of the so-called 'exploiter classes', former aristocrats and White officers, followed by Social Democrats and social revolutionaries, and later by Trotskyites – were, as a rule, unable to emerge from the Gulag system before the 1950s. My interviews include many of this kind. For example, Daria Samaelova was first arrested while still at school, at the age of seventeen, on the grounds that her older brother had also been arrested as a Trotskyite opposition sympathizer. This was in 1927, in the city of Baku in the Caucasus; she was released after two months. But a year later she was arrested again and deported for three years. In 1933 she tried to re-enter normal life and, hiding her past, enrolled as a student in Moscow University. But after a year she was rearrested and exiled to Tartaria. Then in 1936, she was once again rearrested, this time receiving a prison sentence of ten years for Trotskyist counter-revolutionary activity. In 1946, after her release, she was permanently exiled to Kolyma (in the far north-east of Siberia). Samaelova was only rehabilitated after 1956. And far from being a unique case, hers was a characteristic path which hundreds of thousands of others followed. It is unusual only in that she survived such a past to be still alive today, so that I was able to record her history.

Obviously it is impossible to repress the memory of such a fate: that would mean forgetting one's entire life. The effect is rather different: more of a confusion – especially in the memory of prisons and camps – of the superficial distinctions between imprisonment and freedom. Today they all repeat the observation, which is now a commonplace, that the Soviet Union in the mid-1930s was itself an immense concentration camp: even if millions of its people, particularly of the generation born after the revolution, considered their 'cell' the brightest and most beautiful in the world. Thus, those who had served their term and were released into freedom still felt – either consciously or unconsciously – that the Soviet Union itself was a concentration camp, and therefore chose not to return to the 'big world', but instead settled down in Siberia or the far east of Russia, living near the camps, continuing to work on the camp farms on different tasks as exiles. The most far-sighted of them did understand the system. But where could they go, where else could they settle? Ex-prisoners were forbidden to live in the big cities, and in smaller towns a stranger would always be under suspicion. Their fears were sound, for a new wave of repression followed in the 1940s, and those so-called 'recidivists' who had settled down in new places were rearrested and sent off into exile: an exile which is often remembered as scarcely less terrible than the concentration camps, with no work, nothing to eat, and nothing to provide warmth. Indeed, those who were sentenced to the camps in the post-war period – with the exception, of course, of those sent to hard-labour camps – often told me, 'You were better fed in the concentration camps than in freedom.' The camps formed a network spread over Siberia, the far East, Kazakhstan, and so almost the whole country, which was essential to the immense Soviet industrial and agricultural projects, supplying a labour force which therefore had to be fed. Life was certainly tough in these camps, but their objective, in contrast to many of the camps in the repressions of 1937–9, was never annihilation through mass executions or death through starvation. The prisoners in the post-war camps adapted themselves to these conditions, and prepared to spend their whole lives in the camps, to which they had already been typically sentenced for ten to twenty-five years. When release came, after the death of Stalin, it was neither anticipated nor easy, and this is partly why there often is a lack of clarity and coherent perspective, and in some respects confusion, in their reminiscences. For them freedom did not come in a single, swift joyful act. Release demanded trouble, letters, and petitions. Re-entry into ordinary life was slow. They had long struggles to win rehabilitation, a flat, or a pension. In the Soviet situation it was very difficult to perceive the end of repression in an individual's fate, not merely in memory, but simply in real life. For many of them the repressions have scarcely finished even in the most recent years, when they have at last been able to talk openly about their own pasts.

What and how did they remember and recollect, thirty or fifty years ago – and today?

It may sound paradoxical, but we in Russia today are certainly persuaded of how short the span of human memory can be. In the last three or four years we have so thoroughly examined – as well as watched on the screen and heard on the radio – so many reminiscences of the repression, the prisons and the concentration camps of the pre-Stalinist, Stalinist, and post-Stalinist periods, that very quickly it suddenly seems as if this past was always known and remembered. Yet a mere ten or fifteen years ago, when the events of the 1920s–50s were much closer and their witnesses younger, it seemed that everything of the past had disappeared into oblivion, and that living witnesses were lone individuals: for they were still in deep concealment.

The first wave of recollections of the camps and prisons poured out during the Khrushchev thaw, when the first ex-prisoners began to talk about their experiences. Those who came back can be roughly divided into two groups. There were those who wanted to forget what had happened to them. When I first began my recording in the 1970s, I encountered, among the families of ex-convicts who had married and had children after their release, some members who did not know about their wife's or mother's past. But there was another group who right through their imprisonment, sometimes subconsciously and sometimes explicitly, had wanted to remember. A determination had developed in them that what had happened to them and those with them should be fixed in the memory and perhaps later recounted: and this had helped them to survive. Many others who wrote their reminiscences in 'fresh footsteps' in the late 1950s and early 1960s spoke about this. They often took the attitude that if the chance to recollect was missed it would be irretrievably lost to us. Perhaps we can recall the recording of the stories – the fresh stories – in the late 1950s, of those who were waiting in queues at the military prosecution offices to obtain their certificates of rehabilitation. At that time there were some among those returning who undertook Moscow 'lecture tours', orally recounting camp experiences, because interest about the Gulag was so high among the intelligentsia on the other side of the barbed wire. But, in literary form, the facts about the prisons and camps were as a rule tragi-comic. In particular, this was the time when certain expressions and terms from camp jargon began to pop up constantly in conversational language. Nevertheless, the real picture of the repressions and of prison and camp life remained entirely hidden. For beyond imprisonment glimmered a ghastlier fantasy. The reality of the camps had been terrible and fantastic enough, but the whole horror was submerged in the incredibly depressing and petty everyday struggles for survival. This was why the appearance of Solzhenitsyn's novel, *One Day in the Life of Ivan Denisovich* seemed so important. I well remember how, reading it as a schoolgirl, I was above all puzzled: I could not understand what had produced such a powerful impression on my parents. I had expected something horrific, freezing the blood in my veins, but all that Solzhenitsyn offered was hunger, cold, filth, and unmanageable labour, a mere biological existence, in which every rag and every tiny crumb of bread took on an existential significance. But ex-prisoners at last saw a rendering of part of their own lives in the novel, and a stream of recollections poured out with the journal reviews. However, the camp theme was very soon officially prohibited again, while official biographies began to use formulas to symbolize that a person had suffered under the repressions: 'In the 1930s and 1940s he worked in the far North', or 'his life was torn apart in 1937'.

But by now it was already impossible to force all the witnesses to subside again. The books of Solzhenitsyn and the recollections of Evgeny Ginsburg and Varlam Shalamoff were reprinted and broadly circulated in samizdaty. Above all, some ex-convicts were asserting the need to talk about their past and of being together with other survivors. Quietly, those who had been in Kolyma, Vorkuta, or Inta were meeting. Nor was this surprising. Among those repressed under the infamous political Decree 58, especially in the 1930s, were many active city intellectuals. It was well known that in almost every concentration camp a university could have been opened. Links made in the camps were often maintained in liberty. People met together and continued to reminisce or even read aloud their testimonies, which had been introduced as court evidence.

On the other hand, to speak to outsiders brought a fear, a fully justifiable fear, that everything might be repeated. With my informants in the 1970s, I constantly used to find that they became instantly silent on seeing my tape recorder. An additional hindrance was their memory of the false confessions, obtained through physical and psychological tortures by the NKVD – the People's Commissariat of Internal Affairs, the internal security police – which were preserved somewhere in the archives. Only now, after having at last got the opportunity of getting to know some official investigation papers, including the minutes of interrogations, and reading the incredible evidence from their nearest and closest – husband, lover, or friend – have I finally been able to confront what forced victims either to keep their silence or to expunge whole sections of their consciousness. Recently, an archivist told me the story of a woman who applied to him to be shown the papers on her father, who had perished in the late 1930s. When he looked at this evidence he discovered that the unique accusatory material was that of this very daughter, who was then aged sixteen. They had taken her to the interrogation and, already frightened by this, she had used some careless phrase of her father, in an argument with him – just letting off steam – the previous evening. But afterwards, of course, she did everything to put this out of her consciousness – and indeed she 'forgot'.

But the perpetually recurring question was how those who were strong and brave people in ordinary life came to denounce themselves and others. The limit of endurance was very plainly explained to me by Ivan Fitterman, an important constructor at the largest automobile factory in the country, who was arrested in the 1950s and sentenced to twenty-five years as a participant in Zionist plotting. He was in the notorious Sukhanovskaya prison, within 40 kilometres of Moscow, which was intended to destroy all who persisted with resistance: 'If they needed to get evidence from you, they got it. Or they killed you. If you did not sign what you were given, you knew that the moment they waved their hand at you, you might be no longer necessary for their evidence.'

'The investigator responsible for our rehabilitation', recalled Irina Kin, the widow of a famous Soviet journalist shot in 1938, herself imprisoned for ten years in the camps, 'showed me documents about my husband. I knew his handwriting; I read how he denounced himself – and I began to be hysterical. But he said to me, "I thought you were a strong woman."'

For many years people found it hard to understand why the punitive administration so persistently sought these confessions. Probably there is one explanation: that in a totalitarian society in the period of total terror, the general guilt needed to be shared by all – by both victims and executioners.

In general, the problem of who were victims and who were executioners in the Soviet context is extraordinarily complex. It is not a myth that those who were shot sometimes died with the name of Stalin on their lips, maintaining to the last minute their belief that there beloved leader knew nothing of the repression. Those arrested in the early and mid-1930s included a high percentage of believing communists. Many even returned from the concentration camps as convinced communists and rejoined the party, by no means merely for the sake of their pension and privileges, or for an easier way of fitting into normal life – although that was one reason – but because they continued to believe in the excellence of communist ideas, explaining their own misfortunes in terms of mistakes and distortions, and also continued to believe in the personal virtues of Stalin. Lenin remained a sacred image, and all that was necessary, as they would then say, was to return 'to Leninist lines'. The ironic consequence of the Gulag system was that both victim and executioner could share a common ideological platform. Neither the investigators, nor the guards or the administrator of the camps could be ideological enemies for arrested communists. Hence, the first thought of those arrested often was that the arrest must be a mistake, a misunderstanding; that the investigator was not an enemy, like the Gestapo, but a Soviet man who simply needed to be convinced that you were not guilty. It happened in some cases that the NKVD investigators turned out to be acquaintances whom they had met in general friendship, and who by no means turned on full moral or psychological pressure. 'There look, but if we had behaved ourselves well, we could be drinking tea together with you at Mr H.'s', recalled Olga Penzo, a ballerina arrested in 1937.

Hence some of those things seem wholly incomprehensible to someone of a different generation: like those pages in the album of an ex-convict, where I noticed among the photographs from the late 1950s a snap of herself with other women at one of the Crimean health spas. One of these women, it was explained, had been the governor of the camp in which my informant had spent some years. Already in the Khrushchev period they had met again in the spa and were photographed together as long-remembered acquaintances. 'She wasn't the worst from there', Katya Gavralova, who had spent eight years in the Kolyma camp, explained to me – 'there were some much worse than her'.

Now, there are former camp administrators who write letters to ex-prisoners asking them if they will confirm, for their personal records, that they were decent and discontented with the party organization. And the ex-prisoners reply: 'Yes, he wasn't so bad, at least he didn't steal from people, or starve them as much as the governor of the next camp.' It is important to note that among survivors a large percentage survived through being in relatively privileged situations, working in the administrative structure close to camp authority.

None of this is surprising: it was similar in the Nazi concentration camps. The difference was that in the Soviet camps the victims were often identifying themselves with the very regime which was inflicting their repression. Thus I have often heard such views expressed as: 'When I was in the prison or camps I was ashamed in front of young women students, or foreigners, about what was happening in my Soviet country . . .' After the war it was still shameful in front of Latvian women, Estonians, or west Ukrainians. And the source of this shame was in their genuine loyalty to the regime, even in the camp or prison. This is the striking meaning behind the apparently absurd remark in the story of a German woman who came as a political immigrant to the Soviet Union in the 1930s and was arrested there: 'How glad I was that I could participate in the building of socialism at Kolyma, how much more incongruous it would have been for me to have served my sentence in some Nazi prison . . .'

Sometimes the links between the two sides were superimposed quite fantastically. Tamara Galkina was the wife of an important military man, but she fell in love with a young subordinate and went off with him. He had an active career in the NKVD. In 1937 they came in the night but, to their surprise, they did not arrest him, but took her – to her first husband, who was being held in connection with the Tukachevsky case. Her first husband Mikhael was shot, and she herself was sentenced to ten years in the camps. Meanwhile her second husband went into the Gulag as a high-up administrator and at the moment of her release he arrived in Magadan, the capital of the Kolyma region, as a general, one of the chief administrators of the immense network of camps in the far east. He summoned Tamara to him. She knew that after her arrest he had given evidence against her, refuted her, and then divorced her. He now proposed that she should stay with him. She refused. But years later, after her rehabilitation, when he was already retired, they were reconciled, and right up to his death they regularly called on each other, and drank tea together like old friends . . .

However, this NKVD general was an exceptional success among those who were arrested and those who were shot. In the 1930s tens of thousands of the NKVD workers themselves perished. They led the repressions from the start; they prepared the process of fabrication of documentation; and then they imprisoned themselves. There were many occasions in later year when the sometime tormentor stumbled on his victim in a camp where both were imprisoned.

In the Soviet situation it was possible for a man to change his life role several times: to shoot White officers in the civil war, to participate in the crushing of the Kronstadt rising, then to struggle actively against the socialist opposition, destroying social revolutionaries and Trotskyists, and later to lead collectivization and the breaking-up of kulak farms with an iron fist, and finally in 1937 or 1938 to become a victim of repression himself. As late as the 1970s, I still often hear ecstatic and uncritical recollections about participation in the civil war, or in collectivization: everything was good and proper, until they were struck by the sudden blow of their own arrest.

There are some questions which I always put to my informants: at the moment of their arrest, how far did they understand what was going on in their country; when were their eyes opened, if they were opened – on arrest, in prison, in the camps, or even later? Very few of them correctly appreciated what was happening because, as a rule, the earliest people who found themselves under threat, either because of their background or because of their political beliefs, were already overrun by the gathering speed of the machine of terror in the 1920s. The least prepared and most blind were the communist victims of 1937. 'It seemed an inexplicable nightmare', I heard again and again, or 'The only thing which came into my head was "It's a Fascist conspiracy."' 'I scarcely understood anything', recalled Dina Yankovskaya; 'as a scientist, a biologist, when at the beginning of 1939 by a happy chance I found myself released from prison, I threw myself into writing letters to the government: to confirm that all those people in prison with me were innocents, and that the NKVD had been infiltrated by Fascists.' The only surprising thing about her story is that rather than immediately rearresting her, they sent her son to the battle-front. She herself survived the Leningrad blockade, before the authorities, after nearly ten years, recollected her letter and arrested her.

'I understood nothing at that stage,' a Comintern worker, Georgei Rubinstein, told me, 'so that after my arrest my first thought in the Lubyanka prison was "They're testing me through a routine task."'

Not surprisingly, nor deliberately do interviewees evoke how far what was happening in the prisons recalled the theatre of the absurd. The wife of a well-known Soviet aviator, who, like him, was arrested, was forced during her interrogation in the Butyrskaya prison to write her husband a letter just as if she was at liberty: everything was in order, she was well and active, the children were studying, and so on. Other arrested women managed – from their cells – to change their clothing, have their hair done at the hairdresser's, and arrange to see their husbands, who also needed to think that they were free. Understandably, they remember the details of such absurd episodes throughout their lives.

In recollections of the Gulag there is always a great significance in the detail, in episodes, in the fine particulars of life: both because of its continuous meanness and equally because it was on this that life itself depended. As a rule, it is the first arrest or the first cell, which is remembered best of all, probably because it came as such a powerful shock to one who, up to that very moment, had been an innocent person. Often, they still hold the whole view of what they saw in their parting glance as they were marched off, their last look at their old life: a handful of sweets scattered on the table, the teapot on the cooking range, the linen on the washtub, the unfinished report on their last work trip which had seemed so important, or the kind neighbours who had managed to return a borrowed coffee grinder just five minutes before the arrest. Each spare little shred of clothing, the stockings given to someone, the mittens stolen from you, they all remained fixed in the memory for decades.

With the millions of Soviet people who had gone through the camps scattered across the whole country, I never cease to be surprised by the part played by unexpected encounters, meetings, intersections, or coincidences: how a man saw someone, how a woman was in prison with someone else. For example, I remembered an episode from Evgeny Ginsburg's beautiful memoir, *Life's Hard Path*, set in the Butyrskaya prison: 'People peered eagerly into their faces – who were they? What about those four, for instance? In such absurd evening dresses with exaggerated *décolletés*, and high-heeled slippers ... Everything crumpled, pulled at ... That's the guests of Rudzutak. They were all arrested at his house as his guests.' Jan Rudzutak had been a major political and party activist and a Politburo member at the moment of his arrest. What had happened to these women who flashed past in the pages of Ginsburg's book to be devoured by the vast camp system? And then, fifty years later, one of these same women was sitting in front of me; she had been arrested, with her husband, in May 1937 in Rudzutak's dacha. Her appearance in the prison had certainly been absurd. 'They didn't allow us to take in anything – our summer silk dresses and underwear were torn, stuck over our shoulders, our stockings were ripped. At the last minutes before our prison transfer I received money from someone and we bought whatever there was in the prison chest.' So an orange top-shirt replaced a scarf on the head, a green football outfit, trousers, and on her feet the high-heeled slippers disappeared and towels were wrapped around. 'This was how I started the journey in December. It was a pure miracle I survived.'

Over many decades, life in the Gulag gave birth to endless rumours, legends, and myths, most of all of course about famous people – long previously believed executed by shooting in Moscow – who were said to have been seen by someone in some far distant camp somewhere. There were constantly recurring themes and details in such stories. For example, at least four women described to me exactly the same scene: how, many years later, when they were able to see themselves in a mirror again for the first time, the image they saw was the face of their own mother. Even as early as the 1970s, I myself recognized incidents recounted to me orally which were also scenes described in Solzhenitsyn's *Gulag Archipelago* or other printed recollections. But now story-telling about the camps has become so general that recording oral memory has become much more difficult. The vast amount of information pouring out of people often seems to happen through an immolation of their own memories to the point where it begins to seem as if everything they know happened to them personally. As a result, while earlier it had been especially important for me to learn details of their lives in the camps and prisons, now it became much more interesting to catch the 'alienation effect' of being at the same time both witnesses and questioners, of how they were themselves fifty or forty years ago. Especially recently, the moment has come for many – although certainly not all – to make a clear distinction between their present and past selves. The painful wound of semi-rehabilitation and the continuing necessity of silence over long years has now left them. On the contrary, ex-prisoners frequently perceive themselves as bearers of important information. The pain of the past recedes and they – especially the women – can talk about the torture of the prisons almost as if it had not been their own. An English-language teacher, Dina Slavutskaya, after describing to me how she had been forced to stand continuously for three days and nights during her interrogation – a form of torture in which she was forbidden to sit or even lean, and through which she has become lame for her entire life – at the end of her story asked; 'but have I told you something dreadful enough?' 'When I saw the prisoners in Kolyma sifting gold,' another woman told me, 'I vowed to myself that if I survived and eventually came out, I would never wear a single gold piece – but now look at me: look at my ear-rings, my chain, my ring . . .'

So far, I have not referred to the continuing contrasts between the stories told by men and those told by women. As a rule, women describe in much fuller detail the everyday routine of the prisons and concentration camps, the clothing, and the appearance and character of people; they speak more calmly and with more detachment about the tortures and agonies they had to bear; and they are more frank about emotional and sexual life in the camps. Indeed, love in the camps is still one of the most painful and difficult themes to speak about. Women see themselves as generally better able to adapt to imprisonment and they much more often stress the crucial importance of friendships and human relationships in this. They also give more emphasis to family relationships: above all to the tragedy of being parted from their children. Men, by contrast, are more reserved. They more often highlight a moment of personal humiliation. They are more often analytical. Men also usually give more detailed and elaborate descriptions of work, occasionally illustrated by drawings; and they sometimes have a better memory for the names of people they met, and for dates. Hence sometimes, although not always, it can be useful when a man and a woman exchange memories together: a husband and wife, if both are ex-convicts, can add to and correct each other's accounts.

Some of the memories which once were the most painful of all have often now softened. In the 1950s and 1960s, for example, the problem of informers remained very acute. There was of course an immense multitude of people who had helped with the arrests and who had become interrogators in the prisons and camps. Those who returned in the 1950s could very easily meet up with the people who had put them in prison – at work, as guests, or on the street. It was extremely difficult to prove who had informed on them and usually any attempt would only end in public scandal. A strange process is now taking place, one which can be illustrated by an incident which I witnessed myself. At one of the Moscow meetings of the Memorial society, which brought together ex-convicts with those who were studying the history of the repressions, one woman, who had been arrested in about 1939, said to me in a completely calm voice: 'but over there is the man who informed on me'. And she greeted him quite normally. Catching my perplexed expression, she explained: 'Of course we were then just eighteen, his parents were old Bolsheviks who were repressed, and then they tried to recruit me too. And of course he was repressed later on himself.' I felt that what she said was the outcome not of a lack of concern for or forgetting of her past, but of a realization, which now at last had come to people of the shameful things which the system itself had done to them. In such a situation people need to behave in their own different ways but it is very important not to presume that somebody still carries the same moral self-estimation they once bore in the past. It was much more difficult in the past than today. Now survivors, or at least those who have not lost the ability for self-reflection, are often changing their own self-evaluation. 'How could I have agitated for those unlucky women to go to the collective farms?' one of my women informants castigates herself: 'I never asked myself that, when the KGB came for me – I thought they were arresting me again, but instead they informed me of the death of my brother, for whom I had looked for years in the camps – my first thought was not about him, but about myself. I thought, "Thank God, they didn't put me in . . ."'

The question now often arises, especially from younger people, of the possibility of opposition in the concentration camp conditions. It is well known that there were of course major forms of direct resistance in the post-war period, including armed escapes, and eventually after Stalin's death uprisings and strikes in the camps themselves. But it seems to me more important, both from my discussions with the 'last' true witnesses now, and also from talking with them in the 1970s when they were younger, that ultimately the only true form of resistance was a determination to conserve one's humanity. It was sometimes undoubtedly very difficult not to become a camp of wolves, faced with the pitiless law of camp life: 'You die today, I die tomorrow.' And, together with the survivors themselves, we do have now, at last, a final chance of evaluating their past journey, with neither partiality nor anger.

21 The Sahel Oral History Project

Nigel Cross and Rhiannon Barker

Nigel Cross was Research Director of the Sahel Oral History Project, and is now Executive Director of the Panos Institute, London. Rhiannon Barker was Coordinator of the Sahel Oral History Project, and is now working at the Health Education Authority in London. Reprinted with permission from N. Cross and R. Barker (eds), *At the Desert's Edge: Oral Histories From the Sahel*, London, Panos/SOS Sahel, 1991, pp. 1–16. This book was published as part of the Panos Institute's Oral Testimony Programme, which explores and illustrates the potential of oral testimony in the development process and gathers, publishes and amplifies the views and experiences of individuals and communities in the South on specific development themes.

Oral history is both a methodology and an academic discipline. It has not yet been widely used in a development context. One aim of the Sahel Oral History Project was to explore how the application of oral history techniques can assist the development process. By talking at length with farmers, pastoralists, refugees and other groups, we hoped to gain a better understanding of traditional land-use practice, land tenure, farming and pastoral systems, the causes of desertification, and many other aspects of Sahelian life. Our aim was not only to record indigenous knowledge and improve rapport with those with whom SOS Sahel and its partner agencies work, but also to develop a practical methodology which could then be incorporated into development planning, project implementation and evaluation.

We do not claim that *At the Desert's Edge* and its supplementary material will become a seminal text for historians of Africa. In most of the places where we worked, there was no written record to support or contradict the oral testimony. In some instances it was possible to record the first tentative outlines of village histories, but this, though fascinating, was peripheral. The principal aim was to record the perceptions of Sahelian men and women – which are neither right nor wrong – about their changing environment and way of life. All history is informed by someone's testimony – his or her story. We did not set out to accumulate facts, but rather to find the stories, to improve the techniques for their collection and, most important of all, to demonstrate their value and utility.

THE PACE OF CHANGE

Social change in the Sahel has been rapid. Many children now have access to formal education. While this may increase their own economic prospects, it also leads to a loss of cultural continuity. Traditional knowledge is considered 'out-of-date' by young villagers as well as outsiders. Recording traditional knowledge both rescues it from oblivion and demonstrates its value to a younger generation. Environmental and economic pressures in the Sahel have combined to create a period of unprecedented social dislocation. Academic analysis of economic, social and physical change, while it may be objective, lacks the authenticity of first-hand testimony and fails to capture the important subjective aspects of these upheavals.

Not the least of our concerns has been to offer alternatives to the received image of Sahelians as passive, grateful beneficiaries who have been helped to fish or farm (the aid agency cover photo), by giving some 500 men and women – classic development 'targets' – the chance to talk back and to broadcast their experiences, priorities and perspectives.

We have not edited out the tragedies or the disasters as these are graphically described by those who have lived through them, but the same witnesses demonstrate their ingenuity and tenacity, and reflect on the 'good life'. The interviews reveal the complexity of everyday Sahelian life: people's relationship to and care of the environment; the position of men and women on the land and in the household; and changes in family relationships and social customs. As the interviews make clear, these individuals are neither emaciated victims nor happy peasants. They are themselves.

THE PROCESS

The preliminary research, identification of sites, liaison with other agencies and development of a questionnaire were carried out between January and May 1989. The interviewing began that June and continued until October 1990. Over 500 interviews were completed, of which just under half were with women. A small proportion were group interviews, bringing the total number of respondents to more than 650. The project worked in eight countries – Senegal, Mauritania, Mali, Burkina Faso, Niger, Chad, Sudan and Ethiopia – at nineteen sites, in seventeen languages.

From the outset, interview sites were linked to ongoing development projects. This strategy provided participating agencies with new, village-authored extension and evaluation materials and the Sahel Oral History Project with a ready-made base. Although it is never easy for development agencies to provide such support, there was a high level of cooperation. As a control, interviews were also conducted in non-project areas. In general, project sites were easier to work in – the relationship that had already been established between the project and the people proved an enormous asset.

A major consideration in the selection of interview sites was that they should cover a range of tribal, economic and social groups. These were divided into five main categories:

- refugees (political and economic): Eritreans and Tigreans in Sudan, ex-pastoralists in Nouakchott, Mauritania

- pastoralists and agro-pastoralists in Mali, Niger, Chad and Ethiopia
- farmers in rainfed areas in Mali, Burkina Faso, Niger, Sudan and Ethiopia
- farmers in irrigated riverine areas in Senegal and Sudan
- fishermen in Mauritania and Chad

We chose interviewers from extension workers, research students and local journalists; inevitably a mixture of luck, judgment and availability circumscribed our choice. The most successful interviewers were good communicators who had a natural curiosity and interest in the respondents. In terms of grasping the complexity of some of the questions and to ensure effective transcription and translation, a relatively high level of education and literacy was essential. Given the nature of the fieldwork – with the inevitable frustrations created by limited transport, inaccessibility of interviewees and difficult living conditions – the energy and enthusiasm of the interviewer was as important as previous interviewing experience. Undoubtedly the most successful interviewers were those who had a thorough knowledge of the area and, in most cases, had been born and brought up within it. They could, in the fullest sense of the phrase, 'speak the same language'.

Finding the right questions

The first task of the project was to prepare a guide for interviewers outlining a standard methodology, together with a draft questionnaire. Initial research for the guidelines involved consultation with development agencies and academics. An interview outline was tested in Sudan. Further consultation, and feedback from interviewers, led to a number of changes. In addition, discussions were held with development workers on each interviewing site prior to the work, in order to establish their own priorities.

To draw up a questionnaire which can be used effectively in many different countries, even though they share common problems and conditions, is a near impossible task. Questions which would strike a European as being neutral and rather mundane, such as 'How many children do you have?', may prove offensive. To divulge such facts to a stranger may tempt fate – an open invitation to God to take a child away.

A cultural bias in the interview outline was inevitable – we saw the project as having a development education role and so were seeking to inform a Northern public as well as an 'expert' audience. We found ourselves seeking answers to questions which members of the community concerned might never have thought to ask. To balance our concerns, interviewers were given scope to exclude anything they felt unsuitable, and encouraged to include questions of their own design. Similarly, questions were added or subtracted depending on the specific country or site and according to the prevailing political, social and environmental conditions.

Working with women

Most of the Sahelian countries in which we were working have strong cultural and religious influences which tend to restrict the movement of women and inhibit easy communication between the sexes. To avoid marginalising women, one male and one female interviewer were sought for each site. But employing women proved much more difficult than men, largely because of cultural constraints restricting their freedom to travel. Women interviewers had less work experience than men and generally needed more training and confidence building.

Despite the extra work involved, the policy of employing women proved critical to the success of the project. On a number of occasions, as an experiment, men were asked to interview women and women to interview men. Their comments on this experience were enlightening. Women generally found the interviews ran smoothly. The men, on the other hand, appeared at a loss to know what to ask women and their questions quickly dried up. Some said that they found talking to women boring and unenlightening, but it is also possible that male respondents found women interviewers less intimidating than the other way around.

As interviewees, women again required a higher investment of both time and energy. In the first place, they were harder to involve since their domestic chores could rarely be postponed – there was always grain to grind, wood to collect or a meal to prepare, and they preferred to be interviewed while continuing their chores. Men were more inclined to lay down the task at hand, benefiting from a male culture which sets aside time and space for communal debate. They generally talked with greater ease for long periods of time without faltering, whereas women usually needed much more encouragement. Women also tended to reflect less critically on their life situation, attributing their hardships to fate rather than external factors, making it more difficult for the interviewer to follow up further lines of questioning.

Problems sometimes arose from men wanting to take over or disrupt interviews with women. Men would decide that they should act as mediators between their wives (or other female relatives) and the interviewer. In some cases it appeared that the woman was reassured by male encouragement; at other times the consequences were disastrous, with the woman feeling unable to talk about certain issues and the man asserting that he knew the woman's mind better than she. It was also noticeable that men often laughed at the questions to women and the women's responses, whereas they took their own contributions much more seriously.

Training

The time allocated to interviewing in each country was about one month. In this period interviewers were recruited by the project coordinator and the actual interview process was completed on two to three different sites. Within this tight schedule, a short three-day training programme was devised which provided an invaluable component of the work.

The first day of training was spent on a thorough review of the questionnaire outline and guidelines, together with some role play where the new interviewer would test interviewing methods and also play the part of respondent. On the second day the coordinator carried out the first one or two interviews, using the interviewer as an interpreter. The flexibility of the interview structure was stressed, with the coordinator demonstrating the value of follow-up questions. On the third day a sample interview was conducted, transcribed and analysed.

Selection

On each site we sought to interview roughly equal numbers of men and women. Initially, interviews were exclusively with the elderly, but as the project progressed it became clear that it would be useful to include younger people in each sample to allow comparisons between the differing perceptions of two generations.

Before interviewing began, those helping to facilitate the work were asked to identify the different economic, social and ethnic groups in the community, to ensure the interviewers covered as wide a spectrum as possible and were not simply choosing to talk to close friends, neighbours or relatives. While the majority of the interviewees were farmers or pastoralists, we also sought specialist occupations such as midwife, hunter, traditional healer, blacksmith and village chief. In most instances people were contacted through the village chief or head of the women's committee. Although this was often time-consuming, once the interviews were endorsed by respected members of the community, the respondents had greater confidence and were more willing to cooperate. We always took care to stress that there was no material advantage to be gained by participating in the interviews, beyond the intrinsic value of sharing knowledge and experience.

Our method of selection was not statistically random since our sample, averaging perhaps twelve men and twelve women in each community, was too small and the logistics too difficult. Some people were selected by the chief, others by village groups, and some were self-selected. On occasion, people were too busy to talk or were simply suspicious of the questions and unwilling to participate.

In refugee camps, and other situations where a well-established social structure was absent, selection methods were more haphazard. Where a community leader could be identified, the channel of communication was relatively easy. More often the camps, lacking ethnic and social homogeneity, had no elected representatives, obliging us to wander from house to house making our own introductions. Interviewees, however, seemed prepared to accept this rather intrusive approach.

The interviews

The majority of interviews were conducted with individuals, although there were also a small number of group interviews of up to fifteen people. While our main interest was specialised material on the environment and work practices linked to personal histories and anecdotes from individuals, group interviews were useful as they provided a consensus account. Individuals in a group situation are often animated by the discussion to follow through certain lines of inquiry in greater detail. Also, in many Sahelian societies the group is the familiar and preferred forum for discussion, especially with strangers.

Most interviews were conducted in private homes or in the shade of a lone but convenient tree. In some instances the village chief would call people to the village square or to his house. We encountered several problems in interviewing in the open: the heat of the sun rapidly wilts the interviewer and respondent; strong winds interfere with the microphone, affecting the quality of the recording; and droves of curious, often disruptive, onlookers are attracted to the site. Wherever possible we sought shelter and quiet.

Interviews lasted between forty minutes and two hours, although initial introductions, rapport-building, tea ceremonies and other hospitalities often extended the time. Two hours is about the maximum sensible period for such intense dialogue. The interviewer has to be constantly alert, planning the next question, encouraging the respondent to talk and looking for interesting areas of knowledge and experience to examine in detail. Since the 'fatigue factor' is high, no more than three thorough interviews were conducted in one day, with an obligatory break after five days of interviewing.

All interviews were recorded on cassette and interviewers were encouraged to take notes to supplement the recordings. A number of people found the note-taking difficult, complaining that it slowed down the dialogue, distracted them from the questions and meant that they lost valuable eye contact with the respondent. Despite this, we stressed the value of brief notes as a useful means of cross-checking, providing back-up for a bad or faulty recording, and for recording non-verbal expressions and descriptions.

Translation

Following the interviews, the interviewer translated and transcribed the tapes into French or English. Transcription is a tedious and time-consuming process and fraught with problems, to which there are no easy answers. An extension worker from Mali poignantly described the type of problem she faced translating the interviews from Bobo into French. Bobo, she explained, is rich with subtly worded proverbs which cannot easily be translated. She cited the following example: 'If you want to stop the mouse, you must first get rid of the smell from the soumbala spice.'

Apparently the proverb refers to the value of a good upbringing. In the past children were brought up to be polite and obedient and therefore could be relied upon to behave well. Today children fail to receive proper instruction from their parents, and for this reason cannot be blamed for behaving badly, just as the mouse is not to blame for taking the soumbala spice when it smells so enticing. Given the complexity of the proverb, the extension worker finally opted for a gloss which omitted the proverb itself. Indeed, so much of Sahelian expression is laced with proverbs which are often exclusive to a particular group that only members of the group can fully understand the meanings and implications. The outsider is left bemused – for example: 'Les termites sont loin de la lune.'

THE RESPONSE

An analysis of the material collected reveals that the project did not recover as much indigenous knowledge, in its specifics, as originally intended. For instance, recipes for medicines, meals and organic fertilisers, and accurate descriptions of plant uses, changing vegetation, animal numbers and herd composition, are often mentioned only in vague terms. The fact that many rural populations have been made to feel that their traditional techniques for agriculture, veterinary and medical care, are in some way 'backward' and unscientific was undoubtedly a constraint. They are aware that the educated élites, who come on sporadic visits, tend to promote the adoption of new technologies and encourage a more scientific approach to development and conservation. For this reason many are reluctant to divulge methods of animal treatment, land conservation practices, or herbal remedies, which may label them as ignorant or out of touch with the 'modern' world.

Our questions about traditional veterinary practices in a camp for sedentarised pastoralists in eastern Chad met with blank faces, shoulder shrugs, and a denial of the existence of any such systems. It was only after the interviewers began to talk in positive terms about techniques they were acquainted with from other areas that the respondents were persuaded to share their own extensive knowledge.

No time for numbers

Then there is the problem of trying to search for common ground across the different modes of cultural expression. The desire for quantification and specificity that preoccupies research in the North is not an easy notion to convey to a Sahelian farmer. Efforts to find out the number of cattle in his herd will more often than not provoke raised eyebrows, derisive laughter and evasive responses. 'God is generous, I have enough animals to fertilise my fields!' . . . 'We have to make do with whatever God gives us.' The question is comparable to asking Europeans or North Americans for their bank balance or an inventory of their assets. Similarly, the question 'How many hours does it take you to grind your corn?' may be answered, 'I begin when I return from collecting the water and finish when my husband returns from the field.'

Responses which involve reference to figures, dates, weights and times are often spoken in French or English. Because such numerical accuracy is not perceived as relevant, it is not usually contained in the local language. For this reason the accuracy of ages, dates of specific droughts and famines is questionable. Indeed, throughout the interviews phrases such as 'in the past' are always preferred to something more precise such as 'in 1919' or 'in 1940'.

It is difficult to know how such constraints on the collection of indigenous knowledge can be effectively overcome. It may be that the problem lies not so much in the method of collection as in the setting of inappropriate targets. Is there simply too romantic a notion of indigenous knowledge? Such knowledge, after all, is not static but evolves to suit a changing environment. It must be open to the acceptance of new equipment and technologies. Farmers and pastoralists will adapt to whatever method serves them best, be it traditional or modern, old or new; archaic practices are usually retained not from nostalgia but because they still serve some purpose. But, as the interviews make clear, some traditions are retained through inertia or prejudice. There are reactionaries in every culture, but in the Sahel today such conservatism can lead to a cruel lack of development – particularly for women, as evidenced by the widespread resistance to education for girls.

One obvious drawback in employing non-specialist local interviewers is their lack of academic training in the detailed environmental or agricultural field. They could run through the checklist of questions but did not have the specialist knowledge to follow up on detailed points of concern and interest. On one site, in Kordofan, western Sudan, we tried a different approach. The coordinator, herself an agriculturalist working in the region, was briefed by an authority on Sudanese ecology who had worked in the area thirty years earlier, producing the first published botanical and environmental surveys. The questions were more informed, and the ability to cross-check details of change against the written and remembered record led to the interviews being much more specific than at other sites.

However, although a tight interview conducted by a specialist can get closer to accurately recording traditional knowledge, it also moves further away from the respondent's priorities and views. These may sometimes be incoherent or even factually wrong, but they have an integrity of their own. There is, then, a tension between the interview that seeks to focus on indigenous knowledge, and the interviewer who solicits opinion and impressions. For the former the 'facts' are primary and the respondent is secondary – a cipher; for the latter it is the other way round.

Perceptions of change

Despite these reservations, the interviews as a whole, although 'unscientific', describe a wide range of environmental knowledge and traditional farming and pastoral systems. Farmers talk about tried and tested methods of improving soil fertility; pastoralists explain how they control animal reproduction, the pastures preferred by each of their animals and the ideal ratio of males to females. Healing methods and herbal remedies are mentioned in varying degrees of detail. There is a great deal of repetition [. . .] which we have taken as evidence of a consensus about environmental and social change. Some of these 'findings' are new, some confirm hunches and others restate the obvious.

Change is everywhere recorded – no one can be left in any doubt that Sahelians have a thorough understanding of their own predicament, and of the causes of desertification. Whereas thirty years ago farmers were able to grow sufficient crops for subsistence plus a surplus for sale, they are now often cultivating from three to five times as much land in the uncertain hope of a yield that will provide enough for their subsistence. Many of the men are seeking employment in the towns so that their families, left behind in the villages, have enough to eat.

Plant breeders have succeeded in developing new varieties of sorghum and millet requiring a shorter growing season, which are able to take better advantage of the meagre rainfall when it occurs. But the extension services are still woefully inadequate and the costs of introducing new technologies often prohibitive.

Those who had led a nomadic life and lost their livestock through lack of pasture have been forced to settle and attempt to make ends meet by cultivation or by seeking employment in the towns. Many long to return to their nomadic way of life and attempt to rebuild their stocks, preferring sheep and goats (especially the latter), since they reproduce more rapidly and are better able to survive on the scanty pasture than cattle and camels.

The shift from pure pastoralism to agro-pastoralism and herding for wages (from absentee owners) is visible across the Sahel. When – and if – more 'normal' rainfall returns, the pasture will be slow to recover, passing through various stages of rehabilitation before approaching the levels of former years. A prerequisite for any recovery, which is well understood, is for livestock numbers to be kept well below the actual carrying capacity of the existing pasture.

There is clear agreement among those interviewed about the main reason for environmental degradation: inadequate and sporadic rainfall. Man-made factors are also cited: pressure on land due to rising population and the fact that more and more pastoralists, whose herds have been decimated by the droughts, are turning from pastoralism to farming. Bush land is being cleared with increasing rapidity to make land available for cultivation. The increased pressure on land and natural resources has disrupted what was a 'previously amicable relationship between farmers and pastoralists': conflicts between the two are frequently reported.

Although the majority of the interviewees felt that degradation was attributable to climatic change, many were confident that steps can be, and are being, taken to counter the damage. Trees are being planted; the fertility of the soil has been improved by adaptations to traditional farming methods, such as compost holes and bunds to reduce soil erosion and improve infiltration of water.

Patterns of life

It was also our aim to record social and cultural change. In this, the Sahel Oral History Project exceeded its expectations and has established a fuller picture of community history and social evolution than originally anticipated. It has revealed the extent of the breakdown of traditional relationships between groups: adults and children, sedentary farmers, pastoralists and agro-pastoralists, men and women.

Much of the information contradicts received development wisdom and provides ample evidence that many standard generalisations simply do not stand up, or are so general as to be seriously misleading. For instance, the interviews highlight the dangers of generalising about women's position in rural communities. According to Fatchima Beine, president of the women's committee of Abalak village, Niger: 'Before, when natural resources were abundant, women did not have to work so hard. Now, however, women do the same work as the men and during the day they work in the field.' But in Tibiri, another village in the same district, local farmer Sayanna Hatta commented:

> New technologies have helped to lighten a woman's load, she no longer has to spend several hours a day grinding grain due to the presence of diesel-powered mills; there are wells and pumps from which she can collect water. The men plough the fields and if the family don't have enough food then it is the men who have to go in search of supplements.

As always, there are marked differences in circumstances within villages and between communities that are lost in generalisations. 'Years ago all the wood we needed was near. It used to take us only five minutes to collect. Now it's a ten-hour trip, so those who can afford it buy it from the men who sell it in the market' (Rékia, woman farmer, Takiéta, Niger). As far as fuelwood collection is concerned, the gap between women with some money and women without has widened.

In the Nile province of Sudan, married women whose husbands have remained in the area as farmers welcome their improved quality of life: 'Now we don't have to pound the dura, or pull water from the deep well; also our participation in agricultural work has decreased' (Um Gazaz el Awad, Shendi); 'When I was young I used to do some work on my husband's farm. But now women are just sitting at home waiting for the men to bring money to them' (Hajeya Juma Ahmed). But in the same area the widow of a pastoralist has had to work as a paid seasonal labourer and is the sole breadwinner for a family of eight.

The value to projects

Development projects are often caught up in an almost obsessive drive to produce quantifiable results which can be presented to donors as proof of the project's success. In this quest for measureable achievements, other more subjective parameters are either forgotten or ignored. We believe this study, in creating a dialogue between development workers and local communities, has demonstrated the value of improved communication at all levels of project activity.

Each development project associated with the interviews was at a different stage, so it was possible to assess the value of participation throughout the project cycle. In Niger we conducted interviews before the project started; the woman interviewer was subsequently employed by the project to manage the women's programme. In Mali the project was at an early stage, in Sudan about half-way through. It became clear that it is never too late to use oral history as a project evaluation tool, but it is most useful if implemented at the planning stage. In Niger, for example, the interviews were used in the project design and followed through thereafter, and extension workers now set up oral history interviews each time they enter a new village.

Feedback from project sites shows that interviewing work conducted by extension workers has had a number of spin-offs – it is an effective method for creating links with new communities, and also a valuable training tool. The coordinator of the interviewing work in Mali notes in her report that the work provided her with a new training area, from which both she and extension workers have benefited. She concludes:

> The general utility of this research to the project is that it does something to counteract the idea that farmers are ignorant, conservative and fatalistic. Such preconceptions persist amongst our staff, although they are more subliminal than explicit. Little attempt is made to link the techniques we are trying to popularise with the farmers' own experiments. Thus the extensionist appears as a giver of solutions and the farmers' own capacities are undervalued. And, seeing themselves as surpassed, the farmers are less likely to volunteer suggestions, further aggravating the imbalance . . . The more details we have of farmer's knowledge and ingenuity, the more we can hope to counteract these problems of attitude.

In the same vein, a Senegalese non-governmental organisation (NGO), Fédération des Paysans Organisés du Département de Bakel, noted:

> We wanted to participate in this project from the start because we realised that it would be of benefit to our own work . . . We felt that it would be particularly useful to our literacy trainers. In this respect the results have gone beyond our expectations. What might have seemed like a lot of extra work from the outside in fact worked to our advantage. We put our trust in young inexperienced workers and were delighted to discover that they were able to carry out the work well . . . In addition they discovered a rich well

of knowledge. We have decided that we cannot leave it here; we will continue the oral history work in our own project.

Thus not the least of the benefits of employing oral history methods in a development context is the impact on project workers, nearly all of whom have acquired valuable new insights, often into their own communities. If oral history techniques are institutionalised in project work, they can increase understanding and sensitivity towards the participating community.

A two-way process

A major obligation of the oral historian is to 'return the compliment'. When 'outsiders' initiate a programme of research, there should be a commitment to seeking new ways of ensuring that the resulting material is of value to the people who provided it. The NGO Fédération des Paysans at Bakel, for instance, published the interviews in Soninke, the local language, for use both as a local resource and as a tool in their literacy programme.

Perhaps the most immediate and practical value of the Sahel Oral History Project has been in identifying the benefits to projects and project workers of taking the time to learn, through interviews, as much as possible from individual life histories and reflections. Secondly, when such work is collected together, important 'under-researched' areas become apparent and can be followed up to ensure that objectives of the developers take into account the many variations in attitudes and priorities of the individuals who make up the community.

To end with a story from Mali: There was once a village so wealthy that the young people decided to make it a youth village of eternal joy, by killing all the old people. On the chosen day there was a single youth who had pity and hid his father so as not to have to kill him. In the new, joyful village of youth, all were strong and worked for themselves, and there were no old people to feed. One day the village was visited by a delegation from the local government, who suspected that something was wrong. They asked the young villagers if they could make a rope out of sand. Impossible. Wild attempts were made to gather up the soil, to no avail. The youth whose father was alive crept off to consult him. The father advised the boy to ask to see the old sand rope first. Thus the delegation realised that this boy's father at least was still alive, and while the others were punished, he was spared.

22 Leprosy in India
The intervention of oral history

Sanjiv Kakar

Sanjiv Kakar is a Senior Lecturer in the Department of English at the College of Vocational Studies, University of Delhi. Extracted from *Oral History*, 1995, vol. 23, no. 2, pp. 37–45, with permission.

INTRODUCTION

There are at the present time at least two and a half million patients of leprosy in India, who constitute about one-third of the world's leprosy population. Leprosy is prevalent in virtually every state of India, ranging from a mere 1,522 cases in Haryana, to an estimated 272,000 cases in the state of Bihar, while Orissa and Tamil Nadu have the highest prevalence rate in the country.[1] In the early 1980s, with the commencement of the National Leprosy Eradication Programme (NLEP), districts with a prevalence rate of five or more patients per thousand of the population were identified as hyper-endemic, and phased introduction of the Multi Drug therapy (MDT) began. Treatment time is substantially reduced with MDT to between six to twenty-four months for most cases, which represents a significant improvement on the earlier dependence on sulfone monotherapy, which entailed continuous drug intake over several years.

Leprosy is a chronic bacterial infection caused by *Mycobacterium leprae*. It attacks mainly the superficial tissues, especially the skin and the peripheral nerves. If untreated it can lead to physical deformity, such as destruction of hands and feet, nose collapse, and muscular atrophy. Injuries caused to anesthetic areas invite ulceration. With timely and adequate treatment, these deformities can be prevented. Early clinical signs include skin patches of heightened colour with anesthesia, accompanied by sensitivity of nerves and muscular weakness. Diagnosis can be confirmed with skin smear tests and other laboratory investigations.

Where seventy per cent of the population live in rural areas, not surprisingly the overwhelming number of patients are rural. From the Leprosy Control Programme of the early fifties, the rural patient came to be recognised as the focus of the Programme. With the launching of the NLEP, and a target of total eradication of leprosy by AD 2000, the endemicity of a *district* became the criteria for priority-based intervention, and the rural patient, virtually non-existent in colonial records, moved to centre-stage. Oral narrative is the only means for such patients, especially those without access to literacy, to enter into the arena and tell their own story. It is a story that has remained largely untold. Voluminous government records, laden with statistics on endemicity and eradication strategies, form the principal archive for information about leprosy in the contemporary period, but these are unhelpful on the matter of the subjective experiences of a patient when confronted with a disease which carries with it a long history of discriminatory practices. Urban, educated patients who might commit their experiences to writing and thus feature as subjects in their own history are anxious to retain anonymity, and are reluctant to recount their experiences; in this manner they perpetuate the myth that leprosy affects only the poor.

Any engagement with leprosy in contemporary India must negotiate the events of the last century, when western medical systems and practices were introduced; these included the separation of leprosy patients from other ill people, the marginalisation of the hospital, and the concurrent patronage of the asylum for the exclusive confinement of leprosy patients. The Lepers Act of 1898, the major legislation on leprosy of the nineteenth century which authorised such forcible confinement (for vagrant patients only!) remained on the statutes well into this century, until the slow process of repeal spreading over the last three decades finally terminated in 1991, with its repeal by the state of Bihar. Some of the perspectives on leprosy formed during the colonial period have lingered into the present, often intermixed with indigenous systems of knowledge; these include an exaggerated fear of infectivity, and the use of both Indian and western medicine for treatment. It is regrettable that recent scholarship on medicine in colonial India, which might have developed these themes further and suggested deeper correspondences, has bypassed entirely the study of leprosy, and its relationship with the entire apparatus of western medicine, in its scientific, cultural and ideological aspects.[2]

In this paper I attempt to redress the historical lacunae by reproducing interviews with leprosy patients in India conducted over the last few years. Following this, I consider how oral history offers a unique archive for the study of leprosy in contemporary India, as well as providing essential data for any interventionist offensive. Next I [. . .] discuss how oral history can also serve as a guide to our reading and rewriting of the colonial history of leprosy. Finally there are some examples illustrating how this oral history project can in truth benefit from an engagement with colonial sources.

LISTENING TO LEPROSY PATIENTS

This exercise in oral history was undertaken during 1991–93, in four leprosy hyperendemic districts (with a prevalence rate of five or more per thousand of the population) in India: Durg and Rajnandgaon (Madhya Pradesh), Salem (Tamil Nadu), and Cuttack (Orissa). The successes of the MDT have encouraged the emergence of cured patients who are now actively engaged in leprosy control and eradication work. This is a relatively new phenomenon and it signifies a breakthrough in the assault on community prejudice about leprosy; for this reason, of the many patients interviewed, I rely heavily here on the testimony of patient activists. Because written narrative is virtually silent on the woman patient, a special effort was made to interact with women leprosy patients, and with children. As this oral history project relates to a commitment to the eradication of leprosy, it focuses on leprosy endemic districts where the health education offensive has enjoyed some success, so as to consider not only the situation of leprosy patients within a village community, but also its transformative potential. (The NLEP is not equally efficient in all districts, nor are the health education strategies uniform everywhere.) Virtually all the patients who were interviewed had received MDT; some had been declared as Released From Treatment (RFT). Questions related to patient perceptions on contagion of leprosy, transmission, curability, experiences of discrimination, and patient participation in the detection of new cases. Some patients were detected afresh during the course of surveys of schools and far flung villages; they were motivated to begin treatment immediately. Of the many interviews conducted, two have been selected for presentation here.[3]

Durg

Thanwarin Bai is a resident of Khapparwada village. This interview takes place outside her hut, which is virtually on the borders of the village. The leprosy worker who has been visiting this village for several years, and who continues to visit once every month with the mobile clinic, and the District Leprosy Officer are the only others present. Occasionally they must assist in interpreting the local Chhatisgarh dialect. Both are on intimate terms with the patient, who now functions as a 'janbhagidar', literally a social communicator, an inmate of the village who has volunteered to assist in leprosy detection and with monitoring of patient progress.

What were your experiences as a leprosy patient?

Then I was living in another jhopri (hut) but not this one, this I got much later from a government scheme to help those who were very poor. When the villagers found out that I had leprosy they forced me to move out. How long could I hide it, the sores on my feet were visible to all, I had trouble walking, and when bathing in the river the other women would see the patches on my body . . . So I had to go, this was the custom in those days. So I built myself another jhopri on the outskirts of the village, near the cremation site, and I lived there alone.

What about your family, you have a son . . .

What could my son do, he is the barber, the village threatened him with a collective boycott if he continued to keep his mother with him. He has to feed his family. What could he do all alone? He kept me as long as he could, but once the signs become so visible, how long can you hide it?

When did these events take place?
(After some hesitation and consultation with the others) The end of 1987. I lived there alone for some months, my son would bring me food and whatever I needed, I grew food also. Then the leprosy workers came and they brought me the medicine, this was the new medicine, MDT, which had newly come to our village. Then they spoke to the villagers to allow me to return home, but there was no success; they kept coming, and then they formed a swasth samiti (health association) with some sympathetic villagers, and finally I was able to return to the village, and the boycott threat against my son was lifted.

Is your treatment now completed? What was your attitude to the medicine at the beginning? Did you believe that leprosy could be cured?
Now I am RFT. When they first came I said, well, what do I lose by taking the medicine, I have lost everything already, so what will I lose by taking it? I did not really believe that it would cure me, but it was free, so I took it. In fact we did not think at all about cure of leprosy, we thought, why has God cursed me? You think of cure only when you think of illness. But all the same I ate the medicine and then after some months I began to notice the difference.

What is the status of leprosy in this village now (October 1991)?
There are 960 people in the village, including children. There are four cases undergoing treatment. The clinic comes here on the 7th of every month, at 11 a.m., just where you are sitting now. The patients come sometimes on their own, sometimes I have to call them. It is not easy to get them here regularly, and the clinic cannot wait for them, they have to visit so many villages. People should have the sense to look after their own bodies, but they do not.

What is the attitude of the villagers to leprosy at the present time? How do they respond to your detection work?
I have visited every home in the village, I have detected some patients too. I have personally examined the girls and the women, the ones who will let me. Always the leprosy workers are telling me to examine the women, how else will they get examined, the men cannot check women's bodies? Earlier it was the custom to evict patients from the village, now that has changed. People have learned to tolerate patients, but they do not love them. Some of the people abuse me: they say, 'First you get leprosy and you bring shame on this village. Now you detect more cases and you bring more shame.'

You live here alone? Where is your son?
When I returned he wanted me to live with him, but I built my hut here. I will always live here.

You have anesthesia on your feet, why are you not wearing your slippers (micro-cellular rubber)? Have you not been given a pair?

I have no ulcers, you can see . . . I soak my feet in water . . . not everyday, where is the time? I have my slippers in the hut. Wearing every day will spoil them, and where will I get another pair? I got these after a lot of difficulty.

Cuttack

Nirankar Sarangi is a resident of the Gandhipalli leprosy colony in Cuttack. Two leprosy colonies exist side by side; originally on the outskirts of the city, urban expansion has now integrated the colonies with the city. The leprosy colony is indistinguishable from any other shanty colony in Cuttack. Many leprosy patients consider this their home, and live here by choice, visiting their villages for brief periods. The patient speaks only his mother tongue, Oriya, so another resident translates into Hindi.

How old are you?

(Laughs) I don't know for sure.

Can you tell us roughly . . . 50s, 60s?

Not so old. Not yet sixty.

Tell us about this place.

This is a leprosy colony, there is another one nearby also. All the patients here have completed treatment or are under MDT. This is our meeting hall, today you can see that people are watching the test match. It is not always so crowded. We all live together like one family. During the recent elections the politicians came many times to talk with us about our problems. We always support the same candidate, the whole colony votes as one block, so our votes are important to them. We told them about the high cost of living, and about the shortage of the special rubber chappals (slippers).

Tell us your story, from the time that you contracted leprosy.

As a child I lived in Ganteshwar village. I got leprosy when I was very young. I continued going to school but one day because the patches on my skin were so obvious, the headmaster removed me from the school. I continued to live at home, until the age of about twenty-two years. The progress of the disease was slow. Over the years the problems at home kept on increasing. Some of our relatives would refuse to visit our home because of my presence. They were afraid that they would get leprosy from me. A cousin of mine had been married when he was a child; now he was grown up and ready to receive his bride, but her family refused to send her to live with us because . . . of me. All these years I had tried so many remedies from the local doctors, to no avail. We had spent a lot of money also. Finally, in 1956, that is a date that I remember, I left home for the famous

Hathibadi Health Home. We had heard about this, it was a major centre in Orissa state for the care and treatment of leprosy patients. I had only sixty rupees in my pocket, which my mother had given to me. From here I moved to the Leprosy Home and Hospital, here in Cuttack. In those days the treatment consisted of sulfone tablets, and injections of Chaulmoogra oil on the discoloured skin patches. These injections were very painful. Earlier the oil used to be administered orally, which was nauseating, and many patients could not tolerate it. Often we would say, leprosy is preferable to the treatment. I would return home for holidays, and to collect money. Many many years later I had a course of MDT here itself. Now I am cured, but the deformities on my hands and feet will remain with me for always.

Have people's ideas about leprosy changed over the years. Are patients still harassed? How do people view leprosy now?
That varies. Many people still fear leprosy, but it is less than in earlier years. We used to call it the 'bada rog' (big illness) in my village. Now when I go home and meet people they can see that I am cured.

What is the condition of leprosy patients in your village now? Are they receiving MDT?
I don't know.

I will ask you a very important question. Please do not be offended, and answer truthfully. Now that you, a Brahmin, have experienced untouchability because of leprosy, and you know what it means for another to feel polluted by your touch, does it not transform your attitude to the caste system?
For me everyone is equal.

Are you willing to interdine with people from any caste? Including Harijans?
Everyone is the same.

Do you actually do so here?
How can I, even though I have no personal objections, here I am a priest, I am in charge of the temple, so I can only eat food cooked by certain hands . . .

ERADICATION STRATEGIES AND COMMUNITY INVOLVEMENT

Virtually every account of the rural patient underlines the vital importance of the village community. Where the community is hostile, patients have no choice but to cover up tell-tale patches as best they can, for fear of being persecuted: finally these become too pronounced, or deformities set in, and this is the stage when the patient is banished from the village. All this is inimical to the functioning of any leprosy eradication programme, which depends on early detection, (both with a view to ensuring complete cure without the patient suffering any physical deformity, and to render the patient non-infectious as quickly as possible), and timely and regular medication. It is simply not possible for the handful of leprosy workers, mostly non-medical staff to physically verify every single village. Where the vast majority of people do not recognise the early signs of leprosy, only community participation can generate knowledge about leprosy, persuade fellow villagers to come forward fearlessly for treatment, convince them of the efficacy of the Multi Drug therapy, monitor and motivate patients who tend to default (in the early stages leprosy is characterised by an absence of pain and discomfort, so patients do tend to be casual about discoloured, anesthetic skin patches), and care for those cured patients who have deformities and who require simple physiotherapy like regular soaking of feet in water to prevent ulceration. Those who have completed treatment often require a measure of rehabilitation to enable them to make a living.

Oral history can assist in garnering up to date knowledge about attitudes to leprosy and the condition of patients. Interventionist offensives must be devised according to local need, for there is tremendous regional variation even within villages close to each other. While some villages in Rajnandgaon, such as Dhangaon, and Dhorabhata, have supportive communities and patients are not subjected to harassment, in others like Khaprikala villagers fear even to touch the corpse of a leprosy patient for fear of contagion. Nardah village (Durg district) has a level of tolerance which allowed a patient to remain home, and visit the village temple every day, without any hindrance; both patient and community shared the stoic belief that a scourge which emanates from God may be revoked by Him; that this patient was an educated man, a physical training instructor in a regional undergraduate college, who denied himself the benefit of medical treatment, indicates that the health education effort here must necessarily be different from other nearby villages, where very different conditions prevail.

Attitudes to contagion, transmission, and curability vary enormously, as interviews with patients reveal. In Tamil Nadu in the south, sexual promiscuity is often cited as causing leprosy; or else leprosy is attributed to the lick of a long earthworm, locally known as 'monna pambu' (a theory of correspondence identifies the blunted fingers of a leprosy patient with the blunt ends of the earthworm). In central India prejudice can take very severe forms, drawing from a fear that leprosy spreads from casual physical contact, and from a belief that such a divinely originated curse brings shame upon the entire village; this often leads to prompt eviction of the patient from the village. Oral narrative is the only means to learn of local conditions, of patient perceptions, and to devise programmes, including rehabilitation schemes, that suit local needs. Oral narrative is the only means for poor, underprivileged patients like Thanwarin Bai to have their say, and to record their own histories.

Oral history also enables leprosy workers and other medical personnel in the field, far removed from the corridors of power, to record their perspective on official policy. Such perspectives, which emanate from the site where official policy comes into contact with the patient, can offer significant insights. For instance, the official Government of India definition of a leprosy free area is when the incidence of leprosy is reduced to one case per 10,000 of the population. Leprosy workers, however, call for multiple criteria: for a working definition which will help them to achieve this target, one which is concerned with process rather than merely with the end result; they stress factors such as freedom from ignorance, freedom from ulcers (for the care of patients with deformities by the community is a valuable index of the level of community awareness and sensitivity), and freedom from deformity (which would indicate whether patients are detected in the early stages). The unanimity regarding the need for effective treatment of the child patient, and a shared concern that child deformity must be prevented by timely medication and physiotherapy, brings the differences between the official perspective and the field perspective into sharp focus. Child deformity is taken very seriously by officialdom as a signal failure of the Programme, and this often results in suppression of such cases by field staff, for fear of incurring official displeasure; whereas the leprosy workers want definitions that make visible such glaring instances of failure, so as to prevent recurrence, and to enable the child to receive first priority in surgical correction. Interviews with leprosy field workers reveal that for strategic reasons they represent leprosy as being wholly non-infectious, as easily curable, and the medicine as having no side effects. Privately they admit that children are more vulnerable than adults and must be protected; but the only means to protect healthy children is to deny infectivity, so that the child can remain at school and undergo treatment. Any other means only results in suppression of cases. [. . .]

ORAL HISTORY / RECEIVED HISTORY

The patient in the community, surely a crucial category, is denied in the colonial discourse on leprosy. Making this visible is perhaps the most significant contribution of this oral history project to the study of leprosy in colonial India. The dialogue between leprosy in contemporary India based upon oral narrative, and the history of leprosy in colonial India, based upon elite, written sources cannot be an easy one. Even if attitudes toward leprosy have remained largely unchanged over the decades in some quarters, nonetheless historical periodisation cannot be wished away. At the same time, any attempt to reconstruct the condition of the leprosy patient in the colonial period cannot remain within the confines of colonial representation. The narrative of the patient within the community makes visible the very limited nature of the colonial intervention in the case of leprosy, and its wilful disregard for the overwhelming number of patients. The Lepers Act of 1898 provided 'for the segregation and medical treatment of pauper lepers', and it invented its own definition of leprosy by representing it exclusively as 'the process of ulceration';[4] this legal definition of leprosy was not supported by medical opinion at the time. Colonial intervention was confined to urban areas, and only to vagrant patients in advanced stages of the disease; as this exercise in oral history reveals, there are many worlds beyond.

Oral narrative can also help to fill in gaps within colonial histories, and enable a more sensitive use of such histories. For instance, the widespread prevalence of discriminatory practices directed at leprosy patients at the present time serves to problematise confident assertions of colonial officials that such practices were wiped out by imperial writ; one official wrote that 'under the British rule, when law and legal procedure predominate, families or communities have no power in this way to drive a leper from his house and property against his will . . . and so his Honour believes that lepers . . . commonly live in their houses with their families and defy the public opinion of the community'.[5] To take the example of contagion, the oral testimony of leprosy patients can enable a more sensitive reading of colonial records. Patients' testimony reveals that leprosy may be regarded, simultaneously, as a contagious disease and as a curse, thus it is extremely difficult to isolate a single cause for exile of patients. As virulent community hostility often coincides with the process of ulceration, this might suggest that ulceration is regarded as the more contagious phase, were it not for the fact that leprosy patients regularly exhibit their ulcers when begging for alms at pilgrimage sites, and this does not provoke visible panic from the general public. This kind of understanding of the complex nature of popular responses to leprosy is a useful aid in approaching even highly competent and able investigation, such as the *Report of the Leprosy Commission, 1890–91* where this complexity is not recognised, and is read instead merely as a native difference: 'It has all along struck the Commission that though a native on being questioned will, as a rule, state that leprosy is a contagious disease, yet his own acts do not support his statements.[6] Colonial sources are unsympathetic to the problematic encounter between the native patient and western medicine; such paradigms which have continued into the present are especially amenable to elucidation by oral history.

The testimony of the female patient is particularly valuable, and challenges considerably her colonial representation. The female leprosy patient achieves visibility in colonial official records only when her sexuality is perceived as constituting a threat to order within the asylum. There are references to separate wards for male and female patients in the asylums, and to homes set up to receive babies of patients at birth. Beyond this, the female patient simply does not exist, except as an appendage to male patients. Missionary publications, reluctant to comment on sexuality, which has no place in their representation of leprosy in terms of sin and redemption, are doubly silenced on female sexuality. Oral narrative reveals, on the other hand, the trauma of the mother who is separated from her children, or the condition of a wife who is discarded by her husband when he learned that she has leprosy. There are also numerous instances of healthy wives who remain with diseased husbands, even following them into exile. This points to new directions and the need to locate other sources to reconstruct the life of the female patient in the last century. What happened to healthy wives of leprosy patients? Did abandoned women patients remain, alone, on the fringe of the village, or did they join mobile bands and wander from temple to temple, from shrine to fair? Did they remarry? Did they bear children? Why was female fecundity such an issue in official and missionary records? Is this related to the fact that male potency declines with advancing leprosy?

Some of these issues may be contextualised with a reconstruction of the situation of one such patient, based upon interviews with villagers. Her name is Basanteen Bai. Residents of Dhangaon village (Rajnandgaon) remember her, and narrate her story. She married and moved to her husband's home in the nearby village of Asra. A young mother with two infant children, her husband evicted her from their home when he discovered that she had leprosy; this action was supported by the Panchayat, the village assembly of Asra. Basanteen Bai was forced to seek refuge at her parents's home. This incident appears to have taken place some three decades ago. Basanteen Bai's family took her for treatment to the Wesleyan Leprosy Home and Hospital at the district centre. It was a fair distance away, so a degree of anonymity was assured. I was unable to retrieve the records of her condition from amid the meticulously maintained records at this institute. Miss R. Bibbee, the Medical Superintendent reveals that it was fairly common for patients to register under an assumed name. Medical staff at this institute describe the attitude towards the leprosy patient in the sixties: the fear of contagion prevailing even amongst doctors, and the unwillingness of para-medical staff to even touch the patient; how the compounder would wrap up the sulfone tablets in some paper and toss them across the counter to the patient; how the few coins that the patient left by way of payment would be soaked in antiseptic for several hours before anyone would dare to touch them. Whenever she needed a fresh supply of medicine, Basanteen Bai would have to trek many miles; as even today patients frequently complain that medicines get damaged by rain and humidity, it is questionable how regularly she consumed her medication. In spite of this, Basanteen Bai continued with the treatment for some months. Doctors advised her to avoid contact with her children, and specifically to desist from breast-feeding her baby. One morning she wandered off, and threw herself across the railway track that borders one flank of Danhgaon. This story, brief though it is, throws into relief the sterility of official testimony. It also provides an entry point for the analysis of hospital and asylum records.

Colonial sources provide a history of leprosy in nineteenth century India, however fragmentary and ideologically charged this may be, and engagement with this archive can prove fruitful. For instance, the references to patient mobility across the country, and to visits to sites of pilgrimage, point to areas where oral history projects might profitably be conducted, especially as patient mobility is not conducive to uninterrupted medical treatment, and this can locate weak spots in the leprosy eradication programmes that are currently underway. Other documents, such as this letter from the High Priest of the Baidyanath Temple, Bengal, dated 8 May 1889, can serve to explain the rationale behind such congregation at temples:

> Baidyanath means the Lord of the Physicians and it is to Him that persons suffering from incurable diseases resort for their recovery from all parts of India . . . The *Susruta*, a great Hindu medical authority, declares leprosy to be a contagious disease. Another book recommends that bodies of dead lepers should not be burned, but buried in holy places . . . It is therefore clear that it is the duty of the relations of lepers to keep them beyond the reach of their fellows.[7]

Such sources can provide a basis for approaching popular perceptions of leprosy, and in assessing the relations of these to the high Sanskrit tradition.

There are indications that at the present time AIDS is being interpreted in some parts of India through the metaphor of leprosy. The visibility of leprosy in India, coupled with a body of prejudice about AIDS enables this connection to take place. In some villages of Kerela AIDS is being referred to as 'the rich man's leprosy', and patterns of community hostility towards AIDS patients are reminiscent of similar patterns of discrimination and marginalisation meted out to patients of leprosy. Oral history can help to prevent such situations from developing, and enable us to draw upon the experiences of the leprosy eradication effort to ensure that we cope with AIDS whilst remaining human and humane.

NOTES

1 Figures for 1991: 'National Leprosy Eradication Programme Guidelines, 1993', New Delhi, Leprosy Division, Ministry of Health and Family Welfare.
2 Studies on health policy in colonial India make very occasional or no mention at all of leprosy. See R. Macleod and M. Lewis (eds), *Disease, Medicine and Empire: Perspectives on Western Medicine and the Experience of European Expansion*, London, Routledge, 1988; R. Jeffery, *The Politics of Health in India*, Berkeley, University of California Press, 1988; T. Dyson (ed.), *India's Historical Demography: Studies in Famine, Disease and Society*, London, Curzon Press, 1989.
3 [A third interview is included in the original article – eds.]
4 Lepers Act, 1898, also known as Act. No. 111 of 1898, V/8/62, India Office Collections, [the original article includes an additional section on 'Colonial Representations of Leprosy' – eds].
5 H. Maude, Officiating Junior Secretary Govt. of Punjab, to the Officiating Secretary Govt. of India Home Dept., Lahore, 16 December 1889, Rpt. in P.S. Abraham (ed.), *Journal of the Leprosy Investigation Committee*, February 1891, no. 2, London, Macmillan, p. 44.
6 *Leprosy in India: Report of the Leprosy Commission in India, 1890–91*, Calentta, Govt. Printing, 1892.
7 Sailojananda Ojha, High Priest, Baidyanath Temple, Bengal, to the Private Secretary to the Viceroy, dated 8 May 1889, in *Papers Relating to the Treatment of Leprosy in India, 1887 to 1895*, pp. 15–16.

Part IV

Interpreting memories: introduction

Chapters in Part I, 'Critical developments', noted early concerns about the atheoretical use of oral evidence, and the development of more sophisticated interdisciplinary approaches to the interpretation of oral testimony. Ronald Grele urged colleagues to consider linguistic and performative aspects of the interview, and to explore the relationship between individual and social historical consciousness; Alessandro Portelli highlighted the orality and narrative form of interview testimony; and Portelli and Luisa Passerini emphasized the importance of subjectivity and showed how silences and 'false' memories can be illuminating forms of evidence. The authors in Part IV use oral history case studies to demonstrate various approaches to interpreting memories.[1]

Trevor Lummis argued in 1981 that 'the problem at the heart of using the interview method in history still remains that of moving from the individual account to a social interpretation'. While recognizing that studies of subjectivity and social memory have offered one angle on this problem, in the first extract Lummis responds to the concerns of some social historians about the representativeness and reliability of oral evidence. He considers a number of ways in which individual interviews can be used and interpreted, emphasizing the importance of triangulation with other evidence and showing how quantitative methods can enhance the validity of generalizations based on sets of oral history interviews.[2]

By contrast, the second extract by Samuel Schrager demonstrates the more qualitative interpretative approach which has characterized much oral history research. Schrager adapts ideas from folklore, linguistics and literary theory to explore the language and meaning of stories. He uses examples from migrant and labour history to show how historical accounts are generated, sustained and contested within different communities, and urges oral historians to recognize that they are 'intervening in a process that is already highly developed'. Schrager explains how features evident in the form of interview narratives – the relationship between narrator and event, similarities and differences between informants' accounts, and the categories which narrators use to generalize about previous events – can be quarried for evidence about social relationships in the past. Since Schrager's article was published in 1983, social memory and narrative form have become pivotal interpretative interests for oral historians.[3]

Alistair Thomson also grapples with the interconnections between individual and collective memory, showing how the remembering of an Australian war veteran was influenced by subsequent personal experiences and by changes in public commemoration which offered different ways of making sense of past experience. Analysis of the layers of meaning which are threaded through recorded memories not only helps us to understand what happened in the past, but can also show how the meanings of past events have changed over time for individuals and in society. The exploration of Fred Farrall's life history also shows how memory and identity are interwoven: Farrall's identity – as a man and a soldier – was shaped by his war memories and, in turn, his changing personal identity affected how he was able to remember the war.[4]

Thomson notes, however, the ethical dilemmas of interview and interpretative approaches which attempt to deconstruct the ways in which people have composed the memories that they live with. The three extracts which follow explore the relationship between interviewer and interviewee during the interpretative process. The introduction to Peter Friedlander's book *The Emergence of a UAW Local, 1936–1939: a Study in Class and Culture* (published in 1975) was an influential and pioneering exploration of oral history theory and method based on a set of interviews between Friedlander and the trade unionist Edmund Kord. Friedlander was one of the first oral historians to reject the notion that memory is a static resource to be mined for facts, and instead argued for a 'critical dialogue' between interviewer and interviewee: 'in contrast to the static and undialectical procedure of orthodox historiography, Kord and I were continually shaping and reshaping historical concepts to fit the emerging pattern of Local 229, attacking the history from various angles'. This interpretative dialogue 'reacted back on the original source, Kord's memory'. The 'elaboration of a number of hypotheses gave a critical focus to his effort to recall', and his recollections 'became richer and more precise' (p. 315). Friedlander shows how remembering is itself a process of historical interpretation, and that both parties to an interview play an active role in that process.

By contrast, Katherine Borland considers a situation in which an interviewee disputes the historian's interpretation of her memories. Borland had interviewed her grandmother Beatrice Hanson, and produced a feminist interpretation of a story about the young Beatrice at a horse race meeting with her father in 1944. Grandmother Hanson 'expressed strong disagreement' with Borland's interpretation of 'a female struggle for autonomy within a hostile male environment'. Borland asserts the value of researchers' interpretations which are not simply 'a recuperation of original authorial intention', yet she also notes the dangers of attacking 'collaborators' carefully constructed sense of self' and outlines a more negotiated interpretative process, an exchange of understandings which might benefit both parties.[5]

Kathleen Blee describes a research scenario in which such an interpretative exchange was virtually impossible, an oral history of the Ku Klux Klan. Blee shows how the testimony of her interviewees was affected by their political agendas, by retrospective censure of the Klan, and by the desire 'to appear respectable to an oral historian'. Yet she also argues that such interviews are revelatory about motivations and ideologies – 'how and why ordinary people might become attracted to the politics of racial hatred' – enabling historians 'to scrutinize the accounts of political actors, and to probe those experiences, beliefs and narratives that do not fit conventional historical interpretations'. Blee questions the recommended practice of an empathetic interview relationship, and struggles with an ethical concern that she may have empowered her interviewees by helping them 'to construct a narrative that "makes sense" of the Klan and its actions'. This study pinpoints a central tension in the role of the oral historian, between responsibility to the interviewee and responsibility to society and history.[6]

In the final extract in this section, Elizabeth Lapovsky Kennedy demonstrates how her oral history of working-class lesbians in New York State has been enriched by a variety of interpretative strategies which heed the empirical, subjective and narrative qualities of oral testimony. The exquisite storytelling styles of her informants revealed the significance of storytelling in a community which needed to create alternative identities and 'guidelines for living'. By embracing 'the uniquely subjective nature of life stories', Kennedy could explore how her narrators coped with and resisted heterosexism and homophobia, and how individuals 'decide to construct and express their identity'. Cases where narrators' memories were internally contradictory or in conflict with each other 'conveyed precisely the freedom and joy and the pain and limitation that characterized bar life in the mid-twentieth century'. Differences between gay male and lesbian memories of the Stonewall riots (a key event in gay liberation), and the ways in which only some stories were inscribed in the myth or meta-narrative of Stonewall, expressed 'the ambiguous position of women in gay culture' and captured 'the cultural processes of making lesbians and women invisible in history'. Kennedy demonstrates that 'there is a tremendous amount to be learned by fully exploring the subjective and oral nature of oral histories', but her conclusion – that the empirical and subjective values of oral evidence are 'fully complementary to one another' and should not be 'falsely polarized' – is an essential recommendation for all oral historians.

NOTES

1 For overviews about oral history interpretation, see P. Thompson, *The Voice of the Past: Oral History*, Oxford, Oxford University Press, 1988, pp. 101–149 and 217–265; S. Berger Gluck and D. Patai, *Women's Words: The Feminist Practice of Oral History*, New York and London, Routledge, 1991 (especially Part II, Authority and Interpretation, pp. 59–106); and D.K. Dunaway, 'The interdisciplinarity of oral history', in D.K. Dunaway and W.K. Baum (eds), *Oral History: An Interdisciplinary*

Anthology, Walnut Creek, Altamira Press, 1996, pp. 7–22. Dunaway's concern about the theoretical bent in recent oral history (p. 9) is developed by P.K. Blatz in 'Craftsmanship and flexibility in oral history: a pluralistic approach to methodology and theory', *The Public Historian*, 1990, vol. 12, no. 4, pp. 7–22.

2 See also T. Lummis, *Listening to History: The Authenticity of Oral Evidence*, London, Hutchinson, 1987. For comparable approaches, see Thompson, *The Voice of the Past*, pp. 247–251; R. Jensen, 'Oral history, quantification and the new social history', *Oral History Review*, 1981, vol. 9, pp. 13–25; P.S. Li, 'Constructing immigrants' work worlds from oral testimony', *Canadian Oral History Association Journal*, 1989, no. 9, pp. 9–12.

3 On narrative form see: S.G. Davies, 'Review essay: storytelling rights', *Oral History Review*, 1988, vol. 16, no. 2, pp. 109–115; S. Featherstone, 'Jack Hill's horse: narrative form and oral history', *Oral History*, 1991, vol. 19, no. 2, pp. 59–62; R.C. Smith, 'Review essay: storytelling as experience', *Oral History Review*, 1995, vol. 22, pp. 87–91; M.F. Chanfrault-Duchet, 'Narrative structures, social models, and symbolic representation in the life story', in Gluck and Patai, *Women's Words*, pp. 77–92. On oral history and social memory see, for example, J. Bodner, 'Power and memory in oral history: workers and managers at Studebaker', *Journal of American History*, 1989, vol. 75, no. 4, pp. 1201–1221; see also references in Part I, 'Critical developments' (notes 8 and 25).

4 See also, A. Thomson, *Anzac Memories: Living With the Legend*, Melbourne, Oxford University Press, 1994. Other studies which explore the relationships between individual and social remembering, subjectivity and identity, include: L. Passerini, 'Work ideology and consensus under Italian fascism', *History Workshop*, 1979, no. 8, pp. 82–108 (see Chapter 5); R. Grele, 'Listen to their voices: two case studies in the interpretation of oral history interviews', *Oral History*, 1979, vol. 7, no. 1, pp. 33–42; I. Bertaux-Wiame, 'The life story approach to the study of internal migration', *Oral History*, 1979, vol. 7, no. 1, pp. 26–32; A. Bravo, 'Italian women in the Nazi camps – aspects of identity in their accounts', *Oral History*, 1985, vol. 13, no. 1, pp. 20–27; R. Samuel and P. Thompson (eds), *The Myths We Live By*, London, Routledge, 1990; V. Yans-McLaughlin, 'Metaphors of self in history: subjectivity, oral narrative and immigration studies', in V. Yans-McLaughlin (ed.), *Immigration Reconsidered: History, Sociology and Politics*, New York, Oxford University Press, 1990; and A. Portelli, 'The death of Luigi Trastulli: memory and the event', and 'Uchronic dreams: working-class memory and possible worlds', in *The Death of Luigi Trastulli and Other Stories: Form and Meaning in Oral History*, Albany, SUNY Press, 1991, pp. 1–26 and pp. 99–116.

5 Two other examples of interpretative conflict and collaboration within family oral histories are Akemi Kikumura's article in Part II (Chapter 12), and A. Thomson, 'Memory as a battlefield; personal and political investments in the national military past', *Oral History Review*, 1995, vol. 22, no. 2, pp. 55–74.

6 See E. Luchterhand, 'Knowing and not knowing: involvement in Nazi genocide', in P. Thompson and N. Burchardt (eds), *Our Common History: The Transformation of Europe*, London, Pluto, 1982, pp. 251–272; R.J. Grele, 'History and the languages of history in the oral history interview: who answers whose questions and why?', in E. McMahan and K.L. Rogers (eds), *Interactive Oral History Interviewing*, Hillsdale, N.J., Lawrence Erlbaum, 1994, pp. 1–18 and 163–164.

23 Structure and validity in oral evidence

Trevor Lummis

Trevor Lummis was formerly Senior Research Officer at the Department of Sociology, University of Essex. Reprinted from *International Journal of Oral History*, 1983, vol. 2, no. 2, pp. 109–120 (Meckler Publishing). Reproduced with permission of Greenwood Publishing Group Inc., Westport, Conn., USA.

The validation of oral evidence can be divided into two main areas: the degree to which any individual interview yields reliable information on the historical experience, and the degree to which that individual experience is typical of its time and place. The first part of this paper will look at one or two examples in which individual interviews have been used or interpreted. The major concern, however, is to suggest ways in which simple aggregation can be used to assess validity, for as the data in oral history archives lacks the random quality required for formal statistical validity, some acceptable method of generalising from a number of interviews has to be developed. This need not be merely an exercise in positivistic methodology, but the process of structuring data should be part of the interpretative process and might be used to elucidate some of the wider problems of omission and distortion in oral evidence as they relate to the life-cycle and/or wider cultural events.

THE INDIVIDUAL INTERVIEW

The main concern for oral history is the degree to which accurate recall of the past is possible. It is frequently assumed that it cannot, and the following is a typical expression of this view:

> The difficulty lies in the fact that memory does not constitute pure recall; the memory of any particular event is refracted through layer upon layer of subsequent experience and through the influence of the dominant and/ or local and specific ideology.[1]

This is something of an assertion, however, for there seems to be very little certain knowledge of how the brain records and retains information. It is known that when memory fails it is the most recent memories which go first, while early memories remain clear or are even enhanced. I.M.L. Hunter also states that stimulation of the memory and efforts to remember events can lead to the recall of 'hitherto unreported parts of the original'.[2] Both of these factors suggest that memories are not overlaid, but are laid down in the cells as unique traces and can be recalled as such.

Through experience as an interviewer, I distinguish between memory and recall on pragmatic grounds. By memory I mean the fund of information about the past that an informant will readily relate, often as polished stories or anecdotes, which suggests that they have been frequently retold or thought about; as such, they are liable to be integrated with subsequent experience and values. By recall I mean responses to detailed interviewing which prompts dormant 'memories' that are less likely to be integrated into the individual's present value structure. This latter category includes a great deal of circumstantial evidence.

Clearly, a great deal depends upon exactly what it is that the interview is trying to achieve. It is a mistake to discuss interviews as if they are a standard product, since some areas are more difficult to recapture than others. If an interview is part of an attempt at historical reconstruction of daily life, then the validity of an interview can be assessed for its general accuracy by the degree to which it corresponds to checkable details such as wage levels, and how these details compare with other occupations, prices of goods, local facilities, and so on. These can establish that the correct period is being discussed and that the informant has a reliable recall. In other words, the normal process of maximum triangulation with other sources can go a long way toward establishing the general reliability of the interview. Also, a detailed interview covering routine work processes or descriptive details of the home hardly lends itself to systematic distortion. Yet it is from data of this sort that the historian can build up a picture of a situation and the values and relationships which were part of it. The point is that the interviewer can (if necessary) discount the informant's purpose in relating an incident and accept only what is incidental. For example, one informant, in response to a question on the politics of her father, gave the names of the candidates in the 1906 election (which she dated as 1905) and went on to relate her main memory of the election – that she and some friends 'cheeked' the wife of one candidate. Quite incidentally to the main point of the narrative, she relates:

> I remember they had a meeting and we weren't allowed in, us girls weren't. So we walked as far as Dark Lane as they called it and turned round and came back, a lovely moonlight night. February or March time. That's how we used to while away our time . . . (and then comes the point of her story).[3]

In fact, the election took place in January and early February, and her dating of the incident is clearly based on the darkness of the evening; taken with circumstantial detail, the account is obviously based on detailed recall. It is this, rather than the informant's manipulation of emphasis, which is of interest. The few lines cited are full of information of the age and sex exclusion from a village meeting on politics (she was sixteen years old) and on the winter leisure activity of teenage girls – information which is surely more typical than the remembered and reported fairs that are mentioned in response to questions on 'leisure'. Just as a question on leisure will often be revealing of social class boundaries through accounts of who shared the leisure activities and what types of activities were considered as 'too posh',[4] it is possible that circumstantial detail of this indirect nature may have been filtered through present consciousness, although it is unlikely when given in terms of an actual recalled activity peripheral to the subject area. As Paul Thompson[5] has indicated, a person's *interpretation* of events can be affected by the physiological and social process of aging. The perception that there was more friendliness and community in the past might be due more to the failing capacities and social isolation of the elderly than to any substantial difference between then and now in terms of the wider social group. This sort of value distortion can be allowed for by actually assessing the amount of sociability apparent in the informant's account: for example how near they lived to kin, how frequently and under what circumstances they met with relatives and with neighbours, and so on. In other words, the informant's interpretation of the degree to which society has changed need not be the accepted one.

Nevertheless, if careful reading and cross-checking can, in most cases, establish the validity of much of the detail in interviews, it does not solve the problem of omission and suppression.

This is linked to the complex area of the deeper levels of consciousness and communication, and an article by Ron Grele[6] reveals the number of academic disciplines that might be involved in fully understanding an interview. In a subsequent article and conference paper, Grele has presented his analysis of two interviews for their 'underlying structure of consciousness'[7] in order to reveal how the informants construct their own past. His argument also raises the interesting aspect of the use/interpretation that the historian wants to make of an interview (and that may be at an equally subconscious level as the informant). That is, the methodology used to understand and validate an interview will be intimately connected to the underlying historical assumptions: it will likewise shape the nature of the history emerging from it. For this reason, interpreting interviews in terms of individual structures runs the risk of atomising historical interpretation. In his review of *Hard Times*, Michael Frisch[8] focussed on oral history's potential for understanding cultural processes, and the way in which memory becomes history. He noted that Terkel's book was hailed as a 'huge anthem of praise to the American Spirit', in spite of recording the destructive effect of the Depression years on so many people. In presenting individual experiences as separate entities, there is bound to be some denial of history, since such presentations evade explanations based on any process wider than the individual endurance of economic or social processes. Indeed, as Frisch indicates, the interviews are an eloquent testimony as to why the Depression did not produce 'a more focussed critique of American capitalism and culture'.[9]

Grele's attempt to 'understand the people we are interviewing and their historical point of view'[10] through the structure of the interview is a valuable counter to the acceptance of interview data as positivistic 'facts'. What is less clear is the value of establishing the informant's view of the past in terms of historiographical categories. For, in light of Frisch's comment on *Hard Times*, it will come as no surprise to discover that one of the two interviews analysed by Grele reveals 'liberal consensus historiography' and that the other is 'really almost non-historical'.[11] It is difficult to see how many people are going to arrive at any other structure without a specific knowledge of alternative interpretations to the dominant ethos. They may not have been 'formally instructed by the agencies of the larger culture on how they should view their world and their own lives and pasts',[12] but it might also be argued that culture is so all-pervasive that formal action is unnecessary. Grele states that 'Frisch's major insight is to show us how Terkel's respondents in *Hard Times* divorce themselves from history by turning history into biography and thereby personalising events.'[13] I would suggest that this is a mirror-image of the actual process, and that in fact individuals are bound to experience history as biography. It is this personal experience of events which preserves a limited view of history. The two informants analysed by Grele were both activists, and therefore part of that minority which is most likely to develop and hold a more conscious view of history. Yet it is stated of the ahistorical interview that

> Even at that point where it could be historical – her socialism – it retains its basic static nature and, in effect, defines socialism in terms of its own structure, not that of the socialist theoreticians – a phenomena [*sic*] which we may find is generally observable among the American working class.[14]

Given the anti-socialist pressure in American culture since the start of the Cold War, it would not be surprising to find that individuals who were activists in the 1920s and 1930s now relate their part in that commitment and struggle in terms of economic reformism and common-sense fair play. Contemporary values clearly shape the informant's interpretation of their own past, and impose the subconscious historical structure of the narrative. Analysing the structure of the interview will be valuable for understanding the *present* values (and therefore the potential distortions) of the informant, but an informant's present values cannot be assumed to illuminate their earlier values or attitudes. At an early stage in his career, such an informant may well have believed in total revolution and the inevitability of socialism. Since people frequently become less radical as they grow older, oral evidence probably has an inherent tendency to under-report conflict, and history as individual experience seems likely to strengthen that trend.

It may be that (for the present at least) there is no entirely satisfactory method of validating individual interviews. It might be surmised that the more aware of history and politics an informant is, the more likely is the danger of his rationalising an account of the past to harmonize with a present viewpoint.[15]

There is no doubt that remarkable results can come from one informed person. Friedlander,[16] for example, uses ethnic groupings in the work force to

explain aspects of unionisation and solidarity. Nevertheless, as his informant's experience is necessarily located in one of those groups, his account of
the process may be very partial. The virtue of drawing on a number of
interviews is that they provide some basis for cross-reference.

AGGREGATION AND TABULATION

As this procedure has been criticised for being 'positivistic', it should be
stated that the method is not tied to any specific epistemology. Whether retrospective interviewing is capable of establishing 'factual' data, or whether it
can only record an 'interpretation' of previous facts, structuring the evidence
is equally valuable. If oral evidence is to move from a form of biography to an
historical account, it must proceed from an individual to a social experience.
Even if interviews are 'interpretations', it is still necessary to try to establish
how interpretations change through time, their distribution in social groups,
and the reality which formed them. If they cannot be used to contribute to
historical understanding, there is no reason for historians to interview
people. Before turning to the method of establishing the validity of a group
of interviews, however, I would argue that structuring a number of interviews
can contribute to understanding memory – even in the shape of structured
silences.

The notion of 'silences' comes from Luisa Passerini's work which,
although using a large number of interviews with ordinary workers, has
consciousness firmly at the centre of its concerns.[17] Here just two of the
dimensions she uses will be mentioned – the 'silences' on the years under
Fascism and 'inconsistent' answers, which are accounts which make no reference to major historical events and processes. In commenting on her article, a
History Workshop editorial[18] notes that the idea of a collective silence is
supported by work from Germany and that, in the British context, there is
little beyond the anecdotal to be found in oral accounts covering the period
of the General Strike of 1926. The editorial speculates as to whether that
could be the result of a similar silence, or whether it is 'simply that the
"political" impinges on individual lives in very different ways from the
personal'.[19] There are three aspects here, all part of the structure of memory
– the degree to which memories are censored, the reference points for chronology, and the related issue of how the public and private spheres cohere in
the individual consciousness.

That a number of people who experienced Fascism and Nazism should
avoid spontaneous mention of those years is a reasonable proposition. Those
ideologies were in overt political control for only a brief period, and suffered
an overwhelming military and political defeat. I do not believe, however, that
the scant references to the General Strike in Britain can be explained along
these lines. The trade union movement may have been defeated, but it was not
total, and within twenty years trade unions were enjoying greater power than
they had previously experienced. Trade unionism is not a creed or activity

rejected by all progressive opinion, and there is no reason to assume any self-censorship. Nevertheless, the omission is an interesting one, and the answer to this phenomenon probably lies in the distinction between public and private – that is, the link between memory, experience, and how this is structured in the mind. The example cited by Passerini of a narrative which recounted life up to and including World War I and then the period of the early 1920s before moving to World War II reminded me of my interviews with informants from that age cohort. They too relate their early years, their introduction to work, service in World War I, and their return to work. Then, unless there is some dramatic personal event, they jump to World War II. This leads me to speculate on whether the silences noted are due to censorship or, as was suggested above, simply that public events do not impinge on personal narrative and chronology.

Structuring a number of interviews should be one method of determining to what degree silences and omissions of this general nature are due to 'censorship' or because political events pass largely unregarded. Structuring their chronology would be a start, for it seems that most interviews are a mixture of public and private chronology, but that on the whole the public is used only where it impinges on the private. For example, narratives tend to be separated into periods on the basis of personal and familial events – births and deaths, leaving school, changing occupations, moving house, and so on. Public time intrudes mainly where events force a change in private experience, as when war forces changes in occupation, family separation, and geographical movement. A comparison between the chronology of different cohorts should reveal whether this is the case. The date of the private life-cycle events of each cohort will fall into a different period of public historical events. Therefore, a comparison of the silences and omissions of different cohorts should reveal whether public events do impose silences on particular cohorts. Given the required international cooperation, this comparison might be further tested through comparison with cohorts in other countries. The different cultures, stages of industrial development, and political regimes might even reveal which aspect of the public dimension seems to shape consciousness and ideology.

Ultimately, the question of how memory functions may be a problem for medical rather than historical research, but the structuring and analysis of the way in which people do organise their chronology and relate their life to the public domain would provide some guidance for the use of oral evidence.

The possibility of understanding the structure and consciousness of individual interviews through their comparative structure is, however, only one of two dimensions of validity. The other is the degree to which an interview, or group of interviews, might be representative of a wider social group.

The problems of using interviews as if they were a representative sample is an issue which needs to be discussed. At present, historians simply assume that their informants' experiences are in some sense typical of whichever group they come from, the parameters of that group affinity being set by the historian. This may not be an unrealistic process of historical analysis where the evidence is related to a specific piece of research. But the problem of the valid use of oral evidence is going to increase as the number and range of interviews in archives grows. The problem of interpreting oral evidence and its validity becomes linked to the problems of archiving and of selective retrieval. Paul Thompson's project 'Family Life and Work Experience before 1918' took a quota sample of 444 informants based on the census categories of 1911, in order to ensure that the research was broadly representative of the social structure of the period.[20] However, most oral history projects (including the two main additions to the Essex University Archive) are focussed on a particular group or area, and the interviews do not fill a quota but trace and interview those who participated in the particular circumstance. Although each project by itself may have proceeded quite reasonably on the basis of historical common sense, subsequent researchers wishing to use interviews from more than one project need some means of assessing whether the interviews are in any way typical of the group they are studying.

This is essentially a mundane but necessary task, for to make generalisations based on oral evidence is to claim, at least implicitly, that the interviews used are representative. Quantification and generalisation – 'a few', 'the unskilled', 'some', and similar terms – appear constantly in historical narrative and almost as frequently do not indicate at all what evidence affords a basis for such statements. Attempting to categorise and quantify qualitative evidence presents enormous problems. Still, tabulation can provide a means of assessing how representative are a group of interviews, by revealing the level of internal consistency and by demonstrating the degree of conformity to the broader historical picture known from other sources.

Some data are readily tabulated: age, marital status, number of siblings, religion, and political preference can be coded without any great qualitative loss. This allows for an initial comparison with distributions known from other historical sources. The demographic details, for example, can be structured to provide a comparison with what is known about family size and the facts affecting mortality. The tables which follow are taken from data given by informants about the number of siblings and deaths in their family.[21] It should be noted that 'Reported Number of Sibling Deaths' cannot be compared directly with official statistics on births and losses in the family of children up to the age of twelve or thirteen. Table I(A) gives the figures for the whole sample, providing a general baseline. Given the known effect for the period, one should expect a higher mortality rate among those living in urban areas than those in rural areas. Table I(B) shows that the sample conforms to this trend. Table I(C) divides the group into cohorts by decade of birth; the change in sibling mortality is what would be anticipated from a valid sample. The increase in family size was by then falling, although it could represent a local trend since it was a prosperous decade for the local fishermen. Because no figures for the occupation are available, the point remains speculative.

If a sample is conformable to known trends, one can have some confidence that the internal distinctions will reflect real distinctions. This assumption is enhanced by Table I(D). High mortality is associated with poverty and class. So, given that there is a structured differential in income between the status groups, this should be reflected in similar variations in the mortality rate in the sample. And this trend appears much more strongly in fact, than the qualitative material would lead one to expect. Once one is confident that the tables have some significance,[22] they can be used to aid interpretation. Table I(E) is an example. This shows that the families of men engaged in trawling and drifting share similar mortality rates, whereas the inshore fishermen and non-fishermen share similar but remarkably lower rates. As it is known from the interviews that this is not due to income differences, one is obliged to consider other aspects, and the most plausible one is the pattern of work. In the two groups with high mortality, the man is away from home and the woman is left to cope with the family on her own. The other two groups are at home regularly. This focusses attention on the structure of family life and behaviour. Once again, the simple structuring of the data has given insights which were not evident from the qualitative material. For example, the use of corporal punishment in the home to socialise children reveals the same pattern as the mortality figures, and the absence of the male from the home changes the woman's use of punishment rather than that of the man. Thus, one is forced to consider the interaction between work patterns, family life, and the effect that this has on individual behaviour, rather than a simple relationship between poverty and mortality.

Oral evidence is sometimes criticised on grounds that people cannot, or do not, distinguish with sufficient care between their current ideas and those that they held at an earlier period. This is an issue to which there are no simple answers. Once again, however, there is some value in structuring interviews in order to assess the care with which information has been given.

Table II shows the political allegiance of the informants and their fathers. The information is as unexceptional as it need be in order to show its authenticity. If, on the other hand, the few Labour supporters to be found in the occupation and area had been reported in the earlier cohorts, there would have been good reason to suspect careless reporting. In fact, many of the informants report changing to Labour in 1945. The interesting factor here is that this takes place not as a simple shift along a continuum, but has Liberal moving to Conservative and Conservative moving to Labour. This accuracy is important for political history, because it has been claimed since the Ballot Act of 1872 that 'we cannot make precise correlations between electoral behaviour of small localities and the appropriate statistics of personal income, occupation, religious affiliation and so on'. The advantage of oral history is that it does allow for these patterns to be established in great detail. The internal consistency of this very small group is impressive: it shows (in tables not given here) the driftermen, mainly Liberal, and the trawlermen, Conservative, as suggested in contemporary sources, although the sample also shows that this is modified by status. It even demonstrates the commonly

Table I Reported family size and mortality

		Average no. of siblings per respondent	Reported number of sibling deaths	Percentage of sibling mortality	Number of respondents
A	All respondents	8.0 (482)	1.0 (58)	12	60
B	Urban	8.0	1.2	15	32
	Rural	8.0	0.7	9	28
Respondent born					
C	To 1889	9.6	1.3	14	18
	1890–1899	7.0	1.0	14	27
	1900–1909	8.0	0.5	7	15
Respondent's father					
D	Trawling and drifting				
	Owners	8.2	0.8	11	9
	Skippers	8.3	1.3	16	13
	Crew	9.5	2.3	25	6
E	Drifting	8.0	1.3	16	16
	Trawling	9.4	1.6	17	12
	Inshore	6.7	0.5	7	20
	Non-fishermen	8.9	0.8	8	12

Table II Political pattern by decade of birth: respondents and their fathers *

	Conservative	Liberal	Labour	Apolitical	Don't know	Total
To 1870	38% (11)	21% (6)	—	14% (4)	24% (7)	29
1871–1880	53% (16)	30% (9)	—	3% (1)	17% (5)	30
1881–1890	14% (3)	32% (7)	5% (1)	18% (4)	32% (7)	22
1891–1900	35% (9)	15% (4)	8% (2)	15% (4)	27% (7)	26
1901–1910	46% (6)	—	8% (1)	—	46% (6)	13
Totals	38% (45)	22% (26)	3% (4)	11% (13)	27% (32)	120

Note: * The date of birth of the father has been arbitrarily placed twenty-five years earlier than that of the respondent

asserted link between the Church of England and the Conservatives, and the Liberals and Nonconformity.

The structuring of data from one fairly homogeneous group of views is instructive on two levels. It shows that this small accidental sample of elderly informants (mean average date of birth 1897, one-third born in the 1880s) displays an impressive congruence with wider historical trends, even when the interviews are divided into numerous cells. Second, even though the occupation had an unusually high level of cultural identity between the working fishermen and small owners, the structured evidence reveals stratified distinctions in behaviour and attitudes which were not apparent from perusing the qualitative evidence of individual interviews. Thus, structuring the evidence not only provided some grounds for generalising the evidence in the interviews, but actually contributed to a more accurate appreciation of its meaning and to a reshaping of the interpretation drawn from it. The value of such restructuring will, to a large extent, depend on the research problems. In my own case, a great deal of basic historical reconstruction was necessary because of lack of satisfactory documentary evidence on even such basic information as earnings. It was essential to reconstruct in detail the working practices – control of recruitment, crew autonomy, and so on – in order to understand how the occupational values affected industrial and social attitudes and perceptions.

Oral accounts from those who experienced the specific situation provide unsurpassed and irreplaceable evidence for actual behaviour. I am also convinced that there are enormous advantages to be gained if these accounts are as fully biographical as is practicable. For instance, an understanding of the socio-industrial values of the fishermen was greatly enhanced by access to their earlier lives. Many were recruited from the rural hinterland of the fishing ports, and their experience of the material and social conditions of the countryside helps to explain their response to new circumstances. Nevertheless, the problem at the heart of using the interview method in history still remains that of moving from the individual account to a social interpretation.

NOTES

1 'Editorial', *History Workshop*, 1979, no. 8, p. iii.
2 I.M.L. Hunter, *Memory: Facts and Fallacies*, London, 1958.
3 Essex University Oral History Archive, no. 3025.
4 For an example see T. Lummis, 'The occupational community of East Anglian fishermen', *British Journal of Sociology*, March 1977, pp. 51–74.
5 For this and memory in general, see P. Thompson, *The Voice of the Past: Oral History*, Oxford, 1978.
6 R.J. Grele, 'A surmisable variety: interdisciplinarity and oral testimony', *American Quarterly*, August 1975, pp. 275–295.
7 R.J. Grele, 'Listen to their voices', *Oral History*, Spring 1979, pp. 33–42.
8 M. Frisch, 'Oral history and *Hard Times*, a review essay', *Red Buffalo*, n.d., pp. 217–231.
9 Ibid.
10 Grele, 'Listen to their voices'.
11 Ibid.
12 Ibid.
13 Ibid.
14 Ibid.
15 Even in this difficult area, detailed 'reconstruction' of the past can help. Questions on the books they read, whether they were 'then' aware of ideological debates (for example, Trotskyism or Stalinism) and similar detail can make possible some inferences. This line of questioning might be met with 'silences' or evasion, but in an activist this would be eloquent in itself.
16 See P. Friedlander, *The Emergence of a U.A.W. Local, 1936–1939*, Pittsburgh, 1975.

17 L. Passerini, 'Work, ideology and consensus under Italian fascism', *History Workshop*, 1979, no. 8.
18 'Editorial', *History Workshop*, 1979, no. 8.
19 Ibid.
20 For a fuller account of this project see Thompson, *The Voice of the Past*.
21 These tables and many others can be found in Social Science Research Council Final Report, HR 2656/1 by T. Lummis and P. Thompson. Those used here are largely self-explanatory. In Table I(E) the categories refer to three separate types of fishing which imposed distinct work routines, and therefore affected the level of contact with family and community. Non-fishermen were largely manual workers. Table I(D) refers to the status groups in only two of the categories, since the distinctions were not present in the other two.
22 Note that this is not statistical significance. Because of the unknown bias of mortality and so forth, no oral history sample can be a random sample. What is attempted here is the customary process of historical analysis based on the available evidence.

24 What is social in oral history?

Samuel Schrager

At the time of writing Samuel Schrager was a lecturer at the University of Pennsylvania. Extracted from *International Journal of Oral History*, 1983, vol. 4, no. 2, pp. 76–98 (Meckler Publishing). Reproduced with permission of Greenwood Publishing Group Inc., Westport, Conn., USA.

I

When I went to Idaho after finishing college, without knowing what I would do there except work as a fire lookout during the summer, I began hearing old people talk about what had happened in their country, and what had happened to them, in the past. They told stories with an ease and directness that made the early days seem real and compelling, as if they were still in the air. I was struck by a sense that somehow these people were drawing their recollections from one another, that, even though it would never be possible to recover the actual paths by which the stories had developed, they had grown out of a conversation that has been going on since the very beginnings of settlement and that continues whenever there is talk about the memorable past. Whatever gets recalled after all this time stands for a piece of truth that remains about a world that is gone. There are complicated kinds of agreement and disagreement about the nature of this truth, and it gets probed from many angles of vision. But there is no choice about being inside or outside the dialogue. Everyone is part of it, invested with a participant's responsibility for sifting through what he or she has lived.

[. . .] the oral historian is an intervener in a process that is already highly developed. It is a common illusion to think that this is not so, that narrators are creating their accounts for the first time in the course of the interview. In any such performance there is new and unique creation: in the combination of words, the association of ideas, the ordering of incidents, and much else besides, including, perhaps, the production of entirely new narratives. In all of this the oral historian has a participatory role.[1] But here, as in most circumstances of storytelling, most of what is told has been said before in a related form. Obviously, every narrative must have its initial telling – but usually it appears to take place relatively close in time to the events being described. In the form that the oral historian is likely to encounter it, the story has already undergone the progressive structuring of detail that accompanies retellings.[2] For those who think the purpose of an interview is to get beyond already-formed accounts to some deeper truth about the subject, this may seem discouraging. It should not be. An account's previous tellings give it validity apart from the moment of the interview. If it belongs to the teller's repertoire of narrative, it is grounded in his or her life and in the social world in which that life is lived.

What the oral historian does is to provide a new context for the telling of mainly preexistent narrative and then to tape what is said so that parts of it can be separated and utilized later in yet other contexts. [. . .]

Insofar as the documentary enterprise makes recollection appear to be a preeminently personal phenomenon, the product of an individual and an interview, we are deterred from realizing that accounts begin and evolve in the course of social life and come to listeners, researchers, and readers bearing the imprint of earlier interactions. Oral testimony is full of messages about these social realities – messages which often are noted intuitively, and can be grasped more systematically once the narrative character of the testimony is taken seriously. In the following pages I consider three aspects of the composition of oral history that can be quarried for evidence about social relationships: the position of the teller *vis-à-vis* events; similarities and oppositions in different tellers' versions of events; and categories that the teller employs when generalizing and individualizing events. My point of entry will be 'point of view', a literary concept that at first glance seems to address what is most personal about oral history, namely the particular perspective of the teller, but on closer inspection leads as well to whatever there is about oral history that is most social.[3]

II

By point of view I mean the complicated relationship between the narrator and the events described. This involves not only the narrator's own position with respect to what happened, but also the stances he or she takes towards other participants in the events. Attention to point of view in this latter sense is an especially good antidote for narrowly autobiographical conceptions of oral history. It shows that, far from dealing only with ourselves when we tell about the past, we incorporate the experiences of a multitude of others along with our own; they appear in what we say through our marvellous capacity to express other perspectives. You may be the main character in an event you are describing, but you certainly don't have to be. The protagonist can as easily be a member of the family, a friend or an acquaintance, a figure you know of but haven't met, some larger grouping like the residents of a community, or yourself along with some other persons. You may even reach outside the human circle entirely to take the part of an animal, a dwelling, a place. As the action of the narrative progresses, you can change the focus from one character to another. And you can do more than speak on their behalf; you can quote them directly and even impersonate their voices or their thoughts.

As Anna Marie Oslund began her multi-episodic tale of her family's migration from Sweden, she said:

> I was born in eighteen ninety-one. And in eighteen ninety-two, the end of that summer – it was a late summer – my father went to America to find a better life for all of us. It was *hard* all over and he thought he'd try, he'd come.[4]

Already she had introduced two distinct points of view she would be taking as the story unfolded, her own and her father's; and she had hinted at two more, the words 'all of us', alluding to her family as a whole, and 'hard all over', the society of which they were part. In succeeding episodes she described difficulties which beset all of these people – her father trying to make a stake in Idaho so he could send for the family; the siblings being sheltered by kin and neighbors during her mother's illness; herself cleaning fish off the boats during the night to help by earning a few cents; she and classmates going without lunch in school; Idaho homesteaders losing a harvest to rain in the midst of a depression. At the moment of deciding whether to join their father in America, she made the story funny as she assumed the voice of every member of the family in the space of a few breaths:

> And I think on the third time he says, 'Now', he says, 'you come, or I'll have to come and get you, and that would be lots more expensive.'
>
> All right. Mother called her children, little flock together, and she said, 'Do *you* want to go?' She said to Olivia. 'No,' she said, 'no, I don't want to go because life's just beginning, y'know, you get good jobs and things like that in Sweden too.'
>
> And Esther, all her life she has cried: '*Oh yah*' *(whimpering)*, she didn't want to go either.
>
> And then Signe, she just big-eyed and she didn't know much what it was all about at that age.
>
> And I was the last one that she asked. And I said, 'Yeah, I'm going.' '*Ooooww*' *(crying)*, then everybody cried and I cried too *(laughs)*.[5]

Subsequently her point of view entailed new kinds of relationships, in new surroundings – eating candy with her sweetheart in the corner of the railway station before the departure; among the passengers on the boat; with a tall stranger who lifted her up to see the Statue of Liberty and preached to her about becoming American; witnessing the grief of a young mother separated from her brother on Ellis Island. Then came the train ride across the continent, climaxing with the family reuniting in their new home community of Troy, Idaho:

> And there stood my father at the bottom of the steps.
>
> And mother started out first. And Signe, my sister, somehow I kicked her, because I jumped right in my father's arms *(chuckles)*.
>
> And then a few feet away, against the depot, there stood Uncle Storm. Oh, grey haired, y'know, white, y'know, and holding out *his* arms too.
>
> And then we walked to the hotel, the same hotel that is there now. Thompson was the name of the man that owned that hotel at that time.

And they had a special dinner for us because Gabe, my father, has told them that his family was coming. And we didn't get in before about two o'clock in the afternoon on a Sunday.

And oh,
> my,
> the food,
> the meat![6]

Anna Marie Oslund is clearly the center around whom this narrative as a whole revolves, but it would be a mistake to conclude that she is its true subject, given the responsibility she takes for representing the experience of other persons. She tells how individual characters acted in specific situations; she reports their speech, senses their thoughts, and imputes reasons for why they did what they did. She deals with other lives in the course of these events as confidently as she does her own. And yet her understanding is not an omniscience which reduces them to extensions of herself. The other characters retain an undefinability of will and motivation that is based in their reality as persons who existed independently of her and her narrative. Mrs Oslund's responsibility, moreover, does not stop with her characters as individuals: she casts them as members of groups whose actions she also describes. She, her sisters, and their mother form a unit in the absence of the father; all the passengers of the ship are an entity on the sea. The boundaries of other groupings are more flexible, less defined. When she says her father was one of the pioneers caught in the ruin of the harvest, she may be thinking only of the settlers in his immediate neighborhood, but she may also have in mind the circumstances of people throughout the region. When she says she was one of the children who did not get enough to eat, she may be referring to the immediate sphere of her acquaintances, but she may also be thinking of children across the north of Sweden or even beyond. The possibility of broader or narrower degrees of incorporation makes the question of the membership that is being represented open rather than fixed. Insofar as the experience of her characters is seen to be *representative* of that of others, she can be speaking about specific persons directly and about others symbolically at the same time.

My point is that all of us assume such obligations when we are talking about events. It is formally necessary in the construction of narrative for the teller to have some point of view. Scene by scene one has to be speaking from somewhere in order to orient the account, to give coherence to the development of the plot. As the point of view moves with the flow of narration, it traces human relationships. Many of these are in the form of identifications. As a teller I am so closely aligned with myself as a character that the two roles usually combine in a single point of view. I also identify myself with various sorts of groupings for whom I presume to speak as a member, and I have empathy with certain persons on whose behalf I speak out of my understanding of them. My point of view can be given over to representing my characters' relationships to their world and to each other from their points of view, as I perceive them. Of course, not all characters are presented in equal detail: their presence is tied to their role in the unfolding of the plot. And identification is only one of the attitudes that is taken towards characters and their actions. At other moments my stance is ambivalent, or antagonistic, or neutral, or unstated. My point of view as teller registers various sorts of distancing not just by what I say but in intonation and other paralinguistic features – by the way I say it. Yet even when my sympathies are lodged with one character or one value as opposed to another, I may still claim an understanding of the other point of view. Indeed, the plot may depend on my portraying it convincingly.

When we talk of what has happened we draw pictures of our folklife. We act in the capacity of chroniclers for events that converge in our lives and are made history through our interpretations. We give our audience access to these experiences by means of the different points of view we are presenting. By entering for a moment into the perspectives of others, listeners get to feel the social relationships that are inscribed in events. Oral historians, by working to recover these messages and their import, can better understand what the narratives they hear are really about.

III

If we turn to the kinds of ties one person's narrative may have to others' narratives, we will encounter the phenomenon of point of view again, but in another light. There are congruences in the accounts of different tellers which convey commonalities in the events being described. These can occur at any level, including image, plot, and theme; they can be present in the selection of a single word and in the chronicling of a whole life or era. [. . .]

Experience [. . .] comes to make sense by being connected with others' experiences. These connections are not simply preestablished in events. They are recognized, forged, elaborated, and invoked in interaction. Cast as narrative, they constitute an unending reservoir of correspondences that have potential for being held in common.[7]

Anna Marie Oslund's story, for example, can be compared with others' stories about the same subject. To begin with, there is the fact that she even happens to have a narrative about migration. Every person I have recorded in Idaho could also tell how it was that they or their family came to the area. For them this event is a slot that has to be filled with a story – a story which, in accounting for their initial presence in the locality, links together fundamental matters of personal, family, and community identity. By far the most frequent reason given for coming, among both Europeans and Americans, was just the one she gave: to find a better life. Other Scandinavians also had harsh accounts about the suffering going on in the old country, while many Americans recounted comparable hardships in their encounters with grasshoppers, drought, and storms on the arid Plains. The pleasures Mrs Oslund remembers on her arrival – meeting her father and feasting at the hotel – also turn out to be a much more common kind of ending for such a tale than might be imagined. This is how Lola Clyde finished telling of her mother-in-law's move by wagon train from Kansas to Moscow, Idaho in 1877;

> I've often heard Grandma Snow say that oh she was so glad because her mother had come down and was waiting there at Uncle Billy Taylor's house. There was Grandma Stewart waiting for them. And they were *so* delighted to see each other after the long trip.
>
> And Uncle Billy Taylor had come out and said, 'Well now you folks just circle your wagons *right* here and stay. I have garden and my trees were already coming into bearing. And we have milk. And there's lots of water. And you can just stay here while you go and *look* for homesteads.
>
> And I've heard them say that some of them camped there for six months, at the Taylor place, while they looked for homesteads that they could settle on.[8]

According to Mrs Clyde, Billy Taylor was called 'uncle' by many, not because he was a relative, but because of his generosity. I have heard other stories end in this way, as the newcomers, arriving after much privation, are greeted by close kin and by settlers who offer food. These images are typical of the scenes of reunion and hospitality which occur remarkably often when people feel the migration they are telling about was successful. And these scenes in turn seem to embody themes that recur in many other kinds of narratives about life in Idaho: concerns about keeping the family together, and about the support members of the community show for one another.

The point is that the single account belongs to an entire narrative environment.[9] It is only by recognizing its resemblances to related accounts that we can begin to locate its traditionality. Heard in the context of other narratives rather than in isolation, Anna Maria Oslund's story is full of resonances. These are concentrated most densely in accounts on the subject of migration, and they ripple outward through narratives about other events. They are parallels in perceptions of the structure of experience. Speaker and listeners grasp such resonances both explicitly and implicitly, but for the interviewer who is not attuned to the narrative environment, the echoes will be muted or absent.

While migration is an event that persons and families underwent singly or in small groups, there are certain events that whole communities experienced at the same time. These events may also give rise to slots that need to be filled with some kind of account – filled, that is, if the teller has any claim to membership or affiliation with the group that went through the experience. Such an event is the strike which began in the lumber camps of northern Idaho, eastern Washington, and western Montana in July 1917, spreading from there to the Pacific Coast to become the largest work stoppage in the history of the American logging industry. Of the local men I know who were working in the woods during that time, most have nearly identical attitudes about what happened and why. In the words of Dick Benge, a career lumberjack:

> *They didn't want more money!*
>   All they struck for:
>   better conditions.
> You know, before that time we all packed our blankets,
>   pit bedbugs
>   greybacks and all that stuff (*chuckles*).
> Well all they wanted,
>   they wanted to get out of this packing their blankets,
>   and have *beds*
>   *furnished* em.[10]

By 'they' Mr Benge is referring to the IWWs, the Industrial Workers of the World, or 'Wobblies', the union that organized men in the camps and called the strike. Glen Gilder, a farmer who worked in the woods occasionally, described the situation in this way:

> The goddamn lousy bunkhouses. They'd get it cleaned *up*, maybe once every two or three years.
>   Then somebody'd come in with a batch of lice and go through the whole damn bunkhouse.
>   Bedbugs.
>   Oh, hell! They lived a little bit – hell, farmers used to take better care of hogs than Potlatch took care of their men![11]

'Potlatch', the Potlatch Lumber Company, was the main employer in the area. For a third view, here is a statement by Axel Anderson, a foreman for Potlatch and eventually their assistant superintendent for woods operations:

> So I think there, through the Wobblies there, during the war days, the First World War, they did a good job then. Before that time each one of us carried their own blankets. From camp to camp, you know. Well there was no way anybody could keep a camp *clean*. Cause you know they go from one camp to another and then unload their bundle and it might have been full of bedbugs. And they stayed![12]

Given his affiliation with the company, Axel Anderson could be expected to support it against the strike and the union, but his sympathies are the reverse.

Here are three men, each with a different relationship to logging as a means of employment, adopting the same attitude towards the strike. Each of these snippets of talk gives the image of bedbugs continually infesting bedrolls and bunkhouses as the reason it happened. In all I have heard perhaps twenty more men use this sort of imagery to make this point, and in each one of their narratives it serves as just one element in a larger structure which is built on the contrast between the awful conditions in the camps before the strike and the decent conditions afterwards, and turns on the conviction that the IWWs were the agents responsible for the change. Taken together, these elements are a declaration that the motives of the strikers were just, that their actions were necessary. Since these accounts are in essential agreement about the causes of the walkout, the changes it brought about, and the roles of the union and the company, they show an order of congruence that warrants regarding them as a single conception of the strike. This is the core of the oral tradition about the event.[13] Now, a man who utilizes this set of conventions does not thereby commit himself to drawing a given set of meanings from them, nor to phrasing them or using them in a particular way. He embroiders them in his own fashion. In his total narrative about the strike, they need not take up much room: if he were working in the woods when it happened, for example, he might well concentrate his account on specific incidents that occurred in the camps. Still, the presence of the core of the tradition signals an orientation of the whole testimony whose implications extend far beyond the experience of this one event.

There is an alternative interpretation of the strike, utterly opposed to the one we have been considering, and it is the only interpretation the historian will find validated in local written sources. During the period of the walkout the IWWs were vilified by the lumber companies, state and local authorities, and virtually every newspaper in the region. They were accused of being saboteurs, arsonists, and foreign agents. When the strike began, many of them were imprisoned in county jails and makeshift bullpens. As the harvest approached, their opponents organized farmers into 'protective associations' to guard the fields against incendiarism, and after the strike was over they claimed the IWWs had been defeated and gave credit to the lumber companies for voluntarily improving camp conditions. Arthur Sundberg never worked in the woods, having been a sawmiller and mill maintenance foreman in the company town of Potlatch, where anti-IWW rhetoric was intense; nevertheless, he insisted that the IWWs' purpose was to win 'a good meal and a clean bed', and then he addressed the charge that they were 'bolsheviks'.

Well. At the same time – that is, the same period of time – the farmers around the country, there used to be an *awful* lot of smut in their wheat. Boy I've seen the blower on some of these thrashing machines where you'd think that they was burning *coal*. It was the straw coming out, it was just a black cloud of smut.

So every once in a while there'd be a thrashing machine would explode and burn.

Well the *IWWs* done that, see.

Well the IWWs didn't have anything to do with them *farmers*, they were up here in the *woods*! But nevertheless, in all the newspapers – if you go back into the archives of some of these newspapers, you'd see where this thrashing machine, that wheat field burned,

and the IWWs done that!

> And this locomotive jumped the track,
>   and IWWs done that!
> Well they got blamed for an awful lot of stuff that I don't think they had
> anything to *do* with at all.[14]

The insistence that the IWWs were innocent of charges of sabotage is quite common in accounts which support the strike, and the explanation that the harvest fires were caused by highly flammable smut is one I have heard from several people. Those sympathetic to the strike are clearly aware of the contrary position, and some, like Mr Sundberg, represent it even as they refute it in their testimony. When this opposing position is taken into account, it becomes apparent that the oral tradition in favor of the strike must have developed alongside it, and not autonomously. The core elements of the tradition, asserting IWW responsibility for the transformation of conditions, do not refer directly to this other interpretation, but they imply it and are locked in debate with it, having been shaped in part as a refutation of its charges.[15]

Thus the patterning of an event in narrative can mark divergences as well as congruences. This is as true for an experience like migration, which for some ended on a note of bleakness and frustration rather than hope, as it is for an event like the IWW strike. Almost no documentation exists to show how oral traditions emerge regarding such events, but often the process is not hard to imagine. In the case of the strike, I think it is reasonable to assume that people working in the woods already had definite attitudes about their situation which were tested and sharpened during the walkout, that in conversations while it was happening and afterwards they began turning it into story and reaching for understandings about what it meant, and that with distance these became in time increasingly selective renderings that stood for a consensus, and stood against other versions of the event. If this is so, then it was in the course of interaction as well as reflection that lasting conceptions of the experience were shaped. Each person had individually to come to terms with what had happened, and what he said about it had to find some acceptance with listeners. In the continuing dialogue about the event, each person's version was to some extent affected by others. The core of the tradition congealed as their collective point of reference for thinking about the event.

This sharing of perspectives is a form of identification. It is another side of the process of representing points of view which I discussed earlier. There I suggested that we openly express the perspectives of others who are incorporated as characters in our narrative; here we are taking a point of view we share with others and giving it *as our own*. When a man defends the Wobblies he is speaking on their behalf; he is also representing a collective sentiment *about* the Wobblies, even though he claims only to be offering his own view. This raises again the question of the membership which is symbolically represented by a narrative. I have mentioned the indefiniteness of the outer boundaries of many of the groups on whose behalf the teller speaks. This indefiniteness applies as well to the position of the teller in relation to others. When talking to me about the strike, no one made any claim that 'all my logger friends feel the same way', or 'this is a consensus', although when I heard people discussing the event together they were in agreement about it. By asserting only that this is the truth as he sees it, each teller stands on his own authority. Listeners are left to decide for themselves how representative he is, how broadly across the community and the region his perception of events applies.

The representativeness of what he says is limited by the existence of opposing versions of the truth. We have already seen that these divergences register in the more distanced attitudes a teller takes towards some characters and actions and are implicit as well in the language by which congruences are expressed. They appear fully-fledged when different tellers hold contradictory views of an event. When such divergences fall into a consistent pattern, forming a range of positions regarding the experience, they indicate boundaries between groups or tensions within them. The challenge posed for oral historians is to recognize significant instances of agreement and disagreement in testimonies and to trace their distribution. This patterning of sentiments is direct evidence of the way feelings have been structured within the society.[16]

If we want to understand the meaning the past has in northern Idaho, we have to reckon with the fact that, half a century after the 1917 strike, support for it was strong in oral testimony and opposition to it very limited. The main trickle of hostility I found came from high-level management and from law enforcement officials. Full-time farmers, whom I expected to speak warily of the IWWs, seldom had reservations about them, and some even poked fun at the exaggerated fears they felt were abroad during the harvest. A number of people who worked in the woods and sawmills thought that the IWWs were too radical, but they still did not inveigh against the strike. In short, antagonism about the walkout hardly took root, despite the intense campaign waged against it at the time, while sentiment in favor of it has blossomed over time.

Of necessity, my interpretation of the testimony and its distribution must be cursory, but I can mention several inferences I draw from it about group affiliations and conflict. There is compelling evidence that most local men who worked in the woods identified themselves with the migratory lumberjacks who were the backbone of the IWW membership. Most of these local men were ready to quit work, but not to be involved openly in strike actions. They were reluctant to antagonize the lumber company they were dependent upon for the employment that enabled them to make a home in the area. In their contradictory position they could not risk being associated with the union, and yet they felt the IWWs were acting on their behalf, on behalf of loggers as a group. This conviction has spread with time, displacing ambivalent feelings about the strike and whatever inclinations there once may have been to entertain the company's reading of events. It has been taken up by many who were not themselves subjected to harsh conditions in the woods but who identify with the loggers and their situation.

The alliance of interests among settlers and migratory lumberjacks against a combination of corporate, government, and local business and professional interests is etched in oral tradition, but it has gone unrecognized by historians who have studied the strike of 1917.[17] Insofar as the issue has been dealt with, it has been assumed that the IWWs had little if any local support. This view tends to be buttressed by the further assumption that the Wobblies were quite unlike the resident population because they were drifters who were unable to lead normal lives. Such interpretations are typical of generalizations made in scholarship about the IWWs, although some historians are skeptical of their basis. William Preston, for example, argues that the most essential characteristics of the union members and their supporters are still unknown:

> No historian knows how much tacit support for Wobblies existed during their free speech fights and strike activities or to what extent the militant activists represented, then or now, a much larger but historically inert mass of radical protest . . . If little is known about working-class attitudes in general, the characteristics of the I.W.W. minority are equally debatable. What kinds of men and women joined the Wobblies is, of course, extremely significant to the overall judgement eventually made about radicalism.[18]

In his article, however, Preston does not mention oral history as a source of evidence that could address questions of this scale.

No doubt oral testimony is the best single source available, as it is for many facets of life still in memory. Yet it rarely appears at the center of scholarly debate. Reservations still abound about its validity and reliability, and about the feasibility of recording and using it extensively. However well intentioned, these objections hide ideological considerations about *what* aspects of *whose* experiences are to become part of the record. They also imply an oversimplified notion of memory processes, according to which every testimony is to be judged as an independent, more or less accurate, set of perceptions about the real course of events. Oral historians themselves inadvertently reinforce the devaluation of their enterprise when they treat congruences in different people's testimonies as though they were no more than independent confirmations of this kind. The strike of 1917 is but one case of the historical importance that people's memories have because they carry social conceptions, and of the special significance of those correspondences and differences that are deeply and widely held.

The search for these patterns does not end with the study of a single event, however memorable it may have been. The occurrence of the strike took only a moment in historical time, and the narratives about it are but a fragment of a world of talk. To learn about the significance the strike has come to have, we need to know how the ideas which are crystallized in talk about it are expressed in other narratives about other experiences. These events may seem closely related to the strike, as in other stories about working for the lumber company, or far apart, as in stories about coming to Idaho. Still, even in accounts of people migrating to the area, one can hear resonances of the local view of the strike in themes of community support and the struggle for a better future. To follow these connections is to begin to find where particular events fit in the web of feeling that is memory's tracing of a way of life.

IV

The events that are depicted in oral history share, with the groups depicted, an openness of reference that often makes it impossible to pin down just where their boundaries are. Perhaps the testimony deals only with a portion of some larger events; or perhaps it is an instance of a particular class of events; or perhaps it is a composite representation that refers to no specific event at all. The lack of completeness in such testimony is not a defect that could be remedied by more preciseness on the part of the teller. Rather, it is intrinsic to the symbolic potential of discourse, decreed alike by the requirements of communication, by the cognitive processing of perception, and by the nature of narrative itself. To be communicated, as Sapir said, our experience of something is connected with the experience others have of it. To be processed in the mind, as Boas said, experiences are classified 'according to their similarities in wider or narrower groups'. To become the subject of narrative experiences are either individualized or generalized. Scholars customarily call the account of a single experience (or sequence of experiences) a 'story', in contrast to other kinds of statements whose precise relationships to stories are often elusive.[19] [. . .]

From this perspective, oral history is composed of more and less inclusive categorizations of events. At one end of the spectrum are stories about unique instances. At the other end is theorizing which attempts to encompass a potentially unlimited number of instances. In between are many sorts of statements, conventionally known by terms such as 'description', 'generalization', and 'interpretation', which can be said in some sense to be grouping together multiple instances. As narrators we play across the whole range, matching aspects of experience with the capacities of various pieces of memory to depict them. Shifts from one type of statement to another are as effortless as shifts from one character's point of view to another's, and they can happen repeatedly while narrating without drawing any notice.

I can illustrate these distinctions with some of Clara Grove's talk about the evils of liquor and the courage of the pioneers. Like her mother and grandmother, Mrs Grove was active in the Women's Christian Temperance Union for much of her life. The sort of story she most frequently told me about drinking portrayed members of one family or another coping with the male drunkard in their midst. In one of these, she tells of visiting a home when the husband staggers in, reels over the furniture as his young daughter looks on, and apologizes that he has stomach trouble; the mother is out but when she returns she goes upstairs to tend to him, while Mrs Grove excuses herself and leaves. This is the unique instance, the story proper, but it is not all there is to the narrative. Before delivering the anecdote Mrs Grove sketched some aspects of the woman's earlier life, explaining that this was a heart-in-hand marriage. Afterwards she provided a commentary which extolled the wife, both for teaching her children that drinking is an illness and for enduring her husband despite his failings.[20] The story-part presents characters acting out a scene from life; the surrounding statements contextualize this event, putting it in perspective.

Although Mrs Grove used stories to show the impact of drinking on families she knew, she resorted to generalized description when she depicted the organized opposition to drinking. She spoke of the activities of the WCTU in this way:

> Well to go back much earlier than that, back to the very early days after it was organized. The women met in prayer meetings, and then they marched together *to* the saloons to talk with the saloonkeeper.
>
> And we didn't have fancy names for the saloons, and they didn't at that time. A saloon was a *saloon*! And women *did* not visit them. That was almost unknown.
>
> But they would go to the saloons and talk with the saloonkeeper. And some of the saloonkeepers *did* go out of business. Not all of them, but some of them did.
>
> But, at the time that I remember about grandmother: her family worship, every day, always included, 'And put down the wickedness of the *saa-loons* everywhere.' Her family devotion never omitted that. And I presume there were many other people with the same thought.[21]

Mrs Grove is reporting a *schema* of action she finds typical of the WCTU: prayer, followed by marching and an attempt at persuasion, possibly leading to victory. She is claiming that this same sequence of events was repeated on many occasions, and she is giving a summary to cover all these occasions rather than a story about any one of them. She uses the same device with her grandmother's prayer. It may well be that she has no access in memory to any specific time that it happened; rather, all the daily worships have merged in an image of a recurring event. In noting that many others thought as her grandmother did, she is actually generalizing about this generalization. In commenting on the usage of the word 'saloons' and on the prohibition against women visiting them, she cites no single occurrence but a persisting state of affairs. A descriptive passage such as this is concerned with substantial classes of events. And the more abstract the description is, the more events it may be attempting to cover. Take this statement of Mrs Grove's:

> People at that time were more stalwart than they are now and they didn't

become discouraged as much as people do now. They didn't become anything extrovert as much as people do now.
They had a trail that they followed.
And if there was no trail there they *made* one.
And you just couldn't move them like you can people now.[22]

Here her outlook on the people and the era as a whole is posed in the most general set of propositions.

If a story is a unique enactment, then it is apparent that other kinds of statement are just as necessary for narrative to do its work. They are needed to show the usual course enactments follow, the setting in which they occur, and the exegesis they have been given. The most abstract rumination can reach for something as complex as the tenor of an age, but their very scope opens them the more easily to contradiction. Thus there is a gap between the assertions Clara Grove made about people's stalwartness and her images of drunkenness: she knew both to be true, but in philosophizing about the whole she fixed only on the more optimistic side of her understanding. In many of her narratives pioneer virtue went unchallenged, but in many others it was tested and sometimes, at least temporarily, it was defeated. All of these narratives can be said to belong to the same Story, whose stakes are finally the vindication of Mrs Grove's deepest principles in the face of the dark forces loose in the world. It is in fitting together the different forms of her testimony that we discover the special cast her conflicts have taken and the character of the affirmation she has found.

Stories and other kinds of statements are mutually implicative. They challenge and check, suggest and require each other. A story exemplifies a class of experiences; a description hints at the existence of innumerable plots. The connectedness of these forms justifies the belief that what is called 'oral history' is a coherent way of conceptualizing reality, a single *genre* of talk. It also underlies the flexibility we have in giving testimony about persons and groups with whom we have affective ties, for most of the slots that we find ourselves obliged to fill can be handled either anecdotally or descriptively, in one way or another.

V

I have only broken the surface of the question set by my title, but by doing so in several places I hope to have shown an underlying unity: the interdependence of personal and cultural conceptions of the past. I hope too to have shown that in order to learn about this interdependence one has to enter the realm where the narratives have come into being, interpenetrated, and continued to exist.

At the heart of what is social in oral history is the symbolic quality at the boundaries of actions and characters, of the 'I' that stands for the one doing the speaking and the 'we' that designates the speaker's membership in groups.

Intangibilities of reference in these selves, groups, and events reach out to listeners, inviting them to interpret what they are hearing broadly or narrowly, as they wish. A migration story can be a very personal account and at the same time an incarnation of the peopling of an era, the exigencies of pioneering, and the aspirations of all who risk relocating to find a better life. The account of a specific strike in a specific camp can also state the human demand for equity and carry a class's vision of the nature of history in a period and a place. Experience is pulled towards the universal and grounded by the particular: it is mythic and historical at once. Narrative takes shape and power through this interplay, from the first evocation of experience through each subsequent retelling. Listeners, to whom the performance gives news of human nature in action at a historical moment, will connect what they hear to their own lives. Tellers will get from their audience the chance to recover the past, to take advantage, as historians must, of the distance from the events imposed by time so they may reconsider them. A narrative's significance, like its form and its fate, can only emerge as the past passes into the present. Its meanings can never be settled.

NOTES

1 Henry Glassie studies the performance of history within a community in great depth in *Passing the Time in Ballymenone*, Philadelphia, 1982. Richard Bauman reconstructs a community's preeminent storytelling situation in 'The La Have Island general store: sociability and verbal art in a Nova Scotia community', *Journal of American Folklore*, 1972, vol. 85, pp. 330–343. This research is grounded in Dell Hymes' conception of the ethnography of speaking: consult his *Foundations in Sociolinguistics*, Philadelphia, 1974. Also drawing on Hymes, Nessa Wolfson gives linguistic criteria for the performance of narrative in 'A feature of performed narrative: the conversational historical present', *Language and Society*, 1978, vol. 7, pp. 251–237. Robert Georges offers a general introduction to the study of storytelling as an event in 'Toward an understanding of storytelling events', *Journal of American Folklore*, 1969, vol. 82, pp. 313–328. For the oral historian's influence on recollection, see Ron Grele, 'Movement without aim: methodological and theoretical problems in oral history', in R. Grele (ed.), *Envelopes of Sound*, Chicago, 1975, pp. 127–154, and E.D. Ives, *The Tape-Recorded Interview*, Knoxville, Tenn., 1980.

2 Jan Vansina reviews what is known about the structuring that pervades remembering in 'Memory and oral tradition', J. Miller (ed.), *The African Past Speaks*, Hamden, Conn., 1980, pp. 262–279.

3 The approach to point of view in this essay is indebted to the concepts of Mikhail Bakhtin, especially to *Problems of Dostoyevsky's Poetics*. A new translation by Caryl Emerson appeared in 1983 from the University of Minnesota Press.

4 In the following excerpts, punctuation and paragraphing are determined by weighing a combination of speech features: intonation contours, length of pauses, use of particles such as 'well' and 'and' and the semantic sense of the passage. Words are italicized when spoken with special emphasis. Lines are broken when they are especially rhythmic: they are arranged one beneath the other when the parts are spoken in a parallel way, and from left to right when they are not. (Cf. Glassie, *Passing the Time in Ballymenone*, pp. 39–40, 44–45. On the importance of particles

as markers, see D. Hymes, 'Discovering oral performance and measured verse in American Indian narrative', *New Literary History*, 1977, vol. 8, pp. 431–457.) This interview with Anna Marie Anderson Oslund (1891–1979) was recorded on December 14, 1973 in Troy, Idaho. The excerpt is from interview 1, transcript page 2 (hereafter 1:2). Of the excerpts in this paper, Mrs Oslund's and Axel Anderson's were recorded by Laura Schrager and me; the rest, by me. The research was done under the auspices of the Latah County Historical Society, Moscow, Idaho. The collection is located in the Special Collections Library of the University of Idaho in Moscow.

5 Anna Marie Oslund, 1:4–5.

6 Ibid., 1:15.

7 George Herbert Mead propounded the logic of social interaction in *Mind, Self and Society*, Chicago, 1934. For a more recent primer, see P.L. Berger and T. Luckmann, *The Social Construction of Reality*, Garden City, N.Y., 1966.

8 Interview with Lola Gamble Clyde (b. 1900), on December 2, 1974, near Moscow, Ida. 1:30.

9 The idea is an extension of Bakhtin's concept of 'the literary environment': cf. P.N. Medvedev and M.M. Bakhtin, *The Formal Method in Literary Scholarship* (tr. A.J. Wehrle), Baltimore, 1978, esp. pp. 26–30.

10 Interview with John L. (Dick) Benge (1894–1976) on July 17, 1973, on Hatter Creek, near Princeton, Ida. 1:16.

11 Interview with Glen Gilder (b. 1903), on June 28, 1978, at Spring Valley, near Troy, Ida. 6:52.

12 Interview with Axel Anderson (b. 1886), on July 25, 1974, in Spokane, Wash. 2:27.

13 For a brief but crucial consideration of tradition, see D. Hymes, 'Folklore's nature and the sun's myth', *Journal of American Folklore*, 1975, vol. 88, pp. 353–354.

14 Interview with Arthur Sundberg (b. 1899), on August 1, 1975, in Potlatch, Ida. 4:181–182.

15 In Bakhtin's terms this is a 'hidden internal polemic', Medvedev and Bakhtin, *The Formal Method in Literary Scholarship*.

16 The concept of 'structures of feeling' has been developed by Raymond Williams in *The Long Revolution*, New York, 1961, pp. 41–71, and *Marxism and Literature*, Oxford, 1977, pp. 128–135.

17 Studies of the strike include R.L. Tyler, *Rebels of the Woods*, Eugene, Oreg., 1967, and B.G. Rader, 'The Montana lumber strike of 1917', *Pacific Historical Review*, 1967, no. 36, pp. 189–207. The strike is seen in the larger context of IWW history in M. Dubofsky, *We Shall Be All*, New York, 1969, and of Northwest logging in V.H. Jensen, *Lumber and Labor*, New York, 1945.

18 W. Preston, 'Shall this be all?: U.S. historians versus William D. Haywood et al.', *Labor History*, 1971, vol. 12, p. 441.

19 A wide range of scholars has been interested in the connections between stories and other kinds of statement and between the action and non-action parts of stories: cf. K. Burke, *A Grammar of Motives*, Berkeley, Calif., 1969; M. Frisch, 'Oral history and *Hard Times*, a review essay', *Oral History Review*, 1979, vol. 7, pp. 70–79; W.B. Gallie, *Philosophy and the Historical Understanding*, New York, 1968; G. Genette, 'Boundaries of narrative', *New Literary History*, 1976, vol. 8, pp. 1–13; W. Labov, *Languages in the Inner City*, Philadelphia, 1972, pp. 354–375.

20 Interview with Clara Payne Grove (1879–1977), on November 21, 1975, in Moscow, Ida. 3:9–10.

21 Ibid., 3:1.

22 Clara Grove, on December 16, 1975, 4:32.

25 Anzac memories
Putting popular memory theory into practice in Australia

Alistair Thomson

Alistair Thomson is a Lecturer at the Centre for Continuing Education, University of Sussex. Extracted from *Oral History*, 1990, vol. 18, no. 2, pp. 25–31, with permission.

[. . .] According to the 'Anzac legend', during the Great War of 1914–18 Australian soldiers proved to themselves and to the rest of the world that the new breed of Anglo-Celtic men from the south was worthy to rank with the nations of the world.[1] Gallipoli, where the Australians first went into battle on April 25 1915, was regarded as the baptism of fire of the new Australian Commonwealth, and the commemoration of Anzac Day on April 25 each year became the Australian equivalent of American Independence Day or Bastille Day in France (without the revolutionary overtones). [. . .]

This essay focusses on the life and memories of Fred Farrall, one of about twenty Melbourne working class veterans of the Great War whom I've interviewed [. . .].[2] I don't pretend that Fred Farrall was a typical 'digger' [another nickname of the Australian soldiers], far from it. The search for national character has been one of the obsessive dead ends of Australian history-writing, and in this essay I won't be analysing the extent to which the Anzac legend is an accurate representation of the 'typical' Australian soldier.[3] I'm more interested in the interactions between Anzac legend stereotypes and individual soldiers' identities, in the experience of difference as well as conformity, and in the ways that 'typical' can be oppressive. I want to assess the relationship between Fred Farrall's memory of the war and the national mythology which publicly defines his experience as a soldier, and to use his case study to make sense of the general relationship between individual memory and collective myth.

The theory of memory (and national myth) which informs this essay was developed by the Popular Memory Group at the Centre for Contemporary Cultural Studies in Birmingham. The group focussed on the interractions between 'private' and 'public' memories, and used the following approach to individual memory. We compose our memories to make sense of our past and present lives. 'Composure' is the aptly ambiguous term used by the Popular Memory Group to describe the process of memory making. In one sense we 'compose' or construct memories using the public language and meanings of our culture. In another sense we 'compose' memories which help us to feel relatively comfortable with our lives, which gives us a feeling of composure. We remake or repress memories of experiences which are still painful and 'unsafe' because they do not easily accord with our present identity, or because their inherent traumas or tensions have never been resolved. We seek composure, an alignment of our past, present and future lives. One key theoretical connection, and the link between the two senses of composure, is that the apparently private process of composing safe memories is in fact very public. Our memories are risky and painful if they do not conform with the public norms or versions of the past. We compose our memories so that they will fit with what is publicly acceptable, or, if we have been excluded from general public acceptance, we seek out particular publics which affirm our identities and the way we want to remember our lives.[4]

Some critics of oral history have claimed that the fact that we compose our memories invalidates the use of memory by historians. That might be true for oral historians who have sought to use memory as a literal source of what happened in the past. But if we are also interested, as we must be, in the ways in which the past is resonant in our lives today, then oral testimony is essential evidence for analysis of the interactions between past and present, and between memory and mythology.

This approach to memory requires a review of interviewing technique. In my initial interviews with Melbourne war veterans I wanted to see how the experiences of working class soldiers contrasted with the Anzac legend, and used a chronological life story approach as the basis for questions. The interviews did reveal many differences between their lives and the legend, but I was also struck by the extent to which memories were entangled with the myth; for example, some men related scenes from the film *Gallipoli* as if they were their own. Therefore, guided by the ideas of the Popular Memory Group, I devised a new approach for a second set of interviews with some of the same men. In the new interviews I wanted to focus on how each man composed and told his memories by exploring four key interactions: between public and private, past and present, memory and identity, and interviewer and interviewee. The personal information which I had already gained in the first interviews made it possible for me to tailor my questions specifically for each man in terms of his particular memories and identities. If I had not done the original interviews I would have needed to integrate the life story approach with the new approach.

To investigate the relationship between public and private memories I made the public myth a starting point for questions: what was your response to various war books and films, past and present, and to Anzac Day and war memorials? How well did they represent your own experiences; how did they make you feel? We also focussed on specific features of the legend: was there a distinctive Anzac character; how true was it for your own nature and experience? Were you so very different from the soldiers of other armies? I asked each man to define certain keywords in his own words – 'digger', 'mateship', 'the spirit of Anzac' – and discovered that some of the men who seemed to be uncritical of the legend had contrary and even contradictory understanding of its key terms.

Another section of discussion focussed on experience and personal identity: how did you feel about yourself and your actions at key moments (enlistment, battle, return)? What were your anxieties and uncertainties? How did you make sense of your experiences and how did other people define you? How were you included or excluded, what was acceptable and unacceptable behaviour (what was not 'manly'), and how and why were some men ostracised? Of course these memories, and the relative composure of memory, had shifted over time (the past/present interaction), so we discussed how postwar events – such as homecoming, the Depression and World War Two, domestic change and old age, and the revival of Anzac remembrance in the 1980s – affected identity and memory. The new interview approach showed me that how we remember and articulate will change over time, and how this can be related to shifts in public perception.

Another related and difficult focus of the new interviews was upon the ways memories are affected by strategies of containment, by ways of handling frustration, failure, loss or pain. This required a sensitive balance between potentially painful probing and reading between the lines of memory. What is possible or impossible to remember, or even to say aloud? What are the hidden meanings of silences and sudden subject changes? What is being contained by a 'fixed' story? Deeply repressed experiences or feelings may be discharged in less conscious forms of expression, in past and present dreams, errors and Freudian slips, body language and even humour, which is often used to overcome or conceal embarrassment and pain. Discussion of the symbolic content and feelings expressed by war-related dreams suggested new understandings of the personal impact of the war, and of what could not be publicly expressed. And my interview notes about facial expression, body movements and the mode of talking were revealing about emotive meanings of memories which would not be apparent in interview transcripts.

This approach raised ethical dilemmas for me as an oral historian. Interviewing which approached a therapeutic relationship could be damaging for the interviewee as well as rewarding for the interviewer. It required great care and sensitivity, and a cardinal rule that the well-being of the interviewee always came before the interests of my research. At times I had to stop a line of questioning in an interview, or was asked to stop, because it was too painful. Unlike the therapist, as an oral historian I would not be around to help put together the pieces of memories which were no longer safe.

One partial response was to make the interview, and the interview relationship, a more open process. I tried to discuss how my questions affected remembering, and what was difficult to say to *me*. To encourage dialogue instead of monologue I talked about my own interests and role. In some ways this change in my role (limited by the fact that I never gave up my role as interviewer) affected the remembering. Sometimes it encouraged a man to open up to me and reconsider aspects of his life, although others resisted that opportunity. The explicit introduction of my attitudes into the interviews may have encouraged men to tell stories for my approval, though I usually felt that it facilitated discussion and provoked dissent as much as agreement. In Fred Farrall's case that was not such an issue, as by the time we met his memory of the war was relatively fixed. Although over the years we developed a close and trusting relationship, in which Fred's remembering was actively encouraged by my interest, he seemed to tell the same stories in the same ways to his various audiences, including me. Fred's war story had not always been so fixed, and I gradually realised that his memory of the war, and his identity as a soldier and ex-serviceman, had passed through three distinct phases, shaped by the shifting relationship between Anzac meanings and his own subjective identity.

Born in 1897, Fred Farrall grew up on a small farm in outback New South Wales. He didn't like farm work and, inspired by the patriotic fervour which swept the country after the Gallipoli landing, was glad to join a 'Kangaroo March' of rural recruits for the Australian Imperial Force (AIF). He enlisted in an infantry battalion and was sent to France and the Somme in 1916. By his own admission Fred was not much of a soldier. He was young, naive and under-confident, and wasn't very good at fighting and killing. Like many soldiers of all nationalities, he was terrified in battle and miserable in the trenches, and began to doubt his own worth and that of the war itself. His best mates were killed and mutilated at his side, and though Fred survived the war in one piece, he was a physical and emotional wreck:

> When I came home I was admitted to Randwick Hospital for six months to see what they could do with the trench feet condition, and the rheumatism and a nasal complaint that I contracted on the Somme . . . I didn't realise this at the time, but I long since realised it. But I had neurosis, that was not recognised in those days, and so we just had it. You put up with it. And that developed an inferiority complex, plus, really, I mean extremely bad . . . Well, I had reached a stage with it, where, when I wanted to speak I'd get that way that I couldn't talk. I would stammer and stutter and it seemed that inside me everything had got into a knot, and that went on for years and years and years.

From the fortunate, retrospective stance of a survivor who overcame his neurosis, Fred attributes his shell-shocked condition to the effect of constant bombardment on the Somme. He admits that he was unable to express his fear during and after the battle, and was discouraged from doing so: it was not manly or Australian. Many of Fred's stories contrast his own inadequacy with the supposed bravery of other Australians. The legend of the Australian soldier – the best fighter in the war – caused many diggers to repress their feelings, and worsened the psychological trauma of the war.[5]

Fred's condition, and his sense of personal inadequacy, was worsened by his return to Australia.

> I was something like pet dogs and cats that are turned out in the Dandenongs [a mountain range near Melbourne] . . . If anyone was to ask me now what I was like at that time, I would say that in some respects, it could truthfully be said, and I suppose this applied to many others, many others, that we wouldn't be the full quid. In other words, we weren't what we were like when we went away. I don't know whether you've heard Eric Bogle's songs. Well he mentioned that in something he said about Vietnam . . . And then when I got into civilian life, well this was something new, and to some extent it was, it was terrifying. You're out in the cold, hard world. Nobody to look after you now. You've got to get your own accommodation, your own meals. In short, you've got to fend for yourself.

For men like Fred who were teenagers when they enlisted, the social experience of repatriation was especially traumatic. Fred was lucky. Because of his ill-health he couldn't go back to work on the family farm, but a cousin and her digger husband gave him a room in their home in Sydney, and got him back on his feet. He enrolled in a government vocational training scheme to become an upholsterer, but the scheme was badly organised, and though the government subsidised trainees' wages, employers were not interested when the subsidy ended. Fred searched for work for almost two years before he got a job in a motor car factory. I asked him whether his war service badge helped him to get a job. It didn't, and he wouldn't wear it for many years:

> Well, we didn't value it.
> *Why?*
> Well, it'd be hard to explain other than that first of all, we, of course, had been disillusioned. What we'd been told that the war was all about, didn't work out that way. What we'd been told that the government would do when the war was over, for what we'd done, didn't work out either.
> *In what ways?*
> Well, you see, the pensions in the 1920s, unless you had an arm off or a leg off or a hand of or something like that, it was almost as hard to get a pension as it would be to win Tatts [an Australian lottery]. There was no recognition of neurosis and other disabilities . . . And anyway, the doctors that they had in those days, I suppose they were schooled in what, how they were to behave and so they treated the diggers as they interviewed them and examined them as though they were tenth rate citizens. Something like we look upon the aboriginals. There was great hostility between the diggers on one hand and the Repatriation officials on the other.

Fred felt that ex-servicemen were regarded as 'malingerers', and refused to use the Repat. until 1926, when he had a breakdown and had no choice.

Despite this hostility, the war remained a haunting memory for Fred. He chose to marry on the anniversary of his war wound, he named his house after the places where his two best mates were buried, he remembered (and still recites) in exact detail the places and dates where many friends were killed. These private forms of commemoration, which transformed grotesque experience into relatively safe lists and rituals, were Fred's way of coping with the past. Experiences and feelings which he could not cope with were unconsciously expressed in his dreams:

Oh well, the dreams I had were dreams of being shelled, you know, lying in a trench, being in a trench or lying in a shellhole, and being shot at with shells. And being frightened, scared stiff. Here, to now, I didn't know there were so many others like me until I read this book on Pozieres.[6] That most of them had this fear, and when you come to think of it, well how could they be otherwise . . . You don't know when the next shell that is coming is going to blow you to pieces or leave you crippled in such a way that it'd be better if you had been blown to pieces . . . [In the dream] you'd be going through this experience and you'd be scared stiff, you'd be frightened. You'd be frightened, and wakened up, probably, by the experience.

One reason why Fred could not come to terms with his wartime fears and feelings of inadequacy was because he could find no appropriate public affirmation of his experience as a soldier. He found that he could not talk about his war:

Well, well it was a different atmosphere in the 1920s for instance, and the early 1930s. First of all those that were at the war were reluctant to talk about it, and those that were not at the war, didn't go to the war and the women and that, didn't seem to want to hear about it. So the war slipped into the background as far as the average person was concerned . . . I never talked about it. Never. For years and years and years. Now just why that was I don't know. But, the soldiers, generally speaking, were not very enthusiastic about army life and were ever so pleased to get into civilian clothes again . . . When we got back, there was a sort of hostility toward anything to do with the war, by a lot . . . All they wanted to do was distance themselves as far as they could from anything to do with the army, with the Repat., or the war.

Fred shut away his beautifully embossed discharge certificate in a dusty drawer, and he declined to wear his medals or to attend Anzac Day parades or battalion reunions. The nature of Anzac Day and of other public forms of commemoration, and the perceived neglect by the government, was partly to blame for Fred's inability to express or resolve his ambivalence about his war experience. This was not true for all diggers. Many of the men I interviewed describe how they enjoyed the celebration of their digger identity on Anzac Day, and the humorous reminiscence of veterans' reunions. Public remembrance and affirmation helped these men to cope with their past, filtering out memories which were personally painful or which contradicted the legend.

The nascent Anzac legend worked because many veterans wanted and needed to identify with it.

Fred's initial interview explanation of his non-participation is that Anzac Day was a drunken binge, and that he wasn't a drinker. He stresses his own sobriety and complains that the popular 'larrikin' image of the digger – boozer, gambler and womaniser – has not accurately depicted his own experience and view of the AIF. I hadn't expected this response, but it shows how another aspect of the digger steroetype – larrikin as well as fighter – could misrepresent an individual's experience, exclude him from public affirmation rituals, and make him feel uncomfortable about his own identity. Several other old diggers expressed the same unease about the larrikin image which has featured prominently in recent Anzac films, and remembered that even during the war they were made to feel uncomfortable by this behaviour and reputation. Others revelled in the stereotype, which conjured up exciting memories of their own wild youth.

Fred also avoided Anzac Day because its patriotic rhetoric did not match his wartime doubts about the worth of Australian involvement, or the bitterness he felt about the postwar treatment of the soldiers. But the main reason for his non-participation in Anzac ritual was the extreme confusion and distress he felt about the war. The public celebration of Anzac heroes was a painful reminder of his own perceived inadequacy as a soldier and as a man, and Fred was unable to enjoy the solace and affirmation it offered to other returned servicemen.

Although Fred Farrall was traumatised by his memories and identity as an Anzac throughout the 1920s, he gradually found another life and identity in the labour movement, which in turn helped him to compose a sense of his war which he could live with more easily. Fred recalls that he was politically confused after the war, but that a work-mate persuaded him to join the Coachmaker's Union in 1923: 'that was the beginning of my active part in politics . . . [and] sowed the seeds of my socialism that I developed a few years after and have had all my life'. He became active in the union, joined the Labour Party in 1926 and then, unemployed and disillusioned with the Labour government of 1930, he joined the Communist Party. In the labour movement Fred found supportive comrades and gradually regained his self-confidence. The new and empathetic peer group – many of them were ex-servicemen – and eager reading of radical tracts about the war, helped him to articulate and define his wartime and postwar disillusionment. He believes that was true for many other diggers, and cites the example of his friend Sid Norris:

> In that respect, the making of a big change politically speaking, Sid was but one of thousands of diggers who abandoned their prewar opinions of God, King and Empire being worthy of any sacrifice. The bitter experience of what wars were all about, the making of big profits for some people, was a lesson that changed the diggers' political ideas from conservatism to

radicalism. And Alistair, this is one part, or side, of the Anzac legend that has never been dealt with by the writers of the Great War. Maybe you can give it some thought.

Although Fred had not himself made that recognition during the war, in the late 1920s his new political understanding helped him to emphasise particular senses of his experience as a soldier. Thus Fred now ironically stressed the story of an Irish labourer on his father's farm who had warned him not to go and fight in the rich men's war, and he represented himself as an unwitting victim of an imperialist war. He also stressed that the relationship between officers and men in the AIF was not so very different to that between employers and workers in peacetime Australia, and that the diggers were often rebellious towards authority (he recalled one incident in which he and two mates planned,, unsuccessfully, to kill an unpopular officer). These understandings of the war were part of a more radical Anzac tradition championed by some activists in the labour movement.[7] As a proponent of this tradition Fred articulated his disillusionment about repatriation, and deducted that Anzac Day was 'a clever manoeuvre' intended to bring the soldiers back together again and stifle their anger about pensions and unemployment. [. . .]

Fred also became sceptical of the returned servicemen's organisations which controlled Anzac Day. He recalls that the soldiers in the trenches talked about the need to organise for decent conditions after the war, and that he joined the Returned Sailors' and Soldiers' Imperial League of Australia (RSSILA – now the powerful RSL) on the day he was demobbed. But the RSSILA had been created and controlled by an alliance of citizen and ex-servicemen conservatives, and was granted government recognition as the official representative of returned servicemen 'in return for defending the powers that be' (who were frightened by the violence of dissatisfied diggers and the presence of more radical veterans' pressure groups).[8] In the early 1920s Fred's inner turmoil and physical handicaps had probably kept him away from RSSILA meetings, but this alienation was now confirmed by political suspicion:

> In other words it was the officers in somewhat the same position in civilian life as they were in the army . . . It was not an organisation in the best interests of the ordinary digger . . . It was a political organisation of the extreme right wing and there was no place in it for anyone that had any democratic principles.

By the end of the 1920s Fred Farrall had aligned himself against the RSSILA and was fighting with members of the communist-led Unemployed Workers' Movement in street battles against RSSILA club men and the proto-fascist New Guard movement. By 1937 he was a confident opponent of the official legend and its RSSILA organisers, and was arrested for distributing pacifist leaflets at an Anzac Day parade.

Ironically, by the time Fred had consolidated his radical view of the war, the RSSILA's more conservative Anzac legend, which celebrated the triumph of Australian manhood and the baptism of the nation, was well entrenched. Radicals did contest that version of the war – in Melbourne, for example, some ex-servicemen protested that the proposed Shrine of Remembrance would glorify war, and campaigned for the more utilitarian memorial of a veteran's hospital – but by 1930 radicals had lost the battle for the Anzac legend and the label 'radical digger' was a contradiction in terms. Fred Farrall gradually shed his identity as a returned serviceman and settled into the role of 'a soldier of the labour movement'.

Although the labour movement's version of the war did help Fred to feel relatively secure with an analysis of the war as imperial and business rivalry, and his sense of himself as a naive and then begrudging victim, it did not (maybe could not?) help him to express or resolve his traumatic personal feelings about the war. Theories about arms profiteers made him angry, but didn't help him to cope with memories of terror, guilt or inadequacy. Nor could he enjoy the wider public affirmation of Anzac Day, which helped other ex-servicemen feel proud of their war service. Thus, for many years Fred usually ignored his military past and tried to forget his painful memories.

There's a third phase in Fred Farrall's war story. Some time in the 1960s or early 1970s he started to read and talk outside of the labour movement about his war. He attended the annual Anzac Day ceremony and reunion of his old battalion. He pinned his war service badge back in his lapel, and retrieved his discharge certificate from its dusty hideaway and stuck it up on his living room wall (above a more recent photo of himself as the Mayor of the Melbourne municipality of Prahran) After years of silence he now talks eagerly and at length about the war to students, film makers and oral history interviewers. Why?

Fred explains the change in a number of ways. It's partly the renewed interest of an old man about his youth: 'I suppose as you get older you have some sort of feeling for what happened long ago.' He's also enjoying the respect, even veneration, which the few remaining Great War diggers receive, from people in the street who notice an AIF badge, and from Veterans' Affairs officials who tell them it is a 'badge of honour' and pay their increasing medical costs:

> Well, there was a time when it just didn't fit into that picture at all . . . Well, we've never had much over the years of value from that sort of thing so if there is anything now, even to the extent of getting some respect, well I think it's worth doing.

Those comments hint at more general processes. In the resurgence of interest in the Anzacs, the specific and often contradictory experiences of individual veterans are being clouded by a generalised, almost nostalgic version of the diggers and their war. Furthermore, in this modern reworking of the legend aspects of their war experience which were once taboo are now publicly acceptable. The Vietnam War and the influence of the peace and anti-war movement have altered public perceptions of war so that the soldier as victim is a more acceptable character – though he still takes second place to the Anzac hero. Fred can now talk more easily about his experience of 'the war as hell', and of his own feeling of inadequacy as a soldier, because those aspects of the war are portrayed in the history books and films of the 1980s. He marvels at how well some recent Anzac historians and television directors depict the horror and degradation of trench warfare. The personal pleasure of having his experience as a soldier recognised and affirmed after years of alienation was vividly expressed when I asked Fred about his visit to the Australian War Memorial in Canberra (second only to the Sydney Opera House as a national tourist attraction):

> Nearly got a job there. I was there about eighteen months ago, you know, and oh gee, look here, I got the surprise of my life . . . I was treated like a long lost cousin [and was asked to talk about the western front to other visitors]. 'Well', I said, 'I wouldn't mind doing that, but', I said, 'I'm a worker for peace and not for war.' 'Oh', the bloke said, 'you know this place was built as a Peace Memorial and so you're at liberty to express your opinions along those lines as you see fit' . . . So up I went. Well I was there for two or three days really. It looked as though I was going to have, at eighty odd, as though I was going to get a permanent job.

No doubt Fred brought the galleries to life with his stories of the misery of trench warfare – the rain, mud, rats, lice, shellfire, explosions, fear – and felt satisfied that at last his story of the war was being told. And he believed that he was making a message of peace.

Yet in this profoundly important reconciliation with his wartime past, and between his own memory and the public story of the Anzacs, Fred's political critique has been displaced. The War Memorial and war films admit that for the poor bloody infantry 'war is hell', yet they still promote the digger hero and the Anzac legend. Fred is so pleased with the new recognition that he doesn't see how other aspects of his experience are still ignored. He doesn't consider the absence of any depiction of tensions between officers and other ranks in the AIF, or the postwar disillusionment of many diggers, or of the analysis of the war as a business, all important themes in his discussion with me. Fred assumes that any museum depicting the horror of the western front must be a 'peace memorial', but doesn't recognise the political ambiguity of a museum in which little boys clamber over tanks and want to grow up to be soldiers.

Fred's memory still has a radical cutting edge. He still condemns the artificial patriotism of Anzac Day and carries his war medals on Palm Sunday peace rallies, using the new interest in the Anzacs to make his own criticism of war and Australian society. But he doesn't direct that critique at the Anzac writers and film makers who are the post powerful myth-makers of our time. The effectiveness of the 1980s Anzac legend is that it convinces even radical diggers like Fred that their story is being told, while subtly reworking the conservative sense of the war, national character and Australian history into an appropriate form for the 1980s. The 'hegemonic' process seems similar to that undergone by the diggers who did join the RSSILA and Anzac Day back in the 1920s. On each occasion individuals are included and their memories selectively affirmed by the public rituals and meanings of remembrance. That affirmation may be essential for individual peace of mind, but in the process contradictory and challenging memories are displaced or repressed.

Fred Farrall's case study highlights the dynamic relationship between individual memory and national myth, and suggests ways in which oral history can be more than just the 'voice of the past'. Oral history can help us to understand how and why national mythologies work (and don't work) for individuals, and in our society generally. It can also reveal the possibilities, and difficulties, of developing and sustaining oppositional memories. These understandings can enable us to participate more effectively as historians and in collective struggle for more democratic and radical versions of our past and of what we can become.

NOTES

1 'Anzac' stands for Australian and New Zealand Army Corps, though the New Zealanders are usually left out of the Australian legend.
2 The interviews with Fred were recorded in July of 1983 and April of 1987, and the tapes and transcripts of the interviews, together with others from the project, are available in the collection of the library of the Australian War Memorial.
3 For such a critique see my chapter, 'Passing Shots at the Anzac Legend', in V. Burgmann and J. Lee (eds), *A Most Valuable Acquisition: A People's History of Australia since 1788*, Melbourne, McPhee Gribble/Penguin, 1988.
4 See 'Popular memory: theory politics, method', in R. Johnson, *et al.* (eds), *Making Histories: Studies in history writing and politics*, London, Hutchinson, 1982.
5 For an analysis in these terms of the nature and effects of shell shock, see E. Showalter, 'Rivers and Sassoon: the inscription of male gender anxiety', in M.R. Higonnet, *et al.* (eds), *Behind the Lines: Gender and the Two World Wars*, New Haven, Yale University Press, 1987, pp. 61–69.
6 P. Charlton, *Pozieres: Australians on the Somme 1916*, North Ryde, Methuen Haynes, 1980.
7 L.F. Fox, *The Truth about Anzac*, Melbourne, Victorian Council Against War and Fascism, 1936.
8 See M. Lake, 'The power of Anzac', in M. McKernan and M. Browne (eds), *Australia: Two Centuries of War and Peace*, Canberra, Australian War Memorial/ Allen & Unwin, 1988.

26 Theory, method and oral history

Peter Friedlander

At the time of writing Peter Friedlander taught at the Weekend College of Wayne State University in Detroit. 'Theory, method and oral history' first appeared in P. Friedlander, *The Emergence of a UAW Local, 1936–39: A Study in Class and Culture*, Pittsburgh, University of Pittsburgh Press, 1975. Extracted by permission of the University of Pittsburgh Press.

This account of the emergence of Local 229 of the United Automobile Workers is based on a lengthy and detailed collaboration with Edmund Kord, the president of the local during most of its first eighteen years. Because there is little documentary evidence bearing directly on the history of this local,[1] I have had to rely almost entirely on Kord's memory. For this reason I think I owe the reader an explanation of the nature and extent of these discussions and communications with Kord, so that the limitations of this study will be clear.

In December 1972 Kord and I spent eight days together on the east side of Detroit. At that time I took notes of our discussions, and Kord showed me the plant and the surrounding neighborhood in Hamtramck, pointed out the important bars, and described such details as the configuration of workers in front of the gate during strikes. I wrote a draft based on this material and on Tonat's dissertation. I sent this to Kord, along with a set of questions, for comments and criticism. On the basis of his response to these I constructed a further set of questions and sent them to him. Later, in late June of 1973, we spent a week together. This time I recorded our conversations on about eight hours of tapes. These were then transcribed and reordered in a rough narrative sequence and in this form became the basis for the major series of communications: an extensive correspondence occupying seventy-five pages. A draft of the first three chapters was then drawn up and submitted to Kord for comments and corrections. Following this we met for a week in January 1974 and two days in March 1974. Again the conversations were recorded. Finally, to fill some gaps that became apparent in the course of drawing up the final draft, Kord and I had six recorded telephone conversations totaling about four hours. What follows, therefore, is the outcome of a lengthy collaboration extending from December 1972 to March 1974.

The extent of Kord's knowledge of events in the plant varied in relation to the location of those events. Kord, who was a grinder in the torch-welding department, had an intimate knowledge of his own department and a substantial, but less intimate knowledge of the adjacent press departments, based on direct contact and close observation. His knowledge of the front of the shop – front-welding and departments 16 and 18 – was gained mainly through discussions at the time with the activists and leaders in that part of the shop, although he possesses a good deal of direct knowledge even there. However, Kord's knowledge of both the toolroom and the inspection department in the early period of the union's history [. . .] is limited not only by their physical distance from his own department, but also by the resistance to unionization exhibited by these two departments.

Nevertheless, because of the nature of the questions that I sought to answer in this study, the limitations imposed by the character of the evidence have little significance: not only is the necessary information unavailable except in the form of the memories of participants; it emerges only through a critical dialogue.[2] Therefore I did not simply ask questions of Kord or solicit his reminiscences. On the contrary, I sought to bring to bear on Kord's experience a number of theoretical and historical conceptions that I thought critical to an understanding of the CIO – conceptions that I found myself forced to alter as my increasingly concrete information obstinately refused to fall into some of my prefabricated categories.

Even if, for example, a certain amount of 'hard' evidence were available, say in the form of census data for the plant, it would be of almost no use. The census would only distinguish between foreign-born and native-born of foreign or mixed parentage. Yet among the latter, it turns out, there were at least three distinct groups of young, unskilled second-generation Polish workers: (1) those who were helpers in front-welding and who expected to be promoted to welders (the most highly skilled production work in the plant), (2) those unskilled press operators who were in their middle twenties, who had left their parental homes, and who were married or planning to get married, and (3) those who were just out of high school (or who had dropped out) and who were members of neighborhood gangs and barroom cliques. Obviously, this kind of information cannot be gleaned from available documentary evidence.

The same problems emerge in regard to other major questions. What was the subjective, psychological content of relationships to authority, and how did this change in the course of the organizing effort? Who were the leaders: what was the inner structure of leadership, conceived of as a social forma-tion, and how did it emerge from the matrix of social relations in the plant? What was the role of leadership, and to what extent did the leaders act or seem to act independently of their followers? How did the various groups of workers conceive of their struggle for power, and what impact did that struggle have on their personal lives and social outlooks? Until recently, the major current in labor historiography has been frankly institutional in orientation, yet the emergence of institutions is only an aspect of a more complex social process. What are the sources of institutionalization, and what is its relationship to the broader social process out of which institutions emerge? [. . .]

Since this work is almost entirely dependent on oral sources and on memory, questions emerge about the structure and reliability of memory and about the nature of the interview process itself – a problem that occupies the middle (and perhaps hybrid) ground between epistemology and linguistic philosophy, on the one hand, and more orthodox historiography on the other. For the problem that we face arises not so much out of the interpretation of data as in its creation. And because the interview process is above all linguistic, language itself becomes a methodological problem.

Superficially, of course, Kord and I shared the same language: everyday English. Moreover, Kord's cultural and social background is fairly close to that of my own family, so that, even if the results of this study might be called ethnographic, the environment I chose to study was familiar. Thus, in the collaboration that we undertook, I brought my own curiosity, informed and disciplined by a specific body of knowledge, a theoretical framework, and a rudimentary method of investigation. To these Kord added his own background in history and theory, the consequences of his father's Socialist culture, his mother's broad intellectual and cultural interests, his own schooling, his intellectual experience in the Socialist party, and, above all, his experience not merely as a participant but as the architect of Local 229. Because of Kord's cosmopolitan, rationalist background, we were able to establish a theoretical framework within which to discuss and interpret such cultural phenomena as the differences between Polish immigrants and their children. Such a theoretical framework is a vital necessity if a discussion is to get beyond the primitive stage of collecting anecdotes.

Yet in spite of this common ground, we initially had considerable difficulty with language and meaning; for history as a discipline has its own language, its canon of interpretation, its collection of problems occupying the forefront of contemporary inquiry. And my approach, a Hegelian Marxism greatly influenced by phenomenology, linguistic philosophy, and structuralism, at first only intensified this problem. Yet if the work of generating a theoretically meaningful account of the development of Kord's local union was to progress, a common language had to emerge out of our collaboration, one whose logic and terms of description would be clear and unambiguous to each of us, and within the framework of which our discussion could proceed with precision. While explicit discussion of theory would help to clarify the problems that I was concerned with, the actual emergence of our common language, and its verification, came only after months of 'practice'.[3] If at first our discussions seemed unclear and unfocused – if we had difficulty understanding each other – by the mid-point of our collaboration we had arrived at a sufficiently clear language and had eliminated a number of extraneous or irrelevant avenues of investigation, so that both question and answer seemed increasingly to be complementary moments in a more integrated historical discourse involving the two of us. The clarity of theoretical focus that developed, in fact, was an important part of the development of our common language.

It was within this framework of linguistic interaction that 'data' was produced: since few facts existed, we had to create them. This is less arbitrary than it seems. A census enumerator, for example, does not merely collect data. Rather, standing behind him are not only the census bureau and its staff of statisticians, but also a cultural matrix and an administrative purpose which give a specific shape to certain perceptions of family structure, nationality, education, etc. Likewise, a newspaper account is hardly 'factual'; it is a reporter's impression, which is itself the outcome of his predisposition to view people and situations in a certain way. Even the 'obvious' fact that there were a certain number of paid-up members in the union at a particular time is a fact only because someone looked at the situation in a certain way and made an observation. (Even such hard observations can dissolve into a welter of complex, uncertain shadings and contradictory meanings when one begins to focus more closely on the phenomenology of social processes.) If, for example, the designer of the census was oblivious to the fact that Lutheran Slovaks lived in a different cultural, political, and social world than Catholic Slovaks, and that Bohemian Freethinkers were quite unlike both, the resulting category, Czechoslovak, is not only limited in its historical usefulness, but is misleading and mythological.

Thus, the historian who deals with artifacts is restricted to bringing his own intellectual apparatus to bear, not on the object itself (an epistemological fantasy at any rate), but on another object: the result of a previous process of abstraction. The limitations of depending on traditional sources are therefore obvious. [. . .]

But how reliable is Kord's memory? This is a problem that encompasses any oral history project, and it must be dealt with forthrightly. Kruchko has observed that, in his interviews with veterans of the struggle to organize UAW Local 674 in Norwood, Ohio, 'the memories of the men . . . even down to small details, were surprisingly accurate'.[4] I found the same to be true of Kord. The depth and intensity of his involvement was such that even now, thirty-six years later, his remembrances are both vivid and detailed.

Nevertheless, memory does not provide us with the kind of pinpoint accuracy found in documentary evidence. Kord's margin of error in the pre-contract period, he estimates, is of the order of several days to two weeks. Thus, I refer to a meeting which was held during the last part of February, for example. How important such a margin of error is depends upon how well Kord could recall the dramatic sequence of events not only in terms of order, but also in terms of the tempo and dynamic of development. In this regard Kord's memory was generally clear and unambiguous, and he was quite certain of all but a handful of minor points. Nevertheless, in addition to the external verification, which was found in the few sources that relate to Local 229 and which appears in the footnotes [of the book], a system of internal checking was also used. As the broad picture began to emerge in the course of our discussions and correspondence, I in effect 'cross-examined' Kord. In general, the contradictions that I found were relatively minor, more often than not based on misunderstandings. In addition, these contradictions were ironed out early in the course of our work: Kord, having become deeply involved in this endeavor, began to do his own checking. Wherever any uncertainty has remained, it is indicated.

Yet if the contents of memory are simply 'facts' as discussed above, we would find ourselves in the same situation that obtains when dealing with more orthodox sources. But while the structure of memory is related to the structure of perception and the latter is itself rooted in culture, education, and experience (native American informants, for example, are extraordinarily unperceptive about Slavs), memory itself is a vast welter of impressions and feelings, as well as a more structured, rational schemata. Many impressions either were not important to Kord in 1937 or did not appear to make any sense; yet, as we brought them to the foreground their possible interconnectedness and meaning emerged. Furthermore, the elaboration of this matrix of meaning and the gradual construction of the history of the local reacted back upon the original source, Kord's memory. As a consequence, Kord's recollections became richer and more precise, and the elaboration of a number of hypotheses gave a critical focus to his effort to recall. And precisely because memory is richer than the rational narrative superstructure to which it is often reduced, the whole enterprise remained open-ended: there were numerous ways of structuring the material. What it would become depended on how we approached our work, what leads we followed, and what problems concerned us. For example, I continued to press for cultural and psychological data on as many workers as Kord could remember, especially the primary and secondary leadership. Certain Freudian and Weberian concerns led me to ask particular kinds of questions (e.g., about personal habits such as drinking). These questions themselves emerged in my own thought only over a period of many months, and the responses to them were by no means immediately intelligible. I was looking for patterns and relationships. At first, however, the material was necessarily fragmentary; then, after more such questions and answers had accumulated, the material became less fragmentary, but it was still difficult to penetrate. Only gradually did patterns emerge relating some characteristics of personality with certain aspects of the history of the local.

Two further examples help clarify the relationship between memory and theory. In the course of our first series of discussions in December 1972, Kord made a remark about 'new hires' in department 19 (in the spring of 1937). The remark registered, but I let it go by. Later, as we continued to discuss the situation in the plant, 'new hires' came up again. What gave the department where these employees worked its peculiar character was the fact that they were members of neighborhood gangs. Yet what I had at this point was not a concept of a social group, but rather the understanding that very likely these gang kids were in fact a group, that they had to be studied further, and that out of all this a concept might emerge. In the next series of discussions and in the seventy-five pages of letters that I sent to Kord, whenever relevant I brought up questions relating to these young workers. What did they say to the foreman under certain circumstances? What forms of recreation did they engage in? Where did they live, and under what circumstances? What were their attitudes toward the union effort at specific times? How did they react to the five-cent raise? The results of such inquiry are contained in the body of the book.

Another determination I sought out more purposefully. I was convinced that there were significant ethical or moral differences between the Appalachian migrants, the first-generation Slavs, and the wildcatters among the second generation. Twice in the course of our second series of discussions (July 1973) I raised this question. Twice Kord replied negatively. The third time, however, something clicked. Kord briefly but cogently described actual confrontations, quoted typical statements made by representative members of the three groups, and described the interrelationship of these groups within the union and their different relationships to the leadership in confrontation situations. Further, he discussed their varying attitudes toward authority, both that of the management and that of the union leaders, and their conceptions of society, of the individual, and of standards of behavior.

This example illustrates both the obstacles to and the immense potential of this kind of investigation. The process of searching, guessing, hypothesizing, and probing that the historian must undertake depends for its success on the degree to which his collaborator is willing to get involved in these questions. Often the relevance of what I asked was not obvious, and some of the more exciting questions were obscure and even ambiguous. To make sense out of some of my questions required that Kord search his memory for any evidence that might have had a bearing on the question, sort it out, and verbalize it. If these cultural differences were not clear at the time, then Kord's cognitive processes did not organize his perceptions along such lines. Such an organization of perceptions, drawn from the complex welter of memory, was precisely what I asked of Kord. And it was here that a real dialectic unfolded, in the course of which we collectively shaped both concept and perception, batting ideas and observations around, exploring their significance, and conceiving of new questions as material developed.

From the foregoing, it is obvious that, if certain problems are to be explored at all, they must be investigated through the use of oral history techniques: the usual sources that historians traditionally rely upon simply fail to throw any light on some of the most fundamental historical processes. Yet even in those areas of data collection where the census is thought to excel, oral history techniques are far more accurate than any but the most accurate hypothetical census. For example, we have already seen one of the problems with the census – its tendency to amalgamate under a single category (such as Czechoslovak) several distinct and often contradictory social groups. Beyond this, however, even if the ethnic composition of a factory were known to a high degree of precision, its relevance would remain dubious. Of what value would be the knowledge that 30 percent of the workers in a particular plant were Polish, if we knew from previous investigations that this geographical unit was far too large to be meaningful? On the other hand, the response of an informant that a single department, say metal-finishing, possessed a work force that was 90 percent Polish might be off by a few points, or even by as much as 10 or 15 percent, but it would be far closer to the truth than the census estimate, which would be unable to go any farther than specifying that 30 percent of the workers *in the plant* were Polish. When one realizes that each department possessed a very specialized ethnic structure, it becomes obvious that if one is to write the social history of the organization of a factory, one must have this information; and from the standpoint of the historian, such data, regardless of the greater margin of error of this technique, is far more useful and indeed, from a historiographical standpoint, far more accurate than the results of a hypothetical census based on plant-wide surveys.

To meaningfully describe patterns of behavior or to analyze the structure of an event are objectives that often lie beyond the reach of orthodox uses of data, particularly when one's interest shifts from the various intellectual, social, and political elites to the industrial working class. In the present study, for example, a critical union action inside the plant is met with strikingly different positive responses on the part of the first- and the second-generation Poles. Such occurrences provide invaluable materials out of which to develop a sense of the interaction of the various political cultures within the plant – or they even permit one to define such cultures in the first place.

Nevertheless, in the conduct of a series of interviews it is important to maintain a critical attitude. Failure to cross-examine can lead to astonishing reversals of fact. For example, in an interview by Jack Skeels of Frank Fagan, a unionist active in the Murray Body plant during the formative years of the UAW, an entirely different story emerges from that found in my own interviews with Fagan.[5] In the Skeels version, an incident in 1933 in which Fagan organized a petition campaign among thirty welders asking for company-supplied leather armlets to protect their clothing and arms from red-hot sparks resulted in the firing of Fagan and another worker. This event, according to Fagan, 'broke the back of the men'. In this section of the interview, Skeels himself intervened very infrequently, resulting in long periods of unbroken reminiscences which were left to stand as they were, with no effort made at cross-examination or elicitation of detail. Unprepared for what was to follow, I reopened the question of the leather armlet incident with Fagan, mainly in order to investigate the ethnic background of the workers involved and the structure of the event. This eighteen-minute section of the interview began with a discussion of the year. Fagan thought that it was 1935. I told him that in his previous interview he had said 1933. He was unable to remember that interview but began to fix the leather armlet incident in relation to other events finally settling on 1935 as the most likely year. The story then unfolded in great detail; I constantly asked for more bits of information – the names of people, descriptions of the welding process and the problem it posed in terms of burning holes in the welders's shirts, etc. Then I asked Fagan to remember as many individuals as he could who were working on the same line and who got involved in the petition incident. At this point the interview makes for poor reading: long periods of silence, punctuated first by one name – about whom I asked such details as ethnic background and union experience – then by another name, the whole liberally sprinkled with remarks by Fagan that this was a long time back and was hard to remember, yet at the same time that he could visualize all of the welders involved in the incident. Nevertheless, he succeeded in remembering eight others besides himself. He described the incident itself: the misgivings of many of the workers about signing the petition, its delivery, and the response of the personnel manager to Fagan and his coworker Udata as he politely threw them out onto the street. From this point on, however, the story directly contradicts the earlier version told to Skeels. Following the firing of Fagan and Udata, some of the welders began a job action, letting the arcs of flame get too big and burning holes in the automobile bodies, as a result of which production of the entire plant was piling up in the repair shop. The foreman told all the welders to go home and to behave themselves when they returned the next day. Alex Faulkner replied (as was reported to Fagan a few days later) that Fagan and Udata both better be at work too. Within a couple of days the company had gotten in touch with Fagan and rehired him. When Fagan returned to work, however, the other workers wanted to know where Udata was, and Fagan, after a visit to Udata's home, ascertained that Udata had gotten another job, not wanting to return to Murray Body. Only then did the tension subside.

The point of retelling this story is to illustrate some of the pitfalls of writing oral history. Memory is a treacherous thing, as more than one of my informants has remarked. The necessity for cross-examination, digging for details, and even confronting an interviewee with contradictory evidence, is critical. It is important *before* the interview to get deeply into the documentary materials relevant to an interviewee's experience, to anticipate several strategies of questioning, and to be prepared with a battery of questions that are derived from the historian's special understanding of social phenomena. It is equally necessary to be alert to the possibility that an offhand remark may contain an important clue, the consequences of which may be totally unexpected and even contrary to some basic assumptions. In general, the historian must counterpose his *intensive* approach to the *extensive* narrative that tends to be the spontaneous response of most informants. Thus, in the Skeels interviews, there are numerous junctures in which an informant reveals something of critical significance. Instead of interceding and sharpening the focus of the discussion, Skeels let these things go by. In fairness to Skeels, of course, we should remember that many of these theoretical concerns are of recent origin. Nevertheless, as the leather armlet incident indicates, there may be some question about the accuracy of interviews conducted in an expansive narrative style, rather than through intensive cross-examination. [. . .]

NOTES

1 This evidence includes C.S. Tonat, 'A case study of a local union: participation, loyalty and attitudes of local union members', M.A thesis, Wayne State University, Detroit, 1956, which is based on a study of Local 229; a few brief notices which appeared in the *United Automobile Worker* between 1938 and 1940; and a collection of correspondence found in the George F. Addes Papers on deposit at the Archives of Labor History and Urban Affairs at Wayne State University (henceforth cited as Archives).
2 The material contained in the Archives pertaining to Local 229 is sparse. Even in regard to two of the most thoroughly documented locals – Local 51 (Plymouth) and Local 3 (Dodge) – the materials available are of such character as to render impossible any attempt at answering the questions posed in the present study.
3 The problem of language as practice in this sense is one of the central points of L. Wittgenstein, *Philosophical Investigations*, Oxford, Basil Blackwell, 1963.
4 J.G. Kruchko, *The Birth of a Union Local: The History of UAW Local 674, Norwood, Ohio, 1933–1940*, Ithaca, N.Y., New York State School of Industrial and Labor Relations, Cornell University, 1972, p.iii.
5 Interview with Frank Fagan, February 19, 1963, Archives, pp. 10–11.

27 'That's not what I said'

Interpretive conflict in oral narrative research

Katherine Borland

Katherine Borland received her doctorate in Folklore from Indiana University in 1994, and is the founding director of a program in Wilmington, Delaware, that motivates and supports inner city high school students to prepare for college. Reprinted from S. Berger Gluck and D. Patai (eds), *Women's Words: The Feminist Practice of Oral History*, New York and London, Routledge, 1991, pp. 63–75, with permission.

In the summer of 1944, my grandmother, Beatrice Hanson, put on a pale, eggshell-colored gabardine dress with big gold buttons down the side, a huge pancake-black hat, and elbow-length gloves – for in *those* days ladies dressed *up* to go to the fair – and off she went with her father to see the sulky (harness) races at the Bangor, Maine, fairgrounds. The events that ensued provided for a lively wrangle between father and daughter as they vied to pick the winner. Forty-two years later Beatrice remembered vividly the events of that afternoon and, in a highly structured and thoroughly entertaining narrative, recounted them to me, her folklorist-granddaughter, who recorded her words on tape for later transcription and analysis. What took place that day, why it proved so memorable, and what happened to the narrative during the process of intergenerational transmission provide a case study in the variability of meaning in personal narrative performances. This story, or, better said, these stories, stimulate reflexivity about our scholarly practice.

Let me begin with the question of meaning and its variability. We can view the performance of a personal narrative as a meaning-constructing activity on two levels simultaneously. It constitutes both a dynamic interaction between the thinking subject and the narrated event (her own life experience) and between the thinking subject and the narrative event (her 'assumption of responsibility to an audience for a display of communicative competence'[1]). As performance contexts change, as we discover new audiences, and as we renegotiate our sense of self, our narratives will also change.

What do folklorists do with the narratives performed for/before us? Like other audience members, we enjoy a skillfully told tale. But some of us also collect records of the performance in order to study them. Oral personal narratives occur naturally within a conversational context, in which various people take turns at talk, and thus are rooted most immediately in a web of expressive social activity. *We* identify chunks of artful talk within this flow of conversation, give them physical existence (most often through writing), and embed them in a new context of expressive or at least communicative activity (usually the scholarly article aimed toward an audience of professional peers). Thus, we construct a second-level narrative based upon, but at the same time reshaping, the first.

Like the original narrator, we simultaneously look inward towards our own experience of the performance (our interpretive shaping of it as listeners) and outward to our audience (to whom we must display a degree of scholarly competence). Presumably, the patterns upon which we base our interpretations can be shown to inhere in the 'original' narrative, but our aims in pointing out certain features, or in making connections between the narrative and larger cultural formations, may at times differ from the original narrator's intentions. This is where issues of our responsibility to our living sources become most acute.

Years ago, scholars who recorded the traditions, arts, and history of a particular culture group gave little thought to the possibility that their representations might legitimately be challenged by those for and about whom they wrote. After all, they had 'been in the field', listening, taking notes, and witnessing the culture firsthand. Educated in the literate, intellectual tradition of the Western academy, these scholars brought with them an objective, scientific perspective that allowed them, they felt, to perceive underlying structures of meaning in their material that the 'natives', enmeshed in a smaller, more limited world, could not see. Therefore, it is not surprising that general ethnographic practice excluded the ethnographic subject from the process of post-fieldwork interpretation, nor that folklorists and anthropologists rarely considered their field collaborators to be potential audiences for their publications. More recently, some researchers sensitive to the relationships of power in the fieldwork exchange have questioned this model of the scholar as interpretive authority for the culture groups he/she studies.[2]

For feminists, the issue of interpretive authority is particularly problematic, for our work often involves a contradiction. On the one hand, we seek to empower the women we work with by revaluing their perspectives, their lives, and their art in a world that has systematically ignored or trivialized women's culture.[3] On the other, we hold an explicitly political vision of the structural conditions that lead to particular social behaviors, a vision that our field collaborators, many of whom do not consider themselves feminists, may not recognize as valid. My own work with my grandmother's racetrack narrative provides a vivid example of how conflicts of interpretation may, perhaps inevitably do, arise during the folklore transmission process. What should we do when we women disagree?

To refrain from interpretation by letting the subjects speak for themselves seems to me an unsatisfactory if not illusory solution. For the very fact that we constitute the initial audience for the narratives we collect influences the way in which our collaborators will construct their stories, and our later presentation of these stories – in particular publications under particular titles – will influence the way in which prospective readers will interpret the texts. Moreover, feminist theory provides a powerful critique of our society, and, as feminists, we presumably are dedicated to making that critique as forceful and direct as possible. How, then, might we present our work in a way that grants the speaking woman interpretive respect without relinquishing our responsibility to provide our own interpretation of her experience?

Although I have no easy answer to this question, I believe that by reflecting on our practice we can move toward a more sensitive research methodology. In the spirit of reflexivity I offer here a record of the dispute that arose between my grandmother and myself when I ventured an interpretation of her narrative. First, I will summarize the narrative, since the taped version runs a full twenty-five minutes. Then I will present her framing of the narrative in performance and my reframing during the interpretive process. Finally, I will present her response to my interpretation. While I have already 'stacked the deck' in my favor by summarizing the story, reducing it through my subjective lens, my grandmother's comments powerfully challenge my assumption of exegetical authority over the text.[4]

Beatrice began her story with a brief setting of the scene: in the grandstand, she finds herself seated directly behind Hod Buzzel, 'who', she states, 'had gotten me my divorce and whom I *hated* with a passion'. Hod is accompanied by his son, the county attorney (who, Beatrice says, 'was just as bad as his father in another way – he was a snob'). Beatrice's father knows them both very well.

Beatrice, the narrator, then explains the established system for selecting a horse. Observers typically purchase a 'score card' that lists the past records of horses and drivers, and they evaluate the horses as they pace before the grandstand. Beatrice's personal system for choosing a horse depends most heavily on her judgement of the observable merits of both horse and driver. She explains:

> And if I could find a *horse* that right pleased me, and a driver that pleased me that were together . . . *there* would be my choice, you see? So, this particular afternoon . . . I *found* that. Now that didn't happen all the time, by any means, but I found . . . perfection, as far as I was concerned, and I was absolutely *convinced* that *that* horse was going to win.

Beatrice decides to bet on Lyn Star, an unknown horse driven by a young man. She knows that this young man's father is driving another horse in the race. Her father and the Buzzels select Black Lash, a horse with an established reputation for speed.

The subsequent action exhibits an inherent potential for narrative patterning. Sulky races, in which a driver sits behind the horse in a two-wheeled single-seat carriage, are presented in a series of three heats. In other words, the same group of horses races against each other three times during the afternoon, alternating with three groups of horses who race against one another in the same fashion. Normally, drivers act on their own, competing individually against their opponents, but the appearance of a father and son in the same race suggests to Bea the possibility that these two may collaborate with one another in some way. Each heat, from the perspective of the audience, involves three stages: selecting a horse and placing a bet, observing the race proper, and collecting on one's winning tickets. With regard to the particular race narrated, an additional structural element is provided by the repetitive strategy employed by the father and son upon whom Bea has placed her hopes.

In each heat, the father quickly takes the lead and sets a fast pace for the other horses while the son lopes along behind. As the horses turn into the second lap and start their drive, the father moves over to let his son through on the rail (the inside lane of the track) thereby forcing Black Lash, the next-to-front runner, to go out and around him Dramatic tension is produced by the variable way in which this strategy is played out on the course. In the first heat, Lyn Star wins by a nose. In the second, he ties in a photo finish with Black Lash. In the third, the father's horse, worn out by his previous two performances, drops back behind the others, leaving Lyn Star and Black Lash to really race. But because of the way the races have been run, Lyn Star's driver had never really had to push his horse. He does so this time and leaves Black Lash half a length behind.

As a superlative narrator, Beatrice recognizes and exploits the parallels between the observed contest and the contest between observers who have aligned themselves with different horses. She structures her narrative by alternating the focus between a dramatic reenactment of events in the grandstand and a description of the actual race as it unfolds before the observers. Within this structure, the cooperation between the father and son on the racecourse provides a contrast to the conflict between father and daughter in the grandstand.

Before the first heat, Bea's father asks her, 'D'you pick a horse?' And she responds that, yes, she has chosen Lyn Star. At this, her father loudly denounces her choice, claiming that the horse will never win, she'll lose her money, and she should not bet. Beatrice puts two dollars on the horse. When Lyn Star wins, Bea turns triumphantly to her father. Undaunted, he insists that the race was a fluke and that Bea's favorite horse will not win again. Nevertheless, Beatrice places six dollars on Lyn Star in the next heat. By now, though, her father is irate and attempts first to trade horses with her so that she won't lose her money, and then, when she declines this offer, he refuses altogether to place her bet. Young Buzzel, who has become an amused audience of one to the father–daughter contest in the grandstand, offers to take her money down to the betting office. Since Bea has never placed her own bets, she accepts.

With the third heat Beatrice's father catapults their private argument into the public arena, as he asks his daughter, 'What are you going to do this time?' Beatrice is adamant, 'I am *betting on my horse* and I am betting *ten bucks* on that horse. It's gonna win!' At this, Beatrice, the narrator, explains, 'Father had a fit. *He* had a fit. And he tells everybody three miles around in the grandstand what a fool I am too. . . . *He* wasn't gonna take my money down!' So Beatrice commandeers young Buzzel to place her bet for her again. When Lyn Star wins by a long shot, Bea's father is effectively silenced:

> And *I* threw my pocketbook in one direction, and I threw my gloves in another direction, and my score book went in another direction, and I jumped up and I hollered, to everyone, 'You see what know-it-all said! *That's* my father!' And finally one man said to me . . . no, he said to my father, 'You know, she *really* enjoys horse racing, doesn't she?'

To understand how Bea frames her narrative, we must return to a consideration of her initial description of how a horse is chosen. This prefatory material orients the audience to a particular point of view, emphasizing that the race should be understood as an opportunity for racegoers to exercise their evaluative skills in order to predict an eventual outcome. Indeed, the length and detail of this portion of the narrative emphasizes the seriousness, for Beatrice, of this preliminary evaluative activity. This framing of the story gains significance if one considers that Bea's knowledge of horses was unusual for women in her community. Emphasizing the exceptionality of her knowledge, she explained to me that her father owned and raced horses when Bea was a child and 'though I could not go *fishing* with my father on Sundays, or *hunting* with him on any day of the week, for some strange reason, he took me with him, mornings' to watch his horses being exercised.

Additionally, in her framing of the narrative, Beatrice identifies the significance of the event narrated, its memorability, as the unique coming together of a perfect horse and driver that produced an absolute conviction on her part as to who would win the contest. Since this conviction was proved correct the narrative functions to support or illustrate Bea's sense of self as a competent judge of horses within both the narrative and the narrated event. In effect, her narrative constitutes a verbal re-performance of an actual evaluative performance at the track.

What do I as a listener make of this story? A feminist, I am particularly sensitive to identifying gender dynamics in verbal art, and, therefore, what makes the story significant for me is the way in which this self-performance within the narrated event takes on the dimension of a female struggle for autonomy within a hostile male environment. Literally and symbolically, the horse race constitutes a masculine sphere. Consider, racing contestants, owners, and trainers were male (although female *horses* were permitted to compete). Also, while women obviously attended the races, indeed, 'ladies dressed up' to go to the races, they were granted only partial participant status. While they were allowed to sit in the grandstand as observers (and, having dressed up, one assumes, as persons to be observed), they were not expected to engage as active evaluators in the essential first stage of the racing event. Notice that even at the very beginning of the story Bea's father did not want her to bet. Betting is inherently a risk-taking activity. Men take risks; women do not. This dimension of meaning is underscored in the second heat when Beatrice, the narrator, ironically recounts that her father was going to be 'decent' to her, in other words, was going to behave according to the model of gentlemanly conduct, by offering to bear his daughter's risk and bet on her horse for her.

Significantly, as the verbal contest develops, Beatrice displays greater and greater assertiveness as a gambler. Not only does she refuse to align herself with the men's judgement, she also raises the ante by placing more and more serious bets on her choice. From an insignificant bet in the first heat – and here it bears recalling that in racing parlance a two-dollar bet is still called a 'lady's bet' – she proceeds in the second and third heats to bet six and ten dollars, respectively.

In portraying the intensification of the contest, Beatrice, the narrator, endows Beatrice, the gambler, with an increasingly emphatic voice. Her tone in addressing her father moves from one of calm resolution before the first and second heats – 'That's the horse I'm betting on', and 'No, I'm gonna stay with that horse' – to heated insistence before the third heat – 'I am *betting on my horse!*' (each word accentuated in performance by the narrator's pounding her fist on the dining-room table).

Finally, if one looks at Beatrice's post-heat comments, one can detect a move from simple self-vindication in the first heat to a retaliatory calumniation of her father's reputation delivered in a loud disparaging voice – 'You see what know-it-all said! *That's* my father!' Thus, at the story's end, Beatrice has moved herself from a peripheral feminine position with respect to the larger male sphere of betting *and* talk, to a central position where her words and deeds proclaim her equal and indeed superior to her male antagonist. Symbolically underscoring this repudiation of a limiting feminine identity, Bea flings away the accessories of her feminine costume – her gloves and her pocketbook.

If on one level the story operates as a presentation of self as a competent judge of horses, on another it functions to assert a sense of female autonomy and equality within a sphere dominated by men. From yet another perspective, the verbal contest between father and daughter results in a realignment of allegiances based on the thematic contrasts between age and youth, reputation and intrinsic merit, observable in the contest between the horses Black Lash and Lyn Star. When her father (tacitly) refuses to place her bet before the second heat, young Buzzell, whom Bea has previously described as an antagonist, and who has been betting with the older men, offers to place her bet for her. In effect, he bets on Beatrice in the contest developing on the sidelines.

Furthermore, with regard to the narrator's life experience, one can view the narrative as a metaphor for a larger contest between Beatrice and her social milieu. For in the early 1930s Beatrice shocked her community by divorcing her first husband. This action and her attempt to become economically independent by getting an education were greeted with a certain amount of social and familial censure. For instance, Beatrice recalls, when her mother entered the date of the divorce in the family bible, she included the note: 'Recorded, but not approved.' It also forced Beatrice to leave her two young daughters in the care of their paternal grandparents for the five years she attended college, a necessity that still saddens and troubles her today.

My grandparents agree that, in the ideology of marriage at that time, 'you weren't supposed to be happy'. My grandfather relates that his grandmother suffered severe psychological strain during menopause, was committed to a psychiatric hospital, and, while there, crossed her name off her marriage certificate. In a slightly more active form of resistance, Beatrice's grandmother, after injuring herself while doing heavy farm work, took to her bed for several years. However, as soon as her son married, she got up, moved in with him, and led a normal, active life, becoming the strong maternal figure of Bea's own childhood. Bea's mother separated herself psychologically from both her husband and her family by retreating into a strict, moralistic, and, in Bea's view, hypocritical religiosity. For Bea's predecessors, then, a woman's socially acceptable response to an unhappy marriage was to remove herself from the marriage without actually effecting a formal, public separation. Although Bea's first husband was tacitly recognized by the community as an unfit husband – irresponsible, alcoholic, a spendthrift and a philanderer – Beatrice was expected to bear with the situation in order to protect her own reputation and that of her family.

By divorcing her first husband Beatrice transgressed middle-class social decorum and was branded 'disreputable'. The appearance in the present narrative of the divorce lawyer and Bea's negative reaction to him leads me to link Beatrice's performance and status at the races to her previous loss of reputation in the larger village society. In both instances Beatrice had to prove in the face of strong opposition the rightness of not playing by the rules, of relying on her own judgment, of acting as an autonomous individual. I would suggest, then, that the latent associations of this narrative to circumstances critical to the narrator's life, even if not consciously highlighted in the narrative, may reinforce its memorability.

What is essential to emphasize, however, is that this is *my* framing of the racetrack narrative informed by contemporary feminist conceptions of patriarchal structures, which my grandmother does not share. Moreover, after reading an initial version of this interpretation, Beatrice expressed strong disagreement with my conclusions. I quote a portion of the fourteen-page letter she wrote to me concerning the story:

> Not being, myself, a feminist, the 'female struggle' as such never bothered me in my life. It never occurred to me. I never thought of my *position* at all in this sense. I've always felt that I had a fine childhood. It seems, now, that I must have had a remarkable one. To begin with, I had a very strong father figure. Surrounded by the deep and abiding love of my Grandmother Austin (whom I adored); the clear, unfaltering knowledge of my father's love and his openly expressed pride in me, and the definite disciplines set

by my grandmother which provided the staunch and unchallengeable framework in which I moved, I knew absolute security. (The disciplines were unchallengeable because I never had the least desire to challenge them. I would have done anything not to disappoint Grandma or make her feel bad, and I was so very happy and secure that only an idiot would have tried to upset the situation.)

In consequence of all this, as I grew older, the inner strength which that sense of security had built in me, served always to make me feel equal to anyone, male or female, and very often superior. Feminism, as such, was of no moment to me – none at all. Privately, it has always seemed ridiculous, but that's neither here nor there. It makes no difference to me what anybody else thinks about it.

So your interpretation of the story as a female struggle for autonomy within a hostile male environment is entirely YOUR interpretation. You've read into the story what you wished to – what pleases YOU. That it was never – by any widest stretch of the imagination – the concern of the originator of the story makes such an interpretation a definite and complete distortion, and in this respect I question its authenticity. The story is no longer MY story at all. The skeleton remains, but it has become your story. Right? How far is it permissible to go, in the name of folklore, and still be honest in respect to the original narrative?

Beatrice brings up a crucial issue in oral narrative scholarship – who controls the text? If I had not sent my grandmother a copy of my work, asking for her response, I could perhaps have avoided the question of my intrusion into the texts I collect. Discussions with our field collaborators about the products of our research are often overlooked or unreported by folklore scholars. Luckily, my grandmother is quite capable of reading, responding to, and resisting my presentation of her narrative. For my own and my grandmother's versions provide a radical example of how each of us has created a story from her own experience. While I agree that the story has indeed become *my* story in the present context, I cannot agree that my reading betrays the original narrative.

Beatrice embraces an idealist model of textual meaning that privileges authorial intentions. It makes sense for my grandmother to read the story in this way. From my own perspective, however, the story does not really become a story until it is actualized in the mind of a receptive listener/reader. As my consciousness has been formed within a different social and historical reality, I cannot restrict my reading to a recuperation of original authorial intentions. I offer instead a different reading, one that values her story as an example to feminists of one woman's strategy for combating a limiting patriarchal ideology. That Bea's performance constitutes a direct opposition to established authorities reveals for me how gender ideologies are not wholly determinative or always determinative of female identity.[5]

Nevertheless, despite my confidence in the validity of my reading as a feminist scholar, personally I continue to be concerned about the potential emotional effect alternative readings of personal narratives may have on our living subjects. The performance of a personal narrative is a fundamental means by which people comprehend their own lives and present a 'self' to their audience.[6] Our scholarly representations of those performances, if not sensitively presented, may constitute an attack on our collaborators' carefully constructed sense of self. While Bea and I have discussed our differences at length and come to an amicable agreement about how to present them (i.e., the inclusion of her response to my initial reading in the final text), I might have avoided eliciting such a violent initial response from her if I had proceeded differently from the outset.[7]

I could have tried to elicit my grandmother's comments on the story's meaning before I began the process of interpretation. During the taping session itself, however, this would have proved problematic. As I stated earlier, oral personal narratives occur naturally within a conversational context, and often the performance of one narrative leads to other related performances. These displays of verbal art provide an important context for understanding how the narrative in question is to be viewed, and from my perspective it would not be productive to break the narrative flow in order to move to the very different rhetorical task of interpretation and analysis.

Furthermore, during a narrative performance of this type, both narrator and listener are caught up in the storytelling event. Although associative commentary about the stories is common, at this stage in the fieldwork exchange neither narrator nor listener is prepared to reflect analytically on the material being presented. Indeed, the conscious division of a storytelling session into discreet story units or thematic constellations of stories occurs at the later stage of review and study.

Nevertheless, the narrator's commentary on and interpretation of a story can contribute greatly to the researcher's understanding of it. I now feel I ought to have arranged a second session with my grandmother in which I played her the taped version and asked her for her view of its function and meaning. Time constraints prevented me from doing so. I did solicit an interpretation from Bea with not much success after I had written and she had read my initial version of this article. At that time Beatrice insisted that the story was simply an amusing anecdote with no deep or hidden meanings. Although it may be that some narrators are not prepared to interpret their own stories analytically, Bea's reaction may have been due to her sharply felt loss of authorial control.

With the benefit of hindsight, let me review two points that proved especially sensitive for my grandmother. First, Bea reacted very strongly to the feminist identity my interpretation implied she had. Though some might quibble that this problem is simply a matter of labels, the word 'feminist' often has negative, threatening connotations for women who have not participated in the feminist movement. More important, Bea's objection points to an important oversight in my own research process.

When I began the task of interpretation, I assumed a likeness of mind where there was in fact difference: I was confident that my grandmother would accept my view of the story's meaning. After all, she had been very excited about working with me when I told her I wanted to study older women's life experience narratives. She sent me a great deal of material and commentary on the difficult conditions of women's lives in nineteenth- and early twentieth-century Maine, material and commentary that seemed on the surface to convey a feminist perspective. Moreover, she offered her own accounts and stories, some of which dealt with very sensitive matters, assuring me that I should feel perfectly free to use whatever proved helpful to me in my research. How, then, did we, who had a close, confidential, long-standing relationship, manage to misunderstand each other so completely?

The fieldwork exchange fosters a tendency to downplay differences, as both investigator and source seek to establish a footing with one another and find a common ground from which to proceed to the work of collecting and recording oral materials. Additionally, as we are forever constructing our own identities through social interactions, we similarly construct our notion of others. My grandmother has always appeared to me a remarkably strong, independent woman, and thus, even though she has never called herself a feminist, it was an easy step for me to cast her in that role. Although she knew that I considered myself an activist feminist, to her I have always been, first and foremost, a granddaughter. She was, therefore, unprepared for the kind of analysis performed on her narrative. The feminist movement has been criticized before for overgeneralizing about women's experience in its initial enthusiasms of sisterly identification. Yet it bears repeating that important commonalities among women often mask equally important differences.[8]

For Beatrice, another troubling feature of my interpretation is the portrait it presents of her father. Here the problem arises from our different understandings of what the narrative actually is. I approach the story as a symbolic construction and the people within it are, for me, dramatic characters. Thus, Beatrice's father, the antagonistic figure of the story, becomes a symbol of repressive male authority in my interpretation. For Beatrice, however, the story remains an account of a real experience, embedded in the larger context of her life. She brings to her reading of the 'characters' a complex of associations built up over a shared lifetime. From this perspective my interpretation of her father is absolutely false. Whether or not it 'works' for the father figure in the story, it does not define the man. In fact, Beatrice's father was one of the few people who encouraged and supported her during the difficult period after her disastrous first marriage. She remembers her father with a great deal of love and admiration and speaks often of the special relationship they had with one another. Indeed, if anyone was the villain of Beatrice's youth, it would have been her mother, a cold, judgmental woman. Nevertheless, in a written account of the racetrack story composed shortly after the event took place, Beatrice herself remarks that at the track, 'Father and the Buzzels were acting very male', quarreling over the results of the races.[9]

When I sent Beatrice a copy of my essay in which *her* narrative had suffered a sea change, she naturally felt misrepresented. To complicate matters, my original essay contained a great deal of theory that was unfamiliar and at times incomprehensible to her. Embedded in the context of my own scholarly environment, I had not bothered to provide any accompanying explanation of that theory. Thus, if I had 'misread' her text, I also gave her every opportunity to misread mine. I now feel that had I talked to Bea about my ideas *before* I committed them to writing, presented her with drafts, or even arranged to have her read the paper with me so that we might discuss misunderstandings and differences as they arose, her sense of having been robbed of textual authority might not have been as strong as it was.

I am not suggesting that all differences of perspective between folklorist and narrator, feminist scholar and speaking woman, should or can be worked out before the final research product is composed. Nor am I suggesting that our interpretations must be validated by our research collaborators. For when we do interpretations, we bring our own knowledge, experience, and concerns to our material, and the result, we hope, is a richer, more textured understanding of its meaning.

I am suggesting that we might open up the exchange of ideas so that we do not simply gather data on others to fit into our own paradigms once we are safely ensconced in our university libraries ready to do interpretation. By extending the conversation we initiate while collecting oral narratives to the later stage of interpretation, we might more sensitively negotiate issues of interpretive authority in our research.

Quite possibly, this modification of standard practice would reveal new ways of understanding our materials to both research partners. At the very least, it would allow us to discern more clearly when we speak in unison and when we disagree. Finally, it would restructure the traditionally unidirectional flow of information out from source to scholar to academic audience by identifying our field collaborators as an important first audience for our work. Lest we, as feminist scholars, unreflectively appropriate the words of our mothers for our own uses, we must attend to the multiple and sometimes conflicting meanings generated by our framing or contextualizing of their oral narratives in new ways.

POSTSCRIPT

On July 8, 1989, after a ten-month absence, I visited Beatrice and gave her a copy of the present version of this paper for her final comments. She took it to her study, read it, and then the two of us went through it together, paragraph by paragraph. At this juncture she allowed that much of what I had said was 'very true', though she had not thought about the events of her life in this way before. After a long and fruitful discussion, we approached the central issue of feminism. She explained, once again, that feminism was not a movement that she had identified with or even heard of in her youth. Nevertheless, she declared that if I meant by feminist a person who believed that a woman has the right to live her life the way she wants to regardless of what society has to say about it, then she guessed she was a feminist.

Thus, the fieldwork exchange had become, in the end, a true exchange. I had learned a great deal from Beatrice, and she had also learned something from me. Yet I would emphasize that Bea's understanding and acceptance of feminism was not something that I could bestow upon her, as I had initially and somewhat naively attempted to do. It was achieved through the process of interpretive conflict and discussion, emerging as each of us granted the other interpretive space and stretched to understand the other's perspective. While Bea's identification with feminism is not crucial to my argument, it stands as a testament to the new possibilities for understanding that arise when we re-envision the fieldwork exchange.

NOTES

1 R. Bauman, *Verbal Art as Performance*, Prospect Heights, Ill., Waveland, 1977, p. 11. For a discussion of the differences between narrated and narrative events, see R. Bauman's introduction in his *Story, Performance, and Events*, New York, Cambridge University Press, 1986. [Editors note: a number of discursive footnotes have been deleted from the original.]

2 For a discussion of new experiments in ethnographic texts, see J. Clifford and G.E. Marcus (eds), *Writing Culture: The Poetics and Politics of Ethnography*, Berkeley, Calif., University of California Press, 1986, and G.E. Marcus and M.M.J. Fischer, *Anthropology as Cultural Critique: An Experimental Moment in the Human Sciences*, Chicago, University of Chicago Press, 1986.

3 For a discussion of the sexist bias in folklore scholarship generally, see M. Weigle, 'Women as verbal artists: reclaiming the daughters of Enheduanna', *Frontiers*, 1978, vol. 3, no. 3, pp. 1–9.

4 The racetrack narrative I present here forms part of an extended taping session I conducted with my grandmother during a three-day visit to her home in December 1986. A transcription of the full version of Beatrice's narrative appears in my article 'Horsing around with the frame: the negotiation of meaning in women's verbal performance', *Praxis*, Spring 1990, pp. 83–107.

5 Beverly Stoeltje discusses the dialectic between individual behavior, changing environments, and ideals of womanhood in ' "A helpmate for man indeed": the image of the frontier woman', in C.R. Farrer (ed.), *Women and Folklore: Images and Genres*, Prospect Heights, Ill., Waveland Press, 1975, pp. 25–41.

6 Victor Turner views performances as reflexive occasions set aside for the collective or individual presentation of the self to the self in 'Images and reflections: ritual drama, carnival, film and spectacle in cultural performance', in his *The Anthropology of Performance*, New York, The Performing Arts Journal Publications, 1987, pp. 121–132. For a discussion of how personal narratives are tools for making sense of our lives, see B. Myerhoff, 'Life history among the elderly: performance, visibility and remembering', in J. Ruby (ed.), *A Crack in the Mirror: Reflexive Perspectives in Anthropology*, Philadelphia, University of Pennsylvannia Press, 1982, pp. 99–117.

7 In several lengthy post-essay discussions, Beatrice, my grandfather Frank, and I discussed both the story and what happened to it during the process of transmission. After hearing the revised version (in which my grandmother's comments were included), Frank stated that he had learned to see features of the society in which he

grew up that he had never really been aware of before. Beatrice was less enthusiastic about my alternative reading, but agreed that my perspective was thought-provoking. For her, the more general issue of how stories are transformed with each new telling was the most interesting point of the essay, and she expressed a desire to continue working on projects of the same type.

8 Equally serious is the tendency to discount as vestiges of false consciousness attitudes or behaviors that do not fit into our own vision of feminist practice. In a cogent critique of this tendency in feminist research, Rachelle Saltzman demonstrates how women who use sexist-male jokes within their own gender group see this activity as an expropriation for use rather than an acceptance of a belittled female identity, in 'Folklore, feminism and the folk: whose lore is it?', *Journal of American Folklore*, 1987, no. 100, pp. 548–567.

9 Quotation from a letter written to Beatrice's second husband, Frank Hanson, 6 August, 1944.

28 Evidence, empathy and ethics

Lessons from oral histories of the Klan

Kathleen Blee

Kathleen Blee is Professor of Sociology at the University of Pittsburgh. Reprinted with permission from the *Journal of American History*, 1993, vol. 80, no. 2, pp. 596–606.

Many contemporary oral histories are rooted in principles of progressive and feminist politics, particularly in a respect for the truth of each informant's life experiences and a quest to preserve the memory of ordinary people's lives. Feminist scholars have been in the forefront of efforts to elaborate these ideals as methodological principles, seeking ways to dissolve the traditional distinction between historian-as-authority and informant-as-subject and to create what the sociologist Judith Stacey calls 'an egalitarian research process characterized by authenticity, reciprocity, and intersubjectivity between the researcher and her "subjects"'.[1]

Such oral history practices have been designed primarily to study and record the lives of 'people who, historically speaking, would otherwise remain inarticulate'.[2] From this tradition of history from the bottom up has come a rich and sensitive body of interviews with union organizers, feminist activists, civil rights workers, and others whose experience progressive and feminist scholars share and whose life stories and world views they often find laudable.

Historians have paid less attention to the life stories of ordinary people whose political agendas they find unsavory, dangerous, or deliberately deceptive.[3] Oral history is a particularly valuable source of rectifying this scholarly lacuna since right-wing, reactionary, and racial hate groups tend to be secretive and highly transient, limiting the availability and usefulness of traditional documentary sources. But there are few guidelines for using oral history to study the non-elite Right. Traditionally, oral historians have emphasized caution, distance, and objectivity in interviews with members of elites and egalitarianism, reciprocity, and authenticity in interviews with people outside elites. However, this epistemological dichotomy reflects implicit romantic assumptions about the subjects of history from the bottom up – assumptions that are difficult to defend when studying ordinary people who are active in the politics of intolerance, bigotry, or hatred.

The use of oral history to study the far Right also raises more general issues of historical interpretation. The ability of oral history to provide new and accurate insights into the lives and understandings of ordinary people in the past depends on a critical approach to oral evidence and to the process of interviewing. Thus, efforts to formulate an approach to oral history that recognizes the range and complexities of narratives garnered from people outside elites and helps us judge these sources critically can assist historians working with other sources and methods.

In the mid-1980s I interviewed former members of the 1920s Ku Klux Klan (KKK) and Women of the Ku Klux Klan in Indiana. These Klan organizations recruited several million men, women, and children across the United States into a political crusade for white, Protestant supremacy. Although the Klan's anti-Semitic, anti-Catholic, and racist politics ultimately had little effect on a national level, the intense concentration of Klan members in some communities and states allowed the Klan to dictate the outcome of elections, the policies of law enforcement, and the nature of community life in these areas. In Indiana, as many as half a million women and men are estimated to have joined the Klan during the 1920s. In parts of southern and central Indiana where the majority of white, native-born Protestants were Klan members, the Klan controlled nearly every local electoral office, police agency, and school board. In these communities, the Klan terrorized African Americans, Catholics, Jews, and immigrants with sporadic incidents of physical violence and with unrelenting intimidation, boycotts, and efforts to terminate from employment, evict from housing, and expel from the community all those it deemed to be an obstacle to an agenda of white Protestant supremacy. In this article, I use interviews with former Klan women and Klansmen from the heavily Klan-dominated communities in Indiana to examine issues of historical interpretation, which I label as evidence, empathy, and ethics.[4]

INTERPRETING EVIDENCE FROM ORAL HISTORIES

Oral history can open new vistas of historical understanding, but it can also mislead and confuse. Accounts by those who have participated in campaigns for racial and religious supremacy, for example, often are laced with deceptive information, disingenuous denials of culpability, and dubious assertions about their political motivation. But with careful scrutiny and critical interpretation, even these interviews can yield surprisingly informative and complex historical information.

One issue that plagues studies of right-wing extremists is the desire of informants to distort their own political pasts. The evidence that such informants present to the oral historian is at once revelatory and unreliable. It is revelatory because, as Paul Thompson recognized, 'what the informant believes is indeed a *fact* (that is, the *fact* that he or she believes it) just as much as what "really happened"'. But it is also unreliable, as Claudia Salazar notes, because 'to debate matters of politics inevitably forces us to look back from the text to the world . . . This move is fundamental if we want to avoid the entrapments of a purely discursivist stance.'[5]

Historical interpretation always requires attention to the partiality, bias, and distortions of any individual's particular historical account when garnering evidence from narratives of direct experience.[6] But reliance upon narrated accounts and memory for historical understanding of right-wing extremists is problematic on another level. In an important discussion of oral history methodology, Alessandro Portelli notes that 'memory is not a passive depository of facts, but an active creation of meanings'. Meanings are created in social and political contexts; memory is not a solitary act.[7] Thus, it is not simply that narratives constructed by former Klan members to explain their role in one of history's most vicious campaigns of intolerance and hatred are biased by their own political agendas and their desire to appear acceptable to an oral historian but also that informants' memories have been shaped by subsequent public censure of this and later Klans.

The former Klan members that I interviewed all related tales of 'clannish' Catholics and Jews, or offensive African Americans, or troublesome immigrants. The tales were recounted as direct experience but were often indistinguishable from the stories manufactured and disseminated by the Klan to justify its crusade for white supremacy. Related in interviews, however, such tales suggest motivations and a self-consciousness about Klan membership that did not exist for most members when they were members. In the Klan's heyday, few members would have felt called upon to put forth reasons – however distorted – for their desire to ensure white Protestant supremacy. In the homogeneous, overwhelmingly white, Protestant, and native-born communities in which the Klan took deepest root, Catholics, African Americans, Jews, and immigrants were simply 'others' – so far removed from the social and political life of white Protestants that rationalizations were unnecessary. The inferiority and ominous character of nonwhites and non-Protestants were simply assumed in the receptive population in which the Klan sought recruits. Only later, with the Klan under attack, did stories meant to exonerate its participants appear.[8]

But if interviews of extremists can elicit such distorted accounts, the recovery of narrated experience also, paradoxically, offers the possibility of constructing more accurate explanations of how and why people become attracted to political movements of hatred and bigotry. Oral histories can tap into the complexity of political experiences and beliefs more directly than can documentary sources. They allow us to scrutinize the accounts of political actors, and to probe those experiences, beliefs, and narratives that do not fit conventional historical interpretations, in addition to revealing 'the tangible "atmosphere" of events'.[9]

The history of histories of the Klan is a case in point. The voluminous historiography of the 1920s Ku Klux Klan has virtually ignored the role of women in this movement. Standard documentary sources, assembled by contemporaries and historians who assumed that women were politically insignificant, focused entirely on the male Klan. By thus overlooking women's actions in the Klan, historical accounts seemed to confirm that

Klan women were minor, incidental players, offering mere window dressing behind which men carried out the real politics of hatred and bigotry.[10]

Oral histories of former Klan women, however, tell us otherwise. Women played a significant role in the second Klan's vicious campaigns of rumor, boycotts, and intimidation of African Americans, Catholics, Jews, and other minorities. Certain stores, according to my informants, were patronized by Klan women because they were 'known to be owned by Ku Klux Klan members'. In contrast, one former Klanswoman recalls, businesses owned by Catholics, Jews, and African Americans 'were hurt terribly because people wouldn't go in there because the Klan would tell you not to'. Informants discussed these boycotts as informal, almost unspoken community norms that governed majority-white, Protestant, and Klan-dominated communities in the 1920s, as did a man who related growing up with just 'an understanding that if you rented your farm, you better not rent it to a Catholic'.[11]

Moreover, oral histories of Klan women reveal that many held complicated attitudes toward gender, race, economics, and nationalism, attitudes that did not fit traditional political categories, such as reactionary or progressive. Ideologies of Klan women in the 1920s were complicated, blending occasional thoughtful, sometimes progressive, views with rigid adherence to dogmas of nationalism, racial hierarchies, or Christian supremacy. Although they slavishly followed the male Klan's politics of white Protestant supremacy, for example, they charted a different political course on issues of gender and women's rights (the rights of white, native-born, and Protestant women, that is).

While the men's Ku Klux Klan promoted traditional views of gender roles, a separate female organization – the Women of the Ku Klux Klan – praised women's rights organizations, the participation of women in the temperance movement, and the extension of the right to vote to women. It promoted the National Woman's Party, supported the Equal Rights Amendment (ERA), which was first introduced in the 1920s, and celebrated women who 'made it' in traditionally male workplaces.[12]

By manipulating the issue of women's rights in this fashion, the women's Klan attempted to link the interests of white, native-born Protestant women to those of the Klan. Its leaders sought to broaden the Klan's appeal to women while obscuring the Klan's agenda of racial and religious hatred. In documentary sources such revealing ambiguities in the ideology of the Klan are erased. It is through oral historical accounts, subject to critical interpretation, that these contradictions can be recovered and explored.

Moreover, the evidence of oral history is embedded not only in narrative accounts but also in the process of interviewing. An informant's mode of presentation can be scrutinized for clues to the meanings that historical actors gave to their experiences when they occurred; this was the case when informants rushed to assure me that the Klan was 'uplifting', 'just a celebration', 'a fantastic thing', a group that 'gave people a feeling they were doing the right thing'. Modes of presentation can be deceptive – oral history approaches can lead unwary scholars to underestimate the devastating effects of far-right and hate-based politics. Claudia Koonz, in her excellent study of women in Nazi Germany, *Mothers in the Fatherland*, for example, argues that in Germany 'history recorded the "bad things"; memory preserved a benign face of fascism'. Indeed, the muting of past atrocities may be endemic to the epistemology of oral history. As Cynthia Hay notes, 'Oral history has often been criticized on the grounds that it is confined to a cosy view of the past . . . [which can] at best obtain banalities about experiences which were anything but banal.[13]

The benign memories of which Koonz warns arose in many of my interviews with female and male members of the 1920s Ku Klux Klan. But unlike Luisa Passerini, who found the pro-Fascist sentiments of Turin workers disguised within 'declarations expressing dissociation or distance from the regime', I found that my Klan informants, unless pressed, felt little need to obscure their political beliefs. Although many informants recounted being involved in economic boycotts and threats against Catholic, Jewish, and African-American families and their property, none expressed any consciousness of having done wrong; few seemed even to appreciate why they might be viewed as intolerant or bigoted. Except when defending against the historical condemnation of subsequent generations, they felt no need to explain *why* they found the Klan appealing. To them, life in the Klan was normal, a given, needing no explanation. The only puzzle was why later generations regarded 'their Klan' so negatively.[14]

Such mundane reactions are not without value. They can reveal, as well as conceal, the force and terror of this Klan. In areas of the United States in the 1920s the Ku Klux Klan so dominated communities in which white Protestants were the majority that Klan life became inseparable from non-Klan life. With the myriad of Klan weddings, baby christenings, teenaged auxiliaries, family picnics, athletic contests, parades, spelling bees, beauty contests, rodeos, and circuses, it is perhaps little wonder that the 1920s Klan is recalled by former members as an ordinary, normal, taken-for-granted part of the life of the white Protestant majority. For members, the Klan defined the fabric of everyday life, at once reinforcing and dictating relations of kinship and friendship and practices of celebration and sorrow. In the minds of its members, the Klan became understood as little more than 'just another club'.[15]

The political culture and activities of the Klan so closely paralleled the daily lives of my informants that they could assert, without irony, that 'everybody was in the Klan' or that 'it was a fun organization . . . like a Halloween parade. You'd mask up, wear sheets and be entertained.' This led also to eerily abstracted and contradictory statements by informants, like a woman who insisted that 'the one Jew in town, he became part of the community. I don't think anybody ever thought about doing anything to him . . . [but] people didn't go to his store'. That a political movement could urge that Americans 'put all the Catholics, Jews and Negroes on a raft in the middle of the ocean and then sink the raft' and be remembered by its adherents as an ordinary, unremarkable social club is staggering. Hannah Arendt's 'banality of evil' is found here – in the millions of people who joined a crusade of violent hatred so easily, so unreflectively. Oral histories are exceptionally sensitive sources for recording the lack of self-consciousness in historical subjects, the sensation of normality and conventionality that fueled the Klan of the 1920s.[16]

But if oral histories can reveal the depth of such unspoken, unacknowledged, everyday hatred and bigotry, such interviews can also be puzzling. Decades after this wave of Klan activity subsided, its former members struggle in interviews to justify their involvement against history's condemnation, to construct – retrospectively and consciously – a narrative of life in the Klan that will exonerate them in the eyes of their children and grandchildren.

Over and over, I heard implausible and internally contradictory stories of forced enlistment into the Klan. One informant initially claimed that he had no idea what brought him into the Klan, that it was just something that happened to everybody. When I later pressed him to describe his activities in the Klan, he changed stories, declaring that he had been helpless in the face of exceptional pressure to join, and that ' there were so many people leaning on me, I had little choice'.[17]

Narratives of self-justification nearly always included claims that the Klan was necessary, that it remedied civil ills, and that it was provoked by its very victims. Gabriele Rosenthal found that Germans who witnessed World War II but did not face persecution constructed stories that asserted they were victims. A similar pattern is evident among former Klan members who declared, for instance, that devastating boycotts organized in Klan-dominated communities were necessitated by the financial power of 'naturally clannish' Catholics and Jews. Or, that 'the colored people were hard to get along with. The white people got along with everybody.' The lack of reflectivity and the stress on self-justification in these interviews are outgrowths both of the acceptability of these white supremacists beliefs in certain populations at a specific time and of a more conscious effort by partisans to deny the consequences of their political efforts. That denial allowed informants to see their role in the Klan as 'great theater' or 'entertaining, more exciting than Chatauqua'.[18]

EMPATHY AND ETHICS

Oral histories of the far Right also raise questions about empathy and ethics. Daphne Patai, a women's studies scholar and oral historian, notes than many feminist scholars have replaced the 'model of a distanced, controlled, and ostensibly neutral interviewer' with that of 'an engaged and sympathetic interaction between two individuals'. Further, feminist principles of oral history can foster a 'fear of forcing or manipulating individuals into discussing topics they did not want to talk about.[19] While such concerns are often overlooked in interviews with elites, where the relationship between interviewer and informant is assumed to be unequal and possibly adversarial, empathy can also be problematic in oral histories of ordinary people. Here again, principles that serve well for studying sympathetic informants can prove immobilizing with members of hate groups. Would it be possible, or even desirable, to create an empathic environment when interviewing Klan members?

Some argue that the researcher should strive for rapport with any informant to maximize the information that can be garnered from the interview, even at the expense of downplaying or forgoing sensitive topics. Based on his experience interviewing Gerald L.K. Smith, for example, Glen Jeansonne cautions that the oral historian 'should not place himself or herself in an adversary relationship unless it is unavoidable' and that 'it is best to leave the subject a graceful exit and not ask tough questions back to back'.[20]

In my interviews with former Klan members, however, I made few efforts to establish such rapport or to shy away from controversial topics. Indeed, I was prepared to hate and fear my informants, to find them repellant and, more important, strange. I expected no rapport, no shared assumptions, no commonality of thought or experience. Moreover, I expected them to be wary of me and reluctant to express their true attitudes. But this was not the case. Instead of participating reluctantly in the interviews, these former Klan members seemed quite at ease. (This openness was due in part to the fact that I found informants through advertisements in local publications and contacts with local historians and civic leaders. As self-identified former Klan members willing to talk with me about their experiences, they are not necessarily representative of all who participated in the 1920s Klan.)

The apparent ease of rapport in these interviews stemmed largely from the informants' own racial stereotypes. These elderly informants found it impossible to imagine that I – a native of Indiana and a white person – would not agree, at least secretly, with their racist and bigoted world views. Even challenging their beliefs had no effect on their willingness to talk. They simply discounted my spoken objections as 'public talk' and carried on the 'private talk' they assumed was universal among whites.[21]

Moreover, even my assumptions about how I would experience the interviews were incorrect. Far from being the stock characters of popular portrayals of Klan members – uniformly reactionary, red-neck, mean, ignorant, operating by an irrational and incomprehensible logic – many of the people I interviewed were interesting, intelligent, and well informed.

Although it might be comforting if we could find no commonality of thought or experience with those who are drawn into far-right politics, my interviews suggest a more complicated and a more disturbing reality. It was fairly ordinary people – people with considered opinions, people who loved their families and could be generous to neighbors and friends – who were the mainstay of the 1920s Klan. Ordinary women and men sustained this deadly outburst against those they saw as different and threatening.

Oral historians are acutely sensitive to the meaning of silences in the narrative and to barriers to communication between us and our informants.[22] Yet, in my interviews with Klan members it was the *lack* of silence and the *ease* of communication that revealed their world views. Such seeming empathy was fraudulent – supported by my informants' inability to understand that racial politics could differ among those who shared a common racial heritage and by my unwillingness to violate the tenuous empathy that propelled the interviews along. Nonetheless, rapport with politically abhorrent informants can be surprisingly, and disturbingly, easy to achieve in oral history interviews.

Closely related to the dilemma of empathy are ethical issues about the knowledge generated in oral histories of those on the far right. Rarely do researchers question the value of historical scholarship. Indeed, historical research, far more than work in the social, natural, or physical sciences, is often viewed as at least harmless, more often liberating. This is particularly true of the social histories and oral histories that seek to empower contemporary groups with authentic accounts of the lives and struggles of their forefathers and foremothers.

Oral historians agree that people try to make sense of events by placing them in narratives, in story lines.[23] Is it not possible that oral histories may help informants construct a narrative that 'makes sense' of the Klan and its actions? After interviewing a female Nazi leader, Koonz reflected:

> I realized that I had come to get information and she intended to give me a sanitized version of Nazism that would normalize the Hitler state in the minds of contemporaries. She saw the chance to share her views with an American as a way of taking her message to not only a younger generation, but a new audience.[24]

Feminist scholars insist that a researcher cannot be content merely to record another's life story for scholarly publication but must 'return the research' to the subject as a means of empowering the informant and his or her community and thereby leveling the inherent inequality between researcher and subject.[25] But is this ethical principle, too, based on romantic assumptions about the consequences of fortifying the political agendas of ordinary people? Does this principle serve any purpose in an oral history of the Klan?

For this issue, there is no easy solution. It seems obvious that a researcher should not actively *seek* to empower the Klan.[26] But perhaps the nature of oral history research – here eliciting and conducting interviews with former Klan members – itself empowers informants, by suggesting to them, and to their political descendants, the importance of the Klan in American history. An oral historian of civil rights activists in New Orleans wrote of her informants, 'Their interview narratives became monuments to the personal acts of making history. They defined and understood their personal experience as history itself.' The hazards of similarly empowering a political vision of racial and religious hatred are all too clear.[27]

Moreover, interviews and oral histories should not be used uncritically in the study of contemporary racism and political extremism. Here, the case of David Duke – repackaged former leader of the Ku Klux Klan and the National Association for the Advancement of White People – is instructive. Massive media attention to Duke's electoral efforts in the 1980s and early 1990s in Louisiana netted hundreds of interviews with Duke supporters. Yet, taken together, these interviews were dangerously misleading. Those who consented or who even sought to be interviewed were almost uniformly lower middle-class, poorly educated, and inarticulate.

But the near election of a former Klansman to statewide office was not fueled by these people, nor necessarily by forces of ignorance or economic marginality. The structure of institutionalized racism into which Duke tapped, and even the votes that nearly gave him the keys to Louisiana's gubernatorial mansion, lay deep within educated, middle-class, mainstream white Louisiana. Interviews with those unsavvy or unrestrained enough to utter racists sentiments on camera or before a tape recorder are of limited value – and indeed can create a distorted image of racial hatred – unless they are placed in the context of institutionalized racism.

Similarly, the mainstay of the 1920s Klan was not the pathological individual; rather the Klan effectively tapped a pathological vein of racism, intolerance, and bigotry deep within the white Protestant population. My interviews with former Klan members shed light on how and why ordinary people might become attracted to the politics of racial hatred. However, they do not reveal much about racism itself – how it is generated and how it becomes embedded in the institutions of modern society. An accurate and politically effective understanding of the politics of hatred and right-wing extremism must be developed on two levels – as the racial, class, or national prejudices held by individuals and as the institutionalized practices and structures whereby these attitudes are empowered and reproduced over time.[28] In this effort, oral history accounts, used with caution and attention to their limitations, can play a significant role.

NOTES

1 J. Stacey, 'Can there be a feminist ethnography?', in S. Berger Gluck and D. Patai (eds), *Women's Words: The Feminist Practice of Oral History*, New York, 1991, p. 112.

2 R. Fraser, *Blood of Spain: An Oral History of the Spanish Civil War*, New York, 1979, p. 31.

3 Exceptions to historians' inattention to people whose politics they abhor include interviews with Spanish Falange militants and fascists and with Boston antibusing activists. See S.M. Elwood, 'Not so much a programme, more a way of life: oral history and Spanish fascism', *Oral History*, 1988, vol. 16, no. 2, pp. 57–66; Fraser, *Blood of Spain*; and R.P. Formisano, *Boston against Busing: Race, Class, and Ethnicity in the 1960s and 1970s*, Chapel Hill, 1991. The persistence, even increase, in radical Right and racial hate groups around the world today underscores the need to understand the historical attraction of ordinary people to such politics.

4 K.M. Blee, *Women of the Klan: Racism and Gender in the 1920s*, Berkeley, 1991, pp. 4–7, 145–153.

5 P. Thompson, *The Voice of the Past: Oral History*, New York, 1978, p. 138; C. Salazar, 'A Third World woman's text: between the politics of criticism and cultural politics', in Gluck and Patai, *Women's Words*, p. 102.

6 Some recent feminist scholarship, however, argues that the greatest possibility for distortion lies in privileging interpretation over direct experience, resulting in an explanatory circle in which experience confirms interpretation and interpretation describes experience. See D.E. Smith, *The Conceptual Practices of Power: A Feminist Sociology of Knowledge*, Boston, 1990; and P.H. Collins, *Black Feminist Thought: Knowledge, Consciousness, and the Politics of Empowerment*, Boston, 1990. On the advantages of working to 'listen in a new way', bracketing theories that structure 'what to hear and how to interpret', see K. Anderson and D.C. Jack, 'Learning to listen: interview technique and analysis', in Gluck and Patai, *Women's Words*, p. 18.

7 A. Portelli, *The Death of Luigi Trastulli, and Other Stories: Form and Meaning in Oral History*, Albany, 1991, p. 52; J. Bodnar, 'Power and memory in oral history: workers and managers at Studebaker', *Journal of American History*, 1989, vol. 75, p. 1202. See also J.A. Neuenschwander, 'Remembrance of things past: oral historians and long-term memory', *Oral History Review*, 1978, vol. 6, pp. 45–53.

8 Blee, *Women of the Klan*, pp. 84–91, 154–157, 171–173.

9 Fraser, *Blood of Spain*, p. 1.

10 For treatments that give little notice to women in the Klan, see W.C. Wade, *The Fiery Cross*, New York, 1987; and L.J. Moore, *Citizen Klansmen: The Ku Klux Klan in Indiana, 1921–1928*, Chapel Hill, 1991. For descriptions of some women's Klans, see D.H.Bennett, *The Party of Fear: From Nativist Movements to the New Right in American History*, Chapel Hill, 1981; and D. Chalmers, *Hooded Americanism: The History of the Ku Klux Klan*, Durham, 1987.

11 Blee, *Women of the Klan*, pp. 147–153. Anonymous informants in central Indiana, interviews by Kathleen M. Blee, August 26, 1987, August 25, 1987, audiotapes (in Kathleen M. Blee's possession).

12 On the views of the Women of the Ku Klux Klan toward women's rights, see Blee, *Women of the Klan*, pp. 49–57. Some publications by the women's and men's Klans in which these views are evident are *Fiery Cross*, December 14, 1923, p. 9; ibid., August 15, 1924; *The K.K.K. Katechism: Pertinent Questions, Pointed Answers*, Washington, 1924; and *Imperial Night-Hawk*, September 3, 1924.

13 Anonymous informants in central and southern Indiana, interviews by Blee, August 8, 1987, May 13, 1987, August 26, 1987, audiotapes (in Blee's possession); C. Koonz, *Mothers in the Fatherland: Women, the Family, and Nazi Politics*, New York, 1987, p. xix; G.C. Wright, 'Oral history and the search for the black past in Kentucky', *Oral History Review*, 1982, vol. 10, p. 86; C. Hay, 'The pangs of the past', *Oral History*, 1981, vol. 9, no. 1, p. 41.

14 L. Passerini, *Fascism in Popular Memory: The Cultural Experience of the Turin Working Class* (trans. A. Lumley and J. Bloomfield), New York, 1987, p. 129.

15 Anonymous informant in southern Indiana, interview by Blee, August 21, 1987, audiotape (in Blee's possession); Blee, *Women of the Klan*, pp. 1, 163–171.

16 Blee, *Women of the Klan*, p. 150; E. Willadene, 'Whitley County survives the Ku Klux Klan', *Bulletin of the Whitley County* [Indiana] *Historical Society*, October 1987, pp. 3–17; H. Arendt, *Eichmann in Jerusalem: A Report on the Banality of Evil*, New York, 1963.

17 Anonymous informant in central Indiana, interview by Blee, May 13, 1987, audiotape (in Blee's possession).

18 G. Rosenthal, 'German war memories: narrability and the biographical and social functions of remembering', *Oral History*, 1991, vol. 19, no. 2, pp. 39–40; Blee,

Women of the Klan, pp. 150, 156; anonymous informants in southern Indiana, interviews by Blee, May 24, 1987, August 27, 1987, audiotapes (in Blee's possession).

19 D. Patai, 'U.S. academics and third world women: is ethical research possible?', in Gluck and Patai, *Women's Words*, p. 143; Anderson and Jack, 'Learning to listen', p. 13.

20 G. Jeansonne, 'Oral history, biography, and political demagoguery: The case of Gerald L.K. Smith', *Oral History Review*, 1983, vol. 11, p. 93.

21 Claudia Koonz makes a similar point about her interview with Gertrud Sholtz-Klink, chief of the German Nazi women's bureau: 'I wondered that people would be so open in their defense of the Nazi state.' See Koonz, *Mothers in the Fatherland*, p. xviii.

22 Cf. D. Janiewski, ' "Sisters under their skin?": the effects of race upon the efforts of women tobacco workers to organize in Durham, North Carolina', *Oral History*, 1979, vol. 7, no. 2, p. 31. See also Portelli, *Death of Luigi Trastulli*, p. 53.

23 Portelli, *Death of Luigi Trastulli*, p. 52.

24 Koonz, *Mothers in the Fatherland*, p. xxii.

25 For a cogent discussion and critique of this position, see Patai, 'U.S. academics and third world women', p. 147.

26 Even this principle is not always followed. Glen Jeansonne secured an interview with the famous anti-Semitic demagogue Gerald L.K. Smith in part through correspondence that 'consistently stressed to him the importance of his career'. Jeansonne, 'Oral history, biography, and political demagoguery', p. 92.

27 Cf. Salazar, 'A Third World woman's text', p. 96; K. Lacy Rogers, 'Memory, struggle, and power: on interviewing political activists', *Oral History Review*, Spring 1987, vol. 15, p. 182.

28 See S. Harding, *Whose Science? Whose Knowledge? Thinking from Women's Lives*, Ithaca, 1991, p. 214.

29 Telling tales

Oral history and the construction of pre-Stonewall lesbian history

Elizabeth Lapovsky Kennedy

Elizabeth Lapovsky Kennedy lectures in History and American Studies at the State University of New York, Buffalo. © MARHO: The Radical Historians' Organisation. Extracted with permission from *Radical History Review*, 1995, no. 62, pp. 58–79.

Oral history has been central in creating knowledge about lesbian and gay male life before Stonewall. This is particularly true for working-class lesbians whose oppression as women and as lesbians, combined with race and class oppression, has made it unlikely that they leave many written records. However, even upper-class women, unless they were inclined to the literary world, were not likely to leave documents about their lesbianism.[1] Despite the prominence of oral testimony in lesbian and gay history, there has been surprisingly little discussion of the problems and possibilities of the method. Most theoreticians of oral history have come to see the practice as revealing two different but complementary kinds of 'truth'. First, oral history adds new social facts to the historical record. Second, being based in memory, it explores subjectivity – an individual's interpretation of the past.[2] In my own work I have tried to embrace and pursue both kinds of 'truth'. But I have been hampered by the fact that the tradition of gay and lesbian oral history has thought much more about the former, what I will call for want of a better term the 'empirical', than the latter, and has not fully considered the interconnections between the two.

The 'empirical' concerns of lesbian and gay oral history emerged from the desire to document and legitimize lesbian and gay history at a time when most people thought no such thing existed. The spirit of the early gay and lesbian history projects, such as the Lesbian Herstory Archives in New York City, the Buffalo Women's History Project, and the San Francisco Lesbian and Gay History Project, was to grab a tape recorder and go out and record the memories of our elders before they were lost. The urgency with which lesbians and gays went in search of their history, first in grass roots community projects and later in the academy, to reclaim a history before its bearers died, encouraged a focus on dates, places, names, and events. Furthermore, the fervent desire to legitimize their findings, and therefore gay and lesbian history, encouraged a downplaying of the oral and subjective nature of the life stories that were collected. At that time, 'serious' history emphasized objectivity and viewed first-person narratives with suspicion. But this kind of defensiveness is no longer necessary. Most social historians have transcended the polarization between the reliability of social facts derived from written sources – letters, newspaper accounts, court records – and those from oral sources. They have come to understand that many newspaper accounts are based on interviews and recollections, and that letters and diaries are first-person accounts. Furthermore, postmodern thinking has questioned the objectivity of historical accounts, revealing the partiality of all sources. In fact, today in gay and lesbian studies it is 'empirical' work that is on the defensive.

In the past fifteen years the most forward-looking oral historians have come to understand the subjectivity and orality of their sources as a strength rather than a weakness.[3] They have explored how oral testimony – the actual storytelling – conveys unique information and how the subjective – what the past means to a particular individual – adds new dimensions to history. They have also emphasized the interactive process between the historian and interviewee in constructing the interpretation, and have considered the political uses of their work. These kinds of exploration are very appropriate for gay and lesbian history. Not being born and raised in a public lesbian and gay culture, each gay and lesbian person has to construct his or her own life in oppressive contexts, a process that oral history is uniquely suited to reveal. Furthermore, the celebration of the twenty-fifth anniversary of Stonewall, which occasioned the writing of this article, has accelerated the formation of powerful cultural myths about the place of Stonewall in gay life. Self-consciousness about how research methodologies contribute to this process is very timely.

This article argues that while gay and lesbian historians need to continue the 'empirical' uses of oral history – of adding social facts to the historical record, and of analyzing how social institutions change – we also need to expand our understanding of what can be learned from oral sources. First, I will consider how close examination of storytelling styles can reveal information about cultural and class differences among lesbians. Second, I will explore how we can learn more about the meaning of lesbian identity by embracing the subjective. Third, I will discuss the cultural uses of memory in interpreting the gay and lesbian past. And finally, I will examine the constructed nature of oral histories, focusing in particular on how the myths of Stonewall both expand and limit historical research. Together these considerations add new dimensions to the writing of gay and lesbian history and help to clarify the meaning of Stonewall.

LETTING THE STYLE OF STORYTELLING BE EVIDENCE IN ITS OWN RIGHT

My own experience working with the oral histories for *Boots of Leather, Slippers of Gold* was that black and white working-class lesbians were exquisite storytellers. The life stories we collected for the most part were breathtakingly beautiful documents of survival and resistance in very difficult situations. At first my proletarian bias led me to assume that this was because most of the interviews were with working-class lesbians. As active agents in shaping a public lesbian community and identity, working-class lesbians were conscious about their place in history and therefore highly articulate. But as more and more oral histories of middle- and/or upper-class lesbians have been published, as in *Inventing Ourselves: Lesbian Life Stories* or *Cherry Grove, Fire Island*, I have had to revise this perspective.[4] Despite their commitment to a life of discretion and privacy, many upper-class women also tell compelling stories. It seems that a significant number of lesbians are good storytellers, no matter their class or cultural group.

Audre Lorde's *Zami: A New Spelling of My Name*, which the author describes as a biomythography, provides some clue as to why this should be.[5] Although Lorde is writing about a black working-class experience, her insights seem applicable to many lesbians. Because the majority of lesbians grow up in a heterosexual culture, they have no guidelines and no patterns for creating a homosexual life.[6] They, therefore, are constantly creating their lives, developing a biomythography, so to speak. Lesbians who are completely private are no exceptions; they cannot passively accept the traditional structure of a woman's life; they must create their own guidelines for living, and therefore actively engage the process of storytelling.

Because storytelling plays a prominent role in lesbian life, we can scrutinize the style of lesbian stories for what it tells us about the culture of the narrator. Do styles differ significantly and can they provide a new window into class, racial-ethnic, and regional variations in lesbian oppression and resistance? In *Boots of Leather, Slippers of Gold* we marshal all kinds of evidence to make our points, but we never use this sort of analysis of the structure and style of storytelling. To my knowledge I cannot think of any other lesbian and gay oral historians that do so. It seems an appropriate time to open up this new direction of analysis.

Buffalo working-class lesbians who were 'out' in the 1940s and 1950s tell the story of their finding, building, and enjoying lesbian community with excitement and humor. The structure of their stories conveys their connection to audience and community. For example, Arlette, a black fem, remembers how she was intrigued by mannish-looking women the first time she saw them on the street:

> The first time I saw really gay women, mannish-looking women was here in Buffalo, New York. And I didn't know what they were. I really thought that they were men. . . . The first gay lady I saw here . . . to me she was fascinating. I kept looking at her, and I said, 'That's a good-looking guy, but it's a funny-looking guy. . . .' I couldn't never tell if she was a man or a woman 'cause I never got close enough to her, but there was one strange thing, she would have on lipstick. I said, 'This woman's different.' She's got on men's clothes, her hair was very nice, cut short. She treated a lady

like a gentleman would with a lady out, but I said, 'Is that a man or a woman?' So I made it a point to get close enough to hear her voice, 'cause I knew if I could hear her talking I could tell. Then I found out, this is a woman. And I said, 'Golly, got on men's clothes and everything, what kind of women are these?' Then I started seeing more women here dressed in men's attire. I said, 'Well, golly, these are funny women.' Then they kind of fascinated me. What could they possibly do? Everybody wants to know what can you do. I got curious and I said, 'I'm going to find out.'

This small fragment is like a dance of anticipation and curiosity. It captures many of the significant ingredients of black working-class lesbian life: the drive toward and excitement of finding lesbians, the importance of the appearance of studs for creating lesbian visibility, the daring of fems who sought out studs. Most importantly for this analysis, the storyteller makes herself an active participant in the process of discovery of community, telling us explicitly what she said and thought. It also conveys a connection to a wider audience, 'everybody', and the humor is based on the public's curiosity about lesbians. [. . .]

As we listened to and worked with these oral narratives, we realized that these stories were not told for the first time to us, the oral historians, but that they had been shared before with friends at parties and in bars. Sometimes we inadvertently repeated questions to a narrator after several years had elapsed, and we would hear remarkably similar stories, embellished with similar details. This made sense to us because working-class lesbians spent a lot of time socializing together in explicitly lesbian space. Their lives were defined by finding and supporting other lesbians in a hostile environment and by developing strategies to live with some dignity and pride. What better way to accomplish this than by sharing stories about these successes and defeats. Essentially we were tapping into an oral tradition that supported lesbians, allowing them to survive in a hostile environment, very much like the oral tradition of African Americans in the South or industrial workers in Italy.

The content and style of these stories are radically different from those of middle-class lesbians of an earlier time period, who not only did not announce their lesbianism to the world, but also never talked about being lesbians with each other. They therefore never shared stories about lesbian life and community. This tendency can be seen in the life story of Julia Reinstein, an eighty-eight-year-old woman, who lived as a lesbian from 1928 to 1942 in South Dakota and rural western New York. During this time Julia's status as a successful teacher – not her lesbianism – defined her public identity. Nevertheless, she had an active lesbian sexual life, and once she settled down with a partner, she developed a small intimate circle of lesbian friends. The recurrent refrain throughout her story is 'It just wasn't talked about'. [. . .] The silence about lesbianism didn't diminish Julia's ability to construct an interesting and compelling life story, but her stories lack the dramatic flair characteristic of working-class lesbian stories. They have not been fine-tuned over a lifetime or used to engage an interested audience in the comedy and tragedy of being lesbian. Julia's stories were not told at the time the events took place; they have only come to be told recently as the contemporary lesbian community began to seek out the stories of its elders and also as Julia prepared to tell these stories to her daughter. They were not part of bringing lesbianism into the public world, but rather reflect the crafting of a private world where lesbianism could flourish.

The contrast between Julia's storytelling style and that of Arlette [. . .] illuminates the nature of class relations in pre-Stonewall lesbian communities. It provides yet a different kind of evidence for the argument that working-class lesbians took leadership in developing a public community in ways that middle-class lesbians did not. The humor, agency, and community that are part of the fabric of working-class lesbian stories help to confirm the analysis that working-class lesbians were key in laying the groundwork for the Stonewall rebellion and for the gay liberation movement. Furthermore, by looking at the style of storytelling, the reader comes to see precisely how working-class lesbians took leadership: not merely 'what they did', but how, through the sharing of stories, they created a unique community and culture.[7]

TAKING ADVANTAGE OF FIRST-PERSON NARRATIVES TO GAIN NEW INSIGHTS ABOUT LESBIAN IDENTITY: BEING OUT OR BEING DISCRETE

In her work on Italian fascism, Luisa Passerini argues that oral history adds a critical dimension to the study of fascism.[8] Because of the uniquely subjective nature of life stories, she contends, oral histories provide a way to learn about an individual's struggle with the authority of fascism. What make some individuals conform to the arbitrary power of the state while others resist it? How do individuals construct strategies of resistance? Passerini views these as some of the most important questions in history. Her questions about fascism strike me as parallel to questions in lesbian and gay history about how individuals cope with and resist heterosexism and homophobia. How do individuals decide to construct and express their identities?

In the mythology of gay and lesbian history, before Stonewall gays lived furtive, closeted, miserable lives, while after Stonewall gays could be free and open. Stonewall is quintessentially about being out of the closet, about fighting back, about refusing to be mistreated any more. However, the rich subjectivity expressed in personal narratives of lesbians and gay men expands our understanding of the construction of identity, problematizing the concepts of 'hidden' and 'out' and making the division between them less rigid.

In Buffalo, black and white working-class lesbians during the 1940s and 1950s – and I hesitate to extend this generalization to gay men – took leadership in being out. One of the central tensions in lesbian bar life was between those who were more out, more public, and those who were more discrete.

Being out was expressed through butch-fem roles, or by appearing in public as a butch or as part of a butch-fem couple. In *Boots of Leather, Slippers of Gold* we were able to document that between the 1930s and 1950s working-class butches and fems became bolder, took more risks, and actively developed a sense of community and consciousness of kind. Lesbians of the 1940s gathered together on weekends and built a public social life; rough-and-tough lesbians of the 1950s pushed this assertiveness and openness to the point where they wore their men's clothes as much as possible, went out to socialize every day of the week, and fought back when needed. This visibility, however, was not in and of itself liberating because, in the anti-gay climate of the times, it entailed embracing the terrible stigma of being 'queer' of being a 'dyke'. Before the 1970s, lesbian and gay life was based on an insoluble paradox. For most lesbians and gay men, to be out to the public entailed being engulfed by stigma and, therefore, isolated from sustained and meaningful relationships with other than a small group of similarly stigmatized people.

Life stories of the working-class women who were leaders in creating and defending lesbian community express this contradiction: The freedom that comes from socializing with your own kind and pursuing your romantic attractions is always shaped by the pain of being a complete social outcast. The life story of Sandy, whose leadership was undisputed in the 1950s, is riddled with bitterness as a legacy of her struggle to build a lesbian life. The other side of the fun of being with her lovers and friends [. . .] is a feeling that her life has amounted to nothing because of who she is.

> You know it pisses you off, because like today, everything is so open and accepted and equal. Women, everyone goes to where they wear slacks, and I could just kick myself in the ass, because all the opportunities I had that I had to let go because of my way. That if I was able to dress the way I wanted and everything like that I, Christ, I'd have it made, really. Makes you sick. And you look at the young people today that are gay and they're financially well-off, they got tremendous jobs, something that we couldn't take advantage of, couldn't have it. It leaves you with a lot of bitterness too. I don't go around to the gay bars much any more. It's not jealousy, it's bitterness. And I see these young people, doesn't matter which way they go, whatever the mood suits them, got tremendous jobs, and you just look at them, you know, they're happy kids, no problems. You say 'God damn it, why couldn't I have that?' And you actually get bitter, you don't even want to know them. I don't anyway. 'Cause I don't want to hear about it, don't tell me about your success. Like we were talking about archives, you know where mine is, scratched on a shit-house wall, that's where it is. And all the dives in Buffalo that are still standing with my name. That's all, that's all I got to show.

The oral histories from working-class lesbians who were much more cautious than Sandy in the 1940s and the 1950s – that is, they did not always wear men's clothes and were not always willing to physically fight men who insulted them – convey less self-hate and bitterness. Also, those women whose families accepted their gayness did not seem to have as much self-hate and bitterness. Sandy's parents had been divorced when she was young, and she had no relationship with her father and a very difficult relationship with her step-father. Her relationship with her mother was also tense, with little communication and understanding. In contrast, Marty, who came out explicitly to her parents and involved them in her life, seems to have internalized no stigma about being gay. She was unambivalently ebullient about gay life, despite the fact that she has been the subject of many insults and fights due to her appearance and her work as a bartender in a gay bar. Her lovers and friends regularly came to her parents' house for Sunday dinner, and she discussed aspects of her life with her mother, including her relationships. The only time Marty was concerned about discretion was in relation to her family. She avoided activity that would cause her parents unnecessary trouble with their neighbors or their extended families. This evidence suggests that the connection we, the children of Stonewall, make between happiness, freedom, and being out is much too simplistic. [. . .]

These life stories from lesbians in western New York challenge the simple equations of discretion and secrecy with furtiveness, despair, and self-hate, and of openness with liberation and happiness. They suggest that class relations and social position played a very important role in shaping whether discretion was restricting and painful for lesbians in the mid-twentieth century. At least for some upper-class women, being discrete allowed them to live multifaceted lives as teachers and respected citizens and as lesbians. Their families continued to protect their reputations as upstanding members of the community. The severe restrictions on the behavior of all upper-class women made the requirements of discretion unremarkable. In contrast, once working-class women gave up the protection of a marriage, they had little promise of reward – financial stability or community respect – for accepting the social restrictions of discretion. Coming out gave them the excitement of associating with others of their own kind, the ability to find partners when a relationship broke up, and pride in who they were. But the virulently antigay climate of the 1940s, 1950s and 1960s meant that for many their lives could not be multifaceted, but had to be marked first and foremost by the stigma of being 'queer', 'butch', or 'gay'.

These life stories also suggest that the distinction between open and secret needs to be refined to indicate the context in which it occurred – that is, to clarify to whom one was open or hidden – and to specify relationships between parents and children. Although Julia [Reinstein] defines herself as completely discrete, her parents were, in fact, fully aware of her relationships with women and were part of a system of discretion that protected her. Although Marty sees herself as completely open and proud of her life during the 1950s, even with her parents, she felt compelled to be discrete in aspects of her life that would affect her family. She was careful not to do things that would embarrass them with their neighbors or other members of the extended family. Although Sandy was completely open in her daily life, never backing down from an occasion to defend herself as a lesbian, she never fully shared her lesbianism with her family, who she felt would not accept it. These life stories suggest the chillingly simple proposition that when daughters were accepted by their families, as in the case of Marty and Julia, their lives were whole and productive, no matter whether they were discrete or open. [. . .]

UNDERSTANDING MEMORY AS A CULTURAL PHENOMENON

Recent theorists of oral history analyze memory as a part of culture in ways that might be extremely useful for gay and lesbian historians. For example Alessandro Portelli's analysis of oral histories of workers in Terni, an industrial town in northern Italy, vividly shows that oral histories can contribute much more than new information about dates, places, and events.[9] The workers' stories about the murder of Luigi Trastulli – a twenty-one-year-old steel worker – by police varied as to the date; some dated it in 1949, which in fact is the correct date, while many others dated it 1953, at the same time as a mass strike. This inconsistency could be taken to show the unreliability of oral history and the faultiness of memory. Portelli suggests otherwise. Although the stories in this case do not help in ascertaining dates, which can be obtained from other sources, they do relay information about how workers think about their lives and the value they give to dignity and pride. Portelli argues that many people had moved the date to 1953 because in their minds the mass strikes of that time avenged the death of Trastulli. It was too painful to consider that a fellow worker did not die for a major cause, and that his death had not been revenged. Thus oral histories, if sensitively used, can provide a window into how individuals understand and interpret their lives.

This kind of interpretation is essential for gay and lesbian oral history. In writing *Boots of Leather, Slippers of Gold*, which is based on oral histories with forty-five narrators, we came upon many cases where narrators' memories were internally contradictory or conflicted with one another. An example that was significant for the development of our analysis involved disagreement about the quality of bar life. For some narrators, time in the bar was the best of fun, for some it was depressing, and for others it was both. We came to understand that these contradictory memories conveyed precisely the freedom and joy and the pain and limitation that characterized bar life in the mid-twentieth century.

Lesbian and gay history provides fertile ground for the scrutiny and interpretation of memory. For instance, in his book *Stonewall*, Martin Duberman questions whether a dyke started the Stonewall riots by swinging at the police when they ushered her into the paddy wagon, as reported in the *Village Voice*.[10] Some of Duberman's narrators are sure it was a dyke while others are adamantly sure it was not. An appeal to the validity of the written sources does not have much utility in this case because gays and lesbians know how frequently the press can be wrong. In trying to reconcile these different views, Duberman says, there were many things going on at once, and it was hard to know what actually started things off. In fact, Duberman records a variety of views as to what started the riot.

Another way to use the information of the disputed nature of the Stone-wall story is to consider what this disagreement tells us about the contested relationship between men and women in the gay community. The assignment of agency to women by participants in Stonewall is completely in keeping with women's role in the bar community. Lesbians were always known as 'trouble' and respected as good fighters. In the gay imagination, based on the experience of the 1950s and 1960s, it is highly likely that a woman would start swinging. Yet, at the same time, the denial of women as leaders in fighting back reverberates the dominant view of women in heterosexual society as passive with little skill in fighting. It also encapsulates the male-dominated atmosphere in the Stonewall Inn. Women, when there, were made invisible. One Buffalo lesbian who went sporadically to the Stonewall Inn and was in fact there on the night of the riots, but left to meet a blind date shortly before 11 p.m., remembers always being mistaken for a drag queen.[11] The conflicting memories about how the Stonewall riots started concisely express the ambiguous position of women in gay culture and capture the cultural process of making lesbians and women invisible in history.

Given that social constructionists have analyzed the formation of both gay and lesbian identities, there is surprisingly little research on the relationships of gay men and lesbians at any point in history.[12] What struck Davis and me in our research was how many women insisted that men and women got along perfectly in the past unlike today. As our research proceeded, we gathered evidence that suggested that these statements were ideological. Women and men socialized together on some occasions but not on others, and there was always an underlying tension between the men and women in public life, if not in personal relationships. In *Boots of Leather, Slippers of Gold*, we suggest that the narrators emphasized this harmony to highlight how different the situation was in the past, when there was no ideological commitment to differences between gay men and lesbians as there is today. But as I think more about memory and the constructed nature of lesbian and gay identity, I wonder if the narrators aren't affirming the unity of women and men that they saw as important for survival.

CONSTRUCTING THE INTERVIEW AND INTERPRETATION: THE BIASES OF THE STONEWALL METANARRATIVE

Researching the Stonewall riot, like studying any major historical event, reveals both the possibilities and limitations of oral history. To do so we need oral histories to correct the historical record of life before and at the time of Stonewall; we also need to be fully aware of how the myth of Stonewall, as the central event of twentieth-century gay and lesbian history, constructs the nature of the oral histories we collect and the interpretations we derive from them.

Unquestionably, Stonewall is a key moment for lesbian and gay history. It did transform the lives of many gays and lesbians, and it also became the turning point for the rapid spread of a new kind of gay and lesbian politics and movement. But the history is more complicated than that, and oral history has begun to indicate this. Oral histories show that working-class women, who were rendered invisible by the politics of Stonewall, made an active contribution to developing the sense of solidarity and pride that made Stonewall possible. And although Stonewall is quintessentially about being out, many working-class lesbian and gay men were out before Stonewall.

Such correctives to the historical record are extremely important and are unquestionably the strengths of oral history. But at the same time, oral histories have been shaped by the myths of Stonewall. Many scholars in empirical fields have come to question abstract standards of objectivity and to understand the constructed nature of interviews and their interpretation. The general orientation of contemporary anthropologists, feminists, and oral historians is to encourage reflexivity – that is, the conscious identification of the social position of the interviewer and interviewee – and to recognize that knowledge is the result of a dialogue between the two. In most situations, this involves an awareness of the power differentials, due to class and race privilege associated with most researchers. The implications of such an approach are immense, easily a subject for an entire article or book.[13] Here I will narrow my focus and suggest some of the ways in which the centrality of Stonewall in the iconography of most lesbian and gay researchers shapes or biases oral-history research.

By periodizing twentieth-century lesbian and gay life as pre- and post-Stonewall, we are creating a metanarrative, an overarching story, of lesbian and gay history, where we understand bar communities, resort communities and homophile organizations as laying the groundwork for the development of gay liberation politics. By definition, seeing Stonewall as a major turning point in gay and lesbian life commits researchers to a certain vision of gay and lesbian history, one that makes central the creation of a fixed, monolithic gay and lesbian identity, most often understood as white and male. A pernicious effect of this metanarrative of Stonewall is that it tends to camouflage women's voices and make racial/ethnic groups and cultures invisible.

To do an adequate job in revealing lesbian participation in pre-Stonewall life we need to combine homosexual and women's history.[14] Davis and I attempt this in *Boots of Leather, Slippers of Gold*, and although we were successful in placing lesbians at the center of the study, we were not able to escape telling lesbian history from the perspective of the development of a fixed lesbian identity. Rather we explicitly embraced this bias. We were interested in understanding the ways in which lesbian bar communities were predecessors to gay liberation. This beginning perspective was very useful because it allowed us to reveal the ways in which working-class lesbians built solidarity, developed a consciousness of kind, and expressed pride in being lesbian in the 1940s and 1950s. From this, we were able to argue that bar communities provided a tradition of being public to gay liberation and were also a fertile ground in which gay liberation could grow. For a lesbian to swing at the police, as was possibly done at Stonewall, was a mode of being in the world that Buffalo lesbians had already perfected. As important as this perspective was and is to our work, it also limited the work, skewing it towards the necessity of building a stable lesbian and gay identity. I am not so much concerned that work like ours is partial because all research is; rather I am interested in bringing to the fore the people whom the Stonewall myth excludes. A perfect example of the repercussion of our perspective was our unwillingness at the beginning of the research process to interview women who were no longer living as lesbians. We felt that people had to be gay 'through and through'. As a result we missed interviewing many woman who had been fems in the community of the 1940s and 1950s. Who else did our perspective exclude? *Boots of Leather, Slippers of Gold* is a history of survivors: those who were bold and brazen and could survive the stigma and the ugliness of oppression. Some women were no longer able to tell their stories, having been wasted by alcohol or sickness. Others never felt comfortable in the bar community due to the prominence of roles and/or working-class culture and wanted to forget it. When we located potential narrators and asked them to share their memories of lesbian community during the 1940s and 1950s, several people turned us down, expressing some variation of 'what [lesbian] community?' In their minds, the divisiveness outweighed the solidarity and had not allowed them to thrive.

The writings of lesbians of color in the last fifteen years have made amply clear that lesbians of color do not have one single identity, but rather multiple identities.[15] In the case of the African-American lesbians in Buffalo, they were part of the larger bar community, but they also maintained their own African-American house parties and bars. They cannot be considered, nor did they consider themselves, lesbians first and African-Americans or Native American second, or vice versa. Therefore a metanarrative that focuses on the formation of a unitary lesbian identity and politics might include African-American and Native American women, as *Boots of Leather, Slippers of Gold* did, but by definition communities of color cannot be the central focus. We need therefore to orient the interviews and open our interpretive frameworks to multiple centers of lesbian life and to ask fundamental questions about how these varied points interact rather than assume that they fit together in a linear history of Stonewall.

In arguing, as I have done throughout this article, that there is a tremendous amount to be learned by fully exploring the subjective and oral nature of oral histories, I have also suggested that the 'empirical' and 'subjective' should not be falsely polarized. They are fully complementary to one another. I am convinced that gay and lesbian oral history is at a point where, to grow, it needs to fully embrace the subjective and oral nature of its documents. By doing so its 'empirical' goals are not compromised but expanded.

NOTES

1 [See] E. Newton, *Cherry Grove, Fire Island: Sixty Years in America's First Gay and Lesbian Town*, Boston, Beacon Press, 1993; E. Lapovsky Kennedy and M. Davis, *Boots of Leather, Slippers of Gold: The History of a Lesbian Community*, New York, Routledge, 1993.
2 For an eloquent statement of these two truths, see A. Portelli, 'Introduction', in *The Death of Luigi Trastulli and Other Stories: Form and Meaning in Oral History*, Albany, State University of New York Press, 1991, pp. vii–x.
3 See, for instance, L. Passerini, 'Italian working class culture between the wars', *International Journal of Oral History*, 1980, vol. 1, pp. 4–27; P. Thompson, *The Voice of the Past: Oral History*, Second edition, Oxford, Oxford University Press, 1988; M. Frisch, *A Shared Authority*, Albany, State University of New York Press, 1990; S. Berger Gluck and D. Patai (eds), *Women's Words: The Feminist Practice of Oral History*, New York, Routledge, 1991; and Portelli, *The Death of Luigi Trastulli*.
4 Hall Carpenter Archives, Lesbian Oral History Group, *Inventing Ourselves: Lesbian Life Stories*, New York, Routledge, 1989; Newton, *Cherry Grove, Fire Island*.
5 A. Lorde, *Zami, A New Spelling of My Name*, Trumansburg, N.Y., The Crossing Press, 1982.
6 I am grateful to my colleague, Masani Alexis DeVeaux, for illuminating this point in one of her lectures to my gay and lesbian community seminar.
7 I am grateful to Molly McGarry's reader's report for emphasizing this point, and offering this sentence as a way of highlighting it.
8 Passerini, 'Italian working class culture between the wars'.
9 Portelli, *The Death of Luigi Trastulli*.
10 M. Duberman, *Stonewall*, New York, Penguin Dutton, 1993, pp. 197–198.
11 This information comes from a personal communication with Madeline Davis who has spoken directly with the lesbian who frequented the Stonewall Inn.
12 To my knowledge Marc Stein is the only person who has written on this topic. M. Stein, 'Sex politics in the city of sisterly and brotherly love', *Radical History Review*, Spring 1994, vol. 59, pp. 60–93. Esther Newton is also addressing this issue in her most recent work, as evidenced by her paper, 'Baking ziti at the coronation: homophobia, sexism and the subordinate status of lesbians in Cherry Grove', given at the 93rd Annual Meeting of the American Anthropological Association, 2 December 1994, Atlanta, Georgia.
13 And in fact there will be a new book on the subject. E. Lewin and W. Leap (eds), *Doing Lesbian and Gay Field Work, Writing Lesbian and Gay Ethnography*, Champaign/Urbana, University of Illinois Press, forthcoming, in which I have a paper.
14 [See] M. Cruickshank, *The Gay and Lesbian Liberation Movement*, New York, Routledge, Chapman and Hall, 1992; Newton, *Cherry Grove, Fire Island*.
15 See, for instance, C. Moraga and G. Anzaldua (eds), *This Bridge Called My Back: Writings by Radical Women of Color*, Watertown, Mass., Persephone Press, 1981; B. Smith (ed.), *Home Girls: A Black Feminist Anthology*, New York, Kitchen Table: Women of Color Press, 1983; A. Lorde, *Sister, Outsider: Essays and Speeches*, Trumansberg, N.Y., Crossing Press, 1984; and G. Anzaldua, *Borderlands, La Frontera: The New Mestiza*, San Francisco, Spinster's/Aunt Lute, 1987.

Part V

Making histories: introduction

Our final section examines how oral testimony might be preserved and presented to a wider audience: the decisions involved, and what impact this selection and editing process has on the evidence itself. The current vibrancy of the international oral history movement is derived at least in part from the application of personal testimony in a wide variety of 'public' settings: from archives and libraries to books and local history reminiscence groups, from theatres and schools to radio and television, from museums and galleries to the new multimedia. Beyond academia the phrase 'oral history' has become a familiar strap-line on popular history publications and people's history television programmes, denoting accessibility and intimacy. With a methodology rooted in orality, often committed to popular involvement and empowerment, oral history is uniquely placed to take advantage of developments in information technology.

From Canada, Jean-Pierre Wallot and Normand Fortier begin with an overview of the troubled relationship between archivists and oral history. Steeped in documentary sources, traditional archivists (unlike librarians) have been slow to recognize the potential that oral history has for what Jim Fogerty has referred to as 'filling the gaps' in archival collections.[1] Not so in the developing countries of the South, where archivists have readily embraced oral testimony as a substitute for the lack of written archives.[2] Equally importantly, in the former Soviet bloc oral history has emerged as a corrective to state-manipulated archives, taking a key public role (as Sherbakova illustrates in Chapter 20) in rescuing and preserving memories of famine and repression which would otherwise be lost. Whilst few archivists, even in the North, continue to argue that archiving is an essentially passive activity, many more bemoan the lack of resources required to initiate interviewing projects or make recordings publicly available. Resourcing issues are, of course, even more acute in developing countries, where even basic shelving and environmental controls are sometimes lacking.[3] Apart from those rare audio-visual archives that actively collect oral and video history, few mainstream archives view oral sources as a priority and until recently there has been scant attention devoted to cataloguing standards for oral history material.[4] For many archivists and librarians the burning issue has been one of access: of finding the means to make audiotapes and transcripts searchable by users. Although the situation is improving, oral history practitioners have unfortunately been rather cavalier about the technical quality of their recordings. Some have been even worse at documenting their recordings or obtaining legal consent before depositing tapes in public archives and libraries, and this has hampered progress significantly.[5]

Even fewer oral historians have moved into video interviewing, as demonstrated by the remarkable paucity of writings on the subject, particularly outside the United States. In part this relative silence is because videographers and broadcast programme-makers seem notoriously reluctant to expose their methodology to public gaze and debate, whilst the pressures of the television industry provide few opportunities to be reflective and self-critical in print.[6] In Chapter 31 Dan Sipe surveys the field of film and video, stressing the extra layers of historical meaning that can emerge from the visual, and arguing that historians are in danger of relinquishing their role in shaping public history to television producers and film-makers.

It would be misleading to claim that oral historians have never been aware of their archival role. Raphael Samuel's piece (Chapter 32), reprinted here and originally published in 1971, argues that the role of the 'collector of the spoken word . . . is that of archivist, as well as historian, retrieving and storing priceless information which would otherwise be lost . . . his greatest contribution may well be in the collecting and safe preservation of his material rather than in the use he can immediately find for it'. This begs the question: what archival form should this oral record take? For years many oral historians have tended to view a transcript as the equivalent of the original source, and have even been known to destroy the tape once a typescript had been prepared.[7] Fortunately such heinous acts seem to have been banished by the availability of cheaper tape, and by the growing interest in orality and in discourse analysis which requires the tape to be retained. None the less most archivists, librarians and their users find that transcripts speed access, particularly if they are word-processed or, increasingly, if they are linked via hypertext applications to sound and images. Samuel explores the time-consuming and exacting process that is at work in rendering speech into grammatical text: the 'artistry' involved in balancing accuracy against readability.[8]

Moving from the oral to the 'written' raises additional challenges when the editing involves a group or is part of a creative process where the aim is to produce a publication of some kind. Jane Mace has been running community reminiscence and adult literacy and writing groups in London for twenty years, working at the cusp of 'talking and writing'. Here, she details the process of collaborative negotiation that leads to publication, believing ultimately that the final product 'should be one that satisfies the authors, whether I have regrets about some of their choices or not'.[9] This contrasts with Marjorie Shostak's retrospective piece about her pioneering book *Nisa – The Life and Words of a !Kung Woman*, in which the conversion of the oral to the written was, perhaps more typically, firmly in the hands of the researcher. Nisa liked the idea of her words being made permanent (those that 'the wind won't take away') but had little input in the editing of the final book. One reason for this more unequal relationship was the lengthy translation and editing process, marked by the challenge of representing the constant repetition typical of Nisa's form of expression.[10] In the end Nisa gained some cows, Shostak a career.

Both Mace and Shostak raise the issue of the wider 'audience'. Who do the interviewees think they are talking to and who do they think will be reading their story? Apart from the interviewer, are they addressing family members, peer group or posterity? Is the audience they have in mind the same one as the interviewer/writer has in mind? Don Ritchie has pointed out that the authors of some of the best-known 'oral history' books have handled oral evidence 'rather loosely'. Tapes are absent or bear little resemblance to the published text. One of Studs Terkel's interviewees is quoted as claiming that his words had been rearranged 'in such a way that I can't make sense of them'.[11] Does this comment make us read Terkel's books with a new eye, and are we content for him as editor/writer to have licence to interpret and rearrange as he sees fit? As readers we cannot readily compare the written text with the original interview, and in the case of British writer and oral historian Tony Parker, such comparison is impossible because he destroyed his interview tapes.[12]

Maintaining the full meaning and orality of the voice is Peter Read's concern in Chapter 35, which compares transcription, the edited book and the radio broadcast. Although he extols the suitability of radio for oral history,[13] he claims that each form has its limitations in encapsulating the 'total meaning' of an interview. None can convey both memories of time and place, and intimate and emotional moments. By contrast, Read argues, multimedia CD-ROM applications can present every aspect of an interview all at once. Simultaneously a user can listen to the audio or watch a video clip, read a transcript, study a facsimile document or check a map: it is 'more personally-involving'.[14]

Karen Flick and Heather Goodall, through their work with Aboriginal community histories in Australia, develop these ideas further. They explain what led them to interactive multimedia and argue that 'making history' in this way forces historians to 'reflect on and anticipate our audiences' desires, intentions and questions, as well as to consider the context in which the people we have interviewed and recorded were themselves responding to their real or intended audience'. Interactive multimedia history is public history at the cutting edge of popular culture and scholarly enquiry. Access is not necessarily dependent on literacy. People may become involved in a way they never could in the creation and use of a book. Not only can conflicting oral accounts be directly compared but hypermedia applications also allow different meanings to emerge through sound. The problem comes in not allowing the technology to predominate. The metaphor of 'place' which is an obvious starting point for many interactive computer programs (*Windows 95*'s '*Where* do you want to go today?') threatens to swamp the stories about those places. Flick and Goodall outline how they reconceived their multimedia programme as a web of stories: life stories, theme stories, and place stories.[15]

The process of 'making histories' (which Sipe, Mace, and Flick and Goodall describe) is the focus of Alistair Ross's piece, which shows how oral history can encourage children to acquire new skills and 'become historians'.[16] Through a project about a school's wholesale evacuation from London to the Wiltshire countryside in 1939, Ross found that quite young children were able to sift what they heard, compare it with documentary sources and select evidence for a piece of writing. Projects such as this represent a growing worldwide trend in the teaching of history in schools which emphasizes a multi-disciplinary and eclectic approach embracing oral history, both as source material and project work.[17] Students are encouraged to learn by doing. They are being expected not only to consult archives and museums but also to assess them as repositories of public history which have their own histories, and which are themselves shaped by opinions and beliefs. Museums, like archives, are no longer impartial and passive recipients of artefacts, but are now dynamic participants in creating and presenting public histories.

Perhaps as a result of this, museums throughout the world have been particularly active in collecting oral testimony in recent years. For some, oral history has been merely a means of gathering information about material culture, for others it has underpinned community 'outreach' work in which the museum ventures outside its hallowed building.[18] For a few major museums oral history has been central to exhibition design: for example at the People's Story in Edinburgh, Ellis Island Museum in New York, the Holocaust Memorial Museum in Washington, and Hobson Wharf in Auckland.[19] In each case oral history has been used not merely as text but also as sound, explicitly seeking an empathetic response from visitors and encouraging interactivity between objects and experiences. The People's Story was largely created by local people: they decided what they wanted to see in their museum and set about collecting objects and setting up reminiscence groups to achieve it. Recently the voices of tradition in the museum world have been arguing that the function of museums is to preserve and interpret artefacts, that oral history is technically difficult to include in a gallery space, and that it is an expensive luxury that simply cannot be afforded in a climate of public expenditure cuts. But as Anna Green's piece here shows, from the experience of constructing an oral history exhibition in New Zealand, technical problems can be overcome and oral history displays can greatly increase attendance and popular involvement in museums.

At its best oral history can take a major role in both telling us more about our past and in democratizing the study of history. As a process of co-construction it is self-evaluative: conflicts of perception and evidence can be explored as an interview proceeds. Furthermore oral history encourages historians to consider their own motives and the way their presence can shape the evidence as it is generated and interpreted. When oral history is community-based it can be a liberating and participatory force, encouraging a reassessment of long-held beliefs, or fostering new skills, or breaking down racial and ageist stereotypes. As Michael Frisch has remarked, it involves us all 'in exploring what it means to remember, and what to do with memories to make them active and alive, as opposed to mere objects of collection'.[20] In this spirit we close the *Reader* with an inspiring piece by Shaun Nethercott and Neil Leighton about a community oral history play commemorating a strike by carworkers in 1937 in Flint in the United States. Reminiscence theatre has been taken up with vigour in many countries, combining a range of collecting, interpreting, transcribing, writing and performance skills.[21] The Flint play had its genesis as a labour history project, 'recapturing the history of working people, of those left out of the history books'. Interviewing brought generations together to re-create family and community histories; shaping the play through improvization brought the strikers and actors together. What emerged was quintessential oral history: a synthesis of performance, memory and comment.

NOTES

1　J.E. Fogerty, 'Filling the gap: the role of the archivist', *American Archivist*, 1983, vol. 46, no. 2, pp. 148–157. The *Journal of the Society of Archivists* in Britain has almost totally ignored oral history. Elsewhere see D. Ritchie, 'Preserving oral history in archives and libraries' in his excellent book *Doing Oral History*, New York, Twayne, 1995, pp. 131–158; C.T. Morrissey, 'Public historians and oral history: problems of concept and methods', *The Public Historian*, 1980, no. 2; W. MacDonald, 'Origins: oral history programmes in Canada, Britain and the United States', *Canadian Oral History Association Journal*, 1991, vol. 10, pp. 12–24; R. Lochead, 'Oral history: the role of the archivist', *Phonographic Bulletin*, 1983, no. 37, pp. 3–7; D. Lance, *An Archive Approach to Oral History*, London, Imperial War Museum/IASA, 1978; F.J. Stielow, *The Management of Oral History Sound Archives*, New York, Greenwood, 1986; D. Treleven, 'Oral history and the archival community: common concerns about documenting twentieth-century life', *International Journal of Oral History*, 1989, vol. 10, no. 1; A. Ward, *Manual of Sound Archive Administration*, London, Gower, 1990. Oral history in libraries has been discussed elsewhere, but for the British context see C. Cochrane, 'Public libraries and the changing nature of oral history', *Audiovisual Librarian*, 1985, vol. 11, no. 4, pp. 201–207. For the US context see Willa Baum's writings, especially 'The expanding role of the librarian in oral history', in D.K. Dunaway and W.K. Baum (eds), *Oral History: An Interdisciplinary Anthology*, London, Altamira Press, second edition, 1996. For Australasia see M.P. Chou, 'Small windows on the Pacific: oral history and libraries in Australia, New Zealand and Papua New Guinea', *International Journal of Oral History*, 1985, vol. 6, no. 3, pp. 163–178.
2　W.W. Moss and P.C. Mazikana, *Archives, Oral History and Oral Tradition: A RAMP Study*, Paris, UNESCO, 1986, provides a good overview. See also S. Peet and K. Manungo, ' "We have a tradition of story-telling": oral history in Zimbabwe', *Oral History*, 1988, vol. 16, no. 2, pp. 67–72.
3　C.A. Paton, 'Whispers in the stacks: the problem of sound recordings in archives', *The American Archivist*, 1990, vol. 53, pp. 274–280; Moss and Mazikana, *Archives*, pp. 43–45.

4 A major step forward is M. Matters (comp.), *Oral History Cataloguing Manual*, Chicago, The Society of American Archivists, 1995. See also C. Clark, 'The National Sound Archive IT Project: documentation of sound recordings using the Unicorn collections management system', *IASA Journal*, 1995, no. 5, pp. 7–25; and B.H. Bruemmer, 'Access to oral history: a national agenda', *American Archivist*, 1991, vol. 54, no. 4, pp. 494–501.

5 B. Robertson, 'Keeping the faith: a discussion of the practical and ethical issues involved in donated oral history collections', *Oral History Association of Australia Journal*, 1989, vol. 11, pp. 18–29. For discussion of oral history, copyright, ethics and legal consent see the excellent chapter on 'Legalities and ethics' in V.R. Yow, *Recording Oral History*, London, Sage, 1995; also J. Neuenschwander, *Oral History and the Law*, Los Angeles, Oral History Association, 1993; A. Ward, *Oral History, Copyright and Ethics*, Colchester, Oral History Society, 1995.

6 J. Blatti, 'Public history and oral history', *The Journal of American History*, 1990, pp. 615–625; P.M. Henson and T.A. Shorzman, 'Videohistory: focusing on the American past', *The Journal of American History*, 1991, vol. 78, pp. 618–627; P. Thompson and J. Bornat, 'Interview with Stephen Peet', *Oral History*, 1982, vol. 10, no. 1, pp. 47–55; G. Lanning, 'Television History Workshop Project No 1: The Brixton Tapes', *History Workshop*, 1981, no. 12, pp. 183–188.

7 This was a policy, now abandoned, pursued by the Oral History Office at Columbia University. At Essex University in Britain, a survey of academics in 1994 by the Economic and Social Research Council's Qualidata found that 'at least 80% of qualitative datasets . . . were either already lost or at risk, and even of those archived, half had gone to totally unsuitable archives, some without cataloguing or public access . . . material lost or at risk would, at present costs, have taken £20 million to create' (internal report, 1997).

8 Amongst the huge literature about transcription see M. Frisch, 'Preparing interview transcripts for documentary publication', in his *Shared Authority: Essays on the Craft and Meaning of Oral and Public History*, Albany, SUNY Press, 1990, pp. 81–146; S.A. Allen, 'Resisting the editorial ego: editing oral history', *Oral History Review*, 1982, vol. 10, pp. 33–45; Ritchie, *Doing Oral History*, pp. 41–50; Yow, *Recording Oral History*, pp. 227–236; D.K. Dunaway, 'Transcription: shadow of reality', *Oral History Review*, 1984, vol. 12, pp. 113–117; W.K. Baum, *Transcribing and Editing Oral History*, Nashville, American Association for State and Local History, 1977.

9 See also P. Duffin, 'Turning talking into writing', in J. Bornat (ed.), *Reminiscence Reviewed*, Buckingham, Open University Press, 1994, pp. 116–125; J. Bornat, 'The communities of community publishing', *Oral History*, 1992, vol. 20, no. 2, pp. 23–31; A. Progler, 'Choices in editing oral history: the distillation of Dr Hiller', *Oral History Review*, 1991, vol. 19, pp. 1–16.

10 On the problems of translation see M. Andrews, 'A monoglot abroad: working through problems of translation', *Oral History*, 1995, vol. 23, no. 2, pp. 47–50.

11 Ritchie, *Doing Oral History*, p. 102.

12 Tony Parker discusses his approach to editing and writing with Paul Thompson, 'Tony Parker: writer and oral historian', *Oral History*, 1994, vol. 22, no. 2, pp. 64–73.

13 Again, little has been written about oral history and radio, but see D.K. Dunaway, 'Radio and the public use of oral history', in Dunaway and Baum, *Oral History*, pp. 306–320; C. Fox, 'Oral history on public radio: "a match made in heaven"', *Oral History Association of Australia Journal*, 1990, vol. 12, pp. 38–46; H. Molnar, 'Women's oral history on radio: a creative way to recover our past', *Oral History Association of Australia Journal*, 1990, vol. 12, pp. 47–56.

14 W. Schneider and D. Grahek, *Project Jukebox: Where Oral History and Technology Come Together*, Anchorage, Centre for Information Technology,

University of Alaska at Anchorage, 1992; R. Rosenzweig, '"So, what's next for Clio?" CD-ROM and historians', *The Journal of American History*, 1995, vol. 81, no. 4, pp. 1621–1640.

15 On visualizing oral testimony see Joshua Brown's review of *Maus: A Survivor's Tale*, New York, 1986: 'Of mice and memory', *Oral History Review*, 1988, vol. 16, pp. 91–109.

16 See also Chapter 17 in Part III by Eliot Wigginton.

17 A. Redfern, *Talking in Class: Oral History and the National Curriculum*, Colchester, Oral History Society, 1996; also *Oral History*, 1992, vol. 20, no. 1: special issue on oral history in schools. Also B. Lanman and G. Mahaffy, *Oral History in the Secondary School*, Los Angeles, Oral History Association, 1988; and *Oral History Association of Australia Journal*, 1986, vol. 8: special issue 'Oral history, children and schools'. These ideas are also being explored in schools in Eastern Europe – for example see R. Perks, 'National Curriculum', *The Guardian*, 10 December 1991.

18 S. Davies, 'Falling on deaf ears? Oral history and strategy in museums', *Oral History*, 1994, vol. 22, no. 2, pp. 74–84; S. Jones and C. Major, 'Reaching the public: oral history as a survival strategy for museums', *Oral History*, 1986, vol. 14, no. 2, pp. 31–38; D. Hyslop, 'From oral historians to community historians: some ways forward for the use and development of oral testimony in public institutions', *Oral History Association of Australia Journal*, 1995, vol. 17, pp. 1–8; J.K.W. Tchen, 'Creating a dialogic museum: the Chinatown History Museum experiment', in I. Karp, C.M. Kreamer and S.D. Lavine (eds), *Museums and Communities: The Politics of Public Culture*, Washington, Smithsonian Institution Press, 1992, pp. 285–326; B. Factor, 'Making an exhibition of yourself: museums and oral history', *Oral History Association of Australia Journal*, 1991, vol. 13, pp. 44–48.

19 H. Clark and S. Marwick, 'The People's Story – moving on', *Social History in Museums*, 1992, vol. 19, pp. 54–65; R. Perks, 'Ellis Island Immigration Museum, New York', *Oral History*, 1991, vol. 19, no. 1, pp. 79–80.

20 Frisch, *Shared Authority*, p. 27.

21 In Britain: G. Langley and B. Kershaw, 'Reminiscence theatre', *Theatre Papers*, 1981–2, no. 6; E. Dodgson, 'From oral history to drama', *Oral History* 1984, vol. 12, no. 2, pp. 47–53; P. Schweitzer, 'Dramatizing reminiscences', in J. Bornat (ed.), *Reminiscence Reviewed*, pp. 105–115. In New Zealand: M. Harcourt, 'A walk in someone else's shoes', *Oral History in New Zealand*, 1994, no. 6, pp. 14–20. *Oral History Review*, 1990, vol. 18, no. 2, was a special issue devoted to theatre and performance in the US.

30 Archival science and oral sources

Jean-Pierre Wallot and Normand Fortier

Jean-Pierre Wallot has been the National Archivist of Canada since 1985, and served as President of the International Council of Archives between 1992 and 1996. Normand Fortier has been an archivist with the National Archives of Canada since 1992 and edited the *Guide to Oral History Collections in Canada* (1993). Extracted with permission from *Janus*, 1996, no. 2, pp. 7–22.

[. . .] In archival science, the principal debates have borne on the issue of the very inclusion of oral history recordings in archives, and therefore on acquisition of these records, and, more recently, on their creation by archival institutions. In pith and substance, they have paralleled the debates among the more traditional historians, the links between the two professions being so close that they have followed similar paths in this regard.

Archivists' resistance and mistrust is sometimes attributed to the nature of the medium (sound recordings and, now, video recordings), which is so different from paper. These professionals are said to have reacted in the same way that some now are reacting to machine readable archives. On a deeper level, some of the reluctance that archivists have felt with respect to oral sources is tied to the clash between the definition of traditional archival science, which still underlies their practices, despite some exceptions,[1] and the characteristics of oral testimony. In effect, the basic principles of traditional archival science were articulated in the nineteenth century in tandem with the growth of a 'positivist', 'empirical' historiography that pretended to be more exacting, that was concerned with political, diplomatic and military issues. The method on which the system is founded is based on textual criticism applied in particular to official documents and inspired by methods previously developed in diplomatics.[2] Research, it is held, must be based on reliable documents that are subjected to exacting criticism. In this way, it can reveal 'facts' to which one can assign, if not certainty, at least a high probability of truth.

Archival science is based entirely on the concept of records – that is, traces that are generally in written form (but that may also be in iconographic form or in the form of maps, plans and so on) created and accumulated by individuals or institutions in the normal course of their activities. The documents bear witness to actions and transactions between the parties involved, whence their evidential value. They are produced spontaneously to serve purposes proper to their creator(s), to guarantee rights and record decisions, not with a view to informing posterity. Owing to the 'organic' or 'natural' nature of their creation, they acquire qualities of impartiality and authenticity that make them reliable evidence with respect to the action and transactions with which they are connected and that gave rise to them. Under these conditions, archivists play a passive role, except with respect to protecting the integrity of the document; their role consists in preserving the documentary heritage as it was constituted, respecting at once the provenance of documents and the context in which they were created (the link between the documents and their creation, accumulation and use during their active life) and the order they were originally placed in.

In the context of the concepts flowing from traditional archival science and the positivist historiography of the nineteenth century, oral documents appear suspect.[3] An oral document is considered a piece of testimony – that is, an opinion – whose link with the facts seems much less sure than in the case of official documents. The uncertainty connected with the opinion is made worse by its oral nature, in contrast with a written document, which, even when it is originally based on oral testimony, fixes the form and content on a particular date. In addition, in the context of an interview, testimony is solicited from the outside and is constructed explicitly to inform a third party or posterity, so there is deviation from the automatic, impartial reflection of an act. Finally, in most oral history sound recordings, the testimony is not contemporary with the events related, and its recording is sometimes done long after the events: its reliability is at the mercy of memory.

The appearance and then growth of oral testimony and its use bring out the limits of the documentary universe traditionally defined by archival science and history. Even in countries with a written tradition, audio-visual documents, such as videotapes, are sometimes the only 'document', the only evidence regarding facts that are, nonetheless, significant or even spectacular (acts of war, disasters and so on). In addition, some groups, communities, peoples and entire societies have produced and still are producing only very fragmentary written traces. For example, African societies south of the Sahara did not use written documents. Moreover, a majority of the population would not have been able to read them. The main written sources for the study of these countries are connected with colonial powers and the local administrations they established, as well as with explorers, missionaries, traders and travellers from the home country of other nations. These are writings, but they make up a documentary heritage that is highly incomplete, strongly biased by the interests of the colonizing power, difficult to access and based partly on oral sources. The same is true of relations between Whites and Amerindians in America and the Aboriginals in Australia and New Zealand. However, even for the countries of the 'North', is it not ironic that the thoughts of Socrates or in the New Testament, the well-spring of Christianity, have come to us only via oral testimony transcribed later? [. . .]

Even in societies in which the written word occupies a dominant place, documents tell us little about the groups further removed from power, or do so from a very biased point of view (for example, Aboriginal peoples, ethnocultural minorities, women, children, disadvantaged classes, people on the margins of society), about whole layers of social life (for example, domestic life, emotional life, family, illegal activities such as prostitution, smuggling, and clandestine political activities), and even individuals. Generally speaking, oral accounts provide a wider window on day-to-day life and can therefore call into question or enrich institutional history (that of a union, government department or company, for example).[4] Their content, which may relate at times to personal experience, at times to popular tradition, may adjoin myth, recognized now as 'a component much more than the enemy' of history, to use the words of F. Bédarida.[5] Finally, interviews allow for exploration of less-known periods or aspects of the lives of influential persons.[6] They throw light on the informal networks and real decision-making processes (for example, the dealings – without written trace – between the leaders of the various political parties in Parliament), and people's motivations, matters which are just as essential as the results, and can even sound out the 'facts' from a contemporary, and then retrospective point of view.[7]

Sound recordings and, to an even greater extent, video recordings go beyond mere language to bring out personality traits and nuances of meaning, tone and emotion that are lost in writing. They provide access to meanings, to facets of communication that are otherwise inaccessible.[8]

Historians and archivists have discovered – or rediscovered – these fields of study and the contribution of oral sources much later than practitioners in other disciplines. The documentation favoured by traditional archival science yields an incomplete image of the institutions and actors in society and their interactions, emphasizing official instruments, to the detriment of informal processes. Archival science theorists have postulated that the spontaneous creation of documents adequately reflected their creators' activities, without always looking at the process of creation of the documents itself. This approach posed a problem in the early part of this century, and poses even more of a problem today. The technical and economic transformations of the twentieth century, which have led to a veritable documentary explosion, have also led to a qualitative impoverishment of the paper-based documentary heritage. An increasingly large share of communications is done orally, either on the telephone or in person, thanks to improvements in telecommunications and transportation. Individuals – even people of letters – only rarely keep diaries, which, moreover, as with correspondence, do not always reveal the real intentions, motivations and sentiments of their authors.[9] In addition, the increase in the number of new electronic media points to a decline in the stability of the document, which has often become 'virtual',[10] and in the fixedness of the link between document and act (not counting the fact that this technology promotes greater brevity). The growing requirement for democracy and transparency in the political process, and the risk of legal proceedings, can lead those at the top to 'edit' the documents they leave behind.[11] In short, more and more important transactions are done without adequate traces being left behind on paper or, in many cases, in any other medium. [. . .]

Archival science has developed its own concepts in close relation with history, since historians originally were, to some extent, its favoured clientele. The opening up of archival science to new types of documents reflects as much the *evolution* of the disciplines it serves as the *changes that have occurred in the production and accumulation of documents.*

A companion *discipline* of archival science since the nineteenth century, history in the twentieth century has considerably expanded its scope of study, methods and sources. To political, diplomatic and military aspects have been added the economy, social groups, demography, attitudes, the world of the imagination and the symbolic universe. Analysis of decisions, conscious acts and 'events' has been enriched with an examination of structures, as well as conjunctures. Interest has shifted away from the male elites toward women, ordinary people, social classes, those on the margins of society, ethnocultural groups and Aboriginal peoples. This renewal has been accompanied by a growing multidisciplinarity or interdisciplinarity, increased use of 'models' or, more often, 'problematics', greater quantification, and use of serial sources. Methods have developed, moving beyond, though not renouncing, the venerable tradition of textual criticism.[12] Moreover, the diversification of historians' interests has been accompanied by a wider and wider range of archive clienteles: professional historians and other social sciences and humanities specialists, of course, but also geneticists, journalists, radio and television broadcasters, militants, lawyers, genealogists, interest groups, people interested in local or family history, government officials, and so on. In 1989–1990, historians accounted for only 13 percent of researchers registered with the National Archives of Canada.[13]

Upstream, the most significant development in archival science in the twentieth century has, without a doubt, been the emergence of document selection and evaluation as a practical and theoretical necessity.[14] The *documentary explosion* that characterizes the twentieth century makes necessary the destruction of documents and even, in the case of large organizations such as governments, of most documents (at the National Archives of Canada, less than 5 percent of the documentation produced by the federal government is preserved).[15] In principle, this elimination is done only with the agreement of the archivists. This has therefore profoundly modified the role of archivists in relation with the canons of traditional archival science. On the one hand, they are more involved in records management, since evaluation of documents and development of preservation schedules are done in close co-operation with the institutions that create the documents. On the other hand, they must formulate criteria for deciding which documents will be preserved and which may be destroyed.

In other words, today, archivists are no longer just neutral gatherers of a documentary manna that falls naturally into their hands. They 'create' archives by evaluating the huge body of recent documents and choosing to eliminate more than 95 percent, intervening with respect to upstream information management practices, describing to a more or less detailed extent, downstream, certain holdings or parts of holdings in relation to others, and providing or not providing research tools and distance access points. These practices shape access to the archives and therefore, in a sense, the very content of the archives for the public. Moreover, how could archivists have fitted the image of neutral keepers of documents, when, for any evaluation, there is a cultural and social background? This constant phenomenon – history itself has never been neutral and objective, in the strict sense of the word – simply stands out more in this age of information. However, it is appropriate to objectify the process as much as possible.[16]

Now and in the future, the documentary heritage that a society or an era leaves behind will not be the result of an unconscious sedimentation or a sedimentation of chance occurrences – it will be 'constructed', in a sense. Thus, one finds combined the conditions for an overturning in archival science: in the selection process, the main reference point is no longer the document, but rather the human activity for which an account is needed – in other words, the context of creation, the provenance, the function. This contextual approach 'is concerned in the first instance with acquiring knowledge of the context in which information is recorded rather than knowledge of the information contents of the records'.[17] The archivist's task is no longer to manage a pre-existing documentary universe; rather, it is to give an account of institutions and societies, as well as of their actions and transactions, by participating directly in the building of a documentary heritage in which the emphasis on evidence is greater than that on information. All these developments have forced archivists to renew their theoretical arsenal and return to certain basic concepts such as provenance.[18]

Archivists who subscribe to this new paradigm are endeavoring to build a documentary heritage that is as complete, as representative and as revealing as possible. [. . .] They seek to identify the forgotten elements, the silences, the gaps in the documents held by the archives depository, on the basis of its mandate. A first step is the identification of potential holdings that could fill these 'holes'. Some people go further and encourage archivists to participate directly in the creation of documents, for example, through sound or audio-visual recording.[19]

This participation may take several forms. (1) The archives depository serves simply as a *documentation centre* for oral history projects that have been carried out or are underway, thus promoting co-ordination and minimizing overlap between projects.[20] In Canada, most oral archives are kept in archives depositories, although several museums have impressive holdings. (2) The archivist or his/her institution may also *give rise to and support* oral history projects carried out by others: grants, loans of equipment, training, project supervision, assistance in the preparation of interviews through careful selection of supporting documents that will reinforce the survey's reliability and coherence.[21] The archives depository then endeavours to make its priorities coincide with those of the communities and groups undertaking and carrying out projects.[22] (3) The archivist or his/her institution may *directly create* oral sources. These may be secondary sources – for example, interviews conducted with creators of documents when an accession takes place, allowing for the obtaining of details regarding the organization of an institution, the way its documents are filed and the strong points, as well as gaps in the holdings.[23] Given the over-abundance of documents generated by large institutions, and the complexity and insufficiency of the filing systems, such interviews may even constitute 'meta-documents', in the manner of computer systems documentation.

Archivists may also create new projects, designed to complete collections held by the depository, on the basis of a documentation strategy.[24] In so doing, they may sometimes broaden the generally accepted parameters of oral history. For example, they conduct surveys regarding current events, seeking to capture a wide range of points of view. The result is then significantly different from that of retrospective surveys done a few years later.[25] Use of film or video recording today, although not appropriate in all situations, also provides unique opportunities – for example, for visually perpetuating the memory of disappearing occupations, techniques, skills and folklore, as well as gestures and social interaction during ceremonies or group interviews.[26]

There is a lack of unanimity among archivists and creators of recordings regarding the need to create or even simply acquire oral history recordings to balance out (and, in some countries, establish) the documentary heritage. The discussions bear on, among other things, the *validity of the oral archives*.

First of all, there is the matter of the *oral sources as testimony (evidential value)*. Archivists readily acknowledge the evidential value of the recordings – that is, their usefulness for understanding the activities (research, teaching and so on) of their creator. The problem has to do with the failure of the creators of the oral history recordings to deposit them in archives and to document them sufficiently to identify their context. Researchers sometimes equate them with manuscript notes, of purely private interest. Many oral history projects have a specific goal: a publication, radio or television program, or exhibition, for example. Those in charge of the project hold to this primary goal and do not take the necessary steps (description, documentation, depositing in archives) to preserve them in the long term and make them accessible.[27] Some radio or television broadcasters erase the recording in order to be able to re-use the tape.[28] However, research findings can only be critiqued fully when the sources used in the research are available to other researchers. Transparency is needed for any public debate or scientific undertaking.[29] This requirement extends, of course, to the documentation surrounding recordings.

The *informational value* of oral testimony has been the subject of much debate among oral historians and has led to controversy. Archivists, for their part, have wondered about the extent to which recorded oral testimony can be re-used.

A first problem has to do with the quality of the recordings submitted to archives. The widespread use of audiotape recorders and video cameras has led to a proliferation of poorly prepared projects, in which the subjects are badly chosen, the sound quality of the recordings is not good, and the record-ings are poorly documented and executed.[30] The apparent ease with which this technique can be used supports the illusion that the memory of elderly persons, for example, establishes a direct link with the past. However, we know that memory is a living thing, that testimony is a constructed (and therefore selective) account, and that the circumstances surrounding the interview – the *context* – and the way the interview is conducted contribute to this construction.[31] Prior research and careful preparation are needed if such investigations are to be a success. It should be added that the depositing in archives of recordings without appropriate documentation makes evaluation of the recordings very costly and, consequently, proper use of the recordings very difficult.

Over and above the matter of the researchers' preparation and profes-sionalism, one may wonder about the extent to which oral testimony lends itself to being used out of context and in a way not foreseen by its creators. Some people maintain that one cannot foresee future research trends, and therefore cannot deliberately create sources for posterity.[32] Others, while not-ing the difficulty involved in re-using recordings made in response to very specific situations, feel that interviews may be used for more than one pur-pose, on the condition that they contain questions of a more general nature bearing on the context of the subject.[33] In this regard, accounts of people's lives, which are based on a general biographical approach, pose fewer prob-lems.[34] However, truth to be said, a number of these problems are hardly different from those connected with many written documents with which archives are encumbered.

The team responsible for the oral archives project of the Sécurité sociale in France has formulated some interesting methodological proposals with respect to these issues. It distinguishes among three types of project: passive collection of testimonies, with a view to use by future researchers (this is the work of 'archivists', but the authors include in this category the work done by most American 'oral historians'); collection within the framework of a specific research project; and, finally, creation of oral archives. In the latter case, what is involved is the conducting of an investigation on a specific subject and the application of a systematic critical method to what is said, with a view to going beyond the statements prepared in advance and constituting a true body of validated documents.[35]

Finally, over and above the objections in principle, some people note that archives' budgets, which are barely sufficient for the carrying out of archivists' traditional tasks, should not be 'diverted' for the creation of documents.[36] This opinion appears to be debatable, to say the least. Archival institutions serve to document the actions of individuals, institutions and societies. Their level of resources (human and financial) determines the extent to which they can properly carry out their mission. Moreover, everything depends on the type of society, the mandate of a given institution, the institution's budget and the competence of its personnel, and so on. It is clear that, in some countries, the depositories must create oral sources, which constitute a major and even the essential portion of their holdings.

DOCUMENTATION OF ORAL SOURCES

Most of the fundamental debates among archivists focus on the acquisition (and, more recently, creation by archivists) of recordings. Development of the oral documents, once they have been accepted into the archives, raises questions of a more practical nature. This section bears more on archival aspects than on oral history in general. In effect, recordings are acquired and created by libraries, museums, centres for folk studies, radio and television broadcasting companies, and audio-visual centres, as well as by archives. They are often classified and described without reference to archival standards and practices.[37]

Public access to archival documents presupposes proper description. This is an even more essential condition in the case of oral sources, in so far as the richness and the synthesizing nature of documents of this kind (an account of a person's life is not about the economy or politics and so on; it covers all these realities from one perspective) make their consultation difficult and time consuming. For the same reasons, the establishment of proper research tools requires considerable resources, particularly when the recordings arrive at the archives unaccompanied by sufficient documentation. Nevertheless, the requirement of transparency with respect to access to the oral sources used by researchers also extends to this documentation, under the central principle of provenance in archival science: the recording, as a document, bears witness first of all to an interview, not to the subject of the interview.[38] Oral sources depend on the relationship established between the interviewer and interviewee: a complete appreciation of the result therefore depends on a knowledge of the interview and its context (place, presence of third party, relationship between interviewer and subject, and so on).[39]

Of all the factors, it is probably the absence of a proper description that most hampers access to oral archives.[40] A national or regional guide is an indispensable first tool for determining the scope of the oral sources and directing researchers to the institutions most suited to their needs. Such guides do not exist for all countries and require regularly updating if they are to remain useful.[41] At the depository level, the classification and description standards vary considerably; some depositories favour item-based description of the sort used by libraries, while others favour relating the recordings in archive holdings to the creators of the documents – that is, to their provenance.[42] The Canadian archival community is developing description standards and is also looking at the issue on the international level. In all these cases, the depositories are wondering how far to go in describing, particularly with respect to the status of the transcription and the need for it.

Transcription of sound recordings can considerably improve access to those recordings: a transcript can be consulted much more quickly and does not require special equipment. When done shortly after the recording is made, in collaboration with the interviewer and sometimes with the person interviewed, transcription makes it possible to eliminate ambiguities in the testimony. At the first oral history centre, that of Columbia University in the United States, the transcript, reviewed and corrected by the person interviewed, constituted the real document. This reflex, rooted in the tradition of the written word, in a way conferred greater validity on the oral document. The recording was considered a transitional step. Until the 1960s, people even went so far as to erase and re-use the original tapes, which were, it is true, very expensive.[43] Today, nearly all authors consider the sound recording the original document. It is the most complete document, the only one that delivers all the richness of the oral (and sometimes visual) testimony: not only its manifest content, but also, as we saw earlier, the hesitations, tone and traces of emotion, as well as accents and pronunciation.[44] Transcription is difficult work and the results are always imperfect. It is a 'translation' from the oral to the written word.[45] As such, it serves as a tool for research and for publication of testimonies.[46]

The widespread practice of transcription involves very large costs: it is estimated that it takes a qualified person some fifteen hours to transcribe one hour of recording.[47] Today, however, use of computer equipment and word-processing makes it possible to reduce the cost of transcription and facilitates indexing.[48] The decision whether to transcribe depends mainly on the available resources and, no doubt, the degree of use. Moreover, one archivist notes in this regard that archives are not in the habit of providing their users with a transcript of their ancient manuscripts, which are at least as difficult to consult as sound recordings.[49] Transcription may be desirable (though more and more difficult in the case of a large corpus), but archivists have other options – for example, drawing up an indexed list of the subjects dealt with in each interview, cross-referenced to the location of that portion of the recording on the tape. In any event, a proper description is also useful to archives, in so far as it makes it possible to reduce consultation of the recordings themselves, and therefore, reduce the costs connected with equipment and additional copies.[50]

Sound and visual recordings on magnetic media – and even, to a lesser extent, on film, – pose difficult and costly preservation problems. Over and above the requirements with respect to the environment and the handling of the tapes, which are described well in the trade publications, one must take into account the variety of recording formats, which are usually incompatible, and rapid technological change, particularly in the case of video recordings. Consequently, archives have to constantly recopy documents in a common format, since it is hardly possible to maintain a complete inventory of play-back and copying equipment. The advent of optical digital preservation technology points to the possibility of a universal format that could be used for animated images, sound, maps, photographs and other visual documents, as well as for textual material.[51] Unfortunately, the physical stability of the media has not been proven. Above all, the variety of formats and equipment and their incompatibility hardly seem about to disappear. Archivists find themselves faced here with the same problems as in the case of other computer documents.

The depositing of oral history recordings in archives and, above all, public access of these documents create certain legal and ethical problems. Since the situation varies from country to country, only a very general sketch can be given here.[52]

Ownership of an oral history recording depends not only on law, but also on ethics: in some cases, the testimony is considered part of the person himself or herself or of the group to which that person belongs, and can be alienated only under certain conditions.[53] The legal provisions, for their part, may vary, depending on whether it is ownership of the medium or ownership of the content that is involved. Copyright may mean that an individual has the right to control use of the recording by another or the right to derive profit from that use, or may merely signify recognition of the individual's contribution. The problem consists in knowing who holds the copyright (informant, interviewer, organization sponsoring the project, archives . . .?). These questions arise mainly in the case of publication of a transcript or the radio or television broadcasting of a recording, but they can affect access to the recordings by restricting reproduction possibilities. Archives must ensure that the transfer of the recordings is done with all the necessary authorizations, and this is not a simple matter, given the uncertainty in the law. In some cases, participation in an interview is sufficient to establish consent. It is generally preferable that the recordings be accompanied by a written authorization from the persons interviewed or, to avoid the intrusion of a legal document into the relationship of trust established at the time of the interview, by an immediately recorded oral authorization.[54]

A second issue relates to *respect for privacy*, both that of the informant and that of the people mentioned in his or her testimony. Dissemination of the content of some recordings could be harmful to some individuals, and even lead to libel suits. Moreover, this situation is not restricted to oral documents. However, if the archives have participated in the creation of the oral document, they might have to assume some of the liability and suffer prejudice. Any authorization should therefore refer to the restrictions imposed on use of the recordings. In the case of state archives depositories, these conditions, with respect to public documents alone, could be in conflict with access to information laws.[55]

The matter of the costs connected with developing oral sources relates back, in the final analysis, to the funding of archives depositories. Funding problems are hitting archives programs hard and explain in part the poor quality of some projects and of the resulting archives. In 1984, a survey done by the International Council on Archives led to the conclusion that there was chronic underfunding of most oral history or oral tradition programs.[56] This problem is becoming critical for the developing countries, which have only meagre resources to allocate to archives in general.[57] There are some happy exceptions, however. For example, the National Archives of Zimbabwe allocate a significant portion of their budget to oral sources.[58]

CONCLUSION

When life and principles come into conflict, life nearly always wins the day. Oral history as a discipline is relatively new – witness the recent decision of the International Council on Archives to split the audio-visual archives committee in order to create a separate oral sources committee – but its use and popularity are growing. Oral archives exist, and are growing in number, size and quality, as are oral history projects. It can be expected that, in the twenty-first century, there will be an expansion in this field of study. Archivists can no longer turn away, shield themselves behind sophisms of a theoretical sort and refuse to participate in various ways in this effort to document important aspects of life in their societies. They too are affected by the invasion of audio-visual technology as a dominant channel for the dissemination of information and knowledge among all segments of the population. It is not a matter of abdicating the fundamental principles of their discipline, but of extending them and, above all, influencing the creators of oral sources in order that the latter may properly document their projects and sources. If archives collaborate on oral history projects or even take the initiative in some cases, they must, more than anyone else, observe the major principles with respect to provenance, context, evidential value and so on. In addition, their contribution is needed to clarify issues relating to copyright, protection of privacy and right of access, given their long experience in these areas. They must also speed up their efforts to define descriptive standards at several levels and participate in the preparation or updating of oral sources guides, so as to facilitate access to them. The problem of preservation remains untouched for the moment and will require significant investments on the part of institutions and governments.

NOTES

1 'The archivist and oral sources', in *Documents that Move and Speak. Audiovisual Archives in the New Information Age, National Archives of Canada, Ottawa, Canada. April 30, 1990–May 3, 1990. Proceedings of a Symposium Organized for the International Council of Archives by the National Archives of Canada*, Munich, London, New York, Paris, KG Saur, 1992, p. 85.
2 L. Duranti, 'The concept of appraisal and archival theory', *The American Archives*, Spring 1994, vol. 57, no. 2, pp. 328–344.
3 P. Thompson, *The Voice of the Past. Oral History*, Oxford, Oxford University Press, 1978, ch. 2; P. Joutard, *Ces voix qui nous viennent du passé*, Paris, Hachette, 1983, ch. 2.
4 J. Cruikshank, 'Oral tradition and oral history: reviewing some issues', *Canadian Historical Review*, 1994, vol. 75, no. 3, p. 407.

5 Cited in B. Blanc, 'Sixième Congrès international d'histoire orale', at Oxford, 1987, *La Gazette des archives*, 1987, vol. 139, p. 254. See also Cruikshank, 'Oral traditions and oral history'.

6 J.E. Fogerty, 'Filling the gap: oral history in the archives', *American Archivist*, Spring 1983, vol. 46, no. 2, pp. 150–151.

7 D. Aron-Schnaper *et al.*, *Histoire orale ou archives orales? Rapport sur la constitution d'archives orales pour l'histoire de la Sécurité Sociale*, Paris, Association pour l'étude de la Sécurité Sociale, 1980, p. 27.

8 T.L. Charlton, 'Videotaped oral histories: problems and prospects', *American Archivist*, Summer 1984, vol. 47, no. 3, pp. 228–236.

9 Fogerty, 'Filling the gap', pp. 150, 153.

10 In this regard, Hugh Taylor and Cynthia Durance speak of a return to the Middle Ages, to a sort of inclusiveness approaching oral tradition ('Wisdom, knowledge, information and data. Transformation and convergence in archives and libraries in the western world', *Alexandria*, 1992, vol. 4, no. 1, pp. 37–61).

11 Fogerty, 'Filling the gap'. See also H. Jenkinson, *A Manual of Archive Administration*, second revised edition, London, Percy Lund, Humphries & Co, 1966, p. 55; A. Ward, *A Manual of Sound Archives Administration*, Aldershot, Gower, 1990, p. 6.

12 For a quick overview of this subject, see G. Paquet and J.-P. Wallot, 'Pour une méso-histoire du XIXe siècle canadien', *Revue d'histoire de l'Amérique française*, 1980, vol. 33, pp. 387–425.

13 G. Blais and D. Enns, 'From paper archives to people archives: public programming in the management of archives', *Archivaria*, Winter 1990–1991, vol. 31, no. 1, p. 110, n. 4.

14 This concern was for the most part not a consideration for Hilary Jenkinson (*A Manual of Archive Administration*, Oxford, Clarendon Press, 1922), but it already appears clearly in Theodore R. Schellenberg (*Modern Archives: Principles and Techniques*, Chicago, University of Chicago Press, 1956).

15 This is a fairly common proportion in Western countries. See Fogerty, 'Filling the gap', p. 150.

16 J.-P. Wallot, 'Building a living memory for the history of our present: new perspectives on archival appraisal', *Journal of the Canadian Historical Association*, 1991, pp. 271 ff.

17 T. Nesmith, 'Hugh Taylor's contextual idea for archives and the foundation of graduate education in archival studies', in B. Craig (ed.), *The Archival Imagination. Essays in Honour of Hugh A. Taylor*, Ottawa, Association of Canadian Archivists, 1992, p. 16.

18 See R.-H. Biter, 'Les archives', in C. Samaran (ed.), *L'histoire et ses méthodes*, Paris, Gallimard, 1961; H. Booms, 'Society and the formation of a documentary heritage: issues in the appraisal of archival sources', *Archivaria*, Summer 1987, vol. 24, pp. 69–107. Terry Cook has proposed a 'provenance-based structural–functional' approach ('Mind over matter: towards a new theory of archival appraisal', in Craig (ed.), *The Archival Imagination*, pp. 38–70).

19 Fogerty, 'Filling the gap', pp. 148–157; D. Reimer, 'Oral history and archives: the case in favor', *Canadian Oral History Association Journal*, 1981, vol. 5, no. 1, p. 33; D. Lance, *Sound Archives: A Guide to Their Establishment and Development*, London, International Association of Sound Archives, 1983, pp. 177–178; R. Lochead, 'Oral history: the role of the archivist', *Phonographic Bulletin*, November 1983, no. 37, pp. 3–7; C. de Tourtier-Bonazzi, 'La collecte des témoignages oraux', *La Gazette des archives*, 1987, vol. 139, p. 251. Alan Ward, although he assigns archivists a 'reactive' role, concedes their participation in the creation of recordings, comparing it to their involvement in information management in the institutions whose documents they acquire (*A Manual*, p. 14).

20 Archives nationales de France, *Le Témoignage Oral aux Archives. De la collecte à la communication*, Paris, AN, 1990, p. 30.
21 Fogerty, 'Filling the gap', p. 154.
22 G. Berkowski, 'Moving and speaking between the lines: the Manitoba Oral History Grants Program', in *Documents that Move and Speak*, pp. 112–118; E.S. Andrade, 'Oral History in Mexico', *International Journal of Oral History*, November 1988, vol. 9, no. 3, p. 218.
23 B.H. Bruemmer, 'Access to oral history: a national agenda', *American Archivist*, Fall 1991, vol. 54, p. 496; Archives nationales de France, *Le témoignage oral*, p. 30.
24 For examples of oral archives creation programs, see Lance, *Sound Archives*, ch. XII; Aron-Schnapper *et al.*, *Histoire orale ou archives orales*; T.A. Schorzman, *A Practical Introduction to Video History: The Smithsonian Institution and Alfred P. Sloan Foundation Experiment*, Malabar, Krieger Publishing Co., 1993; D. Chew, 'Oral history in the Republic of Singapore', *International Journal of Oral History*, November 1986, vol. 7, no. 3, pp. 206–210; M. Chou, 'Small windows on the Pacific: oral history and libraries in Australia, New Zealand, and Papua New Guinea', *International Journal of Oral History*, November 1985, vol. 6, no. 3, pp. 163–178; S. Mbaye, 'Les archives orales au Sénégal', in *Documents that Move and Speak*, pp. 99–111; Archives nationales de France, *Le Témoignage Oral*.
25 Fogerty, 'Filling the gap', p. 156.
26 As early as 1900, it was proposed that cinematography be used to document systematically the traditional trades that were disappearing. See S. Kula, 'Management of moving-image and sound records', in C. Durance (ed.), *Management of Recorded Information: Converging Disciplines*, Munich, K.G. Saur, 1990, p. 181; T.L. Charlton, 'Videotaped oral histories: problems and prospects', *American Archivist*, Summer 1984, vol. 47, no. 3, pp. 228–236; Schorzman, *A Practical Introduction*.
27 Bruemmer, 'Access to oral history', p. 495.
28 Lochead, 'Oral history', pp. 3–7.
29 D. Henige, 'In the possession of the author: the problem of source monopoly in oral historiography', *International Journal of Oral History*, November 1980, vol. 1, no. 3, pp. 181–194.
30 One of the harshest criticisms of this shortcoming is found in B. Tuchman, 'Research in contemporary events for the writing of history', *Proceedings of the American Academy of Arts and Letters and the National Institution of Arts and Letters*, Second Series, no. 22, New York, 1972, pp. 62 ff.; see also D. Treleven, 'Oral history and the archival community: common concerns about documenting twentieth century life', *International Journal of Oral History*, February 1989, vol. 10, no. 1, pp. 50–58; J. Dryden, 'Oral history and archives: the case against', *Canadian Oral History Association Journal*, 1981, vol. 5, no. 1, p. 35; Fogerty, 'Filling the gap', p. 149; W.W. Moss and P. Mazikana, *Archives, Oral History and Oral Tradition: a RAMP Study*, Paris, UNESCO, 1986, p. 23.
31 Aron-Schnapper *et al.*, *Histoire orale ou archives orales*, p. 67; Joutard, *Ces voix*, ch. VIII; Cruikshank, 'Oral tradition and oral history', pp. 410 ff.
32 Dryden, 'Oral history and archives', p. 36.
33 Fogerty, 'Filling the gap', p. 157.
34 Archives nationales de France, *Le Témoignage Oral*, p. 27.
35 Aron-Schnapper *et al.*, *Histoire orale ou archives orales*, pp. 57–62.
36 Dryden, 'Oral history and archives, pp. 36–37.
37 The *Guide to Oral History Collections in Canada* (under the direction of Normand Fortier, and edited by the Canadian Oral History Association in 1993) gives one a good idea as to the diversity of situations. The preface by Richard Lochead in the *Guide* and the article by Wilma MacDonald ('Origins: oral history programmes in Canada, Britain and the United States', *Canadian Oral History Association*

Journal, (1990, vol. 10, pp. 12–24) describe the relations between archivists and creators of oral history documents in Canada, the United States and Great Britain.

38 Moss and Mizikana, *Archives, Oral History and Oral Tradition*, p. 48.

39 A.G. Quintana, 'The archivist and oral sources', in *Documents that Move and Speak*, pp. 88–89.

40 Bruemmer, 'Access to oral history', p. 495; Lochead, 'Oral history', p. 6; B. Aleybeleyle, 'Oral archives in Africa: their nature, value and accessibility', *International Library Review*, October 1985, vol. 17, no. 4, p. 422.

41 Bruemmer, 'Access to oral history', p. 497. The same author suggests a national (in the United States) five-point program for improving access to the oral history holdings: establishment of a USMARC format for description of the documents; creation of guidelines to ensure uniformity in the MARC AMC oral history documents; establishment of a program of loans between libraries and archives; research into new technologies to facilitate communication of information; and support from oral history researchers for this program of proper access.

42 Moss and Mazikana, *Archives, Oral History and Oral Tradition*, pp. 50–51; Mbaye, 'Les archives orales', pp. 99–111.

43 Joutard, *Ces voix*, p. 75; F.J. Stielow, *The Management of Oral History Sound Archives*, New York, Greenwood Press, 1986, p. 19.

44 Stielow, *The Management*, p. 23; Moss and Mazikana, *Archives, Oral History and Oral Tradition*, p. 58; Archives nationales de France, *Le témoignage oral*, pp. 27–28.

45 These are the words of Philippe Joutard (*Ces voix*, p. 218). See also Archives nationales de France, *Le Témoignage Oral*, p. 27.

46 Moss and Mazikana, *Archives, Oral History and Oral Tradition*, p. 58.

47 This estimate is that of Phillipe Joutard, who notes that American authors give higher numbers (*Ces voix*, p. 217); Paul Thompson suggests an average of six to twelve hours (*The Voice of the Past*, p. 197).

48 Stielow, The Management, p. 89.

49 Mbaye, 'Les archives orales', p. 108.

50 Kula, 'Management of moving-image and sound records', p. 80.

51 Ibid., pp. 79–80. Philippe Blasco and Philipp Pataud-Célerier provide interesting examples of digitalization and use of multimedia computer technology for dissemination of heritage in 'La chaîne du savoir', *La recherche*, July–August 1994, vol. 25, no. 267, p. 815.

52 Moss and Mazikana, *Archives, Oral History and Oral Tradition*, pp. 49, 68–70; A. Bruford, '"My tongue is my ain": report on the Joint Day Conference of the Scottish Oral History Group in Association with the British Association of Sound Collections on Copyright, Confidentiality and Public Access Rights in the Recording and Use of Oral History', *Phonographic Bulletin*, November 1990, no. 57, pp. 16–32; Stielow, *The Management*, pp. 42–51; Ward, *A Manual*, pp. 48–58.

53 Moss and Mazikana, *Archives, Oral History and Oral Tradition*, p. 49.

54 Joutard, *Ces voix*, p. 215.

55 Stielow, *The Management*, p. 48.

56 Moss and Mazikana, *Archives, Oral History and Oral Tradition*, p. 79. For the United States, see Fogerty, 'Filling the gap', pp. 153–154.

57 For example, see M. Faseke Modupeolu, 'Oral history in Nigeria: issues, problems, and prospects', *Oral History Review*, Spring 1990, vol. 18, no. 1, pp. 77–91; P.J. Sehlinger, 'Oral history projects in Argentina, Chile, Peru and Bolivia', *International Journal of Oral History*, November 1984, vol. 5, no. 3, pp. 168–173; M.A. Foronda, Jr, 'Oral history in the Philippines: trends and prospects', *International Journal of Oral History*, February 1981, vol. 2, no. 1, pp. 13–25.

58 Private communication from Terry Cook in the winter of 1995.

31 The future of oral history and moving images

Dan Sipe

Dan Sipe is a historian and filmmaker who teaches at Moore College of Art and Design in Philadelphia. Reprinted from *Oral History Review*, Spring/Fall 1991, vol. 19, nos. 1/2, pp. 75–87, by permission of the Oral History Association.

An epoch in the practice of history is coming to a close. For hundreds of years the printed word has been the dominant mode of communication for the historical profession, in the process shaping its basic assumptions and structures. Today, the printed word is being superseded by a diversity of communication forms with the greatest impetus coming from moving images. As a methodology rooted in multiple modes of communication, oral history can play a pivotal role in accelerating the historical profession's comprehension of this radical shift in the nature of communication. In return, moving images can more fully express oral history's reflexive dimension, which makes more explicit the human role in the creation of history. The relationship between moving images and oral history, always reciprocal, holds particular promise amidst the present revolution in communications.

A challenging manifestation of this change in communication is the rapidly growing disjunction between the practice of professionals based in academia and the practice of history in society. On the one hand we find history professionals who remain deeply wedded to writing, as they examine more areas and fields with more numerous and sophisticated methodologies than ever before. On the other hand, film and video, especially as broadcast on television, have spawned a staggering array of historical works which arguably are the major influence on the public's historical consciousness. Closer to home, consider the number of people creating family and local histories with moving pictures; better yet, note the number of video yearbooks for schools being produced. The glaring contradiction is that these two major trends have intersected very little: professional historians have had limited effect on the history presented through moving images; the changes in communication wrought by moving images have wielded even less influence on the historical profession.

The core of the conundrum lies in the role of communication in the history of history. The historical profession has always been structured around the medium of the written word. Writing and history have been synonymous, as evidenced by the word 'historiography'. Writing is an essential part of the 'deep structure' of the practice of history; it is the form of our content, but in

Hayden White's words, we have not questioned 'the content of our form'.[1]

The practice of history as we conceive of it today began with the transition from orality to literacy, which led to written records and the earliest works we recognize as history.[2] The next great shift came with the advent of the printed word, which transformed society and the practice of history. As the era dominated by the printed word winds down, historians are faced with complicated questions about the use of a variety of mixed and changing forms of communication, ranging from simple audiotape to the promising complexities of videodiscs linked with computers.

The technologies of moving images are changing at a bewildering pace, yet history using moving images does not even have a rubric, a commonly agreed upon title. It is not that moving images have been rejected by historians. The majority of historians seem to find the concept of history using moving images at least somewhat intriguing and a goodly number are enthusiastic; historians seem to be accepting the idea of a relationship between moving images and history. The *Journal of American History* and the *American Historical Review* now print film reviews and articles on the subject, while the major historical associations have film committees, give awards to films, and even schedule sessions at their conventions. Valuable work has been done on the history of film and on analysis of films as evidence for social and intellectual history in journals such as *Film and History*. A very few historians such as Robert Rosenstone, Natalie Zemon Davis, Robert Brent Toplin, Daniel Walkowitz, and John O'Connor have invested time and energy considering the possibilities of film or video for serious, original historical work.[3] New York University, to take one encouraging example, now trains historians in the use of film and video as part of its public history program.

Yet this good will and interest add up to very few historians doing history through moving images. The barrier seems to be that the historical profession is structured around the medium of the written word and is somewhat insulated in its academic setting. And in fact, doing history with moving images presents a substantial challenge to this setting and its assumptions. As Robert Rosenstone notes, history on film and video 'is not history in the sense that academics think of it. It is history with different rules of representation, analysis, and modes of reading and comprehension that we do not yet fully understand.'[4] Moving images contradict the deep structures of the historical profession, and as a result historians do not yet have the training, the institutions, the motivations, the professional structures, or the categories to effectively use moving images. To do this, in truth, would require learning complicated new skills and undergoing a different type of socialization.

Why should historians make this change? Robert Rosenstone has offered an eloquent case for the sheer intellectual and artistic challenge of history using moving images. He suggests that film can offer an alternative that dramatically expands the possibilities of history. While acknowledging recent transformations of the practice of history, he points out that:

We have changed the nature of history radically, but not the nature of the consciousness and hence the form that expresses that history. . . . The opportunity now [exists] for a new way of Seeing the Past. More radical because it breaks with form and not just with content.[5]

When discussing such issues, it is very easy to focus on film only as it affects the presentation or communication of history. But it may be just as important to consider its impact on historical evidence as such. The dominance of writing has been based on its power as a form of evidence – writing has been so central to history precisely because it nearly always creates a document. One writes on a surface which then constitutes a document, a piece of evidence. Moving images also automatically document themselves, and they offer extraordinary evidence. The experiments of Edward Muybridge photographing a running horse with multiple cameras remind us that the medium has its roots in the quest for superior evidence. The videotape of the police assault on Rodney King only reaffirms the potency of moving images as evidence.

However, for most historians motion pictures are irrelevant as direct evidence because none exist for their period. And for a substantial minority of historians of more recent times, film evidence exists as part of a stunning flood of data. Except for historians of film or those social and intellectual historians who use feature films as evidence of the spirit of a period, filmic evidence was also extremely limited until television generated an increased flow. Given the complexities of working with moving images discussed above and the lack of training, support, or rewards from the profession, understandably few historians who could use moving pictures as evidence have taken up the challenge. Historians are thus effectively cut off from utilizing the most powerful communication and evidentiary form of our time. The traditions and structures of the profession seem to militate against any major change. The one powerful exception is the rising field of oral history.

Oral history and moving images have considerable potential synergy. They intersect in two crucial and related ways. First, filmed or videotaped oral history demonstrates the possibilities of moving images as substantive evidence, linked to an interview's explicit articulation but carrying information and documentation in its own right. By encouraging such a focus on image as part of integral historical evidence, visual oral history can help lead historians away from the limited conception of moving images as merely an alternative form for evoking, communicating, or translating written history. Oral history can demonstrate the power of film and video as evidence while moving images provide a new level of evidence for oral history.

Secondly, moving images combined with oral history have a special power to encourage and support a comparative, reflexive approach to history itself. Historians have generally become more familiar with the notion of understanding a work of history as a construction, and of considering the variant ways in which historical works have been and might be constructed. But, ironically, writing has been so central in this that its centrality as a shaper of the construction process itself has been largely assumed and hence unexamined. Other modes of evidence and communication, in combination with or in juxtaposition to written texts, may help to encourage a much-needed examination of the assumptions and deep structures of history as a whole. Film and video can support the emerging reflexivity of oral history practice, and a more consciously developed relationship between oral history and moving images may thus enhance the quality and credibility of both and suggest new directions for historical practice as a whole.

Let us first consider evidence. Moving images with recorded sound constitute not merely supplemental, but definitively superior evidence for oral history, as well as the best example of the potential of film and video as evidence. For most of human history, an interview would be 'recorded' in another memory, or perhaps preserved as an oral tradition in a formalized tale with a memory aid such as a poetic form. Retelling was an indispensable component of such oral history. The written word came to provide a better documentary record, but audiotape has given modern oral history the capacity to revive the oral dimension, in the form of easily generated, mechanically accurate evidence that writing could not match. Oral history has, in effect, reintroduced orality as a mode of research and communication for doing history. Although oral history usually involves secondary orality, that is the orality stemming from recorded sound in a literate culture, it has begun to challenge the monopoly of the written word.[6]

The power of moving images extends this challenge in a number of significant ways that begin with the paradoxical realization that orality, at its core, is not purely a concept grounded in sound. The spoken word is embedded in a setting, a situation, a context. People speak with body language, expression, and tone. They respond to and refer to their setting and to objects. Many people learn to communicate not with the precision or brilliance of their words but with energy and effect – as interviewers often learn when they discover a vibrant interview reduced, in the transcript, to a series of leaden, banal sentences. And in historical research the loss is not randomly distributed: those most diminished by translation from speech to writing tend to be the less educated, the less formally articulate – those who are usually socially and politically the less powerful, the less heard.

The visual dimension of moving images counteracts this tendency, adding layers of expression and evidence as it captures human interaction and settings. In this sense film and video emerge as the most effective ways to record evidence for most oral historical purposes. This is not to say that all or even most interviews must be videotaped, but when the quality of the evidence is crucial and the interview is significant, moving images should be the first choice.

The word 'choice' suggests reflexivity, the second dimension noted above. It has become more widely recognized that what is so unusual about oral history as a historical field is that most of its evidence is not found but generated. Oral historians do more than document memory; they elicit it. In essence, oral history is the collaborative creation of evidence in narrative form between interviewer and narrator, between living human beings. To be fully descriptive historically, oral history should thus document not only the interview's explicit information, but the process itself. The dialogic relationship between interviewer and narrator, the role of memory, and the function of narrativity – all are central to how interviews illustrate the construction of history as a process. And all these aspects are more clearly revealed when moving images are used.

The interaction between the interviewer and the narrator is a crucial dimension of oral history, a point made most compellingly by Eva McMahan.[7] However, such interview relationships are difficult to decipher from a transcript, especially if not specifically discussed. Subtle cues of voice, posture, gesture, and eye contact, all the non-verbal indicators of affect, indicate the quality of a relationship, but few of those cues are generally transcribed. These aspects of an interview that are outside words – the 'unworded' dimensions – are crucial evidence if we take the dialogic aspect seriously. If videotaping is done purely for evidentiary research purposes, the interviewer should probably be included in the image unless there is some clear reason not to. When videotaped, the interviewer yields some control, becoming less of an interpreter while the viewer becomes more of one. Consequently, the viewer is empowered while the narrator's story is less mediated; he or she is in more direct communication with the audience. Interviewers could move to an even more reflexive style by inviting the narrator to reflect on the interview and the interviewer, perhaps at the end of the session.

The richer detail of videotaped interviews also records more fully the expression and process of memory generation. One can watch the external signs of the processes of memory and see whether the interviewer encourages, probes, or challenges the memory of the narrator – stances often communicated non-verbally. Oral historians always face the problematic of memory for history and cannot evade its deepest challenges by dealing with safely distanced memories recorded long ago.[8] The plastic nature of memory requires the fullest documentation of its presentation and for this no other medium can match moving images.

Moving images can also capture the creation and presentation of oral narrative. Oral historians are more likely to recognize narrativity as a mode of discourse because they help create it, and videotaped oral narrative offers particular opportunities for insight into this process. Hayden White, who has done more than any other historian to raise the question of narrativity, sees film as offering an opportunity to find an alternative mode of discourse.[9] In this respect, filmed oral history invokes three far from identical forms of narrativity – the written word, the spoken word, and the filmed word – that can be compared and contrasted for their historical implications. If moving images are used only to document interviews, the spoken word will inevitably have primacy. But when images are edited into constructed presentations, historians must also engage the logic of the filmed word, a primarily visual dimension with its own codes for how evidence can constitute and communicate historical statements.

The concern of oral historians with the dialogic role of the interviewer, memory, and narrativity thus all can be advanced by moving images as an additional mode of communication. Moving images also have more immediate, even prosaic advantages for òral historians. Film or videotape documentation can simplify the work of the interviewer. Instead of trying to conduct an interview while simultaneously grasping the setting, the relationships, and all the other unworded data, the oral historian can concentrate on the interview and study the footage later. The many benefits of using moving images for evidence easily outweigh apprehensions about cost, technical skills, or the effect of a camera on a narrator. More complicated aspects of filming or videotaping usually arise only when shooting for broadcast.

Why, then, have oral historians not become more actively engaged with moving images, even at the primary level of evidence gathering? The *Oral History Review* remains exceptional among the major oral history journals in systematically reviewing films and tapes and in following video developments. The *International Journal of Oral History* gave very intermittent coverage and *Oral History* rarely even mentions moving images. Disappointingly, the 1991 Oral History Association convention offered no sessions devoted to moving images, even though the OHA newsletter regularly reports the availability of tapes and films.

Some oral historians are videotaping interviews and even producing tapes, although they seem to have received relatively little recognition.[10] Some archives now use videotape regularly and accept videotapes as archival material. There is, then, a group of oral historians of undetermined size that recognizes the utility of video. Still, video seems to inhabit some sort of twilight zone: many oral historians at least tacitly accept its value and some even use it, but few deal with it or comment on it systematically. Eva McMahan has a short but thoughtful section in her recent book *Elite Oral History Discourse*, but even the revised version of Paul Thompson's fine overview *The Voice of the Past* fails to deal with film or video in a meaningful way. Since Thompson does give substantial attention to radio and even theater, it is clear that this represents a specific choice not to engage the potential role of moving images in oral history.[11]

More revealing is another significant book, Michael Frisch's *A Shared Authority*, which does deal perceptively with film and oral history. In several essays on films, Frisch adroitly discusses memory, the relationship between an audience and a work of oral history, and the American sense of history. Moreover, he understands film and television as media in subtle ways and assumes the importance and relevance of film and video to oral history. Frisch does not, however, discuss the role of the moving image in and of itself.[12] I suspect that a sizable group of sophisticated oral historians assume and accept a profound affinity between moving images and oral history just as Frisch does. They embrace it so thoroughly that they do not develop it. While their assumption is correct, all the dimensions of the affinity between oral history and film and video need to be examined.

My own awareness of the power of moving images for oral history springs from my work on a major filmed oral history research project documenting the recent history of a village in China.[13] Years of conceptualizing and editing documentary films from powerful interviews in a language I do not speak made me acutely aware of the visual dimension of oral history. The enthusiasm of leading scholars of modern Chinese history for the filmed interviews made me recognize the power of filmed oral history as evidence. Moreover, because everyone involved recognized that the material was singular, our work revolved around shaping the films to represent the interviews rather than using the interviews to illustrate a script. As a historian, I experienced the capacity of filmed oral history to add extra dimensions to interviews and to more fully communicate a narrator's story.

Most of the people interviewed for these films were Chinese peasants, uneducated or little educated, and every word they uttered had to be translated. Yet the films literally let them speak. The dramatic highpoint of *Small Happiness*, the documentary on women in the village, occurs when an old woman confesses to smothering her infant son years before because she had no food for him. But her words are just the bare outline. Her story is just as much told in her anguished expression, her tone, her pauses, her breathing, the way she holds her body.

Transcripts alone could not have communicated, as the combination of words and images can do, the pace, rhythm, or overlapping of interview dialogue. Three older women sitting in a row with bound feet are asked if as girls in pre-revolutionary China they had wanted their feet to be bound. Simultaneously, they erupt that of course, they had wanted to. But it is the rapidity and simultaneity of their response, as well as their affect and tone, that tell us most about their feelings. For these peasants, the quintessential 'unheard' people, the visual dimension is absolutely crucial to their stories, and moving images lessen the mediating role of the interviewer.

It is similarly easy to find examples, in recent films, of how images can help document and unfold complex evidence, rendering transparent the relationship between interviewer and narrator and thus opening to audiences the process of historical construction. *Twenty Years Later* is a Brazilian film made in 1985 by Eduardo Coutinho.[14] The film had its genesis in a radical docudrama that began shooting in 1964 and recreated the murder of a peasant organizer. Many radical peasants including Elizabeth, the organizer's wife, played themselves, with Coutinho serving as director. The coup of 1964 ended the filming, the footage was seized by military, and the participants fled the area. Twenty years later, the footage was returned to Coutinho, now a successful filmmaker. He set out to find the participants and discover what had happened to them, all the while documenting the process of the search. The firm pivots on tracking down the widow who had to give up most of her children and had lived anonymously in a tiny village for years. The cost to this family of their parents' courageous politics is palpable. The wife now eschews politics, with one of her sons leading her through a litany of apolitical views. Silences, pacing, and affect are once again key. The cost to the woman shows on her face. Her banal words are telling precisely because of the lifeless way she presents them, especially when juxtaposed with footage of her earlier incarnation as a firebrand.

In the film Coutinho shows the old footage of the dreary, romanticized docudrama to its erstwhile stars; we see them, and we see them seeing themselves. Moreover, we witness a transformation of the filmmaking style from a heavily directed work to a much more reflexive one. The peasants in the new film are unscripted and undirected. The film crew, and Coutinho as director and interviewer, play their roles openly in front of the camera. Moreover, the wife who lost her husband, her children and her very name is now at the center rather than her martyred husband. Inescapable to viewers is the chasm of privilege between her and Coutinho, between two classes, between artist and subject. Coutinho may restore her name and reunite a tattered family, but these things are gifts that he has the power to bestow. Even though he opposes those with real power in Brazil, Coutinho has prospered and has much more control, much more power than his interview subject. Elizabeth controls only the expression of her memory. If she seems wary and cautious, if she sounds bowed and almost broken, that is her decision. Publicly expressed memory can be perilous; her memory is situational not out of politeness but out of an experience of danger and vulnerability. Any interviewer working from the bottom up has a privileged position, but Coutinho's privilege has a history – to his credit he does nothing to soften or conceal it. No matter how great his desire to empower, to listen, to help, there is a grotesque imbalance between them that film can express clearly and straightforwardly.

This power of the interviewer-historian-filmmaker is expressed in the last scene when the film crew is finally leaving and the woman who has suffered so much, who has been silenced for years and has only cautiously spoken, sees the car pull away. Finally, Elizabeth bursts out with an affirmation of her radicalism. Coutinho, the man with the car, with the camera, pulls away from this old woman; and the positioning, the objects, the affect are central as she finally speaks her mind and redefines herself and the film. It is an extraordinary moment, which even a very capable writer would find difficult to evoke and a transcript could not imaginably convey – but even a mediocre cameraperson would be able to capture it. This scene is emblematic of the power of moving images as evidence and reflexivity, for its ability to capture a density of evidence beyond any other form.

A similarly fine example of how filmed oral history can engage the problem of memory and subjectivity, so central to oral history, is Lise Yasui's *Family*

Gathering, a documentary of the internment of her Japanese-American father's family during World War II.[15] Yasui opens the film with what turns out to be her mistaken memory of meeting her Japanese grandfather as a small child; we see him as she did in numerous home movies. Then she tells us of learning that he died before she could meet him, but that she still feels that in some sense the meeting took place; we ponder the ways in which we 'know' the past: home movies, useful or satisfying memories, our memories of other people's memories. Clearly, memory has a constructed and plastic aspect: we wonder what is the purpose and meaning of Yasui's faulty memory of her grandfather.

She then goes on to tell a tale of the family's internment, with a particular focus on her grandfather's imprisonment without trial as a dangerous person. What sets the film apart is that Yasui documents the process of trying to get information from her family, of pushing to expose their memory of experiences and issues they had never talked about. Finally, late one night, her father reveals to her that the grandfather had committed suicide years after the war, never having recovered from the humiliation of an unjustified imprisonment. So history is about inquiry, and memory is the pivot – both Yasui's naive, constructed memory of her grandfather and the edited, controlled, repressed memory of her family. Throughout, the visual images she offers are central to the tension and paradoxes of these relationships, as she and the family lived them over time and express them in the moment of the film's examination. In this way, the film succeeds powerfully in capturing the complexity of memory as we really live with it.

Filmmakers such as Coutinho and Yasui have almost instinctively used oral history as evidence; their presentations have begun to explore some of the key questions for oral history as a whole. Yet the discussion of the relationship between oral history and moving images is only beginning. As historians come to give increasingly serious consideration to the potential of film and video both as evidence and as a mode for communicating historical narrative and interpretation, oral history has a pivotal role to play: it offers perhaps the clearest route to appreciating the power of filmed and videotaped historical evidence. And it is the historical methodology most open to multiple modes of communication, most able to reveal the reflexive dimensions of the historical process.

The goal is not the overthrow or displacement of the printed word, but rather to have the moving images of film and video recognized as generating discrete modes of discourse with their own ways to encode information, express concepts, and embody ambiguity and certainty. Developed in this way, moving images provide a counterpoint to writing that can reveal the underlying assumptions of much of our historical practice and make transparent some of history's basic methods. Ultimately, this approach is consonant with a conception of history based on multiple methodologies, varied forms of evidence, and diverse modes of discourse. No single approach or form would dominate, but forms could be used fluidly depending on the goals of the historical inquiry, spurring the development of a variety of hybrid forms.

With film and video recognized as a means of actually 'doing' history, the ongoing transformation of the practice of history can continue to advance in some intriguing new ways. Oral history already has nudged the historical profession in new directions; increasing recognition and use of moving images can help it push both inquiry and historical communication even farther. To this end, the time has come for sustained, systematic description, discussion, and analysis of how moving images can work as an integral dimension of oral historical practice.

NOTES

1 H. White, *The Content of the Form*, Baltimore, Johns Hopkins University Press, 1987.
2 W.J. Ong, *Orality and Literacy*, London, Methuen, 1982.
3 For representative pieces by Rosenstone, Toplin, and O'Connor, see the 'AHR Forum' in *American Historical Review*, 1988, vol. 93, pp. 1173–1227. Also, see N. Zemon Davis, 'Any resemblance to persons living or dead: film and the challenge of authenticity', *Yale Review*, Summer 1987, vol. 76, pp. 457–482. Toplin and Walkowitz are among the few historians who are also filmmakers.
4 R.A. Rosenstone, 'Revisioning history: contemporary filmmakers and the construction of the past', *Comparative Studies in Society and History*, 1990, vol. 32, p. 837.
5 R.A. Rosenstone, 'What you think about when you think about writing a book on history and film', *Public Culture*, 1990, vol. 3, p. 64.
6 W.J. Ong, *Interfaces of the Word*, Ithaca, Cornell University Press, 1977, pp. 53–81.
7 E.M. McMahan, *Elite Oral History Discourse*, Tuscaloosa, University of Alabama Press, 1989.
8 D. Thelen, 'Memory and American history', *Journal of American History*, 1989, vol. 75, pp. 1117–1129.
9 H. White, *Metahistory*, Baltimore, Johns Hopkins University Press, 1973, *Tropics of Discourse: Essays in Cultural Criticisms*, Baltimore, Johns Hopkins University Press, 1978, and *The Content of the Form*, Baltimore, Johns Hopkins University Press, 1987, and 'Historiography and historiophoty', *American Historical Review*, vol. 93, pp. 1193–1199.
10 P.M. Henson and T.A. Schorzman, 'Videohistory: focusing on the American past', *Journal of American History*, 1991, vol. 78, pp. 618–627.
11 McMahan, *Elite Oral History Discourse*, pp. 108, 113–117, and Paul Thompson, *The Voice of the Past*, Oxford, Oxford University Press, 1988.
12 M. Frisch, *A Shared Authority: Essays on the Craft and Meaning of Oral and Public History,* Albany, State University of New York Press, 1990.
13 R. Gordon and C. Hinton, *One Village in China* [The Long Bow Trilogy: *Small Happiness, All Under Heaven, To Taste a Hundred Herbs*], New Day Films, 1985–1988. See *OHR* Media Forum discussing this project, Fall 1988, vol. 15, no. 2.
14 E. Coutinho, *Twenty Years Later*, Cinema Guild, 1984.
15 L. Yasui, *Family Gathering*, New Day Films, 1988.

32 Perils of the transcript

Raphael Samuel

Raphael Samuel, who died in 1996, was a founder of the History Workshop movement and journal in Britain. Reprinted from *Oral History*, 1971, vol. 1, no. 2, pp. 19–22, with permission.

The spoken word can very easily be mutilated when it is taken down in writing and transferred to the printed page. Some distortion is bound to arise, whatever the intention of the writer, simply by cutting out pauses and repetitions – a concession which writers very generally feel bound to make in the interests of readability. In the process, weight and balance can easily be upset. A much more serious distortion arises when the spoken word is boxed into the categories of written prose. The imposition of grammatical forms, when it is attempted, creates its own rhythms and cadences, and they have little in common with those of the human tongue. People do not usually speak in paragraphs, and what they have to say does not usually follow an ordered sequence of comma, semi-colon, and full stop; yet very often this is the way in which their speech is reproduced. Continuity, and the effort to impose it even when it violates the twists and turns of speech, is another insidious influence. Questioning itself, however sympathetic, produces its own forced sequences, and the editing of a transcript is almost bound to reinforce this. The writer has his own purposes, and these may be only coincidentally those of his informant; irrelevance (as it appears to the writer) may be patiently listened to, but be given short shrift when he comes to single out passages to reproduce. Then, all kinds of rearrangement may seem to be called for, if the illusion of continuity is to be preserved. The writer may even resort to changing the order of speech, since comparatively few people will speak to a single point at a time (indeed the better the interview, the less likely they are to do so); nor will they always say all the things that they have to say on a subject at one go. The decadence of transcription may become extreme if the writer, not content with mutilating a text, by cuts and rearrangements, then attempts to weave it together again with interpolated words of his own. Thus, the very process by which speech is made to sound consecutive is also bound, in some degree, to violate its original integrity, though the degree to which it does so will depend upon how far the writer is aware of the temptations to which he is prone.

Let me take, as an example of these difficulties, a passage from Ronald Blythe's book, *Akenfield*, a word portrait, in recorded autobiographies, of a Suffolk village. It is an old farm worker's account of a domestic economy in the years before 1914. The picture he gives is a very bleak one, but it is so bleak indeed, so sparing of detail, that one wonders whether, in the original interview, there were not some loose ends which the author has chosen to tidy up:

> There were seven children at home and father's wages had been reduced to 10s a week. Our cottage was nearly empty – except for people. There was a scrubbed brick floor and just one rug made of scraps of old clothes pegged into a sack. The cottage had a living-room, a larder and two bedrooms. Six of us boys and girls slept in one bedroom and our parents and the baby slept in the other. There was no newspaper and nothing to read except the Bible. All the village houses were like this. Our food was apples, potatoes, swedes and bread, and we drank our tea without milk or sugar. Skim milk could be bought from the farm but it was thought a luxury. Nobody could get enough to eat no matter how they tried. Two of my brothers were out to work. One was eight years old and he got 3s a week, the other got about 7s. (p. 32)

In these lines the progress from point to point is relentless. Not a word is wasted or out of place. None of them convey the feel of a household or even, except in the most summary sense, of hardship. No phrase has been allowed to escape 'immediate punctuation'. There are no loose ends and one or two of the sentences read very much like the author's gloss on his informants original word – 'skim milk . . . was thought a luxury'. There are no dialect words or phrases, no grammatical idiosyncrasies, no sense of the personal and individual in this account of a poor home. Everything is in its place and accounted for, but none of it comes to life. I have chosen a particularly bad passage and I do not want to suggest that the rest of the book – or even of the interview from which I've quoted – is as bad as this; if it were the book would hardly have acquired so great a popularity. Usually the interviews are more rewarding, but even so they eschew superfluity and digression so often that one is left with a recurring unease: are we really being told the whole story?

Take, by contrast, George Ewart Evans's recent book, *Where Beards Wag All*. This is also about a group of Suffolk villagers, and is largely made up of their recollections, but you seem actually to hear his informants talking and ruminating about the past, instead of hearing a summary of what they said. Here is an old man who sounds very different from the old man of Akenfield:

> It's like this: those young 'uns years ago, *I said*, well – its like digging a hole, *I said*, and putting in clay and then putting in a tater on top o' thet. Well, you won't expect much will you? But now with the young 'uns today, it's like digging a hole and putting some manure in afore you plant: you're bound to get some growth, ain't you? It will grow won't it? The plant will grow right well. What I say is the young 'uns today have breakfast afore they set off – a lot of 'em didn't used to have thet years ago, and they hev a hot dinner at school and when they come home most of 'em have a fair tea,

don't they? *I said*. These young 'uns kinda got the frame. Well, that's it! If you live tidily that'll make the marrow and the marrow make the boon [bone] and the boon make the frame. (p. 212)

Although both Blythe and Ewart Evans are recording old Suffolk labourers, the voices seem worlds apart. Perhaps this can be explained by differences in method on the part of the writers – either in recording or in transcription or (quite possibly) both. In the one passage we are given mere information; in the other meanings ebb and flow. The speech is ragged at the edges; it twists and turns, gnaws away at meanings and coils itself up. There is a sense of a speaker thinking, wondering, and trying to answer the questions in his own mind rather than those of the reader. Syntax is difficult, but the final effect is memorable.

George Ewart Evans is using as much artistry as Ronald Blythe. He has probably eliminated some hesitations, pauses or repetitions from his quotation, and he has put in punctuation, but he has done this in a way which preserves the texture of the speech. Italics are used to indicate unexpected emphasis, punctuation to bring the phrases together rather than separate them, and occasional phonetic spellings to suggest the sound of the dialect. In other words, the artistry in his transcription is to convey in words the quality of the original speech.

Now that work in oral history is well under way, it would be helpful if there could be some exchange of difficulties and some discussion of method. It is possible that certain conventions can be established, at least among those who recognise each other as fellow-workers in the field, and in time these would begin to exert their effect. It would be helpful if historians could be dissuaded from transcribing speech according to the conventions and constrictions of written prose, if they could make some attempt to convey the cadences of speech as well as its content, even if they do not aim to be phonetically exact. There is no reason why sentences should make an orderly progression from beginning to end, with verbs and adjectives and nouns each in their grammatically allotted place. If the speaker allows his sentences to tail off, or remain incomplete, why should not the transcript reflect this? If his meanings emerge through digression, the transcript ought not to convey the sense of a forced march. The historian ought not to impose his own order on the speech of his informants. He retains the privilege of selection, but he should use this as scrupulously as he would when working from printed sources or MSS., indicating any cuts he has made. Within a quoted text – a long passage such as those I have taken from *Akenfield* and *Where Beards Wag All* – he should stick to the speaker's own order, otherwise he will be in danger of providing a gloss of his own instead of the original text.

The collector of the spoken word – of oral memory and tradition – is in a privileged position. He is the creator, in some sort, of his own archives, and he ought to interpret his duties accordingly. His role, properly conceived, is that of archivist, as well as historian, retrieving and storing priceless information which would otherwise be lost. At present the archive in which his material could be copied or stored does not exist; nevertheless, his greatest contribution may well be in the collecting and safe preservation of his material rather than in the use he can immediately find for it, or the way he writes it up. However intelligent and well thought out his work, it is inconceivable that his will be the only selection of texts that could be made. The information which he brushes aside as irrelevant may be just the thing upon which a future researcher will seize – if he is given the chance. Research can never be a once-and-for-all affair, nor is there ever a single use to which evidence can be put. Historians in the future will bring fresh interests to bear upon the materials we collect; they will be asking different questions and seeking different answers. And the more successful we are in executing our own research tasks, the more likely it is that their work will diverge from our own. Unless recordings can be preserved in their original integrity, and made freely available for other researchers to consult, they will remain locked forever in the preoccupations of the collector, immune to criticism, and incapable of serving as a base for a continuing enquiry.

33 Reminiscence as literacy

Intersections and creative moments

Jane Mace

Jane Mace has been teaching in and writing about adult literacy and community education since 1970. Extracted from Jane Mace (ed.), *Literacy, Language and Community Publishing: Essays in Adult Education*, Clevedon, Avon, Multilingual Matters, 1995, pp. 97–117, by permission of the author and publisher.

A reminiscence group is a group, usually of older, or elderly people who have come together in order to share recollections of their past experience. [. . .] In my experience of setting up and convening six reminiscence groups since 1980, the people who agree to join them do so because they see an opportunity to reflect aloud, with others, on their life experience. They do not, in the first instance, see their role as writers, nor, for that matter, as listeners: but as tellers; and when I and others invite them to take part, we are inviting them to see themselves primarily as oral historians. The work of facilitating such groups means, certainly, encouraging participants to be attentive listeners, as well as narrators; but, in addition, we also invite them to see themselves as potential or actual writers. [. . .]

Reminiscence work, approached as a process which is about literate as well as oral narrative, entails a series of moves between talking, listening, writing and reading. Ever since, as a literacy educator, I first began doing reminiscence work, I have become increasingly fascinated with the meaning of these moves. Neither writing nor speech are as much about *communication* as they are about *creation*: we use language, whether spoken or written, not merely to transmit something ready-made from our experience or thinking, but in order to *create* new meaning and new worlds.

The work of reminiscence, taking this view, is primarily a creative activity. I am interested in how oral accounts may become written texts, through a process in which participants have time to reflect on and develop the first version of a story – and, if they choose to do so, to be able to edit, amend and elaborate on it as a piece of writing. The published version of this process is, by definition, selective (just as any of the earlier interviews, group discussion or written drafts were). For those who make the choice to have their texts appear in print, the process entails, first, reading back a transcribed version of their talk on the page and then deciding how far that written version accords with the version of themselves that they feel willing for others (unknown) to read – rather than for a group or individual (known) to hear.

In this chapter, I want to analyse some of these issues as they occur during the course of a specific approach to reminiscence work with elderly people which I call 'lines and intersections', in order to explore in what ways a move to *writing* changes what was originally an *oral* reflection on experience. [. . .]

Over the period of a reminiscence project's life, I see a series of intersections between what seem to be lines of speech and text, creating and re-creating. At the point where these lines intersect there is a new kind of creative moment. One line, for instance, is that of an individual speaking while others are listening. Another is a group following a text while one person reads it aloud. When such reading causes one of the group to look up and offer their own comment or begin a narrative of their own, I see an intersection, exactly the kind of moment that this kind of reminiscence work is intended to encourage, with the aim of enabling a mutual enrichment between the oral and the written work.

Other examples of what I mean by such intersections are:

• when one person's account of an event (re-read as transcript) is echoed and re-told by another;
• when one member's text is brought in for others to read, following it on a copy as they listen to it being read aloud; and this reading causes another to look up and add her own anecdote or reflection to that of the author.

Two other intersections which interest me are the delayed effects of oral work in a group or an interview, as when

• recollections expressed in speech (in interview or group) stimulate either speaker or listener later to seek out documentary sources (diaries, old reports, letters) to bring back for sharing in a later discussion; and
• when the recollection of the voices and thoughts prompted by talking with others leads an individual, later and alone, to contemplate writing as they have not done before

[. . .] All the intersections I have described depend on a central interconnection: that between the individual interview and the group meeting. Individuals agree to be interviewed; some, but not all of them, subsequently agree to join a group which meets several times; during the group meetings, individuals are given the attention of the whole group. At each stage, the job of the adult educator coordinating the project is to set up these lines and encourage these intersections.

From our observations of our own practice and that of others, Jane Lawrence and I suggested[1] that reminiscence work in an adult education setting tends to follow a series of phases over a period of eighteen months to two years, from outreach and interviewing to an open meeting, after which a group forms and meets regularly, to exchange recollections and prepare some of these recollections to share with others in the form of a display, publication, or performance. This pattern was true for my own work with three such projects: the 'S.E.1 People's History Group' (1979–90), the 'Now and

Then Group' (1981–84) and the 'Cottage Homes Making History Project' (1992–93). [. . .]

Publications from reminiscence work, as I have already said, can only provide a very selective account of the authors' recollections. But their function is not only to provide a slice of social history: in an important sense, the publication from reminiscence activity is the creation of and a souvenir from the reminiscence work itself. Reminiscence work, if it is to convey something of its making, needs to include something in its published work from the interchange which preceded the individual narratives. This both makes the creative moments more visible to other readers, and brings them back to mind to those who were originally part of the group itself. It was for this reason, in one published autobiography, *A Sense of Adventure* by Dolly Davey, that I proposed interleaving Dolly's first-person narrative with extracts from group discussion between Dolly and other group members.

There was a sequence of events (and creative moments) by which Dolly's text evolved between June and December 1979:

1 First, Dolly came to a meeting of the group as companion to an older neighbour, and talked (on tape) to three people.
2 I sent Dolly the transcript, went to see her at her home, and we talked again, on tape.
3 I transcribed this, too, and sent it to Dolly.
4 She read the transcript and wrote some additional pieces.
5 I copied parts of the transcripts and Dolly's writing, and other members of the S.E.1 group read these.
6 At further meetings of the group, Dolly talked some more and her husband, Fred, joined the discussions. Again, I transcribed the tape and returned the transcripts for participants to read.
7 Finally, Dolly and I separately read the whole, I wrote an introduction, and she and I agreed the completed text.

The book which resulted consists largely of Dolly's narrative. In brief, this relates how she left her home in Yorkshire in 1930 to come to London. After four years working as a domestic and lady's maid, she met and married Fred. This is an extract from the text as it appeared in the finished book, when she relates a historic day soon after that:

> It was 18 months after we got married that he was invited to come up to my home, and he did. He rode from London to Yorkshire, on a pushbike. I left on Sunday morning at 10 o'clock on the twelve-and-sixpenny excursion, and he left on the Friday and arrived at my home the same time as I did – just in time for dinner! It was really an achievement, because he had never been up there before, and he didn't know the route. It was one great north road then. There wasn't an M1 or anything like that.[2]

On the same page, immediately after this, we included the following extract from the discussion in which Fred, with Dolly recalled this event for three others of us (Jenny, Gladys and me) in one of the S.E.1 People's History group meetings:

Fred: Her mother said that if we could get there, she might be able to get me a job. We had Eva then, our eldest. The labour money was twenty-eight shillings a week, and the train fare to Stockton was twelve and six. I said, 'We can't afford that. You can go on the train, I'll borrow a bike, and we'll save twelve and sixpence.' Twelve and sixpence was terrific, what you could get for it; and I didn't think no more of it. Borrowed a bike off a boy across the road called Freddie Kippick.

Dolly: You left on the Friday night, I left on the Sunday morning, and we practically met at the door.

Fred: I was about five minutes after.

Jane: Do you remember the journey?

Fred: Yes.

Jane: Was it raining?

Fred: No.

Jenny: You were lucky.

Fred: When would it be, in August? Must have been, because I remember picking Victoria plums by the roadside. The first night I slept somewhere in St Albans, I think it was; and the next night I spent in Doncaster racecourse. Just went off the road, like, and you were on the course. Just put a groundsheet down, and a blanket. I bought fish and chips for threepence, and a bottle of Tizer. And I started off with half a crown.

Dolly: I got there at lunchtime, and my mother was just dishing the lunch up, 4 o'clock.

Fred: I had a terrific ride.

Gladys: All that way on a bike?

Fred: Yes, Dick Turpin had nothing on me, love, by the time I got there.

The combination of Dolly's account with this interchange between her, Fred and their listeners conveys a different sense of the reminiscence process (the intersections and creative moments) than would have been possible with the first-person narrative of Dolly alone. It was that mix of telling and retelling, which was the work of her autobiography [. . .]

Part of my original question remains to be answered? What is the difference (and dilemmas) between oral and written narratives? Who makes the changes to oral transcripts, in order to transform them into written texts? What kind of changes are seen to be necessary? The editorial work is sometimes shadowy; a combination of reminiscence worker/educator and interviewee/author. Both need to see the transcript – or at least that amount of the tape which the transcriber has managed to translate to paper. A next move made by many reminiscence workers (including me) is to offer a draft of what the text might look like if some of the repetitions and (usually all) the interviewer's questions are removed. The interviewee/author then offers their own editorial changes. Some (but in my experience, a minority) reading the transcript of their speech on paper, engage in writing new material, to be added to it; fewer still choose to rewrite the whole thing. (Of the sixteen authors in this position in the Cottage Homes Making History Project, for instance, two women sat down at long-unused typewriters and rewrote much of their texts; a third wrote an additional three pages about earlier work experiences which she felt were crucial to add to the narrative; the rest expressed satisfaction with the text as it stood, apart from minor amendments).

The exercise of editorial control, however, while it entails apparently small decisions of detail, can make significant alterations to an author's meaning and purpose, in any publishing enterprise, and in community publishing it is often the most shadowy stage of the process. It is, therefore, this minority of participants who choose to rewrite their draft texts which interests me; and in this last section we shall look at a set of moves made by one woman and me from our original interview to the transcript of the interview tape, and the 'public' written text of her narrative. I am giving her the pseudonym 'Nora' because, although her final published text, as a stencilled booklet, was public and therefore quotable, I have not had her permission to quote, as I will be here, from the transcript of her interview with me.

Nora was the third of the seventeen people I visited in their homes in Lambeth between January and March 1979. Her completed text was one of four that I typed, duplicated and printed, and of which we circulated and sold a total of 120 copies (including twenty sets lodged with Lambeth libraries). What follows is an account of what she first told me, how I then edited it and how she, in turn, added to it and altered it before it became published. The very first words recorded on the tape of her interview with me were these:

> We used to live up in the top flat till 1940. Then we moved down here. I've sort of grown up here. What was I? Thirteen, when I came here.

In the next forty minutes of our interview, Nora went on to tell me of the other places where she lived, and how she had gone on to work for over forty years as an office worker with the General Nursing Council. She then introduced almost immediately what was to be one of the two main stories in our conversation: the night of the Zeppelin raid (in 1915). There followed, in the interview and transcript, some regret for the changes in the local neighbourhood and shops; some more reference to the Zeppelin raid, and then the account of an incident (her second story) which took place nearly twenty-five years later in the Second World War, when she and her brother were caught in an air raid. She talked then of an unexploded bomb which landed in her street, how everyone had had to be evacuated, and how she had defied the air raid warden and had walked down the street when she came home to get groceries. Finally, we talked about the 1951 Festival of Britain, a reiteration of Nora's feeling of regret at the loss of neighbourliness and shops, and a brief summary of her childhood years.

The first moments of Nora's life, then, actually only came up in the last moments of our interview; and in the transcript, this narrative of her childhood appears on the last page. What she said is in Quote A:

Quote A
Going back to my childhood, we lived at Clapham, and of course there was five of us in the family. My father died a fortnight before I was born. And my mother had the boarding house then, so kept us all. Well, there was a gap – there was the two girls and a boy, then a baby boy died, so there was a gap. And my younger brother and I were the two kids then. And of course the others being older, they had all their friends in and out. And we had quite a happy, oh, I had a happy home. We were never short of anything: I'm not going to say there weren't things we would have liked, but you couldn't get, you saved up for them – because my mother wouldn't have anything on hire purchase.

I sent Nora a copy of the transcript of our dialogue, and went to meet her a week later. She had read it, and wanted to add several things for precision. She also made other comments, as we talked, which I noted down. I undertook to do my own editing on the transcript, ensuring that these additions and comments were included, and later sent her the edited version to read. In my editing, I did two things which until recently I found myself doing consistently in reminiscence work since:

(a) deleted my questions to her; and
(b) changed the sequence of her recollections into a chronology of life history.

When we met again a few weeks later, she had been busy. She had got out her old typewriter, obtained a new ribbon, and had re-typed her own version of the text.

Nora and I, then, both made changes to her original talk with me to a written text for others. Through my editing, the last thing Nora had told me in the interview had become the first paragraph I put in her edited text (namely her summary of early family life, quote A). This replaced what had actually been the first thing she had told me about in the interview – a reference to the flat in which we were both sitting ('What was I? Thirteen, when I came here'). The text, I reasoned then, would be read by others not sitting as I was with her, and would need a different introduction to the author and what she had to say. Now, fifteen years after that interview, I am not so sure. As I suggested at the beginning of this chapter, reminiscence is always a present activity; and autobiographical writing, no less so. Why not begin the narrative with the author's present context?

Nora, in any case, accepted this re-ordering: but chose to amend the wording. I now want to compare what she wrote (and we published) with the paragraph transcribed from her original words. What she wrote is Quote B:

Quote B

I was born in June 1902. My father had died in May *leaving my mother with five children – the four older still at school.* Mother then took in boarders in order **to keep the home going and us all together. We were always encouraged to bring our friends home, and therefore had a happy home life.** We were never short of **essential** things: I cannot say there were not other things we would have liked, but you had to save up for them, because my mother would not have anything on hire purchase. *She was a wonderful mother, and taught us the value of things.*

The key changes Nora made amounted to:

- the *rewording* of four statements (bold type);
- the *addition* of two pieces of information (italic type);
- and the *deletion* of her original version of the number of brothers and sisters in the family: 'there was a gap – there was the two girls and a boy, then a baby boy died, so there was a gap. And my younger brother and I were the two kids then. And of course the others being older, they had . . .'

Nora was working to produce a text for a public readership; she was consciously thinking about the effect of the writing on others. So, for example, to give historical information for the reader, she added the date of her birth. The *change* in this first sentence, however, also had the effect of changing the relationship between her birth and her father's death – which, in the earlier version, was very direct ('a fortnight before I was born'). The *omission* of detail about her as a child, in relation to her brothers and sisters, removes another personal dimension – resonant, perhaps, with old emotions which Nora would rather keep private. She then altered the identity of the children who brought friends home from 'they' to 'we'. This alteration, the change to a passive voice, and the formal connective 'therefore', effectively hid her child self still further from the reader. The change is from 'they had all their friends in and out' to: 'we were always encouraged to bring our friends home'.

Did Nora feel she had portrayed herself as too vulnerable, excluded from her mother's greater freedom with the older children, or from their games? Had she decided she wanted to convey a longer time span than her very early years, to a time when perhaps she too *was* encouraged to have 'all her friends in and out'? Or did she simply want to write what she felt was a more elegant and formal sentence, with less interruption? Perhaps she wanted all three. I do not know: for, at the time, these were not the questions I was asking her.

Tags like 'Of course' and 'as I say', are common features of oral discourse, designed to include the listener in the speaker's knowledge and carry her along in the story's flow; as in: 'And *of course* the others being older, they had all their friends in and out.' In a written text when reader and writer are at a greater distance from each other than speaker and listener, it makes sense to leave it out, as Nora decided to do. But what of the change from 'and we had quite a happy, oh, I had a happy home' to 'and therefore [we] had a happy home life'? Is that hesitant 'oh' in her original voice a sigh of pleasure at recalled happiness? Is it a hesitation, as she remembers sorrow or other feelings which were also there? Or is it an adult's sympathy for her seven-month pregnant mother, suddenly widowed with five children, she herself not yet born (The intonation of her voice on the tape, which I have listened to again recently, could be interpreted in any of these ways.) In any case, in removing the 'we had quite a happy, oh, I had a happy home' Nora also erased past and present emotion, favouring instead a more impersonal and unequivocal assertion for her reading public: an authorised version that she preferred to her original, more ambiguous one.

Nora's final change, from 'any' to 'essential' ('we were never short of anything/essential things') I see as a change to precision. It was a happy home life with everything 'essential' provided for them; but as children, they were short of things they wanted. This time the text gives a glimpse of something that was less vivid in the original interview: the recalled longing of a child for 'inessentials'.

Some of the changes which Nora made to other parts of my edit of her transcript meant, as some of these did, the removal of her own presence in the text. They also took away some of the rhythm and buoyancy which had been in her original spoken version. Here, for example, is what she told me, first, about a cafe breakfast which she and others had enjoyed the morning after they had been turned out of their flats following the fall of an unexploded bomb, when the 'all clear' sirens had sounded. Her original words had been:

> We all went in there, and had breakfast, of bacon and egg, and rolls. I've never tasted bacon so good since. It was marvellous!

In her re-typed version, Nora changed this to:

> We went into the cafe and had breakfast: tea, bacon and egg, and bread and butter. It was a really grand meal and much appreciated by us all.

Her personal pleasure, voiced with enthusiasm, is gone: instead, Nora has chosen the more banal voice of a formal thank-you letter.

While there were losses, however, there was also gains in the transpositions and additions which Nora made to her transcript. In re-reading it, she had seen things she wanted to add, to explain things more fully to a readership she was now holding in her imagination. An important example, from the paragraph she wrote out, is the sentence she added as a tribute to her mother: 'She was a wonderful mother, and taught us the value of things.'

Nora and I both worked on her text: each in a different way, but both taking an active part in its shape, style and tone. Over the years since then, I have changed both my own editorial habits. Sometimes, as with Dolly's book, I have left in some of my own questions in preparing texts for publication; and sometimes I have suggested that texts begin in the middle rather than in the supposed beginning of a life. The important idea that I still work with is that the final text should be one that satisfies the authors, whether I have regrets about some of their choices or not. [. . .]

NOTES

1 J. Lawrence and J. Mace, *Remembering in Groups: Ideas from Literacy and Reminiscence Work*, London, Oral History Society, 1992.
2 D. Davey, *A Sense of Adventure*, London, SE1 People's History Project, 1980, p. 22.

34 'What the wind won't take away'

The genesis of *Nisa – The Life and Words of a !Kung Woman*

Marjorie Shostak

Marjorie Shostak, who died in 1995, was an anthropologist. Reprinted from Personal Narratives Group (ed.), *Interpreting Women's Lives: Feminist Theory and Personal Narratives*, Bloomington, Indiana University Press, 1989, pp. 228–240, by permission of the editors, author and publisher.

This essay about personal narratives is something of a personal narrative in its own right. It explores questions I have asked myself for eighteen years, since I first collected life histories in the field – questions I have never formally addressed in print, or perhaps even fully answered for myself. How best to handle the material, how to present it fairly, and how to find forms suitable for publication – these are some of the problems, both practical and ethical, that I have grappled with. My solutions have been compromises, at best, idiosyncratic constructions bound by the material and by my individual experience. Nevertheless, I offer them here in the hope that they may help clarify these problems for others working in similar ways.

First some background about me and my research. Armed with the life histories of Cora Dubois (*The People of Alor*, 1944) and Oscar Lewis (*The Children of Sanchez*, 1961), I went, in 1969, to the northern fringe of Africa's Kalahari Desert in northwestern Botswana to begin a twenty-month stay with the !Kung San (Bushmen). My goal was to collect life histories, a vehicle through which I hoped the people's experiences, thoughts, and feelings might be expressed. I returned again five years later and stayed five months, continuing this line of research along with others.

What fascinated me about the !Kung was that, although their ways had begun to change, people still maintained much of their hunting and gathering tradition: wild plant foods composed about 65 percent of the diet, and wild game meat the rest. People were seminomadic and lived in groups that fluctuated in composition, usually numbering between fifteen and thirty. Social life was essentially egalitarian, with minimal differentials in wealth, and with no formal status hierarchies or social classes. Work was hard, but there was plenty of time for leisure: women gathered about two to three days a week, and men hunted about three to four days a week. Food was usually more than adequate, sometimes abundant, and only rarely scarce. Children, adolescents, and the elderly were not regularly enlisted in the food quest.

This way of life is similar in many ways to that of our remote ancestors living tens of thousands of years ago, long before the advent of agriculture. This was the context in which our humanity formed and flourished, nourishing the remarkable breadth of human abilities as we know them today. How reasonable or difficult this way of life was is lost in the past, its shadows sketched in archeological sites, on the walls of caves, and in the very presence and persistence of humans on earth today.

The !Kung are one of a very few human groups who have lived in recent times as hunters and gatherers. They are fully modern people, in no sense remnants or leftovers from the past – physiologically, psychologically, or intellectually. All have also had some degree of contact with outside cultures, some for hundreds of years. Nevertheless, even in the most marginal areas – the only ones in which hunters and gatherers now remain – a pattern of life prevails that is likely to be similar, in many ways, to ones followed by hunters and gatherers of the past. Even modern hunters and gatherers living in diverse locales – Australia, central and southern Africa, South America, and the Arctic – share many organizational features.

I was fortunate not to be one of the first anthropologists to study the !Kung San – fortunate because by the time my first field stay was completed, a large body of data collected by other anthropologists and medical scientists was available. Without this work, my own ability to interpret, make sense of, and relate personal narratives – singular voices within a highly varied range – to a more generalized whole would have been compromised.

The life-history interviews were extensive and intimate and were conducted without interpreters. The first hurdle, of course, was learning the language – replete with clicks and tones and bearing no relationship to anything I had ever heard before. I launched my first 'interviews' after about six months. I asked pregnant women which sex child they preferred, polygynously married women what it was like to share a husband, and a handful of women and men – those most likely to tolerate my intrusive questions – their thoughts about marriage.

The results? At this distance it does not seem surprising, but at the time it felt quite devastating: my ambitious questions coupled with still-too-rudimentary language skills led to failures dismal enough that, had I had the inclination to pursue other lines of research, I might have adopted a new stratagem with embarrassing speed. But I didn't (of course), and by the end of the next six months, things had begun to look brighter: my interviewing skills and language ability had improved to the point that a 'research protocol' was developed, one that lasted until the end of my stay.

That protocol was the interview itself. My initial approach was to include anyone willing to talk to me about his or her life. After conducting a number of what turned out to be fairly tense interviews with men, I realized that they felt uncomfortable talking with me about intimate subjects – much as I did with them. Subsequently, I turned my attention solely to women.

By the end, I had invited eight women to work with me. Each set of interviews was introduced in the same way: I explained that I wanted to learn what it meant to be a woman in the !Kung culture so that I could better understand what it meant to be one in my own. I previewed the topics I hoped to discuss: earliest memories, feelings about parents, siblings, relatives, and friends, childhood play, marriage, relationships with husbands and/or lovers, childbirth, parenting, feelings about growing older, and thoughts about death. The women were encouraged to discuss anything else that they felt touched the core of their lives. An interview lasted about an hour, was conducted exclusively in the !Kung language, never included other people, and was tape-recorded. Each woman was interviewed eight or more times.

I tried to elicit specific incidents rather than generalized statements. Discreet memories were more likely to capture the texture of the women's experiences and to highlight the variations among the different women in their life stories and in their interpretations of these stories. The tape recorder was used not only for detail but to enable the reconstruction of how memories followed one another and how words were used; the goal of the final translation was to reflect a sense of the !Kung language, to preserve its nuances, beauty, and subtlety of expression.

There was considerable variation in the women's willingness to be drawn into this process, but overall the interviews were successful: each woman opened a piece of her life to me, and each piece reflected on and deepened my understanding of the experiences of the others. Of the eight, one woman stood out: Nisa.

Perhaps because she was emotionally vulnerable at the time of the interviews, or just because she took pleasure in the process of reviewing her life, Nisa put more effort into our work than did any other woman. She also had exceptional verbal gifts and articulated her story by reaching more deeply into herself and by choosing her words more deliberately than did the others. While I ordinarily was directive with them, Nisa quickly grasped the requirements and took charge; the momentum was often hers. We completed fifteen interviews during my first field trip, and six more during my second. Her story is the one I ultimately translated, edited, and published.

The result is *Nisa: The Life and Words of a !Kung Woman*. A short outline of its structure reflects the way I resolved the questions raised by the material. As I saw it, three distinct 'voices' – or points of view – needed to be incorporated. The first was Nisa's. Presented as first-person narrative, her voice was translated and edited from the taped interviews and chronologically ordered into fifteen chapters, from 'Earliest Memories' to 'Growing Older'.

The second voice was the 'official' anthropologist's, putting Nisa's story into cultural perspective: the ethnographic background to topics Nisa discussed was reviewed in headnotes preceding each chapter of her story. The third voice was my own, not primarily as anthropologist but as a young American woman experiencing another world. This voice was sandwiched on either side of the fifteen chapters of narrative and ethnographic notes. A personal introduction set up the overall framework of Nisa's story, and an epilogue summarized my second field trip, including my final encounter with Nisa and my closing thoughts.

Finding an acceptable balance for these three voices was problematic: it took many drafts before that balance was arrived at. Along the way, I confronted and tried to resolve a number of methodological and ethical questions, which can more generally, perhaps, be understood as questions about the uses of personal narrative, especially those conducted in cross-cultural settings. Five of these questions follow.

1. *Can personal narrative be used as ethnography? Since no person is ever truly representative of a culture as a whole, how should an informant's personal biases and distance from statistical norms be handled?*

One of the first issues I struggled with was how to deal with Nisa's representativeness, or lack of it. Nisa's life experiences were different in many ways from those of most other women: she had no living children, she had been married five times, and she was unusually uninhibited, if not an outright extrovert. I wanted her individual voice to be presented clearly, but other women's experiences were needed to balance it.

The interviews conducted in an identical manner with seven other women provided the broad base I needed: Nisa's experiences were compared to theirs. The base became even broader when material collected by other fieldworkers was included. My position, ultimately, was quite favorable: when Nisa said she first married at age nine, I looked up the age curve of first marriage for girls in one publication, the marriage ceremony in another, and the economic and political considerations involved in a third.[1] I found out, for example, that although on average girls first marry around age sixteen, some, especially in Nisa's generation, married as early as age nine. The headnotes summarized this perspective, enabling the reader to place in context Nisa's sometimes unusual experiences in her own unencumbered narrative.

2. *Can a personal narrative be used even as a true account of the person who is relating it? How dependent is a personal narrative on a particular interviewing relationship?*

Here, a class that I audited, taught by Vincent Crapanzano at Harvard University in the late 1970s, provided guidance. He noted that personal narratives do not exist independently of the collaborative process involved in their collection. People's stories are not in final form, shape, and content, waiting patiently for a glorified mechanic (i.e., biographer, anthropologist, or the like) to open their 'verbal tap', allowing the preformed story to escape. Instead, an interview is an interaction between two people: one, with unique personality traits and interests at a particular time of life, answers a specific set of questions asked by another person with unique personality traits and interests at a particular time of life.

In presenting Nisa's story, I therefore took care to describe our relationship as best I could: an essentially practical one which we both thoroughly enjoyed but which did not involve significantly more time than when we actually were working together. There was no doubt that Nisa, aged fifty and experiencing a difficult adjustment to menopause, filtered her life story through her then-current perspective; there was also no doubt that Marjorie Shostak, aged twenty-four, recently married, a product of the American 1960s, asked questions relevant to a specific phase of her life. I asked Nisa to tell me what it meant to be a woman; her answer was her narrative: selected memories retained through time – real, embellished, imagined, or a combination of all three – which best served her current definition of self. Her narrative thus reflected a finite contract between fifty-year-old Nisa and twenty-four-year-old Shostak; any other combination, no doubt, would have produced a different result.

3. *Can personal narratives be used freely in our own work for our own purposes? Is the collection and publication of personal narratives a boon for researchers while being a thinly disguised 'rip-off' of informants? Where does our ultimate responsibility lie?*

It was less clear for me, not working toward an academic degree, than for most graduate students and faculty what I had to gain by working on Nisa's narrative. Indeed, had I not been personally 'hooked', feeling almost a sense of responsibility for publishing it, the course of my life during the past eighteen years would have been very different. But I *was* hooked, although never without ambivalence.

The first time its value was impressed upon me was soon after I returned from the field and passed around some preliminary translations; they were met with tremendous enthusiasm and encouragement. An article I subsequently published was followed by a call from the Harvard University Press, inquiring about my future plans for writing a book.

It took ten years before *Nisa* was finally published. Work on the book was only one of the reasons it took so long; I was also intensely involved in other projects. By the time I made a firm commitment to completing *Nisa*, I had translated her twenty-one interviews twice: once after my first field trip, and again after my second. Having become more proficient in the !Kung language, I felt I could render more subtle and accurate translations from the original tapes.

However smoothly or roughly my life might otherwise have gone, I have nevertheless clearly profited by having published the book. But what did Nisa gain? The actual interview process seemed a positive one for her, and, in some small way, it may even have helped her. Our initial work took place during an emotionally stressful time: the recent onset of menopause was bringing home the finality of her childlessness; by that time, all of her four children had died.

Talking about her life, reviewing the births, the deaths, the marriages, the many additional loves, the highs and the lows – all while 'teaching' me about life and womanhood – Nisa also took pride in her skillful handling of the situation. She reveled in the knowledge that she was teaching me the 'truth' about life, while others, she would explain, often taught me 'lies'. She benefitted in other ways (as did the other women), with presents and with an agreed-upon payment. Status also accrued to her among the !Kung for being involved with 'anthropologists' work'.

But there was more. Nisa responded to our talk as though she appreciated the chance to contribute to something 'bigger' than what was typically asked for by the anthropologists. She was well aware that I planned to bring the verbatim material I collected back to the people with whom I lived. They, I had explained, would be interested in learning about !Kung women's lives. She approached the tape recorder as an ally, one with tentacles reaching out to worlds beyond her own. She jokingly referred to it as an 'old man' – a symbol, perhaps, of a wise, experienced presence that could receive the full import of all she hoped to say. During the very first interview, she expressed this concern directly: 'Fix my voice on the machine so that my words come out clear. I am an old person who has experienced many things, and I have much to talk about.'

She was also aware of the fragility of talk – and of experience. Reflecting on the interview process itself, she once said, 'I'll break open the story and tell you what is there. Then, like the others that have fallen out onto the sand, I will finish with it, and the wind will take it away.' Perhaps she recognized that with me there was a chance that the wind might *not* take *all* of it away.

Indeed, during the last interview of my first visit, she spoke about my taking 'our talk' with me when I left. She said she would collect more talk and 'save it for me'. When I returned four years later, she reminded me of this: she said she hadn't forgotten her promise and collected things to talk to me about. This and other responses to the challenge of our work suggested that the interviews were a welcome outlet for her, a satisfying and otherwise unavailable avenue for self-expression.

What about more material rewards? When I returned to the field, I spoke to Nisa about my desire to publish her account – something that would not, in fact, happen for another six years. I likened the final book to products for sale in stores, a parallel with which she was already familiar. If it sold, I told her, she would get something out of it. If it didn't, she might not.

Her initial response was, 'If this is what you want to do, that's good. But you're the one who has to do it, not me.' I explained that, indeed, it would be years of my work, but that it was her story. Concerned about her privacy, we agreed that I would use pseudonyms. Together we settled on 'Nisa' and other names. Giving her consent, she said that if the book sold, she would like some cows. I reviewed with her the most problematic stories – those involving violence, and others that might be seen as personally compromising – and asked if she wanted any of the material excluded. She answered without hesitation, 'all our talk, all that this "old man" [the tape recorder] has heard, wants to enter the talks'.

Nisa has received her cows and continues to receive gifts from me. As a result, she has become one of the people with wealth and stature in the changing world of the !Kung. I have contributed additional time and money helping the community she lives with. But where my ultimate responsibility lies in relation to her is still somewhat unsettled. L.L. Langness and Gelya Frank discuss some of the subtleties of the interview relationship.[2] They point out that informants sometimes harbor 'unexpressed expectations' of anthropologists. In the process of receiving attention from outsiders, usually from those with higher status than their own, informants may become vulnerable. They cite the claim of cross-cultural psychologist David Guttman that '[informants] too often experience our transient gestures toward equality as massive seductions', and recommend close supervision of anthropologists not only by experts in their particular field but by – and here they may overestimate the wisdom of these practitioners – clinical psychologists or psychiatrists as well.

These concerns are legitimate, but they can also be exaggerated and even patronizing to informants. In Nisa's case, I think the seduction worked both ways. I didn't enter Nisa's life until she was about age fifty, and when I did, it was for a very short period of time. When I returned four years later, her life in the interim had clearly been fully lived, although she had not forgotten to 'collect' stories for my return. Even if my impact on her was larger than I recognize, my belief now, as then, is that – except for the later financial rewards – I have played an essentially minor and positive role in her life.

That does not justify my shirking from what I see as a continuing responsibility toward her and her community or underestimating what she gave. She offered weeks of her time, telling her story with gusto, courage, imagination, and humor, along with thoughtfulness, occasional sadness, anger, and longing. For me, 'talking her talk with me' and trying to make sense of it involved many years of my life. The ultimate gain for either of us can hardly be considered to be financial. Nisa gave her talk; I tried to keep the wind from taking its beauty away.

4. *How does the editing and translation process affect how personal narratives are used? What factors must be considered when translating, editing, and presenting a personal narrative once it has been collected?*

Shaping Nisa's narrative required considerable discipline and attention to detail. A total of twenty-one interviews – representing between twenty-five and thirty hours of tape, all recorded under less than ideal conditions – were translated twice, a process that was tedious and time-consuming. The initial translations were literal, word-for-word transcriptions written in English, but with unusual expressions noted in !Kung. Following a second field trip, I translated and transcribed the initial fifteen interviews again, along with six additional interviews conducted during this subsequent stay.

These translations were broken into segments, usually the length of a story, and were roughly edited. These segments were then grouped, usually by topic, sequenced into loose chronological order, and more finely edited. Details and embellishments from incidents discussed more than once were combined into one account. To clarify the flow from one story to the next, missing or unclear time markers were inserted (for example: 'Not long after', or 'Some time passed'). All questions of clarification, all diversionary comments, and all directive suggestions on my part were eliminated from the final narrative.

In addition to this editing, an overriding structure needed to be created, a 'literary' one that would grab the attention and maintain the interest of American readers, To that end, I experimented with a number of formats. My first approach treated each interview as its own chapter and followed it with ethnographic and personal commentary. This didn't work: the interviews lacked consistent dramatic and emotional integrity; they didn't stand up well on their own. Comments and asides as well as occasional interruptions from the outside frequently disrupted the flow of talk. Or, the conversation jumped around, restlessly, from topic to topic, settling on a clear direction only half-way through. Or, I would introduce a string of interruptions to clarify the flow of details, or merely to have an unfamiliar word or expression defined. The overall progression of interviews did have an interesting character, but ultimately it was not enough to be the most effective form in which to present Nisa's story.

The main alternative was the chronological presentation – the one I chose because it made sense, not just to me but even in terms of !Kung narrative form. Although they had no prior experience with my specific life-review format, Nisa and the other women had no trouble adopting the chronological approach. In Nisa's first interview, we did a 'once-over', quickly reviewing the grand scope of her life from her earliest memories to the interview-present. The second interview started at the beginning again. Throughout that one, and the next thirteen, we proceeded again through her life story, this time much more slowly, stopping often, touching events in depth, carefully moving forward in time until we reached the interview-present. At the end of each interview, we would discuss where we might pick up the next day. The next day sometimes began with a review of the end of the previous day's interview. More typically, it would start with a recent dream, or Nisa would tell me that she had prepared her thoughts in a certain direction for our talks that day.

The six interviews conducted with Nisa during my second field trip, four years later, clarified material collected during the first trip: we reviewed stories I hadn't previously understood, went over unclear time sequences, added material in areas that had been underrepresented, and reviewed events in Nisa's life during my four-year absence. For both sets of interviews, no constraints on time or on the total number of interviews existed; we determined the end of each one, and the series as a whole, at the point both of us felt her story had been told.

Nisa had her own sense of narrative style. Most of her stories were told with a beginning, a middle, and an end; some were short, others lengthy. Usually, the chronological, or linear, mode I encouraged prevailed, although sometimes she, or I, would jump to a related topic. If I interrupted to ask a question, she might reprimand me, 'Wait, I'm getting to that. Now listen.' At times, the process of narration itself became her focus, as when she described the dissolution of one of her marriages and ended her story with, 'That's all, and we lived and we lived.' An unusually long silence followed. Then she added, thoughtfully, and slowly, 'No, there is something in my heart about this that isn't finished. My heart is still shaking. The story hasn't come completely out. I'm going to talk more about it until it does. Then, I'll go on to another. Then, my heart will be fine.'

The chronological approach also found support in !Kung traditional story-telling. The !Kung exercise sophisticated narrative pacing and sequencing skills in a rich body of oral myths, those describing the time 'in the beginning' – when God walked upon the earth and animals were still evolving from people – as well as in their animal tales, stories of character and intrigue, dependent on chronology and an orderly succession of events. Similarly, frequent recountings of hunts and experiences while gathering require subtle verbal cues and accurate time sequencing. It is possible that had I been less directive, a fairly comparable indigenous narrative form would have emerged.

But with few conventions to guide me, each editing decision was guided by my ultimate goal: to present Nisa's unique experience of life – as expressed in her interviews – as a distinct voice within the context of !Kung culture as I, and other researchers, saw it at that time. Because, as 'objective' as each researcher tried to be, our collection and interpretation of data were inevitably influenced by the intellectual 'umbrella' we shared. (For example, since then, the !Kung's long history of contact with other cultures, which we were aware of but did not emphasize, and the 'myth' of their isolation have come much more to the fore.) My headnotes reflect a view generally shared by anthropologists in 1981, and, in some ways, the narrative material chosen does as well.

As described above, questions of clarification were eliminated, duplicate accounts were collapsed, extraneous story fragments were excluded, and a chronological sequence was imposed. In addition, a small number of stories I didn't understand, and anecdotes and minor incidents about people not central to the themes of the narrative (such as customs of or gossip about the neighboring Bantu-speaking people) were also eliminated. Stories that covered duplicate ground, and that would have impeded the general flow of the narrative, were also left out (for example, dreams that were similar to ones included, or secondary stories about lovers – none important or containing details not already in the narrative; even in its published form, many readers find the narrative too heavily weighted in that direction and find some of Nisa's numerous amorous encounters tedious). There is no doubt that I also held subtle and not-so-subtle biases toward the material.

Nowhere were the editing choices more delicate than in the translation process itself. I would not be honest without admitting that there were times when I was tempted to 'adjust' the narrative beyond what could be considered justifiable. Nisa, as those familiar with the book know, is a strong, earthy, sexual, highly self-contained but not always exemplary character. I was sorely tempted to leave out some of her less appealing traits to highlight those that ennobled her. A slight shift in the translation, so subtle that no one but I

would know, could also have achieved this end. How much grander Nisa
might have appeared had I translated everyday idiomatic speech into literal,
poetic utterances! 'The sun rose' is prosaic; 'The dawn broke open the darkness' is poetry. But if every !Kung child and adult, dull or witty, described the
sunrise in the same standard way, then, when Nisa used those words, my
responsibility was to translate it into standard English – which I tried very
carefully to do as I went along.

Another translation problem was the use of repetition. In a culture with
strong oral traditions, repetition often becomes part of the ritual form. For
example, as one memory ended, Nisa often said, 'and we lived and we lived
and we lived'. (The phrase might actually be repeated several more times.)
Although a more 'literary' expression could have been employed, such as ' a
few moons (or rainy seasons, etc.) passed', Nisa used repetition: it symbolized
the passage of ordinary time, bridged two stories or parts together, and acted
as a dramatic device around which to organize her thoughts – a technique
used widely by other storytellers. In translating her words, such strong strings
of repetitions did not work in English, and I often substituted 'and time
passed', or 'and we just continued to live'. In a sense, this epitomizes the
problem of translation: the !Kung expression conveys a different sense of
time than do the English ones – a sense of the past that is more immediate
and continuing. Instead of losing that completely, I left some of it in, trying
to retain its flavor, but substituted words or reduced the repetitions drastically
to make it work on the printed page.

My editor at the Harvard University Press once asked in jest, but with
telltale nervousness in his laugh, 'You do have interviews with Nisa on tape
. . . don't you?' Ultimately, Nisa's narrative and the assumption of my having
edited our work responsibly and professionally have been accepted on faith.
Not that this faith has been misplaced; it has not. Nevertheless, the handful
of people who could have checked my translations never have. I suppose they
never felt the need; most of them had worked with me in the field, had
evidence of my language abilities, had heard many similar stories themselves,
and had heard enough gossip about the personal nature of my work from the
!Kung themselves that they trusted that I did what I claimed to have done.
Above all, they knew enough about the !Kung to know that Nisa's narrative,
even when it surprised them, rang true.

5. *Can personal narratives be used as a mirror or guide to our own lives?*

If they could not, most of us would probably be much less keen on doing
them. After all, they are difficult to obtain (especially in foreign contexts),
laborious to work with, and tricky to present. Methodological obstacles
are vast: becoming proficient in another language, developing rapport, learning interview techniques, insuring reliability of data, adopting appropriate
sample size, maintaining objectivity, and recognizing one's own biases.
Ethical issues are no less complex: protecting an informant's privacy (within
the community as well as without), educating informants about the collaboration so that they truly can give informed consent, recognizing the informant's

sensitivity toward us and ours toward her or him, and translating, editing, and presenting the informant's 'true' voice in such a way that the
idiosyncratic and the generalizable can be distinguished.

The impetus for surmounting these obstacles came, for me, from the realization that if I didn't do it, no one else was likely to. After all, fewer and fewer
!Kung remained connected to their fast-disappearing hunting and gathering
traditions, and the other anthropologists who worked with them had different
research interests. While a well-told story of any person's life is of value, one
that came from a culture which reflected a most ancient form of human
organization – a form in which all our human potential originally became
manifest – seemed potentially to be of great significance. When I devised my
project, I hoped I would learn from the !Kung what it meant to be human.

The impetus for collecting personal narratives, however, came from an
overlapping but distinct set of issues: recently married, living in the field with
no other outsiders, I found fieldwork much more isolating than life as I had
known it before. I learned much about the !Kung language, their !Kung way
of life, and who they were as people. Setting aside, as best I could, involvement in my own world, I nevertheless remained an outsider, there to interpret and bring back pieces of another way of life. In truth, I was drawn to
interviewing people because I felt lonely; I hoped, perhaps, that 'structured
friendships' would allow me to share in people's lives and feel part of the
community. After initial difficulties, they did just that.

A few years before *Nisa* was published, my literary agent sent part of the
manuscript to numerous publishers. At one house it was rejected because, it
was claimed, Nisa's voice wasn't interesting enough; she sounded as if she
could be 'the woman next door'. Despite the rejection, I was elated. That was,
after all, what I had been hoping for. Nisa – at home, in the Kalahari Desert,
part of a society with no chiefs, no status hierarchies, and minimal inequities
of wealth, semi-nomadic, small-scale, and minimally materialistic (each
person's possessions weigh about twenty-five pounds) – was being mistaken
for 'the woman next door'! Her experiences must reflect something universal,
after all.

My desire to find a guide, someone to mirror my own life, had been
realized. Nisa's voice reverberated not only within me but within others.
Considering her story, perhaps it is not so surprising: a woman living in one
of the most remote areas of the world, facing life with courage, humor, spirit,
and dignity, who, despite repeated tragedy, carried on with a sense of entitle-
ment to enjoy what was yet to come. She had told this story with care and
generosity, a story with echoes of an ancient time, reflecting themes tens of
thousands of years old.

CONCLUSION

One of the people Barbara Myerhoff interviewed for her study of a community of aging Jewish immigrants in California was Shmuel. He had come

to the United States from Eastern Europe early in this century, at a time when pogroms against Jews were rampant. Speaking about life in Poland before it was all 'wiped out like you would erase a line of writing', he said about death: 'It is not the worst thing that can happen for a man to grow old and die.' He continued, 'But if my life goes, with my memories, and all that [the knowledge of a way of life destroyed by Hitler] is lost, that is something else to bear.'[3]

It is for Shmuel, Nisa, and the silent others they represent, as well as for ourselves, that we should continue to record these lives and memories. The ethical and methodological problems may be formidable, but they are small compared to the goal. Indeed, the most important ethical message regarding life histories is not a restriction but an obligation: we should make every effort to overcome obstacles, to go out and record the memories of people whose ways of life often are preserved only in those memories. And we should do it urgently, before they disappear.

No more elegant tool exists to describe the human condition than the personal narrative. Ordinary people living ordinary and not-so-ordinary lives weave from their memories and experiences the meaning life has for them. These stories are complex, telling of worlds sometimes foreign to us, worlds that sometimes no longer exist. They express modes of thought and culture often different from our own, a challenge to easy understanding. Yet, these stories are also familiar. It is just this tension – the identifiable in endless transformation – that is the currency of personal narratives, as they reveal the complexities and paradoxes of human life. As we cast our net ever wider, searching for those close as well as those far away, the spectrum of voices from otherwise obscure individuals helps us learn tolerance for differences as well as for similarities. What better place to begin our dialogue about human nature and the nature of human possibilities?

NOTES

1 R. Lee and I. DeVore, *Kalahari Hunter-Gatherers*, Cambridge, Mass., Harvard University Press, 1976; L. Marshall, *The !Kung of Nyae Nyae*, Cambridge, Mass., Harvard University Press, 1976; R. Lee, *The !Kung San*, Cambridge, Cambridge University Press, 1979; N. Howell, *Demography of the Dobe Area !Kung*, New York, Academic Press, 1979.
2 L.L. Langness and G. Frank, *Lives: An Anthropological Approach to Biography*, California, Chandler & Sharp, 1981.
3 B. Myerhoff, *Number Our Days*, New York, Dutton, 1978, pp. 73–74.

35 Presenting voices in different media
Print, radio and CD-ROM

Peter Read

Peter Read is an Australian Research Fellow at the Australian National University in Canberra. First published as 'What oral history can't tell us: the role of the CD-Rom', *Oral History Association of Australia Journal*, 1994, no. 16, pp. 87–90, reprinted with permission from Peter Read and the OHAA.

The difficulty of transferring oral history interviews to a form which can be shared by others has long been discussed by oral historians. It is a wider problem than how to turn voice into print. How does one render what was essentially a personal, intimate and one-to-one communication to a form which is impersonal, public and one-to-many?

Three alternatives have long been available to the oral historian. The first is the literal transcription; generally the original recording and the transcription are lodged together in an archive such as that of the National Library. Good transcription, though, is highly skilled and prohibitively expensive. Unless one is engaged in interviewing former cabinet ministers, one is unlikely to have transcription provided by the commissioner of the interview. The transcription, like the original tape, will probably have a very small audience unless someone shapes it either into a radio broadcast or a book.

Radio, which bypasses transcription altogether, is the second method of sharing the interview with a wide audience. One would imagine that a good interview will make a good broadcast, but that is not always the case. Radio, it seems, abhors a silence, though silences can sometimes convey as much as words. Pauses longer than a couple of seconds are likely to be shortened on radio, whatever their emotional or dramatic significance. Sentences will vanish and whole minutes of talk will be transposed in the producer's effort to make the good narrative, which has too often been regarded as the same thing as good oral history. Some excellent works have of course come from broadcast oral histories: *Taim Bilong Masta* and *Prisoners of War* are two of many expertly produced and moving programs produced by the ABC's Oral History Unit and a number, such as *Lifeblood of Footscray*, have been produced outside.

But some speakers will seldom make it to the airwaves and some speaking styles will be considered too mannered to use at all. Consider the following verbatim transcription from an interview with a woman born in 1903, as she recalled the opening of the first Parliament House in Canberra in 1927. She had an exceptional memory, a most interesting tale to relate and her words required virtually no editing.

Could you tell me about that Aboriginal man, the very old chap?

Oh yes. There was . . . I can't think of his name, but he was the oldest Aboriginal around Canberra at the time and er, they dressed him up and two police was guarding him. And they brought him to the first row of people at the ropes and they put him beside where I was standing. So when the procession started, of course people were saying, 'Here comes the King and Queen' and he got under the rope and had his hand out to shake hands to the King and Queen. And the police grabbed him, brought him back and put him there and he waved and waved like everyone else. And er, oh, I'd say about an hour afterwards, the Queen and her guard walked down and, er, spoke to the police, and they brought them over to where I was standing and he was sitting, and she shook hands with him and presented him with a tin of biscuits. And he was excited to think that 'the Missis', as he called her, gave him a present and er, everyone around went talking to him and he finished up breaking down and he cried like a child. He had, I suppose, so much attention given to him.

A tape editor would have only to remove the four 'ers' to present the listener not only with a historically important story, but a piece of prose that needs neither correction nor embellishment.

But the interview was no use to radio. Slow delivery and idiosyncratic speech rhythms ensured its rejection by the Australian Broadcasting Commission. And I can understand the reluctance of putting it to air. The pauses *are* very long, the intonation *is* unusual. So this historic tape has not, to my knowledge, been heard or transcribed and read by anybody and, unless someone finds its existence mentioned in the catalogue, it is likely to remain undisturbed in the vaults of the National Library's Oral History Unit.

A further problem, unresolved by either broadcast or printed text, is how to convey to a mass audience the deep emotion of an intimate interview. Some of the most moving interviews in the literature of oral history not unnaturally concern profound personal experience – the torpedoed ship, the brutality of a prison camp, the hunger and despair of the Great Depression. In my own work in Aboriginal oral history, I have recorded stories of massacres, children being snatched by welfare officers, police torture and sexual abuse, not because I was seeking the sensational, but because the speakers were seeking, through me, a wider audience.

The consciousness of a wider audience in no way reduced the intense, sometimes agonised, emotion of the speakers as they related a story of great trauma. In so doing, a relationship was established between the interview and subject in which the interviewer assumed a role not unlike that of a good friend, even a counsellor. It is a relationship which, though temporary, raises a variety of ethical questions and responsibilities which I won't pursue. The point here is how the interviewer can best convey not only the story, but the emotions by which the story was related to the unseen mass audience.

Here is a recent example drawn from my current work, which investigates the way in which non-Aboriginal Australians form and talk about their attachments to particular places. In this extract, a woman describes her former life at Cribb Island, a village on the edge of Moreton Bay. She and her family had lived in the area practically all their lives, until in 1973 they were evicted before the area was levelled for the extensions of Brisbane Airport. Within a year of receiving notice of eviction, the family had, under duress, sold their self-built family house to the Government.

> How did the kids take it, do you think?
>
> Well my second daughter Patricia has never forgiven anybody for it. She said, 'I cannot take my children to see where I used to live, where I grew up, where I was born, and I cannot take my kids to show them where I went to school'. She was very bitter about the whole thing. She's really a motherly mother, if you get what I mean, she likes a . . . the family orientated child . . . child, she's nearly . . . But she's . . . the other children aren't as bitter about it as what Patricia is. She really . . . whenever she talks about it she says, 'I can't take my kids to see where I went to school', she says. 'That really hurts.'

This was a heartfelt statement but, in terms of what was to follow, not particularly emotional. Adapting the passage for broadcast would present few problems, though a text transcriber would ponder how to punctuate the last phrase. 'That really hurts', which is spoken with a rather greater vehemence than the previous sentences. There is no satisfactory way in which the reader – though not the listener – could be alerted to the emotional change.

It was then apparent that the increased intensity of the last phrase was a preparation for a more serious narrative. The woman now took a deep breath and began to describe something which was much more personal and affecting: how she watched the destruction of her family's home:

> The elderly couple I was talking about earlier . . . I used to do their washing and ironing and their grocery shopping and things like that. Got a bit difficult once we had to shift. But I dropped off their groceries and I came around and went past my house. And I saw it being pulled down. And I just stopped the car and I burst into tears. Just seeing them pulling it to pieces, was just . . . something you'd strived [for], and John had worked very hard to get for us. Just to be pulled to pieces. Just terrible. And I know other people felt the same way.

The radio producer, I suspect, might reject the sound version of this passage as too broken, too hard to follow, perhaps even too personal. There are too many pauses and changes in dynamics, though it's interesting to reflect that, if the story of Cribb Island was turned in to a radio drama, the actors would be called upon to heighten the emotion implied in the script with all the dramatic technique they could muster.

The third of the standard forms of presentation of the oral history interview is the edited text or published book. But there are intractable problems, barely apparent in this written version of the interview, which present themselves to the text editor: how, first, to reveal the change in pace and intensity between the first and second passages. An editor should, arguably, try to punctuate the last phrases to convey the intensity of the whispered, agonised, 'Just terrible', followed by the firmer emotional closure by which the speaker was telling the interviewer that she desired to say no more on the subject. A literal rendering of all the spoken words, set out in accordance with the speech rhythms, might be:

> The elderly couple I was talking about earlier . . . I used to do their washing and ironing and their grocery shopping and things like that. Got a bit difficult once we had to shift. But I dropped off their groceries and I came around and went past my house.
> And I saw it being pulled down.
> And I just stopped the car and I burst into tears.
> I just . . .
> Just seeing them pulling it to pieces.
> Was just . . .
> Something that you'd . . . strived, and John worked very hard to get for us.
> Just to be pulled, just to be pulled to pieces.
> Just terrible.
> And I . . . I know other people felt the same way.

Without hearing the sound of the voice, readers might think that the first version is powerful enough in its own right and they would be right. It is obvious that at least one person felt deep emotion at the destruction of Cribb Island and, if that was the intention of the editor, the purpose is achieved. The second version may convey that emotion more clearly, but without the actual simultaneous speech, such spacious setting out can look a little over-dramatic or even affected. But, whichever the version preferred, I think that oral history has failed us. *An* emotion of grief and loss has been conveyed but not *the* particular forms of grief and loss experienced by a particular speaker. Oral history conveys the former well, and that is what we historians, readers and listeners expect of it. But it often fails to carry the particular intensity of the interview because of the gulf between the one-to-one communication and the one-to-many.

We've considered the literal transcription, the radio broadcast and the edited book. Each has its limitations in carrying the total meaning of an oral history interview – that is, both the memories of a certain time and place and what may have been also an intimate, emotional and personal exchange.

The CD-ROM offers a fourth avenue of communication. Recently Jay

Read and I recorded and edited an Aboriginal oral history of the Northern Territory, called *Long Time Olden Time: Aboriginal Accounts of Northern Territory History.* Its original version,[1] published after ten years of lobbying unsympathetic publishers, presented the oral accounts as both a book of transcriptions and a set of tapes, so that one could either read or listen or, ideally, read and listen simultaneously. Though the tape and text formula was a great improvement on text alone, the difficulties were many, not least that if one loses one's place one has to start again at the beginning of the tape. In 1993 *Long Time Olden Time* was released as a CD-ROM, for which the reader needs an Apple Macintosh CD-ROM reader. The most obvious advantage of the electronic form is that one never loses one's place.[2] At the flick of the mouse one can go to page 33 or 133, the cursor alights at the top of the page and the voice starts simultaneously.

There are other advantages of the CD-ROM format. One can use the 'search' facility to find all the stories from a particular area. One can highlight a particular area of the map to bring up an enlarged scale version of the same area. Schoolchildren can type notes or answer questions on one side of the screen. And the potential remains for more advanced uses. An American poetry series has a video of the poet reading a work in the bottom left-hand corner of the screen, while the text of the poem and relevant images are juxtaposed in the rest. Why not have the original verbatim tape on the bottom of the screen and the edited version on the top?

Its easy to get carried away by the techniques and possibilities of electronic razzmatazz. One doesn't want to emulate the early music aficionado who kept on building improvements into his harpsichord to make it sound louder and more sonorous – to find that he'd invented a piano. Movies have already been invented!

The real strength of the CD-ROM in oral history is that it has the capacity to advance a mass audience towards an understanding of the intangible moments of the real interview. Text and sound together, especially when controlled by the viewer, is a much more personally involving form of communication than either a broadcast or a book. We are no longer at the whim of the broadcaster who finds pauses and unusual speech rhythms distracting. The extended, possibly over-dramatic text layout of the second version of the interview above is entirely appropriate when there is the actual speech to listen to at the same time. If the particular intensity of shared moments can be recaptured only in the memories of the participants, the CD-ROM communicates, I believe, a great deal more than standard oral history formats commonly do.

There is an irony in trying to extol the virtue of a non-print technology through the printed word. All I can do here is to reproduce an extract from *Long Time Olden Time* and invite readers to imagine the electronic version of the book, or better still, to try it out.

The story is a familiar one: an Aboriginal woman, removed from her family in the early 1920s, was placed in the Roper River Anglican Mission in the

Northern Territory at the age of two or three. She grew up seeing her parents once a year, at Christmas. She valued Christian stories above all else because, she said, she was taught to 'know about a White God story, teaching us what to do longa White man way, that story. They didn't let us go to mother and fathers.'

Over many years this full-descent Alawa woman ceased to speak her language and one of the most affecting parts of a memorable interview was her attempt to recall the native tongue she had been taught to discard so long ago. On the tape her voice is barely audible, the pauses are excruciating. The story looks so inconsequential. There is no strong narrative, no climax. Thoughts half-begun fade to silence. This extract would be rejected for both broadcast and book.

Nor should that be surprising. The printed transcription, read without the soundtrack, loses so much that it becomes almost a translation from a foreign language. The soundtrack alone is hard to understand. On the CD-ROM the pauses, the almost audible searching of the mind for words long forgotten, are reproduced without editing. The format, I believe, comes closest to allowing us to apprehend the poignant moment at which the tragedy of a personal history and the tragedy of a people's history are shown as one.

Did you call that missionary mummy and daddy?

Yeah, we usually do that. They usually nursing us.

But they call this crow, from this Alawa . . .

Ah, let me think for that . . . ah. They call some . . .

I couldn't . . .

They call . . . ah . . . emu . . . they call it *juwidjuwidi* . . .
Yeah. That's from Alawa.
The kangaroo they call it . . . *girrimbu, girrimbu* . . .
And that *jidbirlirri*, that plain kangaroo out la [longa] plain, the great big one.
They call it then,
just think for that,
they usually call it then.

And that goanna I told you for that.

And the snake they call it *yangala*, that snake.
Yangala.

NOTES

1 P. and J. Read (eds), *Long Time Olden Time: Aboriginal Accounts of Northern Territory History* (book and three cassettes), Alice Springs, Institute for Aboriginal Development, 1992.
2 P. and J. Read (eds), *Long Time Olden Time: Aboriginal Accounts of Northern Territory History*, CD ROM, Firmware, 1993.

36 Angledool stories

Aboriginal history in hypermedia

Karen Flick and Heather Goodall

Karen Flick is a Yuwalaraay community history researcher. Heather Goodall teaches history at the University of Technology, Sydney, Australia. This is an edited version of a paper presented at Apple University Corporation Conference, Brisbane, September 1996.

New media offer historians both difficult challenges and exciting opportunities. There are many obstacles to historical work in interactive multimedia (IMM) format, which range from the need for extremely diverse skills through to the continual technical frustrations of limited size and bandwidth. Yet the capacity of IMM to link different types of content, known as hypermedia, holds out the enticing possibility of having the immediacy of people's voices and faces as they retell their memories engaged with historical analyses from many perspectives, and of relating memory and its expression very directly with other types of historical sources such as print, image and archival sound.

Perhaps even more exciting is the possibility that 'making history' in hypermedia will allow us to open up questions we can use to better understand memory and the way it is used to make and remake the past. For example, the different contexts in which we retell our memories have a major impact on the process of composing our understandings of the past. Interactive media demand that historians consider their audiences in a way that few other media, even film, do. We are forced to reflect on and anticipate our audiences' desires, intentions and questions, as well as to consider the context in which the people we have interviewed and recorded were themselves responding to their real or intended audience. This characteristic of interactive history is just one of the many which defines it firmly as public history, the exciting arena of engagement and negotiations between popular cultures and scholarly inquiry.[1] Interactive multimedia is therefore not only a tool for new presentations of history, but a tool for reflection on our roles and our craft itself.

'Angledool stories' is an on-going joint project by Karen Flick, Yuwalaraay community history researcher from north-western NSW and south-western Queensland and Heather Goodall, a historian at the University of Technology, Sydney. We are exploring how far new technologies, including hypermedia or IMM might be useful in resourcing Aboriginal community history research. The project aims to produce an experimental

CD-ROM to document aspects of the history of Aboriginal people in north-western NSW, from Collarenebri to Brewarrina. These lands include those of the Yuwalaraay, Kamilaraay, Murawari and Ngiyampaa-speaking peoples, who call themselves collectively 'Murris', and many of whom continue to live in the towns of the region. Angledool was once a small town near Goodooga, at the centre of the region, where around 200 Aboriginal people lived before they were forcibly moved to Brewarrina in 1936. There they were held under Protection Board control until many escaped to the other towns of the region in the early 1940s. Memories of Angledool unite the Aboriginal communities of the area, recalling strong community ties as well as the harsh repression of the 1930s.

The 'Angledool stories' CD-ROM project was initiated because we were frustrated with conventional forms of information storage and retrieval. We had questions already formed which led us to choose IMM as a possible solution. Yet we have found that work on the project has generated many new questions for us about history and memory. These questions have involved the relations between memory, history and representation in 'new media', but they have also allowed us to explore some of the awkward realities of cross-cultural research and representations, and some of the continuing pressures of colonialism on communication among indigenous Australians and between them and their colonizers.[2]

PROJECT AIMS

The 'Angledool stories' project is an attempt to draw on research already conducted in relation to the north-western NSW area, the results of which have often been lodged in libraries and archives far distant from the Aboriginal people whose individual and community history is being 'investigated'. We have a strong interest in the recorded audio and video material which tends to focus on life story from the early twentieth century and on traditional knowledge. There has been a fair amount of oral history and culture recorded, in the linguistic work of Luise Hercus and Janet Mathews, which included life story as well as songs and traditional narratives, and in the life history recordings conducted by ourselves and many Aboriginal researchers.[3] But we have found that there is also a wealth of material recorded earlier in written or photographic form, in government archives, personal diaries, missionary papers, pastoral property records and family photographs. We had hoped to be able to bring all of this material 'back home'. But we found, as have many other hypermedia authors, that CDs are only so big and when we try to fit audio and video recordings on, our space shrinks alarmingly. So we have had to be selective and are now trying to offer at least a taste of the many types of cultural and historical material which can be found around the holding bodies of the country which relate to the north-west.

The intended primary audience for this program is the Murri peoples of the north-western region. For those local Aboriginal people, we hope that the completed hypermedia program (and indeed the process of creating the program) will add to existing information about family and community history. We are aiming further to have the program assist Aboriginal community researchers with information about the location of materials and examples of how historical narratives may be constructed and used to explain the past and its relation to the present. We expect that the program will also be of interest to non-local Aboriginal people, but with the different roles of informing them about an area other than their own, with which they may not be familiar, but which will give them case study materials for comparisons with their own area. Finally, we hope that the program will be used by non-Aboriginal audiences, and should inform them by offering insights into Aboriginal experiences and perspectives on rural north-western history and culture.

The project aims to produce the 'Angledool stories' CD-ROM and then evaluate it thoroughly with both Aboriginal and non-Aboriginal audiences, in rural and urban settings, with small groups of users followed up by focus group discussions. This evaluation process will begin with the stage three prototype, now under development and hopefully completed by the middle of 1997. From this we hope to be able to draw conclusions about the strengths and limitations of this medium in resourcing and representing Aboriginal community history. We hope further to observe and record any differences which emerge in the responses of culturally differing audiences in their use of the program.

THE CONCERNS WHICH LED US TO USE INTERACTIVE MULTIMEDIA

Navigation not dependent on literacy

We have wanted from the outset to use the potential of IMM for non-written communication to build a form of representation which did not depend on literacy. Our authorities are often elderly Aboriginal people whose life experiences have demonstrated great courage and resilience. We want them to feel comfortable navigating around this program, and using it as a teaching tool to instruct younger Aboriginal people or non-Aboriginal employees of their organizations. This will be more likely if they feel confident they will not be forced to demonstrate that segregation of the school system in NSW from 1902 until the 1950s meant that many of them were denied the opportunity to learn to read and write. Low levels of literacy are common among the very group whose knowledge and analyses we are seeking to acknowledge and respect. It is therefore an important goal for us to develop a system of navigation which does not suggest that literacy is necessary to hold knowledge or to teach it. For this reason, we are seeking to use the spoken word to convey navigation instructions, in parallel with the continuing importance of an oral culture for passing on historical knowledge in north-western Aboriginal communities.

However, there are some problems with this approach. One is the fact that another consequence of institutional racism in north-west NSW has been poor health and in particular a high level of ear infections and consequent loss of hearing. So while in everyday life people may depend strongly on spoken communication, there is no guarantee that they will be able to hear effectively in the less than ideal circumstances of variable sound reproduction on computers. For this reason, we are moving to develop a navigation system which will depend as much on visual non-written clues as on spoken instructions.

Audience included in design process

We felt that the only way we could develop a program which would be comfortably used by Aboriginal people in the north-west was to include them in the design process. One of the project leaders, Karen Flick, is a member of that community, but we appreciate that IMM communication may be alienating to an Aboriginal audience despite Aboriginal direction, unless we actively explore what seems most comfortable and engaging to the priority audience in the context in which they will use it. For this reason, we have conducted three field trips in the last eighteen months to discuss the project and demonstrate earlier versions of the prototype to north-western Aboriginal communities. During 1996, we began to draw on the expertise of Brad Steadman, an Aboriginal artist who lives in the north-western town of Brewarrina and who has made an intensive study of the traditional graphic styles of the region. Brad has contributed to details of the new version of the prototype currently under development, and has agreed to an ongoing review and commentary role to provide feedback on the project. The necessity of maximising community consultation and involvement in the project reduces the speed with which the program can proceed. The cost of an undoubtedly slow development time has proved well worthwhile so far in that it has allowed an increasingly rich input by Aboriginal people into the design and its content.

Acknowledgement of distributed authorship

There is a need to recognise the many, active family and community history researchers among the Aboriginal communities in north-western NSW. The work of many Aboriginal people has created the atmosphere where the 'Angledool stories' project could be interesting and welcomed by people in many towns in the area and those living away in metropolitan centres.[4] They deserve recognition and acknowledgement, and the hypermedia form should allow this to occur. Just as important, the history of research in colonial circumstances has left a legacy of anger at academic researchers claiming

Aboriginal knowledge as their own, and has also fostered a tendency for Aboriginal researchers to be defensive of their own work, anxious to protect ownership and control from claims, not just by academics but also by Aboriginal people in other towns and communities. These concerns have been expressed as the need to protect Aboriginal intellectual property, but they have also been manifested in tensions between Aboriginal people involved in research projects. This is an outcome of the repressive conditions in which people have had to undertake community research, and it would be a valuable contribution if hypermedia's potential for many voices to be heard and many authors to be acknowledged could play a positive role in reducing anxiety about ownership. A continuously evolving web site may eventually prove to be the most effective form of hypermedia in allaying fears about encroaching claims to authority in relation to family or community histories.

Indication of conflict and disagreement among primary sources

This occurs for many reasons and all are of great interest to historians: for example, there are differences of perspective and interpretation between Aboriginal people and the official reports and explanations of policy found in archives, indicating differing political power and experiences. There are also differences in memory between individuals which arise from different perspectives on events and different interests. Discrepancies arise too between memories and archival sources because the speakers were either poorly informed or actively misled at the time of the events being recalled. Each of these conflicts or discrepancies is an important indication of historical processes and relationships, and needs to be noticed and, where possible, explained.[5] Just as important, discovering such discrepancies is an inevitable part of being a historian, and many of the Aboriginal people who are now so actively researching family and community history have found such discrepancies and are struggling to make sense out of them to fit them into a meaningful story which explains the complexities of the past. If the 'Angledool stories' project is to be useful in enhancing the research and interpretation skills of Aboriginal people at a community level, we must design ways of indicating conflicts and suggesting ways of understanding how they arise and what they mean. Hypermedia allows the building of many links between elements of text, images or sound, and so potentially it can address this problem of contradictory readings and associations between sources in a different way than would a linear, textual explanation of contradiction. We need to achieve this and at the same time to ensure that the program remains simple enough to use without confusion or disorientation.

SOME ISSUES WHICH HAVE ARISEN DURING THE PROCESS OF DEVELOPMENT

Tension between place and storytelling in interface design and in conceptualization

In describing new media, a widespread approach relates interface design to spatial metaphors, and it is an indication of the complex ambiguities of this issue that, as Ulmer[6] has pointed out, IMM is often described using the colonial language of exploration, discovery and capture. There is no question that place has a fundamental role in Aboriginal cultural and social expressions, as it does with other colonized indigenous people.[7] In Australian oral traditions, the knowledge in any narrative or song is frequently structured around the place where events occurred or for which the protagonists are the custodians.[8] It is also true that place is enormously important for the way members of all societies situate and retell their memories of the past.[9] Therefore, our first prototype used a map and the concept of place as the major navigation metaphor. Users of the CD could select a place and find stories, archival text or images about events which occurred there. We used what looked like overlays to attempt to explain the co-existence of various types of knowledge mapped onto the land for different cultural and historical contexts:

- traditional knowledge (including public origin stories for the major sites in the region but also some sound recordings of indigenous languages),
- invasion (events during the period of violent invasion),
- pastoral (life working and living on pastoral stations), and
- 'towns' (living in engagement with the state and local authorities).

However, we became concerned that the metaphor of place was too static to give full expression to what we saw as the striking and dominant characteristic of the history we were engaged in. The form of oral traditions and oral performance of memory is strongly narrative and dramatic. It is, after all, the *stories* about places which are at the heart of what we are doing. And as historians we, ourselves, have a fundamental interest in historical analysis, which is at base the construction of narratives which seek to contextualize and explain cause and effect of change over time. We found in field trips that people were strongly interested in stories, both in narrative, explanatory accounts of events, and also in life stories. They were looking for ways to hear about the life of their grandfather or auntie. The metaphor of place, in the form of a map, awkwardly broke up the narrative continuity of individual life stories lived in many places and of overview analyses of dynamic process which occurred across space and time. So we shifted focus to explore the ways in which storytelling can become a more fundamental part of the structure and form of our program, rather than just the content.

Our next draft, the second prototype, suggests our response which was to reconceptualize the program as having three lobes. Each is a separate way to learn about the past, reflecting different ways that stories are composed from memories and evidence from the past. The lobes, with their provisional titles, are:

1 *Life stories*: in this section the lives of six Aboriginal people from the area were to be represented. We presented edited sections of audio recordings which were to be accessible in chronological order, simulating a linear account of the person's life, and linked with relevant photographs, family tree information and a time-line that linked the individual life with the larger events of the area. This was to resemble the individually focused autobiographical mode of telling about the past.

2 *Theme stories*: in this section, Karen as historian/storyteller would introduce the user to overviews of the major themes or processes which most oral history recordings from the area refer to. These are School Segregations, Children Being Taken Away and Enforced Migrations. Each of these processes generated resistance and protest, which has often coalesced into regional and state-wide political organizations, and this political response will be explored within each thematic overview. This section was therefore like the processes of analysis and synthesis which historians, whether local or academic, must go through to develop contexts for individual memories.

3 *Place stories*: This continued to be the major section of the content, with a series of overlying maps which gave access to the memories of many people who collectively tell the stories of events at each place in the area.

   • In the *Country Map* (or Culture Map) users would find traditional knowledge in the form of stories about relations between people and land and of examples of each of the area's languages.

   • In the *Invasion Map*, there would be accounts of Aboriginal transgenerational memories of conflict and violence over land. The early maps of the region, from the 1840s and 1850s, show the limits of the presence of squatters during the times when fighting was continuing over ownership and access to land.

   • The *Pastoral Map* would allow the telling of the rich history of Aboriginal lives spent living and working on the large pastoral stations of the area (until the 1940s in many cases), through memories, photographs and documentary evidence drawn from pastoral property records.

   • The *Towns Map* would introduce users to the complex history of Aboriginal people's interactions with local townspeople and authorities, and with state government agencies like the Aborigines Protection and Welfare Boards, from the 1880s to the 1960s.

Overall, the graphic design and arrangement of the Place Stories section suggested the collective, social processes of memory, in which people recall through conversations and questions with their peers and with their audiences. This social dimension of memory and the popular, community-level teaching of history has been well recorded in Australian and international social history investigations.[10]

As we begin to design the third prototype, we are interested in Abbe Don's suggestions[11] that narrative forms themselves are a feasible structuring metaphor in hypermedia design, which demands an attention to audience and engagement. We would like to make storytelling, which needs strongly linear forms, an even more dominant structuring metaphor. But a characteristic of oral storytelling is engagement with an audience, which allows for interruption, questioning and comment – which allows, in other words, for interaction as an integral part of the construction of meaning of the story.

This is a process which has been observed at work in many oral cultures, including indigenous Australian and Native American.[12] While we can program some possibilities for interaction into the CD, to address seriously the issues of interaction with the audience and the realization of distributed authorship, we anticipate that we may need a web site. We are now reviewing web sites which we feel achieve the combination of a strong collection of primary source material with the presence of sound analysis and innovative engagement with the audience. So far, the best examples we have come across in the specifically history area include *The Flight of Ducks*,[13] under constant creation by Simon Pockley at RMIT in Melbourne, and *The Valley of the Shadow*[14] from Edward L. Ayers at the University of Virginia. We do not see the possibility of a web site supplanting the 'Angledool stories' project altogether, and currently we see that the *Valley of the Shadow* project team have moved to archive some of their growing site in the form of a number of CDs. However, we feel that a flexible approach which builds on the strengths of each form to fulfil the goals of north-western Aboriginal historians could mean that we have an associated and on-going web site which is complementary to the CD itself.

Considerations of mode of address

When Aboriginal people are telling their families or small, informal groups of other Aboriginal people about their memories of the past, they frequently share humorous anecdotes (although often with a strong political or moral lesson), or accounts of childhood which stress the positive, nurturing experiences of family and community life, sometimes even including the better-liked Protection Board staff.

At public forums, however, Aboriginal people are not speaking about their past as they would to a small family group: instead, they are making an intervention in a pre-existing and ongoing public discourse and debate. That public level of oratory or testimony has to be composed with a sense of audience: who is listening and what are they asking to hear? What needs to be said? At a recent Aboriginal History and Heritage meeting in Sydney, most people's narratives included a major strand about the way the past can prove the intensity of repression and its impact on Aboriginal lives. Another strand was the assertion of people's continued sustaining of traditional lifeways, practices like hunting and visiting important places. Both of these strands can be seen as engagements with a wider non-Aboriginal Australian audience which often demands that Aboriginal people need to prove their 'authenticity' as 'Aboriginal' on the one hand, and also prove that they have suffered in order to justify their demands for recognition and compensation.

It is therefore crucial to consider the importance of the venue and the context in storytelling. There are interactions occurring when people decide how to express their memories of the past, and the level of public exposure is an important factor because it carries with it implications for the audience who will be listening. There are collective forms and shapes to oral narratives as well as individual styles. At a more private or community focused level, Aboriginal people may choose different elements of their memories to shape differing narratives, which may make similarly powerful statements against racism and injustice, but may do it by humorously belittling the white managers, or even by laughing at the misunderstandings by Aboriginal people of white instructions. These forms of oral performance, which have well-understood meanings within Aboriginal communities, are not only less well understood outside but are also not the messages that wider, non-Aboriginal audiences are demanding.

In her study of Flathead Native American storytelling in Colorado, Therese O'Nell has written about similar diversity of storytelling in different contexts and with different audiences. She was initially confused about the meaning of stories about conflicts with whites because they elicited what seemed, to her, to be inappropriately light-hearted responses from Flathead audiences. O'Nell eventually recognized, however, that the meaning lay not only in the content of the stories, although this was important, but in the interactions occurring between storyteller and audience. As she explained it:

> By shifting focus from the story to the act of storytelling, from the narrated event to the narrative event, the significance of the encounter is understood as emerging in an act involving both narrator and listener.[15]

In the new work we are undertaking on 'Angledool stories', we are giving careful attention to the question of the mode of address, and to how we present people's telling of their memories, their stories. This clearly relates to the need to be aware of that wide interaction between Aboriginal speakers and audiences. Questions then include how, if our primary audience is northwestern Murris, we should script Karen's form of address as storyteller: is this a public performance or a more intimate internal community storytelling session? How should we select, edit and frame the oral material already recorded: to emphasize the public performance or an internal community conversational voice? Karen has been very concerned to include the rich diversity of internal community conversational voice, which reflects her experience of memory and place. Should we shape the users' experience so that they engage with both public and community modes? The only way to work this out is through continual discussion and demonstration with the Aboriginal communities involved, to find out what feels comfortable and what feels out of place and awkward. This consideration of mode of address, which has emerged as we began to script and program the prototype, returns us to our design principle of including the audience as much as possible during the design process, in 'formative' evaluation, rather than just in a 'summative' evaluation after the programming is complete.

Our project is also, however, an intervention in the public sphere as well as the private, community-level processes of research and history making. We hope to open up possibilities, perhaps allow some of the complex, active, rich and eccentric stories of Aboriginal history and the history of interactions between Aboriginal and non-Aboriginal Australians to take their place on the public platform as an accepted and desired strand for storytellers and audiences alike.

NOTES

1 For a valuable and perceptive discussion, see D. Glassberg, 'Public history and the study of memory', *The Public Historian*, Spring 1996, vol. 18, no. 2, pp. 7–23.

2 A more extensive discussion is found in H. Goodall and K. Flick, 'History and interactive multimedia: hi-tech gimmick or a new form for community history?', *Public History Review*, 1995, vol. 3.

3 H. Goodall, *Invasion to Embassy: Land in Aboriginal Politics in NSW, 1770 to 1972*, Sydney, Allen & Unwin and Blackbooks, 1996.

4 H. Goodall, 'Working with history', *UTS Review*, May 1996, vol. 2, no. 1.

5 These issues are discussed more extensively in H. Goodall, 'Aboriginal history and the politics of information control', *Oral History Association of Australia Journal*, 1988, and 'Colonialism and catastrophe: contested memories of nuclear testing and measles epidemics at Ernabella', in K. Darian-Smith and P. Hamilton (eds), *Memory and History in Twentieth Century Australia*, Melbourne and Oxford, Oxford University Press, 1994.

6 G. Ulmer, 'Grammatology hypermedia', *Postmodern Culture*, January 1991, vol. 1, no. 2.

7 A North American example is demonstrated in K.H. Basso ' "Stalking with stories": names, places and moral narratives among the western Apache', in S. Plattner (ed.), *Text, Play and Story: The Construction and Reconstruction of Self and Society*, Washington, DC, American Ethnological Society, 1984.

8 See examples in R. and C. Berndt, *The Speaking Land: Myth and Story in Aboriginal Australia*, Ringwood, Penguin, 1988; in D.B. Rose, *Dingo Makes Us Human*, Cambridge, Cambridge University Press, 1992 (from Central Australia); and in K. Langloh-Parker, *Australian Legendary Tales*, Sydney, Angus and Robinson, 1953, (from north-western NSW). These issues are discussed in Goodall, *Invasion to Embassy*, Ch. 1.

9 Glassberg takes up this issue in 'Public history and the study of memory', and it is explored with stimulating perception in W. Cronon: 'A place for stories: nature, history and narrative', *Journal of American History*, 1992, vol. 78, no. 4, pp. 1347–1376.

10 For a comprehensive analysis of these investigations, see P. Hamilton, 'The knife

edge: debates about memory and history', in Darian-Smith and Hamilton (eds), *Memory and History*.

11 A. Don, 'Narrative and the interface' in B. Laurel (ed.), *The Art of Human-Computer Interface Design*, Reading, Mass., Addison-Wesley, 1991.

12 Far Western Regional Land Council, *The Story of the Falling Star*, Aboriginal Studies Press, 1988; Basso: ' "Stalking with stories"'; and T. O'Nell: 'Telling about Whites, talking about Indians: oppression, resistance and contemporary American Indian identity', *Cultural Anthropology*, February 1994, vol. 9, no. 1, pp. 94–126.

13 http://www.minyos.xx.rmit.edu.au/~s9501395/spockley341.html

14 http://jefferson.village.virginia.edu/vshadow/vshadow.html (subtitled: 'Living the Civil War in Pennsylvannia and Virginia', created by a team led by Edward L. Ayers at the University of Virginia and published by the Institute for Advanced Technology in the Humanities).

15 O'Nell, 'Telling about whites, talking about Indians'.

37 Children becoming historians

An oral history project in a primary school

Alistair Ross

Alistair Ross is Faculty Research Director in the Department of Teaching Studies at the University of North London. Reprinted from *Oral History*, Autumn 1984, vol. 12, no. 2, pp. 21–31, with permission.

This article describes how children of 7 to 10 years of age can acquire certain historical skills through oral history work, and suggests that the practice of oral history may have qualities that make it particularly suited to the development of these skills. Two classes, one of 7–8 year olds, the other of 9–10 year olds, were involved in a project that looked at the history of their inner London school and focussed particularly on the school's evacuation to Wiltshire in 1939. Although the work stretched over five months, it was not continuous – Christmas and other priorities intervened – and most of the work was concentrated in two months in the spring of 1983.[1]

Fox Primary School is a local authority maintained school with some 350 pupils, drawn from a wide range of ethnic, national and social groups. There are perhaps more professional parents than are typically found in inner city schools. The building, which dates from 1937, is the third which has housed the school. The school was originally founded as a charity school by Caroline Fox in 1842, and taken over by the London Schools Board in 1876 and rehoused in a new building at the Notting Hill end of what is now Kensington Church Street. This building was demolished in a street widening programme, and the school was moved to its present site, just south of Notting Hill underground station. The local area has changed considerably over the period: there have been particular social changes since the early 1960s that have meant that few of the ex-pupils are still in the immediate locality. Nevertheless, we were able to compile a list of ex-pupils, some of whom were at the old school building in the 1910s.

We had several objectives in choosing the history of the school as a suitable focus for study. The subject would be child-centred, and allow contrasts to be made between then and now. It would be relatively local, so that the social environment could be directly compared. We had already a certain amount of documentary resources: maps and photographs from the local library, extracts from the school log books from the Greater London Council archives. These only provided a skeletal framework, initially of more use to the teachers than the children. It was teachers who had to make an initial selection of materials to photocopy at the archives and teachers who had to direct children in their interpretation of the documents. The decision to include a series of interviews with ex-pupils and ex-staff of the school allowed the children an opportunity to develop a wider range of skills than would have been possible using documents alone. Children were able to handle a much greater volume of material than would have been possible through sources that they had to read. They would be more likely to confront problems of bias and contradiction in what they were told. They would have to make crucial decisions about which material to select for presentation – they couldn't possibly include in their histories of the school all that they heard. Paul Thompson has suggested that some of these values are developed in oral history work by students, and particularly emphasizes the sense of excitement that can be fostered, and the understanding of bias.[2]

We hoped that our programme would develop:

- Children's oral skills, of listening, questioning, talking, discussing and arguing. These skills sometimes seem to be under-valued by parents and teachers, and need as much attention as the more formal language skills of reading and writing, if children are to be fluent communicators;
- Social skills of interaction, discussion and co-operation;
- The development of intellectual concepts of social change, tradition, conflict and cause;
- Skills of empathy with individuals of a different generation;
- Intellectual skills of sifting and selecting evidence, and making informed decisions about editing their sources;
- Understanding of the problems and values of historical evidence, in particular, problems of bias and contradictory evidence;
- Ability to make records and narrative accounts of what had been found.[3]

We planned to start with interviews of people we had invited into school, moving backwards in time until we reached the evacuation at the beginning of the Second World War. The village of Lacock, to which the school was sent, is still the home of many of the families who were hosts to the evacuated children, and we planned to take all our children to the village to interview groups of hosts and ex-village children, to discover if their memories matched those of the evacuees. Our final stage – not reached because of difficulties in tracing ex-pupils – would have been to push back further in time with memories of the 1920s and early 1930s.

Arranging interviews was not as easy as had been anticipated. An ex-teacher, who had started teaching at the school in the late 1950s, was our first interviewee. Two ex-pupils, now local librarians provided details on the 1930s and 1940s. Many children also interviewed their own parents about their school days; although this usually lacked the direct connection with our school, it did give us a useful range of comments on education in the 1950s, and had the added value of giving a useful cross-cultural perspective reflecting the ethnic groups within the class. Interviews at Lacock were somewhat easier to arrange; despite the acquisition of the village by the National Trust, much of the community remains intact. Mrs Copeland, an assistant at the Fox Talbot Museum in the village, collected together a group of more than a dozen ex-hosts and children, and evacuation organisers such as the former billeting officer from the WRVS and the village postmistress. In turn, these led to further evacuees, because we found that many of the Lacock families still kept in touch with their former charges, now all in their fifties. Three ex-evacuees came to the village with us, including one who had not been back since she had returned to London after the war.

Our initial interviews were rather stilted. There was a tendency for the children simply to sit and listen to what the adult decided to tell them. Questioning was hesitant, with children tending to repeat questions already asked and to act as though they were waiting for their turn to speak. This seems to have been a stage at which the children were still a little uncertain of how they were expected to behave: the idea of questioning and discussing things with an adult other than a teacher in school was relatively novel. They were not generally accustomed to discussions in class that required them to collaborate and to listen to each other as well as to the teacher. Many classroom 'discussions', when analysed, are series of dialogues, each between the teacher and an individual child. Children await their 'turn' to speak and don't imagine that the other dialogues are of any concern to them.[4] However, interviews soon became easier in this respect, partly because the children saw that teachers were now in a somewhat different role. We were no longer in control of the information giving process, and the fact that we too were asking questions demonstrated that we were learning as much as the children. Our questions also gave the children examples on which to model their own.[5]

After each interview and discussion we asked the children to produce some kind of written record of what they had found most interesting. This was done partly to provide a record of what had happened, but principally to focus children's attention on the need to select from the extensive range of information given in the interviews, each from 30 to 45 minutes long. This exercise demonstrated one point very clearly. The interviewees had been briefed to try to talk about their own personal experiences and if possible not to generalise about the period. Nevertheless, most of them felt obliged to surround their recollections with more general statements about social and political conditions of the time. Yet subsequent discussions and written accounts almost always focussed entirely upon the personal recollections; statements about the broader context were either not understood or did not attract sufficient attention for them to be recalled. But the personal reminiscence would often be turned into a more general and impersonal statement. For example, on the infant school day in the 1930s:

> In the old Fox School all the young children used to have a rest in the hall after lunch. Each child had a mat as a blanket, all the blinds would be pulled down and the lights be turned off. (Wanda, 10)

There was often a particular interest in the interviewee's opinions and the reasons they suggested for events. Where one child generalised about:

the drill they did every day to teach children to put gas masks on. The younger children had Mickey Mouse gas masks so it would not frighten them. (Emily)

others took away more personal impressions of the gas masks:

he said they smelt rubbery and took a while to get used to. (Tania)

Their appearance and the strong smell of rubber frightened the smaller kids, so they invented the Mickey Mouse gas mask. (Sam)

The evacuation itself was also a subject of interest:

He went with the teachers and the rest of the school. It sounded very exciting, but he didn't like it, so he came back to London to stay with his mum. (Sam)

He hated staying in Lacock . . . He stayed with two other boys with an old lady. His parents fetched him back after only three weeks. (Martha)

Interrogation skills developed. There was one particularly vivid account by an ex-evacuee:

So in the morning we all said goodbye to our mums. We'd been issued with a gas mask in a cardboard box . . . Nobody knew where we were going, we all met at the school, four classes of 11 to 14 year olds. And we all got in the train and went to where we went . . . We didn't know where we were going at all, and all those children didn't know where we were, and nobody wanted us at all.

More vigorous interchanges between children and adults followed this:

Were all the windows taped up?

No, that happened later, when – do you know why all the windows were taped up?

Yes – so the windows wouldn't shatter –

Yes, that's right, and that's something that happened when the bombs dropped, and there were quite a few bombs around here . . .

Again, it was the personal details that dominated the written accounts.

I was only interested by the way they got rid of the children in Henley. They went round Henley in a long line knocking on doors and the people took them very unhappily. Mr Williams was last. He took a home with an elderly couple. He liked them. (Emily)[6]

Most of the girls were picked first. (Jenny)

Most of them chose girls because the girls could do the washing and things like that . . . He stayed there a whole year. When he came back to London all the children were playing in the street because there was no school. (Berta)

Slowly the parents began to think that there would never be bombing so they began to take their children back again. (Sam)

This led to some good empathetic writing when children were asked to imagine themselves as evacuees.

We were lined up: boys in one line, girls in another. I was in the girls' line with my suitcase in one hand and in the other a gas mask and a book for the train journey. I kissed my mum goodbye. We trailed our feet all the way to Paddington Station. I kept repeating in my head 'What's going to happen to me, I wonder, what's going to happen to me' . . . I had never been on a train or in a car before so I was quite worried. We got onto the train . . . (Tania)

At this point we experienced some difficulty in getting enough interviewees and the children were next asked to interview their parents about their schooldays. This had a particular advantage in that it introduced an important cross-cultural perspective, reflecting the diverse national origins of the class:

My father went to a school in Durclar. He did English, Nepalese, Sanskrit, Science and Mathematics. (Pamir)

He told me that in the morning before school a couple of school monitors would go outside and look for boys and girls climbing mango trees or paddling in streams. (Leila)

They went to school in the village. They were in a very big class . . . there were children of any age and one teacher, named Senorita Palma. (Berta)

She went to a school in Malaysia. She was seven when she started. She wore a uniform of a white blouse with a three-pleated skirt, with half a square on each shoulder with a belt. (May-ai)

One parent had been to Fox school itself when young. She had decided views on the nature of modern primary education:

She thinks that Fox school was completely different about thirty years ago. It was strict . . . I think it's strange that my mum thinks the education was better then. Because you would've thought that people thought up new better and advanced ways to teach people. (William)

Personal reflections and opinions began to appear more regularly in children's accounts:

At school in north Germany her first teacher was male, he was very strict.

My mum did reading, writing and maths. She liked geography best though I'm sorry to say she was bottom in everything. (Patricia)

I asked her if the school dinners were nice, and she said 'alright', but I am sure that when she was at school she thought they were disgusting. (Kate)

Then daddy said he liked his school dinners. He hesitated then said that he liked them. I was so surprised. (Karenka)

Personal detail and incident still dominated narratives:

She put her tongue out at the milk woman and the milk woman saw so she ran after her. She went into the toilet and the milk woman couldn't find her. If she was caught the punishment would be having her legs smacked or she would stand in the corner. (Becky)

These parental interviews were, in a sense, 'practice' interviews, but also had a real value in adding new bases for comparison.[7]

The project spread. Two classes had been involved from the outset (though the examples so far have been drawn only from the older class), but some children in other classes also joined in by interviewing their parents and grandparents. One seven year old wrote:

When my nanny was little she went to Portobello Road school. Her teachers wore black and her teachers looked fierce with her hair in a bun though she was very nice . . . She had dinner it was awful as it was cooked by older children learning to cook there . . . (Jessica)

Oral skills were beginning to develop, as were some ideas of change and tradition. These concepts were perhaps more firmly grasped by the older children, for the 7/8-year-old class seemed to employ a deficiency model to compare the past with the present ('they didn't have . . . then', etc.). There was also, I believe, a developing understanding of the nature of historical evidence, though this did not become clear until after the next stage of the project: following in the footsteps of the evacuees to Lacock.

We had seen the Fox school log book for the 1930s, and its final undated entry following the July 9th, 1939 record of Sports Day:

For records of the emergency school opened during wartime, please refer to the temporary log book.

The temporary log book was missing, but the headmaster of the school in Lacock had sent us a copy of his log book entries:

Sept 2nd. War with Germany
Government scheme for evacuating mothers and children from certain areas in event of outbreak of hostilities with Germany was put into operation. War almost certain. 59 children with 5 teachers (including Hd. Master) arrived on Sat. 2nd and were billeted in Lacock. Staff of Lacock school and myself assisted.

3rd Sunday – War declared on Germany. About 400 children and teachers were expected to arrive, but instead 93 mothers with 141 children, mainly from Shepherds Bush arrived at short notice about 12.30 and were distributed amongst residents of Lacock and Bowden Hill . . .

At Lacock there were fourteen people who had agreed to talk with us. We split the children into six separate groups, each interviewing two or three people and reporting back to the others on our return. We did not want to spend all our necessarily limited time in the village on interviews, and each group also toured Lacock Abbey, the former family home of the Fox Talbots, where lessons had been held for the evacuees during the war. Most of the children were accompanied by one of the ex-evacuees, who was able to point out particular places – the cloisters where school milk was drunk, the sacristy where they left their coats, and the rooms where lessons were held.

The shape of the interviews tended to follow that of the previous ones – an introductory narration by two or three adults, then questions and discussion. We found, however, that children were now more ready to focus the adults' attention on particular incidents, and generally to intervene. This was partly due to the development of their interviewing skills, but was also encouraged by having two or three adults together, who themselves tended to interrupt and correct each other; children undoubtedly modelled themselves on the adults. The tendency for a group like this to conform in their narratives, as Paul Thompson suggested might happen, does not appear to have occurred to any significant extent.[8]

The following extracts are from an interview conducted by older children.

Mrs H.   A lot of them were very very friendly, and a lot of them settled and some of them didn't and they went back, they just couldn't settle.

Mrs W.   And we do hear – and now I hear from mine regularly every year, and he's married with three children.

Mrs H.   It's funny, because Edward Small that Mrs W. had here, I was friendly with Lily Small, his sister, that lived down the street, 15 West Street. I was friendly with Eddie too.

Child 1   *Was there anything special, special work, that children had to do when the war was on?*

Mrs W.   I don't know, I don't think so. I do remember this, the children had to grow their own vegetables, we were told, you know, we had to grow as many vegetables as we could in those days.

Mrs H.   Oh yes. And they were allocated a little bit of ground in the Abbey gardens, and they all had a little tiny plot each, and they all had to grow what they could on there.

Mrs W.   'Cos I suppose they had their lessons on gardening and that. And it was surprising what they brought, I know what Eddie brought home, it was amazing, how he got on, not knowing much about gardening and that, but he took to it.

Child 2 *How old were you when Eddie lived here?*

Mrs W. I can't remember, um, going back a good few years now . . . in my thirties.

Mrs H. I know when they were coming I was at the Lacock school, and we were called together to say evacuees were coming and to meet them, and would we be as kind as possible and make them settled. Most people were quite happy about it. Just speaking for myself, I made loads of friends, and we used to get around with them, you know, in gangs. We really made them settled as best we could.

These children had been talking to a wartime host and a woman who was a child when the evacuees arrived. Another group, this time of younger children, talked to hosts and an evacuee (Mrs G.).

Mrs F. They were full of beans, they were too lively for Mrs B., so they were parted. They had to be parted. They didn't stay with the lady what picked them in the first place . . .

Mrs J. And they came to us.

Mrs G. – She's talking about my sister and myself.

Mrs F. Yes, we don't know about the others. They were good – but they were full of beans. And they were with people who were rather old, you see . . .

Teacher *So they were split? How did you pick the children?*

Mrs F. We came up here. I think it was, to the school. We said which we'd like, sort of thing, but it didn't always end up like that . . .

Mrs J. Well, I suppose some would say well, we've got girls, so we'll have girls as well.

Child *When the children arrived, were they different from the village, the children in the village?*

Mrs J. Oh well, there was a difference, the conditions, the surroundings, was different. 'Cos I think the children thought it was a terrible place.

Mrs G. Yes, well the village children used to tell us that they thought all London children were dragged up from the gutter, they called us –

Mrs F. – Oh, did they?

Mrs G. Called us guttersnipes, and things like that, said we lived on bread and dripping . . .

Mrs F. Anyway, there was sure to be a little bit of trouble between the two [groups of] children, bound to have been, because, I expect you see, you all thought 'where are the fish and chip shops?' and things like that.

Mrs G. Oh no!

Mrs F. You didn't?

Mrs G.   Oh no, fish and chip shops weren't something we went to.

Mrs F.   You didn't have them surrounding you?

Mrs G.   No, there weren't thousands of fish and chip shops. But what we couldn't get over was the idea of being in separate houses.

Mrs J.   Oh, I see, separate cottages.

Mrs G.   Yes, everybody had their own house. Quite different to what we were used to in London . . .

Mrs G.   When we got off the train at Chippenham, we had labels tied to our coats, and gas masks, in square boxes, and we went to a hall near the station and were given a carrier bag with apples, an orange, a bar of chocolate and tin of condensed milk, and some Horlicks tablets, and that was supposed to be our rations for the day, to go to the people we were staying with.

Mrs F.   Some of them had never seen apples on trees before!

Mrs G.   I think a lot of the London children went a bit beserk at first.

Mrs J.   Well, that was natural.

Child   *Did any of the village children tease the London children?*

Mrs J.   Ah yes!

Mrs G.   We fought tooth and nail – mostly in the village High Street. One winter, when the snow was very deep on the ground here, Wally chased after one of the boys. The village boys filled their snowballs with stones, and one hit me on the eye. And Mrs F.'s brother Wally, he chased him all the way down the High Street and gave him a good box round the ears when he caught him.

Mrs J.   Well, that's not fair, they used to do that when I was at school, it's not fair.

Mrs G.   But there was a lot of rivalry between the Lacock children and the London children . . .

Mrs J.   Yes . . .

Mrs G.   And Mr Steele [the London headteacher] was always telling us that we had to show them that we were just as good, if not better, and this was why we had to put the panto on . . .

Child   *Were there any really bad fights with the town children and the village children?*

Mrs G.   I think the boys fought quite hard. Boys do a lot anyway, about things, but I think the village boys and the London boys used to get into real scraps.

Mrs J.   But they didn't go about with knives and that like they do now!

Mrs F.   Oh no, nothing like that!

Mrs G.   They just used their fists.

Mrs F.   It was fist fights.

Mrs G.   But there weren't all that many fighting, just sometimes they'd fall out.

Child   *Did the girls fight?*

Mrs G.   No, not really. They were very jealous of each other, because the

London girls used to look at the village boys, you see, and think 'Oh, I like that one!' and the village girls didn't like this, so there was a bit of trouble there.

Mrs F.   Oh, that's gone on the world over, hasn't it!

Mrs G.   We used to admire them, especially if they were beautiful – good cricketers. We used to go to village cricket matches – 'Oh, isn't he lovely, that one?' Probably he was about 25 years old, we used to admire them from afar – we were ten!

Mrs F.   Course, there was a difference in the mothers and that too. When we had the mothers and children, you know, some were very nice and some didn't get on . . .

These interviews gave rise to a much deeper level of discussion back in school, when groups compared notes. Firstly, the younger children simply wrote accounts of what particularly interested them. Some stuck with the prosaic:

Some of the children were homesick. Some of the children settled in but some of them were unhappy. Some mums came to Lacock with their children. All the children wanted fish and chips but Lacock didn't have any . . . (Lucy)

Others picked out the conflict:

The village boys and the London boys had fist fights together. The London children were known as 'guttersnipes' because most of them were brought up in slums. (Caroline)

The other children didn't at this stage know of the account of disputes between the evacuee children and local children. They were asked to prepare initially a list of points mentioned in their interviews, and then to select from this three or four of the more interesting topics to write about. I hoped that this would focus their attention on the problems and difficulties of deciding what to include in a written narrative. Again, the items that evidently struck the children most were those of a highly personal nature: the evacuee who remembered the foul smell of the chicken mash, the extra cheese rations for the coal delivery man, and the way that the family slaughtered its pig after obtaining the necessary government permit.

Nearly every family had a pig. When the time came to kill it they had to get special permission from the government, and they were only allowed to keep the insides and the rest went to the army. (Sam)

If you wore glasses in the war you would have to wear special ones to fit into your gas mask. You wore the glasses not on the outside of the gas mask but on the inside. (Wanda)

When the evacuees came they didn't have enough space in Lacock school, so they took them to the Abbey, in one of its rooms. There they learned lots of things, and one of them was how to grow vegetables. They had a space each in the Abbey's gardens. (Berta)

Personal difficulties predominate in the children's narratives:

Mrs H. lived in Cuckoobridge Farm and took in fifteen children and five mothers, and said that the mothers were the hardest to cope with . . . She put the children in the cheese room. (Tania)

The five mothers didn't want to sleep in the cheese room, they refused to. (Kate)

The hardest thing for the children to get used to was the food, because in the country people eat stews and things like that. (Emily)

At the time of the war most people had toilets at the end of their garden. People were very luck to have a bathroom in their house. Most people . . . bathed in a tin tub by the fire. (Wanda)

The younger children's written accounts were naturally much briefer, and it was decided that the best way to exchange information would be for each group together to tell the others what they had found. It was in this way that they all discovered that while some interviewees had said that the evacuees got on well with their hosts, others had told of occasional street fights.

The conflicting evidence was discussed separately with each class. The older children were ready, at 9 and 10, to offer a series of logical explanations as to why accounts might be different – so many various explanations that one was suspicious that they were anxious not to imply any error, deceit or bias on the part of their interviewees!

Sam	All the people we interviewed said they were arguing. The Fox schoolboys and the Lacock boys. But the other person said that they were perfectly friendly.
Teacher	*Why are the stories different?*
Tom	It might have been different places, in different parts of Lacock.
Martha	But Lacock's not very big at all.
Wanda	It's not possible.
Tania	Mrs B. said she didn't exactly live in the village, she lived about a mile away.
Sam	They might just have remembered different things. Maybe there was lots of friendliness, lots of fighting, and people remembered differently.
Tom	Mr E. told us that they had a concert, and after the concert they were all friendly, because of it. Maybe Mrs H. remembered *after* the concert, and the others before it.
Martha	Yes, what was his name, the headteacher – Mr Steele, put on a concert, a play, and after they were friendly . . .
May-ai	What if some of them [the hosts] had girls [staying with them], and

some had boys. The boys are more likely to fight, and so the people who had girls would have thought they were all friendly, because – and the ones with boys –

Wanda   Yes, we had boys in our group.

We then discussed how we could find out why different versions were being remembered.

Sam   We could ask them. We could say that the other person said something different and did they remember anything else.

Shagufta   We could try and trace one of the Lacock children.

Berta   Mrs W. was one of them. We know.

Shagufta   She'd probably remember best if they were fighting or not.

Martha   What did she say?

Berta   She said they were fighting, arguing. Well, not so much arguing, but she said that the Lacock children thought the London children were sort of dirty and that.

What other sources were available for them to check on events, I asked.

Kate   Look in books?

Edmond   Oh, the school log books. They had to write down the things that happened every day. So we'd find out if they were fighting or not.[9]

How, I asked, would the log book compare as a source to the memories of the people they had interviewed?

Shagufta   Well, talking, they might not remember.

Teacher   *What sort of things do you think people remember best?*

Sam   Something to do with themselves, more than things about outside?

May-ai   Yes.

Berta   Like the pig mash [which stank] . . .

Sam   [On the log book] But they didn't have to remember back. They actually wrote it down while they were there.

Emily   There's more evidence in the log book, they wrote it at the time.

Teacher   *Is what is written in the log book necessarily everything that happened?*

Child   No.

Sam   Because if you wrote down everything it would be hundreds of pages.

Emily   It's the school record, not of outside the school.

Edmond   It's the headmaster. What he knows.

Teacher   *Is there any reason why the head should know about something and not write it down?*

Sam   If it was really bad, then maybe the people who read it would think it was a bad school –

Andre   – if he wrote down that there was nothing but fighting.

Berta   He wouldn't tell everything, but he'd tell most of it.

Emily   He might tell things, but he might sort of twist them a bit, he might sort of twist the truth, so if it was something really bad, a bad fight and somebody got really hurt, he'd maybe say there was a fight but he'd twist it a bit and say 'a grazed knee' or something like that . . .

Leila   Is this book just for anyone to look in, or is it just for teachers?

Teacher   *What do you mean? Why is it important who it's for?*

Leila   He might write things, if the teachers were the only ones who might look at it perhaps he would write the more serious things, or if it was for people from anywhere, who came along to see if they wanted their child at the school, he wouldn't put it all in.

The possibility that the interviewees might have subconsciously altered or mellowed their account for the particular audience was also accepted by many children.[10] But some children still had a certain unwillingness to accept the idea that the people they had met and interviewed might have been biased in their accounts.

Teacher   *Would they tell you a different story than they'd tell each other?*

Sam   No . . . no. 'Cos they've got nothing to hide, really.

Teacher   *How do you know?* (Laughter)

Sam   Well, I mean . . . they hadn't got a school to make it sound good.

Would books from the library present useful information to check or corroborate oral sources?

Emily   They don't tell you exactly about Lacock. They tell you about the whole world, not specifically about a little town. You find out sort of bits, but you wouldn't find out what happened in Lacock.

Leila   It wouldn't tell you about the children, about the people.

Tania   But one book might tell you a bit of information, and another book another, and you can add it up from the different books.

Finally, we discussed how they had selected what to write about. Some children had chosen things 'that we thought would help people reading it to know about evacuees'. Others had chosen what they were told most about, or 'the actual evacuees in Lacock' (i.e not generalisations they had been told). As we talked, it became clear to some children that the people they had interviewed had also been selective in their memories:

they told us what *they* thought was interesting . . .
If they chose the most interesting things, then some of the facts would be missed out. And we've chosen it and written it very shortly, so we didn't get all the details in.

The younger children were not able to distance themselves from the evidence in such a way. They also saw less need to explain why accounts were contradictory – they seemed to almost filter out potentially different stories by a process of selective recall of details that were compatible. For example, on the question of how the London children were received by the Lacock children:

Child 1   One person put a stone in a snowball.
Child 2   They thought they were guttersnipes –
Child 3   – and that they only ate fish and chips –
Child 2   – and they thought that their clothes were very dirty and they were very dirty, and it wasn't true.
Teacher   *How do you know it wasn't true?*
Child 3   Because this lady told us and they tried to be clean and wash their clothes and things like that.
Child 4   The Lacock girls didn't like the London girls because they fancied some of the Lacock boys –
Child 5   – because they were big and strong.
Child 6   The Lacock girls were jealous.
Child 1   We spoke to one of the London girls, she was the one who got hit by a snowball.
Teacher   *Did anyone say that the London children were liked?*
Child 7   Yes, after a while they did.
Child 3   They put on a play and then became friends.
Teacher   *Is this a good way to find out what happened in the past?*
Child 2   Yes.
Child 8   No, It's easier to find out from books and things –
Child 2   – 'Cos books might have been written by people who weren't there and don't know very much about it –
Child 8   – No, but there could be someone who had actually been there; they would know more about it because they know exactly what happened.
Child 2   Yes, but they have to.
Child 3   If you want to know if something's really true, you have to really find out from the people who was there.

We then discussed the reliability of various kinds of evidence. I asked if they could trust people's memories;

Child 4   Sometimes.
Child 3   They forget sometimes.
Teacher   *What kinds of things will people remember best?*
Child 7   Like the plain things. That's what makes their lives.
Child 6   And it's a big thing and it's easier to remember, and that's what all the people remembered clearly . . .
Child 9   You could look if any of them had their diaries. They might have written down things which they remembered when it was the war.
Child 6   But you know which day things happened.
Child 9   The diary is better, because the diary was when it actually happened. Not a book, the book are copies.

When asked how books and diaries differed in their usefulness, several children made very concrete comparisons:

Child 4   Diaries from that long ago are probably all tatty and things, and you couldn't hardly read it.
Child 6   The book is better 'cos it costs more than the diary.

Other children were able to make more profound abstractions on the distinctions:

Child 7   A book will tell you a little about each person, and a diary will tell you a lot about one person, and I think they're both equal.
Child 3   A diary is better than talking to people, 'cos they might have forgotten.
Child 10   Talking is better – they might forget to write the diary.
Child 11   You might not be able to read the writing.
Child 9   They might not remember it. In a diary, it's going to be much more detailed.
Child 3   Probably it will be true because they wouldn't lie to themselves.
Child 10   They *might* be lying.
Child 3   Who'd lie to their own diary?

These younger children had also developed a critical awareness of the nature of evidence, and were prepared to justify different kinds of sources as having varying degrees of reliability. However, they seemed less able to accommodate the idea of bias. Conflicts in evidence were either ignored, with different accounts simply synthesized into one apparently coherent account, or explained away with statements about people forgetting, and so on. The older children seemed much more prepared to accept that people's accounts would be biased, and that this would need to be taken into account when conflicting evidence was found.[11] They were also aware that they themselves were engaged in a process of selecting evidence. By this age (9 and 10 years) they seemed to have grasped the idea that history is only those parts of the past that seem relevant to us, and that many people and stages are involved in making the decision as to what is relevant.

For both groups of children, the project allowed them to gather together a far greater amount and range of material than would have been possible had we relied upon traditional secondary sources. Paul Thompson has made the point that oral communication was the dominant mode of communication up until Reformation Europe.[12] With primary aged children at least, oral communication is still the principal medium: for them, the written word is slower and more laborious.

By allowing children to take on a genuine investigation in this way, giving them access to real data, we encouraged them to act as historians. It seems that the best way to acquire the skills and attitudes that historians have is to practice them in a real enquiry. Oral history presents a rich field for such investigation, and one that is immediately and excitingly available to the young child.

NOTES

1 I am very grateful to many people for help with the work described here; particularly to my colleague Ron Browne, who taught the class of 7–8 year olds. We were both grateful for the help given by our interviewees, and in particular Mrs Copeland and Mr Caunter of Lacock, who helped make so many of the arrangements. Sallie Purkis provided invaluable encouragement.

2 P. Thompson, *The Voice of the Past: Oral History*, Oxford, Oxford University Press, 1978, p. 10.

3 Several of these skills are taken from the various ILEA curriculum guidelines: *History in the Primary School* (1980), *Social Studies in the Primary School* (1980) and *Language in the Primary School* (1978).

4 A. Ross, 'The bottle stopper factory: talking about work', *The English Magazine*, Summer 1983.

5 S. Purkis, *Oral History in Schools*, Colchester, Oral History Society, n.d., p. 7.

6 Some pupils were evacuated to Henley-on-Thames, not Lacock.

7 Purkis, *Oral History in Schools*, p. 8.

8 Thompson, *The Voice of the Past*, p. 116.

9 Only a few pages of the log book were then available, which noted only 'relations between the "resident" and "visiting" Heads and Staff were cordial' (15 Sept 1939). Mr Caunter, current head of Lacock school, later searched the log book at our request and found further references of 'friendly relations . . . between the visiting children and our own' (4th Sept 1940).

10 Thompson, *The Voice of the Past*, p. 100.

11 Ibid., p. 92.

12 Ibid., p. 99.

38   The exhibition that speaks for itself
Oral history and museums

Anna Green

Anna Green lectures in history at the University of Waikato, Hamilton, New Zealand. This unpublished paper was first presented at the US Oral History Association conference, October 1996.

Is it possible to construct a museum exhibition structured around sound and storytelling? This is the question we faced early in 1995, following the completion of a large oral history project on the community of Frankton Junction, New Zealand. Over the previous eighteen months my graduate oral. history class recorded about two hundred life histories with men and women who had lived and worked in this railway community, once the largest railway junction in New Zealand. In addition to the interviews, we had sought permission to borrow and copy photographs of everyday life from family photograph albums. Despite the gradual dispersion of the railway workforce over previous decades, the response was overwhelming, and the oral testimonies and photographs combined to create a rich account of life in a working-class railway community from the 1920s to 1970s. A grant from the Environment and Heritage Fund of the New Zealand Lottery Board then made it possible to return the history to the community in the form of an exhibition.

Determined to make the oral history the central focus for the exhibition, but having no previous experience in museums, I began research with a small team of graduate students, exploring the journals and handbooks on social history in museums. Was it possible to construct an exhibition around oral testimonies presented in audio, not transcript, form? There was virtually nothing to be found on this subject. Stuart Davies's comment in 1994 that 'oral history occupies an ambivalent, uncomfortable and vulnerable position in museums' seemed to be an understatement.[1] For example, a handbook for museum professionals, frequently cited in the British and New Zealand literature, contains one short chapter on oral history. Two-thirds of this chapter is devoted to the inherent unreliability and flawed nature of memory, and the author finally concludes that oral history has limited value and may best be presented, heavily contextualised, in a separate 'library' space.[2]

The journal articles indicated that most social history museum curators continue to perceive oral history as, at best, a useful adjunct to the material object collections. 'History provision without objects would be and usually is something else . . . objects make museums', wrote one museum curator in

1993.³ The role of objects in stimulating reminiscence among visitors has received favourable comment.⁴ But when oral history was incorporated into exhibitions, the spoken word was usually transformed into text on walls, and consequently lost the multi-layered complexities and entrancing vigour of oral narration. On those occasions when oral history remained in its original form, it frequently accompanied a recreation of social or working life and as a consequence sound was defeated by the busy visual panorama and became little more than background noise. None of this does justice to oral history, nor the importance of memory as a living, active engagement between past and present. Memories should not be regarded like shards of pots, inert fragments from a long-dead past. As Michael Frisch has suggested, we need to 'involve people in exploring what it means to remember, and what to do with memories to make them active and alive, as opposed to mere objects of collection'.⁵

To achieve this, the memories must become the central focus of an exhibition or display. The Frankton exhibition team decided to try and construct a museum exhibition using oral testimonies as an oral source: in other words sound and listening would take precedence over sight and looking. We shared the conviction that creating a highly detailed stage-setting can distract visitors from listening to the oral testimonies. Furthermore, we did not wish to allow surviving material objects, or photographs, to determine the direction and content of the exhibition. The oral testimonies focussed upon human relationships at home and at work, drawing upon the whole range of human experience. The photographs, in contrast, primarily recorded special and happy family occasions, or masculine work or sporting culture. Only one set of photographs, taken by a professional photographer of his wife, recorded the experience of married women engaged in household work, in contrast to the strength of these memories in the oral histories. While there were many photographs of children at play, there were none, of course, of corporal punishment, or the ritual exchange of insults on the way to school between Catholics and Protestants. Consequently the themes for the exhibition were derived from the oral histories, and the lack of correspondence between the audio and visual aspects of the exhibition, apparent in nearly every section, was briefly discussed in the accompanying written guide.

THE ORAL HISTORY EXHIBITION

The exhibition was a co-operative venture with the staff at the Waikato Museum of Art and History, whose design, photographic and technical expertise were invaluable.⁶ A special graduate class also worked with me on the exhibition, and their individual and collective contribution to the project is gratefully acknowledged.⁷

The shape of the gallery space, and the desire to create five separate sections to the exhibition, determined the final plan, which is shown in Figure 1.

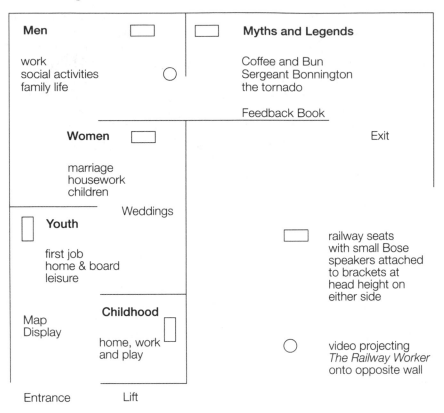

Figure 1 Final plan of the exhibition

TECHNICAL PROBLEMS

The principal technical problem we had to overcome was that of making the oral history accessible and audible, while minimising sound bleeding in a relatively open-plan exhibition. We did not want any barrier, such as the requirement to use earphones, to stand between the visitor and the oral history. Furthermore, it was essential that the visitor was comfortable while listening, and this indicated the need to use seating. We were fortunate to be loaned old red railway seats, temporarily removed from carriages undergoing renovation, by the Waikato Branch of the New Zealand Railway and Locomotive Society. Each seat became an independent sound unit, with the CD player hidden underneath. The oral histories were transmitted through robust bookshelf-sized speakers, with internal amplifiers, attached to brackets at ear-level on either side of the seat. Placing the speakers in this way reduced the volume necessary for comfortable listening, and sound bleeding between sections was negligible. To further emphasise the oral history, the lighting was deliberately subdued. The walls were painted a dark green, and both the railway seats and the surrounding photographs were illuminated by spotlights.

EXHIBITION GOALS

We began with three goals for the oral history exhibition:

- to represent as fully as possible the diverse range of oral testimony;
- to encourage visitors to reflect upon their own memories;
- to enable visitors to contribute their own responses and memories.

The extent to which we were able to achieve these goals was dependent upon a number of factors, including the principles of selection, editing and sequencing developed as we worked our way through the tapes. Following advice from the curatorial staff we agreed that the whole exhibition should only be approximately one hour in length, therefore each of the five sections could only use ten minutes of recordings. This entailed selecting, in total, under sixty minutes of oral history from the three hundred hours or more recorded! For the first four sections on children, youth, men and women, we decided to include material on the three broad themes of family life, work and leisure. With ten minutes' playing time, only two or three quotations could be included on each particular topic. The childhood section, for example, finally consisted of twenty oral history extracts, roughly half a minute each in length.

SELECTION

To represent the diverse range of experience within the oral testimonies with an oral history cohort of this size was going to be an immense problem from the start. Our first decision was to include only firsthand experience as far as possible. This reduced the pool of information on any one theme to more manageable proportions. Sound quality also eliminated some recordings, and played a far greater role in the selection process than we would have liked. We found that it took very little extraneous noise to render a recording unusable for exhibition purposes. A panting fox terrier, chiming clock and intrusive interviewer rendered some oral histories unusable.

But we were still left with many more stories than we could include. Two criteria in particular became central to the choices we subsequently made. The first related to the context – an exhibition – and the need to interest a wide range of people. We tried to choose topics within the themes that would have most appeal to a contemporary audience. Although we agreed that the broad themes of work, family life, and play/community activities should form the internal skeleton for the first four sections, there were of course many different aspects to these themes from which we could have chosen. Stories which appeared to offer the most interesting options for engaging with the present-day audience through lively narration, humour or emotion tended to survive the radical selection process in which we were constantly engaged.

The second criterion was based upon the weight of evidence within the oral testimonies themselves. We decided to make representativeness the major criterion for inclusion. Subjects and perspectives dominant within the testimonies were selected (linked by a minimalist narrative smoothing the transition from one subject to another). This may seem, on the face of it, rather indefensible, particularly in a postmodern world. There were, however, positive aspects to this approach. The choice of representative stories did enable us to strengthen the focus of the exhibition. An example of this is evident in the childhood section. Nearly every interview described incidents of severe corporal punishment, either at school or at home. These accounts are profoundly moving, indicating that experiences of physical violence can remain a source of mental anguish throughout life:

> people always hammered their kids in those days, I mean, God, my mother used to take to me with the bloody stock whip actually and she used to beat the living hell out of me, I mean, . . . just because I bloody well annoyed her, you know. But it was the thing that was done.[8]

> I was the one who always got the hidings, I think, only because I used to answer him back . . . I can remember one occasion when I was up the road where I used to play at the end of Lake Road, which was only just up round the corner, and I was coming home, it was dark, my father yelled out to me, 'hurry up', I said, 'I'm coming', when I got to the back door he was waiting behind the back door and let me have it. I was bruised all over.[9]

The disadvantage of selecting representative stories lay in the risk of stereotyping experience. This was most problematic in the section on women, where housework and motherhood dominated the accounts almost to the exclusion of all else. Gaby Porter has rightly warned us about the risks of representing women's lives with a narrow domestic focus.[10] We had no desire to reinforce a conservative popular belief that a married woman's place is in the home. But it was important that we remained faithful to the experiences repeatedly described in the oral testimonies. These were dominated by descriptions of the hard physical work involved in looking after a house and family of five or six children, prior to the widespread ownership of refrigerators, gas or electric ovens and washing machines. Such accounts make the indispensable contribution of working-class women to the household economy transparently obvious. Heating the copper and washing everything by hand, scrubbing the floors and cooking meals on a wood- or coal-fired stove at irregular times for family members on shiftwork showed that household labour was time-consuming and physically arduous in the middle decades of the century.[11] The contrast with housework in contemporary society is implicit within the testimonies, and challenges facile comparisons with the present.

EDITING

Editing the tapes for inclusion within the exhibition involved both technical and ethical considerations. We were fortunate in having access to the Pro-Tools computer software on which to edit the tapes, but the process took far longer, and was far more expensive, than had been anticipated. To transfer the recordings from analogue to digital audiotape, and edit every oral history extract, took approximately five days. I had budgeted for five hours. The interviews were conducted in the homes of the interviewees, and consequently while the quality of sound was generally quite good, individual voice levels fluctuated enormously. We tried to make the sound levels more consistent, so that listeners would not have difficulty adjusting between loud and quiet voices, but this was only possible to a limited extent. However, we were able to remove interjections, irritating laughter and extraneous noises, when they did not overlap with the voice of the interviewee. While students recording the interviews had been asked to confine themselves to non-verbal responses (smiling, nodding), many did not. Yet those students who engaged actively with the interviewee, through humour and shared interests, created a rapport and environment that appeared to elicit much more lively and extended storytelling. Although these stories required more extensive editing, they became the backbone of the exhibition.

While constructing the exhibition tapes, we were also aware of the need to protect the personal authenticity of people's memories. It is important not to distort the intentions of the interviewee, or alter the tenor of their testimony. Editing the extracts for inclusion on the exhibition tape became a matter of balancing the desire for short, dramatic or effective extracts with the narrator's provision of an explanatory or ambivalent conclusion to these stories. The following example of this dilemma is taken from the section on men, where Matt Andrew discovered that while some celebrated the male work culture, others were less sure:

> – but, again, it was wrapped up with the job you were doing, and as an indication of how you became isolated from your family, I was working in the lounge one night on some papers and an argument developed at the kitchen sink with the son and the daughter and my wife, and I could hear it of course. I thought, now, the next thing that's going to happen is that we'll get Dad. The discussion and the argument went on and it was resolved, and I was still sitting there. I suddenly realised that I had become an extension of the family, and that I was no longer involved in the decision-making process. I was no longer involved in the discipline of it.

The first version of the tape extract ended at this point, and the focus of the story is sharp and clear. However, the interviewee goes on to say:

> And whilst that may be comforting to some people, it was disturbing to the extent that I resolved that I would resign, I would not stand at the next election for national counsellor.[12]

The inclusion of the final statement may have detracted slightly from the impact of the story. But it helps to explain why the narrator chose to retell this particular experience, for it was the catalyst that made him resolve to give up his position within the railway union. In so doing, the attention of the listener is drawn to the narrative purpose which often underlies our stories about the past.

SEQUENCING

The sequencing of the recordings may also enable the curator to illustrate other aspects of storytelling in oral history. This was of particular relevance in the final exhibition section – on Frankton myths and legends – which drew upon the imaginative and collective dimensions of memory. One of the legends concerned the 1948 tornado, which caused considerable damage, and was responsible for the deaths of three people. It was remembered by virtually everyone, and the stories were a combination of direct experience, hearsay and imagination. Jane Moodie wished to illustrate the evolution of community myth, through which accounts of the tornado acquired the patina of repeated narration and were characterised by humour and exaggeration. From the wide range of possible stories, she chose examples which gradually moved from the prosaic to the much more imaginative:

> When the tornado struck we were right in the middle of it and of course the whole roof went off the house, but the ceiling was left and it was just full of about four or five inches of this greasy railway soot. And of course then there was a really heavy rain came after the passing of the tornado, and it just washed all this sticky, dirty, greasy soot just came down the walls and on to everything in the house. It was unbelievable. . . .[13]

> But Mrs Hill down the road actually, they had a rotary clothesline, and her husband was a guard on the railway, and she heard this terrible roaring, you see, and she went outside to see what it was. And here was the clothesline about fifty feet up in the air, going round and round, and round and round, and round, and she had Johnny's railway overalls pinned to the line – and it was going round and round and round, and the overalls were standing straight out.[14]

> Yeah, I was there, right in it. We were playing up in Seddon Park and we went down to Frankton and watched the house where the railway line crossing Lake Road is, my sister and me, and we actually saw the house get picked up and taken across the railway, and the people sitting at the table having their tea.[15]

INTERACTION

Finally, we hoped that the exhibition as a whole would encourage visitors to reflect upon their own lives and memories, and make comparisons with their experiences in the present. In particular, we wondered whether a younger generation would compare the memories of the earlier generation with their own experiences and current orthodoxies about family and working life. The recollections of shift-work, and the havoc it played upon the ability of men to play an active role in family life, have as much relevance now as in the past. Questions such as these were raised within the printed exhibition guide. This provided a brief summary of each section, concluding with a couple of questions intended to elicit comparisons with visitors' own experiences. The section on men, for example, read:

> Shiftwork dominated the daily experience of those men who worked for New Zealand Railways. The long, irregular hours adversely affected their family lives. Jobs on the railways were keenly sought after, however, for these offered both security of employment and opportunities for advancement. A hierarchy based upon skill divided the workforce, while a powerful camaraderie existed among workmates.
> • How would you define the roles of husband and father today? Do they differ from the roles apparent in the memories recounted here?
> • Do irregular working hours have an impact upon your family?

We thought that questions such as these might encourage people to contribute their ideas to the exhibition. Limited resources meant that we could not record oral histories in the museum, and so we opted for a book with written comments at the end of the exhibition.

The book contains pages and pages of comments and memories, from both older and younger visitors. Virtually none directly address the questions posed in the exhibition guide, a lesson perhaps for the didactic curator! Many entries begin, 'I remember', which suggests that the exhibition did encourage the audience to reflect on their own memories or those of their parents or grandparents. Some visitors described encounters they observed within the exhibition space: men and women sharing memories, or sitting on the railway seats and engaging in one-sided arguments with the oral history! Others found the exhibition profoundly moving, with one visitor writing simply, 'I cried, memories of feelings.' Very few entries indicate discomfort with the absence of objects, while many expressed satisfaction with the focus of the exhibition along the lines of the following entries: 'Real history – good to hear people giving their own version of what happened', and 'Wonderfully interesting exhibition, more should be made of oral histories.'

CONCLUSION

Is it possible to construct an exhibition around oral history in an audio form? The Frankton Junction exhibition suggests that the answer is a resounding yes. The oral testimonies communicated directly with each visitor, and conveyed a richness of experience and imagination which was sufficient to capture their interest. The subjects, family life, childhood and work, have resonance for us all. People will sit and listen, if the stories interest them and the environment is comfortable and inviting. There is no need to banish oral history to the walls, listening posts, booths, earphones or, worse still, libraries!

For the museum itself, the exhibition significantly increased attendance and attracted many who had never visited before. However, the human resource devoted to this exhibition far exceeded those normally available to museum staff. Combining the project with my graduate teaching programme, and acquiring external funding, made it possible to record large numbers of people, work our way through the tapes, and construct the exhibition within the space of two and a half years. Returning the history to the community has to be done within a reasonably short time-frame, if most of the contributors are to live to hear it. 'Love, Labour and Legend' was the result of a rewarding collaboration between academic historians and museum staff in the sphere of public history. I hope that there will be many more exhibitions that speak for themselves in the future.

NOTES

1 S. Davies, 'Falling on deaf ears? Oral history and strategy in museums', *Oral History*, Autumn 1994, vol. 22, no. 2, p. 74.
2 G. Griffiths, 'Oral history', in D. Fleming, C. Paine and J. Rhodes (eds), *Social History in Museums: A Handbook for Professionals*, London, HMSO, 1993, pp. 111–116.
3 G. Cavanagh, 'The future of museum social history collecting', *Social History in Museums*, 1993, vol. 20, p. 61.
4 J. Urry, 'How societies remember the past', in S. Macdonald and G. Fyfe, *Theorizing Museums*, Oxford: Blackwell/The Sociological Review, 1996, p. 50.
5 M. Frisch, *A Shared Authority: Essays on the Craft and Meaning of Oral and Public History*, New York, State University of New York Press, 1990, p. 27.
6 In particular, Sally Parker (Senior Curator), Michele Orgad (Exhibitions Manager), Max Riksen (Designer), Stephanie Leeves (Photographer), Kent Eriksen (Exhibition Preparator).
7 The members of the exhibition graduate class were Matt Andrew, Chanel Clarke, Sue Garmonsway and Jane Moodie.
8 Frankton Oral History Project (FOHP), interview 172, tape 1, side B, 39.4 m.
9 FOHP, interview 157, tape 1, side B, 18.6m.
10 G. Porter, 'Putting your house in order: representations of women and domestic life', in R. Lumley (ed.), *The Museum Time Machine*, London, Routledge, 1988, pp. 102–127.
11 See S. Garmonsway, 'Just a wife and mother: the domestic experiences of Frankton women, 1940–1960', Unpublished MA thesis, University of Waikato, 1996.
12 FOHP, interview 022, tape 1, side B: 7.1 m.
13 FOHP, interview 014, tape 1, side B: 17.6 m.
14 FOHP, interview 172, tape 1, side B: 28.2 m.
15 FOHP, interview 187, tape 1, side A: 6.0 m.

39 Out of the archives and onto the stage

Shaun Nethercott and Neil Leighton

Shaun Nethercott is Director of Research for Media Vision and was Artistic Director of the Labor Theatre Project. Neil Leighton was Director of the Labor Theatre Project and teaches politics at Michigan-Flint University. Reprinted from *Oral History*, Spring 1990, vol. 18, no. 1, pp. 61–65, with permission.

It is February 11, 1987. You are on your way to a play commemorating the fiftieth anniversary of the Flint Sit-Down Strike. As you enter the theatre, your expectations are jolted. Instead of simply receiving tickets, you are asked to fill out a membership card for the 'People's Union'. As you wait in the lobby, you are accosted by a long-haired youth who thrusts a copy of a tabloid, the *Flint Auto Worker*, into your hands. Its front page blares 'Autoworkers Win! GM Strike is Settled'. Browsing through what appears to be a union newspaper, you find page three is another front page, this one screaming 'Plant Closings Idle Thousands!' A factory whistle blows, someone hollers, 'time for work', and the crowd begins making its way into the theatre.

Your expectations are again denied. You are not allowed to sit in the auditorium. Instead, you are guided to double doors leading directly onstage. There you are confronted with peculiar arrangements of chairs, platforms, odd bits of furniture and scenery. At the furthest end of the stage, beneath the jumble of rope and pulleys controlling the theatre's fly system, sits a conglomeration of large platforms on which perch broken-down chairs, apple crates, a beat-up chest. Folding chairs ring the platforms, forming banks of audience seating.

Just beyond these dishevelled platforms are two groupings which obviously create the confines of a church and a bar. In the centre of the space, the racks and tools of the shop stand in opposition to the steps and columns of the Courthouse. At the foot of the Courthouse is the store; beyond the store, the tidy, identical platforms which mark the tract housing of Little Missouri.

No one directs you where to sit. Distinct choices present themselves – nooks and crannies on the poor side of town; or the bleachers and rows of little Missouri; or perhaps behind the pews in the church, or at a booth in the bar. If none of those satisfy you, maybe the steps and levels of the Courthouse would be comfortable. If not, there are benches and chairs lining the streets. At no spot in the theatre can you see everything else. Where you sit will determine your experience of the play.

When the play begins, action surrounds you. Sometimes you can neither see nor hear what is happening in another part of town while other events occur next to you. In the church, you'll be asked to join in a funeral; in the bar, you can have a drink while the workers hash and re-hash the events at work. Clashes, triumphs and tragedies which fuel the strike are embedded in daily routine; life goes on with beds to be made, coffee to be drunk, shopping to be done. As you sit in Little Missouri you may be watching Maggie curl her hair, while across the town the Morrises argue whether Tommy should join the union. Next door Chu-Chu reads the *Flint Auto Worker* and drinks himself into oblivion. You experience the play like you would life – or like you would an oral history: your knowledge is experiential, incomplete, and intimate.

You are experiencing a play based on oral history in which oral history provides the model for form, content, and re-transmission of the subject matter. The play was *'37–'87*, the oral histories were those of the sit-down strikers as collected by the Flint Labor History Project. The content was an effort to empower the members of a working class community whose recent ancestors had changed the face of industrial America. Through the medium of oral history as performance we hoped to reacquaint them with their own history and their own class's accomplishments in the building of a once proud city. In this way we sought to mobilize working class people to take greater control over their daily work. Theatre as a means of transmitting the essential understanding of their own past and present experience appeared to be a significant if not ideal, cultural mechanism.

The primary purpose of the Labor History Project, begun in 1978, was the 'recapturing' of the history of working people, of those left out of the history books. The project consisted of four principal investigators, an anthropologist, two political scientists, and a historian.

In a rush against time as the sit-downer population rapidly disappeared, we began interviewing rank and file participants in the great strike. We identified and interviewed over 150 survivors of the strike, including their families, small businessmen, professionals, General Motors supervisors, police, and other community members from the period. In an ongoing course entitled 'Exploring Community History', we trained over one hundred students to conduct family and peer group interviews, thus tracing the latitudinal impact of the strike. In this way the Project aided the children and grandchildren of workers to re-create their family and community histories, thus validating their working class origins and experiences. Believing validation fosters empowerment we hoped to encourage working class people to take greater control of their own work life. We were, in short, practicing 'people's history' as described by Benson, Brier, and Rosenzweig in *Presenting the Past*:

> Convinced that the discovery of and knowledge of one's own history can be personally empowering and a catalyst for social movements, the practitioners of people's history have often experimented with new media and explored topics ignored by mainstream academic histories. In addition, some people's historians have emphasized the *process* as well as

the content of history, striving to make it a partnership between those with historical expertise and those with historical experience.[1]

From the beginning the members of the Labor History Project were interested in several key points of Flint's social history as it related to the Sit Down Strike and its aftermath. First was the question of solidarity, how it was achieved and what had happened to this concept some fifty years later. For example, why were large numbers of rural and southern white workers able to achieve a high degree of militancy if not class consciousness? Little in their background provided a basis for collective action. We discovered that skilled leadership and a small group of left-wing party members, former Wobblies, and others channelled worker unrest to create the recognition of a common plight *vis-à-vis* General Motors.

Secondly, we were interested in the lack of collective memory about the strike. Contemporary workers knew little or nothing about this event. This break in transmission could be traced to a few key sources. Labor history of any sort was consciously 'disincluded' from Flint Community Schools. This practice can be traced to the Mott Foundation's Community School Program, which pumped $100 million into Flint Schools for forty years with specific provisos as to how that money should be spent.[2]

The third element dealt with the actual recording of the strike. The 'official' histories of the strike were the product of white, middle class, male professionals – journalists, photographers, newsreel producers, labor writers, chroniclers, historians. These people, who, even if they were sympathetic to the strikes' cause, did not work in the plant, were not residents of Flint, and often had their own ideological or political axes to grind.

More important, perhaps, was the fact that the sit-downers had done little to transmit their own histories, even to members of their families. Through McCarthyism and its antecedents, many sit-downers were made to feel that the strike and their participation in it was somehow suspect. For many strikers, the Great Flint Sit-Down Strike of '36–'37 was something one didn't talk about. Though one of the central events in American labor history, it became an event without context and without a significance to most people in the very town where it happened.

All these elements raise serious questions about the interpretation of workers' history. We became keenly aware our role should not be one of 'historian' but that of 'facilitator'. We sought to create a partnership between those with historical 'expertise' and those who created the historical event.[3] In other words, we saw ourselves as providing the means by which the transmission of information about the strike could pass from the strikers to the community.

Oral history was thus conceived as a process, not a product. In our efforts to further that process, we used a broad variety of media. The most successful, and problematic, was the creation of a play based on the collected oral histories. We refined the play in consultation with the sit-downers, constantly rewriting and adapting it on the basis of numerous 'interactives' in which various scenes toured union halls, community groups, and local high schools. The play was '37–'87; the project was the Flint Labor Theatre Project; the purpose was the empowerment of Flint's working class.

The voices came to us as from a void. Our task was to fill that void, and make those empty voices live again, so that those who follow can understand what has been gained and lost. We hoped to create an image of the strike onstage that would provide a model for action in the larger community.

First we had to conquer our own ignorance. Books, photographs, magazines, movies, and newspapers supplemented the painful transcription of tapes. Thus, every actor learned at least one life, one voice, very, very well. That voice became a source, our hook into the rhyme of the time.

From these voices we learned of Macedonian chicken soup with lemon, and urinating in a trough because no one could leave the line, and crates of tomatoes offered to the straw boss who soon learned to demand it as tribute. From these same voices we learned that the strike was not a monolith. It was hated and loved, endured and created, exciting and painful, foolish and wise. It was the strategic manoeuverings of the leaders, the manipulation and counter-manipulation of the press, the boredom of those who stayed in the plant, the endless drudgery of those who ran the strike kitchen and rounded up picket lines. It was young wives with little kids wondering how they were going to eat with no money coming in. It was blacks joining the union despite the protests of some whites. It was women using blackjacks and breaking windows, defying the police. It was unlooked-for victory, and crashing defeat. It was all those things and then some. It just depended on where you happened to be.

The only constant was a kind of passion which still reverberated after fifty years. Supporters of the strike could still get angry when they thought of life in the plant, where they were fined for using the bathroom, subjected to name-calling, hitting, and where blacks could be fired for speaking socially to a white. They still shuddered when they recalled seeing their friends' limbs crushed in the jaws of a press, skin scorched by molten iron, or fellow workers collapse from the pace of the assembly line.

These recollections were a shock to the young ears listening to the tapes. The students began to ask questions. One student discovered her grandfather had been a member of the Flying Squadron, a group of militant union activists. While he'd never told his family about his organizing activities, he'd carefully kept his union cap and button, the yellowed pages of a scrapbook, and his membership card stored in a box under his bed. Others discovered aunts and uncles who lived through the strike. At home, students asked their autoworker parents to describe working in the shop. The community began to reclaim its own history.

During the second phase, we began to improvise scenes, trying to discover the life behind the oral histories. Our work followed the model described by Jan Vansina: a performance is built through improvisation on an existing stock of images and forms. Songs were combined with a photographic image, and reinforced with tales from the tapes. As we worked our way into the material, 'bits of tales are combined, sequences are altered or innovated, descriptions of characters shifted, settings placed in locales.[4]

The theatre that is oral history makes its way into our scenes. The performance of the speaker becomes the model for our performance. When Bob Travis, a primary organizer of the strike, described the secret meetings held at the beginning of the organization drive, he couldn't resist acting it out, and neither could we:

> We'd have these meetings when we first started. Secret, so the company wouldn't find out. Spies, you know, everywhere, I remember one – a meeting that is – in a church, north side of town. Guys were nervous about coming, colored part of town, you know . . . We'd cut off the lights and wait in the dark. [Knock on table, then whispering] Who is it? And they'd answer 'Joe – from the stampin' plant' or some such . . . We'd let 'em in and set 'em in the dark. They'd set there for a while and if anyone made a sound, there'd be 'Sh, sh, sh' all round. Finally I'd light a single candle, 'Boys, we got a difficult job ahead of us.' By then they'd be ready to hear whatever I had to say. We got quite a few people that way. (Chuckles)[5]

This speech, complete with action, enactment, and comment is what Brecht would call 'primitive epic theatre'. Even its content is about performance. Travis freely admits, as does historian Henry Kraus, that the danger of spies though real was not extremely high.[6] The silence, the candle, the whispering created an aura of mystery, urgency, and heroism which drew members in as surely as the union message itself.

It became obvious that we could not simply enact or represent the strike. The material wouldn't allow it. There were too many layers of interlocking, self-conscious performance. The actors were performing scenes based on interviews which were themselves a type of dramatic poetry detailing events which were very often specialized performance such as picket lines, demonstrations, speeches.

Oral history is the tale of events, mediated by memory and shaped by performance. It is the time of the interview looking back to the time of the event. Recognizing that feature, we decided our production would be distinctly presentist. The actors never fully shed their eighties selves; they could comment on their characters and the play's events. Costume changes took place in full view of the audience. The lights and mechanics of the stage were fully exposed. There was no effort to realistically represent the locales of the strike. We wanted the audience to be aware of the play as performance, memory, and comment.

Having thus created a complex of scenes guided by oral history and supplemented by documentary research, we began performing for the people most able to evaluate and interpret our work – the sit-downers themselves. In a series of what came to be called 'interactives', those whose lives we tried to present critiqued our work, corrected our vocabulary, and fleshed out our emotional understanding. A remarkable mentoring relationship developed. We'd perform, then ask innumerable questions about the minutiae of life – 'What did you do on a date?' 'Who were your favourite bands?' 'Did you fight with your wife about money?' The sit-downers would laugh and tell great old tales. A few weeks later, at another preview, a phrase, an anecdote, or a detail provided by the strikers had worked its way into the performance. For us and for them, these interactives were the most satisfying experience of the project. Oral history became a process shared across the generations, creating a bond in which the performer, performance, and audience became one.

When the final series of performances opened on the 50th anniversary of the strike (February 11, 1987), a play steeped in the process, form, and content of oral history had been created. Its use of environment, experience and multiple perspective were functions of the personal and idiosyncratic nature of oral testimony. The use of '80s referents and the self-conscious use of performance reflected oral history's dependence on memory and reminiscence.

These formalistic and stylistic choices reflected oral history's strengths and weaknesses. The play, like its source material, was highly dependent upon an understanding of the cultural context in which the testimonies arose. Unlike traditional linear drama or narrative history, the content was not explicitly stated, nor were the causes, effects, and interrelationships spelled out. Oral history and experiential theatre require the audience to participate in the event, and provide their own meaning and interpretation to conflicting information and phenomena. Consequently, both are activating and liberating.

The sit-down strikers and contemporary autoworkers had no trouble contextualizing the play. Their response was one of stimulation and identification. However, those who had not heard of the strike, or had little understanding of factory work because of class or age found the play mystifying.[7] To this audience the exchange of recipes carried equal significance as the passing of strike leaflets. Working class audiences knew the latter as an act of defiance, middle class and young audiences did not.

Thus, the process of transmission fell apart at a critical juncture. Those who needed to know about the strike the most – i.e. those who control information within the community and those who will soon inherit the community – were not reached by this type of performance. They would have learned and understood more had the play been highly contextualized and linear – as the movie *Matewan* had been.

And last, but not least, the use of the '80s referent seemed ultimately a conceit which pointed more to its own cleverness instead of addressing the real issues of memory and perception. The audience needed to know why the actors remained so fully in the '80s. The dual awareness of past and present implicit in the use of oral history is significant; our theatrical solution to the problem was not.

Still, one could say that the Labor Theatre Project was extremely successful within a limited application. It involved students, union members, and strikers in the active reclamation of their history – sometimes with tempestuous results. A group of activists first brought together in one of our interactives formed a powerful coalition which organized a whole series of rallies, pickets and demonstrations – a vivid example of life imitating art imitating life. The impact of the Jobs and Justice Fight-Back Committee is still being felt in Flint.

Although the play was the centrepiece of the Labor Theatre Project we realized it could not have a sustained impact. Therefore we soon decided to create a video production for use in classrooms, over public television and access channels and by other drama groups. A Detroit film-maker who had worked on 'With Babies and Banners' become involved with the project. He shot more than a hundred hours of tape chronicling every facet of the play's production, development, and community interactions. Project members raised more than $50,000 and with the donated talents of several skilled individuals and their television equipment completed the shooting. The video production is now being edited.

The video allows us to add a dimension to the use of oral history, albeit a limited one. Though losing the multidimensional aspects of live interaction, video does continue transmission of community history. It is our hope the video may spur others both in and out of Flint 'to carry it on', and create an equal relationship between history and the community, educators and their constituents, between classes and generations. Ideally oral history, even via television, offers a challenge to the accepted myths of the received culture and provides a means for the radical transformation of the social meaning of history.[8]

NOTES

1 S.P. Benson, S. Brier, and R. Rosenzweig (eds), *Presenting the Past*, Philadelphia, Temple University Press, 1986, p. xvii.

2 The Charles Stewart Mott Foundation was started in 1935 by the largest individual stockholder of the General Motors Corporation and is located in Flint, Michigan. Mott lived in Flint from 1905 to 1973. When he died at the age of 97 he was worth more than one half billion dollars. As might be expected 'the Foundation' exerts tremendous influence over most facets of Flint civic and educational life.

3 As Paul Thompson states, 'the historian comes to the interview to learn: to sit at the feet of others who, because they come from a different social class, or are less educated, or older, know more about something. The reconstruction of history itself becomes a much more widely collaborative process, in which non-professionals must play a critical part.' P. Thompson, *The Voice of the Past, Oral History*, Oxford, Oxford University Press, 1978, p. 11.

4 J. Vansina, *Oral Traditions as History*, Madison, University of Wisconsin Press, 1985, p. 12. For a similar process see the South African production and documentary *Bopha!*

5 Robert Travis, Tape II, 2. Flint Labor History Archives, University of Michigan-Flint.

6 Henry and Dorothy Kraus, *Interviews*, May 5, 1982, Flint Labor History Archives.

For a detailed account of the strike written by the only participant to have written a book see H. Kraus, *The Many and the Few*, second edition, Urbana, University of Illinois Press, 1985.

7 A. Duranti, 'The audience as co-author: an introduction', *TEXT*, vol. 6, no. 3, 1986, p. 243. 'Interpretation is not a passive activity whereby the audience is just trying to figure out what the author meant to communicate, rather, it is a way of making sense of what someone said by linking it to a world or context that the audience can make sense of.'

8 P. Thompson, *The Voice of the Past*, p. 18. Similar other oral history projects would include J. Brecher, J. Lombardi and J. Stackhouse, *Brass Valley Brass Workers History Project*, Philadelphia, Temple University Press, 1982; P. Friedlander, *The Emergence of a UAW Local, 1936–1939*, Pittsburgh, University of Pittsburgh Press, 1975; A. and S. Lynd, *Rank and File, Personal Histories by Rank and File Organizers*, Boston, Beacon Press, 1973.

Select bibliography

HANDBOOKS AND BIBLIOGRAPHIES

Finnegan, R., *Oral Traditions and the Verbal Arts: A Guide to Research Practices*, London, Routledge, 1992.

Havlice, P.P., *Oral History: A Reference Guide and Annotated Bibliography*, Jefferson, McFarland, 1985.

Hayes, P., *Speak for Yourself*, Namibia, Longman, 1992.

Hutching, M., *Talking History: A Short Guide to Oral History*, Wellington, New Zealand, Bridget Williams Books/Historical Branch of the Department of Internal Affairs, 1993.

Perks, R., *Oral History: An Annotated Bibliography*, London, British Library National Sound Archive, 1990.

Perks, R., *Oral History: Talking About the Past*, second edition, London, Historical Association, 1995.

Ritchie, D., *Doing Oral History*, New York, Twayne, 1995.

Robertson, B., *Oral History Handbook*, third edition, Adelaide, Oral History Association of Australia (South Australia Branch), 1994.

Seldon, A. and Pappworth, J., *By Word of Mouth: Elite Oral History*, London, Methuen, 1983.

Thompson, P., *The Voice of the Past: Oral History*, second edition, Oxford, Oxford University Press, 1988.

Trask, D. and Pomeroy, R., *The Craft of Public History: An Annotated Select Bibliography*, Westport, Greenwood, 1983.

Wilton, J., *Oral History in Australia: A List*, Sydney, Oral History Association of Australia (NSW Branch), 1996

Yow, V.R., *Recording Oral History: A Practical Guide for Social Scientists*, London, Sage, 1994.

COLLECTIONS AND REFLECTIONS ON THEORY AND PRACTICE

Bertaux, D. (ed.), *Biography and Society: The Life History Approach in the Social Sciences*, London, Sage, 1981.

Bornat, J. (ed.), *Reminiscence Reviewed: Perspectives, Evaluations, Achievements*, Buckingham, Open University Press, 1994.

Darian-Smith, K. and Hamilton, P. (eds), *Memory and History in Twentieth Century Australia*, Melbourne, Oxford University Press, 1994.

Dunaway, D. and Baum, W. (eds), *Oral History: An Interdisciplinary Anthology*, second edition, London, Altamira Press, 1996.

Evans, G.E., *Spoken History*, London, Faber, 1987.

Ferreira, M. de Moraes and Amado, J. (eds), *Usos & Abusos da Historia Oral*, Rio de Janeiro, Fundacao Getulio Vargas, 1996.

Frisch, M., *A Shared Authority: Essays on the Craft and Meaning of Oral and Public History*, Albany, State University of New York Press, 1990.

Gluck, S.B. and Patai D. (eds), *Women's Words: The Feminist Practice of Oral History*, London, Routledge, 1991.

Grele, R. (ed.), *Envelopes of Sound: The Art of Oral History*, second edition, Chicago, Precedent, 1985.

Kaminsky, M. (ed.), *The Uses of Reminiscence: New Ways of Working with Older Adults*, New York, Haworth, 1984.

Lummis, T., *Listening to History: The Authenticity of Oral Evidence*, London, Hutchinson, 1987.

McMahan, E. and Rogers, K.L. (eds), *Interactive Oral History Interviewing*, Hillsdale, N.J. Erlbaum, 1994.

Personal Narratives Group (eds), *Interpreting Women's Lives: Feminist Theory and Personal Narratives*, Bloomington, Indiana University Press, 1989.

Plummer, K., *Documents of Life: An Introduction to the Problems and Literature of a Humanistic Method*, London, Allen & Unwin, 1983.

Portelli, A., *The Death of Luigi Trastulli and Other Stories: Form and Meaning in Oral History*, Albany, State University of New York Press, 1991.

Samuel, R. and Thompson, P. (eds), *The Myths We Live By*, London, Routledge, 1990.

Schwarzstein, D. (ed.), *La Historia Oral*, Buenos Aires, Centro Editorial de America Latina, 1991.

Thompson, P. and Burchardt, N. (eds), *Our Common History: The Transformation of Europe*, London, Pluto, 1982.

Tonkin, E., *Narrating Our Pasts: The Social Construction of Oral History*, Cambridge, Cambridge University Press, 1992.

Vansina, J., *Oral Tradition: A Study in Historical Methodology*, London, Routledge & Kegan Paul, 1965.

PERIODICALS

Bios – Zeitschrift für Biographieforschung und Oral History [Germany], vol. 1 1988–
Historia y Fuente Oral [Spain], no. 1 1989–
International Journal of Oral History, vol. 1 1980–1990
International Yearbook of Oral History and Life Stories, vol. 1 1993–vol. 4 1996
Journal of the Brazil Oral History Association, vol. 1 1997–
Life Stories/Recits de Vie [UK/France], no. 1 1985–no. 5 1989
Memory and Narrative [International], vol. 1 1997–
Oral History [UK], vol. 1, no. 1 1969–
Oral History Association of Australia Journal, no. 1 1978–
Oral History Forum (previously *Canadian Oral History Association Journal*), vol. 1, 1975/76–
Oral History in New Zealand, vol. 1 1988–
Oral History Review [US], no. 1 1973–
Words and Silences: Bulletin of the International Oral History Association, no. 1, 1997–

KEY PUBLICATIONS USING ORAL HISTORY

Bozzoli, B. with Nkotsoe, M., *Women of Phokeng: Consciousness, Life Strategy and Migrancy in South Africa, 1900–1983*, London, James Currey, 1991.

Broadfoot, B., *Ten Lost Years 1929–1939: Memories of Canadians Who Survived the Depression*, Toronto, Doubleday, 1973.

Fraser, R., *Blood of Spain: The Experience of Civil War 1936–9*, London, Allen Lane, 1979.

Fyfe, J., *The Matriarchs: A Generation of New Zealand Women Talk to Judith Fyfe*, Auckland, Penguin, 1990.

Genovese, E., *Roll, Jordan, Roll: The World the Slaves Made*, New York, Pantheon, 1974.

Gluck, S.B., *Rosie the Riveter Revisited: Women, the War, and Social Change*, Boston, Twayne, 1987.

Haley, A., *Roots*, London, Hutchinson, 1977.

Hareven, T., *Family Time and Industrial Time: The Relationship Between the Family and Work in a New England Industrial Community*, Cambridge, Cambridge University Press, 1982.

Hinton, W., *Shenfan: The Continuing Revolution in a Chinese Village*, London, Secker & Warburg, 1983.

Kay, B. (ed.), *Odyssey: Voices from Scotland's Recent Past*, two volumes, Edinburgh, Polygon, 1980/1982.

Kennedy, E.L. and Davis, M., *Boots of Leather, Slippers of Gold: The History of a Lesbian Community*, New York, Routledge, 1993.

Lanzmann, C., *Shoah: An Oral History of the Holocaust*, New York, Pantheon, 1985.

Lowenstein, W., *Weevils in the Flour: An Oral Record of the 1930s Depression in Australia*, Melbourne, Hyland House, 1978.

Messenger, B., *Picking Up the Linen Threads: A Study in Industrial Folklore*, Belfast, Blackstaff, 1980.

Parker, T., *The People of Providence: A Housing Estate and Some of its Inhabitants*, London, Hutchinson, 1983.

Passerini, L., *Fascism in Popular Memory*, Cambridge, Cambridge University Press, 1987.

Roberts, E., *A Woman's Place: An Oral History of Working Class Women 1890–1940*, Oxford, Blackwell, 1984.

Rosengarten, T., *All God's Dangers: The Life of Nate Shaw*, New York, Knopf, 1971.

Terkel, S., *Hard Times: An Oral History of the Great Depression*, New York, Pantheon, 1970.

Thomson, A., *Anzac Memories: Living With the Legend*, Oxford, Oxford University Press, 1994.

Wigginton, E. (ed.), *The Foxfire Books*, New York, Doubleday, nine volumes, 1972–86

Zhang, X. and Ye, S., *Chinese Lives*, Harmondsworth, Penguin, 1989.

Useful contacts

International Oral History Association
c/o Institut für Geschichte und Biographie der Fernuniversität Hagen
Liebigstr., 11,
D–58511 Ludenscheid,
Germany
Email: Alexander.vonPlato@Fernuni-Hagen.de
Publication: *Words and Silences,* no. 1 1997–

Oral History Society (UK)
c/o Department of Sociology
University of Essex
Colchester
Essex CO4 3SQ
United Kingdom
Fax: 0171–412–7441
Email: Rob.Perks@bl.uk
Publication: *Oral History*, vol. 1, no. 1 1969–

Oral History Association (USA)
Executive Secretary
Baylor University
PO Box 97234
Waco, Texas 76798–7234
USA
Fax: 817–755–1571
Email: OHA_Support@Baylor.edu
Publication: *Oral History Review*, no. 1 1973–

Oral History Association of Australia
c/o Oral History Program
State Library of New South Wales
Macquarie Street
Sydney NSW 2000
Australia
Fax: 02–223–4086
Email: RBlock@ilanet.slnsw.gov.au
Publication: *Oral History Association of Australia Journal*, no. 1 1978–

National Oral History Association of New Zealand
PO Box 3819
Postal Centre
Wellington
New Zealand
Email: Megan.Hutching@dia.govt.nz
Publication: *Oral History in New Zealand*, vol. 1 1988–

Canadian Oral History Association/Société Canadienne D'Histoire Orale
PO Box 2064, Station D
c/o National Archives of Canada
Manuscript Division
Ottawa
Ontario
Canada K1P 5W3
Fax: 613–995–6575
Email: rlochead@archives.ca
Publication: *Oral History Forum* (previously *Canadian Oral History Association Journal*), vol. 1 1975/6–

Oral History Association of Russia
c/o History Department
Kirov State Medical Institute
137 Karl Marx Street
Kirov 610602
Russia

Malta Oral History Society
15/16 Triq I-Imnajqar
Birkirkara
9 Triq J. Pace
Bormla
Malta

Mexican Oral History Network
c/o Dirección de Estudios Históricos
Instituto Nacional de Antropologia e Historia
Apartado Postal 5–119
México D.F. 06500
Email: smithers@servidor.unam.mx

Brazil Oral History Association
Setor de Documentação Orale
Universidade Federal de Pernambuco
Predio do CFCH Av. Academico Helio Ramos s/n
11 andor Cidade Universitaria
Recife, PE
Brazil
Publication: *Journal of the Brazil Oral History Association*, vol. 1 1997–

Programa de Historia Oral (Argentina)
Instituto de Historia Argetina y Americana 'Dr Emilio Ravignani'
Facultad de Filosofia y Letras
Universidad de Buenos Aires
25 de mayo 217, 2do. piso
1002 Buenos Aires
Argentina
Email: schwarzs@mail.retina.ar
Fax: 54–1– 343–2733

Oral History (Uruguay)
c/o History Department
Facultad de Humanidades y Ciencias de la Educacion
Universidad de la Republica
Magallanes 1577
Montevideo
Uruguay
Fax: 598–2–484303

Cayman Islands Memory Bank
The Cayman Islands National Archive
Government Administration Building
George Town
Grand Cayman
British West Indies
Fax: 809–949–9727

Oral and Pictorial Records Programme (Trinidad)
The Main Library
University of West Indies
St Augustine
Trinidad

Oral History Centre (Singapore)
National Archives of Singapore
140 Hill Street
Hill Street Building
Singapore 0617
Fax: 339–5697

Oral History (Sabah)
Sabah State Archives
Bag 2017
88999 Kota Kinabalu
Sabah
Malaysia
Fax: 225803

Oral History Archive (Zimbabwe)
National Archives of Zimbabwe
Private Bag 7729
Causeway
Harare
Zimbabwe

Index